Routledge Handbook of Contemporary Issues in Expropriation

The *Routledge Handbook of Contemporary Issues in Expropriation* reviews the contemporary major issues involving expropriation (eminent domain/compulsory purchase) in an international context.

Expropriation is a right reserved to all governments, and, thus, it has an impact on all societies. This book, the first of its kind, considers the essential issues from the point of view of both developing and developed countries, and their needs for major infrastructure projects. The content covers major issues, principles and policies and includes the experiences of and examples from different countries and regions, including Australia, Asia, China, Europe, India and the USA. Rather than providing an in-depth examination of individual countries' legal systems, the book focuses on international issues, and also provides a reflection on how national experiences can be related to global needs.

Key themes include:

- Nature and quantum of compensation
- Land rights and the acquisition of traditional land rights
- Issues surrounding 'public interest'
- Alternatives to expropriation
- The future: "good practice", debate and reform.

This handbook is an essential resource for students and researchers in the areas of land policy, land law, planning law, property law and rights, and international development.

Frances Plimmer is a Chartered Valuation Surveyor who has spent most of her career in academia, acquiring the degrees of Master of Philosophy in 1991 and a PhD in 1999 from the University of Glamorgan, UK. She was Reader at the University of Glamorgan and Research Professor at Kingston University, UK. She also held an appointment in the Research Department at the College of Estate Management, UK. She was the editor of *Property Management* (1994–2010) and is on the editorial boards of several international research journals, including the *Journal of Property Tax Assessment & Administration* and *International Journal of Housing Markets and Analysis*. Formerly the UK delegate to the International Federation of Geometers' (FIG – Commission 2: Professional Education), she was the UK delegate to and Chair of FIG's Commission 9 (Valuation and Real Estate Management: 2010–2014). She has an international research reputation on the subjects of expropriation, compensation and property taxation, and has most recently been involved in research into the valuation of unregistered land.

William McCluskey is Professor at the African Tax Institute, University of Pretoria, South Africa. He obtained his PhD from the University of Ulster, Northern Ireland, UK. He has held several visiting professorships, including at the University of Lodz, Poland, and University of Technology, Malaysia. He was also Professor of Property Studies at Lincoln University, New Zealand. His main professional and academic interests are in the fields of real estate valuation and property tax administration. He has an extensive publication record within international research journals and has presented widely at conferences. He is a technical adviser with the International Monetary Fund, World Bank, European Union and Food and Agriculture Organisation-United Nations. He has been involved in a number of missions advising on real estate matters in several countries, including Albania, Botswana, China, Georgia, Jamaica, Kazakhstan, Kenya, Kosovo, Lesotho, the Philippines, Slovenia, South Africa, Tanzania and Uganda. He is a Fellow of the Royal Institution of Chartered Surveyors and board member of the International Property Tax Institute.

Routledge Handbook of Contemporary Issues in Expropriation

Edited by Frances Plimmer and William McCluskey

Routledge
Taylor & Francis Group

LONDON AND NEW YORK

First published 2019 by Routledge
2 Park Square, Milton Park, Abingdon, Oxon OX14 4RN
605 Third Avenue, New York, NY 10017

First issued in paperback 2021
First issued in hardback 2019

Routledge is an imprint of the Taylor & Francis Group, an informa business

Publisher's Note
The publisher has gone to great lengths to ensure the quality of this reprint but
points out that some imperfections in the original copies may be apparent.

British Library Cataloguing-in-Publication Data
A catalogue record for this book is available from the British Library

Library of Congress Cataloging-in-Publication Data
Names: Plimmer, Frances, editor. | McCluskey, William J., editor.
Title: Routledge handbook of contemporary issues in expropriation /
edited by Frances Plimmer and William J. McCluskey.
Description: Abingdon, Oxon [UK]; New York, NY: Routledge, 2018.
Identifiers: LCCN 2018010402 | ISBN 9781138811607
(hardback: alk. paper) | ISBN 9781315749167 (ebook)
Subjects: LCSH: Eminent domain (International law) | Eminent domain.
Classification: LCC K3511 .R68 2018 | DDC 343/.0252—dc23
LC record available at https://lccn.loc.gov/2018010402

ISBN 13: 978-1-03-209468-7 (pbk)
ISBN 13: 978-1-138-81160-7 (hbk)

Typeset in Bembo
by codeMantra

For Jonathan and Danny

– Frances Plimmer

Contents

Contents

Contributors

Yeşim Aliefendioğlu is an Assistant Professor at the Department of Real Estate Development and Management, Faculty of Applied Sciences, Ankara University, Turkey. She received her MSc degree from the Department of Agricultural Economics, Ankara University, and her PhD degree from the Department of Real Estate Development and Management, Ankara University. Her research interests include management and conservation of land resources, land resource economics, land acquisition and real estate studies. She also works as the Co-Head of the Department of Real Estate Development and Management at Ankara University. She has worked in many public and private sector research projects on real estate valuation, project appraisal and land management.

Tatyana Baykova is leading legal adviser at the Institute for Urban Economics. She is an expert on legal issues pertaining to real estate, housing, urban planning, property rights protection and public private partnership. She obtained her PhD in Law from the Kutafin Moscow State Law University, Russia. She held the position of deputy chief of the Legal Department of the Ministry of Economic Development of the Russian Federation. She is actively engaged in drafting amendments to town-planning, land management and other federal and regional legislation, and preparing drafts of laws and other legal documents on real estate, housing and urban planning regulation.

Tina Beale is a Lecturer in the Land Economy and Valuation Surveying Division at the University of Technology, Jamaica. Her areas of specialisation are real estate appraisal and valuation, land management and land and property taxation. She was awarded a Commonwealth Scholarship to pursue doctoral studies at the Henley Business School, University of Reading, UK. In 2015, she was awarded the prestigious David C. Lincoln Land Valuation and Taxation Research Fellowship from the Lincoln Institute of Land Policy, Cambridge, MA. She has presented research papers at several international academic conferences.

Jan Brzeski is Director of Research at the International Property Tax Institute and partner in the real estate advisory firm REAS. He is also president of the Polish Association of Real Estate Counsellors. He holds a PhD in Real Estate Economics and Finance from the Royal Institute of Technology, Sweden. He has worked in all aspects of real estate economics, including policy and taxation issues. He has also worked with urban development and management as a Deputy Mayor of Krakow, Poland, and as a Senior Urban Specialist at the World Bank. He was heavily involved in Poland's early reforms of the real estate and housing sectors, and served as Senior Advisor to the Polish Deputy Prime Minister for five years.

Olga Buzu is Head of Real Property Service in the Agency of Land Relations and Cadastre, Republic of Moldova, and Deputy Chair of the State Certification Board for the certification of property valuers. She is also an Associate Professor at the Technical University of Moldova. She holds a PhD from the Kiev Building Engineering Institute and a Doctor Habilitatus in Economics from the Technical University of Moldova. Her main professional and academic interests are in the field of real property valuation and more specifically ad valorem taxation of real property, arrangements for tax appraisal services within the framework of the real estate cadastre, regulation of the valuation services market and the professional development of valuers. She has been involved in a number of international projects as an expert on real property valuation for tax purposes and has participated as a guest speaker in international training workshops.

Mansha Chen is an Urban Specialist at the World Bank. She works on capacity building for local governments on urban management and has developed a series of global learning programmes, including Sustainable Urban Land Use Planning, Transit-Oriented Development, Integrated Urban Transport Planning, Upgrading Urban Informal Settlements, Land Readjustment and Land Market Assessment. She is currently supporting operational projects in the East Asia and Pacific Region, including a land readjustment pilot in Vietnam. She holds both master's and bachelor's degrees in Urban Planning and a bachelor's degree in Economics from Peking University. Prior to joining the World Bank, she was an urban planner in the Chinese Academy of Urban Planning and Design under the Ministry of Housing and Urban Rural Development.

Dzurllkanian Zulkarnain bin Daud is a Professor in the Department of Real Estate, Faculty of Geoinformation Science and Engineering, Universiti Teknologi Malaysia (UTM). He obtained his PhD from the UTM. He has published widely in international research journals and has presented papers at leading international conferences.

Peadar Davis is a Senior Lecturer in Property Appraisal and Management at the Ulster University, Northern Ireland, UK. His gained his PhD from Ulster University and holds master's degrees from Aberdeen University and Exeter University, UK. He specialises in providing research, consultancy and training solutions for property taxation in developing/transitional jurisdictions. Recent property-related work includes advising the World Bank, Food and Agriculture Organisation-United Nations and Ugandan Government on government property valuation process modernisation; advising the Ethiopian Government on appropriate valuation training reform; and advising the Dubai Land Authority on the creation of property market indices. He is heavily involved in European Union (EU) research concerning urban security, resilience, disaster recovery and critical infrastructure protection. He is the editor (Property) for the *Journal of Financial Management of Property and Construction*.

Chengri Ding is Professor at the Urban Studies and Planning Program and National Center for Smart Growth, University of Maryland, USA. His research focus is on urban economics, urban and land policies, urban planning and China studies. He holds a visiting professorship in several universities, including Zhejiang University, Beijing Normal University and Zhengzhou University. He regularly acts as a consultant for the World Bank; Global Business Network; Food and Agriculture Organisation; and several leading Chinese agencies, such as the National Development and Reform Commission (NDRC) and the China Development Bank. He serves on the advisory board of the International Property Tax Institute and is the Founding Director for the Lincoln Institute of Land Policy's China Program. He has published widely in such journals as the *Journal of Urban Economics, Journal of Regional Science, Regional Science and Urban Economics, Urban Studies, Environment and Planning B* and *Land Use Policy*, and is the editor of several books on land and housing policies, urbanisation and smart growth in China. He has been consulting to Beijing Municipal governments on urban master planning.

Richard Grover is currently a part-time Senior Lecturer in Real Estate in the Faculty of Built Environment at Oxford Brookes University, Oxford, UK. He has held various positions at Oxford Brookes University, including Assistant Dean of the Faculty of Built Environment. His main academic interests are in the property markets of transition countries, property rights and property taxation. He has undertaken a number of projects for Food and Agriculture Organisation of the United Nations (FAO) and the World Bank, most recently in Serbia, Turkey and Moldova. He has been the lead consultant on a World Bank project on Property Valuation and Taxation for Fiscal Sustainability and Improved Local Governance in the Europe and Central Asia (ECA) Region.

Abdul Hassan is the Acting Head of School of Land Management and Development at the University of the South Pacific. He received his PhD from the University of the South Pacific. He has published widely in the fields of property taxation and housing. Before joining academia he worked in the public sector with the Valuation Division of the Ministry of Lands of Fiji. He was actively involved in major projects to acquire land for public purposes. While working for the Fiji Government he has also carried out an attachment duty with the Chief Valuers Office in England, and during this period he attended several Land Tribunal cases dealing with land compensation.

Yu-Hung Hong is the founder and Executive Director of the Land Governance Laboratory, where he studies the use of land tools to facilitate open and inclusive decision-making processes for land resource allocation in developing countries. Specifically, he is interested in investigating how governments can recoup land-value increments generated by public investment and community collaboration for financing local infrastructure and durable shelters for the poor. He was the Director of the Samuel Tak Lee Massachusetts Institute of Technology (MIT) Real Estate Entrepreneurship Laboratory that promotes social responsibility among entrepreneurs and academics in the real estate profession worldwide, with a particular focus on China. Dr Hong taught urban public finance and land policies at MIT, where he earned his PhD in Urban Development and master's in City Planning from the Department of Urban Studies and Planning. His research focuses on property rights and obligations, land readjustment/sharing and local public finance. Dr Hong has been teaching urban public finance and land policies since 1996 and publishes on topics related to property rights, public land leasing, land readjustment and property taxation. He is the author of several academic papers and the co-editor/author of eleven books.

Wan Ibrisam Fikry Wan Ismail is a Senior Lecturer in the Department of Real Estate, Faculty of Geoinformation Science and Engineering, UTM. He obtained his bachelor's and master's degrees from the University of Louisiana at Lafayette and Kansas State University, USA, respectively. He received his PhD from UTM. His field of interests include land policies, especially related to paddy land; rural and small town planning; land administration; and development. He is a member of the Mass Appraisal, Housing & Planning Research Group at UTM.

Mohd Nadzri Bin Jaafar is a Senior Lecturer in the Department of Real Estate, Faculty of Geoinformation Science and Engineering, UTM. He obtained his PhD from the Universiti Kebangsaan, Malaysia. He is an active researcher and has published several papers and presented at national and international conferences. He is a member of the Royal Institute of Surveyors Malaysia and member of the Malaysia Institute of Professional Property Managers. He has been the Head of Real Estate Department at UTM since 2012.

Owiti K'Akumu is a land economist and physical planner with a PhD from the University of Westminster, London, UK. Currently, he is a Senior Research Fellow at the School of the Built Environment, University of Nairobi, Kenya. Prior to joining the University of Nairobi, he was with the Ministry of Lands in Kenya, dealing with land and property compensation. He has published several book chapters and journal papers concerning professional land valuation issues in Kenya.

Iwona Karasek-Wojciechowicz is Attorney at Law and Partner in the law firm Karasek and Wejman. She is also Associate Professor of Law at Jagiellonian University, Krakow, Poland. Her professional experience includes, *inter alia*, legal advisory services to clients from the financial sector, global telecoms and mining companies. She has advised on international arbitration and litigation, legal assistance to foreign investors and in numerous instructions on legal due diligence in real estate transactions. She has also collaborated with the World Bank's Doing Business programme on the enforcement of claims, secured transactions and bankruptcy.

Anil Kashyap is Head of the Department of Geography and Environmental Management at The University of the West of England. He holds membership of the Royal Town Planning Institute and the Royal Institution of Chartered Surveyors. He has recently been appointed to the prestigious panel of the International Land Measurement Standard Setting Committee led by the Royal Institution of Chartered Surveyors (RICS), London. He has strong research interests, spanning energy efficiency in built form; resilient, healthy and smart cities; urban regeneration; and infrastructure development and financing. His key strengths are in strategic urban policymaking, innovative development management and funding mechanisms. He has contributed to major research projects funded by the EU and the RICS Education Trust.

Poonam Kashyap is with the Coventry Business School, UK. She holds an MBA and PhD from Ulster University, Northern Ireland. She has published in several leading international journals.

Nadezhda Kosareva has been a President of the Institute for Urban Economics (IUE, Moscow, Russia) since its foundation in 1995. IUE is one of the leading Russian think tanks carrying out research into urban economics, municipal management, urban planning and housing. Dr Kosareva is also Academic Supervisor of the Graduate School of Urbanism under the National Research University Higher School of Economics, Moscow, Russia. She obtained her PhD in Economics from the National Institute of System Studies under the Soviet Union (USSR) Academy of Science. She is a leading expert in housing policy, housing finance, real estate market development, local governance and urban socio-economic development. Dr Kosareva participated in drafting several legislative and other regulatory documents on housing policy, real estate market development and local governance, including the Housing Code, Urban Planning Code and Land Code of the Russian Federation. She is the author of numerous publications on various aspects of housing sector reform in Russia.

Contributors

Lawrence Lai is Professor in Planning, Economics and Law, Department of Real Estate and Construction, University of Hong Kong. He is a member of the Ronald Coase Centre for Property Rights Research at the University of Hong Kong. He has worked as a consultant for the Hong Kong government, served on the Appeal Board of the Inland Revenue and appeared before the Building Appeal Tribunal and the Planning Appeal Board as appointed member. He is an active researcher and has published more than 14 books and 119 refereed research papers.

Susanne Lyon-Josephs is a New Jersey and New York State Certified General Real Estate Appraiser and a Fellow of the Royal Institution of Chartered Surveyors. She is Executive Vice President with Executive Real Estate Seminars and Manager in the parent organisation PATJO Appraisal Services, Inc. Prior to this she acquired over 20 years of real estate appraisal practice experience with the Land Valuation Department (now a division of the National Land Agency) and was Executive Director of the Jamaica National Heritage Trust. She has been a part-time Lecturer on the Land Economy and Valuation Surveying Programme at the University of Technology, Jamaica. She serves as an Assessor of RICS Candidates (North American and Caribbean chapters).

William McCluskey is Professor at the African Tax Institute, University of Pretoria, South Africa. He obtained his PhD from the University of Ulster, Northern Ireland, UK. He has held several visiting professorships, including at the University of Lodz, Poland, and University of Technology, Malaysia. He was also Professor of Property Studies at Lincoln University, New Zealand. His main professional and academic interests are in the fields of real estate valuation and property tax administration. He has an extensive publication record within international research journals and has presented widely at conferences. He is a technical adviser with the International Monetary Fund, World Bank, European Union and Food and Agriculture Organisation-United Nations. He has been involved in a number of missions advising on real estate matters in several countries, including Albania, Botswana, China, Georgia, Jamaica, Kazakhstan, Kenya, Kosovo, Lesotho, the Philippines, Slovenia, South Africa, Tanzania and Uganda. He is a Fellow of the Royal Institution of Chartered Surveyors and board member of the International Property Tax Institute.

John McCord is a Lecturer in Law at Ulster University, Northern Ireland, UK. He obtained his PhD in Law from Ulster University in 2010. Since then he has undertaken a wide range of published research in the real estate and law fields, with a particular emphasis on housing markets performance and analysis, and compulsory purchase. He has also been successful in a number of European Commission-funded projects and reviews papers for a number of international real estate journals.

Mike McDermott has 40 years' real estate valuation and valuation-related experience in the public and private sectors. In the last 25 years he has consulted on land policy-related matters for developing countries, particularly on facilitating land valuations. The greatest challenges with such valuations are often found in the field of compensation for compulsory acquisitions. He holds a master's degree from Western Sydney University, Australia, and a PhD from the University of Technology, Sydney, Australia. He has published widely in scholarly research media and is the author of a book with the working title *Wicked Valuations: People and Landed Property*.

Donald Mengwe is principal valuer in the Department of Local Government Finance and Procurement Services within the Ministry of Local Government and Rural Development,

Botswana. He is Head of the Division of Rating Valuations responsible for the preparation of valuation rolls for rating authorities and providing advisory services on property tax assessment and administration. He has previously served as Principal Lands Officer in the Directorate of Lands within the Ministry of Lands and Housing responsible for property acquisitions and disposals, property management and carrying out valuations for compensation purposes. He received an Honours Degree from Edinburgh Napier University, UK. He served as Secretary General of the Real Estate Institute of Botswana from 2008 to 2011 and as Registrar of the Real Estate Advisory Council, a statutory body regulating the conduct of real estate professionals in Botswana for the period 2006–08.

Thomas Murphy holds a degree in law from Queen's University, Belfast and a PhD from the University of Ulster, UK. He is a former Head of the School of Law at the University of Ulster, where he has lectured since 1999. He specialises in land, property and housing law, his most recent research relates to the law of compulsory purchase in Northern Ireland and he is co-author of the textbook the *Law of Property in Northern Ireland*.

Maxwell Mutema holds an MBA in Real Estate and Construction Management; an MSc in Project Management with Real Estate Appraisal and Development; and a PhD in Land Management and Economics from the University of Reading, UK. He is a qualified Chartered Surveyor with the Royal Institution of Chartered Surveyors. He trained to become a Chartered Surveyor with CB Richard Ellis. His professional valuation work focusses on Africa. He has been a Visiting Lecturer in the School of Real Estate and Planning, Henley Business School, University of Reading. His academic and practice interests centre around valuation, land markets, land administration, property taxation and urban and rural planning. He has participated in a number of initiatives and assignments to advance the valuation profession globally.

Jan Neckář graduated from the Faculty of Law of Masaryk University with a PhD in Financial Law and Financial Sciences. His current research interests focus mainly on issues of tax administration and property taxes. In these fields he has authored several articles and presented at professional conferences. Currently, he is a lawyer and an external Lecturer at the Department of Financial Law of the Faculty of Law of Masaryk University, Brno, Czech Republic.

Washington Olima is an Associate Professor in the Department of Real Estate and Construction Management, School of The Built Environment, University of Nairobi, Kenya. He is currently Deputy Vice-Chancellor (Planning, Administration and Finance), Jaramogi Oginga Odinga University of Science and Technology, Bondo, Kenya. He obtained his PhD from the University of Dortmund in Germany. He has over 30 years of experience in academia, teaching, research, administration and consultancy services. He has an extensive scholarly record, as demonstrated by publications in internationally peer-reviewed journals, working papers and book chapters. He was the President of African Real Estate Society (AfRES) and member of the former German Academic Exchange Service (Deutscher Akademischer Austauschdienst) DAAD Scholars Association and the Kenya National Academy of Sciences.

Ismail Omar is a Professor at the Department of Real Estate Management, Faculty of Technology Management and Business, Universiti Tun Hussein Onn, Malaysia. He graduated in Estate Management from Heriot-Watt University, Edinburgh, UK. He then pursued his Master's of Business in Property at the University of South Australia and completed his PhD in Land Economy from Aberdeen University, Scotland, UK. His research interests are in the areas of land policy, land management and land administration. He has published and presented many papers in national and international journals and conferences. He has authored some 18 books in the field of real estate management.

David Parker is an internationally recognised property industry expert focussing on compulsory acquisition, valuation standards and real estate investment trusts. He is currently the inaugural Professor of Property at the University of South Australia and a Visiting Professor at the Henley Business School, University of Reading, UK, and University Tun Hussein Onn, Malaysia. He also holds a Visiting Fellowship at the University of Ulster, UK; is an Acting Valuation Commissioner of the Land and Environment Court of New South Wales; and is a sessional member of the South Australian Civil and Administrative Tribunal adjudicating compulsory acquisition compensation and rating disputes. He has authored several publications, including the authoritative *International Valuation Standards: A Guide to the Valuation of Real Property Assets* and *Global Real Estate Investment Trusts: People, Process and Management*.

Frances Plimmer is a Chartered Valuation Surveyor who has spent most of her career in academia, acquiring the degrees of Master of Philosophy in 1991 and a PhD in 1999 from the University of Glamorgan, UK. She was Reader at the University of Glamorgan and Research Professor at Kingston University, UK. She also held an appointment in the Research Department at the College of Estate Management, UK. She was the editor of *Property Management* (1994–2010) and is on the editorial boards of several international research journals, including the *Journal of Property Tax Assessment & Administration* and *International Journal of Housing Markets and Analysis*. Formerly the UK delegate to the International Federation of Geometers' (FIG – Commission 2: Professional Education), she was the UK delegate to and Chair of FIG's Commission 9 (Valuation and Real Estate Management: 2010–2014). She has an international research reputation on the subjects of expropriation, compensation and property taxation, and has most recently been involved in research into the valuation of unregistered land.

Tatyana Polidi is the Executive Director and Head of the Real Estate Department at the Institute for Urban Economics, Moscow, Russia. She holds a PhD in Economics from the National Research University Higher School of Economics, Moscow, Russia. She specialises in economic analysis and modelling, mechanisms of housing affordability improvement, registration of real estate, housing finance, land use and urban planning regulation, and rental housing. Her experience includes urban economics, real estate market analysis, reform and introduction of new mechanisms of mortgage lending, legal improvement of regulatory framework in construction, reduction of administrative barriers in housing construction and protection of rights of bona fide purchasers of real estate. She has worked as a consultant for the World Bank and United Nations Economic Commission for Europe in projects on housing market development, registration of real estate and finance.

Michal Radvan is associate professor of financial law at the Department of Financial Law and Economics, and vice-dean for foreign and external affairs at the Faculty of Law, Masaryk University, Czech Republic. He obtained his PhD from Masaryk University. He is the author of several books and has co-authored some forty-five books. He has presented his scientific research in approximately eighty peer-reviewed articles in prestigious international journals and research conferences. He is a member of the European Association of Tax Law Professors and the Information and Organization Centre for the Research on the Public Finances and Tax Law in the Countries of Central and Eastern Europe.

Fauziah Raji is a Senior Lecturer in the Department of Real Estate, Faculty of Geoinformation and Real Estate, UTM. Prior to joining UTM, she was a valuer with the Department of Valuation and Property Services. She holds a bachelor's degree in Property Management (UTM); master's in Urban Land Appraisal (University of Reading, UK); and PhD in Real Estate, UTM. She is also a registered valuer. Her areas of interest include property valuation, Intellectual Property (IP) valuation and property investment.

Salfarina Samsudin is a Senior Lecturer in the Department of Real Estate, Faculty of Geoinformation Science and Engineering, UTM. She obtained her PhD from the University of Ulster, Northern Ireland, UK. She is an active researcher and has published several papers, and presented at international conferences. She is a member of the Land Administration and Development Research Group at UTM.

Cadien Stuart currently serves as a Senior Lecturer in the School of Building and Land Management, University of Technology, Jamaica. She has also served as Head of the School and as Programme Director. She is a member of the Royal Institution of Chartered Surveyors and was attached to the Land Valuation Department (now a Division of the National Land Agency). In addition, she was a member of the body which managed the transition of several departments into the National Land Agency as an Executive Agency. She is a member of the Association of Land Economy and Valuation Surveyors, Jamaica.

Harun Tanrıvermiş is a professor in the Department of Real Estate Development and Management, Faculty of Applied Sciences, Ankara University, Turkey. He received his MSc and PhD degrees from the Department of Agricultural Economics, Ankara University. He has also obtained another MSc degree on environmental management from the International Technological University under the MED-CAMPUS Programme. His research interests include real estate valuation, project appraisal, land acquisition and expropriation, resettlement policies, land and real estate economics, state property management and environmental economics. He has been a staff member at Ankara University since 1991 and has been working as a research specialist and consultant in the fields of real estate valuation, land acquisition, project development and appraisal, and resettlement policies in many public and private sector projects. He is the founder and the Head of the Department of Real Estate Development and Management and the dean of the Faculty of Applied Sciences at Ankara University.

Tambet Tiits is Director General of the Estonian National Land Board. He was manager of the State Land Survey at the time of Estonia's independence and was the Department Director in the new National Land Board. He served as Director of real estate advisory and consulting service during the period 1994–2015. He served as Chairman of the Estonian Association of Appraisers from 1995–2014 and was elected to the board of the TEGoVA (European Group of Valuers Association) from 2003–2006.

Aivar Tomson is Head of Valuation and Research at DTZ Kinnisvaraekspert, Estonia. He has participated in many projects related to valuation and property market analyses in Estonia. He is also a consultant with the Department for International Development, UK (DFID); Finnish Government; FAO; United Nations Development Programme; and the World Bank. He has been involved in numerous consultancy projects in Albania, Azerbaijan, Ghana, Ethiopia, Latvia, Lithuania, Macedonia, Nigeria, Russia, Turkey and Uzbekistan in relation to real estate matters. He is member of the board of the Estonian Association of Appraisers.

Yuzhe Wu received his PhD degree at Zhejiang University, China. In 2004, he was awarded a doctoral fellowship from Lincoln Institute of Land Policy, Cambridge, MA. He was a visiting scholar in University of North Carolina, USA, during the period between 2011 and 2012. He is Head and Professor in the Department of Land Management at Zhejiang University, China. His research activities include urbanisation, land use policy, sustainable development and land use planning. He has published many academic papers in leading international research journals, including *Land Use Policy* and *Cities*. He is on the editorial board of *Habitat International, Journal of Urban Management* and *International Journal of Construction Management*.

Preface

The taking of something which belongs to someone else is theft and is actionable in the courts. However, governments all over the world reserve to themselves the right to take someone else's land subject to two factors:

1   the overriding *"public benefit"*, which justifies the violation of an individual's landownership rights; and
2   the payment of compensation.

The chapters in this book discuss these issues, the legislative powers which governments retain, the definition of *"public benefit"* and the methods of both the assessment and payment of compensation within various geographic locations.

Because the right to and the procedure for the compulsory taking of land are invariably contained in legislation, the adequacy (or otherwise) of the legislation implemented in different jurisdictions is a recurrent theme in these chapters. Also discussed are alternatives to enforced expropriation, which have far fewer negative outcomes.

What is clear in this volume is that the need for large-scale public infrastructure projects is growing around the world, and not every jurisdiction has the necessary legislative and administrative capacity to undertake the entire process (particularly the assessment and payment of compensation) to the satisfaction of the affected parties. When the process goes wrong, the results can be disastrous for the affected individuals and their community and expensive for governments and their taxpayers.

The principles and practice of the compulsory acquisition of land rights is centuries old, and, in some cases, so is the legislation (and therefore the assumed circumstances surrounding the process), which is also dated, expressed in archaic language and inadequate for the growing needs and expectations of modern societies. The chapters in this book demonstrate the range and breadth of the current issues surrounding compulsory acquisition and consider alternative processes. The thorny issue of compensation also receives much attention.

This book discusses the contemporary issues underlying both the need for and details of compulsory acquisition processes, and the adequacy of both the legislation, its administration and the principles and practice of the assessment of compensation to the dispossessed.

The contents of this book are outlined in the following.

In Chapter 1 Grover draws on data collected by the World Bank's Land Governance Assessment Framework to examine processes of expropriation and the payment of compensation. The normal situation is for compensation to be paid only for the loss of certain rights and at a level which is below that needed to maintain current livelihoods. Those having their land taken have limited rights of appeal and can wait long periods before complaints are dealt with. Part of the problem is that developing countries tend to have capacity limitations in areas particularly relevant to compulsory acquisition, such as land administration, land registration and valuation. There can also be governance issues. Corruption and abuse of office, whether governments are ineffectual in implementing policies and lack of respect for human rights have an impact on the conduct of expropriation.

In Chapter 2, Hong and Chen note that land readjustment has been conventionally perceived as merely a tool to assemble adjacent land plots from different owners for efficient land redevelopment rather than as an alternative to compulsory acquisition. Recent applications of this land tool in some developing countries have shown its potential for minimising the use of eminent domain or government compulsory purchase, for facilitating public-private partnership and for encouraging good land governance. Based on actual cases from the developing world and emerging economies, including Angola, Bhutan, China, Colombia, Egypt, Ethiopia, India, Indonesia, Thailand, Turkey and Vietnam, the authors discuss how supporting legislation, organised communities, collaboration between the public and private sectors, and relationships of trust among stakeholders were tested and gradually institutionalised during land readjustment experiments. These phenomena are quite different from the traditional argument that the aforementioned institutional environments must exist prior to adopting this land tool. Although the examined cases are neither exhaustive nor randomly selected, they raise important questions about whether or not land readjustment could facilitate the building of viable institutions and governance for managing land redevelopment, especially in emerging economies. The rethinking of land readjustment could open the door for more applications of this approach in developing countries, replacing the use of eminent domain or state compulsory purchase in land assembly for redevelopment.

McDermott, in Chapter 3, finds that there are massive infrastructure projects being planned across Asia, and many of them will require land expropriations for implementation. Combined, these projects are of such a scale as to change the future of the planet. The Old Silk Road, established over 2,000 years ago, provides a precedent for such a grand assertion as its openings and closings really did change the future of the planet. Now, the vision of a New Silk Road, also known as "One Belt, One Road", is coordinating infrastructure projects towards that change. This chapter has two main parts: first, a description of the Silk Road 2,000 years ago and current plans for its revival, and second, the major contemporary issues associated with achieving this vision within the context of expropriation. To assist the achievement of that vision the author recommends implementing the principle of ensuring persons are no worse off after the expropriations than they were before.

In Chapter 4, Radvan and Neckar focus on a range of contemporary issues, problems, experiences and commentary in the Czech Republic in the area of expropriation. The chapter assumes that the hypothesis *de lege lata* (of the existing law) is sufficient, and there is no need for amendments. This hypothesis is confirmed partially; there are no serious problems with the regulation *de lege lata* concerning expropriation. There are currently no cases of international arbitration with foreign investors as a result of the expropriation of land and buildings in the Czech Republic. The authors contend that if the authorities proceed according to the law, there are no opportunities to prevent expropriation.

In Chapter 5 on Estonia, Tiits and Tomson describe the country's main experiences related to land acquisition for public purposes during the last two decades. They provide an overview of the current regulations, practice and statistics about land acquisitions made by different authorities for various purposes. The practice of land acquisition for public needs has been processed in line with the constitution. The rights are protected by law. The main processes have largely been based on the voluntary acquisition of land, with compulsory acquisition being rarely used. There is a rationale to implement the readjustment process as an additional tool for resolving acquisition issues in the future.

Chapter 6 by Buzu presents a study of the history of immovable property expropriations in the Republic of Moldova. This extends from the period beginning in 1918 until the present day and shows, against the back drop of Moldova's history, how expropriation relates to requisition, confiscation and nationalisation of land. A particular focus has been placed on the essence, procedures, basic underlying concepts and legal and methodological aspects of property expropriations within the framework of projects deemed important for public purposes. The Republic of Moldova is an economy in transit to the market, and for that reason the author describes market valuation methods as well as regulated methods (such as the method based on regulated, standardised (normative) prices of land typical for centralised planning economies) applied to the appraisal of the property subject to expropriation. In addition, the author examines the methodologies applied to determine the amount of compensation payable for damage caused by expropriation of their property. Furthermore, the chapter discusses a number of expropriation case studies in Moldova, identifies the existing methodological and legal problems, and suggests some actions to improve the methodology of determining the amount payable as compensation for expropriation.

In Chapter 7 the authors (Tanrıvermiş and Aliefendioğlu) contend that for real estate acquisition by public institutions for urban development and infrastructure projects in Turkey, expropriation is primarily preferred, and purchase by agreement is the second option. However, since the foundation of the Republic, land acquisition and expropriation compensation for public services and investments has been the subject of constant debate. The increase in demand for public services resulting from economic development also leads to an increase in the need for land acquisition and expropriation. Over the last 16 years, a total of 300,000 hectares (741,300 acres) of land have been expropriated by central and local administrations, and 10 per cent of the central and local administrations budget has been paid to the owners and beneficiaries as compensation. It has also been observed that the transparency of expropriation transactions made by public institutions is problematic and that there are insufficient budgets within the institutions and a lack of qualified human resources, technical infrastructure and valuation databases.

Karasek-Wojciechowicz and Brzeski, in Chapter 8, describe the regulatory framework for the expropriation of real property in Poland. The first part presents the pertinent context and concepts – constitutional, legislative and international as applicable and binding in Poland. The second part presents the core aspects of real property expropriation including purpose, indispensability, beneficiary, residual property and procedures. The third part discusses compensation for expropriated real property, including compensation form and quantity, and compensation decision and its payment. The final part addresses conditions for returning expropriated real property, including where the property is used other than for its intended purpose.

Chapter 9 deals with the UK, and the authors Murphy, McCord and Davis suggest that land acquisition and compulsory purchase powers are conferred under a range of statutes for a wide range of purposes. Whilst it is well rehearsed that such powers must be exercised in the public interest, recent cases and associated developments in common law have highlighted peculiar and controversial issues relating to competing economic and planning interests between public authorities, developers and affected third parties, which have attracted considerable scrutiny. Thus, this chapter explores the key developments and challenges that have arisen in light of recent decisions relating to public interest, planning gain and "private to private" transfers in the legal taking of land and the issue of State Aid.

Tanrıvermiş and Aliefendioğlu, in Chapter 10, argue that in many countries, central and local institutions need to provide goods and services, and make infrastructure investments to meet their increasing needs for food, accommodation, energy and infrastructure due to rapid population growth. Expropriation of real estate which is in private ownership for these public services becomes unavoidably compulsory when public land may be insufficient or unsuitable. In this chapter, the effects of land acquisition and resettlement for selected infrastructure investments in Turkey are analysed based on legal regulations and international standards, and the possible socio-economic impacts as well as the impacts on natural and cultural assets of expropriation activities have been assessed in this framework.

In Chapter 11 the authors, Ding and Wu, present the land institutions governing land requisition in China in a historical context and then assess the practice of land requisition. The chapter illustrates the positive roles of land requisition on local public financing, infrastructure provision and economic growth as well as its negative consequences, such as social unrest, fiscal risks, inefficient and chaotic land development, and housing bubbles. The chapter also uses two cases to show the extremes in land requisition: one reflects inadequate compensation in land taking and the other suggests windfalls. The chapter recommends radical policy reforms that will promote a unified land market of rural and urban areas, address the entitlement of land value increases, promote fair compensation and avoid windfalls in land requisition.

In Chapter 12, Hassan deals with the acquisition of land for public use under Fiji law. In Fiji the right of the State and authorised statutory bodies to acquire or use private land for public purpose is protected under the statute upon payment of just compensation to the affected owners. In this chapter a brief description of the land tenure system in Fiji is provided. The provisions on compensation and assessment procedures are discussed. The deficit in the legislation and how it compares with the policies of the Asian Development Bank and World Bank are highlighted. In 2016, an independent comparative study was completed by these two international organisations on land acquisition policies they adopted against the Fiji Land Acquisition Law. The findings provide a strong incentive for Fiji to look into its policy, particularly on the resettlements of displaced property owners when the larger portion of the land is taken for public use.

Lai, in his Chapter (13), playfully tells a story and reports a dialogue on so-called government "urban renewal" by edict in Hong Kong. Then he interprets the story and the dialogues in terms of the violation of private property rights to land sold as commodities by the government in "urban renewal" projects. The story develops an article published in Chinese in *Hong Kong Economic Journal* in 1991, and the dialogue is a sequel to an essay on zoning appearing in *Cities and Private Planning*, edited by Andersson and Moroni. The real driving force of "urban renewal" as such is capturing unexploited development potential, and reasons to justify that, like "urban decay", are just pretexts. The author indicates ways to ameliorate the issue of the infringement of rights.

In India, the authors (Kashyap and Kashyap) of Chapter 14 note, the magnitude of the infrastructural investment challenge runs far beyond the capacity of the public sector alone, and interventions are required to create the conditions conducive to private sector investment through partnerships models. The purpose of this chapter is to explore the global challenge associated with infrastructure development, resulting from decades of regulatory arbitrage in emerging economies like India. Here, the authors present the land development models commonly used at the neighbourhood level for servicing land with urban infrastructure which is commonly used in pooling land for any small- or large-scale public projects. Land readjustment is used in many countries to reconfigure underperforming land parcels after pooling land and servicing areas with basic infrastructure to achieve coordinated planned development. However, there are challenges in making land available for the implementation of mega infrastructure projects, or the setting up of large industries, through the implementation of master plans, development schemes due to litigations and prolonged disputes in the taking of clear ownership of land.

In Chapter 15 the authors (Daud, Raji, Samsudin, Fikry, Ismail, Jaafar and Omar) find that compulsory acquisition of land is an extreme form of governmental intervention that affects the constitutional rights of landowners. This chapter provides an explanation and discussion on evolving compulsory land acquisition in Malaysia. It explores the policy context of land acquisition, legislation and regulations involved. It also discusses implementation and trends in land acquisition in Malaysia in terms of the broader debates on economic, social and political transformations. It includes a critical discussion on issues and key challenges of the legal, economic, social and political consequences in land acquisition under the Land Acquisition Act 1960. The chapter then discusses the actions taken and best approaches adopted in two selected case studies. The discussion focusses on critical issues associated with or derived from land acquisition projects. The selected land acquisition cases are The Pengerang Oil and Gas Hub project and The Klang Valley Mass Rapid Transit project.

In Chapter 16 the authors (Kosareva, Baykova and Polidi) present a detailed analysis of the institution of real estate expropriation for state and municipal needs, as applied in Russia. The statutory regulation of common grounds and procedures for real estate expropriation, and individual cases of expropriation using special procedures are discussed. The authors also review the most common matters of court practice and legislative issues around applying real estate expropriation mechanisms for state and municipal needs.

Parker, in Chapter 17, notes that, with around A$200 billion committed to infrastructure development by the Commonwealth and State Governments over the next four years, Australia is currently experiencing an infrastructure boom, with the level of compulsory acquisition likely to be unprecedented in Australian history. Following a review of the key Commonwealth and State Government enabling legislation, the compulsory acquisition process is outlined and the notion of "*just compensation*" considered. Alternative heads of compensation are summarised in the context of the NSW Land Acquisition (Just Terms Compensation) Act 1991, including market value, special value, severance, disturbance and *solatium*, with a review of the interaction of heads of claim within the context of the dispossessed owner seeking a notion of value to owner. The acceptability of alternative methods of valuation is considered by the author, with the preference of the courts for comparable sales rather than the capitalisation method, hypothetical development or discounted cash flow approaches. Given the prospective volume of compulsory acquisition to be undertaken in Australia in the next few years, the role of alternative dispute resolution is explored as a just, quick and cheap route to resolution of compensation claims.

K'Akumu and Olima, in Chapter 18, explore the challenges that Kenya has been facing in the expropriation of land for public purposes. It traces the issues from the very territorial beginnings or colonial period circa 1895 to the present day. During the colonial period, there was a problem because of the absence of appropriate laws to apply in the acquisition of private or customary land. This was overcome principally by importing the Indian Land Acquisition Act, use of *fetwa* (Islamic law equivalent to land acquisition law) and the principle of *bona vacantia* (ownerless goods). During the postcolonial period, the main problem has been resistance by landowners, especially fuelled by claims of inadequate compensation, leading to crippling litigation. This problem has persisted during the 2010 constitutional era, as witnessed in the Single Gauge Railway project that has prompted the government to enact the Land Value Index Amendment Bill (2016) in order to control the price of land and curtail litigation. However, this move may not end the government's challenges as it is fraught with illegalities.

Mengwe (Chapter 19) finds that public authorities in Botswana, when undertaking projects which require land for the public good and where there subsists a private interest or right to use the land, may exercise powers of eminent domain under the terms of the Constitution of Botswana 1966; Acquisition of Property Act, 1955; the Tribal Land Act, 1968; and the Tribal Land (Amendment) Act, 1993. As expropriation is seldom resisted, controversies generally emanate from the compensation issue. This is hardly surprising in a society that is increasingly literate, human rights conscious and litigious, and where property owners are asserting their disapproval of inadequate compensation. The chapter describes the compensation laws and the evolution of land tenure which are essential ingredients for determining the quantum of compensation. It also explores different perspectives on the purpose of the constitutional property clause and approaches articulated in commentaries on assessing just compensation. Problems with the current compensation system are highlighted, and recommendations for improvement are suggested. The chapter concludes by suggesting a legislative reform which would put the question of assessment of compensation in the political arena subject to judicial review and achieve a paradigm shift from the individual to an approach that puts an individual in a societal context where a proportionality test plays a dominant role in the assessment of compensation.

Mutema, in his Chapter (20) on Zimbabwe, notes the challenges being faced by the valuation profession, including the lack of academic training, lack of local valuation standards, professional malpractices and inconsistencies, and the virtual absence of competent and capacitated local professional representative bodies to give professional guidance. These challenges are exacerbated by the predominantly informal customary land tenure system in Zimbabwe and most African countries. Customary landownership is characterised by informal land sales, leases and purchases, with resultant price information asymmetry challenges. In the backdrop of these challenges, there is a growing trend of cases involving compulsory land acquisition which needs valuation for compensation, including customary land. This is a result of rapid land-based investments such as infrastructure projects and urban expansion.

Beale, in Chapter 21, finds that the compulsory acquisition of land is a relic of the colonial era in the Caribbean. In this chapter, new institutional economics are used as the theoretical lens through which the subject matter is assessed in five island states in the region. Three components form the core of compulsory acquisition in the selected islands – the public purpose requirement, the conclusiveness of the declaration and compensation. However, the land market of the region differs from other countries because their markets are arguably synonymous to a lattice with a myriad of interwoven formal and informal land tenures. Within such a context, the purchaser not only faces the strategic holdout problem, but the increased complexity of these markets can make the purchaser's transaction costs insurmountable. The findings of the chapter suggest, *inter alia*, that compulsory acquisition is an efficient process in a world of zero or low transaction costs.

Walters, in Chapter 22 on the USA, notes that the Constitution provides that private property cannot be "taken" for public use without "just compensation". Despite this clear and succinct statement, the history of expropriation in the USA has been described as a "massive body of case law, irreconcilable in its inconsistency, confusing in its detail and defiant of all attempts at classification". This chapter provides a brief overview of this history, then provides an evaluation of the Kaldor-Hicks criterion as applied in expropriation. Particular attention is given to the concept of just compensation. Recent research into the relationship between people and places suggests that the traditional view of land and property as simply another economic commodity misses the importance people give to specific places. In light of this "place identity", the possibility of full and just compensation is questioned. An alternative to expropriation that may avoid this dilemma is presented and summarised.

In Jamaica, the authors Stuart and Lyon-Josephs (in Chapter 23) note, the government, in fulfilling its mandate to serve the people, very often is required to take land from private use for public purposes. Across the property ownership landscape, the majority of property interests reflect a high level of informal interests, that is, customary and informal (squatting) tenure. The law in Jamaica states that compensation for the taking of land is payable only to the holder of the fee simple interest. This implies that with land registration levels standing at less than 50 per cent, land acquisition becomes problematic. The acquisition process can become both costly and lengthy. The authors found that although interests may have been valued, other property rights need to be identified and addressed. These include prescriptive rights, for example, where the land has been used by individuals in excess of 20 years. By surveying and reviewing primary and secondary data, the chapter seeks to identify and address issues surrounding the compensation process for compulsory acquisition under the Land Acquisition Act 1947. The chapter accomplishes this through the study of two highway projects in Jamaica.

Frances Plimmer
William McCluskey

Abbreviations and acronyms

Art.	Article
BIT	Bilateral Investment Treaty
bn	billion
ECHR	European Convention of Human Rights
ECtHR	European Court of Human Rights
EU	European Union
FAO/UN FAO	Food and Agriculture Organisation of the United Nations
FIG	International Federation of Surveyors
GDP	Gross Domestic Product
HABU	Highest and Best Use
IVS	International Valuation Standards
IVSC	International Valuation Standards Council
NGO	Non-Governmental Organisation
No.	number
OECD	Organisation for Economic Co-operation and Development
p.	page
Para.	paragraph
pp.	pages
PPP	Public Private Partnership
RICS	Royal Institution of Chartered Surveyors
UK	United Kingdom
UN	United Nations
UN FAO/FAO	Food and Agriculture Organisation of the United Nations
UN-HABITAT	United Nations Human Settlements Programme
US/USA	United States of America
USD	United States Dollar
USSR	Union of Soviet Socialist Republics
VGGT	Voluntary Guidelines on the Responsible Governances of Tenure of Land Fisheries and Forests

1

Compulsory purchase in developing countries

Richard Grover

I compulsorily purchase your land; you exercise eminent domain; he expropriates.

English irregular verb

Introduction

This chapter examines compulsory purchase[1] in developing, emerging, and transition countries. Their principal common characteristic is that their incomes per capita are lower than those of the countries that make up clubs like the Organisation for Economic Co-operation and Development (OECD). They are currently, or were in the recent past, entitled to receive World Bank loans or grants, or were on the OECD Development Assistance Committee's list of countries receiving Overseas Development Aid.

Developing countries, like others, need from time to time to undertake the compulsory purchase of privately owned property rights: for instance, for the construction of infrastructure or site assembly for development projects. However, a characteristic of developing countries tends to be capacity limitations in areas relevant to compulsory purchase. These can include infrastructure, such as land and title registration systems, as well as human capacity, including lawyers, surveyors, and valuers. Land administrations may lack basic resources, like suitable offices and record storage facilities, and vehicles to enable staff to undertake site visits, or have inadequate or poorly maintained equipment or systems whose licenses have expired. At its most basic, compulsory purchase requires the identification of the parcels to be acquired, the persons (legal as well as physical) with property rights over the land, and the nature of those rights. For this to happen there needs to be a cadastre that identifies the parcels and their boundaries and a land or title registry that records rights. Many developing countries do not have well-developed or comprehensive cadastre and land registration systems. Mapping may rely on relatively old analogue surveys rather than being digital, cadastres may not record buildings or accurately reflect what is on the ground, and informal or non-statutory rights may not be recorded in land registries. If those whose property is taken are to receive compensation that ensures they do not end up being worse off as a result, then what is compulsorily acquired must be accurately valued. For this to happen, there must be qualified valuers capable of working to international valuation standards, and who follow internationally recognised codes of ethics and professional conduct.

There may be governance issues, including how well private property is protected and whether there is the ability to have infringements of human rights judged impartially by an independent tribunal. Those whose property is threatened with expropriation should have the ability to challenge the policy and the legality of the action as well as the valuation of their losses. Good governance means that government is well-managed, effective, inclusive, and results in desirable outcomes. In reality it may be discriminatory, inefficient, or ineffective. There may be corruption – land administration is one of the more corrupt areas of government (Transparency International/FAO, 2011). Government may not be open or transparent in decision-making, and policy-making may not be done in a legitimate, accountable, or participatory way. Decisions may not be consistent or predictable, and the government may not be subject to the rule of law.

The literature contains many individual case studies of compulsory purchase in developing countries, but in order to study these issues more closely and draw conclusions about how typical particular experiences are, one needs a relatively consistent set of data about how expropriation is carried out in a number of countries. The data need to be about actual outcomes and not just focus on laws or policies since there may be issues about the implementation of policy. This chapter draws on a particular source: namely the Land Governance Assessment Framework (LGAF) analyses carried out by the World Bank since 2011. These are demanding, in-depth analyses of major aspects of land governance, including compulsory acquisition. A sufficient number of these have now been undertaken to make some rudimentary statistical analysis possible, both of how compulsory acquisition is carried out and the factors that seem to be associated with particular outcomes. The analysis suggests policy approaches that development banks, international agencies, and bilateral donors might take to enhance the governance of compulsory acquisition and, in particular, to ensure that support for other development projects that involve the displacement of populations does not have unintended consequences.

Land Governance Assessment Framework

The LGAF developed by the World Bank is intended as a "diagnostic tool to help evaluate the legal framework, policies, and practices regarding land governance and to monitor improvement over time" (Deininger et al., 2012). LGAF was created because of the "need for well-designed land policies to ensure the security of long-held land rights, to facilitate land access, and to deal with externalities", particularly at times of major change. Governance is defined by the World Bank as "the manner in which public officials and institutions acquire and exercise the authority to shape public policy and provide public goods and services". One of the issues explored is the compulsory acquisition of land by the public sector.

LGAF is intended to be applied in a collaborative fashion to examine various aspects of land governance and to recommend policies for improvement. Data are collected by expert investigators and presented to panels of specialists. The indicators are scored on a scale of A (good practice) to D (weak practice). The process is an iterative one, with the results being subjected to technical validation, the aim being to reach consensus where possible. The key strength is that LGAF does not just examine whether a policy exists or whether there is legislation on an issue but reflects the judgements of those with experience of its effectiveness. LGAF, though, is not designed to compare the performance of one country with that of another, there being no mechanism to ensure that the assessments in one country are scored consistently with those of others. Nonetheless, with this caveat, LGAF can be argued to provide a systematic approach to reviewing how a range of countries approach compulsory acquisition.

LGAF first appeared in 2012, with a major revision in 2013 in response to the publication of the *Voluntary Guidelines on the Responsible Governance of Tenure of Land, Fisheries and Forests* (VGGT) (Committee on World Food Security, 2012) and experience gained from operating the process. The number of indicators was increased from 80 to 116 (World Bank, 2012, 2013). The fundamental approach to collecting data and scoring indicators did not change significantly, and many of the indicators used in the assessments up to 2013 are similar to those used since then.

At the time of writing 39 countries[2] had been through the process, though not every country has been scored on all the indicators. LGAF has been undertaken for twenty-four countries from Africa, six from Asia, five from Central and South America, and four from Europe. Figure 1.1 shows the variability of Gross Domestic Product per capita in terms of international dollars purchasing power parity. This shows that the countries provide a good cross section in terms of development. The countries include former colonies of Belgium, Britain, France, Germany, Portugal, and Spain, parts of the former USSR, and one country that has joined the European Union. They therefore have inherited a range of legal and institutional heritages.

There is a question about how representative the LGAF sample of countries is. There is likely to be an element of self-selection because of the demanding nature of the task and a degree of bias towards those countries in which the World Bank, FAO, or bilateral donors have been active in land projects, such as systematic first registration and the creation of cadastres. In addition the LGAF analyses were not all undertaken at a single point in time, so there is a danger that the strength of some possible associations could be undermined by policy changes that have taken place between the date when the LGAF was completed and that when the data from other sources used were compiled. Caution is therefore needed in interpreting the results.

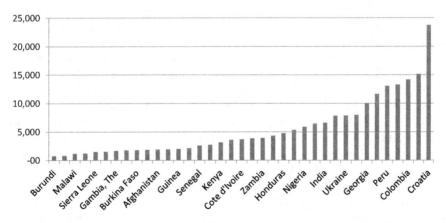

Figure 1.1 Gross Domestic Product per capita in terms of International Dollar Purchasing Power Parity, 2016

Source: World Bank Development Indicators, http://databank.worldbank.org/data/reports.aspx?source=world-development-indicators#.

Alternative compulsory purchase models

Many of the LGAF countries were at one time colonies of European powers. The characteristic legacy from colonialism was a dualistic land law in which colonial written law was superimposed on customary law and practice. Tchawa et al. (2012), with specific reference to the former French colonies of Central Africa, state that "The inability of these [colonial] policies to take local realities into consideration has led to the emergence of multiple systems that duplicate or neutralise each other" (2012, p. 29). The colonial era policy instruments often survived but were applied in ways which were rigid, inapplicable, and ineffective, or the capacity to realise them was lacking. The result could be an amalgam of customary rules, with heavy statutory overlay and confrontation between customary and statutory tenure. Such a dual system was characteristic of Ghana, Nigeria, Tanzania, and Zambia (Bugri, 2012; Adeniyi, 2013; Tenga and Mramba, 2015; Mulolwa, 2016).

The newly independent countries were offered an alternative approach to land management, namely that offered by the Soviet Union. These ideas were spread, amongst other means, by the training of cadres in universities in the USSR and satellite countries like Bulgaria. Central to Communist philosophy was the concept of collective ownership of the means of production, which in practice meant the nationalisation of land. The Second All-Russian Congress of Soviets in 1917 issued a decree on land, which made all land in the Soviet Union the property of the state. The 1936 Federal Constitution placed an absolute prohibition on civil transactions relating to land. The 1936 Soviet Constitution was extended to Estonia, Latvia, Lithuania, Moldova, and Eastern Poland after their annexation in 1940 and became the inspiration for the constitutions and legal structures put in place by the Communist governments of Central and Eastern Europe after they came to power between 1946 and 1949. There were variations between Communist countries, but, in the Soviet system, the tenure rights that existed permitted the tillage of the land and the erection of buildings, with state bodies having rights of operational management.

Compulsory purchase as such could not take place as private property rights capable of being expropriated no longer existed. Rather, the state could withdraw, resume, or reallocate the occupancy or use rights that it had allocated. The withdrawal of land occupancy could result in losses for which compensation was payable, assessed by a commission. However, compensation was generally not paid by the state but by the body to whom the land was transferred (Vondracek, 1975). In other words, the beneficiary directly compensated the loser rather than the state compensating the loser on behalf of society. Losses that could be compensated included the value of expropriated buildings and crops, the costs of reinstatement at another location, the costs of tillage and improvements for which revenue had not been received, and damage to other buildings as a result of the expropriation.

In some newly independent countries, for instance, Burundi and Cameroon, the state was seen as the custodian of land, with the right to manage land resources in the interests of economic and social development. In others, for instance, the Democratic Republic of Congo, a 1972 law granted the state exclusive and inalienable ownership of the land (Tchawa et al., 2012). In Tanzania, after independence in 1961, freehold titles were converted into government leases in 1963 and into granted rights of occupancy in 1969, with all land becoming public land under the trusteeship of the President (Tengo and Mramba, 2015). In Nigeria the Land Use Act, incorporated into the constitution in 1979, vested the management of land with state governors, with ownership being replaced by rights of statutory and customary occupancy (Adeniyi, 2013). In Uganda the 1975 Land Reform Decree declared all land to be public land vested in the state and abolished freeholds and the private estates created for traditional rulers under colonialism, though the 1995 constitution restored land tenures to the position at the time of independence (Obaikol, 2014). Ethiopia's Derg, which ruled between 1974 and 1987, nationalised rural and urban land in 1975 (Gebrewold, 2016).

In recent years expropriation policy has been influenced by two trends. First, the fall of the Berlin Wall in 1989, the collapse of the Eastern European Communist regimes, and the disintegration of the USSR removed exemplars of the Soviet model of expropriation and opened up their property markets to private ownership. This has not followed a universal pattern. Generally, apartments were transferred to their residents either without payment or at a nominal price. Restitution in a number of countries, but not Russia or Poland, has seen the restoration of property expropriated during the Communist period to its owners or their heirs. The land in state and collective farms in Moldova and Ukraine was distributed to their workers, and in Georgia leaseholders could buy the agricultural land they had been occupying from the state at a multiple of its land tax (Egiashvili, 2011; Muliar et al., 2014; World Bank, 2014). The 1987 and 1993 Land Laws in Vietnam reallocated co-operative land to farmer households for long-term use (Vo and Thang, 2013). For officials who grew up under the Soviet system, it can be difficult to adjust to the notion that private owners have to be compensated for the loss of properties over which the state previously had an unfettered right to determine their use.

Second, development banks, international agencies, and bilateral donors have come to adopt a more human rights-orientated approach to expropriation. The Benthamite idea of welfare being the greatest happiness of the greatest number has been replaced by a more Pareto-inspired approach: an increase in welfare can only unambiguously be considered to have occurred when one person is better off in his own estimation, and no one is made worse off. The Hicks-Kaldor compensation test allows for the gainers to compensate the losers, and, if they are still better off, then welfare can be said to have increased. What this Pareto approach rules out is the idea that it is acceptable, for example, for communities in remote upland areas to be removed from their villages so that valleys can be dammed and flooded to produce cheap hydroelectric power that will benefit development.

Between 1970 and 1998 the World Bank is thought to have funded at least 120 projects that involved involuntary resettlement (World Bank, 1998). The adoption of policy OP 710 in 1998 and subsequently OP 4.12 signalled a change in lending policy. Proposals for World Bank funding of projects must now explicitly consider the risk of involuntary resettlement occurring and put in place mitigation measures where these are unavoidable, with the costs forming part of the project. In 1993 the World Bank created the Inspection Panel as an independent mechanism to receive complaints submitted by people suffering harm allegedly caused by World Bank projects. Approximately two-thirds of the cases investigated involved involuntary resettlement, particularly for power and other infrastructure projects (Inspection Panel, 2016). The main issues were failure to recognise risks in scoping a project, livelihood restoration, inadequate consultation, and compensation.

A series of international agreements and declarations to which most governments have signed up have set a framework for expropriation policies and practices. The Universal Declaration of Human Rights (United Nations, 1948) in Article 17 states that everyone has the right to own property and no one shall be arbitrarily deprived of this, and Article 12 says that no one shall be subject to arbitrary interference with their privacy, family, and home. These ideas have been incorporated into regional human rights conventions, which, unlike the Universal Declaration, may offer opportunities for litigation against breaches. For instance, the European Convention on Human Rights,[3] which is binding on the members of the Council of Europe, in Article 1 of Protocol 1 (Council of Europe, 1952) states that every natural or legal person is entitled to the peaceful enjoyment of his possessions and that no one shall be deprived of his or her possessions except in the public interest, as provided for by law and in accordance with the principles of international law. Case law has constrained these powers so that there must be a proportionate balance between the general benefit and the losses to an individual, and these losses should be fairly and promptly compensated (Allen, 2005).

The ideas contained in the various international agreements and declarations have been brought together in the VGGT (Committee on World Food Security, 2012). Section 16 is concerned with expropriation and includes principles such as expropriation only for a public purpose defined in law, respect for all legitimate tenure right holders, that planning and processes for expropriation should be transparent and participatory, that there should be fair valuation and prompt compensation, and that evictions and relocations should not result in individuals being rendered homeless or vulnerable to the violation of human rights. The VGGT has established a framework against which expropriation policies and practices should be assessed and has been incorporated into LGAF.

The process of expropriation

There are two groups of indicators in the LGAF that look specifically at expropriation (World Bank, 2013): those in Land Governance Indicator (LGI) 4.2 consider the justification for and time-efficiency of expropriation, and those in LGI 4.3 examine the transparency and fairness of acquisition procedures and the compensation paid.

If state capture occurs, there is the danger that private interests may use the state's powers of expropriation for their own ends, including the theft of land from citizens and to further their private business interests. If expropriated land is subsequently transferred to private owners, expropriation may fail to serve a public purpose. LGI 4.2.1 asks whether there is minimal transfer of acquired land to private interests, with a score of A being given if less than 10 per cent of the land expropriated in the past three years is used for private purposes, B if between 10 and 30 per cent, C if between 30 and 50 per cent, and D if more than 50 per cent. LGI 13i from the LGAFs carried out up to 2013 is a similar indicator. Figure 1.2 shows that for the majority of countries transfers of land from the public sector to the private sector are minimal, with 22 of the 34 countries for which there is data reporting that less than 10 per cent of the land expropriated in the last three years was used for private purposes.

Limitations on the transfer of expropriated land to private interests do not apply in all cases. In Brazil the transfers to private interests were guided by social policy being transferred to land reform settlements and thence to the landless (World Bank, 2014a). In Ethiopia expropriation can be for public purposes in the widest sense, meaning with no visible limit to the state's power of expropriation. This can include transferring land from one person to another, providing the latter would put it to a better use. For instance, if a new road is constructed, the city can demand that landowners upgrade their buildings in accordance with the master plan, or the land will be transferred to those who can afford to. Although private property is guaranteed by the constitution, property is defined as being any tangible or intangible product that has value and is produced by labour, creativity, enterprise, or capital. Since these cannot create land, land cannot be considered to be private property. The implication is that the state can reallocate land use rights for the land that it owns, though it should pay compensation for improvements made to the land by labour, skill, and capital, including crops and buildings (Gebrewold, 2016). In Ukraine buildings were privatised, but the land under them remained the property of the state. There have been cases in which land

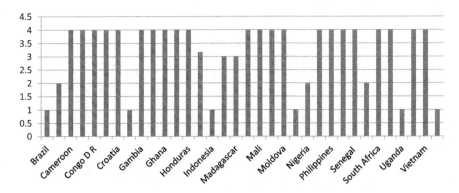

Figure 1.2 Transfers of public land to private interests after expropriation
Source: LGAF.

Note: A = 4, B = 3, C = 2, and D = 1. Countries for which there are no data have been excluded. The figure for India is the average for the six states for which LGAF has been undertaken.

plots allocated to a private party for perpetual use have been expropriated in the name of "public" good and transferred to another private user, and of lease agreements on public lands being cancelled so that the land can be transferred to a private party (Muliar et al., 2014). In India expropriation is used to obtain a "clean" title to land for uses that are not strictly for public purposes and, if clearer records existed, would have been better handled by direct negotiations (World Bank, 2015).

In Nigeria land expropriated for residential purposes frequently ends up in private hands, and the share of agricultural lands acquired by commercial farmers and developers appears to be increasing.

> Indeed, the general view of Nigerians is that expropriation is unfair; it is seen as an example of dispossessing the poor to elevate the rich, since in most cases lands expropriated from lower income groups are allocated to wealthier interests.
>
> *(Adeniyi, 2013)*

In Uganda too it is reported that expropriations are mainly for private interests (Obaikol, 2014). Limitations on transfers of land to private interests can be counterproductive. Transfers to the private sector can result in public facilities, such as for education, healthcare, or recreation, being created, as has been the case in Rwanda (Ngoga et al., 2017).

If the state expropriates land that is then left unused for an undue period, this results in further economic costs in addition to the losses suffered by those whose property was compulsorily acquired. This can happen, for instance, if the project for which the land was taken is delayed or postponed due to lack of finance. LGI 4.2.2 examines whether the acquired land is transferred to its destined use in a timely manner, with a score of A being given where more than 70 per cent of the land expropriated in the past three years has been transferred to its destined use, B where between 50 and 70 per cent, C where between 30 and 50 per cent, and D if less than 30 per cent. This indicator is similar to LGI 13ii, used up to 2013. Figure 1.3 shows that for the majority of countries transfers of expropriated land take place in a timely manner, with 26 out of 34 countries reporting that over 70 per cent of the land expropriated in the past three years had been transferred to its destined use.

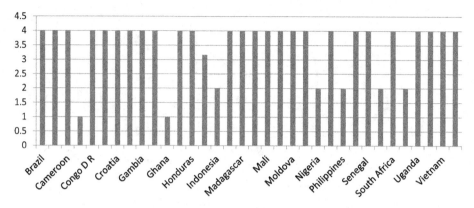

Figure 1.3 Whether land is transferred to its destined use in a timely manner
Source: LGAF.

Note: see Figure 1.1.

Although land may have been transferred to its intended use, there can still be delays in developing that use. For instance, in Ethiopia it is reported that lack of infrastructure, shortage of capital and lack of credit facility, and speculations on the part of the developers can delay development (Gebrewold, 2016). In Ghana the compulsory acquisition of land places a duty on any government agency to have money for compensation. However, only 58 of 713 sites acquired and occupied in the Central Region were fully occupied, with compensation paid and lands fully utilised, whereas in a further 11 cases, sites were fully acquired and compensation paid, though not fully utilised. Excessive land would appear to have been compulsorily acquired that could not be transferred to its intended uses in a timely manner or paid compensation because of lack of resources (Bugri, 2012). In a study of the expropriation laws in 30 emerging economies (15 in Africa and 15 in Asia), Tagliarino (2016) found that 13 of the countries either fully or partially grant reacquisition rights for those whose land is no longer needed for a public purpose, but 17 countries did not, leading, he argues, to a potential risk that excessive land may be expropriated. In Nigeria some lands purchased by the government to curb speculation remain unused for so long that some former owners resell the land to unsuspecting buyers, and expropriated owners who have not received compensation resume occupation of their plots (Adeniyi, 2013).

A key part of the expropriation process is whether the acquiring authority consults with those affected, with the aim of minimising the disruption caused them. If it does not do so, then the process is effectively one of involuntary resettlement. LGAF does not explore this in its indicators. However, Tagliarino (2016) found that in 24 of the 30 countries whose law he examined there was no legal requirement on the government to identify all affected populations prior to expropriation. Although all the countries had laws requiring governments to give notice to affected populations prior to expropriation, only 13 of the 30 required governments to provide information about the expropriation plan, including the reasons for it, and 16 did not require governments to provide any information about the reasons for expropriation. In 17 of the 30 countries there was no legal obligation on governments to undertake public consultations with the affected populations. In just three of the countries whose laws he surveyed (India, Indonesia, and Vietnam) was there a requirement to identify those affected, to inform them about the expropriation, and to consult with them. In four other countries (Burkina Faso, Cambodia, Rwanda, and Tanzania) governments were obliged by law to inform the affected populations and consult with them. As Tagliarino notes, "Consulting the public and affected populations prior to expropriation can benefit governments by generating information that enables socially equitable expropriation decisions" (2016, p. 15).

LGI 4.3.4 examines whether there are independent and accessible avenues for appeal against acquisition. A score of A is given if such independent avenues exist and are easily accessible; B means that they exist, but there are restrictions on their accessibility so that they are only available to the wealthy and those with middle incomes; C means that the avenues are only "somewhat independent and may or may not be accessible to those affected"; and D means that the avenues to lodge a complaint are not independent. LGI 14iv from the LGAFs undertaken up to 2013 is a similar indicator. The pattern here is mixed with 9 of the 36 countries providing independent appeal mechanisms that are accessible and 9 without any independent avenues in which to lodge a complaint. The key is whether such avenues are genuinely accessible rather than being formally provided for in law. Tagliarino (2016) found that 28 out of 30 countries he surveyed had laws that enabled affected populations to challenge compensation in court and through a tribunal, and 21 permitted affected populations to negotiate compensation levels with acquiring authorities.

LGI 4.3.5 examines whether timely decisions are made regarding complaints. For decisions to be timely, they need to be made through a mechanism of first instance, such as a complaint to the acquiring authority, rather than being taken through the courts. Only once the remedies of first instance have been exhausted should cases proceed through the judicial system. If complaints are not dealt with promptly, then this acts as a break on those who are aggrieved by the act of expropriation or the level of compensation being able to pursue the matter by other means. In particular, taking a case before the courts requires resources, whereas making a complaint through a process of first instance appeal requires less means. To be effective, an avenue of first instance must process complaints promptly so that the complainant is either satisfied, can decide whether to drop the case, or pursue it before the courts. Delays are likely to have adverse repercussions on the ability of those affected by expropriation being able to maintain their living standards or status. A score of A is awarded when a first instance decision has been reached for more than 80 per cent of complaints during the last three years; B where the proportion is between 50 and 80 per cent; C where the proportion is between 30 and 50 per cent; and D where less than 30 per cent of complaints are

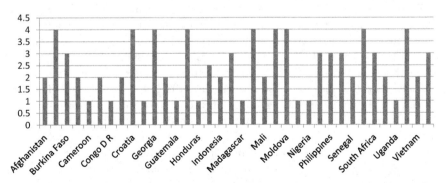

Figure 1.4 The independence and accessibility of appeal mechanisms
Source: LGAF.

Note: see Figure 1.1.

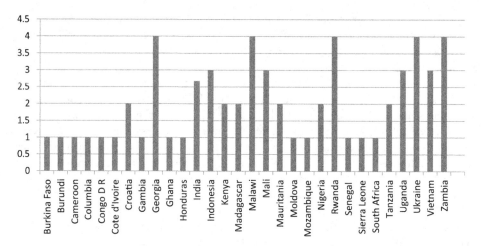

Figure 1.5 Speed with which complaints about expropriation are dealt with by avenues of first instance decisions

Source: LGAF.

Note: see Figure 1.1.

determined within three years. LGI 14v is a similar indicator for the LGAFs carried out up to 2013. The pattern here is that responses to complaints are slow with avenues of first instance complaints disposing of more than 80 per cent of complaints within three years in only 5 out of 31 countries and 13 countries determining less than 30 per cent of complaints during this period. Figures 1.4 and 1.5 indicate that public bodies are generally not very responsive to complaints about expropriation. This could create an atmosphere of impunity in which officials are not held to account for their decisions.

Compensation

LGI 4.3.1 considers whether fair compensation that allows for the maintenance of previous social and economic status is paid in either cash or kind to all those with rights in the expropriated land, regardless of the registration status of the property. The rights under consideration include both ownership and use and access rights. Given how limited the registration of land rights is in many emerging economies, it is important that the loss of unregistered rights is compensated if those affected are not to experience a significant loss of livelihoods. The rights that are compensated have to go beyond those of ownership if there is to be protection of the livelihoods and social status of tenants and other occupiers, those who periodically or occasionally access the land, and those with customary rights of various kinds. The complex livelihoods of the poor can involve gaining entry to land owned or occupied by others for specific purposes, such as gathering or hunting. Nomadic pastoralists and hunter-gatherers may access land seasonally or periodically to exploit natural resources at times when these are abundant. These can be important rights in support of livelihoods, and the exercise of them may be through long usage or custom rather than a registered encumbrance. The implication behind this indicator is that compensation should also include meeting disturbance costs; otherwise the maintenance of economic status could be imperilled. It also explicitly notes that compensation should enable social status to be maintained, implying that compensation is not just about economics.

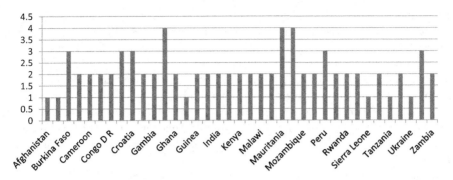

Figure 1.6   Compensation for loss of rights
Source: LGAF.

Note: see Figure 1.1.

A score of A is given where fair compensation that allows for maintenance of social and economic status is paid to all those with rights in the expropriated land, regardless of registration status; B where the level of compensation paid for rights that are not registered does not allow for the maintenance of social and economic status; C where compensation is paid for some unregistered rights, such as to those in possession or occupation, but not for others, such as grazing, access, and gathering; and D where no compensation is paid to those with unregistered rights, such as use or occupancy. In the LGAF carried out up to 2013 indicator LGI 14ii was similar. Figure 1.6 shows that the typical situation is for some unregistered rights to be compensated but not all, though with the level of compensation is below what is needed to maintain the previous economic or social status.

Tagliarino (2016) found that in 18 of the 30 countries whose laws he surveyed, customary tenure holders with formally recognised rights were entitled to compensation. In 21 countries those without formally recognised tenure rights were not, and in 19 countries the users of undeveloped land used for purposes such as hunting and grazing were not entitled to compensation. It has been estimated that 90 per cent of rural lands in sub-Saharan Africa are unregistered (Byamugisha, 2013). In Ethiopia rural land is usually registered, but in peri-urban areas farmers may sell their land informally, and the buyers consequently may not receive compensation, should the government expropriate the land for urban expansion (Gebrewold, 2016). In Rwanda compensation is limited to registered rights and so excludes unregistered ones, such as the renting of a house, grazing, or fishing, compensation for which is the responsibility of the registered rights holder (Ngoga et al., 2017). In Zambia unrecorded rights, such as grazing and gathering of forest products, may not be compensated. Thus the loss of grazing rights due to the establishment of lodges along the lower Zambezi was not compensated, and in Kalimbila village, houses were rebuilt by the mining company, but grazing land fenced off for mine use was not compensated (Mulowa, 2016). In Uganda there have been issues with owners of customary land being compensated for improvements and developments but not for the land itself, even though the tenure is a statutory one, and perennial crops and fruit tress being compensated on a one-season basis rather than the value being capitalised. Problems have been encountered in identifying who should be compensated for the loss of common land or the form of collective compensation, though some communities have secured compensation in the form of boreholes and schools. There have also been examples of the diversion of roads through swamps to avoid the need to pay compensation (Obaikol, 2014). In South Africa there have been the issues of the rights of farm workers and preventing farm evictions (Urban LandMark, 2013). In Georgia, where expropriation has been limited since 1997 to "urgent public needs", and only courts can make decisions on expropriations, there have been concerns about illegal expropriations in tourist zones or areas of cultural heritage without compensation (Egiashvili, 2011). In the Philippines the issue has been the uneven application of compensation resulting in unfairness. National infrastructure projects and those with foreign donors have resettlement action plans and upfront payment of compensation based on market values, but for other projects there is no legal basis for such plans to be prepared or for adequate compensation to be paid (Eleazor et al., 2013).

LGI 4.3.2 examines whether there is compensation for loss of selective rights due to land use changes. In many cases rezoning and changes in the permitted land uses benefit owners by enabling them to convert their land to a more valuable use: for instance from farming to housing. However, this can lead to the removal of those occupying the land or with customary rights over it to make way for development (Devine, 2017; Loperena, 2017). In some cases land use changes may restrict the range of uses to which the land can be put, which can even mean that the land is incapable of beneficial use. For instance, this can happen if an area is designated as a national park or a nature reserve. Those with rights over the land may find that some of these are extinguished, such as hunting, or that they suffer increased losses, for instance from animal predation of crops or livestock from wildlife trespass, or face greater competition with wildlife for scarce grazing or water (Derman, 1995; Spence, 1999; Kantor, 2007; Goldstein, 2013). Although there may have been no loss of land, the rights over it are diminished or constrained in a way that reduces incomes or increases production costs. In effect, some of the rights over land have been expropriated, even if the land itself has not been taken.

The state may also appropriate certain rights, such as mineral or water rights, or grant way leaves that impose costs or restrictions on use, such as pipelines and transmission lines. In Uganda it is reported that the loss of surface rights is compensated but not damage to these caused by the exploitation of sub-surface rights vested in the state (Obaikol, 2014). In some cases, the right to peaceful occupancy will be removed through, for instance, the construction of major infrastructure, like a motorway in close proximity to housing. An equitable system should provide fair compensation in such cases, even where no land is taken. The compensation could, in principle, include mitigation works, for instance noise barriers or animal-proof fencing, or transfers of rights to other land where activities are not restricted rather than a cash payment. A score of A is given where the loss of rights as a result of a land use change is compensated in cash or kind so that people have comparable assets and can continue to maintain prior social and economic status, B means that the compensation results in people having comparable assets but that they cannot continue to maintain prior social and economic status, C means that compensation does not provide people with either comparable assets or the maintenance of prior social and economic status, and D means that no compensation is paid. LGI 2vi is a comparable indicator in the LGAFs carried out before 2013. Figure 1.7 shows that in 16 out of 37 countries no compensation is paid for the loss of rights due to land use changes, with 12 countries providing comparable assets but not necessarily maintaining prior social and economic status.

It is one thing for legislation to require compensation to be provided; it is quite another for it actually to be paid and paid promptly. For this the state must have cash reserves or a land bank from which alternative land can be offered. Without full compensation, those who are dispossessed of their property will be unable to acquire replacement assets, thus

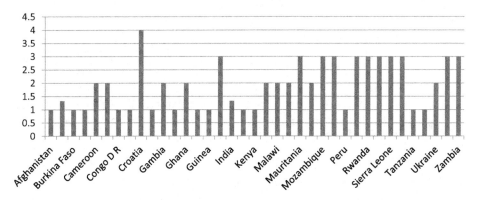

Figure 1.7 Compensation for loss of rights due to land use change
Source: LGAF.

Note: see Figure 1.1.

threatening their livelihoods and social status. LGI 4.3.3 examines whether compensation is paid promptly. A score of A is awarded if more than 90 per cent of expropriated landowners receive compensation within one year, B is awarded where between 70 and 90 per cent of owners receive such compensation, C is awarded if between 50 and 70 per cent of owners do, and D is awarded where less than 50 per cent of landowners receive compensation within one year. Indicator 14 iii from the LGAFs undertaken up to 2013 is a similar indicator. Tagliarino (2016) found that in 16 of the 30 countries he studied, governments are legally required to pay compensation prior to taking possession of land or within a specified time frame, with only seven not establishing time constraints. However, Figure 1.8 shows that most countries are slow in paying compensation to those dispossessed, with 21 out of 37 countries paying compensation to less than 50 per cent of landowners within a year and just 6 paying over 90 per cent of landowners within one year. These figures point to expropriation tending to result in displacement rather than resettlement and to compulsory acquisition being a cause of impoverishment.

In Ethiopia landowners served with expropriation orders must hand over the land within 90 days of the date of payment of compensation, or 30 days, if there is no crop or other property on the land, but the law says nothing about the date of valuation, the payment of compensation, or interest payments if the payment is not made within a reasonable period of time (Gebrewold, 2016). There are government agencies that refuse to pay compensation for no apparent reason, and small towns are reluctant to pay compensation on the grounds of lack of financial capacity. In Rwanda, delays in paying compensation are reported to be due to haste to implement master plan projects, such as the construction of new embassies, a new stadium, or a national airport, combined with limited financial capacity, poor planning, and weak coordination between government institutions (Ngoga et al., 2017). In Tanzania interest is payable on late compensation payments, but the government does not abide by the law (Tengo and Mramba, 2015). By contrast, in Zambia, there is prompt payment of compensation once consensus is reached to avoid changes in political and local opinion (Mulolwa, 2016). In Buliisa, Uganda, Total wanted to get a reputable institution to pay compensation and bypass the government. Perhaps unsurprisingly, the government was not supportive (Obaikol, 2014). These examples suggest that the promptness of compensation payments may

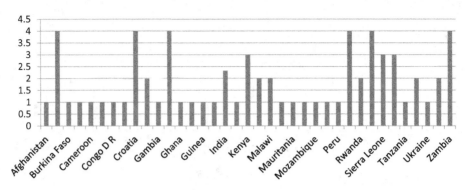

Figure 1.8   Promptness of compensation payments
Source: LGAF.

Note: see Figure 1.1

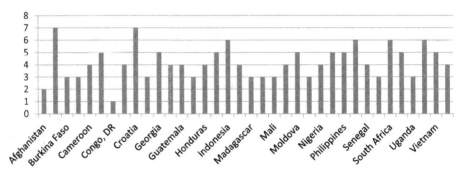

Figure 1.9   The strength of social safety nets
Source: BTI 2016.

depend on who is actually paying the compensation, with foreign private companies being willing to make speedy payments.

The concern is that delays in payment of compensation or the failure to recognise all unregistered property rights as eligible for compensation are likely to result in the impoverishment of those affected by expropriation. Every two years Bertelsmann Stiftung undertakes an assessment of emerging and transition economies for its Bertelsmann Transformation Index (BTI). Evaluation is undertaken on a variety of criteria by expert panels, with a grade being given for each between 10 (excellence) and 1 (poor) (Bertelsman, 2016). Question 10.1 examines the extent to which social safety nets provide compensation for social risks. The results for the LGAF countries for which there are data are shown in Figure 1.9. A score of 4 means that social safety nets are rudimentary and cover only a few risks for a limited number of beneficiaries so that the majority of the population is at risk of poverty. Some 22 of the 36 countries were given a score of 4 or less. Of these 14 were recorded by LGAF as having less than 50 per cent of landowners receiving compensation within one year, and 20 did not fully or did not at all pay compensation of unregistered rights. Only two countries were recorded by the BTI as having a score of 7, meaning that although social safety nets were well-developed, they did not cover all risks for all strata of the population, and so a significant part is at risk of poverty. The implication is that failure to provide adequate compensation for expropriation is not offset by other social safety nets, and so impoverishment is a likely consequence. Expropriation in many countries is involuntary displacement rather than a process of compulsory purchase enabling those affected to acquire replacement assets.

Influences on expropriation policy

The LGAF analyses point to the normal situation in developing countries being for compensation to be paid for the loss of certain rights over land but not others, particularly unregistered rights; for the compensation to be paid below that needed to maintain the economic and social status of those who have land rights expropriated; and for compensation to take a long time to be paid. Only a minority of countries provide an independent and accessible appeal mechanism, and complaints about expropriation are not dealt with promptly by avenues of first instance. By contrast, expropriation appears generally to be used for public purposes rather than to enable land to be transferred to private interests and used for the intended purpose within a reasonable period of time. As there are varied responses from different countries, it raises the question as to whether it is possible to identify the factors that may influence a country's expropriation policy.

It might be expected that there would be issues in the payment of compensation where property rights are poorly protected. Question 9.1 of the BTI examines the strength of property rights. A score of 10 is given where "property rights and regulations on acquisition, benefits, use and sale are well defined and enforced", with property rights being "limited, solely and rarely, by overriding rights of constitutionally defined public interest", and a score of 1 is given where property rights are not defined in law, and private property is not protected. The scores for the countries with LGAF assessments are shown in Figure 1.10. A score of 7 means that property rights are regarded as being well defined, but occasionally there are problems with implementation and enforcement. Although only 10 of the countries had a score of 7 or better, just 6 had a score of 4 or less, meaning they were not safeguarded adequately by law against arbitrary state intervention or illegal infringements. There was no significant correlation between the strength of property rights and whether compensation is paid for all rights, regardless of registration status. This suggests that the issues with the fairness of compensation are not primarily due to an overall lack of protection for those property rights that are formally recognised but, rather, are due to which property rights are recognised.

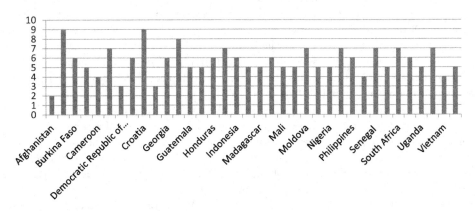

Figure 1.10   Strength of property rights
Source: BTI 2016.

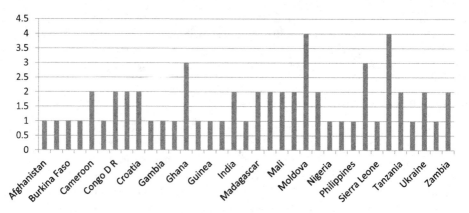

Figure 1.11　Whether registry information is up to date and reflects the reality on the ground
Source: LGAF.

Note: see Figure 1.1

Expropriation processes are unlikely to be fair or efficient if the public bodies responsible are unable to discover who possesses property rights over the land affected. For this to happen records of land rights in land registries and cadastres have to be accurate. LGI 6.3.2 poses the question as to whether the information in the land registry/cadastre is up to date, with a score of A being given if more than 90 per cent of the information they contain is up to date, B if between 70 and 90 per cent is, C if between 50 and 70 per cent is, and D if less than 50 per cent is. LGI 17ii for the LGAFs carried out up to 2013 gives similar information. Figure 1.11 shows that for most of the countries the information in the land registry/cadastre is seriously incomplete, with, for 18 out of 35 countries, it being reported that less than 50 per cent of the information was up to date and only two countries where over 90 per cent of the information was up to date.

In Croatia there are issues with incomplete and outdated entries in registers, and so there can be a difference between what is in the register and what exists on the ground. The recognition of rights in outdated entries can be a long and complex process due to multiple regulations sometimes applying (World Bank, 2016). In Uganda less than 25 per cent of rural areas have been mapped and registered, but 90 per cent of the population lives in them. Approximately 60 per cent of the urban population are slum dwellers living in informal settlements (Obaikol, 2014). In Nigeria registered lands account for only 3 per cent of the land mass and are mainly in urban areas. The land registration system is said to be in a parlous state, with most registries physically insecure (Adeniyi, 2013). Inaccuracies may reflect the fact that the process of systematic first registration is incomplete. In Moldova properties were registered after privatisation, but there has been a lack of systematic surveying of boundaries in rural areas or the delineation of public lands. Weaknesses can also be the result of failure to register property transfers and new construction. What may start off as a comprehensive register after systematic first registration can cease to reflect reality on the ground if these are not recorded. Not all countries require transfers of property rights to be registered. For instance, in Kazakhstan the transfer of land from the state to private ownership has to be registered but not transfers between private owners (McCluskey, 2016).

The World Bank's annual Doing Business survey (World Bank, 2018) examines various indicators of the efficiency of registering properties. It uses a case study of the transfer of a

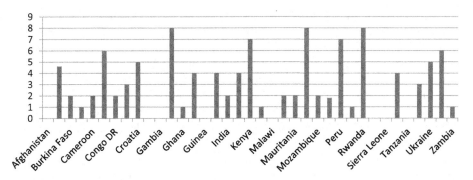

Figure 1.12 Reliability of registration infrastructure
Source: World Bank Doing Business.

warehouse with vacant possession between two domestic companies located in the largest business city. Figure 1.12 shows the results of the assessment of the reliability of registration infrastructure. Countries were scored on a scale of 0–8 on whether titles are kept in digital form, whether there is an electronic database for checking for encumbrances, whether maps of land plots are in digital form, whether there is a geographic information system for recording boundaries, whether the land registry and mapping data is linked, and whether immovable property is identified in a unique manner. Although countries like Georgia and Rwanda scored highly on this index, for most of the countries there are serious deficiencies in the quality of their land registration infrastructures. Byamugisha (2013) reports that 80 per cent of sub-Saharan and South Asian countries still have paper-based systems that are in deteriorating conditions, and 61 per cent of the rest of the world has electronic databases for encumbrances. The Doing Business survey also shows that the geographical coverage of land registries and mapping agencies in terms of the registration and mapping of private plots is poor for most of the countries. On a scale of 0–8, 27 of the 37 countries scored 0.

A possible influence on the accuracy of land registry and cadastre information is the cost of registering property transfers. If costs are high, this may discourage registration, particularly if an informal property market functions effectively without sellers needing to produce formal documentation and buyers being unwilling or unable to register their ownership. In Rwanda, in spite of systematic and sporadic registration, informal transactions were reported to still be taking place, with 32 per cent of transactions in rural areas being registered. A flat fee payment and a lack of awareness of the benefits of registration on the part of landowners appear to be barriers to registration (Ngoga et al., 2017). In Nigeria the costs of first registration are over 5 per cent of the value and include significant informal payments (Adeniyi, 2013). In the Philippines the informal payments needed to secure first-time titling are believed to act as a disincentive, and the cost of transfers is put at 10 per cent of the market value, which includes a capital gains tax at 6 per cent of assessed values and a stamp duty of 1.5 per cent (Eleazar et al., 2013).

The use of mortgages is likely to encourage the registration of property transfers as banks want to be able to register their claims over their collateral. High costs or difficulties in securing building consents can also undermine the accuracy of land registries/cadastres as the uses that they record may no longer be accurate. LGI 6.2.1 examines the cost of registering property. A score of A is given where the cost of registering property is less than 1 per cent of the property's value, B if it is between 1 and 2 per cent, C if it is between 2 and 5 per cent, and D if it is equal or greater than 5 per cent. LGI 18i for the LGAFs undertaken up to 2013 is a similar indicator. Figure 1.13 shows that 16 of the 36 countries have registration costs of at least 5 per cent of the property value and only in three a fee of not more than 2 per cent.

The complexity of procedures can discourage citizens from registering transactions, making land registries and cadastres inaccurate. Figure 1.14 shows the number of procedures required to register a property. There is a significant correlation between the LGAF score on compensation and the number of procedures required to register a property with a Kendall tau of 0.89 ($p < 0.001$), those countries having the least procedures to register a property being those with the more comprehensive payments of compensation.

The evidence suggests that weaknesses in terms of the quality and coverage of land registration and the mapping of private parcels, and the cost and complexity of securing the registration of transactions undermine the ability of countries to pay adequate compensation to those whose land is expropriated. Although there may be formal guarantees in place to protect property rights, such as constitutional rights, the reality behind the way in which they are recorded means that governments in many countries have imperfect information about who should be entitled to receive compensation for the expropriation of their land rights and what those land rights are.

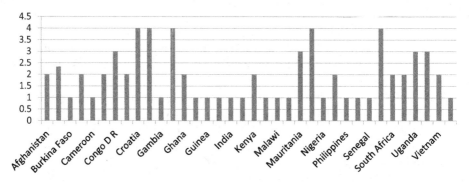

Figure 1.13   The cost of registering a property transfer
Source: LGAF.

Note: see Figure 1.1.

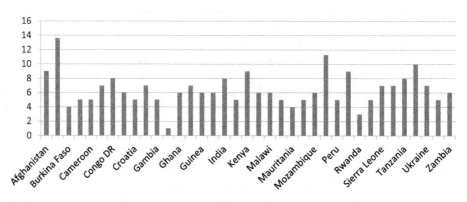

Figure 1.14   Number of procedures required to register a property
Source: World Bank Doing Business.

Influences on compensation policy

It is plausible that compensation is paid promptly when there are independent and accessible avenues of appeal against expropriation. This implies that those with a grievance against the way in which compensation is paid can seek redress. Table 1.1 shows that there is a significant relationship between there being an independent and accessible appeal mechanism and the promptness with which compensation is paid, with a gamma coefficient[4] of 0.46 ($p < 0.005$).

One reason for there to be delays in paying compensation could be corruption or abuse of office by officials, resulting in the compensation due to those whose land has been expropriated being diverted temporarily or permanently. Question 15.3 of the BTI raises the extent to which governments successfully contain corruption. Figure 1.15 shows the score attributed to each country's anti-corruption policies. The key scores are 4, which means that "the government is only partly willing and able to contain corruption", and 7, which indicates that "the government is often successful in containing corruption" with most integrity mechanisms in place "but with some functioning with only limited effectiveness". For 24 of the 36 countries for which there are data, the score awarded was 4 or less, with only 3 scored at 7 or better. The gamma coefficient of the relationship between the anti-corruption policy and the promptness with which compensation is paid is 0.43 ($p < 0.01$), indicating that corruption is likely to be a factor influencing the promptness with which compensation for expropriation is paid.

Question 3.3 of the BTI examines the extent to which public office holders who abuse their positions are prosecuted or penalised. The results are shown in Figure 1.16. A score of 4 means that "officeholders who break the law and engage in corruption are not adequately prosecuted, but occasionally attract adverse publicity". For 19 of the 36 countries for which there are data there was a score of 4 or less. A score of 7 means that "officeholders who break the law and engage in corruption generally are prosecuted … but occasionally slip through political, legal, or procedural loopholes". Only three of the countries achieved a score of 7 or better. The gamma coefficient of the relationship between prosecution for abuse of office and the promptness with which compensation is paid is 0.52 ($p < 0.005$). The statistically significant relationships between anti-corruption policies and prosecutions for the abuse of office, and the promptness with which compensation is paid suggest that corruption and impunity enjoyed by officials is an important factor influencing whether compensation is paid in a timely manner. The levels of the gamma coefficients, though, indicate that there are also other factors involved.

Table 1.1 The Relationship between Avenues of Independent Appeals and the Promptness with which Compensation Is Paid

	Acquired Owners Are Compensated Promptly				
Independent and Accessible Avenues for Appeal in Acquisition	*D*	*C*	*B*	*A*	*Total*
D	7	2	0	0	9
C	8	2	0	1	11
B	2	1	2	2	7
A	4	1	1	3	9
Total	21	6	3	6	36

Source: LGAF.

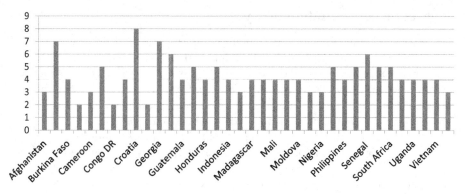

Figure 1.15   Anti-corruption policy

Source: BTI 2016.

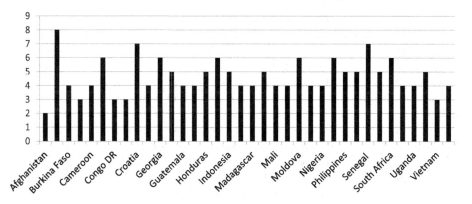

Figure 1.16   The likelihood of prosecution for abuse of office

Source: BTI 2016.

Even where corruption is not a problem in government, inefficiency could still undermine compensation for expropriation. Figure 1.17 uses data from Question 14.2 of the BTI to examine the implementation of policy. The formulation of policy can be good, but if the implementation is poor then policies will be ineffective. A score of 4 means that the government fails to implement *many* of its policies, whereas one of 7 means that it fails to implement *some* of its policies. Some 10 out of 36 LGAF countries, including 7 who failed to compensate at least 50 per cent of landowners within one year, were given a score of 4 or less.

A further potential influence on compensation for expropriation is the efficiency with which property valuations are carried out. Efficient valuations require qualified and experienced valuers who are able to undertake valuations based on market values in accordance with international valuation standards and working within appropriate ethical codes and codes of practice. LGAF does not contain any information about valuation for expropriation but does contain information about the efficiency with which properties are valued for property taxation. If governments have the capacity to base property tax assessments on market values, then they should also be able to assess compensation for expropriation on the same basis. However, if property tax assessments are not based on market values or are not regularly

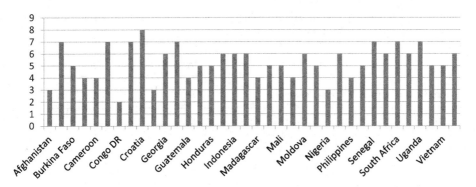

Figure 1.17   The effectiveness with which policies are implemented

Source: BTI 2016.

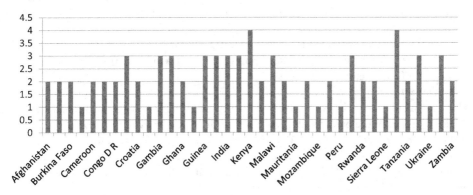

Figure 1.18   The quality of property tax valuations

Source: LGAF.

Note: see Figure 1.1

updated to reflect current market conditions, then it is unlikely that governments have the capacity to value properties for expropriation purposes in a way that would enable the compensation paid to maintain the economic and social status of those losing their land rights.

LGI 7.7.1 examines whether there is a clear process of property valuation for taxation purposes. A score of A is awarded where assessments for tax purposes are based on market values, with minimal differences between recorded values and market prices across different types of users, and where the valuation rolls are regularly updated; B is awarded where tax assessments are based on market prices, but there are significant differences between recorded values and market prices across different users, or valuation rolls are not regularly updated; C means that there is some relationship between tax assessments and market prices, but there are significant differences between recorded values and market prices across different uses or types of users, and valuation rolls are not updated; and D means tax assessments are not clearly based on market prices. LGI 10i for the LGAF assessments made up to 2013 is a similar indicator. Figure 1.18 shows that just 2 of the 37 countries achieved a score of A, whereas 8 were scored at D. It suggests that for the majority of countries, valuation capacity is only developed to a limited extent and that there are significant

Table 1.2 The Relationship between the Valuation Process and the Promptness with Which Compensation Is Paid

There Is a Clear Process of Property Valuation		Acquired Owners Are Compensated Promptly				
		D	*C*	*B*	*A*	*Total*
	D	6	1	1	0	8
	C	10	2	0	1	16
	B	5	4	0	2	11
	A	0	2	0	3	2
	Total	21	9	1	6	37

Source: LGAF and BTI 2016.

differences between tax assessments and market prices. There is a relationship between the quality of property tax valuations and the promptness with which compensation is paid, with a gamma coefficient of 0.34 ($p < 0.05$) Table 1.2. There appears to be an association between the inability to value properties for taxation based on market values and deficiencies in compensation for expropriation, pointing to a lack of valuation capacity as one of the factors affecting compensation.

A problem found across many developing countries is the shortage of qualified valuers, which is linked to few formal university training programmes and difficulties in retaining qualified valuers in the public sector due to the differences between their earnings and those in the private sector (McCluskey et al., 2017). In transition countries valuers may be highly qualified in construction but have limited training in valuation, economics, or finance, resulting in reliance on cost-based methods of valuation rather than on sales or income-based approaches. In Uganda it is reported that 95 per cent of districts do not employ valuers (Obaikol, 2014). In Nigeria the dearth of professional valuers means that most states rely on non-professionals for property valuations (Adeniyi, 2013).

In Rwanda a valuation profession was only established in 2010. Previously the central bank had registered as valuers anyone who applied who had a degree in civil engineering, architecture, or construction. The Institute of Real Property Valuers has improved capacity, but some registered valuers are reported to struggle with valuation methods. Reference prices for land are still being used, although the use of market prices was provided for in a 2010 law. Poor landowners cannot afford valuation fees, which results in them receiving unfair compensation (Ngoga et al., 2017). A USAID study found that there were arbitrary differences in compensation paid that could not be explained in terms of the characteristics of the properties but appeared to reflect the expropriating body. It argued that there was a need for valuers to be properly insulated from external pressures from expropriating bodies to artificially reduce land and other property values (Legal Aid Forum, 2015). In Ukraine, compensation for expropriation was based on normative values rather than on market prices, with evidence of some manipulation of these in order to acquire land at a fraction of the market price (Muliar et al., 2014). In Ethiopia,

One of the common problems experienced in the country is lack of full public participation and the secrecy involved in the determination of property values for compensation and other purposes. Property owners /holders, especially those living in rural areas are usually powerless, with inadequate sources of information, and without access to unbiased valuation organizations.

(Gebrewold, 2016, p. 110)

Valuation committee members are not professionals, and valuation workings and property values are kept secret. If property owners object or disagree, government agents often threaten them for obstructing public development and for acting against "public purpose".

A potential solution to the shortage of valuers is to make use of mass valuation methods to generate values for expropriation, as is done in Slovenia (Žibrik, 2016). This is not without difficulties. For instance, Moldova developed a system of mass valuation based on market values between 2004 and 2012, but this has not been applied to rural housing or agricultural land as systematic registration has not been undertaken in rural areas. Problems were encountered in identifying accurate price data due to capital gains tax being levied on the difference between a base price and the sale price, leading to the base price being reported on registration as the transaction price rather than the true figure (Buzu, 2016).

Influences on appeals policies

If those whose land is being expropriated have access to independent appeals processes that provide prompt remedies, this is likely to result in problems with expropriation and compensation being minimised. If, however, such avenues are not independent, are difficult to access, or take undue time to adjudicate, this can provide an environment in which officials can act with impunity, and corrupt practices can flourish.

The data from BTI Question 15.3 on the extent to which governments successfully contain corruption are used in Table 1.3 to examine whether there is a significant relationship between a country having an independent and accessible expropriation appeals mechanism and a country having an effective anti-corruption policy. The correlation between an effective anti-corruption policy and an independent and accessible appeals mechanism is

Table 1.3 The Relationship between Independent Expropriation Appeals Avenues and Anti-Corruption Policies

Number of Countries		Independent and Accessible Avenues for Appeal in Acquisition				
		D	C	B	A	Total
Anti-corruption policy	2	1	1	0	0	2
	3	3	1	1	0	5
	4	4	4	2	3	13
	5	0	2	3	2	7
	6	0	2	0	0	2
	7	0	0	0	2	2
	Total	8	10	6	7	31

Source: LGAF and BTI 2016.

significant, resulting in a gamma coefficient of 0.52 ($p < 0.005$). Of the 23 countries with a score of 4 on the BTI assessment of anti-corruption policies (meaning that the government is only partly willing and able to control corruption and ineffective integrity mechanisms are ineffective), just four were regarded by LGAF as having independent appeals avenues that are easily accessible. The size of the gamma coefficient indicates that there are also other factors involved in determining whether appeals mechanisms are independent and accessible, but the absence of effective anti-corruption policies seems to influence this.

It is difficult to envisage how an independent and accessible expropriation appeals mechanism can function in countries where human rights, including freedom of expression, are under threat. Those who are adversely affected by expropriation may be too cowed to protest against inequities, and it is unlikely that the political elite, in these circumstances, will permit challenges to its authority to be made through independent appeals processes. Question 2.4 of the BTI raises the extent to which citizens, organisations, and the mass media can express opinions freely. Figure 1.19 shows the responses for the LGAF countries. A score of 4 means that "freedom of expression is often subject to interference or government restrictions", with distortion and manipulation shaping matters of public debate, whereas a score of 7 is given where "freedom of expression is occasionally subject to interference or government restrictions, but there are generally no incidents of blatant intrusions". Some 7 out of 36 LGAF countries had scores of 4 of less, but 16 had scores of 7 or better. There was a correlation between freedom of expression and independent and accessible avenues of appeal against expropriation decisions, with a gamma coefficient of 0.54 ($p < 0.001$).

BTI Question 3.4 examines the extent to which civil rights are guaranteed and protected, and the extent to which citizens can seek redress for violations of these. In other words, the extent to which civil rights are protected and state power is constrained by the rule of law. This is examined in Figure 1.20. The gamma coefficient between civil rights and an independent and accessible expropriation appeals avenue was 0.59 ($p < 0.01$).

It might be expected that if a country has an independent judiciary able to interpret and review laws and pursue its own reasoning free from political influence, this might result in independent appeals mechanisms against expropriation. However, the gamma coefficient between having independent and accessible expropriation avenues and having an independent judiciary as measured by BTI Question 3.2 is not statistically significant. This may be due to the interpretation of expropriation policies being the result of administrative decisions rather than being determined by the courts. The situation in Zambia provides some support

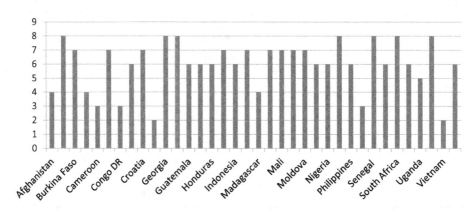

Figure 1.19   Freedom of expression
Source: BTI.

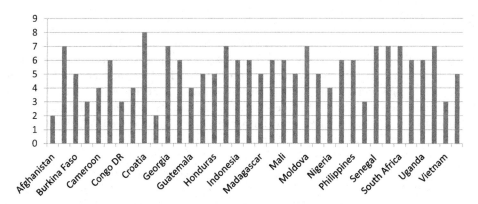

Figure 1.20   The guarantee and protection of civil rights
Source: BTI.

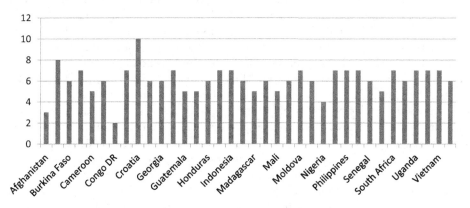

Figure 1.21   Strength of basic administration
Source: BTI.

for this view. Few cases go to law as the bulk of disputes for the poor are arbitrated upon by politicians or civil servants (Mulolwa, 2016).

The quality of government administration does play a part in influencing whether there are independent and accessible appeal mechanisms. BTI Question 1.4 examines the extent to which basic administrative structures exist. A score of 4 indicates that the state is able to do more than maintain law and order, but the territorial scope and effectiveness of its administrative structure is limited, whereas a score of 7 means that basic public services are provided throughout the country, but their operation is deficient (Figure 1.21). There is a correlation between the strength of basic administration and independent and accessible expropriation appeal mechanisms, with a gamma coefficient of 0.38 ($p < 0.025$).

Whether a country has independent and accessible appeal mechanisms against expropriation would appear to be associated with how effective its anti-corruption policies are; whether human rights are respected, particularly freedom of expression; and whether the government is able to provide basic public services throughout its jurisdiction. Expropriation policies do not exist in a vacuum but are likely to reflect the wider relationship between the government and citizens, particularly the extent to which the government is prepared to have its powers constrained by the rule of law.

25

Conclusions

The LGAF analyses suggest that in many developing countries compensation is paid only for the loss of certain rights over land, with the loss of unregistered rights particularly likely to not be compensated. The compensation normally paid is below that needed to maintain the economic and social status of those who have land rights expropriated. Compensation takes a long time to be paid, and in the absence of social safety nets, this is likely to result in impoverishment. By contrast, expropriation appears generally to be used for public purposes rather than to enable land to be transferred to private interests and is used for this purpose within a reasonable period of time.

The evidence suggests that the issues with expropriation have to do with deep-seated issues with land governance. For many countries there is a lack of consultation with those affected and a lack of independent and accessible avenues of complaint. Decisions about complaints are not dealt with in a timely fashion, which when coupled with the limited opportunities for independent complaints can create an environment in which officials can act with impunity. Many of the countries have weaknesses in the information they hold on land rights, with land registries and cadastres not being up to date or matching what is on the ground. These may reflect the costs of registration and complexity of procedures as well as poor infrastructure and incomplete geographical coverage of information about land rights. Expropriation processes can only function efficiently and fairly if governments have accurate information about who is entitled to compensation and the rights that should be compensated. Weaknesses in valuation also undermine the payment of compensation. A lack of independent and accessible avenues of complaint appears to be associated with weaknesses in anti-corruption policies, the failure to prosecute officials who abuse their positions, weaknesses in basic administration, and failure to provide for freedom of expression and guarantee civil rights. These issues suggest that improvements in the efficiency and fairness with which expropriation is carried out do not just depend on technical improvements to land registries and cadastres, and in valuation but also require governments to address deep-seated governance problems, particularly making officials more accountable for their actions and removing the veil of secrecy that allows them to act with impunity.

Data sources

BTI 2016, www.bti-project.org/en/index/
The World Bank Land Governance Assessment Framework, www.worldbank.org/en/programs/land-governance-assessment-framework
The World Bank Doing Business, www.doingbusiness.org/

Notes

1 In this chapter the terms compulsory purchase, compulsory acquisition, eminent domain, and expropriation are used interchangeably, but, as the opening sentence implies, there are subtle distinctions of meaning between them for a native English speaker.
2 Afghanistan, Brazil, Burkina Faso, Burundi, Cameroon, Columbia, Cote d'Ivoire, the Democratic Republic of Congo, Croatia, Ethiopia, Gambia, Georgia, Ghana, Guatemala, Guinea, Honduras, India, Indonesia (Central Kalimantan), Kenya, Kyrgyz Republic, Madagascar, Malawi, Mali, Mauritania, Moldova, Mozambique, Nigeria, Peru, the Philippines, Rwanda, Senegal, Sierra Leone, South Africa, Tanzania, Uganda, Ukraine, Vietnam, Zambia. There is no scorecard for the

Kyrgyz Republic. A draft LGAF assessment was carried out for South Sudan in 2014. In view of the continuing conflict in the country, South Sudan has been excluded from the study.

3 The African Charter on Human and People's Rights in Article 14, the American Convention on Human Rights Article 21, and the Arab Charter on Human Rights Article 31 have similar guarantees of property.

4 The gamma coefficient (Goodman and Kruskal's gamma) has been preferred to the rank correlation measures because the limited number of categories produce many tied ranks.

References

Adeniyi, P. O. (2013), Improving Land Sector Governance in Nigeria: Implementation of the Land Governance Assessment Framework: Synthesis Report, World Bank Group, Washington, DC. http://siteresources.worldbank.org/INTLGA/Resources/Nigeria_Synthesis.pdf.

Allen, T. (2005), Property and the Human Rights Act 1998, Hart Publishing, Oxford.

Bertelsmann Stiftung (2016), BTI 2016: Codebook for Country Assessments, Transformation Index of Bertelsmann Stiftung 2016, Bertelsmann Stiftung, Gütersloh, Germany.

Bugri, J. T. (2012), Improving Land Sector Governance in Ghana: Implementation of the Land Governance Assessment Framework (LGAF) – final report (English), World Bank Group, Washington, DC. Available online at: http://documents.worldbank.org/curated/en/201121504860579264/Improving-land-sector-governance-in-Ghana-implementation-of-the-Land-Governance-Assessment-Framework-LGAF-final-report.

Buzu, O. (2016), "Property Assessment and Taxation in the Republic of Moldova", Land Tenure Journal, volume 2–15, pp. 63–81.

Byamugisha, F.F.K. (2013), Securing Africa's Land for Shared Prosperity: A Program to Scale Up Reforms and Investments, International Bank for Reconstruction and Development/The World Bank, Washington, DC.

Committee in World Food Security (2012), Voluntary Guidelines on the Responsible Governance of Tenure of Land, Fisheries and Forests, FAO, Rome.

Council of Europe (1952), The European Convention on Human Rights. Protocol 1, Paris.

Deininger, K., Selod, H. and Burns, A. (2012), The Land Governance Assessment Framework: Identifying and Monitoring Good Practice in the Land Sector, The World Bank, Washington, DC.

Derman, B. (1995), "Environmental NGOs, Dispossession, and the State: The Ideology and Praxis of African Nature and Development", Human Ecology, volume 23, no. 2, pp. 199–215.

Devine, J. A. (2017), "Colonizing Space and Commodifying Place: Tourism's Violent Geographies", Journal of Sustainable Tourism, volume 25, no. 5, pp. 634–650.

Egiashvili, D. (2011), Improving Land Sector Governance in Georgia: Implementation of the Land Governance Assessment Framework (LGAF), World Bank Group, Washington, DC. Available online at: http://documents.worldbank.org/curated/en/917011504860820976/Improving-land-sector-governance-in-Georgia-implementation-of-the-Land-Governance-Assessment-Framework-LGAF.

Eleazar, F.C., Garcia, B., Guiang, E., Herrera, A., Isorena, L.D., Ravanera, R. and Serote, S. (2013), Improving Land Sector Governance in the Philippines: Implementation of Land Governance Assessment Framework (LGAF), World Bank Group, Washington, DC.

Gebrewold, Zerfu Hailu (2016), Land Governance Assessment Framework (LGAF) implementation in Ethiopia: final country report, World Bank Group, Washington, DC. Available online at: http://documents.worldbank.org/curated/en/747201504859857290/Land-Governance-Assessment-Framework-LGAF-implementation-in-Ethiopia-final-country-report.

Goldstein, N.R. (2013), "Indigenous Rights in National Parks: The United States, Canada, and Australia Compared", Macquarie Journal of International and Comparative Environmental Law, volume 2, pp. 66–87.

Inspection Panel (2016), Involuntary Resettlement, Emerging Lessons No. 1, International Bank for Reconstruction and Development/The World Bank, Washington, DC.

Kantor, I. (2007), "Ethnic Cleansing and America's Creation of National Parks", Public Land and Resources Law Review, volume 28, pp. 41–64.

Legal Aid Forum (2015), The Implementation of Rwanda's Expropriation Law and Outcomes on the Population: Final Report, USAID | LAND Project, Kigali, Rwanda.

Loperena, C. A. (2017), "Honduras Is Open for Business: Extractivist Tourism as Sustainable Development in the Wake of Disaster?", Journal of Sustainable Tourism, volume 25, no. 5, pp. 618–633.

McCluskey, W. J. (2016), "Real Property Taxation in the Republic of Kazakhstan", Land Tenure Journal, volume 2–15, pp. 119–137.

McCluskey, W., Franzsen, R. and Bahl, R. (2017), "Policy and Practice", in Franzsen, R.C.D. and McCluskey, W.J. (editors), Property Tax in Africa: Status, Challenges, and Propects, Lincoln Institute of Land Policy, Cambridge, MA, pp. 29–104.

Muliar, O., Kaliberda, O., Kulynych, P. and Egiashvili, D. (2014), Issues and Options for Improved Land Sector Governance in Ukraine: Application of the Land Governance Assessment Framework in Ukraine – Synthesis Report, World Bank Group, Washington, DC. Available online at: http://siteresources.worldbank.org/INTLGA/Resources/Ukraine_Synthesis_Report.pdf.

Mulolwa, A. (2016), Land Governance Assessment: Zambia Country Report, World Bank, Washington, DC. Available online at: https://openknowledge.worldbank.org/handle/10986/28503.

Ngoga, T., Ntaganda, F., Tushabe, K., Niyonsenga, D., Ingabire, N., and Muvara, P. (2017), Land governance Assessment Framework: Final Report – Rwanda, World Bank Group, Washington, DC. Available online at: http://documents.worldbank.org/curated/en/905231504857005613/Land-governance-assessment-framework-final-report-Rwanda.

Obaikol, E. (2014), Draft Final Report of the Implementation of the Land Governance Assessment Framework in Uganda, World Bank Group, Washington, D.C. Available online at: http://siteresources.worldbank.org/INTLGA/Resources/Uganda_Draft_Report.pdf.

Spence, M. D. (1999), Dispossessing the Wilderness: Indian Removal and the Making of the National Parks, Oxford University Press, Oxford.

Tagliarino, N. (2016), Encroaching on Land and Livelihoods: How National Expropriation Laws Measure Up Against International Standards, World Resources Institute Working Paper, Washington, DC. Available online at www.wri.org/publication/encroaching-on-land-and-livelihoods.

Tchawa, P., Kalambay, L. and Ndihokubwayo, D. (2012), Land Policy in Africa: Central Africa Regional Assessment, African Union-United Nations Economic Commission for Africa-African Development Bank Consortium, Addis Adaba.

Tenga, R. W. and Mramba, J. (2015), Tanzania – LGAF Synthesis Report, World Bank Group, Washington, DC. Available online at: https://openknowledge.worldbank.org/handle/10986/28512.

Transparency International/FAO (2011), Corruption in the Land Sector, Working Paper 04/2011, Transparency International, Berlin.

United Nations (1948), Universal Declaration of Human Rights. Adopted and proclaimed by General Assembly of the United Nations, resolution 217A (III), 10 December 1948.

Urban LandMark (2013), Land Governance in South Africa: Implementing the Land Governance Assessment Framework, World Bank, Washington, DC. Available online at: https://openknowledge.worldbank.org/handle/10986/28524.

Vo, Dang Hung and Thang, Nguyen Van (2013), Improving Land Sector Governance in Vietnam: Implementation of Land Governance Assessment Framework (LGAF), World Bank, Washington, DC. Available online at: https://openknowledge.worldbank.org/handle/10986/28521.

Vondracek, T. J. (1975), "Compensation for Losses Resulting from Acts of Public Policy in Soviet law", in Garner, J. F. (editor), Compensation for Compulsory Purchase, United Kingdom National Committee of Comparative Law, UK Comparative Law Series no 2, London.

World Bank (1998), Involuntary Resettlement: Operational Policy and Background Paper, The World Bank, Washington, DC.

World Bank (2012), Land Governance Assessment Framework: Implementation Manual, 17 July 2012, The World Bank, Washington, DC.

World Bank (2013), Land Governance Assessment Framework: Implementation Manual version 2013, October 2013, The World Bank, Washington, DC.

World Bank (2014), Moldova – Land Governance Assessment Framework (LGAF): Final Report, World Bank Group, Washington, DC. Available online at: http://documents.worldbank.org/curated/en/843141504857423593/Moldova-Land-governance-assessment-framework-LGAF-final-report.

World Bank (2014a), Brazil Land Governance Assessment, World Bank Group, Washington, DC. Available online at: https://openknowledge.worldbank.org/handle/10986/22679.

World Bank (2015), India Land Governance Assessment: National Synthesis Report, World Bank, Washington, DC. Available online at: https://openknowledge.worldbank.org/handle/10986/28513.

World Bank (2016), Implementation of the Land Governance Assessment Framework (LGAF) in the Republic of Croatia, World Bank Group, Washington, DC. Available online at: http://documents. worldbank.org/curated/en/248131504859586732/Implementation-of-the-Land-Governance-Assessment-Framework-LGAF-in-the-Republic-of-Croatia.

World Bank (2018), Doing Business 2018: Reforming to Create Jobs, The World Bank, Washington, DC.

Žibrik, N. (2016), "The Process of Introducing a Modern Real Property Tax in Slovenia", Land Tenure Journal, volume 2–15, pp. 83–99.

2

Reinventing land readjustment

Implications for eminent domain and land governance[1]

Yu Hung Hong and Mansha Chen

Introduction

Cities are centres where people come together to exchange ideas, conduct commerce, appreciate culture, and advance knowledge. Yet the current state of urban development in a myriad developing countries is unsettling, plagued by ongoing inequalities due to uncoordinated urbanisation and housing shortage. In some rapidly urbanising nations, governments lack the fiscal and institutional capacity to build affordable housing and basic infrastructure on vacant land for the growing urban population, resulting in a proliferation of informal settlements and slums (Durand-Lasserve 2006). At the same time, natural disasters and wars around the world have destroyed homes, roads, water and sewage systems, and other public facilities, exacerbating the already limited basic services available to the urban poor.

In some cases, the lack of funding may not be the most formidable problem. Instead, the absence of functional and proactive governance for coordinating land assembly for redevelopment is most challenging (Deininger et al. 2011). The conventional methods—government expropriation and market transaction—are not always the best options. Using compulsory purchase or eminent domain entails high political and economic costs (Hong 2007a, 2008). Public protests, prolonged litigations, or elite capture are common. Acquiring properties through the market is also hindered by potential holdouts, deterring developers from undertaking land redevelopment in inner cities. Socially, both methods lead to the relocation of existing residents, causing major disruption to their livelihoods and the destruction of neighbourhood fabric.

In response to these urgencies, many international aid agencies, such as the United Nations Human Settlement Programme (UN-HABITAT) and the World Bank, as well as governments, scholars, and practitioners, are looking for new ideas or the repackaging of existing ways to build and rebuild cities (Patel, d'Cruz, and Burra 2002). This chapter discusses a long-established land management tool—land readjustment (LR)[2]—and reasserts its often-unexamined potential to build open and inclusive governance structures that begin to tackle these aforementioned challenges of urban development in the developing world.

What is LR?

LR is a planning tool that can support inner-city revitalisation or urban expansion. Its basic principle is to organise landowners and land occupants to act together—in cooperation with a municipality and/or private developer—to pool their land to accomplish a redevelopment project. In return for owners' land contribution to the project, each participant receives, upon completion of the programme, a new parcel proportionate in size or value to the original one. The size of the parcel may be smaller, but the value is greater due to land improvements and public infrastructure created by the project (Hong and Needham 2007). In this way, LR can (1) enable high-density urban development, (2) increase land value, (3) allocate the increased redevelopment value to involved parties equitably, and (4) limit displacement. All these goals are considered comprehensively in a single policy package (Doebele 1982; Hong and Needham 2007).

Different elements of LR can be emphasised during a land redevelopment project, depending on the context. For instance, in the design of an LR project for urban upgrading in an African city where residents do not have legal property rights, policy makers can recognise administratively these squatters' claims to land and allow them to participate in the project (McFarlane 2012). After land is pooled, readjusted, and serviced, the residents are invited back to the neighbourhood to rebuild their homes or receive an apartment unit, sometimes with legal title. This approach allows informal settlers to improve their living conditions and tenure security, and it increases development densities to enable the city to obtain much-needed land space for urban expansion.

LR can also help implement citywide land use regulation incrementally. To ensure that individual LR projects add up to a coherent whole, they must be conducted as part of a comprehensive urban planning process (Doebele 1982). In situations where local governments lack the capacity to execute a large-scale master plan, related LR projects can be implemented in an orderly sequence and at a manageable scale to put into action a coordinated, long-term urban development strategy (Hong and Tierney 2013).

In addition, LR can improve relations between government and its people. As is discussed later, the core principle of LR is to build consensus and cooperation among the parties involved in land redevelopment. These parties include formal landowners, informal landholders, renters, non-governmental organisations (NGOs), national government agencies, city officials, and private developers. The process entails grassroots mobilisation by giving equal opportunities to all stakeholders to participate in the design of the LR proposals. An agreement from the supermajority of landowners is required before LR can proceed, thereby ensuring adequate attention is paid to the needs and concerns of affected residents by the government or private investors.

Last but not least, LR can facilitate land value capture for financing local infrastructure and social services (Doebele 1982). In readjusting land boundaries, land space is created by increasing development densities. This land space can then be sold at market value to raise funds to defray a portion of the infrastructure investment costs. This approach creates a clear connection between development benefits received by landowners and the "price" that they need to pay to make the programme financially viable.

New governance-centered LR approach

To some extent, conventional LR projects are able to achieve some of the aforementioned policy goals. Yet many organisers of LR do not pay sufficient attention to issues related to governance (Sanyal and Mukhija 2001; Turk 2008; Lovering and Türkmen 2011). More importantly, they forget that LR is about a process through which all stakeholders need to be engaged. This is partly because some practitioners perceive LR as merely a tool to facilitate land transactions, and this narrow view has limited the opportunities to use LR to build a self-perpetuating process of involving local actors to engage in land and neighbourhood improvements.

In view of this oversight, we emphasise here the connection between governance building and LR to bring the factor of community engagement and the notion of an inclusive process and a just outcome to the forefront of project design for land assembly.

Our governance-centered LR approach differs significantly from the prevailing argument for the transferability of LR to developing countries. The general belief is that LR should be adopted only if required preconditions exist. These preconditions include, for example, the existence of:

- a participatory planning system;
- a strong sense of belonging to the community among affected parties;
- skilled arbitrators;
- well-functioning legal and political systems to mediate disputes over property transfers;
- technical expertise in land valuation, registration, surveying, and urban design; and
- a buoyant real estate market.

As many developing countries do not possess these enabling factors, some analysts have concluded hastily that LR has very limited applicability to the Global South. This view, however, is based on the misconception that governance and institutions are given and fixed.

We argue that institutions and governance can be created and recreated according to shifting conditions and expectations (Hong and Tierney 2013). Although the application of LR should always be sensitive to the existing institutional environment, it should never be limited by the absence of certain favourable preconditions. Rather, governance and institutional buildings should be treated as an integral component or reform objective of any LR programmes.

It is through LR that organisers can develop a participatory planning system, democratic decision-making processes, and community inclusiveness to make the proposed land swaps viable. Discussions that involve different levels of government, landowners, land users, renters, NGOs, developers, urban designers, and architects will engender an environment of mutual understanding and learning, which in turn reshapes the governance structure for neighbourhood upgrading.

The core aspiration of the governance-centered LR that separates it from other more technically originated LR approaches is its focus on broadening the choice set for all involved parties and encouraging consensus building. In promoting urban development for all, there is nothing more fundamental than to remove obstacles that impede citizens (poor and rich, female and male, young and old) from exercising their right to determine their destinies. Deprivation of their freedom to do that is the worst kind of poverty. Through the governance-centered LR, an implementing agency must foster a social discourse that helps all segments of society learn how to choose freely within a given range of possible options, reconcile differences in their interests, and solve problems collectively. Public and private involvements in facilitating and financing LR must be balanced (Hong and Tierney 2013).

To highlight the practicality of our proposal, we present a comparative analysis of actual experiments in developing countries to ascertain the opportunities of and constraints on our ideas. Selected cases from the developing world and emerging economies, including Angola, Bhutan, China, Colombia, Ethiopia, India, Indonesia, Thailand, Turkey, and Vietnam, are used to illustrate how supporting legislation, organised communities, collaboration between the public and private sectors, and trust relationship among stakeholders were gradually institutionalised during LR experiments. Although these cases are neither exhaustive nor randomly selected, they help raise important questions about the conventional wisdom that LR is only a technical land-assembly tool. The rethinking of the possibilities and limitations of LR could open the door for more application of this approach in developing countries, replacing the use of state powers to take land for redevelopment or urban expansion.

Myth and realities

Based on the experiences of conducting LR in developed countries, scholars and analysts alike have proposed a set of preconditions for adopting this land tool. Since these preconditions play important roles in determining the adoptability of LR in industrialised nations, many analysts consider it impossible to apply similar techniques in developing countries because these conditions do not exist there. However, as is explained later, none of the preconditions for LR are fixed naturally such that developing nations will never be able to apply them in their countries. In this section, we analyse these arguments, separating the myths from the realities. This will help us provide better suggestions for adopting LR in some emerging economies.

It is essential to state at the onset that our observations are based on the research on recent LR practices and experiments in Angola (Cain, Weber, and Festo 2018), Bhutan (Norbu 2018), China (Lin and Li 2018), Colombia (Pinilla 2018), Egypt, Ethiopia (Zekuel and Hong 2108), India (Balakrishnan, 2018), Indonesia (Winarso, Dharmapatni, and Chen 2016), Thailand (Leeruttanawisut 2018), Turkey (Turk 2018), and Vietnam. Thus, we would like to limit our arguments to these countries and avoid any generalisations.

Myth No. 1

An LR legislation is needed prior to the adoption of this tool

Many scholars and analysts alike have argued that countries need LR legislation prior to adopting this approach (Doebele 1982). A prime reason is to empower an implementing agency to legally take land from dissenting landowners when the supermajority of their neighbours has agreed to participate, in order to avoid holdout.

In principle, having some legal rules to guide the operations of LR is a good idea. Yet the procedure for establishing new laws in most developing countries is very long and politically driven. Legislators are often unwilling to take the risk of formalising rules for a new practice that has no precedent in their countries. The potential complications and risks of proposing a special law for LR have deterred officials in many developing countries from experimenting with the idea.

Interestingly, we learned from our selected LR experiences in developing countries that not having special legislation did not hinder implementation of the tool. Examples include Angola (Cain, Weber, and Festo 2018), Bhutan (Norbu 2018), China (Lin and Li 2018), Ethiopia (Zekuel and Hong 2108), and Vietnam. In testing the transferability of LR to their country, project initiators did not try to work with their legislators to establish a special law first. Instead, they started with some pilot projects and then gradually institutionalised the locally generated experiences into some semi-formal rules as additional experiments were conducted in different regions of their country. They also did not try to adopt an LR law based on other countries' experiences. Rather, they learned from their own practices and then came up with enforceable legislation to scale up the application of LR.

Box 1 Land pooling in Bhutan

Thimphu, the capital city of Bhutan, is challenged by a significant urban population increase on top of an already haphazard development pattern and inadequate infrastructure. Since 2003, the city planning authorities adopted the land-pooling approach to cope with these problems, even though Bhutan did not have any legislation that would guide or legitimise the land-pooling practices. Land pooling was intended to reconfigure existing land in such a way that each landowner retained a smaller parcel close to the original location but with improved access to local infrastructure, amenities, and services. It was also intended to avoid the complicated and contentious land acquisition process of eminent domain.

Land pooling involved bringing many different—and even conflicting—interests together to agree upon a redevelopment plan for the city. With extensive public participation and consultation, city officials were able to achieve a unanimous consensus among landowners to contribute a portion of their land for infrastructure development. Based on substantial land-pooling experience, Bhutan formalised land pooling with the adoption of the Land Pooling Rules and Regulations in 2009, which provides a legal basis for land pooling and offers dispute-resolution mechanisms for occupants or landowners unwilling to be part of the process. By then, 12 land-pooling schemes were already approved for implementation.

Source: Norbu (2018)

In dealing with dissenting landowners, officials in these countries did not resort to their power of eminent domain. Rather, they worked hard to convince all landowners either to partake in the project or to transfer their properties to the implementing agency with compensation. In Angola (Cain, Weber, and Festo 2018) and China (Lin and Li 2018), project organisers used eminent domain only as a threat to motivate dissenting landowners to come to the bargaining table. In Bhutan, local officials who were in charge of land pooling in Thimphu worked tirelessly to have unanimous agreement from landowners before they went forward with their land-pooling proposal (Box 1).

Although these LR experiences were not governed by law, these countries were able to transfer their knowledge learned from experimenting with LR to more systematic formal rules and eventually institutionalised these experimental experiences into laws. These laws founded on domestic actual experiences are most effective in guiding local practices.

Box 2 Land readjustment in Turkey

Public LR projects have been implemented in Turkey since the second half of the nineteenth century to deal with inadequate infrastructure and informal settlements. Many legal resources related to LR were established during the time of rapid urbanisation to implement detailed local plans, create serviced urban plots of appropriate size and shape, and provide local services and infrastructure for urban residents.

To make land space available for these public undertakings, a law was established in 1933 to designate the land contribution by owners to be 15 percent of their landholdings. This was later increased to 40 percent in 2003 because the purposes for using contributed land had been broadened from roads and squares to parks, car parking spaces, playgrounds, green areas, religious buildings, police stations, and elementary and secondary schools. The percentage of land contribution and its usage are clearly set in the law. Although these legal rules may minimise uncertainties in some cases, they add rigidity to the negotiation between landowners and the government when these parties are willing to increase (or decrease) land contribution according to varying local preferences and demand for public service levels.

Source: Turk (2007, 2018)

In fact, having a preexisting law does not seem to help the design and implementation of LR if the legal provisions do not reflect the realities on the ground. Some countries have specified in their legislation the landowners' obligation of contributing a part of their landholding to accommodate the public infrastructure construction in their neighbourhood. The intention is to make the amount of land contribution explicit to affected parties, thereby lowering the negotiation costs (Turk 2007; Lovering and Türkmen 2011). For instance, the Egyptian government has stated in its Building Law that landowners could be asked to give up as much as 20 percent of their land to make space available for the construction of public roads and other necessary facilities. Landowners may also have to pay a betterment levy to cover the related construction costs of public goods. Both India (Balakrishnan 2018) and Turkey (Box 2) have similar provisions to delimit contributions from landowners.

Contrary to the original intent of these legal rules, they add constraints and complications to the negotiation between the government and landowners. In some cases, because the supply of infrastructure has lagged far behind demand, municipalities may need landowners to contribute a high percentage of their landholding to build the necessary road network and facilities to serve the increasing population growth. Limiting landowners' contributions to an arbitrary percentage without any consideration of varying local contexts has created inefficiency. On the one hand, places with rapid growth are unable to get the amount of land needed to upgrade their provision of public services. On the other hand, officials in areas that are under less development pressure may take more land from owners than they need, leading to resistance from landowners and failure to implement the proposed project.

Ideally, the land contribution ratio for LR should not be predetermined by the law. Instead, it should be the outcome of repeated discussions and negotiations between landowners and an implementing agency. It should take into account factors such as local preferences, the level of public infrastructure and amenities, specific land and housing market conditions, as well as the proportion of development costs the project intends to recover. There is no "one-size-fits-all" land contribution ratio.

We are not implying that establishing legal rules for guiding the experimentation and adoption of LR is not useful. Laws always play a critical role in institutionalising workable practices on the ground and help scale up LR when the approach has proven suitable for a country. The key message for developing countries is to maintain a certain degree of flexibility with the rule of law when LR is still going through its experimental stage.

How legislation could be conducive to LR experiments

Based on our case studies, we propose possible features of helpful legislation that supports enabling LR in developing countries. First, it will be useful if there is a constitutional provision that recognises land and land value increments created by public actions as social assets. This constitutional order could set the expectation of private landowners that their enjoyment of property rights entails obligations to fulfill the social functions of land. Put simply, when land is needed for public purposes, private landowners should surrender their land to the state for such a public undertaking and receive just compensation (Fischel 2004). This is universally true around the world. The difference is the extent to which these public-private property rights relations are articulated in the law.

For examples, the Brazilian City Statute and Colombian Law 388 have specified clearly, among other things, the social functions of land and the equitable distribution of benefits and costs of urban development (Fernandes 2011). Establishing similar legislations in countries where public officials are considering adopting LR could set the stage for the government to negotiate with private landowners for land contributions to pay for public infrastructure investments. That said, we do not imply that countries where similar constitutional provisions do not exist should amend their constitutions without careful consideration. In most countries, a constitutional amendment is normally a very serious undertaking that entails a very long time for implementation. We recommend experimenting with these ideas incrementally first, and then convincing legislators to change the laws if necessary.

Second, in connection with the social functions of land, it will also be useful if there is a law that gives all citizens the right of access to affordable land and housing. The equal right to shelter, like the rights to education and free speech, is considered a basic human right that can give legitimacy to the government to ask landowners to share their land-related wealth with the society for assisting low-income groups. The redistributive function of land ownership provided by LR can help prevent political and social instability caused by the unequal distribution of land-based wealth. More importantly, this law can set a guideline for government takings of private property for public benefit only. That said, it is important to consider also the fiscal implications of giving all citizens the right of access to affordable land and housing. Governments should try to balance the policy goals of helping the poor to obtain affordable housing with the need to maintain fiscal health.

Another rule that can help achieve the goals of LR is the legal requirement for seeking the consent of the supermajority of affected landowners or occupants to approve the LR proposal. A unique feature of LR is its participatory mechanism for policy decision-making. Unfortunately, when adopting LR, many countries have overlooked this special feature. As a result, communities have lost their chances to learn how to make decisions collectively. LR projects that lack the consent of affected owners are more coercive and controversial. Having a law that mandates the implementing agency to obtain the consent of the supermajority of landowners to approve the LR proposal would avoid this problem. There is no universal threshold for the supermajority requirement. The percentage should be determined based on local contexts and public consultations.

More importantly, if a group of landowners or the local community organises LR as a site-level intervention, the effort must be guided by updated national, regional, and local urban planning legislations to ensure that similar micro-level efforts can add up into a coherent whole. Enforceable detailed plans that are designed based on an updated master plan and national and regional development strategies are indispensable for coordinating LR projects. If these planning functions are not well-developed, LR projects should be at least guided by a generally agreed-upon vision of land use in and around cities.

Myth No. 2

Property rights must be clearly delineated for implementing LR

Another myth about LR is that it requires a clear delineation of property rights (Doebele 1982). Some practitioners believe that without knowing the ownership of land, the implementing agency will be unable to ascertain who has the right to participate in land exchanges. In reality, clearly defined property rights are not always present in developing countries (Gillert 2002; Galiani and Schargrodsky 2010). Current land users might have occupied land informally or do not register their land to avoid high registration costs or the time-consuming bureaucratic procedure. Many practitioners in the Global South have all too often dismissed the potential of LR based on this reason.

We did not find that unclear delineation of property rights was a major hindrance to adopting LR in Angola (Cain, Weber, and Festo 2018), Ethiopia (Zekuel and Hong 2108), and Thailand (Leeruttanawisut 2018). These cases were all related to the upgrading of informal settlements. The self-settlers in some of these cases were driven to squat on public or private lands as a result of involuntary displacements caused by wars and sectarian conflicts or by their inability to find affordable land and housing in urban areas.

Governments in these cases recognised administratively the existence of the informal neighbourhoods as part of their jurisdictions. Informal settlers then verified their occupancy rights based on the knowledge of local representatives and leaders or testimonies from their neighbours. The officially acknowledged and publicly certified occupancy rights immediately protected informal settlers from forced eviction and entitled them to participate in LR if they chose to do so. Recognition of occupancy rights is gaining a lot of momentum nowadays and is generally done through simple legislative procedures such as a municipal government's decree or executive order that observes customary practices.

Box 3 Land readjustment in Angola

In postwar Angola, land has emerged as a critical point of conflict when involuntarily displaced people have sought sites in emerging cities for their new homes or sought to formalise their informal occupations during the civil war. Their lack of tenure security undermines the well-being of the poor and threatens them with mass expropriation. LR was used to mediate these conflicts in Angola despite its limited culture of participation in urban planning practice and weak local governance.

There are at least two well-documented LR projects in Huambo—Bairro Fátima and Bairro Camussamba. The key characteristic of both projects was the *de facto* recognition of the occupancy rights of existing self-settlers. In both pilot projects, the calculations for redistribution and capturing of land value increments were not based on any land-value study, but on an estimate. Thirty percent of the pooled land was used for infrastructure. Of the remaining 70 percent, half was redistributed to previous land occupants, and half was sold, with funds reinvested into basic infrastructure.

Bairro Fátima was perceived to be successful, by all stakeholders, in incorporating the informal settlements into the formally planned part of the city as well as benefiting the occupants because the value of their landholdings increased. It also demonstrated the crucial role played by a local NGO—Development Workshop—in building bridges between the land occupants and the government, convincing the former to participate in the project and securing the backing of the latter.

Source: Cain, Weber, and Festo (2018)

Certainly, these processes could only happen under a "flexible" property rights regime. A rigid property law that only recognises the rights of formal landowners could marginalise the landless in any LR initiatives. This is because only the persons who hold title to the land can participate in the project, formal or informal renters and occupants will be excluded from the decision-making process. These parties are normally the most vulnerable and represent the poorest of the poor who could not afford formal housing and must rent shelter from informal landlords. These marginalised groups will be displaced when their neighbourhoods are upgraded. Some redevelopment initiatives of urban villages in China are illustrative of this serious problem (Box 4).

What are helpful property rights perspectives for LR?

To avoid the aforementioned problems, what would be the helpful legal perspectives on property rights that could facilitate the application of LR? We suggest instituting a flexible legal framework that recognises the diverse land tenure arrangements and property claims of all residents, regardless of whether they are renters or property owners. The law should not just acknowledge and protect registered freehold rights, but should also recognise formal and informal occupancy and leasehold rights (Payne 2001). Self-settlers or renters who have resided in a neighbourhood should be entitled to legal protection from forced eviction. If relocation is inevitable due to redevelopment, occupants and tenants should have the right to claim proper compensation.

Box 4 Urban village redevelopment in China

China is experiencing the largest scale of urbanisation. Guangdong Province became the site of a national experiment with LR, particularly around innovative institutional arrangements, to provide local governments with more flexibility and power to determine the distribution of benefits from land redevelopment. Some of the redevelopment initiatives were led by the village collective and managed by the collective's members, such as Lie De village in Guangzhou.

In Lie De, the city government subsidised the project by waving the collection of the land conversion fee. The collective utilised the revenue generated from auctioning part of its land for commercial uses to pay for the redevelopment costs. Villagers who participated in the project were resettled within the same neighborhood and given extra apartment units to rent out to outsiders to generate income for improving their livelihood. In addition, the village also reserved a piece of land to build a hotel and commercial complex that will also generate income for the collective members.

Higher intensity of land use and an improved living environment raised land values of the rural enclave in the city center that was previously suppressed by both institutional restriction over market circulation and a run-down living environment. Villagers welcomed increases in the value of their real estates, but the hike of rental costs became a nightmare for the migrant population. The demolition of the village and its resettlement with modern and pricy apartment buildings meant that the low-cost housing in which the migrant population resided, along with the social networks for communication and mutual assistance, was completely destroyed.

Source: Lin and Li (2018)

All these changes in perspectives on property relations do not have to be covered in some major constitutional amendments. Instead, they could be adopted by a government decree or executive order. Good examples of how this approach works are found in the temporary administrative recognition of informal settlements by many governments in Latin American countries (Fernandes 2011) and Thailand (Box 5)—which gradually led to the granting of fee simple or long-term leasehold rights through LR (or sharing).

Myth No. 3

LR needs a vibrant real estate market

It is generally true that LR needs a vibrant real estate market to be implementable because one of its objectives is to mobilise land value increments generated by land redevelopment to finance infrastructure investment and neighbourhood improvements. If a project is carried out in a slow real estate market where the demand for land and housing is weak, land values may not increase enough to provide sufficient incentive for landowners and occupants to partake in the project or to cover the redevelopment costs. Certainly, if cost recovery is not the primary objective, this matter is less important.

Box 5 Land sharing in Thailand

The most often used LR-like method that is tailored for informal settlement upgrading is land sharing. Land sharing originated in Bangkok, Thailand, during the 1970s and 1980s as an innovative way to resolve land conflicts between legal landowners and informal settlers. The approach involves the partitioning of a parcel of contested land so that the landowner regains access to a large portion of the original parcel, free of squatters, for redevelopment. At the same time, the informal settlers can stay on or near their present site on another portion of the land, with improved housing and local services and legal tenure.

The Sengki project is considered to be one of the most important and successful cases of land sharing in Bangkok. Sengki is an urban poor community that was upgraded in a participatory manner in partnership with the National Housing Authority of Thailand in the early 1990s. Up until the early 1930s, the land in Sengki that the poor occupied belonged to close relatives of His Majesty, the King of Thailand. The residents rented the land from the Royal Property Bureau (now the Crown's Property Bureau) at below-market rates. In early 1984, the agency that managed the royal property offered to sell a portion of the land to existing residents, and an agreement was reached in 1987. A cooperative was formed to negotiate with the managing agency and the National Housing Authority and was in charge of collecting payments from participating residents and overseeing the implementation of the project.

Source: Leeruttanawisut (2018)

The fundamental operation of LR is to incentivise landowners and occupants to exchange a piece of unserviced land for another serviced plot of higher value, albeit smaller in size. The increase in land value after LR must be sufficient to compensate residents for their loss of land area during the exchange. Thus, a vibrant real estate market will help encourage residents to participate in LR.

That said, there are situations in which a vibrant land market may discourage landowners from partaking in LR projects. This happens mainly in industrialised countries where landowners find selling land to private developers at a high price is more profitable and less risky than participating in LR. Hence, once again, the validity of the argument will depend on the context.

Although it is true that most LR projects need a vibrant real estate market to succeed, this condition does not always benefit the poor. This is especially problematic when the landless are not included in sharing the benefits of land redevelopment. If generating high enough financial benefits for participating owners is the dominating goal, there will be little incentive for the municipalities, the implementing agency, and other stakeholders to keep land prices affordable. If there is no social programme to protect the urban poor, housing could become unaffordable for low- or even middle-income households. Poor neighbourhoods that offer a safe haven to the poor will be gentrified, making affordable housing increasingly less available. An overheated housing market may also create investment bubbles, threatening the stability of the entire economy. These problems occurred in the LR projects in Thailand, China, Turkey, and India.

To maintain housing affordability and lower the chance of gentrification, the government could mandate LR projects to reserve a certain portion of the serviced land for affordable housing. Alternatively, if the implementing agency agrees to build apartment units for existing landowners in return for their land contribution, the government could ask the agency to sell or rent a certain percentage of the housing units to the poor at below market value. This way, renters and other vulnerable groups may not be priced out from the neighbourhood after LR.

Certainly, implementing these remedial proposals may encounter complications. First, they may require the government to subsidize the project or grant an extra density bonus to the developer to build housing units that will be sold or rented below cost. The financial burden of providing affordable housing to the poor should not fall entirely on the shoulder of landowners in the targeted area because it is the responsibility of the entire society.

Second, the process of identifying the right persons who are qualified for the assistance is not trivial. Some people who do not truly need help may take advantage of the system.

Third, mixed-income housing development may not be attractive to would-be homebuyers, thereby lowering the selling prices for the market-rate units. Hence, to make this proposal work, the mindset of the more affluent segments of the population needs to be changed, and the construction materials for the affordable housing units should not be of lower quality simply because they are built for the poor. Both approaches could minimise the chance of segregation.

How to make market work for the poor

The market is a powerful institution for solving urbanisation issues. Yet it will not automatically help us achieve social goals without proper designs. To make the market work for the poor, we need to ensure that all stakeholders are market informed. There should not be a single interest group that monopolises access to the market or its information.

Besides, all market participants, especially the poor, need to understand the financial risks of real estate investment. Property prices are cyclical in the short run. There is no guarantee that investing one's life savings in real property is the best way to generate and store wealth. A possible strategy to allow the poor to accumulate equity, and at the same time to protect them from the investment risks, is to form a housing cooperative, if the local context permits. For example, in Sengki, Thailand, landowners and occupants shared their land for redevelopment, and the informal settlers did not receive a title to the serviced land from the implementing agency immediately after land sharing. Instead, they became members of a cooperative which acted as their legal representative to collectively borrow from a bank to purchase the land from the landlord. Local residents then made monthly repayment to the cooperative over five years, with an option to buy their houses at the end of this period (Leeruttanawisut 2014). This arrangement allowed the poor households with limited financial resources to participate in land sharing while, at the same time, it precluded beneficiaries from cashing in their land hastily, which would possibly have led to massive market displacement and gentrification of the neighbourhood.

More importantly, real estate investment is complex and involves a large sum of capital. Investors, rich and poor, need advice from the professionals. Hence, it is also important to have the government or another reputable entity oversee the integrity and qualification of real estate brokers. They should act as neutral parties to lower the transaction costs of buying and selling real assets. In Britain, estate surveyors are licensed property management professionals whose qualifications and conduct are monitored by the Royal Institution of Chartered Surveyors. It is also important to ensure that services provided by certified real estate brokers are accessible to the poor.

Myth No. 4

Communities must be well organised before adopting LR

As discussed before, LR generally requires the consent of the supermajority of the landowners (or land users in cases of informal settlements) who must work together to design, implement, and supervise the project. Many practitioners are concerned about the potentially huge negotiation costs involved in situations where affected parties have little trust in each other and do not have any past experience of collective action. Thus, some of them have concluded that members of the community must trust each other as well as the government (or the project initiator) and have experience with participatory planning to render the adoption of LR viable (Doebele 1982).

In the developing-country cases that we examined, none of the communities displayed preexisting trust-based relationships prior to the introduction of LR, except Angola. In Angola, the Development Workshop—an NGO—worked with local communities for many years, even during wartime, thus gaining tremendous trust and respect from local residents prior to their introduction of LR to perform postconflict reconstruction of the informal neighbourhoods.

Project initiators in other examined cases did not pick their sites for implementing LR based on the level of trust and cohesiveness of the affected communities. In Bhutan, for instance, landowners were concerned about their self-interest as much as any other landowners in other parts of the world. It was only after public officials had spent years of effort to convince every single landowner of the necessity of balancing self-interest with the communal needs that they were willing to participate in the land-pooling project (Norbu 2018).

In Ethiopia, city officials of Addis Ababa organised countless meetings to solicit inputs from affected slum dwellers before designing their LR project. Based on the opinions gathered from public meetings, they formulated multiple housing options from which residents could select in reaction to the government proposal to redevelop their neighbourhood (Zekuel and Hong 2018).

What these cases have shown is that LR can be adopted in both organised and non-organised neighbourhoods. Indeed, more time and effort will be needed to introduce LR to a community where neighbours do not know each other well. However, that is true for all instruments if we take the proposal of building local governance as one of the key development goals. In fact, a well-organised community should not be viewed as a precondition for adopting LR. Rather, implementing agencies should view community organising as one of the key objectives of LR and develop neighbourhood spirit and collective action through its implementation process.

In terms of organising effort, it is true that communities with homogenous interests may take less time to organise. Yet tailoring organising programmes toward homogenous groups could also run the risk of marginalising the minority and the poor. For example, the majority of LR projects examined here included mostly landowners in the decision-making process. In the Chinese case, only the villagers who were members of the collective that owned the land could share the benefits of redevelopment (Lin and Li 2018). As a result, renters' interests were being ignored. Similar problems occurred in the two projects in Magarpatta and Khed, India, where the interests of the landless and lower caste were not considered when formulating the method of allocating the redevelopment benefits (Balakrishnan 2018).

How should communities be organised?

Given that neighbourhood mobilisation is a key feature of LR, how should communities be organised? There are at least three principles. First, implementing agencies should ensure community participation throughout all phases of the project. The conventional public participation approach is to consult with the affected community at the inception and at the end of the project. Past experiences with this approach have shown that this may be insufficient to help the community generate a sense of ownership of the project, creating a feeling that the consultations are merely token efforts. This happened in Colombia (Box 6), and the Fenicia project in Bogotá aimed to correct this problem (Pinilla 2018). The initiator, which was the Los Andes University, had engaged local communities and other stakeholders in all key decisions throughout the entire planning process. This was to ensure that all concerns about the project, and related opposition to the project, were resolved before the implementation stage. There have been numerous examples in the past where developers received the government's approval of the design of a project but only found out later that they could not implement the plan as a result of strong public resistance.

After the 2004 Tsunami in Indonesia, the reconstruction of the Gampong Lambung, Banda Aceh was a voluntary, community-initiated effort. The community led by the village leader rejected initial help from donors to build housing and instead engaged all the surviving residents to collectively plan and rebuild their community through a participatory LR process (Winarso, Dharmapatni, and Chen 2016).

Box 6 Using LR for urban renewal in Colombia

The *Triángulo de Fenicia* is an urban renewal project in downtown Bogotá within the immediate vicinity of Los Andes University. The project was approved in October 2014 and is still being implemented.

Taking advantage of the fact that the 2003 revision of the Bogotá Land Use Plan (POT) included an area adjacent to the university's traditional campus as part of the areas open to urban renewal, the university decided to play a leading role in formulating the partial plan for the area at the beginning of 2007. Unfortunately, the initial partial plan proposal did not include any public consultation or community participation. By 2010, public resentment of the project was growing, and a social movement organised to defend the neighbourhood from the proposed renewal gained ground in public discussions. In the end, all private initiatives regarding partial plans for renewal were blocked in their processes of formulation and approval.

It was at this moment that an unprecedented process took place within the university. Oscar Pardo, a professor of the business school, argued that an urban project in the zone adjacent to the university's traditional campus should be an opportunity not just for the physical transformation of the university surroundings, but for the social and economic integration of the neighbourhood as well. Under his leadership, a process of raising awareness and negotiations began with those responsible for the initiative. By the end of 2010, Pardo obtained the endorsement of the university authority to modify the project and form a multidisciplinary team of university professors charged with creating a different and innovative workspace for the area. The university team started to build trust with the local neighbourhood, conducted an extensive census of the community, and organised participatory design workshops to define a collective vision of the renewed area.

Source: Pinilla (2018)

Second, implementing agencies must set explicit standards of public participation that are sensitive to local contexts. They include, but are not limited to, who should participate, how often the participants should meet and for what purposes, and what conflict resolution mechanisms should be put in place to deal with disagreements.

As shown from the cases, community participation will only be effective if participants feel that issues discussed at the meetings are significant to them and their families and that their opinions will make a difference in the final decision. Community members will find public meetings burdensome if the gatherings are not well-organised and are dominated by special interest groups. In some situations, separate focus group sessions with minority groups, such as women, youths, and ethnic minorities—who may be hesitant to speak out in public—could be more effective than a big meeting to collect their opinions. It is also important to be sensitive to the cultural differences in expressing disagreements. Not all cultures encourage citizens to confront their neighbours publicly when disagreements emerge. Hence, there should be some informal and anonymous channels for members to voice their opinions privately. Again, there is no one-size-fits-all strategy for systematising public engagement in LR projects.

Third, if a community has not been organised in the past, it may be useful to set up small income-generating activities to attract members to interact and get to know each other. These activities could be a small handicraft workshop that brings together female members to manufacture some small sellable products that they could use to earn extra income. More importantly, it provides great opportunities for them to associate with each other and build trust relations. Similar community activities such as training workshops or sport competitions could facilitate community organising.

Myth No. 5

Stakeholders must trust each other before adopting LR

Some analysts have suggested that LR is not viable if stakeholders do not have preexisting trust in each other (Doebele 1982). This perception is derived from observations of LR practices in Germany, Japan, and South Korea where citizens have great confidence in the capacity and integrity of their government (Sorensen 2000). They also trust their social, legal, and political systems to prevent and punish fraudulent practices. Indeed, it is important that landowners trust their implementing agencies and the system because they are putting their land-based wealth in the hands of other people who promise to return another piece of land of high value in the future. In many developing countries where the rule of law does not govern the nation, it is inconceivable that such property exchanges could take place if there is no trust between the government and citizens and between private developers and local residents.

Ironically, LR has been adopted in many developing countries where there is a lack of trust between the government and citizens and between community members and private sectors. In examining the case studies, there are always landowners who care about individual interests and do not understand their social responsibilities. Some politicians and public officials care more about reelections and job security than their commitments to the society. Some private developers care more about profits than their corporate responsibilities and believe that affordable housing should solely be the mandate of the public sector. In most cases, there may be no overlapping interests that motivate these parties to work together. Thus, it is important to realistically assess and understand the motivations of the parties who engage in collective action to make the win-win outcomes of LR possible.

How can trust be built?

If we can agree that trust-based relationships require a long-term investment from the interacting parties, the key question is how to build trust. Our case studies showed that it is important to find a reputable and neutral broker to initiate the project. If the project is proposed by a government that landowners or informal settlers do not trust, it will require a lot of work to change the perception of the residents before any meaningful negotiations can be carried out. These neutral brokers could be local academic institutions such as the Los Andes University in Bogota, international and local NGOs such as the Development Workshop in Angola (Cain, Weber, and Festo 2018; Brian and Mora 2018; Pinilla 2018), or international development agencies such as the World Bank in Vietnam, that could use their financial and technical support to incentivise cooperation from different stakeholders.

Because a single stakeholder cannot achieve the redevelopment goals alone, the prime function of the neutral broker is to identify mutual interests for involved parties, assign responsibilities to different stakeholders, mediate conflicts, and nurture parties' commitments to their duties. To do that, the broker must maintain a reputation of impartiality in order to gain the trust and respect of all stakeholders. By directing and shaping the interactions among stakeholders, the broker will be able to create substantive dialogues and facilitate collective decisions and actions among these parties. With repeated cooperation and positive reinforcement, trust-based relationships will emerge.

Other common perquisites

It is important that the conditions discussed are examined carefully to tailor the operations of LR to the local contexts. Although there is no one-size-fits-all LR model, our case studies have shown some commonalities that are necessary for adopting LR.

First, it is generally believed that LR is most appropriate for situations in which affected landowners or land occupants have motivation to stay in the neighbourhood. Because they do not plan to move due to their attachment to the community or proximity to their workplace, the idea of property swapping will enable them to return to the same neighbourhood. If residents prefer to move somewhere else and start a new life, purchasing property through voluntary market exchanges or government acquisition may be a better alternative. That said, there have been many LR projects in which absentee landowners were the majority of the interested parties. Under these situations, the negotiation of LR will follow a very different direction because these landowners are mainly interested in maximising the capital gains on their real assets.

Second, it is generally true that financial assistance or bridge loans provided by the government or international development agencies (such as the World Bank, the Asian Development Bank, and UN-Habitat) through central authorities can help facilitate LR, even though part of the project costs can be recovered from land sale.

Third, government's credible commitment to LR is critical for its successful adoption. This is especially true in the cases of Bhutan, Thailand, Ethiopia, and Vietnam where the government was actively promoting the project. This prerequisite is undoubtedly true not only for LR but for all policy experiments. Without the government's long-term support, no policy experiments could survive inevitable setbacks during their trial period. If government commitment is absent, international development agencies could act as honest brokers to facilitate cooperation among stakeholders.

Conclusion: toward a governance-centered approach

As can be seen from earlier discussions, we are suggesting a different focus for conducting LR projects. We are not suggesting a major shift away from perfecting the technical aspects of this land tool. Instead, we want to propose expanding the professional focuses to a governance-centered approach that emphasises the following three factors.

First, LR is a consensus-building mechanism. Given the lack of data and technical expertise in most developing countries, it will be hard to calculate accurately a land exchange formula. Despite this limitation, LR could still be implemented if the stakeholders can agree upon a generally acceptable arrangement for land swapping. Hence, negotiation and consensus building are the operations that actually drive the project, not the scientific estimation of land values before and after LR.

Second, LR should be founded on the idea of creating win-win outcomes for all involved parties. Again, this relates closely to the possibility of building a governance structure that will allow all parties to have a share of the gains; at the same time, no single party will reap the entire redevelopment benefits. LR is not a winner-takes-all scenario.

Last but not least, these two factors require developing reciprocity and the perception of fairness, both of which are fundamental for engendering the collective action required for LR projects. Most people will be unwilling to cooperate if others do not reciprocate their collaborative efforts. To encourage reciprocity, collaborative gestures must be perceived as fair. Because contexts are different, the perception of fairness has to be established through open discussions and mutual understanding. This leads us back to the idea of governance— that is, to design open and inclusive decision-making procedures so that no stakeholders would feel that they were left out from the decision on how to allocate the costs and benefits of land redevelopment.

Notes

1 This chapter is based on the World Bank-MIT joint e-learning course developed by the authors. Similar versions of the course can be accessed via the World Bank Open Learning Campus at: https://olc.worldbank.org/content/land-readjustment-self-paced or edX: www.edx.org/course/entrepreneurial-land-redevelopment-mitx-stl-161x-0.
2 LR is also referred to as land pooling (Minnery et al. 2013; Norbu 8), land sharing (Rabé 2010; Leeruttanawisut 2018), land consolidation (Winarso, Dharmapatni, and Chen 2016), or land reparcelisation in different countries (Sorensen 2000; Turk 2008).

References

Balakrishnan, Sai. 2018. Land Readjustment in Western India: New Conditions and Challenges for the 21st Century. In *Global Experiences in Land Readjustment, Urban Legal Case Studies*, Volume 7. Nairobi, Kenya: United Nations Human Settlements Programme, Chapter 8.

Brian, Isabel and Pia Mora. 2018. *Land Readjustment as Reconstruction Strategy in Chile*. In *Global Experiences in Land Readjustment, Urban Legal Case Studies*, Volume 7. Nairobi, Kenya: United Nations Human Settlements Programme, Chapter 11.

Cain, Allan, Beat Weber, and Moises Festo. 2018. Community Land Readjustment in Huambo, Angola. In *Global Experiences in Land Readjustment, Urban Legal Case Studies*, Volume 7. Nairobi, Kenya: United Nations Human Settlements Programme, Chapter 10.

Deininger, Klaus, Harris Selod, and Tony Burns. 2011. *The Land Governance Assessment Framework: Identifying and Monitoring Good Practice in the Land Sector*. Washington, DC: The World Bank.

Doebele, William A. 1982. *Land Readjustment: A Different Approach to Financing Urbanization*. Lexington, MA: Lexington Books.

Durand-Lasserve, A. 2006. Market-Driven Evictions and Displacements: Implications for the Perpetuation of Informal. *Informal Settlements: A Perpetual Challenge?*, 207.

Fernandes, Edesio. 2011. *Regularization of Informal Settlements in Latin America.* Policy Focus Report. Cambridge, MA: Lincoln Institute of Land Policy.

Fischel, William A. 2004. Why Are Judges So Wary of Regulatory Takings? In *Private Property in the 21st Century: The Future of An American Ideal*, edited by Harvey M. Jacobs. Northampton, MA: Edward Elgar (In association with The Lincoln Institute of Land Policy).

Galiani, Sebastian, and Ernesto Schargrodsky. 2010. Property Rights for the Poor: Effects of Land Titling. *Journal of Public Economics* 94: 700–729.

Gillert, Allan. 2002. On The Mystery of Capital and The Myths of Hernando de Soto: What Difference Does Legal Title Make? *International Development Planning Review* 24, 1: 1–19.

Hong, Yu-Hung. 2007a. Assembling Land for Urban Development: Issues and Opportunities. In *Analyzing Land Readjustment: Economics, Law, and Collective Action*, edited by Yu-Hung Hong and Barrie Needham. Cambridge, MA: Lincoln Institute of Land Policy, Chapter 1.

Hong, Yu-Hung. 2007b. Law, Reciprocity, and Economic Incentives. In *Analyzing Land Readjustment: Economics, Law, and Collective Action*, edited by Yu-Hung Hong and Barrie Needham. Cambridge, MA: Lincoln Institute of Land Policy, Chapter 8.

Hong, Yu-Hung. 2008. Sharing vs. Eminent Domain. *Communities and Banking* 19, 1: 3–5.

Hong, Yu-Hung, and Barrie Needham. 2007. *Analyzing Land Readjustment: Economics, Law, and Collective Action.* Cambridge, MA: Lincoln Institute of Land Policy.

Hong, Yu-Hung, and Julia Tierney. 2013. *Making LR Participatory and Inclusive.* Working paper no. WP1. Cambridge, MA: Land Governance Laboratory.

Leeruttanawisut, Kittima. 2018. *Revisiting Land Sharing in Bangkok: The Sengki Case.* In *Global Experiences in Land Readjustment, Urban Legal Case Studies*, Volume 7. Nairobi, Kenya: United Nations Human Settlements Programme, Chapter 5.

Lin, George C. S., and Xun Li. 2014. Land Readjustment in Urbanizing China: Decentralization, Profit Concession, and Redevelopment of Village Land in Chinese Cities. In *Global Experiences in Land Readjustment, Urban Legal Case Studies*, Volume 7. Nairobi, Kenya: United Nations Human Settlements Programme, Chapter 1.

Lovering, John, and H. Türkmen. 2011. Bulldozer Neo-Liberalism in Istanbul: The State-Led Construction of Property Markets, and the Displacement of the Urban Poor. *International Planning Studies* 16, 1: 73–96.

McFarlane, Colin. 2012. Rethinking Informality: Politics, Crisis, and the City. *Planning Theory and Practice* 13, 1: 89–108.

Minnery, John, Teti Argo, Haryo Winarso, Do Hau, Cynthia C. Veneracion, Dean Forbes, Iraphne Childs. 2013. Slum Upgrading and Urban Governance: Case Studies in Three South East Asian Cities. *Habitat International* 39: 162–169.

Norbu, Geley. 2014. *Land Pooling In Thimphu, Bhutan.* In *Global Experiences in Land Readjustment, Urban Legal Case Studies*, Volume 7. Nairobi, Kenya: United Nations Human Settlements Programme, Chapter 7.

Patel, Sheela, Celine d'Cruz and Sundar Burra. 2002. Beyond Evictions in a Global City: People-Managed Resettlement in Mumbai. *Environment and Urbanization* 14: 159–172.

Payne, Geoffrey. 2001. Urban Land Tenure Policy Options: Titles or Rights? *Habitat International* 25: 415–429.

Pinilla, Juan Felipe. 2014. *A New Approach to Urban Renewal in Bogotá, Colombia: The Fenicia Project.* In *Global Experiences in Land Readjustment, Urban Legal Case Studies*, Volume 7. Nairobi, Kenya: United Nations Human Settlements Programme, Chapter 2.

Rabé, Paul E. 2010. Land Sharing in Phnom Penh and Bangkok: Lessons from Four Decades of Innovative Slum Redevelopment Projects in Two Southeast Asian Boom Towns. In Paper for the Policy Workshop, *Places We Live: Slums and Urban Poverty in The Developing World.*

Sanyal, Bishwapriya, and Vinit Mukhija. 2001. Institutional Pluralism and Housing Delivery: A Case of Unforeseen Conflicts in Mumbai, India. *World Development* 29, 12: 2043–2057.

Sorensen, Andre. 2000. Conflict, Consensus or Consent: Implications of Japanese Land Readjustment Practice for Developing Countries. *Habitat International* 24, 1: 51–73.

Turk, Scene S. 2007. An Analysis on the Efficient Applicability of the Land Readjustment Method in Turkey. *Habitat International* 31, 1: 53–64.

Turk, Scene. 2008. An Examination for Efficient Applicability of the Land Readjustment Method at the International Context. *Journal of Planning Literature* 22, 3: 229–242. The blended learning segment ends.

Turk, Scene. 2014. *Could LR Be Participatory and Inclusive in Turkey?* In *Global Experiences in Land Readjustment, Urban Legal Case Studies*, Volume 7. Nairobi, Kenya: United Nations Human Settlements Programme, Chapter 6.

Viratkapan, V., and R. Perera. 2006. Slum Relocation Projects in Bangkok: What Has Contributed to Their success or Failure? *Habitat International* 30, 1: 157–174.

Winarso, Haryo, Indira Dharmapatni, and Mansha Chen. 2016. Community Empowerment for Successful Land Consolidation-Case Study: Banda Aceh and Denpasar, Indonesia, paper at the 2016 Annual World Bank Conference on Land and Poverty.

Zekuel, Abele and Yu-Hung Hong. 2014. *Urban Redevelopment Experience in Addis Ababa, Ethiopia.* In *Global Experiences in Land Readjustment, Urban Legal Case Studies*, Volume 7. Nairobi, Kenya: United Nations Human Settlements Programme, Chapter 3.

3

Across Asia, if done on the cheap

Mike McDermott

Introduction

Many of the best years of my working life have been spent between Kathmandu and Istanbul. Those adventures began over 40 years ago, when I went on the first of many "Asian Overlands" – mainly 10–13-week hotel and camping coach tours between Kathmandu and London. My job was to look after the passengers (mainly young professionals), which included explaining the sights and cultures along the way through Nepal, India, Pakistan, Afghanistan, Iran, Iraq, Jordan, Syria and Turkey, and from there through Europe to London. The "bible" for that trip for the thousands of hippies that were our fellow travellers along the overland was a book called "Across Asia on the Cheap," the foundational work for the Lonely Planet publishing empire.

Two thousand years before then, the world's economic centre of gravity lay near the centre of that road, where the spice roads from India and beyond met the Silk Road from China in what is now Northern Afghanistan. Now, the world's economic centre of gravity is heading back there from its trek westwards over the millennia, and it is being facilitated by the New Silk Road – the China-led One Belt, One Road (OBOR) initiative (Figures 3.1 and 3.2).

Over the last 10 years, I have been back to several of the countries along Asian Overland and/or the Old Silk Road, but this time as a land policy, institutional, legal and valuation adviser and facilitator, with a strong emphasis on land acquisition and valuation processes in the countries along the way. To research this chapter's identification of major contemporary issues across Asia in this context, I have examined[1] those processes in Nepal, India, Pakistan, Mongolia, Afghanistan, Tajikistan, Kyrgyzstan, Kazakhstan, Uzbekistan, Azerbaijan, Georgia, Armenia and Turkey, and drawn lessons from them.

Many of these countries could benefit greatly from this huge OBOR initiative. As regards the many countries signed up for OBOR – 68 are currently engaged – note that the term "OBOR" is misleading. Just as the Old Silk Road changed directions depending on peace, politics, pestilences and payments (the four Ps), plus the Romans and the Chinese looking to get to one another around the Parthian Empire, so it will be with the New Silk Road. The Chinese are well aware of this, and OBOR is in reality many belts, many roads, many oil and

By far the most rapid shift in the world's economic center of gravity happened between 2000 and 2010.

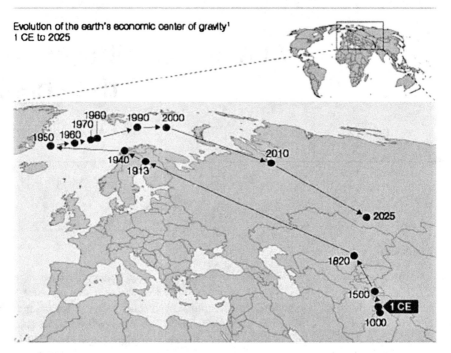

Evolution of the earth's economic center of gravity[1]
1 CE to 2025

[1]Calculated by weighting national GDP by each nation's geographic center of gravity; a line drawn from the center of the earth through the economic center of gravity locates it on the earth's surface. For detailed analysis, see the appendix in the McKinsey Global Institute (MGI) report *Urban world: Cities and the rise of the consuming class.*
Source: MGI analysis using data from Angus Maddison, University of Groningen; MGI Cityscope v2.0

Figure 3.1 McKinsey's evolution of the earth's economic centre of gravity (McKinsey, Dobbs et al. 2012)

gas pipelines and the major maritime routes linking to them. A more recent terminology, the belt and road initiative, is therefore more accurate, but for now "OBOR" is more widely understood. Whatever rubric is used, if all or even most of the proposed developments come to pass, it will be the largest infrastructure project that the world has ever seen.

However, if land acquisition and valuation principles and practices do not meet international best practices, the dream could become a nightmare. In fact, even if they do meet those standards, there could still be unintended consequences. I emphasise that international best practices are not there just to be nice. They are as tried and true as generally practicable, and are there to ensure that as many unnecessary difficulties as possible can be avoided, allowing more time and treasure to be devoted to the necessary ones. Sadly, it would appear that the pain of many of the hard-earned lessons often has to be gone through anew by those who think they know better.

Therefore, this chapter is based on researches of acquisition and compensation principles and practices of some countries now along the routes of the old Asian Overlands and Silk Roads that may be affected by OBOR. It then reports on general issues these studies and my own experience have identified. They indicate that just as those routes chopped and changed

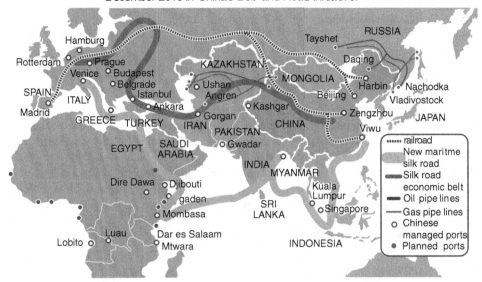

The reviving of the Silk Road
infrastructure projects being planned and undertaken as of December 2015 in China's Belt and Road initiative.

Figure 3.2 The New Silk Road
Source: Mercator Institute for China Studies (MERICS), Berlin.

according to conditions, so do acquisition and compensation practices. But there are now normative principles available for them to enact the most skilful means available. These have been developed worldwide, often at great cost, through long experience and countless cases. Many of these are now linked together in the policy and practice documents of international donors, but there is still a long journey ahead of us to achieve the objective of the "before and after" principle of resettlement and compensation: that *at worst the dispossessed persons should be no worse off after the expropriations than they were before*. Hereinafter, I will refer to this as the "Principle." In this framing, that means providing compensation across Asia that is neither on the cheap nor extravagant, but is just, and which can be seen to be just.

To set the scene for the reader, as a result of my lived experience the following review provides a travelogue: two paragraphs for every country I have researched for this chapter. The first paragraph is about the country 2,000 years ago, when the Old Silk Road was in the first of its heydays and the world's economic centre of gravity was along it. Even though it is now so long ago, a depth of historical understanding may be developed from it which could, in turn, provide insights into current international sensibilities and potentialities. The second concerns its forthcoming role along the New Silk Road (OBOR) where the world's economic centre of gravity is returning. This return is subject to many provisos, one possibly being that the resettlement and compensation processes required do not cause destructive riots, civil disturbances and the like.

As much of it is from lived experience and all of it is high level and only by way of introduction, I do not include reference to sources in the travelogue text, but refer the reader to Peter Frankopan's *The Silk Road: A New History of the World* (2015) as an overall reference source, and because it contains references to other excellent sources. The next section of the chapter then addresses the general problems and issues across Asia identified by my researches either in or of those countries. Finally, the chapter draws its own conclusions, preparatory to the final chapter of this book. Both these later sections contain reference to the sources.

The Silk Road travelogue

Nepal

The Old Silk Road[2]

Two thousand years ago, what is now Nepal was already included in the network of commercial relations of what is now India. The mighty Himalayas were the trade barriers to the north, and impenetrable jungles and other barriers were the trade barriers to the east. At that time Buddhism was prominent from northern India to Afghanistan. Buddhism entered China via the junction of the Silk Road from India to that from China at Balkh, in modern Afghanistan. Buddha's birthplace is in what is now Nepal, and he traversed these trade routes at least as far as Varanasi during his process towards enlightenment. Centuries later, at this time of 2,000 years ago, a strong pilgrimage tradition had been established in Buddhism. By this time, spiritual motives motivated travellers to Nepal from afar, as well as any commercial ones.

The New Silk Road

On 12 May 2017, Nepal signed an agreement to be part of the OBOR agreement. The economic, geopolitical and other consequences of this are yet to be determined, but as India is ambivalent about OBOR they could be serious.

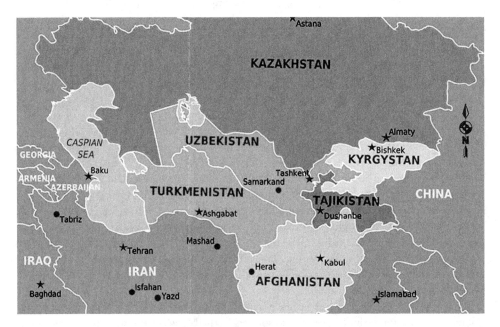

Figure 3.3 The lands of the Old and New Silk Roads from Georgia to China
Source: Central Asia Map by Cacahuate, Wikipedia Commons.

India

The Old Silk Road

At that time, India had the world's largest Gross Domestic Product (GDP) with about 40 per cent of the total; China had about 30 per cent, and the rest of Eurasia had about 30 per cent. India's network of commercial relations already extended from western Europe to the Spice Islands (now in Indonesia). That network linked with the Old Silk Road through what are now Pakistan and Afghanistan. An integral part of that network was what later became known as the Grand Trunk Road, which runs from Bangladesh to Kabul, Afghanistan, and which we used to travel along on the Asian Overlands.

The New Silk Road

At the time of writing, India opposes the OBOR initiative and is countering it with several other initiatives. It realises that it has missed the boat so far with central Asian trade and intends to rectify that. One such initiative is with Japan, and they look together towards establishing an Asia-Africa Growth Corridor (AAGC). One reason is that OBOR involves major infrastructural development in Pakistan, including over territory that India claims as its own. India's overland routes are effectively blocked off by Pakistan to the west and China to the north, and means to circumvent this are by an International North-South Transport Corridor (INSTC). As well as India itself, member states of this proposal are Russia, Iran, Armenia, Azerbaijan, Belarus, Bulgaria (observer status), Kazakhstan, Kyrgyzstan, Oman, Syria, Tajikistan, Turkey and Ukraine. The proposal is that from ports along India's western shore, ships will transport goods to Bandar Abbas in Iran, then head north through Iran to Moscow and St. Petersburg before looping back down by sea again along the western coast of Europe to the Mediterranean, and then through the Suez Canal and the Red Sea to the Arabian Sea, back to India. Rather like the Old Silk Road had routes both north and south of the Taklimakan desert, so with the New Silk Road routes are planned or being considered for the western and eastern sides of the Caspian Sea. The western side would traverse Azerbaijan, and the eastern side would link with the Iran-Turkmenistan-Kazakhstan railway. Feasibility studies indicate that these routes for the North-South Transport Corridor would be much cheaper than current ones, cut the transportation time in half and could thereby substantially improve India-Russia trade. Moreover, with less land to be acquired its establishment costs in terms of expro-priation, resettlement and compensation could be significantly lower than some proposed alternatives (a cost factor routinely underestimated in such projects, often resulting in unjustly low compensation for the powerless).

India is also expediting plans for a South Asian Sub-Regional Economic Cooperation (SASEC) road, which focusses on improving connectivity between Bangladesh, Bhutan, Nepal and India. SASEC itself also enfolds the Maldives, Sri Lanka and Myanmar, and the road is to form part of the Great Asian Highway, a 32-nation initiative under the aegis of the United Nations Economic and Social Commission for Asia and the Pacific (UNESCAP). It starts in Japan and connects South Korea, China, Hong Kong, Southeast Asia, Bangladesh, India, Pakistan, Afghanistan and Iran. From there it goes to the border between Turkey and Bulgaria, west of Istanbul, where it joins with European route E80. The Grand Trunk Road will maintain its prominence from before the time of the Old Silk Road to form part of that highway.

Pakistan

The Old Silk Road

The lands now within Pakistan were of major importance to trade of the time, the afore-mentioned network of commercial relations including the Indus River, at the mouth of which, near modern Karachi, lay the trading post called Barbarikon in Greek (which was the lingua franca of the time along the Silk Road, together with Aramaic) and the port city of Minnagara. This trade route went right up north to connect with the Grand Trunk Road, and to great ancient centres such as Taxila. Exports from there to the Roman Empire included aromatics; herbs and spices; indigo; semi-precious stones; and cloths, including silk.

The New Silk Road

Pakistan is to be a major participant in the New Silk Road, the China-Pakistan Economic Corridor (CPEC) being the "flagship" initiative of the whole OBOR, not only reviving aforementioned feeder routes of the Old Silk Road, but creating new ones. The possibility of the Chinese establishing a naval base in the vicinity of Karachi, not to mention other military support for OBOR infrastructure, dismays the Indians and others. The geopolitical importance of the area to China is clear. The potential sites are close to those globally strategically vital areas, the Persian Gulf and the Strait of Hormuz.

Mongolia

The Old Silk Road

Sitting north of China and south of Siberia, Mongolia's role in the Silk Road was at its height over a thousand years after the time examined here. Some consider that much of the terrible destruction wrought on the great cities of the Old Silk Road was inflicted to ensure the permanency of Mongol dominance over the trade. The invading Mongols reopened the Silk Road in time for travellers like Marco Polo to traverse it.

The New Silk Road

Mongolia is central to the China–Mongolia–Russia corridor of OBOR, and copper from its vast Oyu Tolgoi copper mine is transported along it to China, Russia and Europe. Again, however, there are many geopolitical obstacles that must be overcome. One relates back to the travel of religions along the Old Silk Road. Mongolia's form of Buddhism revered the Dalai Lama, and his visit there greatly upset the Chinese.

Afghanistan

The Old Silk Road

Here, we arrive at the fulcrum of the Old Silk Road, where the commercial networks from what are now Nepal, India and Pakistan, which extended as far south as modern Indonesia, met the Old Silk Road from China in what is now in northern Afghanistan near Balkh, the Mother of Cities, seat of the Greek Bactrian Kingdom established by one of Alexander the Great's generals. The area remained Greek-ruled for centuries, but by this time they had been conquered. However, their Hellenistic influence remained (Mairs 2011). That is, Balkh was the link point of the three regions – India, China and the rest of Eurasia – which produced almost all the world's GDP at the time. Alexander's wife, Roxana, came from the region. It was also the major western city within the Kushan Empire. Under Ashoka the Great, it supported Buddhism in its Empire, which stretched back down to Barbikon in the south, up to the major Silk Road city of Fergana in the north and across the north of India to the east of Mathura, just north of Agra, the eastern capital of the Empire and the legendary birthplace of Lord Krishna. Balkh was razed to the ground by the Mongols, and it never recovered.

The New Silk Road

Due to geopolitical matters – the "Great Game" narrative – in particular those following upon the Saur Revolution in 1978 (which I witnessed from my hotel balcony), Afghanistan is in danger of losing its historic role at the pivot of the great Eurasian trade routes. Furthermore, the combination of its rich mineral resources, serious difficulties in governance and other factors make it a classic candidate for the infliction of a "resource curse."[3] Even so, their spirit is not broken. As mentioned later, under the heading Tajikistan, acquisitions and other works are under way to link northern Afghanistan to OBOR, and work continues on the roads from Pakistan's Khyber Pass to Jalalabad, Kabul, Kandahar and Herat, and a memorandum of understanding has been signed between Iran and Afghanistan for a railway between Kahf in Iran and Herat in Afghanistan. Moreover, Uzbekistan is looking to continue that line from Herat to Mazar-i-Sharif, the modern successor to the nearby ruins of Balkh. Thereby, Uzbekistan could gain access to the Iranian port of Bandar Abbas. The US and India are reviving a "New Silk Road" plan announced by Hilary Clinton in 2011, which means to restore Afghanistan's historic central position for trans-Asian trade. The Chinese, too, recognise the core importance of Afghanistan to trans-Asian trade; the first-ever rail connection between the two countries – albeit not directly (for example, via the Wakan corridor) but indirectly via Kazakhstan and Uzbekistan – arrived in 2016. However, as long as the war there lasts Afghanistan's role will remain diminished, and when the infrastructure bypassing Afghanistan is completed, the diminishing of Afghanistan's role from its centrality of 2,000 years ago may become permanent. With many more fighters entering Afghanistan following their losses in Iraq and Syria, the prospect of peace seems ever more distant.

Kyrgyzstan

The Old Silk Road

The Silk Road began after the second century B.C. Han Dynasty Chinese Emperor Wudi heard of the sacred horses of Fergana, magnificent steeds immortalised in a Han Dynasty statue from the period from the Fergana Valley, which now stretches through Kyrgyzstan, Tajikistan and Uzbekistan. Some say the superstitious Emperor thought these sacred horses may be able to take him to the Tortoise Mountain of Xi Wangmu, Royal Mother of the West, who would then be able to bestow on him the peaches of immortality. Immortality in prospect, and the horses' potential as cavalry horses as well! Wudi could not resist the temptation. He sent off a diplomat called Zhang Qian who, after many adventures, returned to his Emperor who then asked the Ferganese for the horses. When they refused, Wudi put together a huge army, got the horses he wanted and opened up the Old Silk Road. To this day, Zhang Qian is remembered as a hero for his 25 years of exploration and adventure in opening the Silk Road, including years as a prisoner of the Huns (who later conquered to the gates of Rome itself). Zhang Qian should also be renowned at the global scale as a pioneer of our global village.

The New Silk Road

China has over 120 projects planned for Kyrgyzstan, many of which will involve resettlement and compensation issues. Furthermore, a rail link between Uzbekistan and China is mooted – a massive engineering challenge through those formidable mountains; there are both wavering political commitments and alternative routes under consideration, but once again any such development might involve resettlement and compensation issues.

Tajikistan

The Old Silk Road

The Old Silk Road contained many perils. Amongst the most arduous would have been the traversing of the Taklamakan desert and the passes through the Pamirs, one of the massive mountain ranges of the Central Asian Knot. Once accomplished, one could descend into the beautiful country of Tajikistan. Tajikistan has six sites designated by the United Nations Educational, Scientific and Cultural Organisation (UNESCO) in 2014 as World Heritage status because of their role along the Chang'an-Tian Shan corridor of the Silk Road[4] between Kashgar and Samarkand. Another route through the Pamirs went through Tajikistan between Kashgar and Balkh. The furthest of the many cities Alexander the Great founded, Alexander Eschate, is in Tajikistan's part of the Fergana Valley. Scholars generally believe that it is this city that the Chinese received the horses from.

The New Silk Road

Tajikistan retains its geographic centrality along the Silk Road, but not a monopoly of the network. Geopolitical issues get in the way of realising that potential. There is a partly built Turkmenistan-Afghanistan-Tajikistan railway to go underneath Uzbekistan. If successful, the line will also link to the Iranian and Turkish networks to link to Europe to the west, the Arabian Sea to the south and South Asia to the east. However, Tajikistan has suspended its construction pending peace in Afghanistan.

Turkmenistan

The Old Silk Road

One of the great centres of Greco-Buddhist learning, the city known as Merv, was renamed Margiana after Alexander the Great's visit. It grew to be one of the largest cities in the world a thousand years ago, but, like Balkh, it was destroyed by Genghis Khan. Its ruins are now a UNESCO World Heritage site. Nisa, another ancient Silk Road city in Turkmenistan, flourished under the Parthian Empire (the great rival Empire to the Romans at this time) but was destroyed forever by an earthquake at about the time of this Old Silk Road narrative, 2,000 years ago.

The New Silk Road

China has about 154 infrastructure projects planned for Turkmenistan. Also, Turkmenistan's part of the Turkmenistan-Afghanistan-Tajikistan railway has already entered Afghanistan. Moreover, negotiations have begun to link Russia, Azerbaijan, Kyrgyzstan, Uzbekistan and Turkmenistan to Iran, and its seaport of Bandar Abbas – a north-south corridor to complement the east-west OBOR. While I have not included Iran in this travelogue I have traversed it north to south and east to west many times; its potential trade logistics benefits to India are profound. If OBOR, this north-south corridor, and other links are established, Iran's historic role along the Silk Road may even be surpassed to the benefit of Turkmenistan.

Kazakhstan

The Old Silk Road

As mentioned earlier, the umbrella term the "Silk Road" was in fact a number of trade routes carrying many items. I know of no evidence of Kazakhstan's trade routes being dominant in the 2,000 years-ago period we are referring to here: I believe that came centuries after, with the establishment of Turkish Khanates in the region.

The New Silk Road

Kazakhstan is vast: the largest landlocked country in the world, and the ninth-largest overall. It is also large economically; except for Russia, its GDP is bigger than any other former Soviet country. It is now an upper-middle-income country courted by many countries, and received over $20 billion in Foreign Direct Investment in 2016. Called "the buckle of the belt" of OBOR, it looks forward to being a major component of OBOR, both in terms of its infrastructure and its trade. Benefits to Kazakhstan will include access to the Pacific Ocean via Chinese ports. OBOR fits together well with Kazakhstan's own *Nurly Zhol* (Bright Path) initiative, which looks to link such transport and logistics matters with broader socio-economic concerns in Kazakhstan – manufacturing and industry, social infrastructure, small and medium enterprise development, energy supply, public utilities and home ownership.

Uzbekistan

The Old Silk Road

The city of Fergana, the valley of which extends as mentioned to both Tajikistan and Kyrgyzstan, is in modern Uzbekistan. Uzbekistan also has other fabled cities along the Silk Road of that time, such as Khiva, Bukhara and Tashkent (then called Chash). Another of these is Samarkand, over a millennium later the seat of the Empire of Tamerlane. His descendant, Babur, occupied and was expelled from both cities before conquering India and founding the Mughal Empire there. In turn, Babur's direct descendant, Shah Jahan, built the Taj Mahal. James Elroy Flecker's famous poem, *The Golden Road to Samarkand*,[5] reminds us that not only silk but many other high-value portable items were traded along the Silk Road and that the main road extended southwards from there in that period, going into the heartlands of Parthia (modern Iran) via Mashhad and Teheran (then called Rey) to Baghdad, the departure point for Samarkand in Flecker's poem. From Baghdad they would head west to the coast of the eastern Mediterranean such as Antioch, Tyre, Sidon Akko (Acre) and Caesarea via a network of trade routes already ancient then, parts of which were dominated at different times by the Nabateans of Petra and later (in the third century) Queen Zenobia of Palmyra, along such routes as the Kings Highway and the Via Maris,[6] before sailing to Alexandria, Rome, Ephesus, Byzantium and other cities of the Roman Empire. By the time Silk reached the Roman Empire, with all the tolls and trading along the way, it was literally worth its weight in gold. These days, however, rather than revenue from tolls,[7] the value added to the transit countries will arrive (as it did with the pioneering railroads in nineteenth-century US) in terms of added opportunities for exports of produce and the increases of the value of land around the stops along the routes.

The New Silk Road

Uzbekistan marks a differentiation between the Old and New Silk Roads. While 2,000 years ago the Old Silk Road, as mentioned, went south from what is now Uzbekistan to the latitudes of Afghanistan, Iran, Iraq and Syria, the New Silk Road sets a straighter course, across Asia to Turkey.[8] For now, instability afflicts many of the countries the Old Silk Road passed through from Uzbekistan, and once the infrastructure is in place those countries will not regain that role. They will surely link into the network when able. However, one belt of OBOR, a railroad north of all the countries mentioned here, goes through Russia from China's network, and loops back down into Europe south to Spain. Skilfully managed, Uzbekistan itself can look forward to a similar centrality concerning road transport to that it had in ancient times and is looking to rail transport corridors additional to the Russian one mentioned earlier.

Azerbaijan

The Old Silk Road

One of the routes of the Silk Road went from Kashgar, Samarkand, Bukhara and Khiva to the eastern shore of the Caspian Sea, where the products could be shipped to the other side, to modern Azerbaijan. This route could be competitive with the land routes to the south because the sea route often had several advantages, including usually being cheaper. As the Bay of Baku is the best harbour on the western side of the Caspian, it is likely that Baku would have been the port there. However, while there are Greco-Roman artefacts from around this time in the area, there are, as the ruins of Ephesus show, seas that have shifted their shores quite markedly over the millennia, and there is little known of the history of Baku at that time. If such a route existed 2,000 years ago, as it definitely did later, it could have resumed its westerly overland trail from Baku via Colchis and Iberia to the Black Sea, and from thence or its coastline to Byzantium. It is thought that such a route was used by the two unnamed smugglers, possibly Nestorian Christian monks, who presented live silkworms to Justinian I (A.D. 527–565) in Byzantium, by then called Constantinople, and started silk production in the west.

The New Silk Road

The importance of Azerbaijan to OBOR has already been alluded to in the section on Turkmenistan. However, there are other relevant initiatives, such as the Baku (Azerbaijan)-Tbilisi

(Georgia)-Kars (Turkey) line. In Kars, it will connect with Turkey's high-speed Ankara-Erzurum-Kars railway and once again integrate with other networks. Those networks include not only OBOR, but also the Trans-Caspian International Transport Route (TITR), rail and sea routes linking Azerbaijan to the rest of Eurasia as far east as China and west as Ukraine.

Georgia

The Old Silk Road

The aforementioned Colchis and Iberia were the areas where, centuries before, the legendary Jason had gone with his Argonauts in search of the Golden Fleece and the land of the Amazons. By this time it was a restive border of the Roman Empire, fought over between Pontus, Rome and the locals (including between themselves), the Iberians being particularly loyal to Rome at the time. Legend has it that Jesus's disciple Saint Andrew preached in what is now Georgia, doubtless travelling the Silk Road to get there.

The New Silk Road

Georgia was not included in the original plans for OBOR; however, the developing Anaklia Black Sea Deep Water Port Project, the Kars-Tbilisi-Baku railway, which is intended to complete a transport corridor linking Azerbaijan to Turkey, Georgia's strong trade links to the EU and imminent free trade agreement with China hold promise of even improving its historic importance along the Old Silk Road (Figure 3.3). Linking already existing and with planned transport corridors will bring Chinese produce to Europe and vice versa along the straightest path, and about twice as fast as ships can. Once again though, geopolitics could play a pernicious part.

Armenia

The Old Silk Road

Two thousand years ago, Armenia occupied a much larger area than it does today. The Romans gradually defeated the Armenian Artaxiad Dynasty in the first century B.C. At one stage, Mark Antony installed his and Cleopatra's six-year-old son on its throne. Armenia was finally overthrown by the Romans in A.D. 12. Only a few decades before then, its Empire had stretched from the Caspian to the Mediterranean Seas, and as such Silk Roads would have traversed Armenian territory on their treks westward. In 18 A.D. Marc Antony's great-grandson Zeno was installed to rule, and a peaceful period ensued until his death in 35 A.D. Later that century an Arsacid Dynasty took over, and remained until the fifth century. China and Armenia definitely knew of each other by that time, and there is evidence of direct relations between Armenia and China from 1,000 years ago.

The New Silk Road

As with Georgia, Armenia's somewhat parlous geopolitical situation has made welcome the possibility of participation in OBOR. However, it also acts as a deterrent to infrastructure investment. Azerbaijan and Armenia are still at loggerheads over Nagorno-Karabakh, and Armenia's historic conflicts with Turkey remain. However, Armenia is a member of the

Eurasian Economic Union, and its fellow members include Russia, Kyrgyzstan, Belarus and Kazakhstan – powerful and influential friends to have in the region. Even so, again, once infrastructure is in place more geographically efficient opportunities may never be realised.

Turkey

The Old Silk Road

Antioch, the capital of Roman Syria, was one of the great entrepots of the Roman Empire, and 2,000 years ago probably the major Western terminus of the Old Silk Road, as well as the major city of the Via Maris, and, boasting a population of over half a million, the third-largest city in the Roman Empire. From there, the produce could be shipped to the two larger cities, Rome and Alexandria, and other great cities of the Empire, including Ephesus, also in modern Turkey. Some would also have sailed to Byzantium, an independent city state prospering under the Pax Romana, thanks to its extraordinary location and an easily fortified position, both of which allowed it to become the greatest city in Europe for almost a thousand years, until it fell to the Turks on one of the most important dates in history, the 29 May 1453. It then became the capital of the massive Ottoman Empire for almost 500 years. Today, it is again one of the great cities of the world.

Within the Roman Empire, all roads led to Rome. That included the Silk Road, but it led to China as well. Whether or not anyone could traverse the whole span of the Silk Road – and there were many reasons why not – 2,000 years ago people from Petra to Capernaum to Antioch to Ephesus to Byzantium could step on roads that led all the way from Rome to China. And as China's sage Lao Tzu had said centuries before, the longest journey begins with a single step, and the way that can be known is not the way; perhaps such travellers did exist. After all, we only know of Marco Polo's travels because he was imprisoned and found an amanuensis in a fellow prisoner.

The New Silk Road

Turkey is a founder member of OBOR. As mentioned earlier, the OBOR should cut delivery times between Europe and China in half; between Turkey itself, however, and China, the time cut will be even more dramatic – perhaps to one-third the time or even less. The major obstacles in the way of achieving this vision are unquestionably geopolitical, and there is little doubt that powers that do not want it to happen will try to stir up trouble in the hope of delaying or even destroying the initiative. Attention to this aspect is a likely strategy, thereby making the adherence to international best practices as far as is possible in the relevant domain even more important.

The Silk Road travelogue conclusion

To progress the world's economic centre of gravity back towards its position 2,000 years ago, OBOR and the many other development initiatives across Asia will require a significant percentage of total global expropriation over the coming years. As with most of the planet, land is a sensitive issue across Asia, and often at all scales, from personal and households to national and international. As chaos theory confirms, and as do recent political events such as the trigger of the Arab Spring and that of the destruction of the British Empire, under some circumstances large events can snowball from little injustices. The trigger for the

Arab Spring was the self-immolation of the Tunisian trader Mohamed Bouazizi in protest over his treatment by a petty corrupt official. The trigger for the destruction of the British Empire was another petty bureaucrat, a South African railway ticket inspector, ejecting an insignificant-looking little man from a train, despite his holding a first-class ticket. The puny little nobody was a lawyer by the name of Mohandas Karamchand Gandhi. While clearly in each case, those little injustices were not the cause any more than the silk bolt that broke the camel's back, wise governance will attempt to minimise potential for any such grievances to occur in the first place. That is best achieved by justice being done and being seen to be done: no more, no less.

Major contemporary issues in expropriation across Asia

Introduction

One needs a lodestar to comment on major contemporary issues in expropriation across Asia. I have already provided that in the main introduction: the Principle that *at worst the dispossessed persons should be no worse off after the expropriations than they were before.* While simple to state, in practice achieving the two main required goals – the Principle both being achieved, and being seen to have been achieved – can be fiendishly difficult. Moreover, such difficulties may emerge at all the just scales mentioned earlier – scales from personal and households to national and international.

It gets worse. Problems caused at one scale can have major impacts at other scales. For example, policies and legislation at national and international scales can have major consequences at personal and household scales. If they are perceived as inequitable, regardless of whether or not they really are, those perceived injustices can then cause major blowbacks at national and international scales. Whether or not the grievances are legitimate, blowback can be orchestrated by those operating at any scale who may consider it is in their best interests to delay or destroy the project concerned (Roosevelt 1979). Looking at what is at stake along OBOR, it would be unwise to dismiss the possibility of agent provocateurs in this context.

Moreover, on the global scale, the government instrumentalities that must implement these processes, such as land administration and police forces, are often amongst the most corrupt of all forms of governance (Quan 2016).

We are therefore entering a world of potentially wicked problems:

> A wicked problem is a complex issue that defies complete definition, for which there can be no final solution, since any resolution generates further issues, and where solutions are not true or false or good or bad, but the best than can be done at the time. Such problems are not morally wicked, but diabolical in that they resist all the usual attempts to resolve them.
>
> *(Brown, Deane, Harris and Russell in Brown, Harris and Russell 2010, p. 4)*

While therefore not always sufficient, the aforementioned lodestar being achieved and being seen to have been achieved can be amongst the most robust defences against such occurrences. In turn, transparent and accountable adherence to international best principles and practices can be the optimal means of achieving that result. There are several expressions of these principles and practices, but when commenting later, I am primarily relying upon the Asian Development Bank's Safeguard Policy Statement (ADB 2009).

I therefore proceed by examining three topics with major issues along the Silk Roads in particular, and then provide an overall summary of issues in general. The three major topic headings are legal, procedural and valuational.

Legal

The relevant current legislation across Asia dates from 1894 to 2017. Sadly, it cannot be concluded that the age of the legislation is a reliable guide to its compatibility with internationally recognised best practice standards.

In his 50-country desktop survey of the status of the legislation relating to valuation for expropriation, Tagliarino (2017) includes six countries reviewed here – Afghanistan, Kazakhstan, Mongolia, India, Nepal and Pakistan – and the source of the Old Silk Road, China itself. While only a desktop review, and only of the legislation, it provides a practical analytical framework by interrogating the legislation by using the following ten questions (Table 3.1):

The answers to those questions were then placed within three categories: yes, partial or no. The countries whose laws were examined by both this and Tagliarino's study are Nepal, India, Pakistan, Afghanistan and Kazakhstan. To the nearest whole number, those countries averaged four yes, two partial and four no: not a promising situation.

Another major concern is for what purposes properties can be compulsorily acquired. Generalities such as "in the national interest," "national security" and the like can prove to be open doorways to abuse, including corruption and exploitation. It is clear that an articulation of the uses for which properties can be expropriated provides at least some protection against such behaviour. However, even when articulations are made, they may still be illegally extended. For instance, in one of these countries such a list of specific permissible

Table 3.1 List of Compensation Valuation Indicators (Tagliarino 2017)

1. Does the law allow for assessors to follow an alternative approach (e.g., "replacement cost" approach) instead of a "fair market value approach" to calculating compensation in cases where land markets are weak or non-existent?
2. Does the law provide compensation for unregistered customary tenure rights held by Indigenous Peoples and local communities?
3. Does the law establish special protections for women landholders regarding compensation entitlements?
4. Does the law require assessors to take into account the loss of business and other economic activities?
5. Does the law require assessors to take into account the improvements (i.e., attached and unattached assets on the land [e.g., crops, buildings]) made on the land?
6. Does the law require assessors to take into account intangible land values (e.g., cultural, social, historical land values)?
7. Does the law provide affected populations with the right to opt for alternative land instead of compensation in cash?
8. Does the law provide affected populations with the right to negotiate the amount of compensation?
9. Does the law require that compensation must be paid prior to the taking of possession of the land or within a specified timeframe thereafter?
10. Are affected populations granted the right to appeal decisions on the amount of compensation in court or before a tribunal?

uses was provided in the legislation, but one for the provision of parklands, a use often quite clearly in the public interest, was omitted. The government officials concerned just went ahead and did it anyway.

Procedural

A valuer from one of these countries told me that when he was negotiating for compensation under the relevant Act he was told by the official concerned that they had a budget, and the official had no authority to expend beyond it. So even though what the valuer told him made sense, the valuer's client would have to accept the budgeted amount. That is, the valuer's assertion, if confirmed, would mean that the official concerned rated the authority of the budget over that official's legal responsibility to obey the law!

Moreover, that incident occurred in a country with one of the most enlightened pieces of legislation concerning expropriation – "enlightened" not only in comparison with other countries along the Silk Road, but on a global scale. This serves to highlight a major procedural difficulty: the implementation of legal frameworks can involve suites of wicked problems, including but not limited to the valuational ones such as those described later. Under such circumstances, abuses can occur not only by corrupt officials, but also by honest and dedicated officials who have no ability to address the grievances of the dispossessed within the timeframes and budgets demanded of them.

Such procedural difficulties extend well beyond the aforementioned example. In contrast, I have been advised by concerned valuers in another of the aforementioned countries that in one instance the costs of the property acquisitions exceeded the budget for the entire project, which ran into hundreds of millions of dollars. In yet another country mentioned earlier, government officials urged the affected parties to surrender their properties to the state as a patriotic act. However, they remained silent about whether they would provide their own properties as compensation to the affected parties on similarly patriotic grounds.

Lacking both the procedural protocols and adequate training, protocols, information and guidance to effect the relevant policies' principles and laws, even the best officials may find such policies and laws unimplementable, and yet the project must go ahead. What are they to do? In many cases, their natural goodwill evaporates as they are forced to act as bulldozers, not out of malice but from their perspective out of necessity. After all, even when valuations in accordance with international best practices are provided they can differ wildly, with few if any procedures in place to qualitatively assess the valuations towards arriving at a figure in accordance with the relevant policies and laws.

Lack of procedural rigour also results in phantom properties being placed on lists for acquisition (ghost land and buildings or large jury-built premises built when so-called "valuation tables" are used to compensate for buildings on a flat rate per square metre for building types, disregarding their quality), with some or all the compensation going to corrupt officials or related parties. Such are but some examples of the many procedural dilemmas put before officials attempting to perform their roles, presented to be comprehensive but indicative of the procedural difficulties that may be encountered even with the most enlightened policies and laws in place.

Valuational

In its commentary on the transition economies of Eastern Europe and the Commonwealth of Independent States, the International Valuation Standards Council (IVSC) identified several unique economic, legal and institutional characteristics in those countries' property markets. These included:

- A poor or inadequate legal framework that does not allow for the efficient functioning of the property market.
- The lack of published information or difficulty in obtaining information regarding transactional and other data needed for proper valuation.
- Greater volatility of property markets.
- Lack of adequately trained professional valuers.
- Outdated national valuation standards.
- External pressure.
- Excessive or insufficient government intervention (IVSC 2001).

In my experience, these difficulties are hardly unique. They remain endemic within developing countries across Asia, but significant progress has been made on several of these fronts. One of the problems that has to be addressed in opaque markets is the corruption of the valuation process. A valuer from one of the aforementioned countries told me of discovering collaboration between another valuer and the client to defraud the acquiring authority by means of overvaluation, the valuer then getting a cut from the previously agreed figure between the valuer and the client, and the amount the valuer achieved in negotiations with the acquiring authority. Similarly, when compensations are too generous, land invaders such as speculative squatters or legitimate purchasers may intervene to milk the system, with or without collusion by corrupt officials or valuers. In another country, an official claimed that everyone knows what the market value is, so why is it necessary to provide evidence? In still another country, it was alleged that valuers collude with others to provide inflated values and take a cut of the fraudulent profits acquired thereby. When it is difficult to read the market, it is difficult to discern which valuation is honest and which is fraudulent.

The most effective remedy for this is institutionalising not only governmental supervision of valuers but also peer supervision to provide both peer punishment and co-evolutionary mechanisms (Ohdaira 2017). Peer supervision is particularly important for valuers, as one bad valuer can damage the credibility of them all, and credibility is fundamental to a valuer's existence.

In the case of property professionals such as valuers, peer supervision can be enacted by means of establishing institutes of valuers (for example, the Chamber of Appraisers in Azerbaijan). In general these are best established at national level, and in early stages at least, they are checked by government to ensure the high ethical and other professional standards required to elevate valuers to the levels required for court recognition as experts are achieved and sustained. Particularly in this context of compensation for expropriation, it should be noted that it was this need for valuers to be recognised as expert witnesses in courts that required that status in the first place. Already, there are both national and transnational institutes of valuers at varied stages of establishment and activity in the region: for example the Eurasian Association of Appraisers. The largest such transnational institute globally is the Royal Institution of Chartered Surveyors (RICS), which has established boards such as the North Asia Valuation Board to seed this process.

Summary

Across Asia, major deficiencies can be identified almost everywhere in the context of achieving the Principle.

We valuers observe that the highest and best legal use of a property may change when the surrounding environment does. For example, there may be a need for one shopping centre, or one hotel, in a locality. In such a case, once that hotel or shopping centre is developed, there will be no demand for another. When there is no demand, there is no need to supply, and the value of the unused properties reverts to a lower highest and best use, and thereby a lower value. That is, the first out of the blocks in such circumstances wins the race.

While matters are never that simple, they often are almost that simple, as the term "initial advantage" describes in complexity economics: that could well be the case here. Once habits are ingrained, agreements signed, transport corridors established, they are hard, albeit not impossible, to change. Again in valuation, we call that the "ant trail" when it comes to siting shops and offices. Once a critical level of momentum is gained, it may become practically unstoppable.

Given both the international rivalries and consequent urgency of gaining the initial advantage, the authorities may find the temptation to damn those in the way and go full speed ahead too great to resist. However, that would be unwise, as it would seed the ground with legitimate resentments such as those of Mohamed Bouazizi and Mahatma Gandhi mentioned earlier. Again from complexity and chaos theories, this is termed "the butterfly effect," from the observation that a flap of a butterfly's wings may, when the circumstances are right, trigger a cyclone.

The butterfly effect is a universal phenomenon, not confined to butterflies' wings. That is, counter-intuitively though it may be, stupendous consequences result from seemingly trivial causes. Moreover, exploiting internal resentments to gain international advantage is a game as old as empires (for example, see Roosevelt 1979), so the wiser strategy is to minimise such resentments via policies, laws, ethical and transparent principles and practices so that the aforementioned Principle is both achieved and seen to be achieved.

Even then, there may be such blowbacks: the point is to minimise them, thereby minimising the very real dangers they could present to such projects.

In the conclusion to his master's thesis (Section 5.1), Christopher De Gruben, MRICS, also a practising valuer, provided insights into the situation in Mongolia which I consider to be applicable to varying degrees to most of the countries along that span of the New Silk Road being addressed here:

> Capacity building, lack of verifiable and credible data, a poor regulatory environment, unwillingness to pay for high quality valuations, lack of client education all play their role as barriers to the optimum application of IVS.
>
> *(De Gruben 2017)*

Both De Gruben and I share the view of many such valuation practitioners, including those interviewed for his thesis.

An Asian Development Bank Report (ADB 2014) supplied a frame to summarise the major difficulties in Azerbaijan, which I here employ as it is useful for this high-level summary. As this chapter engages at the high level and does not drill down into the situation in particular countries, I will not drill down to specific overall gradings, as Tagliarino (2017) has performed in the legal context. Suffice to say that across Asia I have encountered the best (in the legislative sphere) and the worst (in all spheres) in my experience.

Institutional and technical capacity

One common problem is that even when expropriation laws approach international best practices, the legal framework to enact them – the rules and regulations to implement those laws – still require framing. The saying that "there is many a slip between cup and lip" is particularly appropriate in this space: it's one thing to say what should be done; discerning what can be done, and how, is often a far more complex task.

Moreover, while the lack of valuation capacity mentioned earlier is endemic, there are other disciplines lacking as well. For example, officials who have not been given the training to embark upon such sensitive procedures can be required to expropriate properties, and while they may have the temperament to excel in bureaucratic procedures, they may lack the character required to engage in the process in the firm but fair way such procedures require. Therefore, those tasked with resettlement and compensation procedures must have *trans*-technical capacities, including empathy and understanding, to competently implement the Principle. As Lewis Mumford put it, here we have reached a:

> point at which we utilize the completest developments in science and technics to approach once more the organic. But here again: our capacity to go beyond the machine rests upon our power to assimilate the machine. Until we have absorbed the lessons of objectivity, impersonality, neutrality, the lessons of the mechanical realm, we cannot go further in our development toward the more richly organic, the more profoundly human.
>
> *(Mumford 1934, p. 363)*

That also goes for resettlement and compensation competencies. Under such circumstances, manuals can assist in the implementation of the Principle only with those with the right personal qualities for their respective tasks, such as honesty, emotional intelligence and appropriate temperament, when it comes to resettlement officers, and being able to provide well-researched and articulated valuations without fear or favour, or other corrupt practises, when it comes to valuers. However, like any skill sets, the ones the manuals require take time to achieve expertise in, and costly mistakes involving too little or too generous resettlement and compensation terms can result even with the most competent but particularly with merely mechanical application. Mumford again:

> Those parts of reality that can be reduced to patent order, law, quantitative statement are no more real or ultimate than those parts which remain obscure and illusive. Indeed, when applied at the wrong moment or in the wrong place or in a false context the exactness of the description may increase the error of interpretation.
>
> *(ibid, p. 370)*

Therefore, there will be situations involving doubts that no manual can address, except for people who are capable of more than mere machine thinking. If it is to be one or the other, much international common law directs that the benefit of such doubts should go to those to whom resettlement and compensation is due, not to the acquiring authority. However, over-generous compensation can open up a new can of worms, the prey-to-predator effect, whereby the affected parties mistake consideration for weakness, and exploit the situation for their own enrichment at the expense of the public purse.

Such a manual should set out how to generally best implement the requirements in the relevant legal domain and, if that domain has accepted donor or other recommendations towards international best practices, how these are to be achieved within such laws. These manuals should be individually produced for each such domain and level of governance, and include what is to be done, how it is to be done and in what order. They should include but not be limited to the relevant surveys, not only spatial and tenurial but also social surveys such as censuses of affected parties and their affected properties (including how they and their properties are affected – impact assessment surveys and the like), and identification of vulnerable groups and any others likely to require special concern. Public consolation protocols and procedures should also be included and grievance redress mechanisms established. In many countries courts have years of backlog in their cases, and such local circumstances require addressing the cases at the local level. Remedies may include, but not be limited to, established international alternative dispute resolution procedures, mediation and the like.

Valuation

There are different levels of acceptable valuation accuracy for different purposes. Methodologies such as mass appraisals and valuation tables are generally appropriate for rating and taxing purposes. However, as upheld in common law within legal domains mentioned herein, they are plainly negligent in cases of expropriation. Consequently, if losses occur to either the affected parties or the acquiring authority as a result of such negligence, such losses should be recoverable from the negligent party concerned. This includes cases where the expropriating officers hold themselves out to be professional valuers when they are not. In this context, unless refused access, individual inspection and valuation of each property being acquired is a necessary but insufficient precondition to avoid a charge of negligence. Similarly, a speaking valuation (one leaving the reader apprised of both the evidence and the reasoning of the valuation) is necessary but insufficient. In cases of refused access, it would be recorded in the valuation, and, as in other standard assumptions, disclaimers and qualifications should be mentioned in a speaking valuation so that the reader is able to better assess the valuation on its merits.

In several countries, in the absence of any valuers of a professional status in the kind of property being acquired, values are determined by panels of government officials, despite the clear conflict of interests involved, sometimes with a token representative or two from the affected parties and sometimes not. Such panels may actually achieve a fair and reasonable result, and justice would thereby be done. However, such a panel is hardly the right look for justice being *seen* to done, which under these circumstances is also highly important. Consequently, value juries may be developed in the domain concerned in such circumstances, which are more likely to both achieve fair and reasonable results, and be perceived as doing so.

As with complying with a manual, even when the valuation complies with the prescribed protocols, that does not mean the valuer should be accepted as an expert. That depends on experience and training. This field is not one for inexperienced valuers; only the best should be engaged – a problem when there are few if any valuers in the domain concerned.

As well as land and buildings, to achieve the Principle there are other properties which may need to be separately compensated for in the domain concerned – crops and trees, businesses and the like. In some cultures, for example, a person can own trees and their produce on another's property. The main heads of compensation over and above that for the land and buildings – severance, disturbance, injurious affection and solatium – may require competencies beyond those of a professional real estate valuer to assess. Once again, to achieve the Principle such matters must be taken into account.

Vulnerable groups

The elderly, infirm and other socio-economic groups (for example, single mothers) may require special care for the Principle to be achieved. This is to be accomplished via the head of compensation known as disturbance. Disturbance compensation is to cover all the costs of the relocation, including those of legal, valuational and other advice if required, stamp duties and other imposts that would otherwise not arise, loss of business income and the like. Like the valuations themselves and all other heads of compensation, such costs will vary on a case by case basis.

Livelihood restoration

As with the special needs of vulnerable groups, to achieve the Principle restoration of livelihoods will vary. This comes within the disturbance head of compensation (provided as always that it is allowed within the relevant legislation). It is often impossible to predict exactly how long a particular livelihood will require to be restored and whether or not a particular affected party will be diligent in restoring the livelihood, whether the compensation paid will be abused and a host of other contingencies; however, once the prospects are learnt in the relevant domain and livelihood through experience, a heuristic can be established. For example, generally fruit traders may only need three months to get their livelihoods back, others may need six months and others may perhaps never do so. Once again, general heuristics are acceptable as orienting generalisations, but special circumstances may require special compensation. Generally, skills in judgements of this nature may require expert input; not necessarily valuers, but accountants, other traders or similar capable of providing an opinion of expert status, and generally such skills are often lacking in the less-developed countries along the Silk Road.

Monitoring and evaluation

When we are placed in a bureaucratic role, it is a natural impulse to pay compensation and consider oneself rid of the affected parties. After all, they have been resettled, they have their compensation, so goodbye. However, even when short-term monitoring and evaluation protocols have been established and punctiliously followed over the project and the short-term thereafter, on many occasions that process has been shown not to have achieved the Principle over the long term. Sometimes socially devastating effects have emerged even when all seemed acceptable at the time. Much can be gained in this regard from the sharing of experiences by implementing agencies along the Silk Road and elsewhere, requiring long-term institutional and technical capacities, not just ad hoc ones for the life of the project.

Financial facilitation of the reconciliation of livelihood rehabilitation requirements

This facilitation is generally overlooked along the Silk Road, risking long-term pain for short-term gain. Once again, financial, institutional and technical capacities are recommended for all countries along the Silk Road to ensure the sustainability of fulfilling the Principle.

Simplification of the government approval mechanisms

Einstein's observation that there is nothing more simple than complicating, and nothing more complicated than simplifying, is relevant here. Once again, costly lessons can be avoided by learning from international experiences, but costly lessons can be encountered by simply importing such mechanisms without duly diligent consideration of their local applicability, including the capacities of locals to implement them. Simplicity is only good when it emerges from complex understanding of local circumstances: then, it can be of great benefit to all concerned. Once again, improvements in this regard are recommended even in the most advanced countries along the Silk Road.

Grievance redress mechanism

The aforementioned methodologies include internationally accepted alternative dispute resolution procedures, such as the institution of a Land Acquisition Inspectorate for accepting and reviewing complaints or claims, mediation or the still relatively untried procedure of value juries. While cultural acceptability is vital in grievance redressing, and adjustments may be necessary to be acceptable, procedures to ensure that only the most contentious require the decisions of the courts are highly recommended. Once again, adaptation of international experiences should be considered to save unnecessary pain for all concerned; there will still be more than enough of that without it.

Preparation of a country land acquisition and resettlement framework

If not already prepared, this process is a vital one towards the implementation not only of OBOR but the many supplementary and competing plans currently on the table. There are potentially great improvements in human development along the Silk Road if such projects are skilfully planned and executed, that skill including the empowerment of as many persons in the countries concerned as possible. That objective must not exclude those parties whose properties are to be expropriated: the means must be worthy of the ends.

Conclusion

Those along the Old Silk Road did not only trade in silk and other goods. Of even greater importance to this day, they traded in "duty free" ideas – cultural exchanges by the fire at night, with stories and poems and song, and exchanges of religious, philosophical, artistic and technological knowledge, just as we did in our free-camps in the desert on our Asian Overlands around 40 years ago. Today, there is a new opportunity for those places to learn from one other on a personal basis, not merely via machinery.

However, both personal and mechanical communications, rather than isolated silos in each country having to address blunders that could have been easily avoided by such communication, are required across Asia. In addition to particular circumstances unique to each country, there are also general circumstances applicable in applying just laws concerning expropriation, resettlement and compensation. When it comes to policies concerning laws and their implementing protocols, those learnt from hard experience by international financial institutions can save a great deal of unnecessary conflict. While they may appear to be charitable by the mechanically minded in a hurry to get things done, they are not just that. Rather, they are far more practical than attempts to do things on the cheap. They are tried and tested as the best processes to resolve the aforementioned contemporary issues across Asia, and they have emerged as needed to implement the Principle: not just financially but overall. In implementing that Principle, not only are firmness and fairness essential, but they must be seen to be as such.

It is therefore wise for acquiring authorities to institutionalise engagement with one another, to brainstorm on what lessons they have learnt, and are still to learn, towards implementing the Principle. In so doing, they will do well to emphasise that a merely mechanistic approach simply will not achieve that Principle because they are dealing with human beings for whom, as

Alexander's tutor Aristotle observed around the time of Alexander's conquests along most of the routes that would become the Silk Road, the source of all enmity is the feeling of being slighted.[9]

If they can implement that Principle wisely, it will facilitate the return of the world's economic centre of gravity back along the Silk Road towards where it resided 2,000 years ago, to the great benefit not only of those along the Silk Road but also, as with the Old Silk Road, to the ultimate benefit of us all. If they do not implement the Principle and try to do things on the cheap, Asia may become very cross indeed.

Notes

1 In some cases professionally in the countries concerned, in others only desktop researches.
2 www.thoughtco.com/ancient-nepal-overview-121072.
3 https://en.wikipedia.org/wiki/Resource_curse.
4 http://en.widenews24.com/2016/10/11/unesco-designated-changan-tianshan-corridor-silk-road-world-heritage-site/.
5 www.poetryatlas.com/poetry/poem/119/the-golden-road-to-samarkand.html.
6 One of the major roads of the latter from the Kings Highway passed through Capernaum. Jesus therefore preached along the Silk Road.
7 Tolls would simply increase the viability of the maritime routes over the land-based ones. Already, maritime transport in several contexts is around two to three times cheaper than rail, which is cheaper than road by a similar order. The blocking of the Silk Road through wars, with rewards for victory including such tolls and other taxes, led to the West's discovery of the Americas, and ultimately the rise of the maritime powers, and thereby the British and American Empires.
8 There are plans to restore the historic route through Iran, Iraq and Syria to the Levant, but for now such prospects seem too distant for those countries to be considered in this chapter.
9 Aristotle's Rhetoric, 1378–80, which is available online at: www.bocc.ubi.pt/pag/Aristotle-rhetoric.pdf. He further divides "slighted" into arising from perceptions of any of three feelings being directed at one: contempt, spite or insolence. Being treated as nothing but an object in the way is symptomatic of all three.

References

ADB (2009). Safeguard Policy Statement. Manila, Asian Development Bank: 92.

ADB (2014). Country Assessment on Land Acquisition and Resettlement: Azerbaijan. Project Number: 43288 – 01. Manila. Asian Development Bank.

Brown, V. A., et al. (2010). Tackling Wicked Problems through the Transdisciplinary Imagination. Abingdon, Oxon, Earthscan through Routledge.

De Gruben, C. (2017). Identification & categorisation of barriers to applying International Valuation Standards to property valuations in emerging markets: A Case Study on Ulaanbaatar, Mongolia. MSc in Sustainable Urban Development Thesis, University of Oxford.

Frankopan, P. (2015). The Silk Roads: A New History of the World. London, Bloomsbury Publishing Plc.

IVSC (2001). Valuation in Emerging Markets. International Valuation White Paper, International Valuation Standards Council, 347–356.

Mairs, R. (2011). The Archaeology of the Hellenistic Far East: A Survey. Oxford, Archaeopress.

Mumford, L. (1934). Technics and Civilization. New York, Harcourt, Brace. Fourth printing, March, 1936.

Ohdaira, T. 2017. "A Remarkable Effect of the Combination of Probabilistic Peer-Punishment and Coevolutionary Mechanism on the Evolution of Cooperation." Scientific Reports 7(1): 12448.

Quan, J. (2016). "Land and Corruption." Land Policy Bulletin (4).

Roosevelt, K. (1979). Countercoup: The Struggle for the Control of Iran. New York, McGraw-Hill.

Tagliarino, N. K. (2017). "The Status of National Legal Frameworks for Valuing Compensation for Expropriated Land: An Analysis of Whether National Laws in 50 Countries/Regions across Asia, Africa, and Latin America Comply with International Standards on Compensation Valuation." Land 6(2): 37.

4

Expropriation from the wider perspective in the Czech Republic

Michal Radvan and Jan Neckář

Introduction

Expropriation is a legal institute, which uses the power of law to make changes in property rights. The aim of this institute is to facilitate the transition to desirable outcomes or to impose restrictions to achieve similar ends in relation to the existing property rights which would not be possible without this institute. This chapter focuses on a range of contemporary issues, problems, experiences and commentaries in the Czech Republic in the area of expropriation (including general expropriation rules, the public interest definition, determination of the purpose of expropriation according to individual laws, the time aspect of expropriation, the Material Intention of the Act on Line Transport Constructions, compensations for expropriation and tax impacts, and international arbitration with foreign investors as a result of expropriation). Including the outcome of case law improves the understanding and interpretation of the expropriation institute. At the end, the chapter offers potential solutions to the issues covered. It works with the hypothesis that the regulation *de lege lata* is sufficient and there is no need for amendments. To confirm or disprove this hypothesis is the main aim of the chapter. Concerning the scientific methods, description is used to introduce the legal regulation, analysis to conclude the pros and cons of the existing regulation and case law, and comparison and synthesis to summarise gained knowledge and the present regulation *de lege ferenda*. The professional literature on the expropriation issues within the Czech Republic is limited, and it has been necessary to work with sources for which expropriation is of marginal relevance only. The only exemption to this is the chapter in the book written by Průcha and Neckář (2008).

General legal regulation

The fundamental legal act, which regulates expropriation in the Czech Republic, is the Declaration of Fundamental Rights and Freedoms (published as a resolution of the presidium of the Czech National Council as a No. 2/1993 Sb., as amended), which is a part of the Constitutional order. Article 11 Para. 4 of the Declaration states that expropriation or the restriction of property rights is permissible only in the public interest, on the basis of legislation and for the payment of compensation. According to Article 36 Para. 2 of the Declaration, the expropriation procedure is always under the judicial review.

There are several judgments of the European Court of Human Rights (ECtHR) influencing the decisions of Czech national courts. For example, ECtHT, in the case *Papamichalopoulos and Others v Greece* (24 Jun 1993), "considers that the loss of all ability to dispose of the land ... entailed sufficiently serious consequences for the applicants de facto to have been expropriated in a manner incompatible with their right to the peaceful enjoyment of their possessions". In the case *Sporrong and Lönnroth v Sweden* (23 Sep 1982), the ECtHR stated that "For the purposes of the latter provision, the Court must determine whether a fair balance was struck between the demands of the general (public) interest of the community and the requirements of the protection of the individual's fundamental rights". Such a principle of proportionality was mentioned several times in the judgments of Czech Constitutional Court (e.g., 9 Jan 2008, II. ÚS 268/06) (Šimáčková 2012).

As Article 11 Para. 4 of the Declaration is dealing with both expropriation and the restriction of the property rights, the County Court in Hradec Králové (31 Oct 2000, 31 Ca 82/2000–51) stated that if it is possible to achieve the purpose of expropriation only by the restriction of the property rights, then expropriation is not permissible, that is, the establishment of an easement must be preferred over the expropriation of land.

In the legal regulation of ownership, the constitutional presumption that expropriation or the restriction of the property rights is permissible only in the public interest, on the basis of legal acts and for compensation, is specified in the Civil Code. Article 1038 of the Civil Code (Act No. 89/2012 Sb., as amended), states that the expropriation or restriction of property rights is allowed only in the public interest, if it is not possible to achieve the purpose another way, and on the basis of the Act. The Act sets another condition – the purpose of expropriation. Article 1039 of the Civil Code established the right to compensation for the expropriation: the owner is entitled to full compensation corresponding to the extent to which the owner's property has been adversely affected. Compensation is provided in monetary terms. However, it may also be provided in a different way (other land or structure), if so agreed by the parties.

The expropriation procedure is regulated by administrative law regulations, among which the Expropriation Act (Act No. 184/2006 Sb., as amended) has the meritorious position. On the one hand there are supplementary civil conditions, which are necessary to be satisfied before proceeding with expropriation, and on the other hand, the main principles of the expropriation procedure are set in this Act. The expropriation procedure is executed by public administration. The Expropriation Act specifies the conditions for the expropriation process: the expropriation is permissible only for the stated purpose of expropriation and only to the extent that it is necessary to achieve the purpose of expropriation, as provided for by a special Act. Expropriation is not permissible if the rights to land or the construction necessary to achieve the stated purpose of the expropriation can be obtained by agreement or otherwise. Expropriation is permissible only if the public interest in achieving the purpose of expropriation outweighs the preservation of the existing rights of the expropriated. The public interest in expropriation needs to be proven in the expropriation procedure.

Public interest

The public interest is an indefinite legal concept; it is not defined in the Czech law (County Court in Hradec Králové, 31 Oct 2000, 31 Ca 82/2000–51). From the nature of the term, it can be deduced that it is such an interest that can be classified as general or generally beneficial, or being in the interest of society as a whole. Such an interest cannot be in conflict with the law (Supreme Administrative Court, 23 Oct 2003, 2 As 11/2003–164).

Zemánek (2014) states that

> the position of public interest in the human rights agenda (of the Czech Constitutional
> Court) is somewhat ambivalent: on the one hand, it is a tool giving effect to the guaran-
> tees of fundamental rights where their *status positivus*, ie., guarantee claims against public
> authorities, is invoked, for instance, in the areas of social rights or access to services of
> general economic interest; on the other hand, in necessary cases and to the extent nec-
> essary, it exerts a restricting influence over the exercise of fundamental rights – typically
> in the case of freedom of speech of the media in conflict with the protection of privacy
> of those on whom the media are reporting and who invoke their *status negativus* against
> interference with their private sphere; in the above-described constellation, the public
> interest of informing the public is then a kind of "antithesis" of the liberal essence of
> fundamental rights in a democratic society, based on the rule of law. The role of the
> Constitutional Court is thus obvious: to seek and effectively enforce, at the level of con-
> stitutional law, a fair, i.e., duly substantiated, balance between competing, qualitatively
> mutually incommensurable social values: fundamental rights and public interest. At
> the same time, under conditions stipulated by the constitutional Charter, the European
> Convention for the Protection of Human Rights and Fundamental Freedoms, or the
> Charter of Fundamental Rights of the European Union, as the case may be, the bound-
> aries of fundamental rights and freedoms may be regulated only by law, must apply
> equally to all identical cases, must examine the substance and purpose of such rights and
> freedoms, and must not be used for purposes other than those for which they were laid
> down. The mutual relationship of fundamental rights and public interest is exclusive
> where the two values cannot be fully upheld side by side, and one must (partly) give way
> to the other, but inclusive in those cases where respecting one of the values is a condition
> for the fulfillment of the other. These general maxims generally form a part of constitu-
> tional doctrines in all European countries. However, the interpretation and application
> of these principles in the daily practice of constitutional justice may vary.

The aforementioned ECtHR has provided the State with a high degree of discretion in
determining what constitutes a public interest in terms of expropriation (*James and Others v
United Kingdom* case, 21 Feb 1986). As stated by Czech courts, not every collective interest
can be described as a public interest of society. The term "public interest" should always
be understood as an interest which can be described as generally beneficial (Constitutional
Court, 28 Mar 1996, I. ÚS 198/95; County Court in Hradec Králové, 19 Mar 1999, 31
Ca 71/98).

It is not possible to state in the Act exactly what activities are in the public interest. The
Czech Constitutional Court (28 Jun 2005, Pl. ÚS 24/04) has found such a procedure to be
unconstitutional, to interfere with power-sharing and a violation of the general rule of law:

> The public interest in a particular case should be identified during the administrative
> procedure on the basis of the measurement of a variety of particular interests, after con-
> sideration of all contradictions and comments. The justification of the administrative
> decision must then clearly indicate why the public interest outweighed a number of
> other specific interests. Public interest should be found in decision-making on a par-
> ticular issue (typically, eg. about expropriation) and cannot be determined a priori in a
> particular case. For these reasons, the discovery of public interest in a particular case is
> typically an executive power rather than a legislative power.

The public interest in expropriation cannot be seen only in terms of the interest of the state or state institutions; it can be found, even if it is necessary to allow the use of a private property (County Court in České Budějovice, 20 May 1998, 10 Ca 65/98; Supreme Court, 16 May 2012, 28 Cdo 1857/2011). The public interest can also be seen in the need of society to (fairly) define the rights of owners in their mutual collision, which occurs, for example, in the case of unauthorised constructions (Constitutional Court, 25 Jan 2005, III. ÚS 455/03).

Time aspects of the expropriation procedure

An agreement is always preferable to expropriation. Expropriation is permissible only if the expropriator fails to enter into a contract for the acquisition of the rights to the land or the construction necessary for the purpose of expropriation provided for by law within a period of 90 days. The time limit for the conclusion of a contract with the expropriated party begins on the day following the delivery of the proposal for the conclusion of the contract to the expropriated party. The draft contract must include an expert opinion according to which the expropriator proposes an amount of compensation for obtaining the necessary rights to the land or the construction, information about the purpose of the expropriation (about a specific intent that cannot be realised without acquiring the necessary rights to the land or the construction from the expropriated party), and the warning that if the contract is not concluded, it is possible in the public interest to acquire these rights by compulsory means. The contract must establish the right to return the transferred rights to the owner unless the purpose of the transfer is not commenced within three years of the conclusion of the contract.

If the contract is not concluded, the expropriator may initiate the expropriation procedure. The expropriation office arranges for oral proceedings to take place to consider the evidence. All objections against the expropriation and evidence to prove them may be filed at this oral hearing at the latest. If the expropriation office concludes that the conditions for expropriation are met, it shall decide by separate statements on the expropriation of the rights to the land or the construction, and on the compensation for the owner. The office determines the period within which the expropriator is obliged to commence the necessary work to achieve the purpose of the expropriation. The period may not exceed two years after the decision has come into force, and it may be prolonged only once for an additional two years. The expropriation office determines the amount of compensation and the time limit during which the expropriator is required to pay the compensation (within a period that shall not exceed 60 days after the decision has come into force). If there is an agreement that the expropriated party will provide other land or another building, the expropriation office determines this property and decides how to compensate for the difference in the prices (if any), including the time period for settlement (not longer than 60 days after the previous decision has come into force). In the appeal proceedings, the appeal body may not amend the statement of compensation against the expropriated party or third parties. If a higher level of compensation is legally granted, the expropriator is required to settle the difference no later than 30 days after the decision has come into force.

If the expropriator has not paid compensation within 30 days of the expiration of the time limit or if the expropriator did not instigate the commencement of the purpose of the expropriation within the time limit, the expropriation office shall, at the request of the expropriated party, decide that the expropriation shall be annulled.

The statement on the expropriation of rights to the land or the construction may be reviewed by the administrative judiciary in the proceedings against the decision of the administrative authority, while the statements on the compensation for the expropriation may be dealt with in civil proceedings by civil courts.

Expropriation according to individual laws

Expropriation is permissible only for the purpose(s) specified by law. This purpose is set out in a number of special laws which may also include a different procedure, but usually the expropriation procedure is established under the Expropriation Act.

The most common reason for expropriation is in relation to development and thus construction activity; therefore, the Act on Town and Country Planning and Building Code (Building Act – Act No. 183/2006 Coll.) sets out the rights and duties necessary for the realisation of the structures or of other public benefit works pursuant to this Act. Grounds and structures may be removed or limited, if they are specified within the issued planning documentation and if it refers to

a   public works of transport and technical infrastructure, including the area necessary to ensure their construction and proper utilisation for the stated purpose,

b   a public benefit works, and namely the reduction of damage caused by floods and other natural disasters in the area, an increase of the retention capacity of the area, the establishment of elements of the territorial system of ecological stability and the archaeological heritage protection,

c   structures and measures for state defense and security, or

d   the redevelopment (or reclamation) of an area.

Rights to a property may be removed or limited also in order to create conditions for any necessary access, for the proper utilisation of a structure or for the introduction of an access road to a structure or land. Proceedings on expropriation of the rights to lands and structures, competence as to their conduct and the conditions for expropriation are established by the special regulation.

Under expropriation law, the right of ownership can be (according to the Road Communications Act – Act No. 13/1997 Coll.) withdrawn or restricted to the land or to the construction, or to the right corresponding to the easement to the land or to the building necessary for the construction, repair, modification, modernisation or reconstruction of motorways, roads, main local roads, their parts, ancillaries or related structures. The withdrawal or restriction is also possible in the case of the ownership of the land if motorways, roads or local roads were established on a foreign land.

The Railways Act (Act No. 266/1994 Coll.) allows that, under the Expropriation Act, the ownership of the land or the construction or the right corresponding to a servitude on the land or the construction may be withdrawn or limited for the purpose of the construction of the track.

In relation to the Building Act, the Act on State Monument Care (Act No. 20/1987 Coll.) states that expropriation powers may be invoked if the owners of immovable cultural monuments that are not State-owned permanently neglect their duties and thus endangers their conservation or if they use the monument in a manner contradictory to its cultural and political importance, monument value or technical condition. If an agreement is not reached with the owners on the sale of the monument to the State, the cultural monument may, in the interest of society and as an exceptional measure, be expropriated on the basis of the proposal of the authority of a municipality, with extended competence through a decision of the expropriation authority. If an immovable national cultural monument is to be expropriated, the expropriation proceedings are initiated by the expropriation authority following a proposal of the regional authority. Otherwise, the expropriation process is governed by the general regulations. The expropriation is possible also for creation of a zone for the protection of an immovable cultural monument or of its environment if necessary.

The Electronic Communications Act (Act No. 127/2005 Coll. on Electronic Communications and on Amendment to Certain Related Acts) sets out the possibility of a limit on ownership in the expropriation proceedings for the purpose of establishing and operating the over ground or underground communication lines of a public communications network.

According to the Spa Law (Act No. 164/2001 Sb.), the property rights to real estate can be restricted or real estate can be expropriated only in the public interest, which for these purposes means an interest in seeking and using the resource for medical purposes and in the conservation of resources in order to preserve their qualitative and quantitative properties and health.

Very specific regulations of purpose and situation in which the property rights could be restricted or limited are defined in the Water Act (Act No. 254/2001 Coll.), Mining Act (Act No. 44/1988 Coll.), Nature and Landscape Protection Act (Act No. 114/1992 Coll.) and others.

However, land reforms are not considered as expropriation. The Czech Constitutional Court (27 May 1998, Pl. ÚS 34/97) decided that land does not normally constitute expropriation of property rights in the true sense of the term because they are basically a collective voluntary exchange of ownership rights by the owners concerned. However, for those owners who disagree with the modifications made, the constitutional rules are valid for expropriation or forced constraint of ownership by the extreme criterion of protecting their property. The Constitutional Court notes that land improvements are carried out in the public interest, by law, and it is for the competent authorities to strictly ensure the right to adequate compensation within the meaning of Article 11 (4) of the Charter of Fundamental Rights and Freedoms.

The time aspects of expropriation – new regulation drafting

The inadequate development of transport infrastructure is one of the main reasons for the decline in the Czech Republic's competitiveness, which represents a significant risk for its economic development in the future. The Czech Republic lacks some key interconnections between the regions and connections to neighbouring states (especially in the north-south direction), which have negative effects on the movement of goods (foreign trade and supplies) and in the long run on its economic growth. Effective transportation of goods across the Czech Republic and within Europe is a basic prerequisite for the success of Czech companies by removing trade barriers in the form of transport costs. In addition to reducing barriers to trade, high-quality transport infrastructure has a positive impact on the time involved in transport, which brings both financial- and time savings to those who use the transport infrastructure. Improved mileage reduction also has a positive impact on employment as it increases the flexibility of the labour market and reduces the cost of commuting to work. Another benefit of motorways and express roads can be the diversion of transport from cities and municipalities and the associated positive impacts. By delaying all these outcomes, there are significant economic losses (Ministry of Transport 2014, 5).

Almost one-third of all delays on motorway and express road constructions are caused by the existing legal regulations relating to expropriation. The delay is between 2.5 and 11.2 years, and the loss is approximately CZK 6.3 billion (280 million USD) (Ministry of Transport 2014, 7). The expropriation procedure itself takes only two months, but it is necessary to add the objection proceedings (six months), an action in the administrative judiciary (two years) and cassation complaint (additional two years) (Ministry of Transport 2014, 10). For example, the case of farmer Havránková was resolved after 20 years (ČTK 2014).

The Ministry of Transport prepared a Material Intention of the Act on Line Transport Constructions in 2014. This Act should deal with motorways, first-class roads and all railroads, and it should provide a comprehensive regulation of the construction of line transport constructions and administrative proceedings prior to the issuance of the decision on the basis of which construction will be allowed. The Act would be a *lex specialis* for the issues concerning line transport constructions – a special law to the Building Act, the Administrative Code, the Expropriation Act and so forth. This would remove some ambiguities or duplications, particularly those concerning expropriation and compensation for expropriation (Ministry of Transport 2014, 54–55). It is presumed that land and buildings necessary for line transport construction should be obtained by voluntary buyout from the owners. If such a buyout is impossible, the expropriation procedure may begin. However, the property-law settlement of immovable property on which the line transport construction is to be located will not be a prerequisite for the submission of an application for a line transport construction permission. Based on the principles of effectiveness and economy, the expropriations should be administered directly by the Ministry of Transport (Ministry of Transport 2014, 61).

Inspired by German law, the decision to authorise a line transport construction will (in relation to the demonstration of the public interest in the expropriation procedure) constitute a binding legal opinion, that there is a public interest in authorising a line transport construction permission. This will also remove the currently not quite appropriate legislation, which requires that it is subsequently necessary in the expropriation procedure to prove the public interest in the expropriation, although in the land proceedings and in the construction proceedings, with the participation of the owners of the land in question, it was decided that the line transport construction can proceed through the given land and immovable property (Ministry of Transport 2014, 61). Another new rule inspired by German law states that after the decision to authorise the line transport construction, where it is necessary to commence the work without any delay, and the owner refuses to leave the subject land, the expropriation authority (Ministry of Transport) may pre-register the applicant's permission for line transport construction (Ministry of Transport 2014, 66–67). Even though the Material Intention of the Act on Line Transport Constructions does not anticipate any unconstitutional issues, taking into account the aforementioned case law, it is very probable that there will be cases in front of the Constitutional Court.

Compensation for expropriation and tax impact

As mentioned earlier, the Declaration of Fundamental Rights and Freedoms states that the expropriation or the restriction of property rights is permissible only in the public interest, on the basis of legislation and by the payment of compensation.

The compensation following expropriation is regulated by the Expropriation Act, which lays down the statutory duty that the compensation is provided in principle in monetary terms. On the other hand, the present owner may accept another real estate (plot or a building structure) by agreement. This applies in situations where the object of the expropriation is ownership of a plot of land or a building structure. Possible differences in value between the two units of real estate will be the subject of a monetary settlement.

The compensation is provided based on its market price, if the object of the expropriation is a plot or a building structure. If the object of the expropriation is an encumbrance on real estate, then compensation is provided on the basis of the value of the property right according to the amount by which it increases the value of the dominant land. The market price is a price, which would be set as a sale price in cases of selling the actual or similar property, or it is a price of providing the same or similar services in the market on the date of evaluation. Apart from this, the present owner is entitled to obtain compensation for relocation, compensation concerning the change of the place of business and other losses and costs expended concerning the expropriation and its consequences from the expropriator.

For the current owner, there are also decisive tax consequences associated with the parties' agreement on the voluntary sale of their property or its expropriation.

The expropriator is usually the State because of the requirement for a public interest outcome on the transfer of rights, but it could be a private person as well. The expropriation is the *ultima ratio* or last resort on the restriction of the property rights, and therefore before expropriation, there must be an effort to reach an agreement between the expropriator (most often the State, which is, in this negotiation, represented by the State body) and the present owner. The type of the agreement is not determined by law; it can be a contract for sale, barter contract or any other type of agreement.

The transfer of real estate or a property right is subject to both the real estate transfer tax and income tax, regardless of the fact that the transfer is based on a voluntary agreement, or based on expropriation. But for the present owner, the tax consequences may be different, depending on the way of ownership changes.

Since 1 November 2016, the real estate transfer tax is paid by the purchaser.

If there is an agreement between the parties and the present owner sells the real estate voluntary, the buyer pays the real estate transfer tax and has all the other responsibilities associated with the obligations stated in the Real Estate Transfer Tax Act (for example, submitting a tax declaration and proof of expert opinion). The tax is paid at 4% of the selling price, which cannot be lower than the estimated price.

On the other hand, under the terms of expropriation, the taxpayer is the expropriator, but the tax remains at 4% of the compensation set out in the expropriation decision (the compensation is based on the estimated price with the potential for an increase; therefore, it is not necessary to compare the compensation paid with the estimated price).

According to this regulation, the tax liability is established for the purchaser and the present owner does not have any obligations with regard to the real estate transfer taxation imposed on the transaction. However, the fundamental difference may exist for the current owner in relation to income taxation.

The Income Tax Act (Act No. 586/1992 Sb.) allows the exemption from income tax for the revenue from sales or any other income from real estate, including flats or nonresidential premises if the property has been the present owner's place of residence for at least two years prior to the transfer, or if the compensation received is used to purchase a new residence. This exemption also applies in the case of selling the property, which is owned by the present owner for more than five years, but some restrictions are applied. This five-year restriction period was established as a method to prevent speculation in real estate.

However, the Income Tax Act established the exemption from income tax for compensation received following expropriation no matter how long the current owner has held the property. If the owner of the property, which is the object of the negotiations and will be the object of the expropriation in case of unsuccessful negotiation, had held the plot or a building structure for less than five years and therefore is not exempt from the real estate transfer tax, it is very often, that at the beginning of the negotiations the owner disagrees with a voluntary sale of the plot or the building structure. and instead calls for expropriation.

Thus, in some situations (especially if the present owner has retained the property for less than two or five years), expropriation is a more convenient and less costly solution because the present owner is not required to pay income tax, which is set at 15% of the income.

International arbitration with foreign investors as a result of expropriation

The Czech Republic entered into approximately 80 agreements for the promotion and reciprocal protection of investments (so-called bilateral investment treaties or BITs). These agreements establish standards of investor protection that the host state must meet. These protection standards include, among others, the prohibition of expropriation. Such a prohibition is not universal: expropriation, which is in the public interest, nondiscriminatory, carried out in due process and provides prompt, adequate and effective compensation to the investor, is permitted. The ban on expropriation typically also applies to indirect expropriation, that is, expropriation in which the state does not withdraw the investor's title from the investment, but actually devaluates it.

When referring to indirect expropriation, some BITs concluded by the Czech Republic follow the 1992 World Bank Guidelines on the Treatment of Foreign Direct Investment phrase "measures having similar effect". (For example, the Czech Republic-Albania BIT, Czech Republic-Argentina BIT, Czech Republic-Australia BIT, Czech Republic-Azerbaijan BIT, Czech Republic-Bahrain BIT, Czech Republic-Bulgaria BIT, Czech Republic-China BIT, Czech Republic-Egypt BIT, Czech Republic-Finland BIT, Czech Republic-Georgia BIT and Czech Republic-Guatemala BIT). Others follow the 1967 Organisation for Economic Cooperation and Development (OECD) Draft phrase "indirect" (for example, the Czech Republic-Philippines BIT, Czech Republic-France BIT and Czech Republic-Chile BIT). The different wording has no impact on the interpretation of indirect expropriation. The Czech Republic-Croatia BIT, Czech Republic-United Arab Emirates BIT and Czech Republic-United States BIT contain very precise wording combining the World Bank Guidelines and the OECD Draft. The Croatian BIT provides: "Neither of the Contracting Parties shall take, either directly or indirectly, measures of expropriation, nationalization or any other measure having the same nature or an equivalent effect against investments belonging to investors of the other Contracting Party" (Radvan and Švec in print).

There are no cases of international arbitrations with foreign investors as a result of expropriation of land and constructions in the Czech Republic. Concerning the aforementioned indirect expropriation, with regard to the renewable energy disputes with the Czech Republic (Antaris, Natland, Voltaic Network, Mr. Jürgen Wirtgen, Mr. Stefan Wirtgen, and JSW Solar, ICW Europe, Photovoltaik, WA Investments), investors could claim unlawful expropriation of their investments. Both BITs and Energy Charter Treaty (ECT) include expropriation provisions and may be invoked. The investors can argue that the amendment of the legislation and the imposition of the levy were equivalent to an unlawful expropriation of their investment. Both relevant BITs provisions on expropriation and Article 13 of the ECT provide a guarantee that direct and indirect forms of expropriation of an investment may take place only against prompt effective and adequate compensation, carried out under due process of law, on a nondiscriminatory basis and in the public interest. The opinion of the Czech Constitutional Court (15 May 2012, Pl. ÚS 17/11, paras. 68–71) is noteworthy, although it relates only to the levy. When considering the compatibility of the levy with the constitutional order of the Czech Republic, the Court emphasised that the extreme decline in investment costs has significant negative socioeconomic effects, consisting primarily of a considerable increase in electricity prices for end consumers. For these reasons, the State had to take the necessary steps. The means selected to achieve this aim appear to be reasonable and appropriate because the levy on solar electricity was set so as to continue to guarantee the 15-year period for return on investments, which is established by law. According to the Constitutional Court, photovoltaic operators still have a 15-year period for the return on their investment, even after introduction of the levy (Radvan and Švec 2017).

In the case of *Saluka Investments BV (The Netherlands) v The Czech Republic*, the Tribunal expressed the opinion that the principle that a state does not commit an expropriation from and is thus not liable to pay compensation to a dispossessed alien investor when it adopts general regulations that are "commonly accepted as within the police power of States" and forms part of customary international law today (Permanent Court of Arbitration 2006, 262).

In the case of *Ronald S. Lauder v The Czech Republic*, the Tribunal stated that even assuming that the actions taken by the (Czech) Media Council in the period from 1996 through 1999 had the effect of depriving the claimant of his property rights, such actions would not amount to an appropriation – or the equivalent – by the State, since it did not benefit the Czech Republic or any person or entity related thereto, and was not taken for any public purpose. It only benefited CET 21, an independent private entity owned by private individuals (Uncitral 2001, 203). Such an approach finds the public interest in which the measure is implemented not as a justification, which protects the measure against the designation of expropriation but, on the contrary, perceives the absence of public interest as an argument against the finding of expropriation in the given case (Sekanina 2009).

Conclusion

It is apparent that there are no serious problems with the regulation *de lege lata* in the Czech Republic concerning the expropriation. There are no cases of international arbitrations with foreign investors as a result of expropriation of land and constructions in the Czech Republic. If the authorities proceed according to the law, there are no opportunities to prevent expropriation. The hypothesis stated at the beginning of the chapter has been generally confirmed. The only issue to be resolved is the insufficient development of transport infrastructure. The Ministry of Transport states that almost one-third of all delays in motorways and express roads constructions are caused by the existing legal regulation of expropriations, and that is why the ministry has prepared a Material Intention of the Act on Line Transport Constructions in 2014 as a *lex specialis* for the issues concerning line transport constructions. The draft is inspired by German law. There are two main areas to improve the line transport constructions:

1   The decision to authorise a line transport construction will (in relation to the demonstration of the public interest in the expropriation procedure) constitute a binding legal opinion, that there is a public interest in line transport construction permission; and
2   After the decision to authorise the line transport construction and in case it is necessary to commence the work without delay and the owner refuses to leave the subject land by agreement, the expropriator authority may pre-register the permission of the applicant for line transport construction.

Such a regulation is quite promising; on the other hand, there are some obstacles:

1   Even the Material Intention of the Act on Line Transport Constructions does not anticipate any unconstitutional issues, but taking into account the aforementioned case law, it is very probable that there will be cases in the Constitutional Court; and

2   A political will is missing; after three years there is still no draft of the Act on Line Transport Constructions.

References

ČTK. 2014. https://byznys.lidovky.cz/bitva-o-dalnici-d11-konci-farmarka-havrankova-prodala-posledni-pozemky-1kf-/doprava.aspx?c=A141126_110321_ln-doprava_mmu (accessed 26.10.2017).

Ministry of Transport. 2014. "Material Intention of the Act on Line Transport Constructions". Prague: Ministry of Transport https://albatros.odok.cz/ODOK/eklep3.nsf/form_Programme.xsp?documentId=87870E(accessed 26.10.2017).

Permanent Court of Arbitration. 2006. www.pcacases.com/web/view/101 (accessed 26.10.2017).

Průcha, P. and Neckář, J. 2008. "Expropriation from the Administrative Law and Financial Law Point of View in the Czech Republic". In Real Estate in Czech and Polish Law, ed. Radvan, M. and Liszewski, G. Temida 2. Białystok: PL.

Radvan, M, and Švec, M. 2017. "Czech Republic". In The Impact of Bilateral Investment Treaties on Taxation, ed. Lang, M. Linde. Vienna: AT.

Sekanina, O. 2009. "Nepřímé vyvlastnění v praxi mezinárodních investičních arbitráží". Jurisprudence 2009(8). www.google.cz/url?sa=t&rct=j&q=&esrc=s&source=web&cd=1&ved=0ahUKEwis7ryf4qfXAhUHoqQKHYHjAlAQFggmMAA&url=http%3A%2F%2Fwww.sekaninalegal.eu%2Fdocument_download.php%3Fid%3D54&usg=AOvVaw3RUFygVvS9pztQUrsLZv_5 (accessed 26.10.2017).

Šimáčková, K. 2012. "Komenář k čl. 11". In Listina základních práv a svobod. Komentář, ed. Wagnerová, E. et al. Prague: Wolters Kluwer. (Retrieved from ASPI).

Uncitral. 2001. www.italaw.com/cases/610 (accessed 26.10.2017).

Zemánek, J. 2014. "Public Interest in the Case Law of the Constitutional Court of the Czech Republic". www.constcourt.md/public/files/file/conferinta_20ani/programul_conferintei/Jiri_Zemanek.pdf (accessed 14.11.2017).

5

Acquisition for public purposes and valuation in Estonia

Tambet Tiits and Aivar Tomson

Introduction

History of land tenure

Tallinn, nowadays the capital city of Estonia, adopted Lübeck Civil Law in 1248. Later in the thirteenth century cities governed by the Lübeck law were formed into a powerful trade association, the Hanseatic League. Lübeck law was applicable in Estonia until the nineteenth century. So, the oldest records of owners (archived) are from 1312. The first signs of land registration, which can be considered as the basis for the current system, date back to 1865, when the Russian Empire established the Baltic Private Law Code (*Liv-, Est- und Curländisches Privatrecht*) (Luts, M. 2000, p. 157). The Code included land regulation based on the Land Register (*Grundbuch*) and was similar to the advanced systems in Continental Europe at this time.

Three radical changes took place during the next fifteen decades:

- Land reform relating to rural areas was initiated at the beginning of Estonian independence in the 1920s. Almost all the land belonging to the large landlords was expropriated, leaving them with relatively small land units. No compensation was paid for the expropriated land at first; later, however, a much lower value basis compared to the market value was used (Estonica, 2017). The expropriated land formed the State reserve and was allocated to new farms.
- In the beginning of the Soviet occupation in 1940 all land was nationalised. During the German occupation (1941–1944) ownership rights were not officially restored, but the former owners were allowed to use their land again. With the Soviet reoccupation in 1944, the former owners were not permitted to use their land; nationalisation was followed by collectivisation of agriculture between 1947 and 1949, causing a new redistribution of land.
- Changes in land tenure mainly focusing on the agricultural sector were introduced again in the 1990s at the end of the Soviet occupation before the re-establishing of independence. After Estonia regained independence in 1991, private landownership was

gradually restored. An ownership and land reform was initiated: the legal owners or their heirs were to regain ownership or be compensated for the land illegally expropriated after 16 June 1940.

Legal framework

Estonia is a democratic republic wherein supreme political authority is vested in the people. The activities of Parliament, the President, the Government and the courts are organised in accordance with the principles of separation and the balance of powers. Everyone is equal before the law. No one may be discriminated against on the basis of nationality, race, colour, sex, language, origin, religion, political or other views, property or social status, or on other grounds.

The first legal acts ensuring private ownership were the so-called reform laws that came into force in 1991. The Land Tax was introduced in 1993, and it attracted international attention because of its unusual approach as only the land was taxed and a value-based property tax was implemented in circumstances of nearly non-existent land markets. The laws enabling the functioning of the property market were adopted during the same period: the Law of Property Act and the Land Register Act providing the legal environment for ensuring property rights in 1993, and the General Part of Civil Code Act regulating property transfers in 1994.

These laws were followed by the Land Cadastre Act and the Land Consolidation Act in 1994. Despite its introduction in the beginning of the land reform process, land consolidation stayed out of the focus of the reform process. The Planning and Building Act and the Immovable Expropriation Act were approved in 1995. In this way all regulations necessary for ensuring the property rights and public interests were simultaneously adopted within a four-year period (1991–1995).

Legislation adopted in this period included also regulations on conducting notarial acts, preemption rights, different types of condominiums, the taxation of property transfers, capital gains and so forth. The only major area that remained without appropriate new regulation related to rental relations, however, the Law of Obligations Act was adopted in 2001. Many laws went through numerous changes because of the impracticability the first solutions, or the changing environment.

According to the Civil Code, immovable real estate is a delimited part of land (plot of land). The essential parts of immovable real estate are things permanently attached to it, including buildings, crops, forests and so forth. Real rights relating to a unit of immovable property are essential parts of the immovable.

Real rights are ownership (the right of ownership) and restricted real estate rights: servitudes, real encumbrances, the right of superficies, the right of preemption and the right of security. Ownership is a full legal control by a person over a thing. Ownership includes the right to possess, use and dispose of a thing, and demand the prevention of the violation of these rights and the elimination of the consequences of a violation from all other persons. Only in cases provided by the law, is ownership valid. Only the law or the rights of other persons may restrict the rights of an owner.

It is presumed that information recorded in the Land Register is correct. If, based on information entered in the land register, a person acquires ownership of immovable property or a restricted real right by a transaction, the information entered in the Land Register is deemed correct with regard to the person. The law protects the rights recorded in the Land Register.

The Land Register is public. Everyone has the right to examine its content and receive extracts therefrom pursuant to the procedure provided by the law. Ignorance of information in the land register cannot be an excuse for anyone.

The property system is based on three main public registers: Land Register (legal rights), Land Cadastre (physical and fiscal data) and the Register of Construction Works (building data). These registers are administrated by different authorities, and the basic units in all these registers are different. However, knowing the cadastral code, postal address or land register identifier, it is easy to obtain the necessary data from the different registers. All these data are accessible via internet. The only legally significant data are in the Land Register, while all the other data accessible via the internet are informative by nature.

Land Register is completely digitised: the registry, diary and the deeds. The Land Cadastre covers the country and the boundary map, and a lot more information is available through the web map service (WMS), but the status of the Register of Construction Works is very different. It includes new construction, and this way data has been recorded from the 1990s and represent the most reliable part of this register. There are still big gaps and inaccuracies related to the buildings constructed during the Soviet occupation or even earlier. As there is no systematic actualisation system in place many data are out of date. This fact does not produce any serious legal consequences, but it can be still misleading or even harmful from a technical point of view, which may finally lead to inaccuracies in property values.

Land acquisition stands on two pillars: Notaries and the Land Register. All land transactions should be verified by Notaries and registered in the Land Register in order to become effective. There are different types of immovable property rights, which can be based on landownership (freehold) or right of superficies (leasehold). Similar rights can be related to apartment (including non-residential space) ownership, which contain a physical share of a building together with a legal share of the common ownership to which the physical share belongs (the land and buildings). Thus, there are four different types of immovables.

Land acquisition

Legal background and practice

The property of every person is inviolable and equally protected. Property may be taken from owners without their consent only in the public interest, and in the cases and pursuant to a procedure provided by law, and for fair and immediate payment of compensation. Everyone whose property has been taken in this way has the right to bring an action in the courts to contest the taking of the property, the compensation or the amount of the compensation.

As the land system is based on private ownership, the main part of transactions are related to the legal entities and private persons. The State and municipalities should be also considered as potential owners. The State owns large forest areas including nature conservation areas, highways, railways and some other areas which mainly have certain link to public interests and needs. Municipalities own relatively small areas.

As public interests were not a priority of the land reform in the 1990s and because of changes in public needs over the time, land acquisition by public authorities has been relatively active in recent years. Although public authorities have preemption rights in certain circumstances, they are not eager to use this opportunity mainly because of financing issues. However, this is still an opportunity to solve a relatively limited part of public needs.

The main solution adopted is based on voluntary acquisition, which is an inseparable stage before expropriation takes place. Most cases of public acquisition are resolved on a voluntary basis as typically the land taken is relatively limited in terms of value, and it is just a pragmatic solution for both sides. Expropriation has been rarely used because most often public authorities offer a price which exceeds the market value. Although there is no detailed regulation enabling the price level to exceed the market value, it is still a common practice to increase the payment to an amount equal to the proposed accuracy level of valuation reports. Adding here the time factor, in the case of voluntary acquisition, it is possible to get paid immediately and, as such, it is a favourable solution for the owners.

The definition of expropriation according to the law stipulates that expropriation of immovable real estate is the transfer of an immovable without the consent of the owner in the public interest for fair and immediate compensation. The right of expropriation is strictly limited by the law. Immovable real estate may be expropriated in the public interest for the construction or expansion of buildings belonging to national defence, border guard, police and so forth; for energy production supply; for the construction of public ports and airports, educational and medical institutions, public streets and roads; for the extraction of mineral resources; for the installation of lines; for the creation of access to bodies of water, scenic points of interest, protectable natural and cultural objects; for the establishment of cultural and sporting facilities, cemeteries, public waste disposal sites, buildings necessary for water supply to public water catchments and reservoirs, and sewerage and water purification; and so forth. Expropriation is also allowed for the alteration or removal of buildings which substantially damage their surroundings or scenery if the owner does not do so by a given date.

Expropriation is also permitted in other cases provided by law. This means that there can be some other laws covering expropriation, but today the Immovable Expropriation Act is the main one. It is also permits the owner to initiate expropriation by requesting the State or a local government units to purchase the immovable real estate if restrictions established in public law do not allow its use for its current intended purpose. Expropriation is not permitted if the purpose for which expropriation is requested is achievable in another permissible manner.

Land acquisition for public needs and expropriation are in the hands of different public authorities, but in the context of valuation, it is based on private valuers who hold a special license. This license is issued by the Land Board, but there is a certain link to the authorisation of valuers because the only opportunity to apply for such a license is based on an existing authorisation which is coordinated by Estonian Qualifications Authority—an independent foundation. However, the Land Board or some other central body is not obliged to supervise the process of land acquisition carried out by different public authorities. Municipalities, ministries and other public authorities act themselves by making voluntary acquisitions and preparing expropriation cases.

Based on the current law, the voluntary acquisition process can be handled as a separate part of expropriation system. It is the Immovable Expropriation Act, which deals with this. Public authorities start their action by initiating a voluntary acquisition, and in most cases there is no need for expropriation. Some amendments to the Law were passed in 2005. Before that, the legislation was very clearly in favour of landowners because the only way to achieve improvements in real estate was to initiate and complete the expropriation process. It was a complicated situation for the public authorities because in most cases it was too slow. The amendments which have been in force since 2005 allow for the acquisition process to proceed if the appeal is related solely to the amount of compensation, that is, it is necessary to clarify the rights of the authority to proceed with the process of expropriation, but matters related to the compensation do not influence decisions regarding expropriation. The next step after voluntary acquisition is the agreement process within the framework of expropriation, and only after that will the actual expropriation be implemented.

Statistics

The main purposes for acquiring land for public (State) needs during last decade have been as follows:

1   Almost all of the land acquired by the State has been for road construction and reconstruction. On average there are 260 such proceedings annually. During the last few years there have been slightly more proceedings annually, of which most cases are related to road reconstruction.
2   Reconstruction and modernisation of the State border (strips) started in 2014. The process today concerns about 100 landowners.
3   The State acquires land in nature protection areas provided the protection procedure restricts considerably the use of land. There are approximately thirty such transactions per year.

The above include both voluntary acquisition and expropriation. The number of proceedings related to expropriation have been rather limited. In 2011 there were eight expropriation proceedings, in 2012 there were only three proceedings and in 2014 there were two cases.

Source: Ministry of Finance, Report of state real property: April 2014 and October 2015 (Figure 5.1).

The number of acquisitions made by the State has been relatively stable. At the same time, municipalities have been more and more active. Road Administration which is responsible for road construction has made the biggest number of acquisitions so far. Acquisitions made by the Ministry of Environment (nature protection) and Ministry of Internal Affairs (State border) are the other notable authorities in this context.

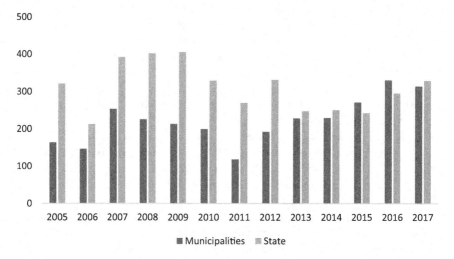

Figure 5.1   Number of acquisitions made by the State and municipalities (1 Jan 2016–28 Nov 2017)

Source: National Land Board.

Table 5.1 Acquisition of lands 2016–2017 for public needs by central administration

Institution	2016		2017 (01.01–23.11)		Total	
	Agreements	Parcels	Agreements	Parcels	Agreements	Parcels
Ministry of Education	3	3	3	3	6	6
Ministry of Defence	22	29	13	19	35	48
Ministry of Environment (Estonian Land Department)	48	52	14	15	62	67
State Forest Management Centre	2	4	0	0	2	4
Ministry of Economic Affairs (Road Administration)	167	175	230	262	397	437
Ministry of Economic Affairs (Maritime Administration)	0	0	1	1	1	1
Ministry of Internal Affairs	34	49	36	48	70	97
Ministry of Finance	1	2	0	0	1	2
Total	**277**	**314**	**297**	**348**	**574**	**662**

Source: Register of State Assets.

Infrastructure development

The main requirements have involved road construction so far. These might be related to the Road Administration in the case of highways and to municipalities in case of smaller roads and streets within settlements. However, in most cases, they concern the reconstruction and enlargement of existing facilities. The main approach is based on the voluntary acquisition of land taken. The buildings on taken land are rather untypical, and in most cases only a small part of land unit is acquired. There are no principal differences between voluntary acquisition and expropriation in the context of the value basis. The payments are based typically on market value, although some other value basis can be used. There has been only a limited number of expropriation cases so far.

The State land may be transferred by way of exchange, and this is permissible also in cases which are related to infrastructure developments. The Road Administration has recently started such a few cases, but none of these have been completed so far. The main rules are settled by the State Assets Act. When the State acquires an immovable property by way of exchange, the difference in the value of the relevant properties is paid to the owner of the acquired property by way of compensation. Where the obligation to pay compensation falls on the owner of the property to be exchanged for a property belonging to the State, the value of the properties to be exchanged may not differ by more than 10%. The difference in the value which is the subject of compensation is paid in monetary form. This regulation has been in force from the middle of 2016, but the first cases are still under way. Although there are no detailed rules about any differences in location, the exchanges have been based on the same or nearly the same location, which simplifies value comparison.

Nature conservation

A remarkably large part of Estonian is covered by different nature conservation regimes. These are mostly related to the forest areas but also include some other areas, and even limited parts of urban areas. Depending on the conservation regime, the land can be owned by the State or private owners. There are different types of protected areas like national parks, nature reserves, landscape protection areas, but there are also banks and shores and certain species which are protected.

Land acquisition by the State is needed in case of privately owned land having extensive restrictions which do not allow the use of land in an efficient way. Although the areas which should be acquired by the State are not large, land acquisition has been complicated because of limited financing. In the beginning of the 2000s, quite large land areas were transferred by exchange, but the process was stopped because of corruption issues; and, as a result, voluntary acquisition has been used as the main approach for approximately the last ten years.

Amendments of the regulation and the procedure

Background

Estonia has gained experience related to the acquisition of land for public purposes over a relatively short period—since the beginning of Land Reform in the 1990s. There are new challenges that need to be addressed. A major project is related to the construction of the railway, "Rail Baltic" (RB). RB is an international fast railway connection from Tallinn to Central Europe. There are preliminary analyses considering a tunnel between Tallinn (Estonia) and Helsinki (Finland), that would also connect Finland with RB from the north. The railway will be built together with Latvia and Lithuania, and there is also cooperation with Finland and Poland. It is the first major cross–Baltic cooperation project. The railway will be electrified and built with the European rail gauge of 1,435 mm (the current rail gauge standard is different from the European Union (EU) standards). It is meant for both passengers and freight, anticipating a maximum speed of 240 km/h (150 miles per hour). It will involve substantial EU funding and the construction should be finished by 2026. The work is divided into three stages and currently, the planning stage is ongoing, although the design stage has also begun (Figure 5.2).

Why is the RB project special in terms of land acquisition?

1   In Estonia such a long, entirely new route corridor is a major project. The experience gained so far comes from road construction and concerns mainly the expansion of already existing roads. Entirely new road sections have been built as well, but the number of landowners involved has been small compared to those affected by the RB. To implement the RB project, the State needs to acquire approximately 650 properties currently in private ownership.

2   The RB route will pass through very different land uses, both in rural and urban areas, as well as through several new development areas. It will also affect already planned development areas, where building work has not yet been started. These lands will not remain directly under the route, but the route will have a broader impact on the whole area.

3   The time factor is also of importance as the land in the RB route corridor must be acquired within a limited period. Thus, negotiations with landowners must also be carried out within limited time frame (three to five years).

4   Discussions have started, regarding whether Estonia needs such a railway at all. A lot of articles are published in the media by opponents, and protests against RB have been organised.

5   Estonian laws have become outdated and need to be amended; the legislative process is, however, time-consuming.

6   There is a lack of experience with reallocation in Estonia.

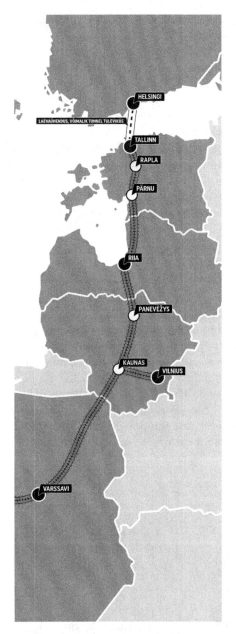

Figure 5.2 Railway from Tallinn to Central Europe (potential extension through tunnel to Helsinki)

Land consolidation for the RB

Land consolidation becomes a relevant tool in the process of land-related issues. Earlier land consolidation plans had been implemented in Estonia only in land reform for the return or the privatisation of land. Reallocation has not been used for improving land use or making it economically more efficient. The necessary regulation and practice for the implementation of the consolidation and readjustment in the process of major infrastructure developments is absent.

Reallocation can be considered when landowners are interested in it. Reallocation could include lands that remain directly under the route corridor, connecting roads and infrastructure, and for which there is available State-owned land. In cases where land consolidation is initiated by the State, the State will cover all the related costs. Farmers in particular are interested in reallocation, because EU payments are area-based, and the farmers are interested in retaining land, not in selling it to the State.

For the implementation of the RB project several legislative amendments have been drafted. These amendments include a simplification of the cadastral and surveying procedures. In addition to other land acquisition alternatives, the aim is to use land consolidation options in order to avoid expropriations. Extensive legislative amendments have been prepared to ensure a successful process. The acquisition of land will include three different processes:

1   Land consolidation process
2   Voluntary acquisition process
3   Expropriation process (as last resort)

Voluntary acquisition and expropriation have been in use in Estonia, but land consolidation is now introduced as an additional process. The basic idea was rather new for the politicians. Consolidation would help to provide sustainable farms, businesses and properties, it will hold land acquisition costs down, and, so far, it has had a positive public impact. The National Land Board is hoping that experiences will support the use of consolidation for the other projects and purposes as well. The National Land Board, when analysing the acquisition case, will first look into the consolidation options. Consolidation includes private properties and lands in public ownership, and this provides the option to minimise the damage which results from land acquisition (Figure 5.3).

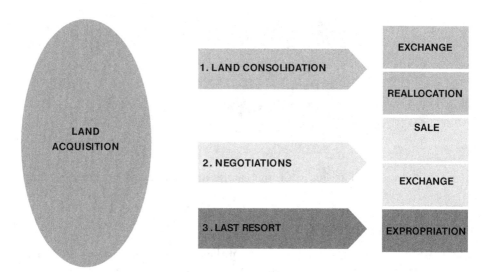

Figure 5.3   Acquisition alternatives and compensation
Source: Authors.

(a)

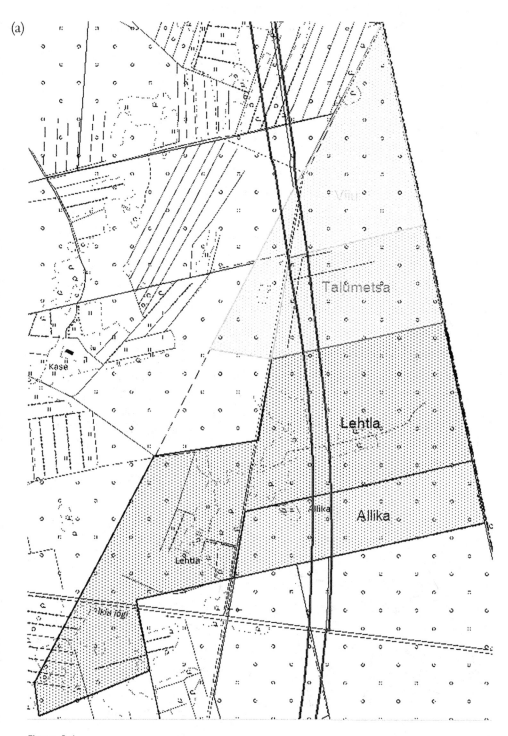

Figure 5.4

(b)

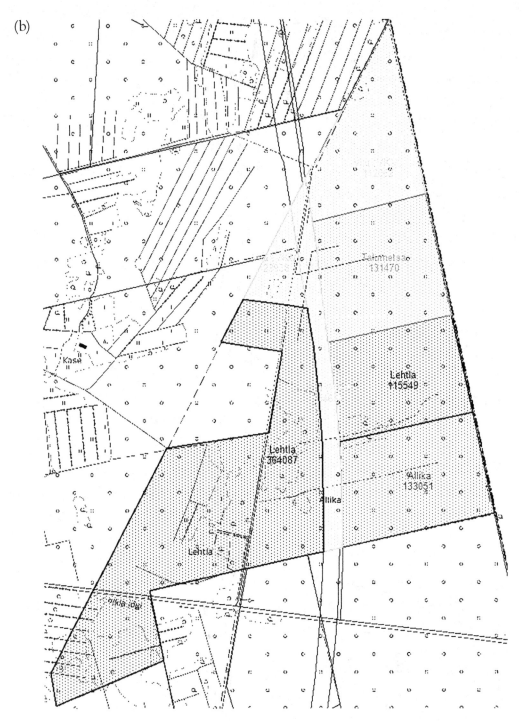

Figure 5.4 (Continued)

Example of land consolidation

Reallocation is considered but only when landowners are supportive. The aim of reallocation is to have private lands on one side of the railway, and to use State land as much as possible directly under the route corridor.

- The current situation is shown on the left-side scheme. Light blue is State forest lands, yellow, green and purple are the lands of three different private owners. The red area is new route corridor for the railway.
- Reallocation is presented on right-side scheme. The lands of the private owners now are on one side of the route. The reallocation is based on the valuation of land and the growing of forests (timber) (Figure 5.4).

Given the support from the farming community for reallocation, and its anticipated positive benefits, the harm caused by land acquisition will be minimised and the process will also in general support the economy.

Conclusions

The practice of acquisition for public needs has been undertaken in line with the constitution. The rights to land ownership are protected by law, and respecting this, the main process has been by voluntary acquisition.

There is a rationale for the implementation of the readjustment process for solving acquisition issues. The Government is now in the process of preparing amendments of the regulation.

References

Estonian Land Board.

Estonica - Encyclopedia about Estonia. Land ownership in Estonia in the 20th century, www.estonica. org/en/Land_ownership_in_Estonia_in_the_20th_century/.

General Part of the Civil Code Act, www.riigiteataja.ee/en/eli/528082015004/consolide.

Immovable Expropriation Act, www.riigiteataja.ee/en/eli/525012017001/consolide.

Land Register Act, www.riigiteataja.ee/en/eli/519062017006/consolide.

Law of Obligations Act, www.riigiteataja.ee/en/eli/524012017002/consolide.

Land Cadastre Act, www.riigiteataja.ee/en/eli/524102014003/consolide.

Land Consolidation Act, www.riigiteataja.ee/en/eli/501122014001/consolide.

Luts, M. Private Law of the Baltic Provinces as a Patriotic Act. 2000 V. pp. 157–167. Juridical International.

Ministry of Finance.

The Constitution of the Republic of Estonia, www.riigiteataja.ee/en.

6

Expropriations of immovable property in the Republic of Moldova

The relevance of expropriations for a socially useful purpose

Olga Buzu

Introduction

The Republic of Moldova is one of the young sovereign states that appeared on the map of Europe after the disintegration of the Soviet Union. Moldova's area is 33,846 square kilometres (13,068 square miles) including Transnistria and 29,683 square kilometres (11,461 square miles) without Transnistria. The population, which was approximately 4,364 million in 1990, has been steadily decreasing at a rapid rate since then because of a demographic decline, the nation's complicated economic situation and the emergence of opportunities to find employment abroad. According to the National Bureau of Statistics, Moldova's 2016 population was 3,551 million.

In recent years, the Government of Moldova has been implementing certain measures to stabilise and develop the national economy, with a major focus on the development of transport infrastructure, construction of engineering lines and networks in rural areas, and the development of drainage and irrigation systems vital for Moldova's agriculture. The implementation of such projects often involves expropriations of immovable property (in most cases land) for a socially-useful purpose.

Key terms and definitions

Expropriation means the action of taking property from its owner for public use or for the benefit of the state or an authority. (*Expropriate* originates from Medieval Latin *expropriates* – separated from one's own [past participle of *expropriare*], equivalent to *ex-* = ex- + *propri(are)* = to appropriate [derivative of *proprius* = proper] + *atus* = -ate). *Expropriation* is often identified with the *nationalisation of private property*. Nationalisation means the bringing of assets (of land, industrial facilities, banks, transports or other private property) under the ownership or control of a nation. Nationalisation or expropriation as broadly understood can take the form of (1) expropriation without compensation (confiscation) or (2) full or partial redemption (requisition) of property. Expropriations can extend to immovable property (for example land, on which a railroad or a motorway will be built) and to movable chattels.

Expropriations of private property were taking place for a range of reasons during the 1930s and 1940s within all territories occupied by Russia's Red Army: including Moldavia, Western Ukraine, Belorussia, Estonia, Latvia, Lithuania, Poland, Hungary, Romania, Bulgaria, Germany (German Democratic Republic).

Confiscation (from Latin *confiscatus* [past participle of *confiscare* – to seize for the public treasury], equivalent to *con-* = con- + *fisc(us*)= basket, moneybag, public treasury) means a particular case of expropriation understood broadly, as the action of depriving one forcibly of all or a part of one's property without compensation and the transfer of that property to the public domain for a number of reasons (as a sanction applied for a crime or for an administrative or civil infringement, etc.).

Requisition (from Latin *requsitio* = a searching) means the type of expropriation where central or local governments take property from their owners and provide them with compensation at the value of that property.

In the Republic of Moldova, requisition is a civil law category and one of the possible reasons to forcibly deprive owners of their property (Law on Requisition, 2002, Art. 1). According to that Article, the requisition of property is the measure of last resort whereby competent authorities or public administrations demand from public institutions, public and private companies and individuals the surrender of certain of their movable chattels or immovable property provisionally in accordance with the aforementioned law. Requisitions can be performed in the event of a natural catastrophe, a major accident, an epidemic, an epizootic outbreak and other emergencies as a result of which authorities may decide to take private property from their owners in order to promote the public interests. Requisitions take place according to the procedure and on the conditions established in the law and involve the payment of compensation of the value of the property to their owners.

Expropriations for a socially useful purpose differ significantly from requisitions from the legal point of view as well as in practical terms. The law on expropriations for socially useful purposes was enacted in Moldova in 2000 (Law on Expropriation, 2000). That Law interprets this type of expropriation as the transfer of property and property rights from private owners to public owners, the transfer of public property owned by an administrative-territorial unit to the entire nation or the transfer of property rights to the entire nation or to a certain administrative-territorial unit in order to facilitate nationwide or local community services in accordance with the law, subject to the prior payment of fair compensation for the damage and loss sustained.

The history of expropriations in the Republic of Moldova

Expropriations are not a new concept in Moldova's history. During the twentieth century, the territory of the current Republic of Moldova used to be a part of several countries successively, witnessing different political regimes – some of which were directed against the population and enforced on the people of Moldova against their will.

In the early twentieth century, Moldova was a part of the Russian Empire and known as Bessarabia or the Bessarabia province. Then it was a part of Romania between 1918 and 1940. Moldova was a part of the Soviet Union from 1940 until 22 June 1941 – the day the Second World War involved that country. During the Second World War it was a part of Romania again until August 1944. Moldova became a soviet republic in August 1944 and remained a component part of the Soviet Union until 1991 when it proclaimed its sovereignty as an independent state.

Broadly speaking, Moldova has witnessed expropriations of property on several occasions because of its frequently changing political systems; those expropriations were large-scale and of different types. The Soviet rule was proclaimed in the province of Bessarabia on 1 January 1918. Moldovan peasants and workers welcomed the Decree on Land adopted by the second all-Russia congress of the Soviets (people's councils) in October 1917 and treated it as a guide to action (Decree 1917). Land owned by major landlords, including monasteries was confiscated within the shortest possible time. The aforementioned Decree introduced new principles underlying ownership and the use of land. It abolished private ownership to land and nationalised all land and its subsurface resources. Only the land of minor peasants and Cossacks was exempted from confiscation. Community-level peasant committees and regional soviets (councils) of peasant deputies were granted the authority to manage and control land use. Land tenancy and use of hired labour to cultivate land were banned. All citizens were granted the right to use land, provided that they tilled it personally or jointly – as a family or as a partnership. Thus, all land was made public property. In the period from late 1917 to early 1918, peasants were transferred approximately 1.5 million "dessiatinas" (approximately 1.6 hectares or 2.7 acres) of land for use free of charge. However, the application of soviet laws did not last long. The First World War was not yet over, when in early 1918, Romania (which fought alongside the Entente, the tsarist Russia's ally in that war) formed a coalition with the Russian tsarist army (at that time consisting mainly of officers because most soldiers had sided with the people's councils) and took control of a part of the former province of Bessarabia. The Austrian and German armies came to support these actions a little later. By mid-March of 1918 Romania was controlling all the territory of the current Republic of Moldova, as well as areas on the left bank of the Dniester and the territory which is now the Odessa region in Ukraine.

Soviet laws were restored within these territories in June 1940 when the Soviet Union peacefully took Bessarabia under its control as an outcome of the negotiations between Germany and the Soviet Union. In August 1940 the Presidium of the Supreme Soviet of the Union of Soviet Socialist Republics (USSR) adopted the Decree on the nationalisation of banks, industrial and commercial enterprises, railroads and water transport as well as telecommunication facilities in Bessarabia (Decree on Nationalisation, 1940). That Decree proclaimed all production capacities in existence at the time to be public property. Bessarabia became part of the USSR. All major industrial enterprises and power stations, as well as large commercial enterprises and wineries, medical, social, cultural and educational facilities, large hotels, large tenement buildings and so forth, were nationalised. The nationalisation process was progressing in industry, transports, telecommunications and commerce rapidly, and the process had actually been completed before October 1940. About 500 industrial enterprises were nationalised in Bessarabia.

Agriculture was also affected by major reforms. The Decree on the Restoration of the Soviet Laws Regarding Nationalisation of Land in Bessarabia (Decree on Restoration, 1940) issued by the Presidium of the Supreme Soviet of the USSR on 15 August 1940 made all land, complete with its subsurface resources, forests and waters, public property, that is, the wealth of all citizens, and banned private property rights in land. This Decree was enforced with similar promptness between June and November of 1940, and as a result, 163,000 hectares (400,000 acres) of land were confiscated from major landowners, and subsequently 134,000 hectares (330,000 acres) of that land were transferred to non-landed or land-poor peasants for their possession and use. In parallel, land was also taken from some of the wealthier peasants. The outcome of that process was the expropriation of about 105,000 hectares (260,000 acres) of ploughed land (together with unharvested crops) and 2,800 hectares (7,000 acres) of orchards and vineyards. After land, expropriations were extended to working animals and productive livestock, agricultural machinery and tools.

The Second World War had interrupted these political and economic reforms in Moldova, but they continued after the war was over. The transition from individual farms to collective farms began in 1946. This process was characterised with the pressure on wealthier peasants, pushing them out of all spheres of economic life. Farms of wealthier peasants accounted for a minor portion of all individual farms (only 2.1% in 1947),[1] and by early 1949 there were less than 1%, and during 1949 wealthier peasants were eliminated as a social class. Most of the wealthier peasants and their families fell victims of political repressions and were exiled from Moldova to Siberia and Kazakhstan. Their entire property (including livestock, tools, machinery, crops, orchards and vineyards) was expropriated, confiscated or taken from them in other ways and transferred to collective farms at no cost.

Many years later, most of the exiled individuals were exonerated and allowed to return to where they used to live. However, their confiscated property was not returned to them, nor were they paid any monetary compensation for its value. Having just become independent and sovereign, the Republic of Moldova enacted a law exonerating all victims of political repressions in 1992 (Law 1225, 1992). According to that Law, all those who had suffered from political repressions became entitled to claim back their property which had been confiscated, nationalised or otherwise taken from them. The Law did not extend to the land, forests and perennial plantations that had been nationalised according to the standard procedure all over the country. Thus, although that Law gives the victims of political repressions exonerated at a later stage the opportunity to claim back the physical property taken from them, the State actually provides compensation at the value of that property assessed according to the market prices prevailing at the time the decision is made to satisfy the application for restitution. According to Moldova's laws, the value to be compensated is the current market value of the confiscated property assumed to be in the state in which it was at the time of confiscation. In other words, a retrospective property valuation has to be performed in such cases. The process of paying monetary compensations to victims of political repressions is still underway.

During 1950–1991 the term "expropriation" had a rather vague and abstract meaning for Moldova because all land (with the aforementioned exceptions) was public property notwithstanding its destined use. There was no private ownership of immovable property during that period. Consequently, there were no definitions for the terms such as "market value", "real estate market", or the "sale and purchase" of land.

This situation changed dramatically in 1991 when Moldova began its transition to market concepts in all economic spheres, and began privatising buildings and structures. The right to own immovable property privately was guaranteed by the Law on Property (Law 459, 1991). The Law on Privatisation (also enacted in 1991) provided the legal framework for transfers of public property to private owners.

The legal framework for expropriations

At present, the laws of the Republic of Moldova allow expropriations solely for socially useful purposes. The Constitution of the Republic of Moldova (1994) says (in Article 46): Private property rights and their protection are guaranteed by the State, and that no one's property can be taken unless it is needed for public purposes in situations described in the law and for which prior fair compensation is paid.

The Civil Code of Moldova (Civil Code, 1992, Art. 316) also includes a rule stating that private property is secure and describes situations and conditions making expropriation permissible. This Article says in particular that "no one shall be forced to surrender one's property other than in a situation of public need and subject to prior fair compensation". Expropriations adhere to the procedure established by the law. Public authorities may use the land under any real estate for projects of major public interest, subject to payment of compensation to the owner for the damage to soil, plantations and structures and for any other damage caused by public authorities.

In addition, the Civil Code requires that that the amount of such compensation for damages be determined in agreement with the owner or by the courts in the case of a difference of opinion. In such situations the decision to take private property from its owner cannot be enforced before the pronounced judgement becomes *res jucata*.

The entire set of legal rules concerning expropriations is covered by Moldovan Law no. 488 of 18 July 1999 on expropriations for a socially useful purpose ("Law").

Expropriation targets are subdivided into those of national importance and those of local importance.

Targets of expropriation of national importance include:

a   Immovable property (land, mineral resources, water basins, forests, buildings, structures and other site-specific property that either cannot be moved or becomes damaged and unfit for its intended use if moved);
b   Rights to possess immovable property for a term of up to five years, unless the parties agree otherwise;
c   Property rights and personal non-property (moral) rights directly associated with an invention which can make a considerable contribution to the nation's defence and security interests;
d   Cultural, artistic and historical treasures of extraordinary importance for the national identity of the public; documents certifying the nation's statehood;
e   Property rights to the flora and fauna species for which Moldova's outdoor spaces are a natural habitat and an area for the development and reproduction of species which are on the verge of extinction – where there is a genuine threat that a certain species may become extinct.

Expropriation targets of local importance include immovable property and property rights thereto similar to the ones described earlier. In the author's opinion, the subdivision of expropriation targets into those of national and local importance is not very obvious, and its necessity has not been substantiated in the Law with sufficient clarity. Moreover, the Law says that expropriations may extend to movable chattels on the implementation of fundamental laws in the case of an emergency (war, hostilities, or the suspension of civil government).

The Law also mentions the possibility of expropriating only a part of a land holding, of a building or of a structure. Where a socially useful purpose dictates the necessity to expropriate a part of certain immovable property and the property owner files an application with the court, requesting full expropriation of the property, it is up to the court to decide whether it is possible to expropriate only a part of the concerned property. The entire property has to be expropriated where it is not possible to expropriate only a part thereof.

The parties involved in the expropriation process are: the expropriated party on the one side and the expropriator on the other. The expropriated party is the property owner or the holder of other property rights to the target of expropriation. The State (represented by its competent authorities or by parties explicitly endowed with the relevant authority under the law) is the expropriator in respect of nationally important targets and locally important targets.

It should be pointed out that expropriations are only allowed in Moldova for a socially useful purpose, which is understood to mean (Law 488, Art. 5.1):

a   Geological surveying and prospecting;
b   Extraction and processing of mineral resources;
c   Construction of facilities for the generation of electric power;
d   Construction of transport routes and of structures required for the maintenance thereof; the construction, aligning and widening of streets;
e   Construction of communication lines, heat supply, sewage, electric power supply, water supply and gas supply lines;
f   Building of structures intended to protect the environment;
g   Construction of dams to control the water level in rivers and water reservoirs and to prevent floods;
h   Construction of weather stations, seismic stations, safety alert systems, contingency management systems and systems intended to warn the public of natural hazards;
i   Earthworks to prevent subsurface soil erosion; irrigation and drainage systems;
j   Sites for the construction of: housing for the public housing sector; educational establishments; medical, cultural, sports, social protection and social security facilities; other publicly owned social facilities; office buildings for public administrations, courts, embassies, consulates, missions of foreign and international agencies;
k   Sites for the laying out of public parks and cemeteries; sites for the accumulation and burial of waste;
l   Modernisation of urban, residential and industrial areas, of the existing architectural complexes in accordance with urban development plans for the concerned settlement which have been duly approved by the respective local public administration;
m   Preservation, protection and restoration of monuments, historical complexes and landscapes, national parks, wildlife preservation areas and natural monuments;
n   Prevention of natural calamities: such as earthquakes, floods, landslides, avalanches;
o   Ensuring of the nation's defence and security; maintaining public order;
p   Preservation and protection of cultural, artistic and historical treasures of extraordinary importance for the national identity of the public; of documents certifying the nation's statehood;
q   Preservation, protection and ensuring the reproduction of endangered species as well as of plants, animals and other wildlife species on the verge of extinction.

A socially useful project of national importance is any project implemented to achieve the nation's objectives and to benefit the entire nation or a major part of the nation's population. A socially useful project of local importance is any project implemented to achieve community objectives and to benefit the entire local community or a group of communities within the concerned administrative-territorial unit.

The organisation declaring a project to be a socially useful project is the national parliament, in the case of national importance projects, and the local government (public administration) of the concerned administrative-territorial unit, in the case of projects of local importance.

If the expropriation target is located in more than one region (administrative-territorial unit) or in more than one municipality, the parties deciding on the expropriation are the regional or municipal governments of the concerned administrative-territorial units.

The party initiating the pronouncement of a socially useful project is the public authority which submits this proposal to the relevant competent authority according to the procedure prescribed by the Law.

A project can only be declared a socially useful project after preliminary research which is performed by a committee established, respectively, by the national government or by the local government of the concerned administrative-territorial unit(s) – depending on the classification of the expropriation target.

This preliminary research is intended to identify the project components which substantiate the project's national/local importance and to verify the existence of social, economic, environmental or other background conditions demonstrating that the implementation of the project is necessary and that the project should be included in the urban planning and territorial development plans duly approved in accordance with the law.

The document formally proclaiming the project to be a socially useful project of national/local importance is made known to the public through its posting by the local government of the territory where the expropriation target is located and its publication in the official gazette of the Republic of Moldova (*Monitorul Official*).

The procedure for submission of expropriation suggestions

After the project is declared to be socially useful, the expropriator takes steps to submit an expropriation application within 10 days of the declaration.

The expropriating authority notifies the target owner affected by the expropriation in writing who then becomes entitled to claim immediate and fair compensation.

The expropriation notice has to include the text of the expropriation application and has to be given to the individuals and entities holding exercisable rights over the expropriation target, to describe the terms and conditions for compensation of damages and the procedure for the transfer of the property and of the relevant property rights or, if applicable, for the cession of the relevant property rights.

Where housing or land is expropriated, the owner has to be offered a title to replacement housing or to a replacement plot of land, respectively. If the value of the offered replacement housing/land is less than the value of the expropriated housing/land, the expropriator pays the owner the difference in value between the expropriated property and the offered replacement property.

After they are notified of the forthcoming expropriation, the owner(s) and the holder(s) of other exercisable rights to the expropriation target are required to take steps to conserve the target.

The expropriated party is entitled to make a counter-offer in response to the received notice of expropriation. This counter-offer is a document formally stating the claims of the expropriated party regarding the expropriation terms and conditions. The counter-offer should be submitted to the authority making the expropriation offer within 45 days of the service of the expropriation notice.

The authority making the expropriation offer registers the submitted counter-offers and makes a note regarding the compensation offers made for damage and other claims of the target owner(s) or of the holder(s) of other exercisable rights to the expropriation target.

The specifics of forcible deprival of land are also covered in the Moldovan Law on Normative Price and the Procedure for the Sale and Purchase of Land (Law 1308, 1997). Different from the Law on Expropriation, this Law says that the national government can forcibly deprive owners of land by agreement with the concerned local public administrations in order to satisfy public needs for land. The Law differentiates between expropriations of arable and non-arable land. Article 15 of the aforementioned law states that landowners can be deprived of their land for agricultural purposes by virtue of the need to establish public agricultural production units (for research or pilot projects). The Law emphasises, however, that owners may only be forcibly deprived of their land for non-agricultural purposes by virtue of major public needs, such as the construction of an industrial facility or a road; the laying out of a telecommunication line; the creation of a special purpose facility; the building of a waterworks and the implementation of other water development projects; the extraction of mineral resources; community development; the construction of a cultural, educational, medical, sports or recreational (integrated) facility; or the creation of a natural or historical monument.

The Moldovan Law on Normative Price and the Procedure for the Sale and Purchase of Land provides sufficient details regarding the rights of individuals and entities forcibly deprived of their land in order to satisfy public needs for land (Law 1308,1997, Art. 16). The Law imposes an obligation on the government to offer the owner a replacement plot of land instead of the land which has been forcibly taken. If the quality of land offered as a replacement is lower than the quality of the forcibly taken land, the landowner is entitled to compensation for the damage caused by the exchange. The damages are compensated in monetary terms if the landowner does not agree to the exchange, or if the government has no appropriate land to offer as a replacement. All disputes emerging out of or in connection with the forcible deprival of land are settled in accordance with the procedure prescribed by the law.

Value of expropriated property: theoretical and legal framework

It is necessary to examine the meaning of the term "value" in respect of the expropriated property for the determination of the amount payable as compensation for the damage suffered by the owner. There is no uniform opinion concerning this matter, and no uniform approach has been established by Moldova's laws and regulations, which circumstance gives rise to multiple disputes and complaints from the affected individuals and entities whose property has been expropriated.

Thus, Article 17 of the Moldovan Law on Normative Price and the Procedure for the Sale and Purchase of land states that compensation for the damage caused by the forcible taking of land is payable on the basis of market prices, but in any case it cannot be lower than the standard price computed using the price rates established by the aforementioned Law (Law 1308, 1997, Annex, Line II).

If the relevant local public administration and the landowner cannot agree the market price of the land, the price is set by the court on the basis of the opinions of independent experts.

The Law on Expropriation for a Socially Useful Purpose describes the procedure for the determination of the amount payable as compensation for damages (Law 488, 1999, Art. 15). If the owner of the expropriation target does not think the amount offered by way of compensation is fair, the court creates an expert panel which has to include one person representing the expropriator and one person representing the expropriated party.

The amount payable as compensation is determined according to the actual value of the immovable property or of the property rights to be expropriated and dependant on the damage suffered by the owner(s) or by the holder(s) of other exercisable rights.

The expert panel and the court determining the amount payable as compensation have to consider the price at which similar immovable property and the rights thereto exchange hands within the relevant locality as at the date of the expert opinion, as well as the damage suffered by the owner(s) or, as the case may be, by the holder(s) of other exercisable rights having taken into account the evidence submitted by them.

The experts determine separately the amounts payable as compensation to the owner(s) and to the holder(s) of other exercisable rights.

Where land is expropriated, the amount payable as compensation cannot be less than the normative price which is computed on the basis of the price rates established by the Law on Standard Prices and the Procedures for Sale and Purchase of Land.

Compensation is paid after the parties reach an agreement. Where such agreement is absent, the court pronounces a judgement to transfer the amount awarded by the court to the expropriated party's bank account within 30 days of the day on which the court decision becomes final.

Cultivated land may only be taken from the owner after the crops are harvested – unless the amount awarded by way of compensation also includes the value of unharvested crops.

In the case of creditors with higher ranking priority claims or of other creditors identified by court, their claims are satisfied according to the compensation procedure and depending on their rights. The amounts payable to creditors as compensation are determined by the court.

The damages or compensation paid reflects the actual value of the concerned immovable property and losses suffered by the property owner because of its expropriation.

Where land is expropriated, the awarded amount may not be less than the standard price of the land.

Moldova's Land Code (Land Code, 1991) also prescribes certain approaches and forms for the compensation of damages sustained by landowners. According to Article 93 of the Land Code, the damages from the permanent or temporary deprivation of land, from the imposition of limitations on the landowner's rights, or from land impairment because of the activities exercised on that land by other enterprises, institutions, agencies or individuals are also subject to compensation in full (including any loss of profits) to the landowner who has suffered those damages.

Compensation for the damages is payable according to the statutory procedure by the enterprises, institutions and/or agencies which are allocated the expropriated land as well as by the enterprises, institutions and/or agencies whose activities limit the rights of the parties possessing the relevant land (because of the establishment of protective belts, buffer zones and/or restricted areas for diverse facilities), and which cause impairment to nearby land, prevent any intended use of nearby land or cause lower yields or impaired quality of agricultural products.

All disputes arising from or in connection with compensation for losses and the determination of the amount of the damages subject to compensation are settled in general courts or in state arbitration courts.

The Land Code describes a broader range of situations where compensation is payable for damages. In particular, such situations include:

- Compensation for damages to agrarian and/or forest industry producers and of loss of profits to enterprises, institutions and agencies because of the delayed return of the land;
- Compensation for damages to agrarian and/or forest industry producers from the permanent or temporary deprivation of land.

Although these descriptions do not directly include the term "expropriation", the Land Code actually describes the expropriation situations, and in doing so, the Land Code makes a reference to the relevant laws and regulations. Article 94 of the Land Code says that the terms, conditions and procedures of expropriations for governmental and public needs of land and real estate owned by individuals and entities are regulated in special laws that ensure the protection of property rights.

But what does the Land Code say about the amounts payable as compensation?

In case of the delayed return of productive land, the enterprises, institutions and/or agencies to whom that land has been transferred for temporary use are required to compensate the landowners for losses to the agrarian and/or forest industry producers and for loss of profits during the period the land was used in excess of the pre-established term – to the amounts and according to the procedure prescribed by the Law.

Compensation for losses caused to the agrarian and/or forest industry producers (because of the withdrawal of arable and/or forest land from agricultural and/or forestry production or because of the allocation of arable and/or forest land for temporary use for any purpose other than for agricultural and/or forestry production purposes, or because of a limitation of land possession rights or the impairment of soil quality caused by the activities of the concerned enterprises, institutions and agencies or by uses other than the intended use of the concerned land) shall be payable to the national Treasury and allocated to ensure the restoration and development or to improve fertility of the concerned land. Compensation for such losses shall be payable in addition to compensation for damages.

These losses are subject to compensation in full according to the rates approved by the national government.

Losses in agrarian production are compensated by the concerned governmental, cooperative and public agribusinesses – enterprises, institutions and/or agencies – in the event they have located a construction project on the irrigated or drained land or the land under perennial plantations or the plough-land or any other land with a soil quality ("bonity") of more than 40 points which has been allocated to them.

Funds paid as compensation for losses in agricultural and/or forest industry production may only be allocated for financing of the projects of construction and assembly, planning and exploration, land surveying and development of new land, the prevention of soil erosion and landslides, the improvement of soil fertility and of agricultural and forestry productivity – according to statutory procedures.

The Moldovan laws establish the rates and procedures for the assessment of losses and for the use of the funds paid to the treasury as compensation for such losses, and also the list of enterprises, institutions and agencies exempted from payment of compensation for such losses.

Moreover, the Land Code regulates compensation for damages caused. Such damages are subject to compensation in full, including the loss of profits.

Thus, the compensation payable for expropriated land comprises two components: (1) the market value of the expropriated land; and (2) the loss of profit from the use of the land.

It can be concluded from this analysis of Moldova's laws, that legal acts of the Republic of Moldova identify the following value types for the purposes of regulating the amount of compensation payable for immovable property expropriated for a socially useful purpose:

- Market value;
- Actual value;
- Standard price of land;
- Damages;
- Loss of profits.

The legislative acts currently applicable were developed and enacted during different periods of time, thus, the author believes it would be of interest to examine the economic content of the value types mentioned in these documents and the methodologies established for their determination.

The term "market value" was introduced in Moldova's legal and regulatory framework in the early 2000s, that is, when Moldova enacted the Law on Appraisal Activities and Title VI of the Tax Code: Tax on immovable property. The definition for the term "market value" was taken from the 1998 European Valuation Standards (EVS). The definition has not been revised or amended since then, and the term currently used still has the meaning allocated to it in the late 1990s. Thus,

> market value is an estimated amount for which the property being appraised should exchange on the date of valuation between a willing buyer and a willing seller in an arm's length transaction after proper marketing, wherein the parties had each acted knowledgeably, prudently and without compulsion.
>
> *(Law 989, 2002, Art. 1)*

It can be concluded from an analysis of the most recent versions of the International Valuation Standards (IVS) and the EVS that the definition has not undergone any major changes since.

Although the term "actual value" of property can be found in Moldova's laws and regulations on numerous occasions, no official definition has been provided for this term. However, if an assumption of its meaning is made based on the logic of its use, the meaning would be identical to that of the term "market value". The term "actual value" appeared in Moldova's laws and regulations in the early 1990s when the first sets of rules were developed for property appraisals for privatisation purposes and the market appraisal methodologies or the term "market value" were not generally use in the country. On the other hand, it can be assumed from the most recent IVS versions that "actual value" demonstrates more similarity to "fair value" – which latter term seems to be closer in its meaning to "actual value" than to "market value" *a fortiori*. It should be pointed out that expropriations were mostly performed in rural areas and outside major settlements, that is, in locations where the immovable property market was at an early stage in its development and where veritable information about the concluded immovable property transactions was hard to access. Nevertheless, the author believes that the Law on Expropriations for a socially useful purpose means "market value" when speaking of "actual value", because the term "fair value" has not as yet gained any formal recognition in Moldova's laws and regulations concerning appraisals of immovable property.

Meaning and definition of the term "normative price of land"

The term "normative price of land" dates back to 1997 when Moldova enacted the Law on Normative Price and the Procedure for Sale and Purchase of Land, which was quite a progressive law for that time.

The State was the only owner of land in Moldova in the early 1990s. Land could not be sold or purchased and there was no land market. However, Moldova was privatising its housing, commercial and industrial facilities rapidly during that period – and each case of immovable property privatisation gave rise to a paradoxical situation where the building or the structure had a private owner, but the land on which it stood was owned by the State.

So, it was necessary to introduce an easy method which would be understandable by all parties involved in the privatisation process for the determination of the basis of value for the forthcoming transactions to privatise land under privatised buildings. It was also necessary to know the basis of value in order to be able to fix rent payable for the use of land by tenants.

These considerations resulted in the term "normative price of land" as the unique know-how of the former Soviet Union republics. The normative price of land was used for the following purposes:

a   To be able to sell and purchase land, including land under privatised property, or property to be privatised, or private property or construction projects in progress;
b   To be able to contribute publicly-owned land under property of the types mentioned in (a) to the share capital of the entity owning that property, on the decision of the general meeting of shareholders and upon approval by the landowner, as the latter's investment in the entity;
c   To reclassify land from agricultural land or forestry land into a different category and to withdraw land from agricultural production;
d   To perform actions of the forcible deprivation of land;
e   To determine the value basis in land tenancy relationships.

Naturally, the normative price of land was an abstract idea at the time the aforementioned law was enacted, and the original intention was to use it only during the transitional period from the start of the land privatisation process until the emergence of the "over-the-counter" land market. According to the aforementioned law, "the normative price of land is a measure unit for land valuation; this measure unit is the national currency equivalent expressing the natural and economic capacity of land" (Law 1308, 1997, Art. 2). The Law established a method for computation of the standard price and that method had to be applied during the exercise of any relationship concerning land, irrespective of the nature of the landownership. The tariff rates for the computation of the normative price of land were established using the arbitrary measurement unit "point per hectare" on the basis of the qualitative and quantitative land characteristics registered in the cadastre. The original intent was for the Parliament to make adjustments to these tariff rates using a certain index on the suggestion of the government and depending on the inflation rate. The Law requires that the costs of the engineering development of the land be added to the standard price of land in settlements (excluding land plots attached to houses) and of land under industrial, transport and other non-agricultural facilities.

The following general formula was approved to compute the normative price of land:

$$NP = B \times T \times S$$

where
NP = normative price;
B = average soil fertility ("bonity") determined for the actual city, town or village (community) or for a particular piece of land, as the case may be; soil fertility is expressed in points per hectare of the land area;
T = tariff rate for the computation of the standard price of land (in Moldovan Lei for 1 point per hectare); and
S = area of the land for which the standard price is computed.

Table 6.1 Tariff rates for computation of normative land prices, in Moldovan Lei for 1 point per hectare

#	*Purpose for computation of the normative price*	*Tariff rate*
1	Sale and purchase of agricultural land, land attached to the house and garden plots	621.05
2	Forcible depriving of agricultural land, land plots attached to the house and garden plots	1242.08
3	Reclassification of land from the categories: agricultural land and forest land; withdrawal of land from agricultural production	19,873.34
4	Sale and purchase of land in settlements (excluding land plots attached to houses)	19,873.34

Source: The table was produced on the basis of Annex 1 to the Moldovan law on normative price and the procedure for sale and purchase of land.

The party determining soil fertility is a specialised surveying contractor. In Moldova, a major contractor of is the State Planning Institute for Land Management. Table 6.1 shows the tariff rates established for computation of normative land prices.

The normative prices of land under industrial or transport facilities and under structures of other types, and the normative prices of non-agricultural land are computed on the basis of the average weighed soil fertility for the entire country.

If the land to be sold is used in a production process and located under a privatised facility or a facility to be privatised or private property or a construction project in progress, the normative price computed on the basis of the tariff rates in Line 4 of Table 6.1 shall be multiplied by the following adjusting factor:

- 0.9 for the city of Chisinau;
- 0.7 for the towns forming part of the municipality of Chisinau;
- 0.5 for the villages (communities) forming part of the municipality of Chisinau;
- 0.5 for the cities of Balti, Bender and Tiraspol;
- 0.4 for the other settlements forming part of the municipalities of Balti, Bender and Tiraspol;
- 0.2 for the towns of Cahul, Causeni, Comrat, Edinet, Hincesti, Orhei, Ribnita, Soroca, Ungheni, Anenii Noi, Criuleni, Ialoveni, Straseni;
- 0.1 for all other towns; and
- 0.02 for villages (communities).

The normative prices computed for agricultural land, land plots attached to houses and garden plots on the basis of the tariff rates in Line 1 of Table 6.1 is multiplied by 0.3 as the adjusting factor. This rule does not apply to computations of rent payable for a tenancy on agricultural land.

It is important to note here that the statutory tariff rates for the computation of the normative prices of land are rather high, and result in much higher values than the market prices of agricultural land. Figure 6.1 shows a map of Moldova with the normative price of land for each region. This is an indirect reflection of the current soil fertility levels, which are the highest in the north of the country and register a clear reduction in the nation's central and southern parts.

The State Enterprise Cadastre has performed an analysis of the agricultural land sale prices, and it has demonstrated that the market prices for this type of immovable property

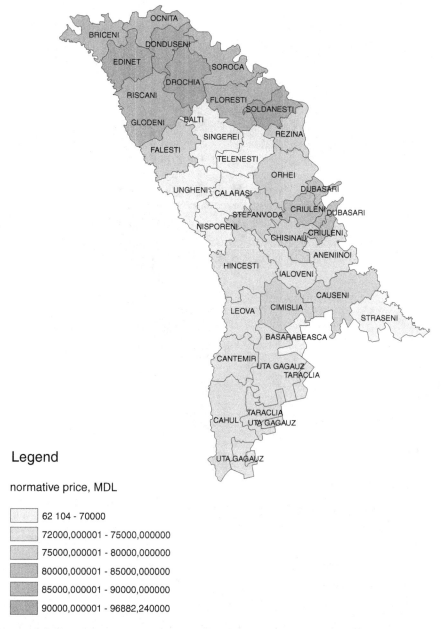

Figure 6.1 The normative prices of land for regions of the Republic of Moldova
Source: Produced on the basis of the 2016 Land cadastre information.

are mostly rather low in Moldova and tend to vary within a broad range throughout the country (Figure 6.2). The difference between the normative prices and the market prices of land is very high. The market prices for agricultural land in the municipality of Chisinau are 10- to 40-fold of the selling prices paid for land in Moldova's regions. Obviously, these prices should not be treated as an adequate reflection of the consumer's value of agricultural

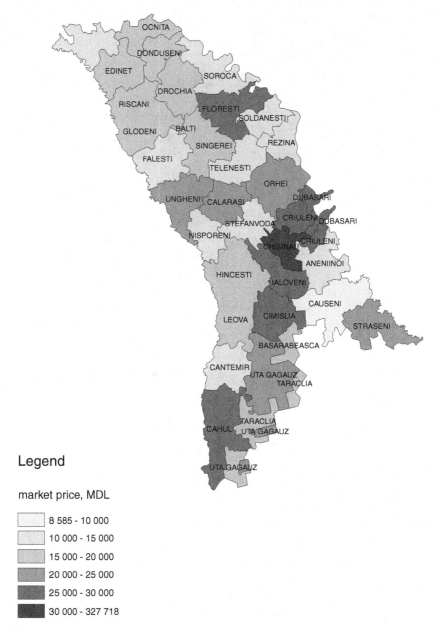

Legend

market price, MDL

	8 585 - 10 000
	10 000 - 15 000
	15 000 - 20 000
	20 000 - 25 000
	25 000 - 30 000
	30 000 - 327 718

Figure 6.2 The average market prices for agricultural land for regions of the Republic of Moldova

Source: Produced by the author on the basis of the 2017 State Enterprise Cadastre data.

land. Rather, this difference can be explained by the greater attractiveness of land as an investment target closer to the capital city being the largest economic hub and cultural and political centre in the country.

The situation described earlier can be illustrated by an example of the difference between the normative price and the market prices of agricultural land in the Cahul region in the south of Moldova. The Cahul-Giurgiulesti railroad was constructed in that region some years ago, and the implementation of the construction project made it necessary to expropriate about 200 units of agricultural land and plots attached to residential houses in certain villages located along the bank of the Prut river. The average market price charged for 1 hectare of agricultural land in that region is MDL 29,000 (MDL 11,750 per acre),[2] whereas the standard price computed for 1 hectare of such land for the purposes of paying compensation for the expropriated property was MDL 72,000 (MLD 29,150 per acre). In other words, the standard price of agricultural land was almost 2.5-fold of its market price in the Cahul Region. Obviously, a difference that big offers some space for potential bargaining where the amount of compensation payable for the expropriated land is determined by negotiations between the expropriating authority and the owner(s) of the property to be expropriated.

The size of compensations payable for damages

The term "damages" is defined in Article 14 of the Civil Code of the Republic of Moldova (Civil Code, 2002). That law also establishes the main rules governing the payment of compensation for damages. The person whose rights have been infringed is entitled to claim full compensation for the damage suffered as a result of this infringement. "Damages" include the expenses incurred or to be incurred by the person whose rights have been infringed in order to restore the infringed right, as well as the loss or damage to that person's property (actual damage) and lost profit that the person would have received otherwise, that is, if the right had not been infringed (loss of profits).

Comments to the Civil Code (Comments, 2002) point out that compensation for damages is treated as a universal remedy and as a means to protect civil rights. Compensation for damages can be combined with other remedies available to the party adversely affected.

Actual damage is understood to include the actual expenses incurred by the expropriated party at the time of expropriation, as well as that party's future expenses necessarily incurred in order to restore the lost right to the expropriated property, that is, additional expenses. Moreover, the actual damage includes damages from any loss or destruction of the property (i.e., loss of its value in use).

Loss of profits means the amount of income which the owner would have obtained from continued the ordinary operation of the property if it had not been expropriated.

In all situations where compensation is claimed for actual damages or for possible future damages, it is necessary to prove the existence of a cause-and-effect link between the amount of damages claimed and the expropriator's actions. This requirement also extends to situations where compensation is claimed for loss of profits. The adversely affected party bears the burden of proof to substantiate the amount claimed as compensation for loss of profits resulting from the expropriation of the concerned property and to demonstrate the cause-and-effect link between the loss of profits and the execution of the expropriation.

For an estimate of the loss of profits, it is important to establish the fairness or probability of profit that the affected party could have obtained from the continued ordinary operation of the expropriated property. "Ordinary operation" is understood to mean its operation in a typical market environment not affected by any unforeseen factors or *force majeure* events. The party affected by the expropriation becomes entitled to claim in addition to compensation for damages, the profit gained by the expropriator and remaining after the payment of compensation of the damages, as the case may be.

Generally, compensation for damages caused by expropriation comprises three components:

- Value of land without improvements;
- Value of the existing improvements or of their reinstatement;
- Loss of profits caused by the withdrawal of the property from its operation.

The following discusses in more detail how each of the components of compensation is estimated.

The value of land without improvements is appraised using a market approach, more often than not, using a sales comparison approach. A mandatory condition prerequisite for the use of this approach is the existence of a sufficiently developed land market and the availability of verifiable information on prices for which similar properties have changed hands.

The value of the existing improvements or of their restoration is assessed most often using a cost-based method, in order to take into account the specific features of the expropriated property more fully. A market-based approach can also be used to that end, but it will yield a market value of the improvements. As market values of immovable property have been lower than replacement values in many rural areas of Moldova during the last seven to eight years, the use of a particular valuation approach depends on whether the owner of the property being expropriated wants to acquire an existing property (building, structure, land under perennial plantations) or to construct a similar building/structure or to plant perennial crops independently from scratch on a new piece of land.

The actual damage from the expropriation of a vineyard is assessed using a cost-based method and the following background data: the quality, state, age and yield capacity of the vines on land to be expropriated; the selling prices per metric tonne (1,000 kg) or the selling prices per 100 kg of the harvested grapes; vineyard maintenance costs and so forth. An estimate should be performed to calculate the indirect costs which the owner of the expropriated vineyard would have to incur in order to reproduce ("replace") that vineyard elsewhere.

Typically, the party calculating the owner's loss of profits caused by the withdrawal of the property from operation is the central authority or the local public administration in charge of the expropriation of the concerned property for a socially useful purpose. It should be pointed out here that Moldova lacks an officially developed and approved methodology for the assessment of the damage suffered and profit lost by the owner as a result of expropriation of the owner's property for a socially useful project. However, certain experience has been accumulated of performing such calculations. These can be illustrated in the three aforementioned situations as examples of calculating the loss of profits by the owner of an expropriated property.

1   The expropriated property is land destined for agricultural use on which its owner is currently growing annual crops. In this situation, the loss of profit is calculated for a period of one or two years (i.e., the time needed to plant, to grow and to harvest the crops).

2   The expropriated property is agricultural land under perennial crops. It is assumed in such situations that the loss of profits is the aggregate income from the future sales of harvested crops for the next five years (i.e., sufficient time to plant a new orchard and for it to grow until its trees reach a fruit-bearing age).

The authority assessing the loss of profits caused by the expropriations of agricultural land is the Ministry of Agriculture. The loss of profits are the estimated total losses caused by the owner's inability to harvest and sell crops for a certain number of years.

The data on the average yield capacity of the main agricultural crops grown by private farms and family farms can be obtained from the National Statistics Bureau of Moldova. This information is available to the general public, and it is presented broken down by year and by agricultural crop (as statistics year books). The principle underlying the calculations for loss of profits is to determine the annual income from the assumed sales of a certain crop, which the owner is no longer able to obtain because his land has been expropriated.

3   Where the expropriated property is land destined for a construction project and the building(s)/structure(s) located on that land, the loss of profits is assessed as the total income the owner was not able to obtain as rent from tenants of that building/structure.

Examples of expropriations for socially useful purposes in the Republic of Moldova

A separate law is adopted for each specific project involving expropriations to describe the general background, the area of land required for the relevant socially useful construction project and the location of the land to be expropriated.

Construction of the Revaca–Cainari railroad

The authority responsible for acquisitions of the necessary land for the construction of the railroad was the Agency of Land Relations and Cadastre. Land was acquired under the relevant Government Resolutions (no. 1417, 2004; no. 104, 2005). The land which had to be expropriated was located in several settlements along the railroad route at the same time. The total number of the land units to be expropriated was 471, which included agricultural land and garden areas adjacent to plots of land attached to houses. The market for agricultural land was still at its early developmental stage at that time, and the authorities had no available sources of reliable information about actual land transaction prices. For that reason, all owners of the land to be expropriated were offered a standard price for their land. Most owners (455) agreed with the offer on the spot and were paid monetary compensation for their land. However, 16 owners did not want monetary compensation. They requested instead replacement land from the public land pool managed by their local public administrations. Furthermore, these owners of the expropriated land wanted larger areas of replacement land because their expropriated land was more fertile (had a higher "bonity") than the land in the public land pool. An agreement was finally reached after lengthy negotiations. The National government issued Resolution (no. 709, 2007) to make 7.9 hectares (17 acres) of land state property available and to allocate 9.8 hectares (22 acres) of agricultural land from the reserve public land pools of the concerned local administrations for distribution to these 16 owners. Only one owner was not satisfied with the replacement land allocated to him from the reserve pool of the local administration: he claimed monetary compensation in addition to that replacement land for the difference in land fertility. A little later, he started claiming loss of profits from the cultivation of his expropriated land for a period of three years. The litigation dragging on for three years, and only in 2010 was the expropriation of land for the construction of the Revaca–Cainari railroad deemed completed rather successfully. In that particular case, the duration of the expropriation process had been six years (2005 to 2010).

But expropriations are not always successful – even though the major strategic infrastructure to be constructed under the project are of vital importance for the public and for the entire national economy.

Construction of the international free port in Giurgiulesti

Land expropriations for the construction of the international free port in Giurgiulesti are a spectacular example of the failed expropriation of agricultural land.

In 2005, the parliament of Moldova adopted the Law on the International Free Port in Giurgiulesti (Law no. 8 of 04.03.2005), and it was published in Moldova's official gazette *Monitorul Oficial*. This port was to remain a free port for 25 years in order to accelerate economic development in the southern regions of Moldova, to ensure the nation's transport and power and to promote international trade. The Law identified land within the borders of the project site for that international port to be public property, and the borders and the conformation of the international port's grounds was documented on cadastral maps in accordance with the cadastral law.

The intention was to build the international port on 120 hectares (296 acres) of land. The port grounds were to comprise:

a   An oil terminal and oil refinery;
b   A cargo storage facility;
c   A passenger port; and
d   An area for the future development of the international port.

The aforementioned Law identified the site of the international port as a first priority development site for the Republic of Moldova. To ensure the integrated development of the site, the National government leased the site of the international port to a general contractor for development on the terms and conditions established in the investment agreement on the international free port in Giurgiulesti.

In 2008 the government adopted Law no. 176 which identified the project to construct the international free port in Giurgiulesti as a socially useful project of national importance. Enactment of that Law suspended all outstanding transactions involving the land to be expropriated for the implementation of that project, and with all buildings and structures on that land.

To ensure implementation of that Law, the Agency of Land Relations and Cadastre of the Republic of Moldova was authorised to make the required arrangements for the conclusion of land purchase contracts with the owners of the land covered by the engineering project of the future port, and thus to expropriate all private agricultural land located within the borders of the site.

The general contractor was transferred 55.23 hectares (136 acres) of the public land required to enable the contractor to construct and ensure operation of the port. However, the initial project envisaged the expansion of the port's grounds by a further 35.06 hectares (86 acres) of private land owned by certain residents of Giurgiulesti. The construction project documentation was improved at a later stage, and now it envisaged development of still further 29.7 hectares (71 acres) of privately owned land. As soon as it became known that the site of the international grounds would expand and the State intended to expropriate additional private land for that extension, the owners of that land filed compensation claims incompatible with Moldova's laws and regulations. The owners of the concerned land said they would only agree to sell it to the State for a given price, which was much higher than the market value of that land and several-fold the standard price calculated for the land to be expropriated.

Acting in accordance with the Law, the State Committee for the Settlement of Disputes arising out of or in connection with expropriations of land conducted separate negotiations with each of the concerned owners, attempting to resolve all issues raised, but its efforts failed to achieve the desired outcome. Therefore the Agency of Land Relations and Cadastre (which was the authority in charge of resolving the problem on behalf of the government) had to submit the dispute to the court for settlement. In 2011, it initiated a separate litigation in the Cahul district court against each of the concerned landowners, seeking a court judgement regarding the amount to be paid to them as compensation for resulting damages. The National Treasury allocated MDL 3 million of public funds for the payment of compensation for that damage. The 43 landowners filed their statements of claim with court. Although these claims have been considered for more than nine years, at the time of writing, the dispute is still very far from settled.

Court hearings have had to be rescheduled several times for reasons attributable to the expropriated owners because they have refused to agree with the amounts offered to them as compensation. On their part, they submitted to court the valuation reports they had ordered in respect of their property to be expropriated. Those reports indicated property values which were almost fivefold the amounts offered as compensation to the owners by the State.

The Agency applied to the Board for the Certification (i.e., licensing) of Immovable Property Valuers with a request to review the submitted valuation reports on land to be expropriated for their fairness and quality. The Board identified some major errors in those reports. The valuer who had issued the reports and who was notified of the board's opinion, acknowledged having made the identified errors and the Board withdrew his immovable property valuer license. As result, the court found all those valuation reports inadmissible as evidence and appointed a panel of court experts to produce a report with an estimate of the damage caused to the expropriated owners.

It should be mentioned here that Moldova lacks a clear and accepted algorithm for making estimates of amounts payable as compensation in accordance with Article 15 of the law on expropriation. This is one of the reasons that the court was not able to decide on this matter; another reason is the complexity and length of the legal expert review, which is mandatory in such situations. Only one of the 43 landowners involved in that litigation concerning the amounts to be paid as compensation has meanwhile agreed to accept the standard price for his land as monetary compensation for its expropriation.

At the same time, courts in other districts of Moldova where expropriations of immovable property were also taking place for socially useful projects have taken a very responsible approach to the consideration of such disputes and imposed an obligation on the parties in dispute to arrive at a decision within a limited period of one month, in view of major importance of the relevant cases.

Conclusions and suggestions

Moldova's economy is currently at the stage when its new productive and economic relationships and trade contacts with Western and Eastern Europe are emerging and taking shape. Development of an up-to-date transport infrastructure, the implementation of intensive farming methods in agriculture and the growth of settlements inevitably lead to the necessity to expropriate private property of individuals and companies for socially useful projects.

Moldova has a legal and regulatory framework for expropriations of property for socially useful projects. However, the current laws do not cover all possible expropriation situations which involve the assessment of the damage caused to the owner of expropriated property. For this reason, courts often lack the required tools to arrive at a final judgement regarding the amount to be paid as compensation for damages caused by expropriation – and so litigations can go on for years, and the necessary expropriation cannot be performed in accordance with the project plans.

In the author's opinion, all problems associated with expropriations of property for socially useful projects can be subdivided into three categories: (1) problems arising from the need to improve the legal framework for such expropriations; (2) problems as to how exactly such expropriations should be organised; and (3) problems arising because of a lacking methodology for the determination of the amount payable as compensation for the expropriated property and the assessment of damage caused to the owner. The author makes the following suggestions intended to facilitate solutions of these problems.

The laws of the Republic of Moldova do not provide sufficient details concerning the exact organisation of the expropriation process and the protection of the rights of owners whose property are to be expropriated. It would be necessary to impose (at the level of the relevant legal acts) an obligation on the central authorities and local public administrations to perform awareness-raising activities by reaching out to the community in order to explain the necessity of the scheduled expropriations and to emphasise the resultant social and economic benefits for the entire local community or for the entire Republic. The laws should provide more details concerning the procedure for appealing against the decisions of expropriating authorities and establish the rights and obligations of each party involved in appeal proceedings as well as the role to be played by local authorities. In the author's opinion, it would also be necessary to set a more acceptable maximum term for appeal proceedings in order to prevent the adverse impact of lengthy litigations on national projects for the construction of engineering, transport or social infrastructural facilities.

The owner of property to be expropriated is quite often left with the task to face court one-on-one when proving the amount of damages caused by the expropriation. The costs the expropriated owner has to incur in such situations are high: according to the Civil Code, the owner bears independently (and often repeatedly) the expenses to prove the amount of loss of profits, the market value, the exact soil fertility of the land and so forth. The valuer's fees as well as the costs of litigation, of court expert reviews, of soil research and of technical expert reviews of the buildings add up to a considerable amount. So, the applicable laws should be amended to compensate the owners for their costs in the event that the court finds the appellant's calculations of the amount payable as compensation to be correct.

The author believes that property expropriation activities could be organised better in the case of expropriations for socially useful projects by imposing an obligation on the relevant central authorities and local public administrations to be more proactive in their outreach to the community, and in particular to owners of the property to be expropriated (i.e., to hold meetings and discussions, to publish guides and manuals, to run awareness-raising campaigns, and in particular campaigns in mass media).

The sites of new projects of national importance are often located close to settlements in rural areas where there is no real estate market for all practical purposes, or where such a market is underdeveloped, which translates to a lack of relevant market infrastructure, data, real estate agents or other professional market participants. In such situations it is a very complicated task for the owner to challenge the amount offered as compensation from the State – and even the engagement of a professional valuer to appraise the market value of the expropriated property will not guarantee a beneficial outcome in every case. The author thinks that in such situations, the local authorities should also inform the community about selling prices at which similar immovable property change hands and provide advisory support regarding all expropriation matters, in particular regarding determination of the amount payable as compensation.

The concerns emerging in respect to the development of a methodology to determine the amount payable as compensation for damages are as follows. Moldovan laws establish different approaches to the determination of the quantum of compensation, and on multiple occasions the terms and definitions used are in conflict with one another. The current methodology developed in mid-1990s to assess the amount of damages suffered does not reflect the market value of the expropriated property. Notwithstanding the seeming ease of these calculations, the author does not believe the methodology currently used in Moldova takes into account the owner's entire damages incurred from the expropriation of property. In the author's opinion, the approach to the calculation of the resultant damages should differentiate between situations where property is expropriated permanently for a socially useful project, and where damages are caused to the owner because of the temporary dispossessed of property.

An analysis of Moldova's laws and regulations on the expropriation of property for socially useful projects and on the calculation of amounts payable as compensation has demonstrated that the formulas underlying calculations of the amounts payable as compensation do not take into account many types of the expropriated owner's losses and expenses.

The methodology currently in effect disregards the social status and moral satisfaction inherent in the ownership of certain immovable property, on top of purely economic benefits. For example, an owner may feel personal satisfaction and pride to own certain real estate, or possibly owners may have inherited land from their ancestors and it has an added value to them because it symbolises their family legacy, provides a continuity of "place", and so forth. The author believes the methodology currently used to calculate the amount of compensation for suffered damage should be improved to take account of the social, personal and ethical implications of owning the property to be expropriated.

The National laws do not pay sufficient attention to the matter of calculating the amount of compensation for damage suffered in the event that the expropriated property is land and improvements located on that land. In such situations, the market value of the relevant improvements cannot always be treated as a fair reflection of the owner's loss. The valuer appraising the market value of such property applies the valuation approaches recommended by the International Valuation Standards and by National law. The market value of property reflects its usefulness or merits from the market perspective, that is, in the eyes of a large number of sellers and a large number of buyers; and as a result, the first approach is most often the market approach (*sales comparison method* in Moldova's laws). However, the Moldovan real estate market is not uniform; its different sectors are at different stages of development. In most cases, construction costs are higher than the current market value of real estate in rural areas and in small towns. That is why a substantiated valuation methodology should be developed to determine which approaches would be optimal in each case for a more exact calculation of the compensation amount.

In the author's opinion, two valuation methods (the cost method and the sales comparison method) should be used to appraise the market value of an integral complex of immovable property, that is, land and the improvements (buildings, structures) located on that land. An appraisal of perennial plantations should take into account the expenses required to plant the orchard/vineyard as well as the costs of their maintenance (pesticides, fertilisers, etc.). Information should be available on each perennial crop – concerning its planting system, depreciation (presented as tables) and the average annual yield capacity of diverse fruit crops.

The author suggests using the capitalised present value of income flows for the period of the property's assumed operation (which is no longer possible because of the expropriation) in situations where loss of profits has to be projected for a period longer than one year. The calculations should be based on the assumed net operating income. That would involve the need to consider fluctuations in the selling prices of the concerned crops during the projected period, changes in the depreciation charges on perennial crops during the projected period and changes in the flows of operating incomes.

It would be possible to overcome conflicting legal provisions on the calculation of amounts payable as compensation to owners of expropriated property through the development of a National property valuation standard for expropriations of property for socially useful projects. The availability of such a standard will make it possible to suggest diverse models for the assessment of the value of expropriated property and the evaluation of loss of profits for different property types in markets at differing stages of development. Such a standard should be developed in collaboration with international associations of valuers to be able to make use of best international valuation practices in this area.

The author believes that the completion of the mass tax assessment efforts of immovable property in Moldova will be a solution for the issue of adequate and fair market valuation. This valuation type is sufficiently well developed in Moldova. Many types of immovable property have already been appraised (mostly the property located in urban areas because market development levels are higher there). The property types that have not yet been entirely registered and consequently not entirely assessed are agricultural land, residential houses in rural areas and special purpose facilities. It is expected that Moldova will implement a World Bank project in the next few years to complete the mass valuation efforts and to perform revaluations of all types of immovable property. It can be expected therefore that all immovable property will be assessed for tax purposes in the near future. The assessed tax value of immovable property differs somewhat from its market value because of the sketchy nature of all mass valuations – but it is still an indication of fair value of property. Mass assessments of all types of immovable property will enable the establishment of an adequate pricing level for similar properties located within the same geographical zone – and so owners of immovable property are likely to have a positive attitude towards such assessments. Timely revaluation efforts at statutory intervals are an important aspect ensuring correspondence between assessed value and market value.

Notes

1 History of Moldavian Soviet Socialist Republic, p. 407.
2 MDL is the Moldovan Leu, equivalent to 0.05 EUR approximately.

References

Civil Code of the Republic of Moldovano 1107 of 06.06.2002, Monitorul Oficial on 22.06.2002 (Issue 82–86, Item 661).
Constitution of the Republic of Moldova of 29.07.1994, Monitorul Oficial on 29.03.2016 (Issue 78, Item 140).
Comments to the Civil Code of the Republic of Moldova, 2002: Book I, Articles 1–283.doc // https://app.box.com/s/4jmkb6v3j4.
Compulsory Purchase and Compensation. A Guide to Compensation Agricultural Owners and Occupiers // https://www.finance-ni.gov.uk/sites/default/files/publications/dfp/Agriculture%20compensation%20Guide%202017.pdf.
Decree on Land Adopted by the 2nd All-Russia Congress of the Soviets (People's Councils), 26.10 (08.11). 1917 // http://www.hist.msu.ru/ER/Etext/DEKRET/o_zemle.htm.
Decree of Presidium of the USSR Supreme Soviet on 15.08.1940 On Nationalisation of Banks, Industrial and Commercial Facilities, Railroads, Water Transports and Communication Facilities in Bessarabia // https://goo.gl/iVtB5a.

Decree of Presidium of the USSR Supreme Soviet on 15.08.1940 on Restoration of Soviet Laws on Nationalisation of Land in Bessarabia // https://goo.gl/SL6Zsq.

Glossary of Agricultural Terms // https://dic.academic.ru/dic.nsf/agriculture/811/%D0%94%D0%95%D0%A1%D0%AF%D0%A2%D0%98%D0%9D%D0%90.

Government Resolution no. 1417 of 21.12.2004 on Allocation of Land, Monitorul Oficial on 31.12.2004 (Issue 242–245, Item 1620).

Government Resolution no. 104 of 02.02.2005 on Measures to Implement the Construction Project Revaca–Cainari Railroad, Monitorul Oficial on 04.02.2005 (Issue 20–23, Item 156).

Government Resolution no. 709 of 25.06.2007 on Land Transfer and Exchange, Monitorul Oficial on 06.07.2007 (Issue 94–97, Item 752).

History of the Moldovan Soviet Socialist Republic (История Молдавской ССР). Chisinau: Stiinta, 1984, 552 p.

Land Cadastre of the Republic of Moldova, 2016. Materials of the Agency for Land Relations and Cadastre.

Land Code of the Republic of Moldova no. 828 of 25.07.1991, Monitorul Oficial on 04.09.2001 (Issue 107, Item 817).

Law no. 459 of 22.01.1991 on Property,Monitorul Oficial on 30.06.1991 (Issue 3–6, Item 22).

Law no. 488 of 18.07.1999 on Expropriations for a Socially Useful Purpose, Monitorul Oficial on 20.04.1999 (Issue 42–44, Item 311).

Law no. 1308 of 25.07.1997 on Normative Price and the Procedure for Sale and Purchase of Land, Monitorul Oficial on 06.12.2001 (Issue 147–149, Item 1161).

Lawno. 1384 of 11.10.2002 on Requisition of Property and Community Work, Monitorul Oficial on 27.12.2002 (Issue 178–181, Item 1352).

Law no. 1225 of 08.12.1992 on Vindication of Political Repression Victims, Monitorul Oficial on 30.12.1992 (Issue 12).

Law no. 989 of 18.04.2002 on Appraisal Activities, Monitorul Oficial on 16.07.2002 (Issue 102, Item 773).

Law no. 8 of 17.02.2005 on the International Free Port in Giurgiulesti, Monitorul Oficial on 04.03.2005 (Issue 36–38, Item 116).

Statistical Databank of the Republic of Moldova//http://statbank.statistica.md/pxweb/pxweb/ro/40%20Statistica%20economica/40%20Statistica%20economica__16%20AGR__AGR020/AGR020100.px/table/tableViewLayout1/?rxid=5360837a-13b5-4912-a2e0-12892e96d2ab.

The Market Prices for Agricultural Land for Regions of the Republic of Moldova in 2017. Materials of the State Enterprise Cadastre.

7

Legal and institutional fundaments of expropriation and compensation issues in Turkey

Harun Tanrıvermiş and Yesim Aliefendioğlu

Introduction

As a result of the increase in communities' needs, the services that are expected from the state are also swiftly diversified, and there is a rapid increase in the requirements of public institutions for technology, qualified staff and funding. To achieve the high growth rate in developing economies, real estate (land, buildings and easements) acquisition and expropriation has assumed critical importance in the framework of neo-liberal economic thought. Public and authorised private institutions are bent upon large-scale land acquisitions for industry, trade and infrastructure investments (Khan 2014). In order to provide public services, such as health, education, security, transportation, water and sewerages infrastructures, public authorities may need to acquire a certain quantity of land. Easement rights and cheap ways of land acquisition are used if the method is adequate for the projects. Therefore, because of the insufficiency of necessary land or the inadequacy of its own land assets (state-owned land), the authority in question may be obliged to acquire privately owned land. In this case, land acquisition can be purchased formally by agreement, or in the case where negotiations in the framework of a formal land purchase fail, the acquisition may be achieved through expropriation or compulsory purchase for the realisation of the public interest or good.

Although, the public interest or good is commonly accepted as the fundamental basis for an expropriation or compulsory purchase, conditions of its practice around the world and the restrictions on private rights – after acquisition – vary from one legal system to another (Ferlan et al. 2009; Sumrada et al. 2013). Beyond these differentiations, in practice, there is a lack of internationally standardised expropriation procedures and unified principles for fair compensation (FAO 2008; Karlbro 2001; Viitanen et al. 2010; Sumrada et al. 2013). In addition, the problem with land acquisition for the provision of public interest goods through the doctrine of eminent domain is that it has failed in many cases to bring significant socio-economic advantages and interventions with respect to the incidence of acquisition and the entitlement to compensation (Khan 2014). The other issues of expropriation of real estate for public purposes are the manner in which these acquisitions are conducted on the one hand and the methods employed and types of compensation which are provided to former owners on the other hand. Many projects have failed or took more time in their implementation and therefore their realisation because of the refusal of landowners to concede their real estate. Some projects carried out for the public interest have had undesirable consequences such as unemployment, loss of income sources and social structures being adversely affected. This situation may lead to conflicts between former owners and the project-conducting authority, as a result of which the project realisation may be hampered. Despite all the arguments to explain the failure or the success of land expropriation or compulsory purchase, the legal framework underlying this mode of purchase and the capacity of the institution in charge to conduct the necessary land acquisition and the provision of public interest in question appear to be the cornerstone in the accomplishment of an effective and successful public interest outcome without negatively affecting the local populations or society.

Land acquisition is required in every country for public services, infrastructure and superstructure investments, and different methods are used in the process of land acquisition. For the acquisition of real estate in large quantities necessary for the implementation of development projects, methods such as expropriation, purchasing, zoning, land consolidation, easement, donation and leasing are used. However, each real estate acquisition method is regulated by different laws, and the implementation stages, procedures, valuations and the payment of compensation associated with each of the methods differ.

Expropriation processes frequently used by public institutions in Turkey are carried out according with the principles defined in the Turkish Constitution and Expropriation Law No. 2942 and the purchase methods in accordance with Public Procurement Law 4734. When there are issues regarding the implementation of the aforementioned methods, possible solutions are sought by the judicial organs and well-established precedents of the European Court of Human Rights (ECtHR), and efforts are made towards improving the efficiency of land acquisition.

The required real estate for infrastructure investments must either be owned by the public or transferred to the public domain. However, public institutions generally do not possess large and suitable real estate holdings sufficient to respond to all the requirements that may arise. Although real estate transfer and acquisition of such real estate with compensation or free of cost among public institutions is possible and easy, acquisition of real estate under private ownership takes a long time, the acquisition costs are high and the satisfaction levels of all affected stakeholders are low. When the mandate of the provision of public services is considered, there is an obligation to transfer the ownership of real estate not owned by the public to the ownership and management of the public institutions using public powers or via other means.

During work conducted toward land acquisition for public services and the compensation of landowners, there are discussions in terms of the nature of investment, the nature of the investing institution (public, private and international initiatives) and the location of investment (rural or urban) in Turkey. The execution of construction works within public investment through both direct procurement and contracting, as well as land acquisition and expropriation in projects where construction work is carried out with alternative financing options, is necessary. In particular, for projects carried out by foreign institutions or international initiatives through models such as build-operate-transfer (BOT), build-operate and public-private partnership (PPP), the existence of public interest in land acquisition becomes a matter of debate.

Under the Turkish Legal System, real estate ownership and use, intervention in ownership, the regulation of residential construction and infrastructure projects are regulated by the Constitution, Law No. 2942 and different laws for public and private sectors. State and public entities have the right to expropriate privately owned real estate for the public interest through making an up-front payment of its value. The valuation of land, businesses and other assets affected by the expropriation process; the compensation payable to affected persons; the monitoring and evaluation of work at the beginning of the project's operation period; and the development of mitigation measures when required are neglected in many countries. Beyond that, the methods used in the valuation of the expropriated real estate, valuation conditions, the validity period of the valuation, the applications of interest rate, the payment of compensation for non-pecuniary damage come to the fore. The issues experienced in these areas cause major disputes between the owners and the competent public institutions in the expropriation process (Tanrıvermiş et al. 2004; Tanrıvermiş and Aliefendioğlu 2015), with owners applying to the ECtHR with a claim for more compensation in cases where the local judicial process has been exhausted. The value of the expropriated real estate is expressed in many countries as 'fair value', 'fair compensation' and 'full replacement value', and the ECtHR decisions also make reference to the criteria underpinning these terms (Gemalmaz 2006; Aliefendioğlu and Tanrıvermiş 2016b). Moreover, it should be emphasised that in Turkey, different valuation approaches are defined for expropriation and real estate acquisition according to the type(s) of real estate involved. As a result, instead of proper valuation methods for 'fair compensation' considerable subjectivity and uncertain aspects underpin the implementation of the valuation criteria. As a result of the diversities of practices and the fact that many projects failed because expropriation and compensation processes have been mismanaged, international organisations, especially financial, undertook the elaboration of Standards Performance for the projects they finance (IFC 2012; EBRD 2014).

In this study, the basic principles and problems in real estate acquisition and expropriation practices for public investments have been defined, and in the second stage, the principles of valuation applied to the expropriated real estate based on their types, and the methods for calculation of compensations have been examined within the context of Turkey. The methods of real estate acquisition and compensation calculation for large-scale fixed capital investments have been evaluated in terms of national legislation and international standards as well as the economic, social and environmental impacts they cause. The problems encountered by public administrations, owners and other stakeholders, as well as the incongruity of national regulations with international standards, have been identified and the measures to be taken to improve the country practices are presented. In this context, land acquisition as defined in local regulations, the improvement of valuation practices and the identification of rights holders to be compensated during the land acquisition phase of projects were evaluated. In addition, real estate acquisition, expropriation and compensation principles to be implemented within the framework of performance standards in case of infrastructure projects receiving funding from international organisations were compared with practices in Turkey. The results of this study, prepared on the basis of research into the legislation and literature, as well as stakeholder interviews, are also significant because they allow the identification and effective implementation of policies to improve the land acquisition process for infrastructure investment in Turkey as well as in many other countries that display similar characteristics. In the conclusion section of the study, legislation and practice results are evaluated and solutions for the problems identified recommended

Real estate acquisition methods for infrastructure projects: the relationship between public investment and public interest

Investments should represent improvement of the existing human and financial capital to increase national income and ensure economic growth. Therefore, to achieve the aim of ensuring the development of the nation in an balanced way, the intervention of public authorities through investment in infrastructure and other resources becomes inevitable. The most important and most powerful vehicle for the direct intervention of the public is undoubtedly infrastructure investments. In the use of public investments to reduce regional disparities, the state spends more financial resources on a relatively underdeveloped region than the revenue generated from that area. This way, such regions can become more attractive to industry and commerce through the elimination of basic infrastructure problems or by increasing the production capacity with relevant investments (Genç et al. 2007; Kalem 2015).

The main purposes of public investment can be listed as ensuring a maximum contribution to growth, supporting private-sector investments, reducing interregional disparities and increasing employment opportunities and public welfare. Priority in public investment is given to areas such as education, health care, drinking water, sanitation, science and technology, energy, transportation and irrigation, and infrastructure investments (such as highways, ports, airports, railway station complexes, potable water, irrigation and power generation dams, pipelines and thermal and nuclear power plants), and these have significant impacts on economic and social development. While most public investments are not profitable financially, it is necessary to use public resources because they are acceptable from economic or social perspectives, and the interests of private firms in these investments is usually not possible without public support or contributions.

While the acquisition of the lands required for public investments and services can be achieved through zoning, consolidation, purchasing, expropriation, donations and other means, often expropriation and purchasing methods are used. According to Expropriation Law No. 2942, in cases where the public interest requires additional expropriation by the public entities of real estate owned by real and private legal entities, under the authority clearly defined in legislation, expropriation in favour of private corporations and institutions is also possible. There are occasions where the acquisition of real estate may be required for such purposes as social benefits, public interests and public purposes; education, health and recreation facilities from which individuals can benefit; infrastructure and public services.

The Turkish Constitution of 1982 stipulates that everyone has the right to own real estate, and this right may only be restricted by law based on the grounds of public interest. According to Turkish Civil Code No. 4721, ownership is a right *in rem* that gives the owners the authority to use, utilise and control their real estate as they wish within the framework of the rule of law. Expropriation is a process that ends the authority of an individual to maintain the possession of real estate. The right of the owner to real estate may be handed over for a public interest such as health, public order, social justice, equality, economic and social development, solutions of important social issues, communication and an effective settlement policy. In this context, the process of expropriation can be described as a competent authority forcibly taking possession of real estate owned by natural or legal persons to perform a public service which aims to serve the public interest, paying its value up-front (or in instalments if certain conditions are met) through the procedures set forth in the relevant legislation (Böke 2003; Tanrıvermiş et al. 2016).

The right of public administrations to acquire real estate necessary for the purpose of performing public service or public undertakings through expropriation has been defined in the Constitution, Law No. 2942, as well as in legislation governing the duties and powers of the different public institutions. Since the main reason and purpose of expropriation is the execution of public services or enterprises, as a result of infrastructure projects financed in recent years, it has been observed that the relationship between 'public service' and the concept of 'public interest' has become a subject of debate. Whether the services provided by some public institutions are 'public services', and land required for the services in question can therefore be acquired through expropriation, are often matters of discussion. This problem is especially apparent in projects funded with the BOT and PPP models, and with expropriation in favour of private individuals and institutions. Because of the very high financing costs of projects implemented through BOT and PPP models and their high-tech requirements, they take a long time to be achieved by the public sector. With the aim of accelerating local development and raising the service quality, it is clear that investing in these models will be of benefit to the general public. However, it is noteworthy that the operating rights granted to eligible companies in the BOT model, and the rental periods and prices in the PPP model, and guarantees granted by the state in both models have become issues of debate.

Large-scale fixed capital investments such as highways, bridges, airports and ports are of interest to the Turkish private sector as well as to foreign investors. The BOT model is used for the financing of projects such as Istanbul's Third Bosporus Bridge and the Northern Motorway, the Marmaray rail transport project, Istanbul's third airport, Çanakkale Harbour Bridge and Gebze-Izmir Motorway, while the PPP model is preferred for health-care investments. The growing interest of foreigner companies in toll road, bridge and tunnel investments contributes to the shortening of the investment period and the resolution of financial problems. For example, the Gebze-Orhangazi-Izmir Highway Project providing access between the provinces of Istanbul and Izmir is one of the large-scale fixed investments built under the BOT model, and because the route passes through fertile farmland and plantations in the western part of the country, the expropriation process was difficult and the costs were very high. As a result of the high efficiency of land affected by the project, agriculture generating economic revenue in the area and the nature of the project, land prices demanded by real estate owners were higher.

While the financing of public investment projects with BOT or PPP models in general has positive outcomes in favour of public institutions, local people affected by the projects and mainly engaged in farming are adversely affected both economically and socially. Apart from land consolidation, the standard method of expropriation used in land acquisition for the projects, the physical and economic resettlement of the households adversely affected by the project are neglected, and the methods of land acquisition and compensation are not consistent with international standards. Also, according to Article 6 of the Agrarian Reform Law No. 3083 on the Landscaping of Irrigation Areas, up to a 10% contribution can be deducted from public and private land within the boundaries of the consolidation area, in accordance with the project's characteristic for places to be used by the general public, such as channels and roads. According to Law No. 3083, what is meant by 'places dedicated to public use', such as roads and channels, are to be allocated for project purposes. Considering that large-scope projects such as motorways cannot be part of the implementation of land consolidation projects in irrigation areas in this context, it has been ruled by the Council of State that charging a contribution fee of up to 10% from places within the consolidation project for highway construction, or places to be considered in the scope of the implementation project, is not in accordance with the purposes of Law 3083 (the Council of State Office 17, numbered decree absolute: 2015/3602), and the administration in charge has restarted expropriation work for all road routes.

The share of the investment budget varies between 2% and 3% of the total gross national product in Turkey, and with the use of alternative financing mechanisms resulting from insufficient internal savings of large-scale fixed capital investments, the projects need to be completed in a short time (Aliefendioğlu and Tanrivermiş 2016a). Owners of real estate frequently criticise the use of expropriation, particularly in projects constructed with models such as BOT, build-operate, restore-transfer and PPP, on the grounds of the length of the operation times of projects; they emphasise that expropriations are conducted in favour of real persons and private legal entities and that there is no public interest involved. On the other hand, because of the construction and future running of many energy and mining projects within the scope of the licenses granted to private individuals and companies, the relevant ministry acquires land through expropriation in cases when the acquisition of the required real estate through a (formal) purchase by agreement fails. Although conducting expropriation in favour of private individuals and institutions is explicitly defined in legislation under the authority granted by special laws, significant problems are encountered in the perception of these regulations by those affected by the project and the real estate acquisition process. Regardless of the financing method, it is obvious that transportation projects will increase traffic fluidity and shorten transit times significantly. In addition to shorter travel times and fuel savings, reducing accidents and increasing the comfort of travellers because of the improved quality of the road, the investment would be beneficial for the general public.

Expropriation includes the stage from the conception of the public interest project to the registration of the acquired land in the name of the public entity which has conducted the whole process. Furthermore, the concept of public interest or utility which should justify expropriation of privately owned land according to Turkish legislation must be approved by the legislator, that is, the Turkish Republic National Assembly, or at the local level, the local legislation assembly (according to Articles 5 and 6 of Law No. 2942 and the fifth Article of Law No. 4650). After the validation of the expropriation project, all information about the land to be expropriated, that is, the total superficies, the ownership statute, the owners and their addresses, is collected through the related Cadastre and Title Deed General Directory. This step is very important in the determination of an expropriation methodology and the amount of compensation to be paid.

Evaluation of real estate acquisition methods and practices

The methods of acquiring lands required for the realisation of public services vary based on laws defining the duties and powers of public institutions and land use purposes. Although land acquisition applications are permitted within various laws, zoning development practices in urban areas and land consolidations in rural areas, specific expropriation and purchase methods on both sides are often preferred. Apart from these, real estate acquisition by such means as rights of servitude, rental and donations are also possible.

In order to acquire land required by local and central governments to provide services to the city, from parcels within the zoning application (according to 3194 Zoning Law), a Development Readjustment Share (DOP) of up to 40% is deducted, and the land obtained in this way must be used for common services and facilities associated with these services such as primary and secondary schools by the Ministry of Education, roads with controlled access except for highways, waterways, squares, parks, playgrounds, green areas, places of worship and police stations. When land acquired by public institutions through a DOP is insufficient, is in specific areas where zoning cannot be implemented or is in rural areas, expropriation is required for the acquisition of land necessary for public investments. For places in rural areas identified and declared as land consolidation application areas under Law 3083, a contribution deduction of up to 10% can be made from land in private ownership, according to the project's characteristics and for investments that will be used by the general public, such as roads and channels. In addition, the use of the lands obtained through the participation share deduction at the land consolidation stage for investments in rural areas, to which adjacent parcel owners and other people living in these areas do not have access, are not considered appropriate with regard to the expectations of owners and the methods of land acquisition, zoning and land consolidation practice principles, principles of equity and the scope of the rights to real estate. In summary, there seems to be a requirement to select the correct methods in the integration of lands required for social and technical infrastructure projects for the public to ensure that real estate rights, ethical values and social justice are fulfilled and satisfied.

With the agreement protocol first signed in 2012 between the General Directorate of Highways and General Directorate of Agricultural Reform, it has been decided that land consolidation and transportation projects should be addressed together, disintegration of the aggregated land should be prevented and the expropriation costs reduced. For example, for the 406 km (252 miles) of the route of the Gebze-Izmir Highway Project, it has been proposed that 80% is to be expropriated, and the rest (1,150 hectares (2,841 acres)) is to be acquired from private individuals through a land consolidation project. As a result, one-fifth of the total area to be expropriated in the project is planned to be acquired through consolidation. However, as the result of a delay by the court, expropriation work has restarted, and while construction work has already started, the land acquisition process has not yet been completed.

In the acquisition of private real estate necessary for infrastructure projects, generally expropriation can be made in accordance with Law 2942 or purchased in accordance with Law 4734 on Public Procurement. In accordance with the provisions of Law No. 2942, purchase, easement, full and partial expropriation, the transfer of real estate between two public bodies, confiscation, free use and other methods can be used to acquire the necessary land. Many laws cite the two basic regulations that are mentioned, and even agreements related to energy projects built according to international conventions specify that land acquisition should be performed in accordance with national legislation. Public investments are observed to be built on public interest fundamentals and on the condition that private properties are expropriated in exchange for the payment of compensation. Public institutions have preferred to carry out expropriation in real estate acquisition for many infrastructure projects, despite the high financial burden of the process, for such reasons as the legal basis of the practice, ease of application and provision of fast results if preparations are done well. However, a system for analysing the income and living conditions of the households affected by the project in the pre- and post-project periods and a monitoring and evaluation system have not usually been established.

Therefore, and according to the legal status of real estate subjected to acquisition, methods of acquisition vary, and the implementation stages, procedures, valuations and the payment of compensation of each of the methods differ. In this context, the expropriation processes frequently used by public institutions in Turkey are carried out according to principles defined in the Turkish Constitution and Expropriation Law No. 2942, and the purchase methods in accordance with the Public Procurement Law No. 4734. Also, to complete these two legal frameworks regarding methods for real estate acquisition by public entities, possible conciliations or statements can be found through national judiciary organs and international organisations such as the ECtHR.

In the Constitution of the Turkish Republic, while private ownership and inheritance are defined in one part (Article 35), the conditions for the expropriation of real estate under private ownership for public interest or utility and nationalisation are defined in another

(Article 46). According to Expropriation Law No. 2942, for public utility or interest purposes, the government through public legal entities is given the authority to undertake the expropriation process, the estimation or determination of the compensation amount, the registration of the expropriated real estate and servitudes in the name of the relevant public authority, the transfer process of unused real estate among public administrations, mutual (reciprocal) rights and related responsibilities, and the management and resolution of issues related to these process. As a principle, only real estate under private ownership can be subjected to expropriation or compulsory purchase. Because of the compulsory nature of the action, the terminology of "seizure" is also used to qualify the process. In a case where a public institution is in need of real estate held by another public institution, a temporary or permanent allocation, transfer, rent or grant can be undertaken between two public entities, and usually this is done without compensation.

A comprehensive legal framework for the valuation and payment of expropriation compensation has been established in Turkey. Expropriation procedures are intensive, costly and problematic. These problems depend on the location and properties of the project, the affected land tenure, land use, income sources of the affected persons and other factors. In settlements where the main source of income is (irrigated) land and livestock or there is no other income source, the impact of taking irrigated land and pastures for the implementation of a project will be much higher and may even involve prohibitive costs compared to projects affecting nonagricultural lands.

In addition to privately owned land, the use of public land is required for investment projects. According to Meadows Law No. 4342, 'meadows' are lands excluded from registration, and are public lands for the benefit of people of the village or town. Meadow land required for expropriation is taken out of the 'meadow and rangeland' classification by the commission in governorship in the province and can be used by the relevant authorities after registration on behalf of the Treasury. Meadows cannot be reclassified as such even after being temporarily expropriated. For the use of forest land, the Forestry and Water Affairs Ministry's permission is required (in accordance with Forests Law No. 6831), and compensation must be provided for the damage to forests. Forest lands are protected by Law No. 6831, and restrictions are imposed on persons regarding their use of the forest both individually and jointly. In relation to State forests or in case of necessity or public interest, permission can be granted to real and legal entities in return for compensation, for those made and/or operated by the State free of charge for a period of 49 years and this period can be extended up to 99 years. In addition, within the framework of Mining Law No. 3213, Turkish Petroleum Law No. 6491, Natural Gas Market Law No. 4646, Electricity Market Law No. 6446 and other regulations, acquisition of real estate for mining and oil exploration, operation and transport stages, electricity production, distribution and oil production is possible.

According to the Mass Housing Law No. 5543, in the expropriation for the construction of facilities related to airports, factories, economy and defence, resettlement of persons who had to leave their residences due to a partial or complete change of ownership is undertaken, including the reinstatement of the former standard of living of those who will be obliged to leave their homes. Enforceability of Law No. 5543 may require a physical relocation or a major reduction in income and livelihood resources. Law No. 2942 prescribes the compensation of landowners and possessors, and Law No. 5543 takes families benefiting from land as its basis. Therefore, State support to be provided in accordance with Law No. 5543 envisages the provision of housing and land that will be adequate for the family and granting of the required means as per their former livelihood resources.

Expropriation methods and Operation of expropriation

In almost every country, the concept and the scope of expropriation or compulsory purchase are explained in a specific legal framework. In the Turkish Legal System, the compensation is calculated according to the regulations, and the entire process of compulsory purchase must be in accordance with legal dispositions. Article No. 46 of the Turkish Constitution designates the framework of expropriation, thus: (i) expropriation is conducted by the State or relevant public legal entities, (ii) expropriation is undertaken for the provision of public utility or interest, (iii) compensation is paid in cash, (iv) only privately owned real estate is subjected to a total or partial taking, and (v) the expropriation process must not conflict with the methods and fundaments of other laws. Law No. 2942 defines the nature of the public entity which can undertake expropriation and its responsibility in the conduct of the process of the expropriation. Regarding compensation, the Constitution recommends that for privately owned lands expropriated within the framework of agricultural reform; high-scale energy, irrigation and other infrastructures projects; planted forest; the protection of coastal zone; and tourism activities, the compensation amount is to be paid by instalments, while for other projects, the compensation is paid as a cash lump sum.

However, in the case of the latter, the payment will be made before the expropriation process starts and, in the case of instalment payments, when the public authority who conducts the expropriation process misses an instalment deadline, the beneficiary will be paid interest at the highest rate, according to the national debt.

In the expropriation process, the administration that conducts expropriation takes a decision on the nature of the public interest purpose, and then various characteristics of the required real estate are identified. The administration makes a scale plan that shows the boundaries, surface areas and types of real estate and resources to be expropriated, and thus the land to be expropriated is determined with certainty. In places with a cadastre, the records relating to the units of real estate are investigated, and information (including volume, area, page and parcel number, name of owner(s) in the title deed) on the real estate is noted in the plan. At this stage of plan preparation, sufficient funding is obtained by the management, primary valuations for expropriation with the purchase method will be made by the appraisal commission established within the management structure and the expropriation completed after reaching an agreement with the owner. If no agreement can be reached, the valuation procedures for the registered lands are performed by experts appointed by the court.

Different methods can be used in the expropriation process. However, with the amendments in Law No. 4650 of 2001, it has become mandatory to initially use the purchasing method for expropriation and to prepare adequate funding before the start of its implementation. After the decision regarding the public interest and expropriation, the administration establishes one or more valuation commissions, each consisting of three persons from its own organisation. The administration may reach agreement with the owner over the value to be arrived at by the valuation commission and purchase real estate, resources or easements on them. Real estate, rights or easements purchased in this fashion are deemed to have been expropriated from the owner through purchase and, as a result, appeals against expropriation and compensation are not possible.

The commission arrives at the value of the takings by using experts and institutions' reports; sales values received from local real estate trading offices; or, when necessary, industry and chambers of commerce, in addition to the criteria in Articles 11 and 12 of Law No. 2942. Article 11 of Law No. 2942 stipulates that only the income method of valuation be used, and the use of fair sale values is seen as a major contradiction to the income method for administrative valuation commissions. The efficient and effective operation of commissions and the completion of expropriation processes in a short time are not easy because of the lack of a valuation infrastructure. On the other hand, it is observed that administrative commissions do not always use the valuation methods defined by law, and valuations are not conducted based on scientific principles. Some public administrations prepare commission reports after receiving research and consultancy services from departments of real estate development at universities and from valuation firms, and thus ensure that the process is more transparent and accountable.

The administrations appoint one or more reconciliation commissions to conduct and finalise the purchase or exchange transactions over the purchase price through negotiation. The administration notifies the owner in writing that it intends to purchase the necessary real estate, rights or resources through barter or exchange without specifying the price determined by the valuation commissions. In the event that the owner or their representative responds to the administration within 15 days, negotiations take place. If an agreement is reached on the value or exchange that does not exceed the administration's original valuation, a memorandum of conciliation that contains all the legal and actual properties and expropriation value of the real estate is arranged and executed by the owner or their representative and commission members. Within 45 days of the date of execution of the memorandum at the latest, the due amount is made available for payment by the administration, and the owner notified to submit a waiver on behalf of the administration in the land registry. Upon the grant of the waiver in favour of the administration by the owner or representative, the compensation will be paid, and thus the expropriation process is completed.

If expropriation is not performed by this purchase by agreement procedure, the valuation will be made by the court and the land registered in the name of the administration. The administration applies to the civil court of the location where the land is situated with a petition, including the valuation and other data and documents annexed to it. The petition requests the determination of the value of the land and a decision regarding the registration of the land in the name of the administration in return for payment of the determined value in advance or in instalments if the required conditions are met. The court determines the day of the hearing within 30 days of the date of filing and annexing the lawsuit petition and a sample of the documents submitted by the administration. The court notifies the owner of the real estate of the date of the hearing or, if the address of the owner cannot be found, through notification by publication. The administration is also notified of the date of the hearing (Kalabalık 2003).

The court announces the expropriation with a summary of documents in a local newspaper (if any) where the real estate is situated and in one of the national newspapers. During the hearing, the judge invites the parties to agree on the value of the real estate. In case of agreement between the parties, the judge considers this to be the purchase price and the related transactions will be carried out in accordance with the provisions for a purchase by agreement. If the parties cannot agree, the judge fixes a discovery date within 10 days and a hearing date within 30 days of the first hearing, and an expert committee conduct a discovery to determine the value of the real estate in the presence of all those concerned. The declaration of the highest civil authority (mukhtar) of the place where the real estate is situated will also be taken in the discovery. The expert committee appointed by the court are obliged to determine the value based on the valuation report prepared in accordance with valuation standards accepted by the Capital Markets Board and taking into account the statement of relevant parties, reflecting all the elements mentioned in Article 11 of Law No. 2942 and addressing each element in the report individually.

If the parties cannot agree on the land value, the judge convenes a new committee of experts if required to settle the dispute within 15 days. According to the type and nature of the land to be expropriated, an expert committee of at least three will be established and at least one of them must have a master's degree or doctorate in real estate development or be a licensed appraiser (in accordance with No. 6362 Capital Market Law dated 12 June 2012). The areas of the experts' expertise are determined by taking into consideration the nature of real estate to be expropriated. Taking into account the reports and statements of the parties and experts, the judge will pronounce a fair and equitable expropriation compensation or payment. This decision is notified to the land administration and the bank where the money is to be deposited. Upon the agreement of the parties, the administration will have 15 days to pay the determined expropriation value (depositing the payment in the appropriate bank and submitting the receipt of the deposit). Where necessary, this period may be extended once by the court. Upon submission of the receipt proving that the expropriation compensation or payment is deposited in the name of the owner by the administration, or showing that such amount has been allocated by the bank for payment to the right holders that may emerge in the future where the current owners cannot be determined, the real estate will be registered in the name of the administration and the expropriation compensation will be paid to beneficiaries. The registration of the judgment is the final step, although, the parties have the right to appeal the provision concerning the compensation amount (Kalabalık 2003; Tanrıvermiş et al. 2004).

In areas where cadastral works have not yet been completed, it is necessary to begin the process by drawing up a map of the real estate to be taken. To determine the lands to be expropriated, upon application of the administration that is to conduct the expropriation, the highest civil authority of the location (mukhtar) appoints two regular and two substitute members, who take an oath in the magistrate's court and are requested by the administration to conduct the expropriation. In determining the real estate, the highest civil authority (mukhtar) or a representative and two members of the elders' board must also be present. These kinds of land identification works and payment are shaped by Article 29 of Law No. 2942. The administration that is to conduct the expropriation will need to identify the real estate, the owners of that real estate (according to the land registry) or the possessors if there is no land registry records and their addresses. To this end, the administration may use title deeds, population and tax records or conduct other external research. However, it should be emphasised that cadastral work in Turkey is 99.5% completed, and, therefore, land for infrastructure projects with no entry in the cadastre would be rare (Tanrıvermiş 2016).

Instead of an expropriation payment, it is possible for the administration to transfer a land holding as recompense to the owner. However, in the exchange through the transfer of a piece of land it is necessary for the owner to agree to such a transfer. According to Law No. 2942, in the case of the owner's acceptance, instead of monetary payment, part of the administration's real estate which has not been allocated to public service and which may cover this fee partially or completely may be given. The value of real estate that will be given instead of expropriation compensation will be determined by the tendering commission of the administration and, in case such a commission does not exist, by a commission established for this purpose. The difference between the values of real estate units will be paid in cash by the relevant party. The value of the real estate that the administration may give to the owner in exchange of expropriation may not exceed 120% of the expropriation value. It is noteworthy that public institutions rarely opt for barter practices because the public institution requesting the barter has to conduct valuations for both the real estate that is to be given and received, and the existence of an upper limit for the difference between the values of both real estate, amongst other reasons.

In the Turkish Legal System, there are different types of expropriation, and this plurality is based on the type and scope of project and the rapidity of the expropriation process. In recent years, many expropriation projects have been conducted under the qualifier of "urgent expropriation" supported by legal instrument, (especially in Article 27 of Expropriation Law No. 2942). It has recently been observed in Turkey that the Council of Ministers' decisions are taken to acquire land using the urgent expropriation application in almost all fields including urban development, transformation, energy and infrastructure projects. Under Law No. 3634, in the expropriation of real estate for national defence or in situations of urgency determined by the Council of Ministers Decisions, or in extraordinary situations as envisaged by special laws, upon the request of the relevant administration, a court may decide on the seizure of real estate under the principles set forth in Article 12. Such a taking is based on the value of the real estate to be appraised by experts selected in accordance with Article 15, upon which the determined value will be deposited in a bank in favour of the owner. However, any procedures apart from the valuation must be completed later under the rule of urgent expropriation. It is obvious that the valuation methods to be used for the procurement method and employed in valuation processes that will be conducted by both the commissions to be established within the administration and the expert boards to be selected by the court will be the same. The public institutions are observed to prefer the urgent expropriation application in order to avoid the obligation to conduct expropriation using the valuation and purchase method defined in Article 8 of Law No. 2942, because it reduces their administrative responsibilities and allows them to obtain the right to enter the land within a maximum of 1 month before filing a value determination and registration lawsuit.

There may be a public interest in expropriation of the whole or a part of real estate that is required for a public service or enterprise that the administration is obliged to implement. If after expropriation of a portion of land it is determined that the remaining part of that land has become unusable, expropriation of the remaining part may be requested by the owner. If it is not possible for the owner to utilise the remaining land, the owner will have the right to ask for a full expropriation of all of the land. When the administration conducts expropriation, it must allocate that real estate to its intended purpose and public interest. Under Law No. 2942, in the case where the administration takes no action to achieve the purpose for which the land was taken, the owner has the right to take back the expropriated real estate. If the administration that has conducted the expropriation does not make any operations or erect any facilities in line with the purpose of expropriation or if the real estate is left as it is without being allocated to meet public interest within 5 years from the finalisation of the expropriation cost, the owner or their heirs may repurchase the real estate by paying the expropriation compensation plus interest accruing from the day they had received the payment. The right to repurchase must be exercised within 1 year of the right in question arising.

Assessment of real estate valuation and compensation methods and comparison with international standards

Debates regarding the valuation of expropriation compensation have been ongoing in Turkey since the 1920s, and significant changes in the methods and approaches to be used in real estate valuation have been made in the Constitution and legislation. The Constitution of 1924 stipulated the determination of expropriation compensation to be based on the current price (or market value). However, in the Constitution of 1961, the concept of "just compensation" was established as the basis and this concept was defined as "market value" by the Constitutional Court. The Article of the Constitution relating to value estimation was amended with Law No. 1488 dated 1971, and Paragraphs 2 and 3 were added to this Article. With this arrangement, the value declared by the land owner for property tax purposes was introduced as the maximum value for compensation purposes. New changes were made in Expropriation Law No. 6830 in parallel with the Constitutional amendment in 1971. In the 1971–1976 period when the Constitutional amendments were in effect, there was significant turmoil in terms of the method that must be applied in the case of land value estimation. After the removal of this in 1976, the valuation of land was based on an equivalent comparable value and income, and the obligation to take the tax value declared by the owner in line with the procedures and formats described in the Real Estate Tax Law as the higher limit was also removed (Tanrıvermiş et al. 2002).

The Constitution of 1982 stipulated that calculation styles and procedures were to be determined in the light of the owners' tax declarations by official authorities as at the date of expropriation, based on unit values of real estate and construction cost calculations and other objective measures (Art. 46). With the amendment to the Constitution made by Law No. 4709 in 2001, the measures related to the determination of expropriation compensation were abolished, and the principles and methods for the calculation of expropriation compensation were specified by law (Art. 46). The rationale for this amendment is to ensure that just compensation is paid in expropriation cases and to prevent financial injury to individuals in terms of the applied interest rates.

Expropriation procedures acquired a very complex nature with Law No. 2942, as a result of which the ambiguous aspects of the valuation process have multiplied and rational decision-making has been made more difficult. The determination of the expropriation value of real estate is based on rationalised valuation reports taking into account all related factors, such as type and sort of real estate, surface area, all the qualities and elements that may affect the value of real estate and the value of each such characteristic, the owner's tax declaration, if any, any valuation made by authorities as at the date of expropriation, the net income that the real estate or resource in question may generate in the location and under the pertaining conditions, relative sales values compared to examples of sales without a special purpose that took place before the day of expropriation for land plots (or urban plots), official unit prices and building cost calculations and depreciation shares, and any other objective criteria that may affect the value of real estate. Law No. 2942 enforces the classification of real estate as rural and urban land plots, and buildings. However, valuations in many countries are based on market value regardless of the type of real estate, and international financial institutions require the addition of full replacement costs in addition to market value. Many problems exist in the field of valuation of real estate according to the type of real estate acquisition, and these are summarised in the following section.

Valuation principles and practices based on expropriation methods

Expropriation of the whole of a unit of real estate is called full expropriation, but the concept of full expropriation is not used in Law 2942. In land acquisition applications, the whole or a part of a plot may be required for public benefit, or it may be necessary to establish an easement over the plot. According to Article 12 of Law No. 2942, three different situations can arise regarding the possible value change in the remaining parts of partially expropriated plots. These can be summarised as follows:

i. If, after the expropriation of a part of the real estate holding, the value of the non-expropriated part is not changed as a result of the expropriation, compensation is the amount corresponding to the value of the expropriated real estate based on the valuation according to the principles stated in Article 11 of the Law numbered 2942.

ii. If the value of the non-expropriated part is reduced as a result of the expropriation, this reduced value is determined and added to the expropriation value of the part taken.

iii. If an increase in the value of the retained land results from the expropriation, the amount of the increase is determined and the expropriation compensation is determined and reduced by the increased value (as per Article 11 of Law No. 2942). The reduction to be made in this situation may not be more than 50% of the value of the part actually seized.

Although there is no special provision in the legislation regarding the real estate which is entirely expropriated, special arrangements are made regarding the real estate subjected to partial expropriation where the owner retains land after expropriation. However, in the Turkish Legal System, parcel integrity is taken as the basis instead of farm enterprise integrity in the valuation studies to be carried out regarding partial expropriation. If only one part of a parcel is expropriated, the subsequent decline or increase in the value of the remaining part is analysed, and the right to request compensation by the owner for the deterioration of the integrity of the farm enterprise after the expropriation of the whole of a plot has not been specifically regulated. In many projects, if a single parcel of a household is expropriated, the use of other parcels outside the expropriation area is negatively affected and the compensation for the change in living conditions and income is inherently neglected; this approach can even be seen as a cost-effective land acquisition model.

In partial expropriation, the value decrease and/or increase related to the remaining parts is assessed according to the principles stated in Article 11 of Law No. 2942. If the part that is not taken is suitable for utilisation according to the zoning legislation, the expenses and costs required to bring those damaged facilities, such as buildings, boundary walls, sewerage systems, water, electricity, gas lines, and machinery, back to their previous state of use by the owners will be added to the expropriation compensation. Such costs and charges are not taken into account in determining the amount of damage to the retained land stated in item (ii). If the part remaining after expropriation is not suitable for use, where the administrative court cases against the expropriation proceedings are not filed, and upon the written application of the owner, within 30 days from the notification of the expropriation decision, the remaining part must also be expropriated.

The fundamental problem in the valuation of partially expropriated parcels is the examination of whether there has been a change in the value of the part that remains after expropriation (Murray et al. 1983; Tanrıvermiş and Doğru 2004). The change in value in the remaining part depends on the conditions of use in the post-expropriation period. Partially expropriated parcels are especially common in transportation projects, and in order for a decrease in value to take place, the opportunity to use it as in the pre-expropriation period should be reduced or completely lost. An increase in value may also be observed for reasons such as the fact that the remaining part after the expropriation is facing a road or an irrigation line. In order for value reductions to occur in expropriation transactions for highways and State and provincial roads and railways, the right to access the remaining part of the plot should be removed, the demand for the real estate should fall and an apparent (negative) value change should emerge.

In expropriation practices carried out by different public institutions, it is often observed that there is a problem in the analysis of the increase or decrease in the value of the remaining part, or the project cannot be applied to the land, and the value decline is determined without analysing the remaining part properly; however, even if the plot is expropriated for irrigation, provincial and State road construction and riverbed rehabilitation, the value of the remaining part is not increased. Another important problem is observed in the determination of the depreciation in the remaining part, and it is not possible to determine the value decrease ratio according to the share of the expropriated part in relation to the total area of the plot. The critical threshold in the analysis of the increase or decrease in the remaining part is 50%, and the remainder of the plot with a value decrease above this ratio has to be expropriated as well. This practice also eliminates the needs of administrations, which are expropriating particularly for railways, roads, pipelines, irrigation and drainage canals, over time. Similarly, if the value increase in the remaining portion exceeds 50% of the seized portion, a reduction of only 50% of the independently seized portion is allowed, which is of particular importance in terms of the protection of the social status and property rights of owners. If the part remaining after expropriation loses its functionality, it becomes obligatory to expropriate the remaining part.

While ownership rights of real estate may be partially or completely expropriated, the right of an easement over the real estate may also be established. Instead of expropriation of the real estate, if it is sufficient for the authority's purpose, an easement can be established compulsorily on a specific part, height, depth or resource of the land. In the calculation of the value of the easement, as in the case of partial expropriation, the land and lot values are compared before and after the project and the impairment resulting from the establishment of easement right is taken as its value. According to the basic principles of ownership law, it is only possible to establish transmission lines such as for power, water, gas, oil or sewerage, or to build a tunnel, cable car, viaduct or a bridge underneath or over the land, by establishing easement rights. However, (with the paragraph added to Article 99 of Law No. 6552 dated 9 October 2014 and Article 4 of Law No. 2942), on condition that the right of the owners to use the property is not prevented, that necessary precautions for the safety of life and property are taken, and based on public interest, arrangements have been made that remove the need to establish easement rights for cable cars and similar transport lines over real estate and for all types of bridges and subways and similar rail transport systems and tunnel construction underneath real estate. As the public investments mentioned inevitably restrict the right of ownership of the property and negatively influence its market capital and rental values, it may not generally be possible to ensure that "the right to use the property of the owners is not prevented and necessary precautions for the safety of life and property are taken" as defined in the legislation. Thus, although the easement is not established for the aforementioned investments, it is considered that the rights of the owners to take legal action for compensation in respect of the loss of rights is possible following the Decision of the Constitutional Court dated 14 May 2015 and numbered decree absolute 2015/49. Since there is no right to an easement for the public investments which are explicitly mentioned in the law, the monetary amount that the owners can claim for their losses of property security or value will be clearly defined as compensation but not property value.

Especially in cases of partial expropriation, it is noticed that the analysis of the value change in the remaining part and the analysis of the possible change in the plot value after the establishment of the easement right cannot be performed rationally. In any event, it has been found that institutions conducting pipeline, water and sewerage, and transportation projects have not conducted research on possible value changes resulting from land acquisition nor have they produced 'good practice' guidelines. Indeed, it seems that each institution tends to use different methods and approaches to land acquisition and that there is no unification or standardisation. It is evident that the value increase is generally not calculated for the retained parts of the plots, which often do gain some advantages, such as frontage to the roads and irrigation channels in the post-expropriation period, and that the owners are granted unfair advantages in this way. On the other hand, there are many instances where the rate of depreciation is chosen based on an assumption rather than rational analysis of the depreciation occurring in partial expropriation and the establishment of easement rights, and the generally calculated expropriation compensation is much higher than it should be (Tanrıvermiş 2008; Aliefendioğlu and Tanrıvermiş 2016b). It should be emphasised that the approaches mentioned are not in line with international valuation standards and the compensation of the owners cannot be settled according to rational principles. Owners generally argue that in particular the cost of an easement right is very low compared with full expropriation value. It is absolutely necessary to inform the owners that the right of easement is for a limited period of time (usage rights are for 49 or 99 years) only. In the event that the remaining parts of the partially expropriated plots and the plots for which the easement rights are established become totally unusable following the establishment of the rights, the owner has the right to demand the expropriation of the entire plot.

Assessment of land valuation principles and practices

Under Law No. 2942, the revenue value of the land must be determined with a basic capitalisation formula. The revenue value of the land (V) is equal to the value to be found by dividing the average annual income (R) by the current capitalisation ratio (r): $(v=R/r)$. In this way, the value of land is established by the accumulation of all the envisaged average annual net incomes of the land until the time when the expropriation process places (Murray et al. 1983). To arrive at the net income of the land, land rental and production costs, excluding rental reserves, must be calculated. Since accounting records are non-existent in farm enterprises, there is considerable difficulty in obtaining physical and monetary data relating to agricultural production costs, product yields and income calculations at farm and village levels. Another important difficulty is experienced in determining the capitalisation rate. As a result of the country's economic and structural nature, it is necessary to determine the capitalisation rate to be applied in land markets with the market approach $(r=R/V)$ at the provincial, district and village levels, and based on the various land types (Tanrıvermiş et al. 2004; Tanrıvermiş and Şanlı 2008).

The current use, the state of the land, as well as the yields, sales, production costs and revenues of the widely grown crops, are not rationally analysed. It has been found that it is impossible to consistently analyse the average annual income of the land, and that the distinction between irrigated and arid land is based on assumptions rather than on the actual state of the land. This is due to the lack of accounting records in farms and the inadequacy of the parcel-scale data held by the agriculture and cadastral agencies regarding land use, revenues and costs. While the income method is based on solid economic assumptions, significant problems are also encountered in analysing the revenues of the lands and the appropriate rate that can be used for the capitalisation of the estimated revenues (Rehber 1999). The capitalisation rates of the lands are primarily based on assumptions and personal convictions rather than the current capitalisation rates based on land types, and the principles of the capitalisation theory, which is the basis for the income method, is neglected. Under these circumstances, there is a requirement to audit the reports of the valuation commissions within the administration, and expert witnesses must be assigned by the courts and comprehensive field studies made in order to verify the validity of the resulting values (Tanrıvermiş 2008; Tanrıvermiş and Aliefendioğlu 2015).

Depending on the location and uses of farmland, differences between the value of land revenues and the market value emerge. The income method remains insufficient for the valuation of lands surrounding particularly big cities and in coastal areas made available for settlement. In these areas, land income, which is the main basis of the income method, often ceases to be a factor in determining land values. Although the expropriation value found in line with the income method in the valuation of lands with potential land plot characteristics on urban-rural area borders may be increased up to 100%, taking the objective criteria in law into consideration, this is not a consistent practice. In the present circumstances, in the implementation of the income method in regions where lands in the process of transition are situated, an approximation of the appreciated land values to current market values through the identification of land values that may be accepted or desired by owners, if not to the real market value of such lands, may be useful for reducing the number of disputes frequently observed in practice. However, efforts in this direction will always involve subjectivity.

The problems caused by working conditions exacerbated by the approaches of the managers of the administration to the expropriation-related matters, and the problems arising from employing persons who are not experts in the field of real estate valuation and expropriation units of public institutions, do not allow for local-level land valuation based on detailed scientific research within the administrations. This structure complicates the process of valuation based on the income method for lands. In order to facilitate the work of administrative valuation commissions and to ensure that land valuations are conducted based on objective criteria, the conducting of scientific studies to determine average annual net incomes and applicable capitalisation rates as per land types at local levels by professional persons and institutions is required and mandatory. As the opportunity of using valuation reports received from subject-qualified experts and firms when required is also provided to commissions in Turkey, it will be possible to greatly reduce valuation problems in expropriation and resolve the problems of the administration by supporting the formation of an accredited private-sector that independently conducts valuation activities, ensuring that such organisations are available to provide advisory and consulting services to administrations (Tanrıvermiş et al. 2004).

Assessment of urban plots and buildings valuation principles and practices

The type of parcels located within municipalities, included in the zoning plan implemented by the municipality, benefiting from municipal services and having residential surroundings, are considered to be "urban plots" The values of such land will be determined by the sales value as at the day before expropriation, and comparative sales analysis is used for this purpose. The comparables on which the valuation is based should show the same qualities and characteristics of the real estate in question, but when such comparables are unavailable, sales made in previous years of different quality, in different places and regions, will be used, and the valuation will take into consideration differences in quality, region and time as well as any superior and inferior aspects of the real estate. If there is a building on these plots, the value left after deducting the value of buildings will be taken as the basis for comparison. The valuation commission and experts must examine the selected plots individually; they must specify the superior and inferior aspects, should not be content with a general comparison and if they conclude that the real estate units could not be compared, they must explain in detail the reasons for this. According to the expropriation legislation, the value or market method is to be used for the valuation of expropriated real estate. For the transactions of lands to be comparable, the land units must bear similarities in terms of all the qualities that affect land values such as location, shape, physical structure of soil, length along the road, the type of road on which the land is located, width of the street and restrictive regulations (such as floor limit, usage ratio of the land) imposed (Tanrıvermiş 2016).

It has been observed that in the valuation of parcels considered as urban plots, incorrect operations were performed by dividing the standard value by the land area in expert reports received by the court, while ignoring the real estate zoning plan functions and development rights. It has also been observed that in expert reports prepared in many provinces, generally it is the precedent with the highest unit value which is selected for the valuation, and with the application of this unit value to the estate in question, "the real estate is assumed to be several times more valuable than the precedent in terms of urban services, infrastructure, regional development speed and structuring advantage". As a result, the appreciated value of the real estate is much higher to an extent that could be defined as exorbitant. It has been determined that in cases of both land and urban plot expropriation, incorrect operations were made and valuation work performed is considered not to be in accordance with international valuation standards and scientific principles.

Valuation done through official unit prices at the date of expropriation for buildings is defined in legislation, and this process completely ignores usage patterns and the revenue of the building. In the cost analysis, integral parts and add-ons are included in the value of the buildings. Cost calculations are determined according to the unit prices as at the official date of expropriation. In the cost analysis, all features of the structure must be specified and a detailed report providing the opportunity for comprehensive checks must be presented. For the construction costs calculation, depreciation from the date of the building's construction to the expropriation date (or notification date) is calculated and subtracted from the cost of rebuilding, and thus the present value of the building is determined. If the owner's real estate consists of dilapidated or ruined buildings, the value of the rubble is subtracted from the current building cost value to determine the expropriation compensation. If these buildings remain in the administration's possession, the value of the rubble is not deducted from the cost of building. If there are goods and materials to be removed from the building, such as machinery, then the costs of their dismantling and removal will be paid to the owner, but the necessary expenses for their reinstallation will not be paid. The compensation payment for buildings is not consistent with the full replacement cost defined in international standards, and the amount paid is not defined as 'fair value' in the theory of valuation.

Comparison of real estate valuation practices with international criteria

Article 46 of the 1982 Constitution, in cases of public interest, allows for the expropriation of real estate under private ownership. In the framework of Law No. 2942, a certain amount of compensation is paid to persons who can prove that they are owners or possessors of real estate being expropriated for the public interest, and regarding public lands, to the relevant public institutions, within the framework of the principles set forth in the law. It is not possible to pay compensation to land users who are not also owners or possessors of real estate or to people who utilise the land in other ways. For persons who use or jointly utilise public lands, no payment of compensation is available. Since expropriation procedures and the payment of costs are tied to certain time periods and the use of land is not possible without paying for its value, expropriating institutions have been obliged to be more attentive in this regard

(Tanrıvermiş and Aliefendioğlu 2015). In recent years, the urgent expropriation procedure has often been used by central and local governments, and free access to the land has been obtained without waiting for the completion of the valuation and land registration case; however, this practice leads to relatively higher expropriation costs.

According to Law No. 2942, expropriation compensation is paid to those whose lands have been transferred and such compensation is based on the (income) value and market value of the land; in addition to this, compensation is paid for the damage to the assets fixed on the land. However, (under Law No. 2942) expropriation compensations may only be paid to persons who have rights over the land. For the development of roads, organised industrial zones, new housing, urban renewal and development plan projects, while a requirement to carry out new expropriations emerges, an increase in the value of real estate that will be expropriated can also occur. When it comes to the expropriation of properties whose values have increased as a result of the development of a region, the payment to municipalities and governor's offices based on such increased values will also be unfair. The administration carries the real burden of development and the owners have not made any direct contribution to the increased value of real estate resulting from the development (Kalabalık 2003). Therefore, in the assessment of expropriation compensation, it is convenient to ignore the value increases originating from the development and to base compensation on the value of the real estate prior to development.

It also calls attention to the fact that in Turkey, the method of calculating the amount paid to the owner of the expropriated real estate is not compatible with international valuation standards, the decisions of the ECtHR and the performance standards of international finance institutions. First, Article 46 of the 1982 Constitution of Turkey states that fair compensation is to be paid for the expropriation of real estate, and this concept is known as "market value" or "fair market value" in the theory of valuation. ECtHR decisions requires that the payment of the market value of the 'goods and properties' expropriated should be made, and the ECtHR interprets the concepts of 'goods and property' independently from the domestic law norms of the member states. In appeals, the Courts tend to accept the "value" that the state infers from administrative procedures and actions, legal regulations or judicial decisions, regardless of the social and economic context, in the scope of the property (Gemalmaz 2006). In Turkey, although Article 46 of the Constitution stipulates that just compensation for the expropriated real estate be paid, Article 11 of Law No. 2942 stipulates that expropriation compensation is to be calculated as income in relation to land characteristics, as market value for real estate of land lot characteristics and as net cost for buildings. It is observed (in Article 11 of Law No. 2942) that such classifications as commercial businesses, economic values and social rights do not exist, and the concept of market value only applies to real estate of urban plot characteristics by law.

The principle of proportionality is violated through legislation and practices, and property rights are limited. Primarily, it is possible for the administration to receive information from experts and institutions as set out under the law; to approach expropriation processes through scientific and international criteria; to process valuation procedures related to expropriated real estate considering the balance between the individual and public interest; and to practice fair, quick, reasonable and equal expropriation for all beneficiaries without the need to resort to such processes as urgent expropriation and land consolidation. In expropriation by force, (in essence without the owner's consent), redressing the balance is achieved, (as required by Article 46 of the Constitution and Article 1 of the European Convention of Human Rights (ECHR) Additional Protocol No. 1), by the payment of fair compensation of the real estate in accordance with the principles of fast and fair satisfaction with a fair trial.

While restricting property rights, the protection of goods and the property of right owners should be respected; provisions that are non-arbitrary, determined by law, predetermined, accessible and containing certainty should be applied in property rights restrictions, and they should be imposed on individual property rights, in favour of general interest, and the need to be individual and should not overload the valuation process nor the process of procedures and lawsuits. Care must be taken to have proportionality and balance in the protection of property rights and the requirements of the general interest.

The owners are observed to be dissatisfied with expropriation based on such assumptions as a result of losing their income and/or jobs and the destruction of social and cultural assets, and do not consider, the amounts paid to be sufficient. Similarly, institutions and courts with the authority to expropriate also complain about the functioning of the process and the excess of the workload. In particular, owners in rural areas, people who have no income and means of livelihood other than crop and livestock farming activities, even if they have received the entire cost of the expropriated real estate, tend to consume the expropriation money they receive in nonproductive areas in a short time, and households who have lost their land and other means of livelihood settle in the suburbs of large cities and cause great social problems. The first example in Turkey is that of the Baku-Tbilisi-Ceyhan Cure Oil (BTC) Project, as a result of which compensation of the revenue loss that could be caused by damage to public common areas, except for the real estate value of the households affected by the project, was supported with social projects, and many contributions have been made by service deliveries to the affected settlements. Financial institutions demand the development of certain projects in order to minimise the negative impacts on persons resulting from the related projects, to assist them in rebuilding their lives or businesses and to ensure that they maintain their livelihoods (Tanrıvermiş and Doğru 2004).

Real estate acquisition for public investments can have positive or negative impacts on the local community and owners affected by the project. As mentioned before, there is more than one method to acquire land for realising public investments. The method of acquiring land depends on the purpose of the project to be developed, the surface, the type of landownership and land use status and the regulations in place before the acquisition. Forced or ill-planned resettlements can cause irreversible consequences such as the destruction of existing modes of living and production, impoverishment and environmental and social stresses. To avoid or to minimise these outcomes during land acquisition, project-related countries and/or international financial institutions such as the International Finance Corporation (IFC) established a standard called "Land Acquisition and Involuntary Resettlement Standard" to be followed by their clients or investees (IFC 2012). Also of relevance is the standard contained in the Land Acquisition and Involuntary Resettlement and Economic Displacement (2014) in the framework of European Bank for Reconstruction and Development's (EBRD's) Performance Requirements (PRs).These standards are described in Performance Standard 5 of both financial institutions. According to this performance standard, involuntary resettlement refers to both physical displacement and economic displacement resulting from land acquisition associated with a client's/investee's operations. These standards are developed according to the intention of the client throughout the life of the investment financed by the bank, and in this case, the government is seen as a third party involved in the facilitation of land acquisition and resettlement, as well as in the determination of the compensation. Furthermore, the idea behind these standards is that the adverse impacts that improperly managed project-related land acquisitions can have on displaced and host communities suggest avoidance of involuntary resettlement or in cases where involuntary resettlement cannot be avoided it should be conducted in such a way as to minimise those impacts. These standards, conditional on the existence of legal proof or otherwise of the people and of the land they own or use, distinguish those (i) who have formal legal rights to the land or assets they occupy or use; (ii) who do not have legal rights to land or assets but have a claim to the land that is recognised or recognisable under national law; or (iii) who have no recognisable legal right or claim to the land or assets they occupy or use.

In the case of involuntary resettlement, two displacements are considered: (a) physical displacement and (b) economic displacement. Thus, the physically displaced are considered to be people who lose their shelter or legally owned lands and are obliged to be relocated in another area. The economically displaced are people who lose their assets or their income sources or other means of livelihood due to an interdiction of access to the land after the acquisition. In addition, these displacements can be partial, full, permanent or temporary according to the nature of the project and the nature of rights of displaced people (The World Bank 2002; IFC 2012; EBRD 2014).

In the case of physical displacement, the performance standard recommends compensation at the full replacement cost of the land and assets of all people affected by the project, with particular attention paid to the needs of poor and vulnerable people. Also, when people are required to move to another location, the client (who conducts the project) must provide choices from among feasible resettlement options, including adequate replacement housing or cash compensation, and provide relocation assistance suited to the needs of the displaced people. In addition, if displaced persons have a legal right or legally recognisable right, they should be offered the choice between compensation in kind, that is, a real estate with equal or higher value, secure tenure, equivalent or improved characteristics and cash compensation if applicable. Even in the case of legally non-recognisable rights, people should be offered the choice of options for adequate housing with secure tenure so that they can resettle legally without having to face the risk of forced eviction.

In the case of economic displacement, those people concerned should be compensated for the loss of their assets or access to assets at full replacement cost. Furthermore, if land acquisition affects commercial buildings, compensation includes (i) the cost of the reestablishment of the commerce elsewhere; (ii) the loss of net income during the period of transition; and (iii) the costs of the transfer and reinstallation of plant machinery or other equipment. Considering the range of displaced persons, if they have a legal right or a legally recognisable claim, they should be offered the option to choose between a replacement real estate of equal or higher value and cash compensation at full replacement cost. In the case of economically displaced people who do not have a legally recognisable right, they should be compensated for the loss of assets (such as crops, irrigation and other improvements on the land) rather than offered land in exchange.

Another issue with the compulsory purchase of land and the assessment of compensation is the valuation processes undertaken to determine the values of properties subject to acquisition, and also those to be given in compensation in the case of compensation in kind. The realisation of many projects has been hampered by people refusing the amount of compensation in the case of cash compensation or the real estate offered in terms of compensation in kind. Even if IFC and EBRD standards recommend compensation at full replacement cost, there is not enough information related to the valuation process. Actually, it is because that part of the process is left to the valuation expert's experience and knowledge that contradictions related to value are frequent. In many projects, the valuation is usually delegated to some "experts" who have insufficient or no background or experience in terms of international valuation standards such as those provided by the International Valuation Standards Council (IVSC) and the Royal Institution of Chartered Surveyors (RICS), both of which are taken into account by the International Financial Report Standards (IFRS) and the International Accounting Standards Board (IASB).

Furthermore, the concepts of "full replacement cost" as described in IFC and EBRD's standards and "replacement cost" in RICS and IVSC's standards are different on some practical points. In fact, the "replacement cost" in RICS and IVSC standards refers to the "price that a participant would pay as it is based on replicating the utility of the asset, not the exact physical properties of the asset" (IVSC 2017). In the determination of the replacement cost, it is recommended to determine the actual physical deterioration and all relevant forms of obsolescence affecting the building, then deduct this figure from the total cost of the subject asset. In a case where the depreciation and obsolescence represent a great part of the total cost, the residue may not be enough to maintain or to improve the standard of living of the displaced person. It is especially at this point where there is a shadow area between the replacement cost as defined in the IFC and EBRD's standards and the RICS and IVSC's standards. While the principle of those international financial institutions is that compulsory purchase should avoid hardship and the impoverishment of people affected by land acquisition and project forecast, the professional valuation standards are considered to be implemented in a free market without pressure from any party in the market. Another aspect which differentiates the concept of replacement cost in the case of compensation on expropriation for the public interest is that it is recommended to be full replacement cost, including the loss of net income during the period of transition and the costs of transfer and the reinstallation of plant, machinery or other equipment; this aspect is not considered in the case of RICS and IVSC standards (IFC 2012).

The main differentiation between countries in expropriation and compensation processes lies in the nature and process the compensation. On one side international financial institutions (IFC and EBRD) in their Standard Performances differentiate people who have legal proof of rights, those who have any claim that can be legally recognisable and those who fall within neither case but who use the land; on the other hand, they recommend compensation at full replacement cost for people leaving or using the land to be expropriated. However, in many countries, and especially in Turkey, these principles seem to be ignored, and in many cases people are evicted by force from the land they claim to own or use. From these last issues comes the refusal of the amount or type of compensation that the project authority proposes to landowners or users. The problems encountered at this stage have usually hampered project completion deadlines.

Furthermore, even if under the Standards Performance of international financial institutions the scope of the compensation may appear to be more acceptable in terms of human rights, the lack of precision related to valuation standards may lead to an underestimation of the value of real estate to be expropriated. Another issue with valuation methods are the concepts used to qualify the value in the case of expropriation or compulsory purchase (Table 7.1). Based on IVSC and RICS standards, the value of property for the purpose of expropriation may be seen in terms of a "forced sale" which arises when the owner/vendor is subject to external legal factors or personal commercial factors. In that way, the legal factors may be seen as compulsory purchase or expropriation of privately owned property by legally a authorised public authority.

In cases where expropriation is carried out for a project, a Resettlement Action Plan (RAP) should be developed and the population whose lives and production systems are adversely affected should be provided with compensation for land, housing, infrastructure and other losses. The affected group is defined as all those with the use of or moral/traditional rights over the land and other assets; the absence of a title deed or any other legally valid document is not a justification for the non-payment of compensation. According to the international standards, those who are adversely affected and have by any manner use rights on land must be compensated without

Table 7.1 Comparative Analysis of Compensation Measurement

Institutions and Nations	Definition and Valuation Basis for Compensation	Valuation Methods and Observation
IVSC and RICS Standards	A forced sale of property is usually undertaken in the case where a loan or mortgage is not paid back.	Here the real estate is put on the market with the idea that the value should be at least equal to the value of the loan provided. Here, instead of considering utility by the owners, the value will be more dependent on the ongoing market conditions. In this sense it may be different from the case of compulsory purchase. Also forced sale is not usually undertaken by a public (State) authority.
IFC and EBRD Performance Standards	Full replacement cost and consideration of all people who have any claim on the land.	The determination of real estate valuation depends of the recommended expert's experience in valuation.
Turkish legal system	Calculation of compensation varies according to the type of real estate and confusion in the methods and ignorance or misuse of international valuation standards.	The valuation of real estate is required for classifying assets such as rural land, urban land and buildings. Rural land value is based on income approach, urban land is assessed by using comparable sales analysis, and building values are based on cost of reproduction minus depreciation.

Source: EBRD 2014; IFC 2012; IVSC 2017 and The World Bank 2002.

having to prove their rights. The valuation process of the real estate affected by the project needs to be carried out at full replacement or substitute cost. The assessment of the monetary value of some losses, such as public services, trading partners, fishing, grazing and access to forest land is not easy. Therefore, every attempt should be made to ensure access to equivalent and culturally acceptable resources and income opportunities. The resettlement plan should also cover land allocation to protect the livelihoods of sensitive groups or culturally acceptable alternative income strategies (The World Bank 2002; EBRD 2014).

There are significant differences between the legal regulations underpinning real estate acquisition and the assessment of compensation in Turkey and the international standards. First of all, while in Turkey individuals are expected to prove that they are the owners or possessors in order to receive payment of compensation, the performance standards envisage that people who use the land in any way and who obtain income from it must be compensated regardless of whether there is a legal basis for their right to benefit from the land. Second, the principle was formulated requiring the compensation of all assets, including full replacement value and transportation costs. As a matter of fact, the international standards are directly concerned with the income of people from the land and accept that any practices that may lead to a reduction in such an income should ensure full compensated. In accordance with Law No. 5543, those who are deprived of their land, totally or partially, as a result of expropriation, as well as those who have lived in the related settlement for three years and do not have any other lands, may benefit from a resettlement plan and related incentives, on the condition that they can no longer make a living because they have been deprived of the land or will have to relocate. In the international standards, however, a physical relocation will not be compulsory, and even if the livelihood of the person is not impeded, they should be compensated if they are affected in any way.

It is observed that in Turkey, amongst the international finance institutions, public and private sectors often take advantage of such sources, particularly those of the IFC and EBRD, and the institutions in question have requested the preparation of land acquisition and resettlement action plans within the scope of directives in the first instance, and in the recent years, of performance standards. Funded by the IFC, the BTC Project is a large and multinational project planned to transfer Azerbaijani oil through a pipeline to be built throughout Azerbaijan, Georgia and the Republic of Turkey to the Mediterranean where it will be put on the international market. In the BTC Project, it was agreed that "land acquisition and expropriation procedures [would] be performed according to the domestic rules of law"; however, with the resettlement agreement prepared, illegal users, fishermen and parties ineligible according to domestic law, along with title deed holders, were also compensated. The rights of the property and the individuals holding the land by ownership (under Law No. 2942) are recognised, and there is no right to the payment of compensation to those using meadows, pastures and forest lands. With resources transferred to the RAP fund for projects financed by international sources, revenue losses that are not possible to recover under the Turkish Legal System, costs and the payment of other reimbursement are made. Unlike the projects funded from domestic resources, which are related to a reduction in the income of owners and holders of other land rights, reducing the social impact of the implementation of expropriation is targeted through social investment programmes for the affected settlements.

New opportunities provided by international projects in terms of expropriation and valuation include the payment of both the land value to the relevant administration and the payment for loss of income to the village or neighbourhood administrations where it is identified that they benefit from the land on the route. In particular, for pipeline projects, after the completion of construction in pastures, meadow and forests, it was determined that normal grass yield could not be secured for an average of 3 to 5 years, although this varied according to climatic and soil conditions. In above-ground plants, an assessment of 20 years' annual grass yield loss has been made. The second major new practice is paying for loss of income to fishermen engaged in fishing in internal and coastal waters, resulting from the restriction of the right to benefit from such resources. Third, tree, product and asset prices were paid to those who illegally used public and private land. Fourth, people were informed about valuation. The negative side of the expropriation and cost assessment approach applied in the Project is that owners and users in the settlements on the project route are inclined to expect the implementation of the same standards in other projects, and therefore expropriation prices rise artificially and the opportunities for conciliation reduce (Aliefendioğlu and Tanrıvermiş 2016b).

Approximately 7.04% of the total investment amount (1.31 billion USD) in the BTC Project consisted of expropriation expenses (99 million USD). If the 3.4 million USD resource allocated to the RAP fund is taken into account, the proportion of the total payment made to the public and private landowners, possessors and users within the scope of the Project is 7.28% of the investment cost. Under these circumstances, it appears that product, tree and asset prices for the users of public and private land and income losses paid for public lands had no significant impact on the total investment amount. Compared with other investments in Turkey, although the price paid for the land was higher than in the marketplace, it was revealed that the share of the land supply expropriation expenses in the total investment amount was quite low; that in many projects, this ratio was 30%; and that there were even investment projects in which such expenses had reached 50% and 70% (Tanrıvermiş and Doğru 2004). Given that the total area of land expropriated was 3,105 hectares (7,672 acres), it appears that one hectare (2.471 acres) of the land was supplied at an average of 3,188.41 USD. The average expropriation cost is sufficient to explain why unit land values are above the market value. It needs to be emphasised that the ratio of the expropriation cost to the market value of the land in all of the provinces on the Project route varies between 100% and 200% (Aliefendioğlu, and Tanrıvermiş 2016a), and although it conflicts with theoretical principles, the value income exceeds the market value, and this value is higher than the fair market value.

Assessment of the implementation of expropriation and compensation

The requirement for the State to have adequate budget provision for expropriation brings the economic characteristics of compulsory taking to the foreground. However, the real estate acquisition by public institutions and expropriation spending are not determined according to methods of acquisition but are announced each year. In relation to this aspect, expenses of expropriation were identified by examining the last 10 years of final accounts laws. In Turkey, in the period of 2006–2016, the share of the expropriation payment in the government's investment budget was on average 8.55%; the share of local governments in the investment budget was 12.97%; and the total expropriation costs of central and local governments in the total investment budget was 10.1% (Table 7.2). When compensation payments, interest and other expropriation costs paid by all the public bodies for lands confiscated without expropriation are added to this amount, it is inevitable that the share of the total payments within investment allowance will double. Also it should be borne in mind that among the expropriation costs revealed by the archival research made, there was no payment specifically made from the funds other than the budgetary requirements!

According to the analysis results of the macro data, there is a linear correlation between the overall economic growth trend and the share of the budget earmarked for expropriation in the investment budget. In times of economic crisis, the budget earmarked for expropriation decreases; however, for a quick exit from the crisis, the public needs to make investments and stimulate the market by its spending. According to the research results, low funds were appropriated for expropriation, real estate required for the investments in this period was used in construction works without being expropriated, and in the following years, high amounts of confiscation compensations were paid. Essentially, this approach is not cost-efficient for the administration and is incompatible with the responsibilities of the administration for the protection of property rights.

It has been identified that in the last 15 years, public institutions have expropriated about 300,000 hectares (741,316 acres) of land for different purposes and that land requirements have rapidly increased because of increasing large-scale public investments. For private institutions, especially the Petroleum Pipeline Corporation (BOTAŞ), Turkey Electricity Transmission Co. (TEIAS) and the Turkey Electricity Distribution Corporation (TEDAŞ), the share of the land on which easement rights were established in the total expropriation area varies between 72% and 84% per year. Other investor state institutions often conduct full and partial expropriation. Among the investor state institutions, in terms of the amount of land expropriated, institutions such as the General Directorate for State Hydraulic Works (DSİ), BOTAŞ, General Directorate of Highways (KGM), Turkish Republic Directorate General of State Railways (TCDD), Turkey Electricity Transmission Co. (TEIAS) and TEDAŞ are at the top of the list, and the share of the amount of land expropriated by these institutions

Table 7.2 Development of the Share of Expropriation Expenses in Investment Expenditures in Turkey

Years	Central Government Investment Costs (1000 TL)	Central Government Real Estate Acquisition and Expropriation (1000 TL)	Share of Expropriation and Real Estate Acquisition (%)	Years	Municipal and Provincial Special Administration Investment Expenditures (1000 TL)	Municipal and Provincial Special Administration Real Estate Acquisition and Expropriation (1000 TL)	Share of Expropriation and Real Estate Acquisition (%)	Share of Land Acquisition in Investment as Total of Central and Local Administrations (%)
2006	12,097,713	666,297	5.51	2006	9,928,863	1,036,164	10.44	7.73
2007	13,003,480	639,571	4.92	2007	12,328,370	1,128,518	9.15	6.98
2008	18,515,893	1,873,134	10.12	2008	13,649,093	1,153,131	8.45	9.41
2009	20,071,509	2,251,001	11.21	2009	11,878,975	916,076	7.71	9.91
2010	26,010,306	1,653,437	6.36	2010	13,035,045	1,551,390	11.90	8.21
2011	30,905,295	3,147,487	10.18	2011	15,981,759	1,737,691	10.87	10.42
2012	34,365,315	2,733,041	7.95	2012	19,058,729	2,591,822	13.60	9.97
2013	43,767,278	3,346,973	7.65	2013	27,579,220	3,365,129	12.20	9.41
2014	48,200,817	5,088,032	10.56	2014	23,470,800	5,391,426	22.97	14.62
2015	57,199,129	5,419,980	9.48	2015	25,807,619	5,432,317	21.05	13.07
2016	59,444,060	5,991,460	10.08		20,560,031	2,953,998	14.37	11.18
Mean			8.55				12.97	10.08

Source: Ministry of Finance, General Directorate of Public Accounts Records.

in relation to the total expropriated land reaches the level of 90% (Aliefendioğlu and Tanrıvermiş 2016a; 2016b).

In order to control and reduce investment cost increases caused by infrastructure investments, it is necessary to develop real estate acquisition methods without the payment of compensation. High amounts of expropriation costs are paid for infrastructure investments, and these kinds of projects create physical barriers to agricultural land. With a protocol signed between the General Directorate of Highways and the General Directorate of Agricultural Reform, displacement of parcels corresponding to highway routes by consolidation projects with the surrounding public land by consolidation can be provided, and also it is possible to reduce expropriation expenses and to prevent unnecessary expropriation by arranging the remaining parts which fall outside the road route in existing expropriation practices and parts which are mandatorily expropriated parcels by consolidation. Consolidation of land along the route of transportation projects as well as consolidation of parcels remaining from expropriation will facilitate access to sources of income and also prevent victimisation of owners. Under this protocol, in three investment projects, the Ankara-Niğde Highway, Istanbul-İzmir Highway and Malatya North Ringroad, a total of 387,918 hectares (958,566 acres) of land was consolidated, and as a result, the expropriation cost, which had been 380 million TL,[1] was reduced to 226 million TL. A 327 km (203 mile) section of the Ankara-Nigde highway, 75 km (46 mile) section of the Istanbul-Izmir highway and 30 km (18 mile) section of the Malatya North Ringroad were acquired through land consolidation, and in these three projects, 154 million TL savings were obtained by public institutions (Öçalan 2015).

The construction cost of the Gebze-Izmir Highway Project was determined to be 9.0 billion USD, the expropriation costs 466.35 million USD in 2009 prices and the share of the expropriation costs in the total investment budget was estimated to be 5.18% (Ministry of Transportation of Turkey 2007). However, this is expected to reach 15% for reasons such as the impossibility of acquiring the section of the project route covering fertile lands by consolidation, which has required that expropriation procedures start again, litigation expenses and the value finalised by the court's decision being much higher than the market value. Excluding the construction period of the project, the eligible firm has been given a 22 years and 4 months operating period. The land required for toll road, bridge and tunnel constructions is to be acquired by expropriation and consolidation. For the 406 km (252 mile) route of the project, a total of 12,000 parcels will be expropriated. The land required for the project is approximately 5,500 hectares (13,590 acres), of which 3,500 hectares (8,648 acres) are private property and the remaining 2,000 hectares (4,942 acres) are public lands. Almost all the parcels affected by the project are actually used as farm or forest land and there are structures on only 240 parcels. Through a protocol executed by and between the Ministry of Food, Agriculture and Livestock, and the General Directorate of Highways, the land required for the project is targeted to be taken through a land consolidation project, although this approach is under frequent criticism by landowners, farmers' organisations and other stakeholders.

When expropriation practices for transportation projects, issues and their impact on the investment cost are evaluated, free land acquisition through such methods as land consolidation and zoning applications is found to be advantageous. Moreover, upon the conclusions reached by a collective consideration of the results of interviews with property owners and other stakeholders in the villages where lands are to be acquired by consolidation in the Gebze-İzmir Highway Project, as well as the lawsuits appealed to the State Council, it has been shown that land acquisition through participation share deductions of up to 10% from lands in the ownership of private individuals in the consolidation areas would not be appropriate for such large-scale and comprehensive projects as highways. Also, that toll roads should not be part of land consolidation projects because of the restriction of access to highways for adjacent areas and the granting of toll-only access rights to users. The outcomes of the interviews conducted with the managers of the non-governmental organisations that took part in the judicial stage explicitly demonstrate that such practices conducted without the consent of the owners of the property in order to reduce expropriation expenses destroy social justice. As a result, the project has been annulled by the relevant judicial bodies, and land acquisition for toll roads through land consolidation has been cancelled on the grounds that this is clearly inconsistent with the objectives set forth in Law No. 3083. However, the administration has started the standard expropriation procedures, but because the required expropriation practices have not been completed despite the near completion of the road construction, the administration is at risk of facing confiscation without expropriation lawsuits.

Consequently, it has emerged that construction of such infrastructure projects that divide agricultural lands and settlements, and adversely affect transport links on the lands and rural settlements through contribution shares that would be obtained through consolidation projects conducted in order to retain the integrity of agricultural lands and access to agricultural lands with regard to social aspects is unacceptable. It is obvious that additional amendments should be made to the laws on zoning development and consolidation applications in order to avoid causing a speculative increase in land values as a result of new transport projects. The preference for land acquisition in transport projects with methods which avoid compensation, such as zoning and consolidation is found not to conform with scientific principles and procedures, social values and fairness. The preferred course of action should be the acquisition of the lands required for the project through expropriation and then the consolidation of the fragmented agricultural lands. In cases where access rights to land are restricted, a replanning of the settlements must be preferred. It seems mandatory that the investor public institution should revise the specified works under the scope of a RAP and adopt land acquisition and compensation principles that are in harmony with the international standards for economic resettlement.

The structural characteristics of rural and urban land markets in Turkey do not allow for rational land acquisition for projects. Certain structural characteristics, such as the lack of an established data network throughout the country for the recording of statistical data at local, regional and national levels related to the actual values in purchase and sale transactions following the completion of cadastral works, land and building leases, income and costs by use of agricultural land, the lack of identified and published records of applicable capitalisation rates observable at province/district levels and insufficient institutionalisation in the area of valuation, do not allow for a rational valuation nor for an audit of the results of the valuation process. When the approach of the managers in public institutions toward expropriation, insufficient real estate development and valuation experts in administrations and problems caused by working conditions are added, it is observed that valuations are not prepared based on scientific research at the local level in administrations.

It is noteworthy that the problems encountered in real estate acquisition and expropriation by public institutions include legislation-related problems, budget deficits, a lack of human resources and inadequacy of the data network. The absence of adequate resources at central and local administrations and the requirement to initiate projects resulting from political pressure lead to confiscation without expropriation, which has been found to create a significant financial burden as well as undermining the confidence of the public. The usability of methods such as development right transfer, exchange and purchase along with expropriation in real estate acquisition is possible, and with the new regulations that should be enshrined in legislation, the use of more reasonable means should be encouraged instead of real estate acquisition involving high costs. Serious problems are being faced in the use of real estate acquisition methods, the implementation process and the payment stages, and these problems are seen as the main reasons for the failure in the completion of investments within the envisaged period (Aliefendioğlu and Tanrıvermiş 2015; 2016a; Tanrıvermiş and Aliefendioğlu 2015).

Although the valuation of real estate and other assets required for projects and compensation for the affected people apply globally, it is observed that there are many problems for authorised bodies in Turkey, as well as in many developing countries There is a need for the preparation of good practice guides, ensuring the transparency of the process of real estate acquisition and the adequacy of compensation paid to the affected households through cash and non-cash means. In addition to the lack of an established infrastructure for real estate valuation for all purposes, lack of conformity of the methods used in the valuation process and those used by experts reflecting the international valuation standards and valuation science is also a matter of debate. Also, when the fact that different persons and institutions apply different practices is added to the mix, it is clear that the quality and conformity in valuation methods, data and approaches used in valuation to acceptable standards are not ensured; this situation leads to major problems in almost every project involving public institutions and real estate owners.

Main problems related to expropriation and compensation payments

In the focus group studies conducted with the executives of the central and local administrative units authorised for expropriation, the issues related to real estate acquisition and expropriation were analysed. Among the main problems encountered are project development and planning practices not being given enough time, failure to provide adequate financial resources in a timely manner, executives being indifferent to and ignorant in subjects of property rights and expropriation, expropriation practices taking too long and cases usually resolved unfairly, inadequate and obscure parts of the expropriation legislation and provisions conflicting with international regulations, the failure to establish adequate data infrastructure in public administration and the lack of a well-functioning real estate market and valuation system. In addition, because of the lack of sufficient funds at municipalities, confiscation without expropriation is often preferred, and this imposes a significant financial burden in addition to damaging confidence in the municipality. These problems could be classified under the titles of 'approach' problems to expropriation and property issues, legislation issues, budget insufficiency, human resource insufficiency, valuation infrastructure and data network organisation insufficiency (Aliefendioğlu and Tanrıvermiş 2015; 2016b; Tanrıvermiş and Aliefendioğlu 2015; 2017):

1   **Problems in the Approach to Expropriation and Real Estate Issues:** The right to property is protected under the Turkish Constitution and Civil Code, and only responsible or authorised public institutions are granted the power of expropriation of and intervention in private real estate rights, and only on the basis of public interest. In practice, it is observed that the managers of responsible and authorised institutions sometimes fail to consider the protection of basic human rights (such as right to

property), and though not vital for the project, they resort to expropriation, confiscate real estate without compensation and thus neglect the negative impact of expropriation on the owners. Where the scope of expropriation, which has a crucial influence on the living conditions of people, is too broad, and particularly if it impacts on a village and even the district as a whole, it can generate common problems for an important part of the community. Unless far-reaching public policies and resettlement action plans toward the elimination of such issues that can be defined as the social and sociological aspects of expropriation are put into action, it is not possible to create awareness among local people about the attention which should be paid to the protection of local community peace, security and the protection of rights to property and the right to life. The versatility of the proprietary rights, particularly in projects where loss of property rights also means loss of livelihood and living space, requires the establishment of replacement living environments and such resettlement must be supported by economic and social considerations. Ignoring this poses great danger in terms of public authorities and officials, and may lead to the emergence of social loss and damage at a much larger scale than the public benefits to be obtained by development underpinning the expropriation.

2   **Issues Originating from Legislation:** Preparations needed to start work on the expropriation process, especially the criteria to be used in the determination of the existence of a public interest and the criteria to be used in the analysis of the type of the real estate are not explicitly identified in the legislation. Among the primary controversial issues and the issues that lead to the prolongation of cases as a result of objections, are: failure in the actual distinction between rural land and urban plots during value determination, a lack of regulations in the legislation related to the situation of the real estate in terms of planning, cadastre and the land register, its counterparts according to the State of the current use and, if any, the appropriate method of income and expense analysis, could be listed, and it can be observed that they usually lead to incorrect operations.

The obscurity of the legislation on which the rural and urban plots distinction is based and the lack of detailed research carried out for this purpose do not usually allow for rational valuation. Multipurpose projects which require expropriation, with resettlement elements (such as large land acquisition, access roads and tunnels), usually involve more than one ministry or public institution. Although the responsibilities and authorities of the institutions are clearly defined in the legislation, generally because the institutions cannot engage in simultaneous operation, the desired results from the project are delayed, and it is inevitable for the affected people to react. As a result, existing legal regulations include general provisions and remain inadequate in today's circumstances. In addition, even a single miscommunication with a single administration can lead to noncompliance between governmental administrations and institutions and disconnection of the institutional link. Additionally, the legislation needs to be revised and strengthened according to the land acquisition policies and good practice guidelines currently implemented by the ECtHR and the international financial institutions.

In recent years, the development of primarily transportation and urban transformation, infrastructure and superstructure investments has gained speed. As a result, an increase in the expropriation practices of public institutions and in the number of the cases has been observed. Owners usually file for cancellation of acquisition procedures in the

Table 7.3 Total Number of Cases in Civil Courts in Turkey and Number of Expropriation Cases

Years	Total Number of Cases	Expropriation Cases	Share of Expropriation Cases in Total Number of Cases (%)
2009	1,729,980	38,502	2.23
2010	1,810,201	37,197	2.05
2011	1,870,830	52,090	2.78
2012	1,708,497	51,409	3.01
2013	1,954,803	55,724	2.85
2014	2,142,665	55,306	2.58
2015	2,167,986	61,196	2.82
2016	2,213,353	70,990	3.21

Source: www.adlisicil.adalet.gov.tr/istatistik.

administrative judiciary in obligatory cases, and the administration file actions with the judiciary for the determination of value and the registration of the real estate that could not be obtained by purchase. In Turkey, between 2009 and 2016, there was an increase in the number of expropriation cases filed with the administrative judiciary compared to the rate of total case numbers (Table 7.3), and it is observed that the conclusion of cases usually takes a long time. As a consequence, the achievement of the investments within the time anticipated are adversely affected. In addition to the expropriation cases, when confiscation compensation cases are filed following land acquisition without expropriation and cases filed for the cancellation of expropriation practices are included, it is seen that the number of the cases has at least doubled.

The number of the cases filed in 2016 in the administrative courts was 190,525, of which expropriation cases were 1,977, confiscation without expropriation 172 and disputes relating to expropriation procedures were 557. The share of the cases relating to expropriation in the total number of administrative cases was found to be 1.42%. The share of cases related to expropriation in the total number of administrative and judicial cases in Turkish courts was 3.04%.

Cases where real estate cannot be acquired by negotiations with the owner and the value is determined by the court, increases the time factor of real estate acquisition, and also its costs. It has been revealed that the value settled by the court is much higher than the value determined by the administration or the value applied by independent experts through service procurement. Identification and registration procedures of the expropriation costs of real estate by the court are usually completed within 1–2 years; and because of the length of this period, many public institutions take a decision to confiscate the land by Cabinet Decree, which can be achieved within 1 month for urgent expropriation. In such circumstances, investments flow from this decision, and valuation and registration of land are carried out simultaneously with the construction of the project. Currently, about 70,990 expropriation value determinations and registration cases are still being heard in courts, 93.38% have been adjudicated and it has been found that generally the conclusion of the cases takes 2 years.

3 **Issues Originating from Budget Insufficiencies:** One of the major problems encountered in the projects involving the compulsory acquisition of land is the public 'institutions' lack of sufficient financial resources. Public administrations need expropriation in order to provide services to the individuals to whom they are required, and

one of the main obstacles they face is the lack of financial resources. The provision of adequate financial support to public administrations for expropriation is one of the fundamental requirements for effectively achieving the public interest (Köycü 2006). With the amendment to Law No. 2942 by Law No. 4650 in 2001, a regulation was made stipulating that administrations cannot initiate expropriation practices without first ensuring adequate funds. Similarly, according to Public Procurement Law No. 4734, construction works cannot be initiated before the completion of the land provision, real estate acquisition, expropriation and zoning procedures, if necessary, and application projects. Despite these two basic regulations, problems in expropriation caused by lack of funds have been unresolved, and it can be observed that projects without sufficient funds are awarded a contract and that construction works have started. Under these circumstances, the confiscation of private land without expropriation becomes an obligation, and this leads to the undermining of confidence among owners in the public administration.

4   **Lack of Qualified Human Resources:** There have been some recurrent problems over the recent years in expropriation practices. Among these problems are, primarily, that commissions established in administrations and those serving on the committees of experts chosen by courts do not having specialist knowledge in the field of real estate and asset valuation, and lack practical experience. As a result, valuation procedures are carried out mostly without audit. Both in public institutions and in committees of experts, experts with undergraduate and graduate education in real estate development and management and certified appraisers are required. However, in the absence of such experts many provinces and rural areas have little choice but to select experts from neighbouring provinces and to appoint instructors from real estate development and management departments of universities as experts in specialty cases. In this way, there is a reduction of the number of reports not based on technical and scientific aspects, and valuation in accordance with objective principles and international standards, and the protection of the rights of all stakeholders achieved. Another problem area is that pressure groups at local level, having expectations of interest in important infrastructure investments, try to create high land values by putting pressure on incumbent committees of experts and courts. Though small in number, some cases of an increase in compulsory land acquisition costs have resulted in this way. In such cases, the solution is the mandatory selection of experts from neighbouring provinces and universities.

5   **Insufficiency of Valuation Infrastructure and Data Network Organisation:** It can be observed that increased values of expropriated real estate usually cannot be defined as 'fair value', and in many projects, the assessed value of the land is higher even than the market value. Landowners are generally dissatisfied with the estimated and paid expropriation value, while administrators of public institutions recognise that expropriation value exceeds the real market value of land. This problem causes delays in investment projects and increases the costs of the investment. This situation is the result of a lack of developed valuation standards, a lack of the institutionalisation of real estate expertise and significant valuation errors. The structure and operation of land markets, the lack of professional standards and an insufficient number of qualified appraisers, along with the main problems in the implementation of valuation methods, lead to the prolongation of operational and valuation processes of expropriation as well as delays in the completion of public investments; increases in investment costs; and, naturally, based on the model of recovery of costs, increases in service prices.

In rural and urban real estate markets because actual purchase and sale transactions are not recorded and real estate ownership is usually shared, the land acquisition process is often slow and costs are relatively high. Thus, it is necessary to establish a database of physical attributes and the financial values related to the acquisition of real estate used in each project, and provide a basis to apply a benchmark in valuation procedures. Integrating amounts and costs of land acquisition of public institutions with a data network or, more importantly, with the land registry which will make it possible to share the results of previous studies and to reduce possible valuation errors to a minimum.

In Turkey, procedures of preparing guides for land acquisition and expropriation in public administrations and performing situation analysis and valuation procedures before the start of the work and informing stakeholders are often neglected. However, in recent years, interest in developing alternatives to standard expropriation approaches and improving land acquisition processes has increased. In addition, resettlement action plans need to be prepared for households and settlements forced to move, and efficient practices involving resources allocated from the project budget should be provided. In order for those who have been displaced as a result of expropriation to establish their businesses again, supported for obtaining bank loans and business development should be available, thus providing them with a share from the real estate values to be increased after investment. Although theoretically this approach will be successful in the future, the possibility of success is seen to be weak with risks involving establishing companies, limited entrepreneurial talent, inexperienced participants and inequality in access to information (Lindsay 2012). In order to restimulate interest in depressed areas in city centres, focusing on the mentioned areas in order to re-establish their commercial attraction is one of the most important issues. For this purpose, the consolidation of land in municipalities or of private persons, the transfer of development rights and for other purposes, business development, and the ways to establish new settlement areas will be necessary. Similarly, in transformation projects to be applied in slum prevention areas, appropriate real estate valuation before and after the projects, proper determination of improvement costs and precautions taken to ensure the previous inhabitants adhere to the project area are considered obligatory.

The elimination of negative issues resulting from expropriation practices by three basic main solutions seems possible. The first is ensuring that the enacting regulations address the system's shortcomings. Along with this, many problems, including primarily practices related to value and problems in the judiciary, will have to be resolved. The second is the need to take precautions in order to resolve the problem of insufficient financial resources, one of the main causes of all setbacks faced in practice. The third and perhaps the most important is related to the vision and efficiency of political and administrative authorities. It is emphasised that attempts by political authorities and administrative bodies to use expropriation for purposes other than public interest, behaviours such as bringing private interests and political and personal animosity to the forefront may lead to results that disturb social peace (Köycü 2006).

Conclusion and recommendations

The process of land acquisition in the construction of public infrastructure is critical for site selection and project appraisal phases. In many countries including Turkey, there are occasions where acquisition of land may be required for purposes such as benefits to society, public interest and public purposes; including education, health and recreation facilities;

infrastructure; and other public services. In addition to land acquisition via zoning practices in urban development areas and infrastructure projects, land acquisition is possible
by expropriation, exchange, donation and purchase. However, because zoning cannot be
applied in the old settlement areas of cities, land acquisition by expropriation and donation
for renewal and transformation projects becomes inevitable (and particularly in the case of
expropriation) result in higher costs. Apart from these, land acquisition and expropriation
processes for transportation investments such as public transport, railway transport, subways
and cable cars, as well as drinking and usage water and sewage projects, progress in quite a
problematic manner. The highway projects developed and land acquisitions realised based
on land consolidation (instead of expropriation) are invariably criticised by landowners,
and courts cancel some of these projects. It seems to be a requirement to select the correct
methods used in the integration of lands required for social and technical infrastructure
projects for the public to ensure that real estate rights, ethical values and social justice are
fulfilled and satisfied.

Expropriation is often preferred for public investments in Turkey, and State, public legal entities and local administrations are able to partially or totally expropriate real estate
in private ownership for the public benefit by paying in advance the price of such real estate. During 2000–2016 in Turkey, public institutions expropriated approximately 300,000
hectares (some 740,000 acres) of land and about 10% of the central and local administration
investment budget was paid to owners in the form of compensation. In some municipalities, the share of compensations for expropriation, and confiscation without expropriation,
within total expenditures may be higher because of public transport, subway, and urban
renewal projects.

There is a requirement for public institutions with the legislative power to expropriate
to make project development and public benefit decisions, provide adequate appropriations,
make scaled plans for expropriation, identify the owners and users of real estate, survey the
sites, establish valuation and settlement commissions, conduct expropriation first by means
of purchase and if there is no compromise, determine cost, and file registration cases. In the
case of judicial proceedings, the appraisal is made by an expert panel selected by the court
and if the determined price is paid within 15 days, the real estate is registered in the name
of the relevant public administration. Because of the concentration of administrative works
and transactions, urgent expropriation decisions have been taken in many projects in recent
years and the lands are entered onto, and other actions are completed later. Alternatively,
immovable properties are acquired through confiscation without expropriation. Despite the
existence of many relevant court decisions (the Court of Appeals and the Constitutional
Court) including the ECtHR decisions, and although the expropriation process has been
described in detail in the legislation, many problems are encountered by public administrations during land acquisition and expropriation phases and the finalisation of expropriation
cases take a very long time.

It is commonly observed that the owners are not satisfied with the estimated and paid
compensation. The amounts paid for expropriation in many projects are higher – for a variety of reasons – than the actual real estate market value. The structure and functioning
of rural and urban land markets, and issues in the implementation of valuation techniques,
extend the operation and cost analysis process of expropriation and lead to delays in public
investments. Moreover, valuation principles set forth in the expropriation legislation do not
comply with the performance standards of international financial institutions. International
financial institutions demand from public and private institutions that apply for project loans,

that the compensation and consideration of transport costs and compensation based on the replacement value be prepared, regardless of the nature of the ownership rights of people affected by the project. In addition, they require the preparation of compensation for legal and illegal uses of public land (pasture, forest land, tenants, sharecroppers and occupiers' use of water resources) and a RAP for people and groups affected by the project. In order to facilitate the financing of public investments with credits provided by international institutions, it seems necessary to reorganise the legislation on real estate acquisition and expropriation processes and to ensure its compliance with international standards.

Land acquisition for large infrastructure projects in almost every locality may affect the assets and quality of life of the people living in the areas in question in a positive and/or negative way. Various expropriation methods are currently used to acquire the land required for public investments and there will be a need to implement a standard method of expropriation in land acquisition for infrastructure projects and to analyse the post-expropriation changes in the economic and social situation of the households affected by the project, as well as the potential changes in the natural environment. Regarding the valuations carried out in the process of the acquisition of real estate required for the projects, following a primary analysis of real estate by type and characteristics, the valuation of real estate is based on the market value for building lots, on income value for lands, and on the net cost for buildings, and compensation based on these values are paid to the owners and possessors. However, it is not possible to compensate sharecroppers, illegal users, or tenants who cultivate lands that belong to others and "Treasure Lands" without a contractual relationship. Important differences in compensation calculation methods are observed both between countries and between country practices and international standards (such as those of the IVSC and policies of international financial institutions).

Despite all the regulations for the assessment of expropriation costs, problems in this field are rapidly increasing. Conducting valuations on rural lands based on income, on urban lots based on market value, and on their complementary parts based on income, market value, and cost methods has become a legal requirement. However, the related regulations are observed to contain many contradictions and there are also significant problems in terms of operation. The land and land-lot distinction is made directly based on agricultural directorate, municipality and title deed registry data and according to the previous judicial decisions, if any, before the field work is carried out in the project area. Valuations are based on previous transaction analysis in land-lots and on the frequently used alternative systems, product yields, product prices and production costs in lands. The results of research carried out in this specialism show that average yields, revenues and costs of the plots in a given investment project generally differ from those of the relevant agricultural organisations. Judicial bodies demanding income and cost analyses to be made using only the data of agricultural organisations not only fail to comply with basic valuation standards, but also fail to reflect the conditions and realities of the country. However, if each plot is to be assessed in its original condition, together with the net income that can be generated where the land is used as desired, analyses of yield, cost and income according to the type of land on each plot and in the surrounding land becomes mandatory. Since even this simple fact of valuation may not be widely understood in Turkey, there is no sense in mentioning basic valuation standards.

In public institutions, the number of technical stuff having theoretical and practical knowledge of valuation is quite limited, sometimes non-existent. The essential thing to do is to train technical staff and experts assigned in value assessment commissions within administrations on valuation methods and to improve their qualifications, reduce the number of important problems encountered in this field, and prevent expropriation from being a means of unjust enrichment (or impoverishment) by the reduction in compensation. Particularly thanks to the complete amendment of the provisions of Law No. 2942 relating to expert choice in 2016, the appointment of individuals with specialised knowledge in real estate development to the committees and providing basic training will be useful in terms of increasing the quality of valuation practices. In Turkey, as in many developed countries, individuals who complete vocational training programmes on expertise provided by research institutions, and who reinforce their knowledge level and the adequacy of their experience by certification should be added to the list of experts; and experts' reports prepared in relation to urban areas should be continuously monitored and evaluated. In practice, technical staff who usually prepare valuation reports which reveal unacceptable final value definitions inconsistent with international standards, should either be required to re-take their vocational training or should be removed the list of expert.

It is seen that a well-functioning infrastructure has yet to be established for real estate valuation in the areas outside valuation practices for capital markets. It is necessary to revise land acquisition processes for public investments and the valuation system according to the international standards and national good practices. A certain quality of standard may not be achievable for reasons such as the valuation committees established in public administrations and the expert committees selected by the courts facing significant challenges in the acquisition of data required to undertake a valuation; the presence of significant errors or deficiencies in the methods implemented in the valuation process or in the application of these methods; the absence of a flow of information between appraisers; the lack of an established audit, and the systems of reward or punishment. As a result, sales values of rural and urban plots that are found to be actually traded in advance of the valuation date, land income and capitalisation rates are often chosen at random and based not on detailed research but on the subjective ideas of individuals. Institutionalisation of valuation procedures will allow the use of data based on the results of research carried out periodically in each region, instead of subjectively conducted activities, and such procedures can be standardised across the country.

In projects implemented by different institutions in Turkey, expropriation take a long time, and interest rates are applied to the value because valuation and registration usually takes 1–2 years. Because of the lack of an established valuation system to support the assessment of the compensation of owners of rights in real estate, and the different expropriation valuation practices of different institutions, sometimes the public institution and sometimes the individuals affected by land acquisition and expropriation are being victimised or overly rewarded. The gain of one and the loss of the other are always high on the agenda, and the issues exceed even national boundaries and are escalated to the ECtHR. Valuation practices for expropriation purposes and valuation and registration cases can occupy the judicial system for years. In expropriation practices conducted by different public institutions, it is observed that land acquisition and expropriation costs anticipated for projects usually remain below the actual expropriation costs at the end of the project. In this light, expropriation is moving away from being a method to be adopted both by the owner and the administration. Developing a real estate management policy which will allow for the protection of the right to property for each citizen in an equivalent measure, and adopting implementation of methods other than expropriation in land acquisition for public investments should be achieved.

There are significant differences between legal and institutional approaches towards expropriation and resettlement processes in Turkey and the approaches of organisations such as international financial institutions. These differences arise both in the calculation of compensation and in the identification of people to be compensated. In Turkey, valuation for fixing the level of compensation is based on the type of the real estate: transactions are realised over the income value of the rural land, the market value of the urban plots and the net cost value of the buildings. Payment of the net cost regardless of whether the building is a commercial business or not causes a significant loss for owners. Second, while compensation to only the landowner and possessor was considered, according to the performance standards of international institutions, in case of damage to any activity generating income for the person using the land or its resources in some way and/or in case of the prevention of access to sources of income, compensation of these losses is necessary, regardless of the ownership rights. These arrangements are particularly important in projects to be financed by foreign sources. For reasons such as the widespread trespass on publicly and privately owned properties in Turkey and the incomplete cadastral works, in the case of the implementation of performance standards principles, the land value of the investments will increase and many investments may no longer be feasible.

It is often argued not only by the administrators of public institutions, but also by other stakeholders and owners affected by the projects, that expropriation procedures are problematic and costly. In order to conduct land acquisition and expropriation processes in less problematic ways, information infrastructures, especially cadastral bases, must be adequately equipped in terms of the quantity and quality of data. For reasons, such as the lack of data related to land use at district, village and even parcel scale levels; products grown; average product yields; input use and costs; unknown actual land purchase; and sale values and rents paid, land valuation based on income is very difficult. Additionally, the capitalisation rates of lands appropriate to their type at district, village and even locality levels are not known, and under these circumstances, it is not possible to revise land valuation procedures and valuations conducted by valuation commissions and experts. Second, some problems are experienced in the classification of the type of the real estate to be expropriated as rural and urban land plot. Increases of up to 10 times are observed by changing some classifications, such as parcels which are within the municipal boundaries, outside the scope of the development plan and actually farmed plots to be considered as rural and urban land plots and showing possible use patterns for the future at the revenue value appreciated (objective criteria). As a result, all the principles of capitalisation theory are neglected and the income approach turns out to be meaningless. Similarly, it was found that precedent sales were involved in land valuation studies, and that the evaluation of development rights and use cases and comparative sales analysis studies have not been conducted in an acceptable manner. It is understood that valuation procedures are conducted without taking into consideration the age, class and depreciation of buildings. Furthermore, because of phenomena such as issues related to parcel and buildings ownership, errors in addresses and lack of information in urban areas, rational valuation also requires additional expertise.

It is not unusual that public investments divide settlements and cause the disintegration of parcels and farm enterprises in rural areas. Taking only parcel integrity as the basis in the assessment of compensation, or taking business integrity and access to income opportunities into consideration can cause significant problems for the affected households and settlements. Urban settlement planning practices of large-scale investment projects and the implementation of these projects in rural areas together with land consolidation can make a positive contribution to the quality of the social and economic conditions of people living in those areas. Especially in public investments by land consolidation, agricultural land is protected either by no or very little expropriation practices, and this also protects rural people who earn their livelihood directly from the land from being expropriated and displaced. When expropriation is conducted, the lives of the people in this area are affected in an irreversible way. Project-affected people often take their expropriation payments, migrate to cities and give up on the jobs or businesses where they live. On some occasions, they even fail to use the expropriation payments in accordance with their purpose; this leads to great social and family problems. Conducting upper-scale planning work at regional and country levels and, following this, at the stage of making land use planning, considering available and possible projects of transport, airport and residential area development of the institutions related to infrastructure investments, developing and applying infrastructure projects eligible for land use decisions should be ensured. Particular attention should be paid to the protection of natural resources, especially to productive agricultural land. In this context, consolidation projects for improving agricultural infrastructure and increasing the capacity of the agricultural business will also make an important contribution to the proper execution of infrastructure investments. One of the primary expenses of public investments is costs associated with large-scale expropriation.

Note

1 Turkish Lira.

References

Aliefendioğlu, Y. and Tanrıvermiş, H. 2015. "Kentsel Dönüşüm Sürecinde Taşınmaz ve Proje Değerleme İşlemleri ve Sorunlarının Analizi: Kayseri Büyükşehir Belediyesi Sahabiye ve Fatih Mahalleleri Dönüşüm Projesi Örneği Çerçevesinde Değerlendirme." *Uluslararası Sosyal Araştırmalar Dergisi* 8(39): 736–769.

Aliefendioğlu, Y. and Tanrıvermiş, H. 2016a. *Evaluation of Land Acquisition and Expropriation for Investment Projects in Turkey within the Framework the Turkish Laws and International Standards: The Case of Baku-Tbilisi-Ceyhan Crude Oil Pipeline Project.* Royal Agricultural University Working Paper. UK.

Aliefendioğlu, Y. and Tanrıvermiş, H. 2016b. *Assessment of Land Acquisition and Expropriation Process for Infrastructure Investments and Urban Development Projects in Turkey.* 5th International Symposium of the European Academy of Land Use and Development (EALD), 1–3rd September 2016. Ljubljana, Slovenia.

Böke, V. 2003. *4650 Sayılı Kanunla Değişik 2942 Sayılı Kamulaştırma Kanunu ve Kamulaştırma Bedelinin Tespiti Davaları (Expropriation Law No: 2942 Amended by Law No: 4650 and Cases of Determination of Expropriation Cost).* Seçkin Yayınları. Ankara. Turkey.

European Bank for Reconstruction and Development (EBRD). 2014. *EBRD's Environmental and Social Policy.* Retrieved from www.ebrd.com/what-we-do/strategies-and-policies/approval-of-new-governance-policies.html.

Ferlan, M., Lisec, A., Ceh, M. and Sumrada, R. 2009. "Acquisition of real property for public benefit". *Geodetski vestnik* 53(2): 276–290.

Food and Agricultural Organization (FAO). 2008. *Compulsory Acquisition of Land and Compensation.* FAO Land Tenure Studies 10. Food and Agricultural Organization. Rome, Italy.

Genç, Ö. and Ertuğrul, E. 2007. *Altyapı Yatırımlarının Finansmanı.* Türkiye Kalkınma Bankası A.Ş. Ekonomik ve Sosyal Araştırmalar Müdürlüğü. Ankara, Turkey.

Gemalmaz, B. 2006. *Avrupa İnsan Hakları Sözleşmesinde Mülkiyet Hakkı.* Beta Yayınları. Istanbul, Turkey.

International Finance Corporation (IFC) World Bank Group. 2012. *Performance Standards on Environmental and Social Sustainability*. Retrieved from www.ifc.org/wps/wcm/connect/topics_ext_content/ifc_external_corporate_site/ifc+sustainability/our+approach/risk+management/performance+standards/environmental+and+social+performance+standards+and+guidance+notes.

International Valuation Standards Council (IVSC). 2017. *International Valuation Standards 2017*. London.

Kalabalık, H. 2003. *İmar Hukuku Dersleri (Planlama, Arsa, Yapı, Koruma) [Zoning Law Courses (Planning, Housing, Building, Protection]*. Seçkin Yayıncılık A.Ş. Ankara, Turkey.

Kalem, A. 2015. *Türkiye'deki Kamu Yatırımlarının Özel Sektör Yatırımlarına Etkisinin İncelenmesi*. T.C. Kalkınma Bakanlığı Yatırım Programlama, İzleme ve Değerlendirme Genel Müdürlüğü Uzmanlık Tezi, Yayın No: 2922. Ankara, Turkey.

Karlbro, T. 2001. "Compulsory Purchase and Restrictions on Land Use: Principles of Compensation in Swedish Law". *Meddlande* 4(88): 1–2.

Khan, M.I. 2014. "Some Observations on Compensation and Productive Capital Base Depreciation of Land Acquisition Affected Farmers." *Excellence International Journal of Scientific Research*. Retrieved from www.researchgate.net/publication/279836846.

Köycü, H.K. 2006. *Türkiye'de Kentsel Toprak Politikalarının Uygulama Aracı Olarak Kamulaştırma*. T.C. Ankara Üniversitesi Sosyal Bilimler Enstitüsü Siyaset Bilimi ve Kamu Yönetimi (Kent ve Çevre Bilimleri) Anabilim Dalı, Yüksek Lisans Tezi. Ankara, Turkey.

Lindsay, J.M. 2012. "Compulsory Acquisition of Land and Compensation in Infrastructure Projects." *PPP Insights* 1(3): 1–10.

Ministry of Transportation of Turkey. 2007. *Gebze-Orhangazi-Bursa-Balıkesir-Manisa-İzmir Otoyolu (İzmit Körfez Geçişi Dahil) Projesi Yap-İşlet-Devret Modeli Çerçevesinde Ekonomik ve Finansal Fizibilite Etüdü*. General Directorate of Highways. Ankara, Turkey.

Murray, W.G., Hariss, D.G., Miller, G.A. and Thompson, N.S. 1983. *Farm Appraisal and Valuation*, Sixth Edition. The Iowa State University Press. Iowa.

Öçalan, N. 2015. *Kamu Yatırımlarında Kamulaştırma Yerine Arazi Toplulaştırması İle Arazi Temini*. http://docplayer.biz.tr/11131377-Kamu-yatirimlarinda-kamulastirma-yerine-arazi-toplulastirmasi-ile-arazi-temini.html, Retrieved date 11/22/2015.

Rehber, E. 1999. *Tarımsal Kıymet Takdiri ve Bilirkişilik*. Uludağ Üniversitesi Güçlendirme Vakfı Yayınları No:139, Bursa, Turkey.

Sumrada, R., Ferlan, M. and Lisec, A. 2013. "Acquisition and Expropriation of Real Property for the Public Benefit in Slovenia." *Journal of Land Use Policy* 32(2013): 14–22.

Tanrıvermiş, H. 2008. *Türkiye'de Tünel, Köprü ve Viyadükler İçin Kamulaştırma Tekniği ve Değerleme İlkeleri ve Uygulamaların Değerlendirilmesi [An Evaluation of Expropriation Techniques and Valuation Principles and Practices for Tunnels Bridges and Viaducts in Turkey]*. Ankara Üniversitesi Basımevi. Ankara, Turkey.

Tanrıvermiş, H. 2016. *Gayrimenkul Değerleme Esasları*. SPL Sermaye Piyasası Lisanslama Sicil ve Eğitim Kuruluşu, Lisanslama Sınavları Çalışma Kitapları Ders Kodu: 1014 (Konut Değerleme Sınavı, Gayrimenkul Değerleme Sınavı). Ankara, Turkey.

Tanrıvermiş, H., Akipek Öcal, Ş. and Demir, E. 2016. *Gayrimenkul Mevzuatı*. SPL Sermaye Piyasası Lisanslama Sicil ve Eğitim Kuruluşu, Lisanslama Sınavları Çalışma Kitapları Ders Kodu: 1019 (Gayrimenkul Değerleme Sınavı). Ankara, Turkey.

Tanrıvermiş, H. and Aliefendioğlu, Y. 2015. *A Study on Identification of Real Estate of Land Plot Characteristics and Analysis of Expropriation Values in the Yusufeli Dam and Hydroelectric Power Plant [A Study on Identification of Real Estate of Land Plot Characteristics and Analysis of Expropriation Values in the Yusufeli Dam and Hydroelectric Power Plant]*. Ankara Üniversitesi Fen Bilimleri Enstitüsü Taşınmaz Geliştirme Anabilim Dalı Yayın No: 22. Ankara, Turkey.

Tanrıvermiş, H. and Aliefendioğlu, Y. 2017. *Principles of Land Acquisition, Expropriation and Compensation Calculation for Infrastructure Projects in Turkey and An Analysis of Key Issues"*, Paper Prepared for Presentation at the "2017 World Bank Conference on Land and Poverty. The World Bank, March 20–24, 2017. Washington DC.

Tanrıvermiş, H. and Doğru, N. 2004. *Türkiye'de Yasalar ve Uluslararası Kuruluşların İlkeleri Çerçevesinde Kamulaştırma Süreci ve Bedel Takdiri: Bakü-Tiflis-Ceyhan Ham Petrol Boru Projesi Örneği [Expropriation Process and Valuation under Legislations and the Principles of International Institutions in Turkey: The Case of Baku-Tbilisi-Ceyhan Crude Oil Pipeline Project]*. Türkiye VI. Agricultural Economics Congress, pp. 183–196. Tokat, Turkey.

Tanrıvermiş, H., Gündoğmuş, E., Birinci, A. and Ceyhan, V. 2002. *Türkiye'de Tarım Arazilerinin Kamulaştırma Bedellerinin Tespitinde Karşılaşılan Sorunlar ve Çözüm Yolları*. Türkiye 5. Tarım Ekonomisi Kongresi, 18–20th September 2002. Erzurum, Turkey.

Tanrıvermiş, H., Gündoğmuş, E. and Demirci, R. 2004. *Arazilerin Kamulaştırma Bedellerinin Takdiri Tarım Arazilerinin Kamulaştırma Bedellerinin Takdirinde Kullanılabilecek Kapitalizasyon Faiz Oranları, Arazi Gelirleri ve Arazi Birim Değerleri*. EDUSER Limited Şirketi. Ankara, Turkey.

Tanrıvermiş, H. and Şanlı, H. 2008. "Tarım Politikalarının Arazi Değerlerine Etkilerinin Değerlendirilmesi [An Evaluation of the Impact of Agricultural Policies on Land Values]." *Türk Kooperatifçilik Kurumu, Üçüncü Sektör Kooperatifçilik* 43(1): 88–111, Ankara.

The World Bank. 2002. *World Bank Policy on Involuntary Resettlement Policy Directive (OD 4.30)*. Washington DC.

Viitanen K., Falkenbach, H. and Nuuja, K. 2010. *Compulsory Purchase and Compensation Recommendations for Good Practice*. International Federation of Surveyors (FIG), FIG Commission 9-Valuation and the Management of Real Estate, November 2010. Denmark.

8

Regulatory framework for expropriation of real property in Poland

Iwona Karasek-Wojciechowicz and W. Jan Brzeski

General context and concepts

The Polish legal system belongs to the system of codified law. The sources of law in this system, as compared to common law, are acts promulgated by qualified bodies, most typically the Parliament. Consequently, the presentation of expropriation regulations requires an introduction to the sources of relevant legislation. In the Polish legal system the courts typically resolve individual disputes between parties and their decisions are not binding on other courts regarding similar disputes. Nevertheless, over longer periods of time involving disputes, especially when considered by the Supreme Court, certain common views of case-law are developed, adopted and used by other courts (especially lower-level courts). This does not preclude some courts from departing from these prevailing views, even by the very Supreme Court in specific cases deemed to be affected by special circumstances, although it happens relatively rarely. This is why it is useful in some places to make references to rulings by the Constitutional Tribunal and by the Supreme Court. There is also another element besides legislation and case-law that brings additional knowledge about Poland's regulatory framework regarding the expropriation of real property – the legal doctrine developed within the academic aspect of law. References are made in places to legal doctrine as it can influence court rulings and legislative resolutions.

Hence, in the Polish legal doctrine expropriation is deemed to take place whenever property rights, in full or in part, are compulsorily taken away from a person (natural, legal) possessing them. However, actual regulations on expropriation, similar to other legal systems, reject such a broad understanding and considerably limit the scope of this institution.

Constitutional context

The list of the sources of law on expropriation regulations begins with the highest authority embodied in the Constitution (of the Republic of Poland). Article 21 of the Constitution reads: "Section 1: The Republic of Poland protects ownership and hereditary rights. Section 2: Expropriation is allowed only for public purpose and for just compensation". There is doctrinal and case-law agreement that the constitutional protection pertains not only to property rights vested in physical objects (e.g., real estate) but also to rights vested in intangible assets such as corporate shares and intellectual property. However, there is no full agreement, in neither case-law nor commentaries, regarding whether the constitutional protection extends to partial property rights; and the Constitutional Tribunal has not resolved this issue in an unambiguous way.

Expropriation, in the constitutional sense, covers the involuntary taking of ownership of real estate for public purposes and for the benefit of a public body. Consequently, this institution does not include punitive purposes (confiscation), which are covered in other regulations. Also, the compulsory taking of property rights for the benefit of a non-public body, as well as for the protection of that body's private interest, is not covered by the expropriation regulations (e.g., enfranchisement of cooperative members taking over the assets of cooperative or local government bodies). However, the Constitution influences indirectly all forms of the compulsory taking of property rights extending into the realm of private property interactions. Article 21 of the Constitution (Sec. 2) "radiates" on the private realm by commanding other laws to impose the principle of just compensation in cases of the compulsory taking of property rights for the benefit of private bodies.[1] The rest of this chapter is focussed entirely on expropriation in the strict sense, omitting cases of the compulsory taking of private property rights by a private body for its benefit, as in cases of the compulsory purchase of shares (stocks) in the "squeeze out" procedure.

The wording of Article 21 of the Polish Constitution does not specify whether expropriation is limited to the compulsory taking of individual property rights through a single act (applying separately to each expropriated owner), or whether it can take a form of general act pertaining to broadly identified subjects (of expropriation). In this matter the Constitutional Tribunal, and hence doctrinal view, is not uniform. In one of its rulings the Constitutional Tribunal argued that one cannot exclude a mechanism of statutory expropriation, since the constitutional meaning of expropriation may be applied to every compulsory taking regardless of its form. This view allows for the inclusion of compulsory taking pertaining to notionally defined group of subjects. The Constitutional Tribunal, however, makes a caveat that such an interpretation does not confer full discretion to legislators in applying various forms of compulsory taking. Only the individual mode of compulsory taking provides for procedural guarantees, especially the right to court process. Nevertheless, the Tribunal has ruled in other instances, that "expropriation (…) is linked to compulsory taking of limited/partial or full property rights through an individual act pertaining to a concrete property for the benefit of a concrete body. This act leads to State acquisition of property ownership, or other property right, in real property owned by a non-State property through a strictly formalised administrative procedure".[2] This leaves out the concept of "nationalisation", which encompasses large-scale compulsory taking in broad sectors of the economy, enabled by special laws.

It should be noted that the Polish Constitution sanctions compulsory taking not only for realising public purpose (Art. 21, Sec. 2), but also for other purposes listed in Article 31, Sec. 3, some of which may coincide with a public purpose. These other purposes include security and public order, protection of the environment, health, public decency or rights and freedoms of other people. These purposes may be realised through not only expropriation but also nationalisation or sequestration, and not necessarily with compensation. There is a lively ongoing debate on the need for compensation in such cases, but this is not directly pertinent to expropriation as such, and is not considered further in this text.

As mentioned earlier, constitutional limitations on expropriation extend beyond the compulsory taking of real property. Ordinary legislation may also confer on the public executive bodies the power to expropriate non-real estate assets. However, the existing legislation allows for expropriation of only those rights that are vested in real property. Consequently, the remainder of this text is devoted to expropriation of real property.

Legislative context

The main legislative act regulating expropriation of real property in Poland is the *Land and Property Management Law (August 21, 1997)*, henceforth UGN.[3] Chapter 4 of the UGN deals with expropriation and contains Articles 112 to 142. Chapter 5 of the UGN deals with compensation for expropriation and contains Articles 128 to 135. Chapter 6 of the UGN deals with the return of expropriated property and contains Articles 136 to 142. The UGN regulates the basic procedures of expropriation.

Expropriation principles, partly differing from the UGN, are introduced by a number of specific acts pertaining to particular types of investments (especially linear properties) or to individually enumerated investments. Among these Acts one should note, *inter alia*, the *Act (April 10, 2003) on specific principles for the preparation and realisation of investments in public roads*,[4] and the *Act (March 28, 2003) on railway transport*.[5] Issues not covered in the specific Acts are regulated by the UGN as to basic principles and procedures of expropriation. There is no room in this text to discuss the specific Acts, although some references are made when discussing specific issues.

International context

In addition to "domestic" national regulations of expropriation, Poland is obliged to observe an international agreement, partly touching on expropriation issues – the European Convention on Human Rights (henceforth ECHR). Polish courts are obliged to act in accordance with the ECHR provisions, and in the case of violation parties may seek protection from the European Court on Human Rights (henceforth ECtHR). According to Article 1 of Protocol 1 to the Convention,

> Every natural or legal person is entitled to the peaceful enjoyment of his possessions. No one shall be deprived of his possessions except in the public interest and subject to the conditions provided for by law and by the general principles of international law. The preceding provisions shall not, however, in any way impair the right of a State to enforce such laws as it deems necessary to control the use of property in accordance with the general interest or to secure the payment of taxes or other contributions or penalties.

At the general level, the protection rendered by the ECHR as formed by rulings of the ECtHR is similar to that provided in Poland's Constitution. Differences exist at the level of the specific interpretation of some specific issues and the scope of compensation. Understanding of property ownership, as specified by the ECtHR rulings over its many years of activity, is much broader than that of Poland's Constitution as it covers a wide range of asset interests with specific economic values. The ECHR extends its protection over partial interests *in rem*, personal rights in intangible property, as well as private and public claims and at the extreme also expectancy rights.

The ECtHR case law has established three principles related to Protocol 1 to the Convention: (i) the principle of peaceful enjoyment, (ii) just compensation for compulsory takings and (iii) national regulations on property use which comply with the general interest. An important issue is the imperative of a "just balance" between the public interest and the protection of private property. In particular, it calls for "reasonable proportional relations" between the means and ends when a particular compulsory taking is executed. The concept of "public interest" is understood broadly to include issues of a political, economic and social nature. The ECtHR thus gives much freedom to domestic legislatures in articulating the range of issues belonging to the implementation of social and economic policies, and relies on domestic legislatures to rule what is "public interest", unless such ruling starkly departs from the basis of reasonableness.

Additional sources of international regulations are embodied in the Charter of Fundamental Rights of the European Union, which is consistent with the European Convention on Human Rights. In its Article 17 the Charter establishes that "no one may be deprived of his or her possessions, except in the public interest and in the cases and under the conditions provided for by law, subject to fair compensation being paid in good time for their loss".

Finally, Poland has signed almost 80 bilateral investment treaties (henceforth BITs). They all have very similar wording, using the same set of clauses as they are patterned after a model treaty developed by Organisation for Economic Co-operation and Development (OECD). These treaties provide protection to foreign investments by strongly restricting expropriation opportunities by the host country (Poland). In case of a compulsory taking, investors may lodge a compensation claim with the international arbitrating tribunal, which is not bound by the case law of the host country.

BIT protects foreign direct and indirect investments (e.g., share and stocks in Polish companies). Typically the scope of a BIT provides guarantees to foreign investors as to (i) non-discrimination, (ii) fair and just treatment, (iii) full protection and security of investments and (iv) no expropriation or nationalisation. BITs do not define these terms and conditions, but have been formulated through rulings of the international arbitration tribunals. Specifically, in the context of expropriation, a "sole effects doctrine" has been formulated, which states that the only criterion for evaluating whether a host country's "behaviour" constitutes "expropriation" is the factual negative impact on the investor's assets. The host country will then bear compensatory responsibility even if it has acted without expropriation intention. In order to qualify as compliant with a BIT, an expropriation would have to be done for public purposes, in a non-discriminatory way, according to domestic laws, and with payment of appropriate (just) compensation. The only reason for non-payment of compensation may be in the case of *force majeure* or in a state of necessity as understood in international law, that is, in situations when it is necessary to maintain public order or to protect national interest regarding national security issues.

Expropriating real property

According to Article 112 of the UGN, expropriation can be applied only to ownership rights, land usufruct (perpetual leasehold) rights or other lesser rights *in rem*,[6] all vested in real property. Not all categories of real property may be subject to expropriation. The lead principle is that expropriation may apply to real property located in specific areas earmarked in local zoning plans for public investments, or real property declared as a site of public purpose investment.

There are few departures allowed from this principle: (i) in the case of the installation of transmission lines (as defined in the UGN); (ii) in the case of the temporary access to property in order to perform maintenance, renovation and repairs of transmission lines; (iii) in the case of necessary limitations on the use of property connected with the exploration and extraction of mineral resources encompassed by mining property; and (iv) when the taking of property is necessary because of *force majeure* or a sudden need to prevent considerable damage. Expropriation is allowed, subject to these exceptional situations, only when the area of the subject property has been earmarked for a public purpose in one of the two land-use planning documents: (i) the local land-use zoning plan, or (ii) a public purpose siting decision.

The local land-use zoning plan is a widely recognised local legal act, which binds a given area to the location (siting) of a public purpose investment with the specification of land development conditions. If such a zoning plan has not been adopted for the subject area, the location (siting) of public purpose investment is embodied in an individual public purpose siting decision. Such a decision has to be issued by a pertinent body prescribed in the *Act (March 27, 2003) on spatial planning* in Article 56,[7] if the public purpose intention is in accordance with separately issued specific regulations. Expropriation is then a tool for carrying out those intentions embodied in the planning documents.

Expropriation may encompass whole units of real property or a part. One may also expropriate a fraction of joint ownership of a subject property, but only if the beneficiary State or local government unit already owns the remainder fraction of joint ownership rights. While expropriation may not be applied to a property ownership held by the State, one may expropriate land (leasehold) usufruct rights or lesser rights *in rem* vested in State-owned land (UGN Art. 113, Sec. 2). Expropriation may also be applied to property lacking a registered title and a clearly identifiable owner (UGN Art. 113, Sec. 4–6).

Expropriation through UGN takes or limits rights *in rem* – full ownership, land (perpetual leasehold) usufruct and lesser rights. Expropriation may not be applied to "obligation rights" such as rental, leasehold and a right of use, and a management/possession right held by a public organisation without the status of a legal person. The UGN states that such rights, established or "inherited" by the expropriated owner, expire three months after the effective date of expropriation (UGN Art. 123, Sec. 2). Expiration of these rights does not attract compensation, and any reconciliation related to the expiration is made between the relevant parties as, for example, between landlord and tenant.

The final effect of expropriation is the transfer of ownership rights to the beneficiary State or local government unit. This takes place on the effective date of the expropriation decision (UGN Art. 121, Sec. 1). In the case of lesser rights *in rem*, these are transferred onto the beneficiary State or local government unit, or, if non-transferrable, they expire. In the case of land (perpetual leasehold) usufruct, the transfer of this right takes place on the effective date of expropriation if a body other than the beneficiary established the usufruct right.[8] In the case where the beneficiary is the body that established the usufruct right, this right expires on the effective date of expropriation so that only an unencumbered ownership right remains (UGN Art. 121, Sec. 2).

Limitations of rights *in rem* (as opposed to their annulment) can take two forms: (i) time unspecified for the suspension of part of these rights (UGN Art. 124),[9] or (ii) time specified for the suspension of the full rights (UGN Art. 126).[10]

In cases of preventing danger, the inflicting of damage or inconveniencies disturbing owners or usufruct (perpetual leasehold) rights holders of adjacent (abutting) properties due to expropriation or its consequent land-use change on the subject property, the expropriation decision has to include mitigating provisions such as requisite easements and obligatory construction and maintenance of appropriate facilities paid for by the expropriation beneficiary (UGN Art. 120).

Expropriation purpose

Article 21 of the Constitution allows expropriation solely for public purposes. Rulings of the Constitutional Tribunal have defined the public purpose as "exclusively that what serves the people, is commonly accessible or constitutes a public good of all of society or a regional community".[11] Expropriation is in the direct interest of the beneficiary public body, but indirectly also in the interest of the whole society or regional community. The Constitutional Tribunal emphasises that "the sacrifice borne by the expropriated is justified and constitutionally legitimised only because it is necessary and indispensible to achieve a specified public purpose".[12]

The ordinary legislation has not given the expropriation beneficiary freedom to identify what is a public purpose instead, it has provided a catalogue of enumerated public purposes (UGN Art. 6) in terms of functions, activities and facilities.[13] However, this enumerative catalogue may be expanded through the recognition of other public purposes identified in other legislative acts.

Expropriation indispensability

Expropriation is allowed if a given public purpose cannot be achieved in any way other than the compulsory taking, in full or in part, of the requisite property rights vested in the subject property (UGN Art. 112, Sec. 3). The indispensability of expropriation is also subject to evaluation through a consideration of the circumstances identified in UGN Article 137 as to when the subject property becomes dispensable for expropriation purposes and when it should be returned if already expropriated (see Part III). This requires consideration of an appropriate time horizon, which is defined (in UGN Article 137) as seven years from the inception of the public-purpose investment activity with effect from the effective date of expropriation. It also sets the deadline for completing this investment at no later than 10 years from the effective expropriation date. If these time scales are deemed excessive, as concluded from the submitted investment documentation, the expropriation application will be ruled as being premature.

Expropriation beneficiary

The Constitutional Tribunal has ruled that "in order to qualify as a public purpose, it is essential to consider the character of the intended use rather than the legal form of the beneficiary that will realise the public purpose".[14] Consequently, it is possible to have a private beneficiary of expropriation for the realisation of a public purpose investment. Although expropriation may, as a rule, be made for the benefit of the State or a local government body (UGN Art. 113), ordinary legislative acts may exceptionally allow expropriation for the benefit of a private entity. For instance, in accordance with UGN Article 125, expropriation may be made for the benefit of a private enterprise, which has obtained concessionary rights for qualified exploration, identification or extraction of mineral resources since this activity is recognised as a public purpose in UGN Article 6. Similarly, expropriation may be made for the benefit of a private enterprise that has been given permission to undertake the installation, maintenance and repairs of transmission facilities (defined in Art. 124 and Art. 125 of UGN).

In addition to the aforementioned direct expropriation for the benefit of a private entity, it is also possible that the State or local government may, after having taking ownership of the expropriated property, hand over the completed development of the subject public purpose investment to a qualified private body.[15] It is essential that the investment is made in order to realise the public purpose, regardless of the entity achieving it. Engagement of public resources is not relevant for the expropriation decision, as the public purpose investment may be financed entirely from public resources as well as entirely from private resources. This view is prevalent, although there have been rulings stating that the public purpose can only be recognised when it is realised by public bodies or incorporated entities owned by them, including public-private partnerships.[16]

Buyout of residual property

As already mentioned, it is provided that only part of the subject property may be expropriated (UGN Art. 113) and needs to be subdivided (UGN Art. 116, Sec. 2, Pt. 3). If the subdivision makes it impossible for the expropriated owner to use the remaining property according to its present use, or to its present zoning qualification, the owner (or usufruct holder) may request that the remaining part of the property (after subdivision) be bought out by the expropriation beneficiary. This "buyout" right does not apply to adjacent (abutting) properties that may, nevertheless, suffer from the same detrimental influences as the remaining part of the expropriated property. However, a doctrinal argument has been made in several instances that all properties detrimentally affected should qualify for such a buyout.

The buyout request is possible also in the case of short-term expropriation when the compulsory taking is made in the case of *force majeure* or in an emergency, and it is needed to prevent considerable damages (Art. 126 UGN). After this short-term period, the expropriating authority is required to return the subject property to its previous condition. If the owner (or usufruct holder) is not able to enjoy the property in its present use or in accordance with allowed use, the owner may request a buyout by the beneficiary. Common courts handle disputes related to this issue, including relevant compensation claims.

Expropriation procedure

Expropriation is the measure of last resort after all other means towards realisation of public purpose investment have been exhausted and failed. This refers mainly to negotiations on acquiring necessary property rights through a market-based voluntary sale-purchase transaction. These negotiations may include an offering of a "replacement" property. Expropriation proceedings may begin only after 2 months of fruitless negotiations.

Article 116 of UGN specifies what is needed for the preparation of the expropriation "application": (i) details of the subject property, (ii) public purpose to be realised, (iii) area of the subject property (or its part) that is to be expropriated, (iv) its current use and the state of development of the subject property, (v) replacement dwellings and their provision to the "expropriated tenants", (vi) owner or any usufruct holder of the subject property, (vii) persons holding lesser interests *in rem,* (viii) the replacement property if such is to be offered and (ix) other relevant circumstances.

Documentation attached to the expropriation application includes (i) documented records of negotiations regarding compensation for the "taking" of the subject property, (ii) a graphic and text extract from the local land-use zoning plan (in the absence of a zoning plan, a decision on the location of the public-purpose investment), (iii) a land survey map showing pertinent data about land subdivision – in case of partial expropriation, (iv) extracts from real estate title register showing the ownership title and other pertinent records, (v) in the absence of such extracts, a statement by the relevant court that the subject property does not have registered title, and (vi) an extract from the National Real Estate Cadastre.

The expropriation application is submitted by a County Head (*Starosta*), acting on behalf of the State or on behalf of a local government unit. The expropriation application may also be submitted by an entity that will carry out the intended public purpose investment on the subject property. The "applicant" registers a caveat against the subject property at the relevant land (title) registry. If the expropriation does not materialise, the applicant is obliged to remove the caveat.

The next step is the administrative hearing conducted by the County Head regarding the expropriation. If in a given time frame no other persons register claims to the subject property, the County Head issues a decision about the acquisition of the subject property by the State or local government unit that applied for expropriation powers. The decision is announced in accordance with the Code of Administrative Procedures. Compensation for the expropriation is established in accordance with regulations stipulated in Chapter 5 of UGN and is held on deposit by the court for a maximum of 10 years.

The expropriation decision should contain the following (UGN Art. 119): (i) the determination of a public purpose, (ii) the identification of the subject property, (iii) the description of property rights being expropriated, (iv) the identification of the owner or perpetual leaseholder, (v) the identification of people holding lesser rights *in rem* to the property, (vi) the obligation to provide replacement dwellings/premises and (vii) the calculation of compensation amount.

The transfer of the expropriated property rights takes place on the effective day of the final expropriation decision. In the case of perpetual usufruct the leasehold interest is terminated on the effective day of the final expropriation decision. The subject property may remain in use by the expropriated owner through appropriate leasing arrangements and upon the owner's application, as long as the public purpose for which the expropriation took place is not being realised (UGN Art. 121).

However, there may be a need to take immediate possession of the subject property or to restrict its use. The County Head may limit the use of the subject property by issuing special permits for specific uses: draining pipes, conduits for liquids, steam, gases, energy and so forth in cases when the owner or leaseholder does not agree to this, after prior negotiations regarding the matter. The special permits may be issued for a period of no longer than 6 months. The restriction and its possible damages to the subject property qualify for compensation to the owners/leaseholder (or other possessor), which is either agreed between the parties within 30 days, or the County Head initiates procedure for estimating compensation. The permitted use has to be compatible with the local zoning plan or, in case of its absence, with the decision on the location of the public purpose investment. If the activities permitted by the County Head render impossible further use of the property in its current manner, the owner or leaseholder may demand an outright purchase of the property by the State.

In the case of *force majeure* or in case of emergency (preventing significant damage), the County Head may issue a decision permitting possession of the subject property for a period of no longer than 6 months (UGN Art. 126). After this period the entity that took possession of the subject property is obliged to return it in its previous condition and to pay compensation for taking possession including possible damages. The compensation amount is either mutually agreed within 30 days of taking possession, or the County Head initiates the proper procedure to estimate compensation amount.

Compensating for expropriated real property

Compensation form and quantity

The expropriation of property ownership rights, land usufruct (perpetual leasehold) rights and lesser rights *in rem* requires the payment of compensation at the value of the taken (lost) rights. If there are lesser rights *in rem* on the expropriated property the compensation to the owner (or usufruct holder) is reduced by the amount equal to the value of these rights (UGN Art. 128, Sec. 2). Alternatively, the holders of the lesser rights *in rem* may also be separately expropriated (if this is required for the achievement of the public purpose) and hence compensated accordingly.

Compensation is payable also for the following additional damages inflicted by the expropriation decision: (i) easements and related nuisance impacting adjacent (abutting) properties, including inconveniences created by the altered use of the subject property; (ii) limitations on the use of adjacent (abutting) properties resulting from the installation of drainage conduits and linear transmission infrastructure, including its maintenance and operations facilities; (iii) obligations imposed on the subject property owner, usufruct holder and holders of lesser rights to make the property available for maintenance and repairs on the transmission infrastructure; (iv) limitations on the use of the subject property stemming from permissions issued for the installation of road/traffic signs and signals on existing buildings, including the installation and maintenance of appropriate pedestrian walkways within building perimeters; (v) limitations on the use of the subject property to facilitate exploration, identification and extraction (mining) of mineral resources; and (vi) the temporary taking of the subject property in case of *force majeure* or emergency needs to prevent considerable damages. In all these cases compensation should be calculated as the value of inflicted damages (e.g., forgone income from business activities). If these damages result in reduced property value the, compensation amount is increased by this loss (UGN Art. 128, Sec. 4).

In each case of compensation (including the case of restricted use) the amount is calculated according to the condition, land-use function and value of the subject property as of the effective date of the expropriation decision. In the case when the expropriation decision is issued separately from the compensation decision (permitted exceptionally), the compensation amount is determined, as a rule, according to the condition and land-use function as at the date when the expropriated rights are taken (or limited).

The determination of the amount of compensation payable is made after obtaining an obligatory opinion of a (licensed) real estate appraiser (valuer). This amount is based on the market value of real property and takes into account the property type, its location, property use, land-use zoning designation, condition and current level of prices for similar properties. The value of the subject property is based on its current use if the use for which it is expropriated does not confer a higher value. If the use of property for the expropriation purpose confers a higher value (highest and best use (HABU)), the compensation amount is assessed at this alternative (and more profitable) use.

If the type of subject property is not traded on the market the compensation amount is based on a replacement cost value (rather than market value). This requires that the property value be composed of two components: value of land and value of improvements. The valuation of the land component follows Article 134 of UGN, while the valuation of improvements is based on the replacement cost of a new building, reduced for depreciation, reflecting the age and obsolescence of the subject property. In the case of compensation for agricultural and forest-covered lands, the valuation is based on a specific methodology for such types of agricultural assets.

Compensation takes, as a rule, a form of monetary payment. In-kind compensation in the form of "replacement" property is also possible and has to be agreed with the expropriated owner or usufruct holder. The compensatory property is taken from the real property inventory held by the State (in case of expropriation by the State) or from that held by local government (if it is the beneficiary). In the case of a value difference between the expropriated and compensatory properties, the amount of the difference is paid in monetary terms.

Compensation decision and its payment

Compensation is determined by County Heads (*Starosta*) as part of the expropriation decision issued by them. In exceptional cases the compensation decision may be issued separately: (i) if requested by the expropriated owner or the entity realising the public purpose investment, (ii) if the compulsory taking has occurred without the determination of compensation or (iii) in other special circumstances listed in Article 129 of UGN.

Payment of compensation is made in one instalment not later than 14 days after the relevant decision. In the case of immediate possession requested by the expropriated owners/leaseholder, an advance payment is made of 70% of the compensation amount and not later than 50 days. The compensation amount is subject to indexation for the period between relinquishing possession and the payment date (UGN Art. 132). If the payment of compensation amount is delayed, Civil Code regulations apply with penalty interest being charged. The expropriated owner, or usufruct holder, may also apply for additional compensation for inconvenience caused by the delay.

In exceptional cases the compensation amount is paid as a deposit into court if (i) the expropriated owners refuse to accept the payment or the transfer of payment is impeded, if or (ii) compensation pertains to a property with a "clouded title". The amount of the compensation payment is subject to indexation for the period between the decision and the payment dates (more about this in the earlier section on compensation).

Returning expropriated real property

General remarks

The obligation to return the expropriated property in case the public purpose is not being realised, or the subject property is no longer indispensable for this purpose, is a necessary consequence of Article 21 of the Constitution even though it is not stipulated as such. This has been confirmed by interpretative rulings of the Constitutional Tribunal so that the constitutional guarantee of private property rights regains its protective power (Art. 21, Sec. 1). Retaining ownership of the subject property in the hands of a public body is constitutionally unjustified, which leads to the conclusion that the property should be returned to the expropriated owner or usufruct holder.[17]

The Constitutional Tribunal, however, seems to be taking a more nuanced view on the obligation to return the expropriated property. In some of its recent rulings, it was proposed that the obligation to return the property is justified only if the public purpose was not realised on the subject property. This, however, does not mean that the public purpose is implicitly assumed to continue forever. If, for example, after the expropriation of land, a public school was built and used for a number of years and then closed for demographic reasons, and the building was then made available for commercial uses, this would not violate the ruling of the Constitutional Tribunal that there were no longer any grounds for returning the subject property to the expropriated owner.

Nevertheless, UGN regulates the issue of returning expropriated property by allowing the expropriated owner (or successors) to request the return of the property. However, it is not clearly stated whether this right extends also to usufruct holder (perpetual leasehold), but the Constitutional Tribunal has confirmed this right.[18] In such a case an issue arises about what is going to be returned to the usufruct holder and how such a return is to be achieved, since upon expropriation a perpetual leasehold is typically terminated, and the beneficiary is given a free and clear property title unencumbered by the usufruct. A more doctrinal view holds that one should grant a new usufruct (perpetual leasehold) with similar conditions as the terminated one, specifically for the same number of years as the remaining period of the terminated usufruct.[19]

Use of property for other purpose

According to current regulations (UGN), the expropriated property may not be used for any purposes than those stipulated in the expropriation decision, unless the expropriated owner (or successor) does not request the return of the subject property. In case the beneficiary takes up an intention for such a "non-conforming" use, the expropriated owner (or successor) has to be duly notified together with information about the possibility of requesting its return (UGN Art. 136, Sec. 1, 2, 5).

The notion of "other purposes" includes not only a different economic purpose and use but also the ownership (or usufruct) transfer of the subject property to another *bona fide* body (person). In this case, the expropriated owner (or successor) may demand only the payment of compensation.[20] However, this limitation does not hold if the subject property is transferred on the basis of lease, rent or gratuitous possession or any other obligatory rights.

No request for property return is possible if the previous owner sold the subject property during the obligatory negotiation procedures which avoided the use of the expropriation procedure.

Property unused for intended purpose

In practice there may often be undesirable situations where an expropriated property remains unused for the stated public purpose, or pertinent investment remains too long in the "preparatory" phase. In order to avoid such situations, the UGN gives the expropriated owner the opportunity to request the return of the property as being deemed redundant for the stated public purpose. Article 137 of the UGN specifies that a property is deemed to remain unused for the expropriated purpose if (1) 7 years have passed since the expropriation decision and no works/activities have been initiated; or (2) 10 years have passed since the expropriation decision and the expropriation purpose has not been realised. If the expropriation purpose has been realised on a specified part of the subject property, the remaining part qualifies for return to the expropriated owner (usufruct holder).

The issue of whether the subject property is redundant for the stated public purpose is a disputed issue. Much depends on how precisely the public purpose is articulated in the expropriation decision. Broad definitions can lead to controversial interpretations as, for example, "development of a residential housing estate", within which different types of investments can be realised, including commercial ones (e.g., retail centre) that may be considered "social infrastructure", and all these investments can be linked functionally to the broad public purpose (in the expropriation decision).

The request for the return of the expropriated property (or its part) is submitted to a County Head (*Starosta*), who manages the procedure and issues the final ruling on a return, refusal of return, repayment of compensation or the return of replacement property (if any). Repossession of the subject property takes place, as a rule, in its current state and condition as at the repossession date (UGN Art. 139).

If the expropriated property (or its part) which is subject to return (to former owners/leaseholder) is encumbered with a leasehold or other possessory rights, these rights expire on the day of the issuance of the final decision to return the property. In the case of rent, lease or other user occupancy arrangements, these rights expire 3 months after the return decision (UGN Art. 138).

As mentioned earlier, in some cases, the return of the subject property is not possible, specifically when there are *bone fide* purchasers or usufruct holders. A request for return is also not possible in the case of investments of a special character even if made at variance with the public purpose specified in the expropriation decision. An example is a public road built on the property subject to a request for return. If the land for this road was expropriated, its transfer to other ownership is impossible (including its return) since public roads have an inflexible structure of ownership and management/maintenance.

Procedures for returning the property

The request for the return of property is handled through administrative procedures concluded in the relevant decision issued by a Country Head (UGN Art. 142). The right for return is passed onto successors of the expropriated owner only through testate procedures, which means that this right may not be transferred to a third party through a contract for sale, unless it is explicitly agreed to by the beneficiary (of expropriation).[21] If the expropriated owner does not respond to the notice about the possibility of a return within 3 months, the right to request the return expires (UGN Art. 136, Sec. 5). However, in the case when the expropriated owner initiates a return request, rather than responds to the notice, there are no deadlines for making pertinent submissions.

It is debatable, whether the right to request the return of property is subject to the statute of limitations since this right belongs to the domain of civil law (that uses the statute of limitations). There are arguments against limitation both on doctrinal grounds and in case law, and acceptance of this view means that the request for the return property may be submitted at any time.[22]

In any case, the conditions permitting the return of the subject property will not occur unless the expropriated owner returns the expropriation compensation (with the appropriate indexation as per UGN Art. 5) and/or the replacement property (UGN Art. 136). This is included in the return decision issued by the relevant County Head that specifies the time deadlines for the return of compensation amount and/or the replacement property. The maximum amount of indexed compensation may not normally be higher than the market value of the subject property as at the return date (UGN Art. 140).[23] If the subject property experiences value growth or a decrease as a result of activities undertaken by the beneficiary directly after the expropriation, the indexed compensation amount is adjusted to incorporate these value changes as at the return date. The estimation of these value changes is made between the property values as at the expropriation date and as at the return date. Changes in land-use zoning (if any) and in the surrounding area are not taken into account.

The expropriated owner (or successor) may request that the return of the indexed compensation amount be spread over a period of time but not longer than 10 years. Instalment conditions for this are included in the return decision issued by relevant County Head. Instalments are subject to interest charges based on a discount rate used by the National Bank of Poland.[24] The State or local government body can secure their (instalment) claims through appropriate instruments including mortgage liens for the owned amounts, thus encumbering the returned subject property.

Notes

1 Constitutional Tribunal ruling on May 29, 2001, K 5/01.
2 Constitutional Tribunal ruling of December 9, 2008, K 61/07, OTK-A 2008, Nr 10, poz. 174.
3 Sometimes translated as Real Estate/Property Management Act –*Ustawa o gospodarce nieruchomościami z dnia 21 sierpnia 1997 r., tekst jednolity z dnia 14 grudnia 2016 r., publ. Dz.U. z 2016 r. poz. 2147 z późniejszymi zmianami).*
4 Pol. *Ustawa z dnia 10 kwietnia 2003 o szczególnych zasadach przygotowania i realizacji inwestycji w zakresie dróg publicznych (tekst jednolity Dz.U. 2017.1496).*
5 Pol. *Ustawa z dnia 28 marca 2003 o transporcie kolejowym (tekst jednolity Dz.U. 2016.1727).*
6 Lesser rights *in rem* include right of use, easement, collateral, mortgage lien and cooperative right of possession.
7 Act (March 27, 2003) spatial planning and management –*Ustawa o planowaniu i zagospodarowaniu przestrzennym (tekst jednolity Dz.U. 2017.1073 ze zmianami).*
8 Two situations are possible: (i) usufruct was established by the State, and the local government is the expropriation beneficiary or (ii) usufruct was established by the local government body, and the State is the expropriation beneficiary.
9 As in case of necessary installation of transmission infrastructure.
10 As in the case of encroaching on a property due to *force majeure* or emergency need to prevent considerable damages.
11 Ruling of the Constitutional Tribunal (June 16, 2015) –*wyrok TK z 16.6.2015 r., K 25/12, OTK-A 2015, Nr 6, poz. 82).*
12 Ruling of the Constitutional Tribunal (December 13, 2012) –*wyrok TK z 13.12.2012 r., P 12/11, OTK-A 2012, Nr 11, poz. 135).*
13 For example: exploration, identification and extraction (mining) of mineral resources; exploration or identification of underground reservoirs for storing carbon dioxide (CO_2.)
14 Ruling of the Constitutional Tribunal (December 17, 2008) –*wyrok TK z 17 grudnia 2008., P 16/08, OTK-A, Nr 10, poz. 181. Authors' translation.*
15 Ruling by the Highest Administrative Court –*wyrok NSA z dnia 15 maja 2008 r., II OSK 548/07, LEX nr 503449).*
16 Act (December 19, 2008) on public-private partnerships –*ustawa z dnia 19 grudnia 2008r. o partnerstwie publiczno-prywatnym, tekst jednolity Dz.U 2015, 696 ze zmianami).*
17 Ruling by the Constitutional Tribunal (December 13, 2012) – wyrok TK z 13 grudnia 2012 r., P 12/11.
18 Ruling by the Constitutional Tribunal (April 3, 2008) – wyrok TK z dnia 3 kwietnia 2008 r. (K 6/05).
19 Bończak-Kucharczyk, 2017, 136, 12. Land and Property Management Act, Updated Commentary.
20 Ruling by the Supreme Court (September 15, 2015) – wyrok SN w uchwale z dnia 15 września 2015 r., III CZP 107/14.
21 Resolution of the Supreme Court (April 18, 1996) – uchwała SN z dnia 18 kwietnia 1996 r., III CZP 29/96).
22 Bończak-Kucharczyk 2017, 136, 8. Land and Property Management Act, Updated Commentary.
23 If market value cannot be established (lack of comparable sales data), then property replacement cost is used.
24 Interest rate charged by the National Bank of Poland for lending to commercial banks.

9

Legal implications of takings

A UK common-law perspective

Thomas Murphy, John McCord and Peadar Davis

Introduction

The common law has a long tradition of vigilance against the arbitrary taking of property by the Crown/state, a tradition that can be observed not only in UK domestic law but also further afield, for example, in the development of the Fifth Amendment to the Constitution of the United States of America (US) and Article 1 of the First Protocol to the European Convention on Human Rights (ECHR). It has accordingly been observed that in the UK, expropriation/compulsory purchase is essentially a creature of statute.[1] Compulsory purchase powers are provided under a wide range of statutes for a wide range of purposes, but the vast majority[2] are exercised through a common procedural framework. However, the UK consists of four nations: England, Scotland, Wales and Northern Ireland, each with its own devolved legislature, and thus, to varying degrees, its own specific laws. In many respects, the operation of the law of land acquisition and compulsory purchase in terms of the legal theory, case law authority and vagaries of day-to day practice are broadly similar across these jurisdictions. That said, the procedural framework remains disparate and fragmented, with striking differences observed not only in matters of detail but in some fundamental procedural aspects relating to the compulsory acquisition of land, compensation and the interference with property rights.[3]

Across the UK there is an array of statutory provisions which enable public authorities to acquire land for a variety of purposes such as urban redevelopment, regeneration and infrastructure provision. Broadly speaking, the acquiring authority will be able to acquire most land either compulsorily or by agreement where it is satisfied that such land is required for development and/or redevelopment, relocation of population or industry, or urban improvement and that it is in the public interest and expedient to acquire the land for such purposes. It is also the case that any acquiring authority seeking to exercise a power to acquire land must comply with specific procedural requirements related to the exercise of that particular power, which includes consultation with the local authority. In the circumstances where acquisition is to be by compulsory means, the acquiring authority must also comply with the general procedural framework laid out in statute.

In the vast majority[4] of instances, compulsory purchase is governed by the Acquisition of Land Act 1981 and takes the following form: first, a power provided in a General Public Act of Parliament, such as Section 226 of the Town and Country Planning Act 1990 (TCPA), will allow a relevant public authority to (generally) acquire land for a specific purpose; second, having identified specific land to acquire for that purpose the authority in question will make a Compulsory Purchase Order (CPO) which will only take effect if, third, it is confirmed by the relevant Secretary of State, who must, if there are any objections which are not withdrawn, hold a public inquiry.[5] Compulsory purchase powers must be exercised in accordance with the terms of the General Public Act from which they emanate and, additionally, Section 23(2) of the Acquisition of Land Act 1981 allows a person aggrieved by a CPO to challenge its validity in the High Court on the ground that a "relevant requirement" has not been complied with. Section 24(2), in turn, empowers the court to grant relief if satisfied that the interests of the applicant have been "substantially prejudiced" by the failure to comply.

This is a summary of "classic" compulsory purchase. However, it is worth noting that while in layman's terms property and land are synonymous, in fact land is merely the subject matter of property rights. That being the case the actions of the State may impinge upon (and take) property rights without physically taking/interfering with the actual land. A classic case is planning blight, where State decisions relating to a particular area have the effect of reducing the value of a particular piece of land in the vicinity. Similarly, the modern state imposes regulatory control over land use, and, in certain cases such regulatory control may amount to a taking of property rights. Such instances may be described as "compulsory purchase in reverse" and, in the UK context, may justify the owner of the land issuing, respectively, a blight notice or a purchase notice, in effect requiring the State to purchase the land. A detailed discussion of planning blight and purchase notices by the authors is to be found in *Property Law and Planning*[6] and is not considered in detail in this chapter. Alternatively, however, the State may overtly take some property rights – in particular wayleaves and easements – that do not involve taking (significant) physical control of the land.

Perhaps the best and most oft-cited summary of the law on compulsory purchase in the United Kingdom is the statement of Lord Denning MR in the Court of Appeal decision in *Prest v Secretary of State for Wales,* where he opined that

> It is clear that no Minister or public authority can acquire any land compulsorily except the power to do so be given by Parliament: and Parliament only grants it, or should only grant it, when it is necessary in the public interest. In any case, therefore, where the scales are evenly balanced — for or against compulsory acquisition with the decision — by whomsoever it is made — should come down against compulsory acquisition. I regard it as a principle of our constitutional law that no citizen is to be deprived of his land by any public authority against his will, unless it is expressly authorised by Parliament and the public interest decisively so demands: and then only on the condition that proper compensation is paid.[7]

So, there must be a power provided by Parliament, the power must be exercised in the public interest and only where, on the facts of the case, the public interest "decisively" demands, and proper compensation must be paid. That these are requirements is not in doubt, but what precisely they mean has not always been clear and the following discussion explores key developments and clarifications of the law.

Whilst this all seems relatively straightforward, land acquisition and compulsory purchase is a broad, complex and technical area of the law, and, in the context of a chapter such as this, it is not possible to provide a comprehensive discussion of the subject in its entirety.[8] Nonetheless, given the diverging legal structures and regionally nuanced differences in development track, what is clear is that the common law plays an ever more vital role in providing much-needed clarity and consistency to the interpretation of emerging issues related to land acquisition, compulsory purchase and compensation. Consequently, this chapter focuses on the major contemporary issues and challenges that have arisen in light of recent decisions relating to public interest, planning gain and private to private transfers.

A principle of constitutional law: public interest, compulsory purchase and "private to private" transfers

The fundamental basis of compulsory purchase is that the *state* has an underlying right to acquire land from the private landowner, but this is subject to strict requirements. In particular, as noted earlier, this must only happen if, in the words of Lord Denning, "the public interest decisively so demands". A key question then is what exactly is in the *public interest*? That is a very broad question and has been considered in depth elsewhere, but a particular issue that has proven to be notably controversial in other jurisdictions, especially in the US, in this context has been the use of expropriation powers by public authorities for (in essence, immediate) transfer to a private developer, who, in turn, facilitates economic development in the public interest (whilst potentially making a significant, non-public, profit). The "takings clause" in the Fifth Amendment to the Constitution of the US provides that

> No person shall be... deprived of life, liberty, or property, without due process of law; nor shall private property be taken for public use, without just compensation.

The interpretation of "public use" to mean "public purpose" by the Supreme Court in *Kelo v City of New London*[9] (thus allowing the practice) has proven highly controversial, provoking much academic debate. In the US the law of takings is very much a "constitutional" matter: a question of fundamental rights.

The development of the takings clause in the US Constitution can be traced from common-law origins and the consequent writings of, in particular, John Locke, so a similar reaction to this phenomenon might be expected in the UK. A cursory examination of recent UK case law seems to confirm this hypothesis: the two major compulsory purchase judicial decisions since the turn of the century, the decision of the House of Lords in *Standard Commercial Property Securities Ltd v Glasgow City Council (No. 2)*[10] and the decision of the Supreme Court in *Regina (Sainsbury's Supermarkets Ltd) v Wolverhampton City Council*[11] were both concerned with the use of compulsory purchase powers to facilitate development by companies. A more careful analysis (of both of these cases and more generally) tells a different story. In fact, the judicial reaction to this (widespread) phenomenon in the United Kingdom has been muted, and perhaps this should not really be such a surprise. The UK has never had a written constitution, and the key unwritten principle of the unwritten constitution is the principle of parliamentary sovereignty. Parliament has long been providing powers that deliberately and overtly serve to transfer land from private ownership to public ownership and back to (different) private ownership. In fact, particularly in the nineteenth century, it was common for Parliament to facilitate the creation of national infrastructure, in particular the railway network, by giving compulsory purchase powers directly to relevant companies.

In *R. H. Galloway v The Mayor and Commonalty of London*,[12] a key House of Lords decision of that era (cited in key modern cases), Lord Cranworth LC considered that public bodies should accordingly be judged by a more generous standard than private enterprises in this context:

> Now, it must be observed that the Legislature, in providing for such an object as that of widening and improving the streets of the *Metropolis*, has to deal with a subject totally different from that of enabling a body of adventurers to form a railway. In that latter case, the persons seeking the aid of Parliament are bound to show that what they are proposing to do is of such public importance as to make it reasonable that they should be enabled so far to interfere with the rights of private property as to compel the owners of the land required for the railway to sell it to them at a fair price. The Legislature has no concern with the question as to how the persons embarking in the undertaking are to obtain funds to pay for the construction of the railway. The railway will become the property of the speculators, and will itself repay them (at all events, it is anticipated that it will repay them) by the tolls levied on it, the outlay they have made. But in the case of a public body, like the Mayor and Corporation of the City of *London*, undertaking improvements in the *Metropolis*, the matter is very different. When they have made a new or widened an old street, they will necessarily have incurred a very great expense for which they can get no return. The new or improved street is dedicated to the public, and, unlike the railway, yields no profit to those by whom it has been made. In order to meet this difficulty, and to enable corporations to reimburse themselves, the course has been to authorize them to take compulsorily, not only the buildings actually necessary for forming the streets or other projected improvements, but also other neighbouring lands and buildings, the value of which, and the proper mode of dealing with which, the Legislature considers to be connected with and dependent upon the projected improvements.[13]

While this reasoning seems binary – either private or public acquisition – it should be noted that the land in question in that case was going to be, in turn, sold to a private profit-making entity, and this was considered unobjectionable by the House. That central assumption has never been fundamentally challenged and certainly not in the aforementioned recent decisions, both of which were set in the context of planning gain.

Buying planning gain?

A criticism of public authorities is that they are inherently inefficient by comparison with the private sector and slow (or unable) to identify and maximise opportunities that arise in the course of their work. In the context of planning, significant opportunities might theoretically exist for a sharp-witted planning authority to exploit: if a developer is seeking permission for a large project, would it not make sense that they provide, or pick up the cost of ensuring, all relevant infrastructure relating to the development is completed (for example, roads and sewers)? Large developments often have an impact on the appearance of the surrounding area, so perhaps the developer could compensate by providing landscaping and trees to replace those destroyed? Perhaps, going beyond mere compensation for loss of amenity, a wildlife sanctuary might be constructed to actively promote conservation in the local area, a key objective of the local authority? However, why stop there – the local council would have built a new leisure centre but has to date been constrained by lack of budget – it would be very helpful if the developer did this for them. In fact, the development is going to be very lucrative and developers should not be greedy – why not just write a large cheque and leave it with the local authority to be used at their discretion for the "public good"?

Some of these seem sensible and reasonable – precisely the sort of things that a public authority acting in the public interest should be demanding. Some others may pause for thought – if the requirement in question (large cheque) is a material consideration in the decision to grant planning permission, what weight has been given to it by comparison to other material considerations, such as the development plan or the views of the Environment Agency? In *R v Westminster City Council, Ex p Monahan*[14] Staughton LJ stated,

> The other extreme arises from the axiom of Lloyd LJ in *Bradford City Metropolitan Council v. Secretary of State for the Environment [1986]...* that planning permission cannot be bought and sold.
>
> Suppose that a developer wished to erect an office building at one end of the town A, and offered to build a swimming-pool at the other end B. It would in my view be wrong for the planning authority to regard the swimming-pool as a material consideration, or to impose a condition that it should be built. That case seems to me little different from the developer who offers the planning authority a cheque so that it can build the swimming-pool for itself—provided he has permission for his office development.

Lord Brown in *Standard Commercial Property Securities Ltd v Glasgow City Council (No. 2)*[15] expressed unease at the potential ramifications:

> I find deeply unattractive the proposition that, almost inevitably at the expense of some beneficial aspect of the development scheme, the authority should be seeking to make a profit out of the exercise of its statutory powers of acquisition.

Any unease in this respect could only be compounded if the developer happened to be in direct competition with a rival and the local authority used compulsory purchase powers to acquire land belonging to the rival for their (favoured) developer, who just happened to be providing the planning gain sought. This raises important considerations of what exactly is meant by legitimate planning gain and how such gain can be secured.

Planning conditions as a means to planning gain

The imposition of planning conditions is the most longstanding device for achieving planning gain. Under Section 70(1) of the TCPA 1990 a local planning authority in granting planning permission may, subject to sections 91 and 92, do so "...either unconditionally or subject to such conditions as they think fit". This is *prima facie* a very wide discretion, and the courts have long imposed limits upon it. In *Pyx Granite Co Ltd v Ministry of Housing and Local Government*[16] Lord Denning said (of what is now Section 70 of the 1990 Act),

> Although the planning authorities are given very wide powers to impose 'such conditions as they think fit,' nevertheless the law says that those conditions, to be valid, must fairly and reasonably relate to the permitted development.

In *Newbury District Council v Secretary of State for the Environment*[17] the House of Lords held that in order to be valid, such conditions would have to:

a   Be imposed for a planning purpose, not any ulterior motive,
b   Fairly and reasonably relate to the development in question, and
c   Not be so unreasonable that no reasonable authority could have imposed them (*Wednesbury* unreasonable[18]).

Ground (a) relates to the scope of town and country planning as a legal concept.[19]

Ground (b) requires that there must be some specific and tangible link between the condition and the site in question and also between the permission and the condition. In the *Newbury District Council* case, planning permission had been granted by the local planning authority to allow a change of use of hangars, previously used to store civil defence vehicles, to store synthetic rubber for a 10-year period, provided that at the end of the 10 years the hangars would be demolished. The House of Lords found that the Secretary of State was consequently entitled to conclude that this condition was not sufficiently related to the temporary change of use for which permission was granted as planning permission was not actually necessary in this case and, even if it had been necessary, the demolition was not required until the 10-year period of use (to which the permission related) was over and that therefore an enforcement notice should be quashed. Similar decisions involving conditions relating to demolition of ancillary buildings in the context of permission for change of use have occurred in *Delta and Design and Engineering Ltd v Secretary of State for the Environment and South Cambridgeshire DC*[20] and *Tarmac Heavy Building Materials Ltd (UK) v Secretary of State for the Environment, Transport and the Regions*[21]; thus, while it may not be impossible to impose conditions of this type, it will certainly be difficult.

A condition that work must be carried out on land not owned or controlled by the applicant will generally be void,[22] though a condition to ensure that off-site infrastructure work such as roads or sewers are completed will be valid.[23] However, that is a matter of degree.

Ground (c) has been typically applied to ensure that property rights are protected. In *Hall & Co Ltd v Shoreham-by-Sea Urban District Council*[24] the offending condition was that an access road had to be constructed on the developer's land at the developer's expense and then dedicated to the public. It is irrelevant that the developer actually suggests that the condition be imposed.[25] In terms of planning policy Paragraph 206 of the National Planning Policy Framework provides that conditions must be:

a   Necessary,
b   Relevant to planning,
c   Relevant to the development permitted,
d   Enforceable,
e   Precise, and
f   Reasonable.

While these are not legal requirements *per se* they will (as planning policy guidance) be a material consideration and, if *ignored*, a consequent decision would be unlawful[26] and, in general, it may be concluded that planning authorities are significantly limited in their capacity to impose planning conditions, both in this respect as well as by the tests laid down in *Newbury District Council v Secretary of State for the Environment*.[27] Consequently, planning gain is now achieved primarily through planning obligations.

Planning obligations, planning gain and the Infrastructure Levy

Section 106(1) of the TCPA 1990 provides that

> Any person interested in land in the area of a local planning authority may, by agreement or otherwise, enter into an obligation (referred to in this section and sections 106A and 106B as "a planning obligation"), enforceable to the extent mentioned in subsection (3)—
>
> a restricting the development or use of the land in any specified way;
> b requiring specified operations or activities to be carried out in, on, under or over the land;
> c requiring the land to be used in any specified way; or
> d requiring a sum or sums to be paid to the authority (or, in a case where section 2E applies, to the Greater London Authority) on a specified date or dates or periodically.

Section 106(3) provides that

> Subject to subsection (4) a planning obligation is enforceable by the authority identified in accordance with subsection (9)(d)—
>
> a against the person entering into the obligation; and
> b against any person deriving title from that person.

Effectively, a developer may either unilaterally or by agreement with the planning authority enter into an enforceable obligation in respect of land. Planning permission will be required, but the planning obligation will be a material consideration in determining that application. While planning authorities are strictly limited in terms of the conditions that they can impose on grants of planning permission in terms of planning gain (such as the building of new roads), planning obligations provide a way around this. The developer could take on an obligation to, for example, fund the construction of a new road to relieve traffic flow in the general area, and the planning authority could take this into account as a material consideration in the awarding of planning permission. Under Section 70(2) of the TCPA 1990,

> In dealing with such an application [for planning permission] the authority shall have regard to the provisions of the development plan, so far as material to the application, and to any other material considerations.

A significant question is to what extent does the law on planning gain (as applying to planning conditions) apply to such obligations – in what circumstances is a commitment to such an obligation a material consideration for the purposes of deciding a planning application?

In *R v Plymouth City Council, Ex p Plymouth and South Devon Co-operative Society Ltd*[28] two competing supermarket chains each proposed significant planning obligations. Sainsbury's offered approximately £3.6 million worth of gain in terms of *inter alia*, a tourist information centre, an art gallery display facility, a birdwatching hide, an £800,000 contribution towards a park-and-ride facility, and up to £1m for infrastructure works to make another site suitable for industrial use. Tesco similarly offered the development of crèche facilities for working mothers, a wildlife habitat, a water sculpture and land for a park-and-ride facility. The Court of Appeal found that (unlike the position with conditions) such benefits did not have to be *necessary* to the decision as to whether (or not) to grant planning permission in order to be material considerations. It was sufficient that they were planning benefits, and in this case they did reasonably relate to the particular development as the park-and-ride facility would, for example, counteract an increase in traffic caused by the development.

Thus, these planning gains were found to satisfy the "fairly and reasonably related to the development" test in *Newbury District Council v Secretary of State for the Environment*.[29] In the subsequent case of *Tesco Stores Ltd v Secretary of State for the Environment*[30] the House of Lords went one step further and found that a planning obligation could be a material consideration even if it did not reasonably relate to the development in question (so long as it had some connection) – it simply had to relate to a planning matter and must not be perverse. The County Council considered that a link road to relieve town centre traffic congestion was necessary for Witney, Oxfordshire and Tesco offered £6.6m to fully pay for it. In terms of physical proximity with the proposed link road there was a tenuous relationship with Tesco's application for planning permission for a superstore (it would potentially contribute to more congestion), but the Secretary of State concluded that the offered obligation was not reasonably related in scale to the increase in traffic likely to be produced by the superstore. The House of Lords concluded this was a material consideration but that the Secretary of State in this case had rightly taken it into account, albeit affording it (as he was entitled to do) little weight. Lord Keith summarised the position as follows:

> It is for the courts, if the matter is brought before them, to decide what is a relevant consideration. If the decision-maker wrongly takes the view that some consideration is not relevant, and therefore has no regard to it, his decision cannot stand and he must be required to think again. But it is entirely for the decision-maker to attribute to the relevant considerations such weight as he thinks fit, and the courts will not interfere unless he has acted unreasonably in the Wednesbury sense … An offered planning obligation which has nothing to do with the proposed development, apart from the fact that it is offered by the developer, will plainly not be a material consideration and could be regarded only as an attempt to buy planning permission. **If it has some connection with the proposed development which is not *de minimis*, then regard must be had to it. But the extent, if any, to which it should affect the decision is a matter entirely within the discretion of the decision-maker** and in exercising that discretion he is entitled to have regard to his established policy.[31]

In summary the *Tesco* case established that in order to be material only the first and third tests laid down for conditions in *Newbury* had to be met: the obligation must have a planning purpose and must not be *Wednesbury* unreasonable but need not fairly and reasonably relate to the development in question. Nevertheless, in order to be a material consideration an obligation will still have to have *some* connection, with Lord Keith adding,

> An offered planning obligation which has nothing to do with the proposed development, apart from the fact that it is offered by the developer, will plainly not be a material consideration and could be regarded only as an attempt to buy planning permission.[32]

On this theme Lord Hoffman stated,

> … to describe a planning decision as a bargain and sale is a vivid metaphor. But I venture to suggest that such a metaphor (and I could myself have used the more emotive

term 'auction' rather than 'competition' to describe the process of decision-making process in the *Plymouth* case) is an uncertain guide to the legality of a grant or refusal of planning permission... in a case of competition such as the *Plymouth* case, in which it is contemplated that the grant of permission to one developer will be a reason for refusing it to another, it may be perfectly rational to choose the proposal which offers the greatest public benefit in terms of both the development itself and related external benefits ...[33]

Lord Hoffman's comments acknowledge that there are serious concerns about this system as it effectively allows developers to "buy" planning permission. The Planning Act 2008 introduced a new mechanism, the Community Infrastructure Levy (CIL), that may facilitate planning gain in a more transparent and systematic manner. Essentially all but very small developments will have to pay a charge based on the number of square metres of the development. This system does not replace the system of planning obligations but works in parallel to it. It also interacts with it. *Tesco* affirmed that in order to be a material consideration an obligation did not have to be necessary to make the development acceptable in planning terms but that, in practice, so long as it has been considered it can legitimately be dismissed according to (more restrictive) planning policy (which provided that it must be necessary). Planning policy was simply another material consideration which had to be taken into account in the decision-making process, but which could be offered the weight deemed appropriate by the Secretary of State. That position has now been changed in respect of many developments by Regulation 122(2) of the Community Infrastructure Regulations 2010. Regulation 122(2) placed the government's planning policy tests into law for all developments from 6 April 2010 on which the CIL is *capable* of being charged: "anything done by way of or for the purpose of the creation of a new building, or anything done to or in respect of an existing building".[34] In respect to any such development it will be unlawful to take into consideration any obligation that does not meet all of the following tests:

a   Necessary to make the development acceptable in planning terms,
b   Directly related to the development, and
c   Fairly and reasonably related in scale and kind to the development.

Thus, for many developments (but not all) the *Tesco* decision seems to have been statutorily reversed. The rationale is that the Levy is designed to ensure that the wider infrastructure costs of a development are met in a standard and transparent manner, thus leaving planning obligations to cover only the situations where action (not merely a financial contribution) is necessary to make the application acceptable in planning terms.

This application of the CIL regulations was considered in *R. (on the application of Thakeham Village Action Ltd) v Horsham DC.*[35] The local authority approved an application for the construction of 146 houses on a site formerly occupied by a mushroom-growing enterprise which included an obligation by the developer to provide £3.75m to facilitate the continuation of the business on another part of the site. Dismissing a challenge to this decision on the basis that *inter alia* this was an attempt to "buy" planning permission contrary to previous cases on Section 106 obligations and the new CIL Regulations, the court found that economic benefits can be material considerations. In this particular case the land in question had been a single site for many years, and while the application would result in the creation of two sites (housing and mushroom production) there was a strong connection between these, both in terms of physical proximity and in terms of economic reality as the proposals for both sites were mutually dependent – one could not happen without the other. The continuation of mushroom production and thus the continued employment of people in the area was most definitely a proper planning purpose, and planning obligation in this case was fairly and reasonably related in scale and kind to the development.

It is against the background of this (not always wholly clear) area of law and policy that the most significant compulsory purchase cases of recent years have arisen.

Compulsory purchase and planning gain

The application of compulsory purchase powers in general is not without controversy. In *Galloway v Mayor and Commonalty of London*[36] Lord Carnworth said,

> The principle is this, that when persons embarking in great undertakings, for the accomplishment of which those engaged in them have received authority from the legislature to take compulsorily the lands of others, making to the latter proper compensation, the persons so authorised cannot be allowed to exercise the powers conferred on them for any collateral object; that is, for any purposes except those for which the legislature has invested them with extraordinary powers.

Similarly, in *Prest v Secretary of State for Wales*, Lord Denning stated that

> I regard it as a principle of our constitutional law that no citizen is to be deprived of his land by any public authority against his will, unless it is expressly authorised by Parliament *and the public interest decisively so demands*...[37]

In respect of many significant developments the role of the planning authority is not restricted to simply deciding whether or not to approve a planning application. Frequently the planning authority will exercise statutory powers to compulsorily acquire the land for the developer. While public bodies have a wide range of compulsory purchase powers, for a wide range of purposes under a wide range of legislative provisions, a key power is contained in Section 266 of the Town and Country Planning Act 1990:

226 Compulsory acquisition of land for development and other planning purposes

(1) A local authority to whom this section applies shall, on being authorised to do so by the Secretary of State, have power to acquire compulsorily any land in their area— (a) if the authority think that the acquisition will facilitate the carrying out of development, redevelopment or improvement on or in relation to the land or; (b) which is required for a purpose which it is necessary to achieve in the interests of the proper planning of an area in which the land is situated.

(1A) But a local authority must not exercise the power under paragraph (a) of subsection (1) unless they think that the development, redevelopment or improvement is likely to contribute to the achievement of any one or more of the following objects— (a) the promotion or improvement of the economic well-being of their area; (b) the promotion or improvement of the social well-being of their area; (c) the promotion or improvement of the environmental well-being of their area.

Having acquired the land under Section 226 the local authority may, in turn, dispose of it to a developer under Section 233:

233 Disposal by local authorities of land held for planning purposes

(1) Where any land has been acquired or appropriated by a local authority for planning purposes and is for the time being held by them for the purposes for which it was so acquired or appropriated, the authority may dispose of the land to such person, in such manner and subject to such conditions as appear to them to be expedient in order— (a) to secure the best use of that or other land and any buildings or works which have been, or are to be, erected, constructed or carried out on it (whether by themselves or by any other person), or (b) to secure the erection, construction or carrying out on it of any buildings or works appearing to them to be needed for the proper planning of the area of the authority ...

(3) The consent of the Secretary of State is ... required where the disposal is to be for a consideration less than the best that can reasonably be obtained ...

So the general thrust of modern UK legislation positively encourages "private to private" or "back-to-back" transfers. However, the application of these particular powers in the TCPA 1990 in tandem (perhaps unsurprisingly) raises particular issues. This is particularly true where two or more potential developers are in competition for a particular site and is magnified where one (or more) of the unsuccessful competitors actually owns, or owns part of, the site in question. In deciding whether to exercise the power of compulsory purchase and in favour of which competing developer issues of planning gain come to the fore.

It is these very powers that were considered by the Supreme Court in *Regina (Sainsbury's Supermarkets Ltd) v Wolverhampton City Council*[38] and (broadly) equivalent Scottish provisions that were considered by the House of Lords in *Standard Commercial Property Securities Ltd v Glasgow City Council (No. 2).*[39] Accordingly, the casual observer might be forgiven for imagining that either of these cases must be some sort of "British *Kelo*" – a fundamental analysis of how and where to strike a balance between property rights and the public interest. They are no such thing.

Standard is an important case but in the relatively limited sense that the House of Lords found in respect to the (broadly) equivalent Scottish legislation that it was legitimate for a local authority to enter into a "back-to-back" agreement with a "preferred" developer. The land in question was a rundown part of the Buchanan Street/Bath Street area of Glasgow city centre, and the city council agreed to assemble the site by compulsory purchase (from various owners) in return for the developer agreeing to indemnify against all costs incurred: thus the council made neither a profit nor a loss (as if the developer themselves had compulsorily purchased the land). In terms of disposing of the land the council was under an obligation not to do so other than at the best price or on the best terms that could reasonably be obtained. The House of Lords accepted that "best terms" could legitimately include planning gain as well as cash benefits and that the gain in question could include off site benefits. However, the particular benefits in question, integration of public art into the development and improvements to areas of adjoining streets were considered to relate directly to the site and to flow directly from the development. As the protagonists in the case were competing developers, the real issue was the quality of the decision making of the local authority in terms of *to whom* the land should be ultimately transferred. A further issue that has also arisen following from the *Standard* case may be that a particular case may potentially fall foul of European Union (EU) rules on State aid, which is considered in more detail later.

Likewise, the *Wolverhampton* case (in particular) looks initially promising but is troublesome; the supermarket chain Sainsbury's owned 86% of a site and the local authority used the powers outlined earlier to transfer ownership of the site to Tesco, their commercial rival: cue outrage. However, the identity of the protagonists is indicative of the real issue: both rivals wanted the site for commercial development and both needed the local authority to exercise their powers in order to acquire it for them. This was not a challenge to the power of the State to acquire property for commercial interests, but it was a complaint that the public authority had favoured the wrong party, making the wrong decision by taking into account inappropriate considerations: specifically the offer by Tesco to redevelop a second, commercially unattractive site which the Council had been unsuccessfully trying to find a developer for. Thus the most apparently significant case on compulsory purchase in the United Kingdom for many years is not really about compulsory purchase at all. Compulsory purchase merely provides the context for an analysis of the law of legitimate planning gain – the nature and extent of the obligations that a planning authority can extract (for example to contribute to the cost of roads and other infrastructure in the vicinity) from a developer in return for permission to carry out the development proposed. In that context the *Wolverhampton* case is highly significant as it extended the law of planning gain to decisions to exercise compulsory purchase powers for planning purposes. While the Supreme Court made appropriate mention of the sanctity of property rights, the ultimate conclusion, that the particular decision to use Section 226 of the TCPA 1990 in this case was unlawful, is explicable only by detailed analysis of the law on legitimate planning gain, an analysis that is beyond the scope of this chapter.

State aid

State aid is generally considered to be an economic advantage derived through the selective use of State resources and which is therefore liable to distort competition.[40] Under State aid law, distortion of competition means that the public measure increases the economic strength of its beneficiary as compared with other competitors or that the State support measure puts at a disadvantage other market players.[41]

Article 107(1) of the Treaty on the Functioning of the European Union (TFEU) contains a prohibition to the granting of State aids in the internal market (save in so far as it is permitted by other Treaty provisions) providing that

> Save as otherwise provided in the Treaties, any aid granted by a Member State or through State resources in any form whatsoever which distorts or threatens to distort competition by favouring certain undertakings or the production of certain goods shall, in so far as it affects trade between Member States, be incompatible with the internal market.

Although the relevance of State aid to the law of planning and compulsory purchase is not immediately obvious, compulsory purchase procedures and issues have increasingly become viewed as an area of law where State aid issues have been introduced.[42]

Notionally, the sale of publicly owned land and buildings below market value could meet the four criteria of Article 107(1) TFEU, thereby amounting to an impermissible State aid. Therefore, the "Commission Communication on State aid elements in sales of land and buildings by public authorities"[43] provides for two approaches to preclude the existence of State aid and ensure that the relevant land is sold at market value, and consequently does not contain State aid. First, by an open, marketed and transparent bidding process, which accepts the best bid and second, through independent valuation to establish market value in accordance with accepted market practice and valuation standards. Further methods of determining market value may be employed although they will not benefit from the assumption that no State aid is involved.[44]

Domestically, ss.123(2) and 127(2) of the Local Government Act 1972 provide that land owned by local authorities is required to be disposed of "for the best [consideration] that can reasonably be obtained". As such, where publicly owned land is disposed pursuant to such provision, it follows that there is no State aid. In the alternative, the difficulty arises where reliance is placed upon the legislative provisions which allow publicly owned land to be disposed of for less than that consideration, giving the potential for State aid which will need to be assessed.

Whilst it is true that compensation for expropriation will not be an impermissible State aid,[45] in the domestic planning and compulsory purchase context it is not necessary to search too far to uncover various State aid challenges and issues related to the grant of planning permission and compulsory purchase orders made in order to facilitate private developers. Indeed, examples of such claims in the planning aspect are glimpsed at in *R. (on the application of Bow Street Mall)*,[46] a challenge to the grant of outline planning permission for a shopping centre in Lisburn, seemingly contrary to planning policy. In this case, the High Court of Northern Ireland rejected the suggestion that the grant of planning permission was a State aid because "there was no transfer, relinquishment or depletion of state resources".[47] More recently, in *Brown v Carlisle CC*,[48] Collins J considered this issue in a challenge to the grant of planning permission for the erection of a freight distribution centre at Carlisle Airport where the permission was for what was described as an "enabling development". In reaching the same conclusion given in *Bow Street Mall*, albeit for a different reason, Collins J held that

> the exercise of a power which only the state or a public body such as a local authority which is in the same position can exercise will not amount to state aid.[49]

Thus, the grant of planning permission will not by itself constitute State aid.[50] Whilst the case law appears to be definitive on this matter, questions remain about whether s.106 obligations entered into by a developer in connection with the grant of planning permission give rise to State aid. According to Maurici and Sargent, there is a sound basis for concluding s.106 and s.106A are unlikely to give rise to State aid.[51] In considering the circumstances where less is being offered via s.106 contributions than would otherwise have been required in connection with the development, they aver that this is principally because decisions made about the level of contributions to a development are concomitant with the overall planning considerations in granting planning permission.[52] Likewise, the conclusion of no State aid will arise in the situation where planning permission is granted with a s.106 obligation actually having been entered into and making provision for various contributions and where the developer then later seeks to be released from some or all of the obligations under s.106A. Similarly, it has become increasingly commonplace for objectors to compulsory purchase orders to argue that confirmation of the order would involve State aid. Whilst this has included the suggestion that the use of CPO powers is itself State aid, the line of case law authorities indicates this is not a sustainable argument[53] and certainly not if one follows conventional practice where there is indemnification of the costs incurred by the authority from the developer.

As for compensation, the key State aid arguments appear to pivot on whether the land has been obtained at undervalue and nuanced considerations of statutory compensation and marriage value. Ultimately, whether such compensation issues will result in an impermissible State aid issue will first depend on the particulars of the agreement between an acquiring authority and developer of the consideration of the compulsorily acquired land; whether that is the best that can be achieved and perhaps overage provisions. Coming back to the provision under s233 of the TCPA 1990, in disapplying the obligation to achieve best value by expressly excluding the usual disposal limitations pursuant to s.123 of the Local Government Act 1972,[54] there is a statutory requirement to achieve "best consideration" or consent of the Secretary of State for land transfer. In these circumstances, the assessment of what satisfies best consideration has been considered by the court in *R. (on the application of Safeway Stores Plc) v Eastleigh BC*,[55] where the court held that

> For my part, I would have formed the view that it was plain that s 233(1) was directed to a very specific set of circumstances of disposal and that s.233(3) required the consideration for that disposal to be judged by reference to the purposes of the disposal. So if there were to be a rival bidder offering more but for a different purpose or for no purpose at all other than to thwart the proper planning of the area, it would be appropriate for the council to ignore that extra financial potential and doing so would involve no breach of s.233(3). The elimination of s.123 applications by virtue of s.233(8), coupled with the fact that any other approach would undermine s.233(1)'s purpose, seemed to me to make that matter entirely clear. There is therefore, in my judgment, a very important distinction between s.233 and the approach that follows under s.123. It is quite clear that the sort of considerations material to s.233 are immaterial to s.123.

Likewise, as noted, the outcome in the *Standard* decision indicates that the local authority can have regard to the planning objectives for which the CPO is being used, meaning an authority could reject a higher offer for land it has acquired if that offer does not deliver the planning objectives for which the land was acquired. Also material to this aspect is the extent to which there is any marriage value which may potentially fall foul of EU rules on State aid, falling outside Article 107(1) as being a measure justified by "the nature of the general scheme". In such circumstances, the legislative framework would certainly appear to suggest so, the case law implying that disposal requires determination of best consideration to proceed on the basis of whether the terms are the best that could reasonably be obtained so as to secure those planning purposes.

Notwithstanding this, the issue is further complicated by the fact that the United Kingdom is leaving the EU, and the precise relationship with the EU and with EU law thereafter remains shrouded in mystery for the time being. This also has possible relevance to the ongoing application of the ECHR.

Article 1 of the First Protocol ECHR

While the United Kingdom does not have a written constitution, the effect of the Human Rights Act 1998 has been to, in essence, incorporate the main provisions of ECHR into domestic law. Article 1 of the First Protocol (A1P1) of the ECHR provides,

> Every natural or legal person is entitled to the peaceful enjoyment of his possessions. No one should be deprived of his possessions except in the public interest and subject to the conditions provided for by law and by the general principles of international law.

The preceding provisions shall not, however, in any way impair the right of a state to enforce such laws as it deems necessary to control the use of property in accordance with the general interest or to procure the payment of taxes or other contributions or penalties.

A1P1 is thus arguable in any domestic proceedings against a public authority, such as a local authority attempting to utilise Section 226 of the TCPA 1990 in order to facilitate a back-to-back agreement with a developer. In a recent article Maxwell[56] has described A1P1 as a "paper tiger" in the face of private-to-private transfers of land using compulsory purchase powers. Taking that analogy one step further, tigers are notable for their ability to move around unseen, and the same is true of A1P1 in compulsory purchase cases – the reader is broadly aware that it exists, but it is largely invisible in the reasoning of the UK courts to date. That said, the requirements of A1P1 are frequently to be found in the basic principles of domestic compulsory purchase law, to which consideration is now given.

Powers: proper purpose

As noted earlier, in the vast majority of cases an "enabling" Act will provide the power to compulsorily purchase the land in question. Such legislation will specify the purposes for which the power may be exercised, and the courts have long insisted on construing the extent of such powers strictly. The classic expression of this principle comes from the speech of Lord Cranworth LC in *R. H. Galloway v The Mayor and Commonalty of London*[57]:

> The principle is this, that when persons embarking in great undertakings, for the accomplishment of which those engaged in them have received authority from the Legislature to take compulsorily the lands of others, making to the latter proper compensation, the persons so authorized cannot be allowed to exercise the powers conferred on them for any collateral object; that is, for any purposes except those for which the Legislature has invested them with extraordinary powers.[58]

In that case the respondents had entered into an agreement to sell the land of the plaintiff to a company whilst the Act that was going to provide them with the powers to acquire and dispose of the land in question was actually passing through Parliament (and thus not in force). Upon the relevant legislation entering into force, the plaintiff attempted to prevent the expropriation by arguing that the respondents were not proceeding on the basis of the purposes of the legislation but rather for the extraneous purpose that they were contractually bound to do so (and fettered by the terms of the contract). The House of Lords concluded that when the land was to actually be acquired the relevant legislation was in force and that the proposed acts of the respondents were fully in line with it. As noted, Lord Carnworth considered that a more flexible standard applied to public bodies than private enterprises in this context,[59] a sentiment expressed again by the House of Lords almost a century later in *Simpson's Motor Sales (London) Ltd v Hendon Corporation*,[60] with Lord Evershed observing that "we are here concerned with a responsible local authority having public duties to perform and not with the promoters of an intended profit-making business...".[61] The Corporation had made a CPO, confirmed by the relevant Secretary of State in 1952, for the purposes of building nine residential flats on a site. For various reasons the Corporation did not proceed to enforce the CPO until 1959, by which time it had concluded that the site would need to be developed as part of a larger project and that such a (larger) development was not likely to proceed in the "foreseeable future" and the plaintiff contended *inter alia* that the change in circumstances made the original decision to make the CPO *ultra vires*. The House of Lords did not agree, and while Lord Evershed appreciated that a local authority could (with agreement) abandon a compulsory purchase order he could find no evidence of abandonment in this case nor evidence of the Corporation proceeding according to some purpose beyond the scope of the statutory power:

> The compulsory purchase order of 1952 became finally effective and not subject to challenge and I cannot therefore think that an equity arises to have it, in effect, set aside on the ground that a similar compulsory purchase order might not have been confirmed by the Minister seven years later.[62]

Conversely, had the specific purpose (in the words of Lord Evershed) "evaporated"[63] *prior* to the confirmation of the CPO, it would have been vulnerable to this type of argument as demonstrated by the recent Court of Appeal decision in *Grafton Group (UK) plc and another v Secretary of State for Transport*.[64] A compulsory purchase order for a disused wharf had been made by the Port of London Authority, but planning permission for development of the site had been refused by the local planning authority. Nevertheless, following an inquiry, the Secretary of State had confirmed the CPO as the inspector had judged that there was a sufficient probability of an alternative scheme being proposed for which planning permission would be granted. The owners of the site successfully challenged the confirmation decision under Section 23 of the Acquisition of Land Act 1981, Ouseley J ruling that the Secretary of State had not had legally sufficient evidence on which to conclude that a subsequent alternative planning application would be approved and that in any case it would have been unfair to have confirmed the order on a different basis from what was originally promoted. Accordingly, the compulsory purchase order was itself quashed (not merely the confirmation of the order). On appeal it was concluded that while the inspector had exercised his planning judgement and the Secretary of State did therefore have legally sufficient evidence, nevertheless the case had otherwise been decided correctly. In regard to unfairness Lord Justice Laws quoted favourably the following passages from the judgement of Ouseley J[65]:

> The inspector's questions revealed nothing specific about the basis upon which he might recommend that the Secretary of State dismiss the planning appeal and confirm the CPO. He did not ask questions about whether a redesign could be accomplished with only a minor reduction in throughput if any, or records no answers if he did. He did not suggest that that was the basis upon which he might recommend confirmation of the CPO and dismissal of the appeal …[66]
>
> The inspector's questions did not make the confirmation fair in the circumstances. The relevant point is not whether the questions revealed the possibility of there being two different decisions, for they certainly did that; and the persistence of the inspector in asking it of so many witnesses meant that that was clearly something in his mind. The real point is whether, knowing of that possibility, Grafton had a fair chance to address the basis upon which the CPO was eventually confirmed without the planning appeal being allowed. It did not.[67]

Thus while the Court of Appeal was willing to accept that the inspector was justified in reaching a judgement that a successful planning application was possible, at no stage was it argued by the Port of London Authority that an alternative design might be adopted, and thus the CPO was confirmed on a basis other than that on which it was put forward.

However, whether that is so may be a matter of degree. In *Procter & Gamble Ltd. v Secretary of State for the Environment Secretary of State for Transport, Secretary of State for Energy and the Tyne and Wear Development Corp.*[68] the Tyne and Wear Development Corporation was established to regenerate a designated area. A competition was held for proposals to develop a 12-hectare (30 acres) strip known an as East Quayside and containing a building belonging to the plaintiff. The winning developer was awarded outline planning permission and a CPO was made "for the purpose of securing the regeneration of part of the Tyne and Wear Development Area". Subsequently, the highway authority made objections which resulted in the plaintiff's land being earmarked for the purposes of road widening. The plaintiff contended that as far as their land was concerned, the CPO was confirmed for a different purpose (road widening) from which it was made (regeneration and/or the particular scheme for which planning permission had been given). While the Court of Appeal agreed that a CPO made for one purpose could not be confirmed for another, it was necessary to determine the actual purpose for which it had been made. In this case the Order had been made for the purposes of the regeneration of East Quayside, not merely the particular scheme as specified in the planning permission, and the inspector had concluded that (as a result of the objections raised by the highway authority) highway improvements were reasonably necessary for the regeneration of East Quayside. Accordingly, the purpose for which the CPO was confirmed was the same as the purpose for which it was made:

> ...the means of achieving the regeneration or redevelopment of an area will almost inevitably alter with the lapse of time if only in order to accommodate requirements which hitherto were unforeseen. The accommodation of the requirements of the highway authority in the present case is a good example of the process of change.[69]
>
> The means of achieving the expressed purpose had plainly changed between making and confirmation from an office development to a road improvement but in my judgment the expressed and actual purpose remained constant.[70]

A different conclusion had been reached in the earlier, in some respects similar, case of *Meravale Builders Ltd v Secretary of State for the Environment and Another.*[71] In this case it was proposed to use Part V of the Housing Act 1957 to acquire land in order to construct 450–600 houses. However, the scheme included a proposal to use part of the land to allow the highway authority (also the housing authority) to construct an extension of an interchange to a major road, thus creating a through route between the major road and the city. Wills J concluded that Part V of the Housing Act 1957 included

> Powers to provide such accommodation include powers to provide such facilities for the residents as the Secretary of State considers beneficial, and if land has been acquired as a site for houses under section 96(a) the housing authority may construct on it "public streets or roads" [s. 107]. The question at once arises: is that a power without limitation, or is some restriction to be inferred limiting the power to construct roads to those which are reasonably necessary to the proper lay-out of any land acquired as a site for housing?[72]

In view of references in subsequent sections to the construction of streets and road "for the purposes of the operations" he concluded that the power was indeed limited by implication to roads that must fairly and reasonably relate to the provision of housing accommodation. On the facts the local authority could not have been compelled to construct this road as a condition of being allowed to construct the houses, and accordingly

> ...it seems to me impossible to say that the acquisition of the land for constructing the Glen Road extension was reasonably and fairly incidental to the provision of housing accommodation. The purpose, which the authorities have never for a moment sought to conceal, was to construct on the land a road which would serve a function independent of the provision of housing accommodation, namely a principal traffic route link between the built-up area to the north and east of the city and the Plympton by-pass. That was a purpose for which, in my judgment, the Plymouth City Council had no powers under Part V of the Act of 1957. Since the order was made for a purpose which was in part, albeit a relatively small part, not within the council's powers, the confirmation was not in my view within the powers of the Secretary of State and the order must be quashed.[73]

In essence the local authority was attempting to extract a sort of planning gain from themselves in the form of "two birds with one stone" – planning gain is thus a recurring theme.

Reasons and transparency

Not only must there be broadly a legitimate purpose for compulsory purchase in principle, there must also be a compelling case in the circumstances of the case for the exercise of compulsory purchase powers – Lord Denning in *Prest*. In order to allow those affected to evaluate the merits of a decision and whether it is susceptible to legal challenge, the decision-maker must give those affected adequate reasons for the decision. Under Section 23(2) of the Acquisition of Land Act 1981 a CPO can be challenged by virtue of a failure to address a relevant requirement. A "relevant requirement" includes any requirement of rules made under the Tribunals and Inquiries Act 1992. As the Compulsory Purchase (Inquiries Procedure) Rules 2007 were made under the Tribunals and Inquiries Act 1992 and include a duty to give reasons, the duty to give reasons is consequently a "relevant requirement". In *South Bucks District Council and another v Porter (No 2)*[74] Lord Brown outlined the duty to give reasons in the (analogous) context of planning decisions:

> The reasons for a decision must be intelligible and they must be adequate. They must enable the reader to understand why the matter was decided as it was and what conclusions were reached on the "principal important controversial issues", disclosing how any issue of law or fact was resolved. Reasons can be briefly stated, the degree of particularity required depending entirely on the nature of the issues falling for decision. The reasoning must not give rise to a substantial doubt as to whether the decision-maker erred in law, for example by misunderstanding some relevant policy or some other important matter or by failing to reach a rational decision on relevant grounds. But such adverse inference will not readily be drawn. The reasons need refer only to the main issues in the dispute, not to every material consideration. They should enable disappointed developers to assess their prospects of obtaining some alternative development permission, or, as the case may be, their unsuccessful opponents to understand how the policy or approach underlying the grant of permission may impact upon future such applications. Decision letters must be read in a straightforward manner, recognising

that they are addressed to parties well aware of the issues involved and the arguments advanced. A reasons challenge will only succeed if the party aggrieved can satisfy the court that he has genuinely been substantially prejudiced by the failure to provide an adequately reasoned decision.[75]

The courts will not be concerned that the decision-maker came to the *"right"* conclusion, simply that they considered the correct factors – material considerations – and the basis of the decision must therefore be clear. This can be problematic where, in the context of confirming a CPO, the Secretary of State comes to a different conclusion from the inspector who has chaired the public inquiry, an issue that has recently been addressed by the Court of Appeal in *James Joseph Horada (On Behalf of the Shepherd's Bush Market Tenants' Association) & Others v Secretary of State for Communities and Local Government and Others*.[76] In this case the local authority had approved a planning application for the redevelopment of Shepherd's Bush Market and then exercised its powers of compulsory purchase under Section 226 of the TCPA 1990 to make a CPO for the purposes of acquiring the site for the developer. In this case, with over 200 objections the Secretary of State was required to hold a public inquiry chaired by a planning inspector prior to consideration of whether to confirm the CPO. Under Section 226 (1A) a local authority must not exercise this compulsory purchase power:

> … unless they think that the development, re-development or improvement is likely to contribute to the achievement of any one or more of the following objects—
>
> a the promotion or improvement of the economic well-being of their area;
> b the promotion or improvement of the social well-being of their area;
> c the promotion or improvement of the environmental well-being of their area.

On the evidence presented over 10 days of the public inquiry the planning inspector concluded that the proposed development failed to sufficiently satisfy these criteria in a number of respects, and her report recommended that the CPO should therefore not be confirmed. Nevertheless, the Secretary of State subsequently declined to follow the recommendation of the inspector and confirmed the CPO. The issue before the Court of Appeal was the extent to which the Secretary of State needed to provide reasons for departing from the recommendation of the inspector. Lewison LJ noted that in the context of confirming a CPO the Secretary of State (and not the inspector) was the decision-maker and thus it could not be said that he was conducting an appeal or review of the inspector's decision. Nevertheless, while there was a reluctance to impose a standard that a Secretary of State would have to meet when disagreeing with an inspector, the key issues were:

i *Did the Secretary of State correctly identify the principal important controversial issues, and if so*
ii *Did he give adequate reasons for disagreeing with the inspector?*

How these apply in any given case will often turn on the specific facts of the case. However, in *Horada* the inspector had, in essence, considered that the expressed objective of the local authority was to provide "the requisite financial as well as physical conditions for an independent, small-scale, diverse and ethnic mix of traders and shopkeepers to continue trading at the market… as far as possible *during* and *after* the redevelopment process".[77] Having reviewed the relevant planning conditions and the content of Section 106 planning obligation that were designed to meet this objective, she took the view that a level of certainty was provided during the construction period but that no certainty was offered thereafter because one of the key measures, a rent freeze for existing stall holders, would end at this point and because there was no indication of the proposed size, form or location of replacement stalls which would, in turn, affect rents, economic viability and thus the future of the existing businesses. The Secretary of State in his decision letter simply considered that "sufficient safeguards are in place" and that "the council will ensure" that the relevant policy requirements would be met. This was not adequate:

> In short, although it is clear that the Secretary of State disagreed with the inspector's view that the guarantees and safeguards were inadequate he does not explain why he came to that conclusion. I do not consider that requiring a fuller explanation of his reasoning either amounts to requiring reasons for reasons, or that it requires a paragraph by paragraph rebuttal of the inspector's views. But it does require the Secretary of State to explain why he disagreed with the inspector, beyond merely stating his conclusion that he did. The two critical sentences in the decision letter are, in my judgment, little more than "bald assertions". The Secretary of State may have had perfectly good reasons for concluding that the guarantees and safeguards were adequate. The problem is that we do not know what they were. In those circumstances I consider that the traders have been substantially prejudiced by a failure to comply with a relevant requirement.[78]

A key argument by counsel for the developer had been that the Secretary of State's decision letter had to be considered as being addressed to a well-informed readership, who would have been aware of the reasoning behind the recommendation of the inspector, and thus by implication the reasoning of the Secretary of State, in coming to a different conclusion. Lewison LJ, however, considered that in this case the readership would have to have been "not only well-informed but also psychic".[79] Lord Thomas of Cwmgiedd, CJ summarised the position as follows:

> 57 I also agree. I add a short observation to underline how important it is that reasons for decisions should be explained in terms the citizen affected can understand. Although the citizen can be taken to know the factual background and in this sense be well informed, the citizen affected by a decision is entitled to an explanation of the reasons in plain English which the citizen can understand.
>
> 58 It is very easy for any expert, whether the person be a lawyer or other professional, to speak in terms that are familiar to other experts in the field. That is, however, not a permissible approach when explaining the reasons for a decision to others, however well informed those others may be in the sense I have described. Experts must therefore guard against speaking in terms which can only be understood through the intermediary of a lawyer or other professional.
>
> 59 In this case, it was particularly important that a proper and easy to understand explanation be given by the Secretary of State for rejecting the Inspector's recommendation. The livelihoods of the traders are put at risk by the proposed development. The Inspector has given her reasons on a matter of vital concern to the traders in a way that could readily be understood by them. The Secretary of State must explain his decision in the same readily understandable way.[80]

Conclusion

In considering the legal context of takings it becomes clear that the statutory requirement for a clear public purpose has become further enshrined by case law, and that the definition of this has been regularly tested, notably in terms of public takings to facilitate private schemes. Concerns regarding such "public to private" deals have led to considerable scrutiny of the planning process which frequently "abuts" the issue of compulsory acquisition, notably the issues of "planning gain" which can range from provision of specific on-site public goods, through off-site public goods to cash payments to authorities with little direct hypothecation. Such developer contributions raise serious concerns regarding the validity of the processes – particularly where they constitute "bids" in an eventual "bargain" which may prejudice directly affected parties. This interaction between market forces and state actors, often with considerable economic interests involved, also "trips" concerns relating to the wider regulations concerning State aid to industry, which need careful consideration on the part of public authorities to overcome as they attempt to foster economic activity and provide vital public infrastructure. Finally, the operation of such fundamental state powers – closely examined in both written and unwritten constitutions internationally – requires full clarity concerning the justification of use – to the understanding of the everyday person who is often directly affected by such schemes – coining the adage that, in terms of the operation of public takings, justice must not only be done, but must be seen to be done.

Notes

1 Though potentially, in time of war, the Crown retains prerogative powers to expropriate property without statutory authority for defence of the realm. Cf. Burmah Oil Co Ltd v Lord Advocate [1964] AC 75.
2 Certain private or local Acts of Parliament both authorise the acquisition of land and specify the land to be taken.
3 For convenience, this chapter focuses on the law and procedure as it applies in England but will make reference, where relevant, to specific differences in the other constituent parts of the United Kingdom.
4 Certain private or local Acts of Parliament both authorise the acquisition of land and specify the land to be taken, for example, the Channel Tunnel Act 1987.
5 In Northern Ireland, Article 87(1) of the Planning (NI) Order 1991 enables the acquiring authority to acquire most land either compulsorily or by agreement. Where acquisition is to be by compulsory means then the acquiring authority must also comply with the general procedural framework laid out in Schedule 6 of the Local Government Act (NI) 1972 (as amended) for making a vesting order. Paragraph 6(1) of Schedule 6 provides:
…a Vesting Order shall operate, without further assurance, to vest in the council, as from the date on which the Vesting Order becomes operative (in this Schedule referred to as "the date of vesting"), an estate in fee simple or such other estate (if any) in, to or over the land to which it relates as is therein specified, freed and discharged from all claims or estates whatsoever (except as is specified in the order).
6 See: Thomas Murphy, John McCord and Peadar Davis, 'Property Law and Planning in Northern Ireland' in: Stephen McKay and Michael Murray (eds) Planning Law and Practice in Northern Ireland (Routledge, 2017), pp. 206–246.
7 (1982) 81 LGR 193.
8 For a detailed consideration of the subject in its entirety in the UK context, see Barry Denyer-Green, Compulsory Purchase and Compensation (10th edition, EG Books, 2013); Michael Barnes, The Law of Compulsory Purchase and Compensation (Hart Publishing, 2014) or Guy Roots QC, James Pereira, Michael Humphries and Robert Fookes, The Law of Compulsory Purchase (2nd edition, Bloomsbury Professional, 2008).
9 545 US 469 (2005) (Sup Ct (US)).
10 (2007) SC (HL) 33.

11 [2011] 1 AC 437.
12 (1866) LR 1 HL 34.
13 At 45.
14 [1990] 1 QB 87 at 122.
15 (2007) SC (HL) 33 at para 75.
16 [1958] 1 QB 554 at 572 (reversed on other grounds [1960] AC 260).
17 [1981] AC 578.
18 A reasoning or decision is Wednesbury unreasonable (or irrational) if it is so unreasonable that no reasonable person acting reasonably could have made it. (*Associated Provincial Picture Houses Ltd v Wednesbury Corporation* [1948] 1 KB 223).
19 See, for example, *R v Hillingdon London Borough Council*, ex parte Royco Homes Ltd [1974] 2 QB 720.
20 [2000] JPL 726.
21 [2000] PLCR 157.
22 *Ladbrokes Ltd v Secretary of State* [1981] JPL 427.
23 *Grampian Regional District Council v Aberdeen District Council* (1983) 47 P&CR 633.
24 [1964] 1 WLR 240.
25 *Bradford Metropolitan Council v Secretary of State for the Environment* (1987) 53 P&CR 55.
26 *Times Investments Ltd v Secretary of State for the Environment* [1990] JPL 433.
27 [1981] AC 578.
28 67 P&CR 78.
29 [1981] AC 578.
30 [1995] 1 WLR 759.
31 [1995] 1 WLR 759, 764, 770.
32 [1995] 1 WLR 759, 770.
33 [1995] 1 WLR 759, 782.
34 Planning Act 2008, Section 208. Section 209 provides that Regulations may specify exceptions.
35 [2014] EWHC 67 (Admin); [2014] Env LR 21 (QBD (Admin)).
36 (1866) LR 1 HL 34, 43.
37 (1982) 81 LGR 193, 198.
38 [2011] 1 AC 437.
39 [2006] UKHL 50; (2007) SC (HL) 33.
40 State aid is a wide subject with a number of practitioner texts devoted entirely to the subject. For an authoritative consideration of State aid issues which are specifically relevant to the planning and compulsory purchase context, see: James Maurici QC and Heather Sargent, 'State aid in planning and compulsory purchase order cases', (2015) Journal of Planning & Environment Law 621.
41 Gianni Lo Schiavo, 'The role of competition analysis under Article 107 Paragraph 1 TFEU: the emergence of a "market analysis" assessment within the selectivity criterion?' (2013) European Competition Law Review400.
42 James Maurici QC and Heather Sargent, 'State aid in planning and compulsory purchase order cases' (2015) Journal of Planning & Environment Law 621, 635.
43 [1997] OJ C209/03. Note that the Communication applies only to the sale of publicly owned land and buildings; it does not apply to the acquisition, letting or leasing of land and buildings by public authorities, which transactions may also meet the TFEU Art.107(1) criteria.
44 See: *Seydaland Vereinigte Agrarbetriebe GmbH v BVVG Bodenverwertungs-und-verwaltungs GmbH* (C-239/09) [2011] 2 CMLR 24 at para [39]. See also: *R. (on the application of Lidl (UK) GmbH) v Swale BC* [2001] EWHC Admin 405, at para [18].
45 *Italy v Commission* (T-53/08) [2010] ECR II-3187. See also: See: *Commission v Netherlands* (C-279/08) [2011] ECR I-7671.
46 *R. (on the application of Bow Street Mall)* [2006] NIQB 28.
47 Ibid., at [83]–[86].
48 *Brown v Carlisle CC* [2014] EWHC 707 (Admin).
49 Ibid., at [58].
50 See also: see *Muller v Bundesamt etc* (C-451/08), [2010] 3 CMLR 18 where, at [57] the court observed, "It is not the purpose of the mere exercise of urban-planning powers, intended to give effect to the public interest, to obtain a contractual service or immediate economic benefit for the contracting authority ...".

51 James Maurici QC and Heather Sargent, 'State aid in planning and compulsory purchase order cases', (2015) Journal of Planning & Environment Law 621, 635.
52 Ibid.
53 A useful explication of the case law is provided by Collins J in *Brown v Carlisle CC* [2014] EWHC 707 (Admin).
54 See: s.233(8).
55 [2001] EWHC Admin 457.
56 Douglas Maxwell, 'Article 1 of the First Protocol: a paper tiger in the face of compulsory purchase orders for private profit?' (2017) Journal of Planning and Environment Law 1337.
57 (1866) LR 1 HL 34.
58 At 43.
59 At 45.
60 [1964] AC 1088.
61 At 1122.
62 At 1126.
63 At 1127.
64 [2017] 1 WLR 373.
65 [2017] 1 WLR 373,389.
66 Ibid., at para [165].
67 Ibid., at para [158].
68 (1992) 63 P&CR 317.
69 At 326, per Mann LJ.
70 At 326, per Mann LJ.
71 (1978) 36 P&CR 87.
72 At 94.
73 At 95.
74 [2004] UKHL 33, [2004] 1 WLR 1953.
75 At [36].
76 [2016] EWCA Civ 169.
77 At [30].
78 At 54.
79 At 49.
80 At 57–59.

10

The impacts of land acquisition and resettlement activities of infrastructure investments on natural and cultural heritage and social and economic life

The case of Turkey

Harun Tanrıvermiş and Yeşim Aliefendioğlu

Introduction

Expropriation of real estate [land, buildings and easement rights (or servitudes)] is the process by which the government takes possession of private real estate for the public good or for the greater interest of the country. In general, the legal system provides the state with the right to take real estate for public use and benefit. This includes eminent domain, compulsory purchase, and expropriation based upon public interest (Atahar 2013). In fact, it is the power of sovereignty that justifies the taking over of real estate by the government under the principle of eminent domain in many countries (Atahar 2013; Maitra 2009; Viitanen and Kakulu 2009). The foundation of ownership of real estate within Turkey is defined in Art. 35, and the provisions for land acquisition and expropriation are mentioned in Art. 46 of the Constitution of the Turkish Republic; the framework of ownership is defined in Civil Law No. 4721, and the principles and practices of expropriation are contained in the Expropriation Act No 2942.

Real estate ownership and use, interference in the ownership status of real estate, realisation of investments in infrastructure, and the regulation of settlements are comprehensively regulated by the Constitution, Expropriation Law No. 2942 and Settlement Law No. 5543. Public investments are carried out through the expropriation of private real estate, involving the payment of the value of private real estate. Rural and urban settlements are thereby established, and the properties necessary for public services are acquired. In principle, the expropriation and resettlement processes in infrastructure investments should be carried out together. The construction and operation phases of infrastructure projects that divide lands and settlements adversely affect transport and other links between lands and settlements. Therefore, projects requiring the acquisition of a high number of large parcels and settlements which are vacated as a result of a disaster or health and security risks must be physically reconsidered within the scope of resettlement.

In Turkey, resettlement activities are conducted for a variety of reasons such as disasters, infrastructure investments, security, health, and the reorganisation of settlements. The acquisition of large quantities of real estate required for the implementation of development projects (such as dams, airports, motorways, industrial zones, industrial parks, urban development and the transformation of areas) is usually carried out by methods such as expropriation, purchase, servitude and renting. The requirement to implement the standard method of expropriation in real estate acquisition for infrastructure projects, to analyse the post-expropriation changes in the economic and social situation of the households affected by the project, as well as the potential changes in the natural environment, constitutes the main themes of the resettlement policy. Competent authorities may need to resettle communities as part of a land acquisition process to acquire land for a business project, and in almost all cases, owners and users are opposed to the land acquisition (Atahar 2013). Land acquisition for large infrastructure projects in almost all localities may affect the assets and the quality of life of the people living in the areas in question in a positive and/or negative way (Aliefendioğlu and Tanrıvermiş 2016; ENCON Co. 2005; İSTEM Co. 2009). In line with international requirements and domestic demands, resettlement practices tend to become the main element of the investment decision, project development, and implementation stages in many countries.

The first regulation on settlement works in Turkey was made by Law No. 2510 dated 21 June 1934, pre-dating those of many other countries. Certain amendments were made to this legislation in 1970 by Law No. 1306, and the basis of the changes was the offering of settlement opportunities to families who had lost their means of living and production. Law No. 5543 was enacted on 26 September 2006, replacing Law No. 2510 because of its ineffective implementation. With Law No. 5543, principles of application and precautions to be taken, resettlement rights and liabilities which related to immigrants and nomads, those whose real estate rights are expropriated, security and disaster risks, settlement activities that should be undertaken in areas with disaster risks, the physical arrangement of settlements in villages, as well as the resettlement rights and obligations of those who have been resettled were rearranged.

By incorporating legal regulations, international standards, and scientific principles, resettlement can be viewed as the planning, implementation, and monitoring/evaluation work that must be carried out with the formation of an interdisciplinary working team and with the participation of many public and private institutions (Özkalaycı and İçten, 2005; Tanrıvermiş and Doğru 2004). However, it is noteworthy that the country's legislation and standards differ in the approaches to the issue and their means of implementation. Despite the legal and institutional frameworks establishing resettlement activities, and the institutionalisation of the subject completed for purposes such as health, disaster, and security risks, the construction of public projects, the regulation of migrants and village settlements, settlement projects, and impact assessment work were often neglected until the 1970s (Aliefendioğlu and Tanrıvermiş 2016). As a result of the neglect of legal instruments and the weakness of sanctions, the difficulties of public institutions working together, and adopted public policy for these purposes, only projects financed by external loans have been successful. Public institutions have preferred to carry out the acquisition of real estate through expropriation for many infrastructure projects, despite the high financial burden of the process, for such reasons as the existence of the legal basis of the practice, relative ease of application, the use of the purchase method, and fast results which can be achieved if preparations are done well. However, a system for analysing the income and living conditions of the households affected by the project in the pre- and post-project periods and a monitoring and evaluation system have not been established, and activities aimed at mitigating the negative socioeconomic effects have been neglected. Moreover, even when the value of the expropriated real estate has been paid in full, people in rural areas, who have no income and livelihood other than crop and livestock farming, tend to consume the expropriation money they receive for nonproductive outcomes and in a short time., As a result the families who have lost their land and other means of production settle in the suburbs of large cities and cause great social problems (Aliefendioğlu and Tanrıvermiş 2016; Tanrıvermiş and Doğru 2004).

In the context of physical resettlement, it is inevitable that the economic and social structures of the households whose settlements have been involuntarily changed will be negatively affected. It is also noticeable that large-scale resettlement works inevitably affect the cultural life that had been established some years ago. While no funds were allocated for the protection of natural and cultural assets in general, especially in the infrastructure investments built in the pre-1990 period, it is noteworthy that since the 1990s, the protection of natural and cultural assets has been given special importance with the enactment of Environment Law No. 2872 in 1983; Law No. 2863 on the Protection of Cultural and Natural Assets in 1983; Law No. 5366 on Renovation, Protection, and Survival of Historic and Cultural Immovable Properties in 2005; and the Enforcement of the Environmental Impact Assessment Regulation in 1993. Until the last three decades, the completion of large-scale fixed capital investments in as short a time and at the lowest cost possible was accepted as the basic philosophy. However, after the 1990s, in line with the enacting of environmental protection legislation and the increasing environmental awareness of the people, it has been found that resources are now reserved for the preservation of movable and immovable cultural assets through environmental impact assessment studies and the preparation and implementation of action plans to mitigate the adverse effects of the projects.

In this study, the principles of land acquisition and resettlement for public investments are examined. The impacts of infrastructure investments on natural and cultural assets, especially projects built for basic purposes such as energy, irrigation, the supply of drinking and utility water, and for socioeconomic life, are evaluated in the second stage. Moreover, resettlement practices and activities in selected large-scale fixed-capital investments have been examined in terms of legislation, international standards and the loss of the natural and cultural assets they cause. Approaches of efficient planning and the implementation of large-scale infrastructure projects that avoid, or at least minimise, the losses of natural, economic, social, and cultural assets as far as possible, and a critical analysis of existing policies, have been undertaken. In addition, resettlement action plans in projects financed by international organisations and the possibilities for developing similar action plans for projects financed with national resources have been evaluated. Also, by considering the outlines of this study, the dilemma existing between national polices for natural and cultural asset protection on the one hand and the preferences for investing in public infrastructure, key issues in resettlement policies, practices, issues, analysis, and solutions on the other is discussed.

Implementations of real estate acquisition, expropriation, and resettlement, and issues in infrastructure investments

Real estate acquisition methods and expropriation for infrastructure investments

Different methods are used to acquire properties for infrastructure investments in Turkey. Among the acquisition methods that cause a change of real estate ownership and require registration are expropriation, purchase, donation, exchange or swap, land consolidation, zoning application, and the establishment of a servitude. Almost all of these methods are regulated by different laws. For example, public procurement and land acquisition are both regulated by the Public Procurement Act No. 4734 (Article 22/e – direct procurement) and the Expropriation Act No. 2942 (Article 8 – expropriation by purchasing method), but the process of acquisitions and valuation works within the context of these regulations is also different. Apart from the methods listed in the first group, it is possible to acquire land with processes such as allocation (temporary or indefinite), leasing (up to 10 years), provisional occupation or the establishment of a servitude (up to 10 years), and an administrative servitude, and such acquisition does not require registration or a change of ownership.

Expropriation is the compulsory purchase of privately owned real estate through procedures defined in legislation in order to enable the provision of public services aimed at the public interest, in exchange for compensation (either as a one-off payment or in instalments if the necessary conditions are met). For expropriation, first the relevant administration makes a public interest resolution; afterward, the identification and inventory of real estate to be acquired are undertaken. Scaled plans including the boundaries, area, and type of the real estate to be expropriated are prepared, and thus the part to be expropriated is determined. In places where a cadastre exists, whether or not the deed registry record reflects the real estate, it is investigated, the data regarding the real estate (such as place, volume, page, parcel number, and area in title deed) are put onto the plan. Once the public benefit resolution is adopted, the scaled plan is prepared, addresses of the owners determined, and sufficient funds are provided by the administration. Acquisition of the land is made by the method established within the administration, and at a valuation set by a valuation commission, and the expropriation of land is made through negotiations with the land owner. The determination and valuation of properties where negotiations with the owner have been unsuccessful, or where properties are repossessed, are carried out by the experts appointed by the court. In land acquisition and expropriation, there are various methods such as (full) expropriation, partial expropriation, expropriation through exchange, urgent expropriation and the creation of a servitude, as well as reimbursement, and payment is based on the same principles.

In cases where expropriation cannot be made through the procurement procedure, the relevant public institution makes an application with the information gathered and documents (Art. 7) to the local court where the real estate is located to determine its value, pay the determined value up-front (or in instalments if the conditions are met (Art. 3)), and have the real estate registered in the name of the administration (Art. 10). Determination of the price and the registration process are usually completed within 1–2 years. Because of the length of this process, many public institutions prefer to have resolutions passed by the Council of Ministers for urgent expropriation, and thus enable confiscation of the real estate within a maximum of one month (Art. 27). Investments for public purposes begin with the resolution and the cost determination, and registration hearings are carried out simultaneously with the construction process.

In the Turkish Legal System, the value of the expropriated real estate is paid only to the owner and possessors, if any, and it is not possible to pay those who occupy and use public land (Tanrıvermiş and Doğru 2004). There are significant problems in the determination of real estate, its classification according to usage patterns, type (rural or farmland or urban lot) analysis, and the valuation processes. According to the legislation, it is necessary to determine the total expropriation value of farmland by using the income capitalisation method, the market value of the urban plot, and a cost analysis of buildings as well as the values of trees and crops, if any. The expropriation values calculated according to the income method for land in rural areas are generally lower than the market values of the land and buildings, and it is not possible for the owners to replace the acquired asset with the amount of money paid (Tanrıvermiş and Aliefendioğlu 2011, 2015). However, international standards require land-to-land compensation or in-kind payment and full replacement cost of assets to be paid as an indemnity (ADB 1998; IFC 2001, 2012; The World Bank 2002; Tagliarino 2016).

Problems such as the quality of valuations, the inadequacies of technology, paucity of qualified specialists and resources, the length of time that lawsuits take, and the fact that they often end with decisions against public institutions are adversely affecting both the satisfaction levels of the owners and the land acquisition process for the project. On the other hand, the central land acquisition and resettlement policy of international financial institutions is to compensate all owners (users, tenants, partners and occupants of rangelands, forests, and water resources), and to use the full replacement cost approach in valuation and compensation processes for the financing of investments, regardless of the legal claims on the real estate (IFC 2012; The World Bank 2002). The process of expropriation and resettlement according to international standards was implemented for the first time in Turkey in the Baku-Tbilisi-Ceyhan Crude Oil Pipeline Project, and this provided considerable experience in adapting international standards to domestic conditions, and, as a result, the sensitivity of public administrators in this area has increased (Aliefendioğlu and Tanrıvermiş 2016). Although it has frequently been argued that in many projects land acquisition and resettlement in accordance with international standards adversely affects the feasibility of projects, and despite the payment of compensation at international standards in the said projects, the share of land acquisition in the total cost was limited to only 7.04%, and according to the Turkish Legal System the said share saw an increase of only 1.5–2.0 points.

Assessment of resettlement: practices and legislation

When displaced by projects, a people, often lose almost everything, from livelihoods to kinship ties, even their identity (Mathur 2016). The term "settlement" is used to describe the provision of housing to meet the social, cultural, and economic needs of a household and the provision of financial income to sustain and improve their lives. Development projects are implemented in rural areas, and families in these areas earn their living through crop production and livestock farming. As a result, it is necessary to prepare resettlement plans with the contribution of many institutions and disciplines, and with the aim of providing the households affected by the development projects, put into practice for public benefit and even the benefit of society, with the same level of income and living conditions they enjoyed before the project, and of minimising the social and psychological problems. In these circumstances, resettlement policies require that a resettlement action plan be prepared to rebuild their shattered lives.

In Turkey, implementation principles of consolidation and the regulation of the physical settlement of immigrants coming from abroad, (such as people whose land was expropriated, nomads, villages whose locations were changed for national security reasons), were outlined first in the Settlement Act No. 2510 dated 14 June 1934 and later in the Settlement Act No. 5543 dated 26 September 2006. Resettlement and the reinstatement of the former standard of living of those who are obliged to leave their homes is compulsory according to Law No. 5543. Under international standards, involuntary resettlements may be either physical or economic or both at the same time. Physical displacement is the actual physical relocation of people, resulting in a loss of shelter, productive assets, or access to productive assets (such as land, water, and forests). Economic displacement results from an action that interrupts or eliminates people's access to productive assets without physically relocating the people themselves (IFC 2001, 2012). However, both the Acts No. 2510 and No. 5543 only deal with physical resettlement, and exclude economic resettlement, which includes compensation for the changed economic and social structure and access to income sources caused by the acquisition of real estate for the project. Only within the scope of the Regulation on the Expropriation of Real Estate Adjacent to the Expropriation Site in Expropriations for the Construction of Dams, published in the Official Gazette dated 6 August 1985, is expropriation of adjacent properties possible after the formation of the lake area, in cases where the social, economic, or settlement order of the area is worsened or cannot be utilised economically and socially. This only occurs if the applicant applies to the relevant authority and the situation is verified as a result of on-site inspection after the affected person decides to apply to the court. Apart from these, it should be emphasised that the evaluation of requests for economic resettlement can only be possible if the project is carried out according to international standards, the loan agreement is approved by the Turkish Parliament, and the land acquisition in the agreement is specifically made in accordance with international standards.

According to Act No. 5543, agricultural and nonagricultural settlement work can be carried out by the government, and the settlements are transferred by means of loans for the affected houses. The scope of the main applications and implementation principles according to the legislation are briefly explained in the following section.

The settlement of persons whose real estate is expropriated

Because of the construction of dams and hydropower plants, areas adjacent to dams, protection areas, airports, roads, railways, industrial and commercial establishments, economic and defence-related facilities, the preservation of historical and natural assets, or the application of special laws by public institutions and organizations: (i) households that have to leave their land as a result of their land being partially or totally expropriated; and (ii) in the case of households who settled on the expropriation site at least three years before the beginning of the calendar year in which the settlement work started are resettled at places determined by the Ministry of Environment and Urbanisation, if they so demand. However, households who have abandoned their land before the beginning of the settlement planning studies and have land to be expropriated cannot be resettled. Within three years retroactively from this date, households who disposed of real estate without a compelling reason and who do not purchase real estate at equivalent or greater value are not resettled, even if they have left their houses.

Those who are settled in areas expropriated by public institutions and organisations, and are affected by the expropriation, but do not want to be resettled somewhere else by the State, can be resettled within their village boundaries by the Ministry upon written application and with the agreement of the relevant governor and the assent of the Ministry of Interior. In cases where entitled families do not agree to be settled at the places indicated by the Ministry, their status of entitlement is cancelled by the Local Settlement Commission. However, in this process, it is observed that only occupants of real estate and residents of dwellings affected by the project in the last three years are covered. This approach contradicts international standards in terms of scope.

Physical settlement arrangement

The arrangement of physical settlements in rural areas is achieved according to plans and projects prepared in accordance with the settlement legislation for (i) the relocation of villages that cannot be developed *in situ* because of the inconvenience of the location and settlement units that are found to be costly for infrastructure services to a more convenient location; (ii) the consolidation of neighbourhoods, suburbs, hamlets, and the like scattered within one or multiple willing village or village boundaries at a new location; (iii) additions to the new settlement area on the request of households not exposed to the disaster in disaster-affected villages; (iv) the preparation and confirmation of the plans for the villagers to be removed, consolidated, and the improvement in the physical settlement and the selling of land to eligible beneficiaries from areas reserved according to the approved village development plans; (v) researching the types of residential buildings, farm buildings, social facilities and settlement models suitable for the climate, social and economic conditions of the country, the building materials, facilities and the preparation of the projects in the form of technical assistance and giving them to the willing villagers and the provision for them of social, cultural, administrative, the economic construction of buildings and facilities and in-village infrastructure; and (vi) in villages where transfer, consolidation, and physical settlement improvement services are completed, loan services to households who sold reserve land, and those building their own houses.

In cases of necessity, cash loans can be given for housing and business premises, with the borrowing conditions to the eligible families as set out according to the principles and procedures stated in the Regulation on Settlement Law Implementation published in the Official Gazette dated 2 December 2007. The purpose of the loan is to support the construction of residential and commercial buildings in the planned settlement area, and the loan instalments to be used according to the construction level are determined by the Ministry. It is possible to give credits for residences, agricultural buildings, and facilities on the condition that they do not exceed 120 m² (1,290 square feet), and a maximum of two types of projects can be implemented in the same settlement, with a commitment to abiding by the provisions of the plan and project, and with an allowance for controlled use.

Special facilities are available for the purposes of ensuring development in villages, encouraging consolidation, transfer to suitable settlements, the consolidation of villages fragmented for any reason or neighbouring villages and improvement of physical settlement, the application of a village development area adjacent to the village centre, the establishment of planned central village settlements, the development of regional architectural structures and modernisation, those who have been living in the village for at least one year and considered as families. Where these conditions are confirmed by investigations carried out by the Governor or District Governor, such people can purchase land in the planned new settlement location. The size of land to be sold will be large enough to cover needs like housing, stables, and barns for a farming household but shall not exceed 2,000 m² (21,500 square feet).

In villages where implementation was carried out according to the Act No. 7269 (for Assistance to be Provided due to Disasters Affecting Public Life dated 15 May 1959), the holdings of families who stay in their old settlements can be consolidated within the administrative boundaries of the village. However, if the implementation is carried out (in accordance with Act No. 7269) outside the administrative borders of the village, the holdings of the remaining household members may be consolidated in the centre of the village it has become a part of, or in the new settlement, where the entitled households are settled (in accordance with the Law no 7269), in the event of the village's legal entity having been abolished. In the transfer, consolidation, and implementation of the village development area, to be carried out under the law in order to develop a central settlement, housing, farm infrastructures, and other buildings and facilities can be constructed by the State, provided that 30 or more members of the village accept the necessary loans. If the construction of residences and farm buildings by the State is not accepted, or if the number of the house-holds is less than 30, separate loans to be determined by the approval of the Minister can be issued to a minimum of five families for the construction of residences and farm buildings and infrastructures.

Real estate that may be used for resettlement (under the Settlement Act No. 5543) cannot be selected from land within military jurisdictions nor from security zones designated for the purposes of the provisions of special laws or the Military Forbidden Zones and Security Zones Act dated 18 December 1981 and No. 2565 and those allocated for national security purposes. However, in case of necessity, such real estate can be used in accordance with the advice of the relevant institutions. However, in the case of settlement implementations to be carried out in special project areas (determined by the Council of Ministers) identified because of disaster risk or in conflict with science, arts, and health laws, the settlement of the families living in the areas in more favourable locations or within the scope of a return to the village projects, forest, or pasture land (determined by the Council of Ministers) on the basis of the rights and obligations set forth in the Decision of the Council of Ministers for the relevant project can be carried out at locations in the private ownership of the Treasury or at new settlements deemed suitable under the jurisdiction and disposition of the State.

Entitlement of nomad and migrant groups

Those not engaged in established agricultural activities and not dependent on a fixed and permanent residence, who make their living by immigrant livestock activities, who migrate between spring and summer pastures according to natural and climatic conditions, who have sustained this lifestyle for generations, who are related to one another, who carry out their animal breeding activities as a group and who are defined as nomadic families, are now entitled to resettlement.

This entitlement does not extend to the following: those who are in breach of the defini-tion (in clause (c) of Para. (3) of Article 3 of Act No. 5543); those who have settled themselves or been resettled as ancestors and household members in any manner by the State; those who have been provided with land; those who have assets other than livestock (according to definitions of nomads in the Law); those with a total value of these assets exceeding the total of 18 months of the gross amount of the monthly minimum wage in force at the date of the determination; those who do not reside in tents and similar environments and who live in any other dwellings, even if rented, in the months of November, December, January, or February; those who own dwellings; civil servants; contract workers; permanent and unemployed workers; short-term workers for seasonal wages, except for immigrant livestock and nonresident agricultural activities; those who are registered with the Social Security Institution; or who engaged in trade and income-generating businesses such as tradesmen, craftsmen, merchants, or are engaged in any business other than animal husbandry.

In the legislation, the concept of "immigrants" and their ownership of rights are also specially regulated. Settled immigrant families of Turkish descent who are affiliated with Turkish culture and come from abroad through special laws are now entitled to benefit from the legislation. However, those who are not deemed settled immigrants, following inves-tigations held (in line with sub-clauses (d) and (f) of Paragraph 1 of Art. 3 of the Act, and Paragraphs 3 and 4 of Art. 6), and those who did not request settlement within two years of arrival in Turkey (in accordance with Article 10), cannot be entitled. However, it should be emphasised that it is not possible to investigate the rights of over 3 million asylum seekers, especially Syrians in Turkey, within the scope of the legislation.

Ownership for the purposes of national security

Families who live in settlements that will be settled for the purposes of national security are also entitled to benefit from the resettlement provisions (in accordance with the terms and conditions stated in the decision of the Council of Ministers to be taken in accordance with Art. 13 of Act No. 5543). However, based on the Decision of the Council of Ministers, those who have not been registered as residents for at least one year before this date and who do not comply with the terms and conditions specified in the decision cannot be entitled to resettlement.

Resettlement implementation: types and problems

There are two main methods of resettlement in Turkey, according to legal regulations: government-assisted resettlement and village relocations through credit support. These main methods of settlement are described briefly in the following section.

Principles and procedures of government-assisted resettlement

According to the legislation, entitled households can be settled for agricultural or nonagricultural purposes. In determining the income levels of those who lose their livelihoods in the loss of their original settlements or who will be settled for agricultural and nonagricultural purposes, the qualifying basis is 18 times the gross amount of the monthly minimum wage in force for workers older than 16 years. In order to establish the fact that persons are obliged to abandon their real estate as a result of its expropriation, it is imperative that the settlement unit is fully expropriated or that the real estate of the particular household is expropriated if the settlement unit is partially expropriated. However, for those whose real estate is partially expropriated or those who own no real estate, their living standards and the conditions of the land not expropriated are taken into account and investigated by a technical delegation consisting of at least three persons from professions such as surveying, construction, agriculture engineering, or economics. Whether the interested parties will lose their livelihoods as a result of the expropriation of part of their land is determined through a unanimous vote, and implementations are carried out according to the report.

For those people forced to leave their settlements as a result of the expropriation of real estate, initially immigration acceptance centres or public buildings allocated by the relevant governorate are used in the provision of their accommodation. In the event that accommodation needs cannot be met in this way, rent allowance up to 30% of the 30-day gross monthly minimum wage in force for workers older than 16 years can be made for provisional accommodation, on an amount to be determined per household with the approval of the Minister.

As a result of investigations by the Ministries of Foreign Affairs and the Interior, the procedures for immigrants who are considered eligible, collectively eligible immigrants, and immigrants deemed to have settled are carried out under the supervision of the Ministry and the relevant governor. In addition, necessary measures shall be taken by the Ministry in order to meet the care, nutrition, and housing needs of immigrants accepted into the country as collective residents. The settlement of immigrants brought into the country according to special laws and considered to be settled is subject to the relevant provisions of the Law.

Accommodation, food, fuel, and medical assistance (provided under the third para. of Art. 9 of Act No. 5543) are met by the State from the date the immigrants crossed the country's border, or from the date of temporary acceptance of the resettlement for expropriation of the real estate by the State, in immigration acceptance centres or public buildings and facilities prepared by governorships in coordination with the Central Settlement Commission. In the event that these benefits cannot be provided in public buildings, outright monthly aid is provided to families in order to help them become productive for up to 12 months, starting from the date of entry into the country for immigrants, the date of temporary resettlement of those who had properties expropriated, and the transfer dates of those to be resettled for national security reasons and nomads.

The transport costs of families to be moved from old settlements to provisional and permanent settlement areas are covered by the State within the framework of the respective transportation projects. In addition to transportation costs, food expenses are paid per person. In return for real estate granted to the beneficiaries, debiting is done based on the expropriation or the purchase prices of the real estate, the construction costs for the structures, and fair market values for the Treasury's land. However, for real estate that has been expropriated, purchased, and developed for the purpose of settlement, and which has not been transferred or retrieved for whatever reason within a period of one year, debts are charged based on the fair values as at the date of the grant to new beneficiaries. The costs of infrastructure facilities in the settlement areas, economic, social, cultural, administrative, and common use facilities, facilities set up for similar purposes, and construction plans and technical assistance-type projects are not included in the debts.

From the amount of total debt calculated by adding the debt provided to the settled persons for real estate to equipment and operation loans issued and their interests, the expropriation compensation is deposited in the Central Accountancy Unit Account of the Ministry and updated according to rates of change in the minimum wage until the date the debt is deducted. If the deposited expropriation compensation is more than the total amount of the debt, the surplus is returned to the person concerned. If the specified amount of debt is more than the expropriation value deposited on behalf of the household, the remaining amount of debt is charged. The debts of the real estate given to those settled are to be collected with no interest over 15 years in 5 equal instalments, with the first instalment due in the 60th month following accrual of the debt.

The allocation of real estate given for the purpose of settlement is annotated accordingly in the title records of the real estate, with a note that for a period of 10 years from the date of assignment, it cannot be sold, donated, used as security for a loan, have the title annotated with a promise to sell, or repossessed. If the persons to be settled do not sign the loan agreement in person or by means of a representative within 60 days from the date of notification, their entitlement is revoked without any other conditions having to be met. However, in the event of there being documented compelling reasons why the signing has not taken place, (such as natural disasters, long-term treatment, detention, and similar cases), this period of time for signing the loan contract will start from the date these reasons have no longer apply. Families settled by the government are granted loans on demand, and the development of their economic activities is supported.

Village relocation with credit support

The village relocation with credit support method is the most preferred by those affected by the project and the institution responsible for resettlement. For this type of resettlement, a sufficient amount of land is allocated from the land owned by the relevant Ministry, and a development plan of the village concerned is prepared or commissioned. Social service facilities are constructed, and lots subdivided for each household from this land for residential buildings, agricultural structures and facilities are transferred to the beneficiaries for payment in advance or in five equal instalments over a maximum of five years. The most important difference between this method and settlement by the government is that affected families seeking resettlement have the opportunity to assess expropriation value for their real estate without any restrictions.

Types of resettlement and issues in implementation

The procedures and principles related to the identification, study, mapping operations, preparation of development plans, registration of plots, application procedures, and the announcement of land sales for new settlement areas are determined in accordance with the Ministry's instructions. Land within the new settlement area within the scope or provision of the State; the surplus land of one or more villages, towns, and cities which are in public use and whose purpose has changed; land generated by the drying of lakes and marshes and the infilling of rivers; land obtained by rehabilitation of alkaline, stony, and similar soils; and locations excluded from titles within the cadastre are registered in the name of the Treasury and made eligible for settlements.

In order to determine the fair value of real estate subject to loans and of real estate to be purchased, a valuation commission consisting of three technical personnel is established under the chair of the relevant provincial incumbent or a person to be appointed by them. In addition, a conciliation commission is appointed in accordance with the third paragraph of Art. 8 of the Expropriation Act dated 4 November 1983 No. 2942. If the real estate in the new settlement area is acquired or expropriated by the Ministry, the prices of the lands to be given to eligible families will be added to the values of roads, common areas, and areas reserved for social structures, and the entitled families will be debited based on the values in question.

If agricultural areas in the settlement areas are acquired by the Ministry through purchase or expropriation, the value of agricultural land to be given to eligible households will be calculated with the addition of in-field roads and areas for common use. The entitled families are debited based on these values. The values of land and lots acquired by the Ministry by means other than purchasing or expropriation are determined by the valuation commission. If the improvement, development, plotting, and application services to be provided for the settlement land and lots are made by purchasing services, such costs will be added to the total value.

In the legislation and in practice, two types of resettlements, namely, agricultural and urban, are achieved according to the demands of dwellings affected by public projects. The first is agricultural resettlement, and this type of implementation seeks to benefit farmers. Such individuals to be resettled must fall within one of the following: (i) their house or land is expropriated in its entirety while their livelihood was earned by farming, (ii) their land is wholly expropriated, but excluding their house, (iii) part of the land is expropriated while their livelihood is earned farming and there is a lack of opportunity to replace that livelihood in the un-expropriated land available, (iv) for those who make a living through partnership, tenancy, or agricultural labour, and whose house is expropriated, (v) their house is expropriated and they are unable to make a living with their un-expropriated land, (vi) those who do not have land and make a living through partnership or tenancy, and (vii) those who make a living as agricultural workers and have no real estate. If there is a demand from a household meeting one of these conditions, the necessary planning for their settlement in rural areas is undertaken.

The second is urban resettlement, where residents are resettled upon request in housing units built by the State. Those who will be resettled in urban areas must be (i) arts or crafts people with residences and workplaces in their expropriated real estate, (ii) arts or crafts people with workplaces on their expropriated land, (iii) arts and crafts people without a residence or workplace, (iv) farmers in areas where there is agricultural overpopulation and who want to be settled in urban areas, and farmers who cannot be provided with land to operate a farming household with a sufficient income, and (v) those who want to or have to learn a craft or occupation, and those who have a craft or occupation but wish to work in another.

Enforceability of Law No. 5543 requires a physical relocation along with a major reduction in income and livelihood resources. Act No. 2942 envisages compensation for individuals who prove that they are landowners or possessors of land, and Act No. 5543 is based on the families utilising the land. Therefore, State support to be provided in accordance with Law No. 5543 envisages the provision of housing and land that will be adequate for the household and the required means of earning a living. Furthermore, unlike Act No. 2942, Act No. 5543 also applies to persons who have proven that they have been established for at least three years in settlements affected by the project, even if they do not have ownership of the land. In such cases, instead of using the compensation of expropriation, resettlement is preferred through gratuitous aids and appropriate credits.

The main principle here is the provision of resettlement sites on similar conditions after the baseline study has been made and the existing settlement status and income levels of the families determined, and ensuring that the standards of living and income levels of the affected households in the project are at least equal to, and if possible higher than, the pre-project situation. In this case, it is essential that families living in rural areas and deriving income from agriculture are resettled in agricultural areas, with households living in or having the capacity to live in urban areas settled accordingly. A detailed resettlement action plan, a timeline (flow diagram), and an adequate budget are required in order to achieve all of these goals.

Expropriation and the implementation of settlements include approaches and practices that complement each other in terms of methods and results. In the case of government-assisted settlements, a fund is created based on the estimated value of real estate to be expropriated and lost by the affected households in the project, and all their settlement needs are met by the State. In village relocations with credit support, resettlement is made through facilities and guidance provided by the government, such as land type, project type, consultancy, guidance, and long-term low interest loans. The selection of the resettlement method most suitable for the specific locality, determined through analysis and the evaluation of data collected by observing, surveying, and interviewing in the project area before the preparation of the plan, as well as considering the preferences of families affected by the project, are determining factors in deciding upon the method of settlement.

While the impact of land acquisition for some projects is rather limited, other projects such as dam construction directly and/or indirectly affect many settlements. In projects for the construction of highways and railways, drinking or irrigation water pipelines, and oil and natural gas pipelines by authorised public institutions, the real estate is divided in a strip map fashion in principle, and the land acquisition process is completed with practices such as expropriation, zoning application, or land consolidation. However, if plots are required in a certain location for projects such as airports, settlement areas, and dam and lakes, expropriation is preferred, and resettlement for such projects is also inevitable. Resettlement services seek to ensure that there is no adverse effect on the environment of those affected by development projects for the benefit of the public, and to help those relocated to attain at least the level of income they previously had, as well as post-settlement impact assessment studies. Such resettlement plans reduce to a minimum the social problems that may occur during the execution of the main project and allow the projects to go into operation at planned times by avoiding the delays and cost increases that may be caused by social problems. However, resettlement works focus on households, while expropriation practice is based on the occupants of registered real estate or its repossession. In the Turkish Legal System, the expropriation and appraisal processes are carried out at the plot scale without taking into consideration farm enterprise integrity or households. Negative influences such as the obstruction of transport links between settlements and plots in the post-project period, the inability to use plots outside the expropriation area, the increase of transport costs and the negative impact on the infrastructural investments of the settlements, and their lack of repair and maintenance during project management inevitably adversely affect the farming income and social status of affected households post-acquisition. However, the fact that government-assisted settlement is based on households instead of individuals is also appropriate for the socioeconomic structure of the Turkish people.

Resettlement plans are of interest to many organisations because of their comprehensive nature and are achieved by ensuring coordination between these organisations. Unplanned and poorly coordinated resettlement plans lead to increased costs, a failure to meet expectations, and eventually face unpredictable settlement problems. Social problems caused by expropriation used in land acquisition in projects involving the development of land and water resources are felt throughout the country. For this reason, and with legal arrangements related to the protection of natural and cultural values being made, and with the World Bank and other international creditors including them as compulsory investment preconditions, resettlement works have been carried out within the General Directorate of State Hydraulic Works (DSİ) since the beginning of the 1990s. First, in 1995, the Resettlement Coordination Committee, composed of the representatives of the relevant institutions, was established under the chair of the State Planning Organisation (now the Ministry of Development), with secretariat and rapporteur duties fulfilled by the DSİ in the commission's work on DSİ projects. Furthermore, in the resettlement works, the requirement for the DSİ General Directorate to be responsible as the main project executive agency was included in the development plans of the country (DSİ 2016; Özkalaycı and İçten 2005).

While households affected by the projects who are not landowners and who will receive low expropriation rates prefer government-assisted settlement, those with high expropriation rates for real estate may prefer to be resettled through village relocation. The landowners who have received expropriation compensation can purchase land divided according to the development in the designated resettlement area, while receiving on demand loans to the amount specified in the regulation. In addition to the infrastructure of the resettlement site being built by the government, the houses to be built are given to the beneficiaries free of charge. Resettlement Action Plans on the methods by which the affected families are to be resettled, and information, consulting, monitoring, and evaluation services to ensure that the best choices are made at each stage of the project implementation, must be prepared by professional experts (specialists in various fields such as engineering, economics, real estate development, statistics, and sociology); it is compulsory for experts from different disciplines to work together in this process.

That compensation for land expropriated in the Turkish legal system is paid only to the owners and possessors of the land, if any, with no compensation being paid to those who merely occupy and use public land, which is incompatible with the standards of international financial institutions. Many international financial institutions require compensation to be paid to all owners and users (users, tenants, partners, and occupiers of pastures, forests, and water resources), irrespective of landownership, for the financing of investments (IFC 2001, 2012). This approach is seen as a new practice for land acquisition and resettlement processes in Turkey. Instead of considering the physical and economic displacement together in the process of land acquisition and expropriation for projects, only physical resettlement is taken as a basis. In particular, organisations such as the World Bank the International Finance Corporation (IFC), the International Bank for Reconstruction and Development (IBRD) and the European Bank for Reconstruction and Development (EBRD) in project financing are directly concerned with income derived from the land, and consider that any implementation that will cause a reduction in income must result in compensation for such a loss. Likewise, it is envisaged that individuals or communities will be reimbursed if they lose their sources of income or if their access to sources of income becomes restricted, which is defined as economic resettlement. International financial institutions are developing policies to ensure that any negative impact of the relevant project on the people in question is minimised and that these people are assisted to restore their lives or businesses and to resume their livelihoods. Although this approach is often perceived as a rescue or welfare improvement practice, it also bears the nature of "development programmes" as well as "involuntary resettlement" schemes because the production and living systems of affected people are disrupted.

Similarly, in the valuation process of the real estate affected by projects, instead of business integrity, plot integrity is the basis, and the change in household income before and after the project and the potential adverse effects are not taken into consideration. However, the monitoring and evaluation of the impacts of expropriation and resettlement processes following the launch of the projects and the plans of action aimed at mitigating any negative effects are also neglected. It is possible, for example, that the reserves of dam reservoirs formed after water retention restrict access to the land and lead to a deterioration of the environmental, social, and economic structure of local settlements to the point where they become uninhabitable. In such a case, the occupants may demand expropriation of the plots formerly excluded from the expropriation area. However, if the obstructed plots are outside the expropriation corridor, the owners must legally seek compensation for the loss of land value or land income according to the general principles. As a requirement of changing economic and social conditions and international standards, an analysis of the pre-existing economic, social, and environmental situation of the location should be conducted at the feasibility stage of large-scale infrastructure and superstructure projects by both public and private institutions, and accordingly, it is considered necessary to prepare a Resettlement Action Plan, including monitoring/valuation works during the period from the beginning to the end of the project and post-project, to allocate funds for this purpose and to implement mitigation measures effectively.

Resettlement policies and evaluation of resettlement practices in major areas

In Turkey, official data on resettlement works carried out by different public institutions such as the Ministry of Environment and Urbanisation, the Ministry of Forestry and Water Affairs, the Prime Ministry Disaster and Emergency Management Presidency, and the Mass Housing Administration are not compiled and published. For this reason, a comprehensive data collection study on the resettlement works carried out by public institutions and the Ministry of Environment and Urbanisation in the last 50 years has been conducted by researchers. Based on the results of this study, the following has been evaluated generally according to the subjects of resettlement practices (DSİ 2016; Ministry of Forestry and Water Affairs of Turkey 2016; Ministry of Energy and Natural Resources of Turkey 2016; Ministry of Environment and Urbanism of Turkey 2016):

Resettlement practices in coal reserve areas

According to the activity report of the Ministry of Energy and Natural Resources in Turkey, there are a total of 14 coal reserves (Ministry of Energy and Natural Resources of Republic of Turkey 2016). Land acquisition and expropriation are compulsory in settlements where open pit (or open cast) mining is carried out within the scope of coal reserve works. Particularly in the Western Anatolia Region, in open pit mining cities, resettlement became compulsory. Similarly, for the evaluation of coal reserves in the Kahramanmaras Province, Afşin and Elbistan Districts, the great majority of the affected households in the two provinces were resettled.

Between 1979–2016 in Turkey a total of 453 families were resettled, 86 (18.98%) in rural areas and 367 (81.02%) in urban areas (Table 10.1). However, land acquisition in coal and other mining areas is by expropriation, and no resettlement action plan is prepared or impact mitigation practices applied; also the restoration of mining land or nature restoration work is often neglected.

Resettlement practices related to forest areas

According to the 2015 activity report of the Ministry of Forestry and Water Affairs, there are 22,343 forest villages in Turkey, and the population living in these villages is determined as 7,096,483 (Ministry of Forestry and Water Affairs of Turkey 2016). In general, land assets are evaluated as scarce, with income sources limited, transportation links poor, and opportunities for socioeconomic development insufficient.

According to the records of the Ministry of Environment and Urbanism, a total of 1,116 households of 1,223 families in forest villages in the following cities were resettled Trabzon (Çaykara), Ankara (Nallıhan), Isparta (Eğridir), Afyon (Bolvadin), Hatay (Yayladağı), Balıkesir (Dursunbey), Samsun (Vezirköprü), and Bursa (Mustafa Kemalpaşa). Among the households resettled, 1,074 preferred to live in rural areas, with 92 preferring to live in urban areas, and it can be seen that the households subjected to resettlement generally preferred to be resettled in their own provinces (Table 10.1). Since forest villages are high in number, and a large number of households live in villages, it does not seem possible in the short or medium term for all affected forest villages to be resettled.

Resettlement practices for earthquake-prone villages and from health risks

Turkey is located in the Alp-Himalaya earthquake zone, one of the active seismic belts of the world, and 42% of the country's surface area is located on the first degree earthquake zone. During the Republican period (1932 to 1945), there occurred a total of 118 earthquakes with a magnitude of 5 and over. In these earthquakes, a total of 81,972 people lost their lives and 572,312 buildings were seriously damaged. A total of 1,158 people lost their lives in earthquakes in 1983 (Biga and Erzurum-Kars), and 3,326 buildings were seriously damaged; three people lost their lives in the 1984 Balkaya earthquake, and 570 buildings were seriously damaged. Recorded as the most serious disaster of the nation, the Marmara

Table 10.1 Distribution of Resettled Households Related to Selected Project Implementation Areas in Turkey (1970- +)

Years	Resettlement Rationale	Indicators	Number and Ratio (%) of Affected Households	Number and Ratio (%) of Affected Households That are Resettled by Their Own Means, Not by the State	Number and Ratio (%) of Affected and Settled Households	Number and Ratio (%) of Affected and Settled Households Based on Settlement Type		Percentage of the Affected Households in Total by Application Areas (%)
						Agricultural	Urban	
1979–1999	Settlement Units Remained in the Coal Reserve Area	**Quantity**	453	–	453	86	367	3.40
		Rate (%)	100.00	–	100.00	18.98	81.02	
1973–2002	In-Forest Settlement Units	**Quantity**	1.223	57	1.166	1.074	92	8.75
		Rate (%)	100.00	4.66	95.34	87.82	7.52	
1983–1984	Settlement Units on the Earthquake Zone	**Quantity**	833	–	833	833	–	6.25
		Rate (%)	100.00	–	100.00	100.00	–	
2008–2014	Nomads (Domestic)	**Quantity**	1.161	–	1.161	273	888	8.72
		Rate (%)	100.00	–	100.00	23.51	76.49	
1983–2016	Immigrants (Relative Communities Living Abroad)	**Quantity**	1.966	277	1.689	1.188	501	12.68
		Rate (%)	100.00	14.09	85.91	60.43	25.48	
2006–2015	Compulsory Settlement	**Quantity**	78	–	78	3	75	0.59
		Rate (%)	100.00	–	100.00	3.85	96.15	
1976–2016	Settlement Units Affected by Dam Site and Remained Underwater	**Quantity**	7.956	16	7.940	4.294	3.646	59.61
		Rate (%)	100.00	0.20	99.80	53.97	45.83	
1976–2016	**TOTAL**	**Quantity**	**13.670**	**350**	**13.320**	**7.751**	**5.569**	**100.00**
		Rate (%)	**100.00**	**2.56**	**97.44**	**56.70**	**40.74**	

Source: Calculated based on the data obtained by the researchers from the records of the relevant public institutions.

earthquake occurred on 17 August 1999, with a magnitude of 7.4, causing great loss, especially in Istanbul; Kocaeli; Sakarya; and Bolu, Bursa, Zonguldak, Eskişehir, and Yalova provinces. According to the damage report, the Marmara earthquake severely damaged 66,441 houses and 10,901 workplaces, 67,242 houses and 9,927 workplaces suffering medium damage, and 80,160 houses and 9,712 workplaces were mildly damaged; 17,479 lives were lost, and 43,953 injured. It is known that 79.41% of the approximately 15.8 million people affected by the earthquake were relocated in urban areas, with 20.59% relocated in rural settlements. The fact that the earthquake occurred in regions where major industrial centres were located and where buildings and population density were relatively high accounts for the serious levels in material losses and loss of life. Approximately three months after this earthquake, 763 people lost their lives in another earthquake with a magnitude of 7.5, with the epicentre in Düzce Province (Hayrullahoglu et al. 2017). Finally, the Van-Erciş-based earthquake on 23 October 2011 and the Van-Edremit-based earthquake of 9 November 2011 caused destructive damage to the structure stock of the region, resulting in many fatalities. As a result of the 23 October and 9 November 2011 earthquakes, a total of 644 people lost their lives, 1,966 people were injured, and 252 people were rescued from the wreckage.

In Turkey, while, on the one hand, compulsory earthquake insurance is implemented, on the other hand, the Mass Housing Development Administration had invested in the construction of permanent housing which was demolished after the earthquake. In this way, normalisation of economic and social life can be achieved in a relatively short period after the earthquake in urban areas. However, the damage caused by the earthquakes in rural areas usually remains unnoticed, and the affected rural areas cannot take advantage of the benefits provided by public and private institutions' in the same way of the urban population. In rural areas, the earthquakes cause damage to housing and agricultural buildings, as well as the death of animals that are the main source of income for the inhabitants. Whatever the risk of earthquake, the resettlement of village dwellings is implemented. In 1983 and 1984, resettlements were carried out in nine earthquake zones, and a total of 833 families were resettled through these projects. It can be seen that all of the household dwellings whose occupiers were involved in agricultural were resettled (Table 10.1).

There is often a need for resettlement to avoid health risks and pothole formation. For example, after it was found that the volcanic stone and natural materials used for housing constructions in the Tuzköy, Karain, and Sarıhıdır villages of the Nevşehir Province caused peritoneal and lung cancer, the villages, mostly from Tuzköy, decided to be relocated, and they have been resettled in a recently constructed village. However, since the number of the buildings constructed for the people living in the risky areas was insufficient, some villagers continued living in their old houses, and it was found that work in other villages was still continuing. According to the results of a focus group, because the construction was only of residential buildings for the households in the newly built village, and not barns and other facilities for livestock, which was the main income source of the households before resettlement, the villagers had not moved because resettlement would have affected their income and therefore their living conditions negatively.

Another risk to life is potholes occurring in Central Anatolia because of the decrease in water level each year, caused by the use of groundwater for irrigation. Large and small potholes are observed to form in many settlements, especially in the Karapinar District of Konya Province, and the rapid growth of potholes (crustal deformation) caused by drought and the rapid withdrawal of underground waters is threatening the lives of both people and animals. The existence of numerous registered and unregistered wells in the closed basin of Konya and the uncontrolled use of groundwater will necessitate the resettlement of many households to avoid the dangers of pothole formation. In the same region, it was found that there were requests to move villages in Çankırı Province and to resettlement of them because of pothole formation.

Settlement practices of nomadic families

There is a considerable size of the population excluded from established agricultural activities, which makes a living by migratory animal husbandry activities, without being dependent on fixed and permanent housing. It is necessary that people of nomadic cultures who do not have a permanent residential location should be settled, for various reasons. In Turkey, six groups leading a nomadic life have been converted to a fixed life-style since 2008. Households in the Tekeli Nomadic group in Kahramanmaraş Province were settled in 2009; in 2010, about 33 households were settled on real estate purchased at the provincial centre, two for agricultural resettlement sites, and the remaining 31 by urban resettlement. In the same year, 28 existing housings in the Central District of Siirt Province were settled by urban settlement. In 2011, 22 families in the Tekeli Nomadic group from various provinces and villages of Kahramanmaraş Province were resettled in the Kızıleniş District of Kahramanmaraş Province, by agricultural resettlement practices. In 2012, one family in Kahramanmaraş Province was placed in a housing unit purchased in the city centre within the framework of the urban settlement policy. In the 2013, all the families in the Malamirza group from various districts and villages in the Siirt Province were moved to houses in Siirt Province, Evren Street through urban settlement practice. In the same year, one family from the Tekeli Nomadic group in Kahramanmaraş Province was resettled in the city centre. In 2014, two families from the Tekeli Nomadic group in Kahramanmaraş Province were resettled in houses in the city centre by urban settlement plan. In 2016, 86 families from the Karakulak group and 86 families from the Kosan group were settled in Diyarbakır province, about 86 households from the Sarıkeçili group in İçel Province and 672 families from the Beggare-Kasreken group were settled in Şanlıurfa Province, and nine families from the Musarşan group were settled in Şırnak Province, and the resettlement works were completed. A total of 1,161 households of nomadic peoples were resettled, 273 of these (23.51%) preferring rural settlements and 888 (76.49%) preferring urban settlements (Table 10.1).

Settlement practices in migrants' groups

Migrant groups were initially settled in the first metropolitan cities of the country, but after the 1990s, cities such as Antalya, Muğla, and Tekirdağ emerged as new centres of attraction. Particularly with the impact of the 1999 Marmara earthquake, there was a reduction in the trend in migration to İstanbul and the Kocaeli provinces. With the expansion of industrial areas, Mersin, Bursa, and İzmir Provinces are now standing out as areas of attraction for resettlement.

It is understood that households were regularly moved within Turkey between 1983 and 1990. In this period, about 786 of the total 991 Afghan families were settled by agricultural settlement and 205 by urban settlement in Kayseri, Tokat, Gaziantep, Şanlıurfa, Van, and Hatay Provinces. In 1997, all 180 Ahiska families were settled in urban areas of the Iğdır Province. In 2000, 128 Bulgarian families were settled in rural areas of Çanakkale Province. In addition to this, from 2016, a total of 595 Ahiska families were settled in Erzincan Province, and 72 families were settled in Ahlat District. In the period within the scope of

211

this study, 1,188 (60.43%) of the total 1,966 immigrant families and 501 (25.48%) households were settled by rural and urban settlement, respectively. It was determined that the remaining 277 families were resettled by their own means (Table 10.1).

Families subject to mandatory settlement practice

In Turkey, mandatory settlement practices can also be observed. In Tunceli province alone, mandatory settlement practices were carried out between 2006 and 2015. A total of 64 families in 2006, 2008, and 2009 were settled in Kocaeli Province, Hereke District, mandatorily. As a result, it has been found that of the 78 families, 3 (3.85%) benefited from agricultural and 75 (96.15%) from urban settlement practices (Table 10.1). The main reason for this kind of displacement is often conflict issues within settlements, such as landownership, common land use, and sharing the same dwellings.

Resettlement practices of villages affected by watershed projects

Land and water development works include energy and water supply and irrigation, which are closely correlated with local development. A total of 595 dams have been constructed and are operated by the DSİ General Directorate in Turkey, 203 of which are classified as 'large' and 392 of which are classified as pond dams. While the general purposes of the construction of dams are categorised into energy, irrigation, and personal use dams are generally constructed for multiple purposes, such as flood protection, fishing, sports, and recreation. When analysing the dams constructed by the DSİ General Directorate, it has been found that 475 of the dams were completed and put into operation before 2000, and 120 started to operate on and after 2000 (Ministry of Forestry and Water Affairs of Turkey 2016; Yiğitbaşıoğlu 1996).

In Turkey, since a significant portion of the population depends on agricultural activities, and because of the importance of agriculture in the economy, water is a vital resource. Important settlement locations around lakes and rivers were established many years ago, and it is unavoidable that some settlements that are important from historical and cultural perspectives will be submerged because of the waters that accumulate during dam construction (Akargül 1998; Bakırcı 1997; Sonmez 2012). The number of affected settlements and households, especially on large-scale projects, has reached a considerable size, and in some projects the district as a whole has to be relocated. For this reason, in large-scale projects such as dam construction and power plant construction, new settlement areas have to be built by the government for the affected families. Particularly in the last three decades, it has been seen that people and families affected by large infrastructure projects are not victimised but are provided with better conditions, primarily employed in positions required in the dam construction, and importance is given to agricultural production and the protection of social and cultural values.

When the dam investments are examined, it is found that resettlement programmes were carried out in the residential areas of 62 projects. For example, 50,800 hectares (125,500 acres) of land remained within the lake area of the Keban Dam and Hydroelectric Power Plant (HEPP) Project, a project started in the 1960s and completed in 1975. About 94 settlements in the project area were completely vacated, including the buildings and lands, while 121 settlements were partially affected by the project (Appendix, Table 10.3). This situation is evident in the seven sample project fields selected as examples and having an important place in the economy of the country. Within the scope of the projects for the development

Table 10.2 Investment Amounts, Expropriation Costs, and Expropriation Areas in Selected Water and Land Development Projects

Selected Projects	Construction Dates	Purpose	Investment Amount (Million $)	Expropriation Area (m²)	Expropriation Cost (Million $)	The Share of Expropriation Expenditures of Total Investment Costs (%)
Keban Dam and HEPP Project	1965–1975	Power Generation	783.00	508,000,000	198.00	**25.30**
Atatürk Dam and HEPP Project	1981–1992	Irrigation, Power Generation, and Drinking Water	3,560.00	538,000,000	508.57	**14.30**
Birecik Dam and HEPP Project	1993–2000	Irrigation and Power Generation	1,142.00	58,000,000	218.00	**19.09**
Yortanlı Dam and HEPP Project	1993–2011	Irrigation	67.44	4,457,436.48	4.96	**7.35**
Ilısu Dam and HEPP Project	2008–2015	Power Generation	16,270.00	178,860,000	2,748.00	**16.89**
Yusufeli Dam and HEPP Project	2012–2019	Power Generation	207.60	16,922,700	160.19	**77.15**
Deriner Dam and HEPP Project	1998–2012	Power Generation	1,387.19	4,730,675.60	111.40	**8.03**

Source: Calculated based on the data obtained by the researchers from the records of the relevant public institutions.

of all soil and water resources carried out in the Republican period, it was determined that approximately 400 settlement units remained totally underwater and that the settlement areas mentioned were included in the resettlement programme. The total number of households affected was 7,956 and, within the framework of resettlement programmes, 7,940 of these households were settled in new rural and urban settlements in accordance with their preferences (Table 10.1).

On examining the official records of authorised public institutions, 13,320 (97.44%) of a total of 13,670 households affected for different reasons were included in the scope of resettlement. It was found that 7,751 (56.70%) of the households that benefited from the resettlement plan were settled in rural settlements, 5,569 in urban settlements, and 350 families found new settlements through their own means (Table 10.1). It has been found that the total expropriation expenditure of the seven large dam investments selected for comprehensive analysis, including resettlement, varied between 8.03% (Deriner Project) and 77.15% (Yusufeli Project) of the total project cost, although the variation in the proportions in question remained at more reasonable levels of 8.03–25.30% if the physical displacement of the Yusufeli District population of about 23,000 is excluded from the scope of the statistics (Appendix, Table 10.2). The share of the expropriation cost in the amount of investment varies greatly depending on the nature of the construction site, the type of dam, and the affected

Table 10.3 Expropriation Areas, Affected Settlements and Households, and Conservation Activities in Selected Water and Land Development Projects

Selected Projects	Number of Parcels	Parcel Area (m²)	Number of Settled Villages and Households	Cultural and Natural Heritage Conservation Work
			Characteristics of Expropriation Areas	
Keban Dam and HEPP Project	Total 59,000 parcels were expropriated in the lake area, and a total of 6,605 households had 30,414 people living in the project area, of which 4,961 households (23,236 people) had to be moved	The total expropriation area is 508,000,000 m2 and the expropriated parcels consist of irrigated lands, orchards, and vineyards	Total 258 municipal villages and hamlets in 9 districts of the Elazığ, Tunceli, Erzincan, Malatya, and Sivas Provinces were affected by the dam. Of these, 94 municipal and villages were completely inundated, and 1 province, 3 districts, and 115 municipal and villages were partially affected. The remaining 23 settlement units were not affected	A total of 158 units of cultural heritage were identified including 21 caves, 7 cemeteries/graves, 15 flat settlements, 78 tumuli, 7 churches, 2 mosques, 2 tombs, 4 inns, 2 hammams, 1 madrasa, 1 traditional house, 1 mill, 4 castles, 6 bridges, 1 ancient road, 3 architectural remains, and 3 different buildings in the affected area
Atatürk Dam and HEPP Project	In the project area, 9,098 parcels were expropriated in a total of 158 settlements	The expropriation area is 538,000,000 m2 and the expropriated parcels consist of irrigated lands, orchards, and vineyards	In the expropriation area, 115 villages and 43 neighbourhoods and district centres were affected and Samsat and Kahta Districts were subject to large-scale resettlement	In addition to district settlements and cultural assets, Şanlıurfa Lidar Tumulus remained entirely in the lake area until 1987, and while archaeological studies started at the Adıyaman Tille Tumulus in 1979, it also remained completely under the dam waters until 1987 due to the project
Birecik Dam and HEPP Project	The lake area covers Birecik, Nizip, Halfeti, Araban, Yavuzeli, Bozova, Adıyaman centre, and Besni Districts, and 7,167 parcels were affected by the project	The expropriation area is 58,000,000 m2, and the expropriated parcels consist of irrigated lands, orchards, and vineyards	Halfeti District centre and Kavunlu village remained underwater in the lake area and the inhabitants were resettled	The Zeugma ancient city and ruins and Halfeti Ulu Mosque remained underwater in the project area

Project				
Yortanlı Dam and HEPP Project	In the dam lake area, 489 parcels from 6 villages were expropriated	The expropriation area is 4,457,437 m2, and the expropriated parcels consist of irrigated lands, orchards, and vineyards	Of the 6 affected villages, only 13 households were affected in the Çaltıkoru village, and 13 villages were not resettled	Immediately after the dam construction tender, the DSI signed a protocol with the Ministry of Culture and Tourism and the General Directorate of Antiquities for excavations to be carried out in the lake area of the dam in order to save and document historical monuments. With the protocol signed on 4 May 1994, the rescue excavations were started on 17 October 1994 by the Bergama Museum Directorate
Ilısu Dam and HEPP Project	The total number of parcels subject to private real estate in the area of expropriation is 16,782, all of which are being expropriated	The expropriation area is 178,860,000 m2, and the expropriated parcels consist of irrigated lands, orchards, and vineyards	According to the determinations, 6 districts and 47 villages belonging to the provinces of Mardin, Sirnak, Siirt, and Batman remained in the dam reservoir area, and they were affected to a great extent by the project	Archaeological excavations only in 14 sites in the Ilısu reservoir, which houses about 300 archaeological sites and the ancient city of Hasankeyf. With the completion of the dams, excavation work is usually stopped and archaeological sites buried in the waters
Yusufeli Dam and HEPP Project	Total 14,687 parcels in the project area will need to be partially or completely expropriated	The expropriation area is 16,922,700 m2, and the expropriated parcels consist of fields and orchards	In the project area, 14,687 parcels and structures on them were affected in 19 villages and the district centre. A total of 1,692.27 ha of land within the boundaries of the 33 km2 lake area have remained within the boundaries of the expropriation area	It was determined that the Yusufeli District centre would be relocated elsewhere in the project area, but the local people do not approve of moving the district centre, and for this reason, the new settlement site selected is not found appropriate. No cultural assets that need to be protected in the project area were identified. It is clear that wild animals will be adversely affected, and the fertile alluvial plains in the riverbeds, which are very scarce in the district, will be completely destroyed because of the resulting lake area
Deriner Dam and HEPP Project	A total of 8,088 parcels will have to be expropriated for the project	The expropriation area is 4,730,675.60 m2, and the expropriated parcels consist of irrigated, orchard, and vineyard lands	Total 30 villages within the boundaries of the Central, Ardanuç, and Yusufeli Districts in the Artvin Province are being affected; 20 villages are partially affected, 7 are greatly affected, and 3 are completely affected. There are no settlements areas in the project for which resettlement work is being conducted	7 cultural properties including two mosques (Zeytinlik and Oruçlu Mosques), two tombs (Upper and Lower Tomb), one mansion (Şükrü Ağa Mansion), and two historical bridges (Berta Bridge and Ferhatlı Bridge) remained in the dam lake area

Source: Based on the analysis by researchers from the records of relevant public institutions.

land, and when resettlement becomes compulsory, it becomes one of the reasons for the increase in the cost of real estate acquisition. It is observed that social development projects are not implemented for families subject to resettlement in large-scale investment projects, though such practices are required for the economic and social restoration of the households affected by resettlement, and it is also considered necessary to make regulations to impose an obligation to allocate funds specifically for this purpose in each project.

Effects of resettlement practices on the protection of natural and cultural heritage and socioeconomic life of affected households

The rapid increase of population in developing countries directly affects the demand for food, energy, and dwelling areas, causing a change in land use in both rural and urban areas. The change in land use in rural areas is highly dependent on factors such as increases in agricultural productivity growth and population density (Tanrıvermiş 2003). Population increases in urban areas causes the transformation of agricultural land, meadows, and forest land near cities into settlements. The increase in the number of households and the population in rural areas lead to an increase in demand for agricultural production areas, and where land in rural areas suitable for agriculture has reached its marginal limit, an increase in production is achieved by the intensive use of inputs such as improved seeds, agricultural chemicals, irrigation, mechanisation, and mixed feed on the one hand, and the transformation of forest and meadow land to cultivation activities on the other hand (Brown 1979; Tanrıvermiş and Bülbül 2007).

In the economic development process, energy demand also shows a rapid increase, and especially by industrial and commercial enterprises which have to use energy at as low a cost as possible in order to protect their competitiveness. In addition to hydropower and thermal power plants, it is necessary to use wind, solar, and geothermal resources together in order to meet the rising energy demand in the country. The poorly balanced distribution of non-renewable energy resources and increasing industrialisation in the world make energy production necessary from all sources; increasing energy demand is generally met by HEPP and thermal power plants in countries such as Turkey. In Turkey, irrigation and energy dams also cause important problems such as the loss of fertile farmland, siltation, flora and fauna and species loss, ecosystem deterioration, and migrations; in addition, local economic and social life are affected directly when settlements remain underwater.

Assessment of spatial changes

After dam constructions, primarily spatial changes are observed in the settlement areas. The evacuation of the area where the lake is to be formed and the dam constructed primarily requires partial or total removal of the existing settlements. Examples include the replacement of Samsat (Adıyaman) as a result of the construction of the Atatürk Dam, and the involuntary resettlement of Halfeti (Şanlıurfa) with the construction of the Birecik Dam. The same is also true for Artvin Province, Yusufeli District, which had to be moved because of the Yusufeli Dam and HEPP Project (Çotur 1990; Gök 2001; Gök and Yazar 2011; Sönmez 2012; Tonbul 1990; Tanrıvermiş and Aliefendioğlu 2015).

Samsat, whose foundation predates the Hitites' arrival from Central Asia, was evacuated in 1988, and moved 10 kilometres north of the old district settlement during the construction phase of the Atatürk Dam. The recorded conquest by the Assyrian King Salmanassar III in 855 BC, Rumkale and Halfeti Districts became two settlements affected by the dam lake as a result of water accumulation in the Birecik Dam in 2000. Since a large part of Halfeti District was inundated, it was forced to relocate, and today the district lies 8 kilometres (5 miles) east of the old Halfeti settlement area (Bakırcı 1997).

Another case of the flooding of settlements in Turkey with the construction of dams is the case of the Keban Dam. After the construction of the dam, 94 municipal villages were completely inundated, and 1 province, 3 districts, and 115 municipal villages were partially affected (Appendix, Table 10.3). A total of 50,800 hectares (125,500 acres) of land were inundated by the dam lake, and the households that had to relocate were resettled in the rural and urban areas of different provinces and cities. In the same way, one district centre (Yusufeli) and seven villages were totally affected, 22 villages largely and 32 villages partially affected as a result of the dams to be built in the Çoruh River Basin. It has been observed that at least 20,000 people in the Çoruh Basin had to leave their settlements after dam construction and had to be resettled; according to the study conducted in the region, the local people reacted adversely to the project at a high level, and the project was not acceptable from a social perspective (Sever 2005; Tanrıvermiş and Aliefendioğlu 2015). As a result of the Derbent Dam, which was put into operation on the Kızılırmak in the Bafra District of the province of Samsun in 1991, 200 households and an area of 17 square kilometres (4,200 acres) of agriculture including the ancient city of Ikiztepe, dating back to 4000 BC, were inundated.

The displacement of settlements causes many infrastructural, economic, and social problems. The fact that people have to abandon the settlements that they have lived in and shaped for many years causes them to adapt with difficulty to new settlements. In addition, since the land in the old settlements where agricultural production dominated and from which income sources were derived, the economic balance of the households deteriorates as the money in question cannot be directed to efficient investments, even if the expropriated land values are higher than the market value. The results of the research show a deterioration in the social and economic structures of the households that had to be resettled as a result of the many dam projects; the failure of monitoring-evaluation and mitigation works, anticipated in the international standards, mean that public investments have had a negative effect on the quality of the lives of citizens. It has also been found that resettlement practices in rural and urban areas are carried out in accordance with the demand of the people affected by the project and resettled, but resettlement practices in urban areas are more successful than those in the rural areas. In addition, if the households in rural areas are placed in urban areas within the scope of resettlement, the families often faced significant economic and social difficulties (Aliefendioğlu and Tanrıvermiş 2016; Bakırcı 2016; Orhan and Gök 2016), and it would be beneficial to provide business development and skills training for individuals affected in such a resettlement process which are suitable for the conditions, and to credit business development activities.

The effects of infrastructure projects should not be considered only in terms of events that causes a settlement to move. It can be seen that the effects of dam investments are not only related to economic activities, but also have negative effects on various other social and cultural aspects of the community. It is evident that the problems of the resettlement process are mainly related to the economic and social uncertainties that may arise in the new settlements and that those who have problems integrating with the local community after resettlement opt to move again to other settlements. It should be noted that the first settlements were generally established close to lakes and rivers (Akargul 1998; Tunçdilek 1986; Tümertekin and Özgüç 1997), which often have many ancient and historical settlements in their environs, with the consequent and significant cultural loss caused by inundation of those settlements during dam construction. Such cultural losses should be evaluated.

Zeugma with the construction of Birecik Dam, Hasankeyf (Mardin) when the Ilısu Dam was put into operation, and the ancient city of Allianoi (İzmir) with the construction of Yortanlı Dam were all inundated. Zeugma was an ancient city founded by the generals of Alexander the Great and later by the Syrian King Selevkos Nikator on of 2,000 hectares (4,950 acres) on the banks of the Fırat River within the borders of the village of Belkis in the Nizip District of Gaziantep Province, and it received the name "Zeugma", which means getaway, in the 1st century BC under Roman domination. Approximately 30% of the ancient city, with its statues, reliefs, and constructions belonging to the Romans and 100,000 Bulla (seal print), was left under the waters of Birecik Dam, and the remaining 70% was affected by the risk of collapse and slipping because of the nature of the clay of which the land is composed (Sönmez 2012). At least 20% of the old settlement area of Hasankeyf District, which has an historical heritage of about 6,000 years from the Sumerians to the Ottomans, had been inundated after construction of the Ilısu Dam. A large part of the city that was moved to a new location has been transformed into a cultural park. The main problem in this settlement is not its displacement, but the fact that the settlement will be flooded with the loss of a great cultural heritage. Planning for its rescue has been undertaken, and it has been decided that many of the historical buildings which would otherwise be under the dam waters will be moved by local and foreign experts and placed in the Hasankeyf cultural park (Aliefendioğlu 2016). In the newly established Hasankeyf District, an "Archaeological Park and Air Museum" has been established on the right and left sides of the city, and it is planned to transform this into a tourism attraction centre with park areas. Of course, how well these studies and projects will proceed, and how the relocated historical structures and cultural assets will reflect their older characteristics, is another controversy. In particular, it is noteworthy that conservation specialists have paid close attention to the preservation of ancient artifacts onsite and that the practice of relocation is generally not acceptable as an alternative to onsite protection.

The ancient city of Allianoi at Paşa Ilıcası Mevkii, located on the border of the Bergama District of İzmir, in the northeast of Bergama, in the vicinity of the Yortanlı Dam, is now completely below the level of water collection at the dam. It is estimated that the history of this settlement dates back to prehistoric times and features buildings and other structures belonging to the Roman and Byzantine periods. When the targeted maximum water level is reached at the Yortanlı Dam Lake, the Allianoi ancient city will lie under 17 metres (55 feet) of water. In order to prevent the complete disappearance of this ancient city, solutions such as injecting concrete into the impermeable plate down to the main rock in the east and west areas, and preventing Allianoi from submerging by the installation of curtain walls have been produced (Sönmez 2012).

Assessment of changes in natural environment

Excavation works during the construction phase of dam and HPP projects with multipurpose investments, such as energy, irrigation, water, flood prevention, fishing, sports, and recreation, are also carried out together with works such as buildings, service roads, the dam body, and tunnels. All kinds of excavation works in the construction phase cause vegetation damage, the degradation of slope balances, mass movements, and other kinds of erosion, and especially an increase in the severity of the decomposition activities that develop rapidly on solid rocks, with the decomposition process resulting in the thickening of the debris cover (Turoğlu 2005). These effects continue even after completion of the construction, with the erosion and sedimentation control studies carried out around the dam lake area extending the life of the dam and preserving its environmental quality (Sönmez 2012). Species loss and the destruction of flora and fauna, loss of agricultural land, and changes in water catchment are summarised as the most important changes in the natural environment.

a   **Destruction of flora and fauna:** The dam consists of a collection of a large body of water, behind a wall built in front of a valley, where the river valley is at its narrowest. The size of the lake depends on factors such as the scheme, the amount of water it carries, and the width of the basin. The area covered by the dam lake should be bare, and surface cleaning is carried out during the dam construction, which results in the loss of plant species. Riverbeds are important habitats especially for rare species of tree, endemic plants, and some animals (Akkan 1990; Turoğlu 2005; Yıldırımlı 2005). During field experiments, the plants in or near the riverbeds are destroyed, and the animals forced to move. Another problem is the effects on the climate after the formation of the dam lake; however, it seems that there are no significant differences in the climate characteristics of neighbouring settlements after the construction of dams with large storage volumes, such as Keban, Atatürk, and Karakaya. (There are some minor differences in the values at the extremities, but these differences do not cause a significant change in the climate of the settlements) (Şengün 2007). However, dams are expected to cause significant loss of plant and animal species as they cause climate change during operational periods. It should be emphasised that for affected pre-dam settlements such as those in Eastern and Central Anatolia regions in a continental climate, there is a slight softening in climate characteristics, especially in winter (depending on the change in the values of relative humidity, maximum and minimum temperature), after dam construction.

In the area of the Deriner Dam and the HEPP Project, especially where the slope is between 70% and 100%, excavations and excavation materials have been randomly left, causing destruction in the natural habitat and scarce vegetation, and leading to increased erosion (Toker 2010). Moreover, because of the excavation materials, erosion control and afforestation works are prevented, which makes a further increase of the erosion rate inevitable (Figure 10.1). Roads opened as a result of the construction of the dam, as well as manufacturing operations and water retention, restrict the movement areas of hook-horned mountain goats (Rupicapra rupicapra), which has a wide habitat around the Yusufeli District (Figure 10.2). In addition, as a result of road construction work, forest areas that were previously inaccessible or difficult to access have become more approachable, resulting in the increased threat of illegal logging (Toker 2010).

Figure 10.1   General view of the Deriner Dam lake area

Figure 10.2 A view of the land before and during construction stage of the Deriner Dam lake area

b **Narrowing of agricultural lands:** Generally, alluvial flats form on the floors of river valleys in different sections. With dams built in front of the rivers, water collects behind them. The fertile alluvial areas around the river, which will be inundated by dam construction, are places where agricultural activities are concentrated. The lands on the alluvial plain are rich in organic materials and saturated with water, and the availability of irrigation allows increased variety in agricultural product and the production of two or more products each year. In arid and semi-arid regions, a greater need for water increases the importance of these areas, and valley floors in these areas constitute the main source of income and livelihood. Alluvial plains incorporating large projects provide advantages such as energy and irrigation throughout the region in the short term, but they cause the loss of agricultural areas at the local level and completely change the economic life of the people living in these settlements. Failure to take account of the direct or indirect effects mentioned in the assessment compensation is also considered to be among the reasons for local people reacting negatively to the project.

c **Possible changes after water catchment:** As the dam starts to collect water, an artificial lake forms behind it and a new base level is formed for the stream that empties into this lake. As a result of this new base level, many changes will take place in its accumulation, and especially erosion activity, which, in turn, leads to many changes in the ecosystem of the region (Sönmez 2012). The gully caused by maximum water stress by the dam lake areas gives rise to a need for additional protection areas on the water surface, resulting in the loss of land in the settlement area and an increase of unused land area.

Assessment of changes in economic and social structure of affected households

Issues such as the age and gender distribution of the population affected by infrastructure projects, the availability of income sources and nonagricultural income sources, the land assets affected by the project and its share in the total productive land, the share of agricultural income in the household income, and so on explain the magnitude of the effects of infrastructure projects. Where the project area selected is outside the settlement, households affected by expropriation with lands outside the project area, and a very small part of the total processing land is affected by the project, the impact of expropriation on the socioeconomic structure of the households remains minimal. In addition, the fact that the project does not require the resettlement of inhabitants is one of the reasons for the low level of impact of land acquisition and expropriation. The potential for a negative impact of development projects on local land markets may arise in the absence of irrigation water demands by farmers both in lake areas and in downstream settlements, in parallel to the water catchment and energy production. The fact that there is more than one power plant in many rivers, where the river is managed from the centre and integrated water resources management have not yet been developed, does not allow the development and implementation of effective strategies for the balanced use of water resources for energy and agriculture. For example, it is not expected that the power plants will adversely affect the landowners during the summer season, when agriculture is intensive, because of the establishment of 5–6 power plant projects on Savrun River (Osmaniye) and the generation of the power plants in the winter period (Tanrıvermiş and Aliefendioğlu 2011). However, the fact that the power plants are operated at night during the summer and that irrigation water cannot be supplied to the lower parts of the river causes irrigation failure and the loss of agricultural productivity, as a result of which the owners often file compensation claims.

Acceding to those households who demand resettlement in rural areas and wanted to maintain their traditional farming way of life becomes important in terms of facilitating the adaptation of the households to new settlements, since income and lifestyles in the pre-project period and settlement are largely based on agricultural activities. For example, it will be suitable for households whose basic livelihoods are agricultural activities such as fruit and vegetable growing to be resettled in places where irrigation is possible so that they can continue with these activities in their new settlements; they should be supported in the new settlement areas by the provision of seeds and seedlings matching the climate conditions. Care should be taken to ensure that the households in upland settlements have the qualifications to host fisheries and rural tourism in order to enjoy the benefits of the landscape in terms of livestock activities, water resources, lakes, and rural settlements to be built around the coastal zones.

In the new Hasankeyf District of Ilisu Dam and HEPP project, where resettlement works are in progress, the protection area is underwater together with the ancient city, which has been in existence for 12,000 years as the cradle of many civilizations. In the new district settlement, the public institution buildings which cannot meet the needs of the people, such as social, cultural, health, education, religion, and security, are designed and rebuilt in accordance with modern standards. Since the residences in the district centre cannot meet all of modern life's needs, the houses in the district are being constructed in a more modern style and with an eye to environmental concerns, unlike those in the existing settlement. The average size of the new accommodation was determined to be 135 square metres (1,450 square feet), reflecting the average household size (Figure 10.3). The

Figure 10.3 Hasankeyf former settlement (left) and new settlement site (right)

new district settlement is established on a larger area of 294.86 hectares (728 acres) compared with the existing settlement (50.82 hectares (125 acres)). In the new residential area, there is 78.7 hectares (194 acres) of green areas accounting for 27% of the residential area (Aliefendioğu 2016). However, the area of pasture and agriculture will remain under the lake area, so the people of Hasankcyf have luxury houses, but the land to be cultivated and the pastureland is reduced, making the people of the district worried about their sources of income. As a result of the dam, the Dicle Valley will negatively affect approximately 70,000 people in settlements that provide livelihoods such as crop production and livestock farming.

Where entire village settlements are expropriated, the effects of the projects on the social and economic lives of the inhabitants are deeper. For example, until 2012, when the Deriner Dam began to collect water, thus inundating the village areas, searches for new settlements continued. In this period, some of the village residents preferred to use the expropriation compensation for the new settlement area and some used it to acquire housing in urban areas, especially in the province of Artvin. Changing the location of the villagers has also caused a change in residential architecture and building materials. The relatively high income level of families with improved transport facilities has increased the tendency to use contemporary building materials in rural houses in the Oruçlu and Zeytinlik villages, which have been resettled because of their location in the lake area (Ceylan 1995). All of the buildings in the new settlement have a contemporary look, far removed from traditional architecture. Although moving away from traditional architecture and housing culture, disagreements (Gök and Yazar 2011; Tanrıvermiş and Aliefendioğlu 2017) are common incidents, and it is an obvious indication of the economic and socio-cultural changes that the rural households themselves choose to use the expropriation payment in this way. It is conceivable that an agreement will be made between the relevant public institutions and the villagers, before construction in undertaken on any area of land, and the village will be built with the support of the state (Orhan and Gök 2016).

In infrastructural projects carried out in many provinces and regions, it has been observed that the expropriation costs paid to the owners are spent rather than invested (Aliefendioğlu and Tanrıvermiş 2016; ENCON Co. 2005; İSTEM Co. 2009). In accordance with the provisions of the Constitution and Law No. 2942, expropriation compensation is generally paid in cash, and applications for an exchange of land, or land instead of that defined in the legislation, are not preferred either by the administration or the affected persons. In addition to providing consultation and guidance to the local public concerning the rational use of the expropriation sums paid to the rights holders, it will also be mandatory that the investment of the households in the new settlement area of their village be encouraged and supported in various forms (such as tax exemptions in some areas, project and material aid to those who will build houses); RAP preparation and implementation will be mandatory to realise these objectives. The resettlement action plan should definitely target the work of resettlement in rural and urban areas according to the demands of locals, and it should be kept in mind that the administration of resettlement in urban areas is more successful than the practices in rural areas. It is observed that families from rural areas who are resettled in urban areas meet with various difficulties in terms of accommodation (finding residences and workplaces) and socioeconomic issues (such as employment, income generation, transportation, neighbouring, and lifestyle); and it is known that households that were involuntarily resettled have problems adapting to the new local community.

Conclusion and recommendations

Population growth in many countries has led to a rapid increase in the need for food, shelter, and energy. However, fertile land resources are being used for nonagricultural purposes, such as the location for urban settlements and infrastructure investments. The pressure from rapidly increasing population growth, along with faster than expected growth in urbanisation, industrialisation, and transportation activities, impedes the protection of prime agricultural and farm land vital to meet the increasing food needs of the country, especially with rapid population growth. As is the case in the rest of the world, in Turkey, agricultural lands, and particularly irrigated lands, are continuously monitored, and the results are declared successful; however, it is not possible to find a source on the existence of land that has lost its fertility due to nonagricultural use, salting, or some other cause. Moreover, within the country, fertile farmland, and even forests and meadows in the immediate vicinity of all major cities, are disappearing. Even those areas that need to be protected by zoning plans are not in fact effectively protected.

Most infrastructure investments consist of projects for the transportation, energy, mining, large-scale farming, urban development, and tourism sectors. The return period on the investment amount for dams are relatively short, especially with dams built for such primary purposes such as energy, irrigation, and water supply, and attempts to increase the economic profitability of the projects are made by providing limited opportunities to the affected dwellings. Dams have been one of the main sources of increased energy production in the industrialisation period, and it is seen that spatial and socioeconomic changes in the settlements affected by the dam construction were neglected until the 1990s, because the completion of investments were to be achieved at the lowest possible cost. Along with this, and besides adding to the country's economy, many projects have also contributed significantly to the pace of social and economic development, creating employment in the local areas, thereby increasing income levels, and thus increasing living standards in different regions. On the other hand, dam construction also leads to many physical and human problems at regional level, and indirectly throughout the country. With dam construction, energy production and irrigation facilities have increased and some of the floods and flash floods have been brought under control. In contrast, with dam construction, many important cultural and natural heritage resources and fertile agricultural lands remain in the lake area. In many investment projects, it has been decided to carry out the classic benefit-cost analysis instead of an environmental benefit-cost analysis, and consequently, instead of long-term and sustainable economic income and social equilibrium, short-term income is taken as a basic decision criterion.

Real estate acquisitions and expropriation activities in large infrastructure projects have differing methodologies in almost every country, and there is as yet no globally accepted standards and guidelines for good practice. Furthermore, it is observed that each country adopts separate approaches and implementations toward the households negatively affected by such projects. In Turkey, only 2.56% of the 13,670 households affected by major infrastructure projects in the last 50 years have opted for settlement through their own means and the remaining households have been resettled by public institutions in urban and rural areas. Despite the fact that the majority of the projects examined involve the settlement of less than 50,000 inhabitants, the fact that 40.74% of the resettled households have preferred urban settlement is mainly the result of the diminution in economic importance of agriculture as the main source of income and livelihood, the difficulties of living in rural areas, and the age and needs of the population in the resettled households. For the dam lake areas, it has also been found that resettlement may not be necessary, thanks to better route selection for the national and international oil and natural gas pipelines, and road and railway projects. However, in the Turkish Legal System, it is only physical resettlement that is understood within the concept of resettlement, and loss of income and any decrease in access to income sources after the implementation of infrastructure projects are not considered within the scope of settlement, compensation is paid only on the request of the households and is based on general principles. Because many international financial institutions have declared procedures and policies regarding real estate acquisition and resettlement in the course of extending credit, and as this is regarded as the international standard today, resettlement action plans are prepared only for projects financed by foreign resources, where it is obligatory to implement them.

Real estate acquisitions for most of the major projects to date have been regarded only as an expropriation problem, which is not sufficient to ensure social justice. No matter how high the expropriation cost in the case studies examined, the process results in the dissatisfaction of the local people affected by the dam and the reimbursed costs cannot be utilised rationally. In this respect, it would be illogical to think that there would be no adverse environmental effects of dam projects leading to large-scale spatial and socioeconomic transformations. The main goal here should be to identify the means for predicting and minimising possible adverse outcomes and ensure their effective implementation. It is necessary to analyse the project process effectively for this purpose, to contribute to the development of society, and to increase the prosperity of the people through the preparation and implementation of comprehensive resettlement action plans and the determination of environmental effects in a real sense and not merely to fulfil administrative requirements.

The efforts made for the protection of the nation's historical, cultural, and natural heritage and the investments required for economic development are fast proving antithetical. For example, to date, only 3.30% of the archaeological remains in the lake areas of the Keban, Atatürk, and Karakaya Dams, built to increase watering opportunities for agriculture and to produce electricity, have been saved. However, the preservation of irreplaceable natural and cultural assets, and their availability to future generations, are the basic environmental responsibility of the individual and the state. As Sönmez (2012) emphasises, forms such as valleys, caves, volcanoes, and cliffs, which are examples of geological periods and geomorphology dating back millions of years, belong to the world, and city remains and historic buildings, which are located within the geography of ancient and historical periods, are humanity's heritage for future generations. In the light of this, in order to preserve the heritage of thousands of years of civilization, public authorities should be very careful in project development and implementation processes, and the potential negative impacts of projects should be well defined, the affected groups examined, and appropriate mitigation measures developed and implemented. In fact, if there are people affected in each infrastructure project, it should be compulsory to prepare and implement resettlement action plan and allocate resources from the project budget for this.

In Turkey, the resettlement of households – affected by activities such as real estate acquisition for infrastructure development; energy and mining investments; and the rearrangement of settlements for safety, the avoidance of potential disasters, and health risks – in rural and urban areas has become compulsory. Especially in the dam and HEPP projects and the resettlement practices in mining and disaster areas carried out until the 1990s, sufficient care was not given to the protection of natural and cultural assets. However, in the dam and HEPP projects built after the 1990s, an emphasis has been placed on the excavation and conservation activities for the preservation of the nations cultural heritage, the exhibition of the recovered artifacts, and the preservation of artifacts that are impossible to relocate. In the last

10 years, large dam and HEPP projects and mining and energy projects have been the subject of intense debate. Many settlements are being relocated, and the local people have reacted by laying the blame for their economic, social, and cultural losses on the resettlement processes; land acquisition and expropriation processes are therefore progressing slowly because of the negative reactions of local people. The share of the project costs for the reconstruction works carried out in the samples examined was relatively low (except in the Yusufeli Project, where the resettlement of an entire district was inevitable), and the main reason for this was found to be related to insufficiencies in the development of social projects for the households affected by public authorities, project implementation, business development programmes, and monitoring and evaluation studies.

According to the research results, while realisation of investments in the short term with costs as low as possible was accepted as a basic philosophy pre-1990, it has since been observed that environmental impact assessment studies and activities aimed at the protection of cultural assets have been conducted, in parallel with the formation of environmental protection legislation and an increase in the public's environmental awareness. However, it is imperative to allocate more resources to such issues as the destruction of fertile lands on riversides formed by alluviums carried by river waters for many years, the post-project prosperity of resettled people and the shift in neighbourhood relations, and the prevention of the destruction of social values and cultural assets. In cases where real estate acquisition for investment projects and the physical relocation of the settlements become inevitable, a planned resettlement policy should be implemented and resettlement activities carried out in rural and urban areas according to the demands of the affected households. It has been found that resettlement practices in urban areas are more successful than those in rural areas; however, those relocated in urban from rural areas have encountered difficulties from the perspectives of accommodation and socioeconomic issues in the post-resettlement period. The results of this research are of special importance in terms of showing the dilemma between preserving the natural and cultural assets in the countryside and public infrastructure investment preferences in many countries. Research results demonstrate that activities such as the selection of settlements for migrants, the determination of the size of the land and the housing units to be built, and the amount of the loan, management of space-person relations, settlement implementation methods, monitoring and evaluation studies, and impact mitigation methods are interest areas for real estate development and management experts, and it is clear that special consideration should be given to the employment of such specialists in organisations implementing policies related to land acquisition and resettlements.

A comprehensive analysis of the lands to be used for infrastructure and superstructure projects should be made, and in projects where fertile agricultural land must inevitably be used, the lost land assets must be included in the cost of the project and the land losses should have a key role in the decision-making process. Losses of alluvial lands in river basins and coastal deltas must be constantly monitored and evaluated, and the implementation of projects that cause minimum fertile alluvial land losses should be preferred as far as possible. Rapid industrialisation and urbanisation have placed various problems on the agenda, one of which is the deterioration within balances in the ecosystem. Disturbances in the ecosystem directly and indirectly affect human life and settlements. Epidemic diseases, global warming and climate change, environmental pollution, and the problems they create are examples of these. Project selection, development, and implementation should be made possible by considering the pressure of big dams on the ecosystem in order to ensure the sustainability of local economic, natural, and social structures as well as the preservation of natural resource assets and the quality of human life. In addition, a regular settlement plan should be made and developed containing new functions over and above those already available in and consistent with those in the settlements vacated. Otherwise, it is observed that people in the evacuated settlements inevitably tend to relocate again after the initial resettlement because they cannot continue the economic activities and social life they had before the project, nor can they integrate into the new settlement; these irregular migrations also cause problems that are impossible to solve in big cities.

References

Asian Development Bank (ADB). 1998. *Handbook on Resettlement: A Guide to Good Practice*, ADB, Manila: Philippines.

Akargul, E. 1998. *Anadolu Kültür Tarihi*. Türkiye Bilimsel ve Teknik Araştırma Kurumu, TÜBİTAK Popüler Bilim Kitapları 67, Ankara: Turkey.

Akkan, E. 1990. *Fırat Havzası Barajları ve Çevreye Etkileri*. Fırat Üniversitesi Coğrafya Sempozyumu 14–15 Nisan 1986 Elazığ, Fırat Havzası Araştırma Merkezi, Elazığ: Turkey.

Aliefendioğlu, Y. 2016. "Kentsel Kesimde Kamulaştırılan Taşınmazların Değerleme İşlemleri ve Sorunları Üzerine Bir Araştırma: Hasankeyf İlçesi Örneği". *Uluslararası Sosyal Araştırmalar Dergisi* 9(42): 1338–1361.

Aliefendioğlu, Y. 2017. *Koruma Statülerinin Taşınmaz Piyasaları ve Değerlerine Etkileri Muğla İli Örneği*, Lambert Academic Publishing, Germany.

Aliefendioğlu, Y. and Tanrıvermiş, H. 2016. *Evaluation of Land Acquisition and Expropriation for Investment Projects in Turkey within the Framework of the Turkish Laws and International Standards: The Case of Baku-Tbilisi Ceyhan Crude Oil Pipeline Project*. Royal Agricultural University Working Paper, Cirencester, Gloucestershire: UK.

Atahar, S.A. 2013. "Development Project, Land Acquisition and Resettlement in Bangladesh; A Quest for Well Formulated National Resettlement and Rehabilitation Policy". *International Journal of Humanities and Social Science* 3(7): 306–319.

Bakırcı, M. 1997. "Türkiye'de Yer Değiştiren Şehirlere Yeni Bir Örnek: Samsat". *Türk Coğrafya Dergisi* 32: 355–365.

Bakırcı, M. 2016. "Barajların Mekanın Yeniden Organizasyonuna Etkileri: Melen Barajı Örneği [The Effects of Dams on Spatial Reorganization: The Case of the Melen Dam]". *Marmara Coğrafya Dergisi* Sayı: 33 (Ocak – 2016): 439–464.

Brown, L.R. 1979. *Yirmidokuzuncu Gün Dünya Kaynakları Karşısında İnsan İhtiyaçları*, Worldwatch Enstitüsü Yayını, Arpaz Matbaacılık, İstanbul: Turkey.

Ceylan, S. 1995. *Artvin Yöresinin Coğrafî Etüdü*, Atatürk Üniversitesi Sosyal Bilimler Enstitüsü, Doktora Tezi, Erzurum.

Çotur, S. 1990. *Keban Barajının Fırat Havzasına Etkisi*, Fırat Üniversitesi Coğrafya Sempozyumu. 14–15th April 1986, Fırat Havzası Araştırma Merkezi, Elazığ: Turkey.

ENCON Co. 2005. *Ilısu Barajı ve HES Projesi Yeniden Yerleşim Eylem Planı Final Raporu Ana Metin*. Enerji ve Tabii Kaynaklar Bakanlığı Devlet Su İşleri Müdürlüğü Yayını, ENCON Çevre Danışmanlık Ltd.Şti, Ankara: Turkey.

General Directorate of State Hydraulic Works (DSİ). 2016. *Activity Report 2015*. Ankara: Turkey.

Gök, Y. 2001. "Erzurum-Kars Depremi'nden (1983) Sonra Yeri Değiştirilen Yerleşmeler". *Doğu Coğrafya Dergisi* 7(5): 145–158.

Gök, Y. and Yazar, M. 2011. "Afetlere Maruz Kalan Yerleşmelerin Yer Değişiminde Karşılaşılan Sorunlara Bir Örnek: İspir Madenköprübaşı Beldesi Elmalı Mahallesi". *Doğu Coğrafya Dergisi* 16(26): 73–94.

Hayrullahoğlu, G., Aliefendioğlu, Y. and Tanrıvermiş, H. 2017. *Deprem Sonrası Kentte Oluşacak Sorunlara Dirençli Kent Yaklaşımı İle Çözüm Aranması: Marmara Depremi Örneği*, In: Kentsel Politikalar, Palme Yayıncılık, Ankara: Turkey, pp. 290–304.

IFC (International Finance Corporation). 2001. Handbook for Preparing a Resettlement Action Plan. Washington, DC, https://openknowledge.worldbank.org/handle/10986/15240 License: CC BY 3.0 IGO.

IFC (International Finance Corporation). 2012. *Performance Standard 5: Land Acquisition and Involuntary Resettlement*, IFC, Washington, DC.

İSTEM Co. 2009. *RAP Completion Audit – Livelihood Restoration Questionnaire Results.* İSTEM Gayrimenkul Değerleme, Araştırma ve Teknik Hizmetler A.Ş., Ankara: Turkey.

Maitra, S. 2009. "Development Induced Displacement: Issues of Compensation and Resettlement– Experiences from the Narmada Valley and Sardar Sarovar Project". *Japanese Journal of Political Science* 10: 191–211.

Mathur, H.M. 2016. *Resettlement Planning: Reversing Displacement Impacts of Development Projects.* In: Assessing the Social Impact of Development Projects, (Ed.) H. Mathur Advances in Asian Human-Environmental Research. Springer, Cham: Switzerland, doi:10.1007/978-3-319-19117-1_13.

Ministry of Forestry and Water Affairs of Turkey. 2016. *Activity Report 2015.* Ankara: Turkey.

Ministry of Energy and Natural Resources of Turkey. 2016. *Activity Report 2015.* Ankara: Turkey.

Ministry of Environment and Urbanism of Turkey. 2016. *Activity Report 2015.* Ankara: Turkey.

Orhan, F. and Gök, Y. 2016. "Baraj Yapımı Nedeniyle Yeri Değiştirilen Yerleşmelere Örnek: Oruçlu ve Zeytinlik Köyleri (Artvin) (Example of Resettlement Due To Construction of the Dam: Oruçlu and Zeytinlik Villages (Artvin))". *Eastern Geographical Review* 21(35): 131–148.

Özkalaycı, Z.E. and İçten, H. 2005. *Yeniden Yerleşim Planlamaları ve Devlet Su İşleri Genel Müdürlüğü'ndeki Uygulamaları [Resettlement Planning and Its Applications at General Directorate of State Hydraulic Works].* TMMOB Harita ve Kadastro Mühendisleri Odası 10. Türkiye Harita Bilimsel ve Teknik Kurultayı, Ankara: Turkey.

Sayhan, S. 1999. "Kızılırmak'ın Hirfanlı Baraj Gölüne Döküldüğü Mevkiide Aktüel Sedimantasyon ve Alüvyal Şekillenme Süreci". *Türk Coğrafya Dergisi* 34: 419–443.

Şengün, M.T. 2007. "Son Değerlendirmeler Işığında Keban Barajının Elazığ İklimine Etkisi". *Doğu Anadolu Bölgesi Araştırmaları* 5: 116–122.

Sever, R. 2005. *Coğrafi Açıdan Bir Araştırma: Çoruh Havzası Enerji Yatırım Projeleri ve Çevresel Etkileri.* Çizgi Kitabevi, Konya: Turkey.

Sönmez, M.E. 2012. "Barajların Mekân Üzerindeki Olumsuz Etkileri ve Türkiye'den Örnekler [The Negative Impacts of Dams on the Environment and Their Examples in Turkey]". *Gaziantep Üniversitesi Sosyal Bilimler Dergisi* 11(1):213–231.

Tagliarino, N.K. 2016. *Encroaching on Land and Livelihoods: How National Expropriation Laws Measure up Against International Standards.* World Resources Institute Working Paper Washington, DC: USA.

Tanrıvermiş, H. 2003. "Agricultural Land Use Change and Sustainable Use of Land Resources in the Mediterranean Region of Turkey". *Journal of Arid Environments* 54:553–564.

Tanrıvermiş, H. and Aliefendioğlu, Y. 2011. *Sayan Regülatörü ve Hidroelektrik Santrali İle Enerji Nakil Hattı Projesi Kamulaştırma Alanında Arazi Değerleri Kamulaştırma ve İrtifak Bedellerinin Tespiti Üzerine Bir Araştırma.* Ankara Üniversitesi Fen Bilimleri Enstitüsü Taşınmaz Geliştirme Anabilim Dalı Yayın No: 5, Ankara: Turkey.

Tanrıvermiş, H. and Aliefendioğlu, Y. 2015. *Yusufeli Barajı ve Hidroelektrik Santrali Kamulaştırma Alanında Arsa Vasfındaki Taşınmazların Tespiti ve Kamulaştırma Bedellerinin Analizi,* Ankara Üniversitesi Fen Bilimleri Enstitüsü Taşınmaz Geliştirme Anabilim Dalı Yayın No: 22, Ankara: Turkey.

Tanrıvermiş, H. and Aliefendioğlu, Y. 2017. Principles of Land Acquisition, Expropriation and Compensation Calculation for Infrastructure Projects in Turkey and An Analysis of Key Issues, Paper Prepared for Presentation at the "2017 World Bank Conference on Land and Poverty", The World Bank, March 20–24, 2017, Washington DC: USA.

Tanrıvermiş, H. and Bülbül, M., 2007. "The Role of Agriculture in the Turkish Economy at the Beginning of the European Union Accession Negotiations". *Journal of Applied Sciences.* 7(4):612–625.

Tanrıvermiş, H. and Doğru, N. 2004. *Türkiye'de Yasalar ve Uluslararası Kuruluşların İlkeleri Çerçevesinde Kamulaştırma Süreci ve Bedel Takdiri: Bakü-Tiflis-Ceyhan Ham Petrol Boru Projesi Örneği.* Türkiye VI. Tarım Ekonomisi Kongresi, Tokat: Türkiye, pp. 183–196.

The World Bank. 2002. *World Bank Policy on Involuntary Resettlement Policy Directive (OD 4.30).* Washington, DC

Tonbul, S. 1990. *Elazığ ve Çevresinin İklim Özellikleri ve Keban Barajının Yöre İklimi Üzerine Olan Etkileri.* Fırat Üniversitesi Coğrafya Sempozyumu 14–15 Nisan 1986 Elazığ, Fırat Havzası Araştırma Merkezi, Elazığ: Turkey.

Toker, E. 2010. *Borçka ve Deriner Barajlarının Çoruh Havzasında Neden Olduğu Arazi Kullanım Değişiminin ve Arazi Tahribatının İrdelenmesi.* Artvin Çoruh Üniversitesi Fen Bilimleri Enstitüsü Orman Mühendisliği Anabilim Dalı, Yüksek Lisans Tezi, Artvin: Turkey.

Tunçdilek, N. 1986. "Türkiye'de Yerleşmenin Evrimi". *İstanbul Üniversitesi Deniz Bilimleri ve Coğrafya Enstitüsü,* İstanbul: Turkey.

227

Turoğlu, H. 2005. *Trabzon-Sarp arası Karadeniz Aklanı Doğal Ortam Özellikleri ve İnsan*, İber Matbaacılık, Trabzon: Turkey.

Tümertekin, E. and Özgüç, N. 1997. *Beşeri Coğrafya İnsan-Kültür-Mekân*, Çantay Kitabevi, İstanbul: Turkey.

Viitanen, K. and Kakulu, I. 2009. "Global Concerns in Compulsory Purchase and Compensation Processes". *International Federation of Surveyors Article of the Month – February 2009*, www.fig.net/resources/monthly_articles/2009/february_2009/february_2009_viitanen_kakulu.pdf.

Yıldırımlı, Ş. 2005. Munzur Dağları, Türkiye'nin 122 Önemli Bitki Alanı, (Eds.) N. Özhatay, A. Byfield ve, S. Atay, WWF Türkiye, Doğal Hayatı Koruma Vakfı, İstanbul: Turkey, pp. 316–319.

Yiğitbaşıoğlu, H. 1996. "Türkiye'deki Barajlar". *Ankara Üniversitesi Türkiye Coğrafyası Araştırma ve Uygulama Merkezi Dergisi* 5: 171–181.

11

China's land acquisition under marketisation

Chengri Ding and Yuzhe Wu

Introduction

China's remarkable economic growth since 1978 has been in tandem with rapid urbanisation. Urban population accounted for only 17.9% of the total population in 1978. That number increased to 57.35% in 2016.[1] This outstanding pace of urban growth is manifested in both massive rural-city migration and urban spatial expansion. The growth rates of urbanisation in the pro-reform period translated into annual rural-city migrants of 10–15 million. The built-up areas expanded from 6,720 square kilometres (2,595 square miles) in 1981 to 49,000 square kilometres (18,919 square miles) in 2015.[2]

This enormous scale of China's urban spatial expansion has had two profound policy challenges as well as implications. One is associated with land-lost peasants and the other with the loss of farmland. Both are associated with land requisition to meet the land demand for industrialisation and urbanisation. On the one hand, the amount of land requisitioned by the State was 2,879.86 km² (1,112 square miles) in 2002, primarily on farmland,[3] and the number kept rising. By the end of 2011, the amount of requisitioned land was 3,958.43 km² (1,528 square miles) (Qian and Mou, 2015). So there was total of 1,078.57 km² (416 square miles) of land requisitioned over nine years, which means approximately 120 km² (46 square miles) was requisitioned per year. On the other hand, peasants who lost land have been another issue generating public concerns. It was estimated that the accumulated land-lost peasants amounted to around 50 million by 2008 (Bao, 2008), and what is worse is that many of them were not satisfied with the compensation paid as a result of the land requisition. A survey conducted in 2011 shows that 64.39% peasants opposed land requisition because of the unsatisfactory level of compensation (Ji and Qian, 2011). However, it is projected that the total land-lost peasants will reach 100 million by 2020, if China's cities continue to grow at the current pace. Land-lost peasants become the number one factor for social unrest in rural areas.

Because land requisition is the primary source of land supply for urbanisation, an enormous amount of farmland land has been lost in the process. For instance, about 16.667 million hectares (41.2 million acres) of farmland was lost during 2003–2011, and about 40% of it was due to non-agricultural construction.[4] The pace of rapid urbanisation has alarmed the central government over its concern for food security. Accordingly, China has adopted a series of policy instruments and measures on farmland protection to achieve self-sufficiency in grains. The most famous farmland protection policies include the designation of basic cultivated land districts, the adoption of a dynamic farmland balance (which virtually is zero-net loss of farmland policy), and a vertical system of land use planning (Ding and Cao, 2017). China has also undertaken land requisition reforms to ease social unrest associated with land-lost peasants.

It is then interesting to ask the following questions: what are the issues with land requisition in China? How have those issues emerged? What are the institutional settings that distinguish China in land requisition? What are the interests as well as the expectations of different stakeholders (peasants vs. officials) regarding requisition? What are the challenges that the land policy reforms should undertake in the future to resolve land issues? What are the lessons to be learned here?

These questions are too broad to be addressed in a single chapter. The following focuses therefore on a general framework of land requisition and preliminary assessment, and presents two cases of surveys on land requisition to illustrate the complexity of land requisition problems.

Land institution on land requisition

Land ownership and markets

China has a distinguishing land institution (Ding, 2003; Lin et al., 2014). Land ownership is geographically defined. The State owns the land in cities and towns, while rural communes collectively own rural land. The State ownership refers to developed or zoned land, while planned land for development is either ready for land requisition or has been requisitioned. Rural land within the administrative boundaries of cities and towns belongs to collective communes.

China introduced a Land Use Right System (LURs) in the early 1990s to provide access to the State's land for private investors, developers, and users. The LURs is virtually a public land leasing system, developed after the Hong Kong model. Under the LURs, private users and investors can lease, transfer, rent, and mortgage land-use rights on the State-owned land. The objectives of the development of LURs are to introduce market mechanisms in resource allocations to improve economic efficiency, to correct government failures in allocation, enhance land management, rationalise land development and land use, minimise the negative consequences of the land tenure system, and promote urban construction and economic development (Ding, 2003). What is distinguishing China's LURs is that it applies only to State land, implying that LURs apply to land markets only in cities and towns, not in rural land. In other words, rural land is prohibited from land development unless it is first converted into State ownership. The land markets which exist only in cities and towns and in which the State owns land, have two outstanding policy implications: one is associated with a two-phase, sequential land development process in rural areas in which land ownership conversion is a prerequisite in the first phase and actual land development itself is the second phase; the other is associated with a rural-city dichotomy of land markets, which is similar to the "*hukou*" system in which geography is used to determine socioeconomic classes. Denied land development rights, peasants in rural areas are basically denied the opportunity to share in the economic prosperity from urbanisation and industrialisation, as manifested in the high rural-urban income gaps.[5]

In State-owned land, there are two kinds of land transactions that define two levels of land markets. One is the sale of land-use rights and the other is the transfer of land-use rights (Ding, 2003). The former defines the "first" level of land market where municipal government, as a representative of the State, sells land-use rights to buyers for a fixed period through auction, tender, or negotiation and collects land conveyance fees in a lumpy, up-front fashion of public land leasing. The transfer of land-use rights defines the "second" level of land market. In both "first" and "second" levels of land markets, the price of land-use rights depends on land-use type, location, land-use density, and neighbourhood externalities. The State controls land markets through its monopolisation of the first level of land markets (or its monopolisation of land supply). The government is not involved in the transfer of land-use rights except for land registration, legal protection, and taxation (Walker and Li, 1994).

Land requisition

According to China's land institution, land requisition is an essential process in urban spatial expansion. This gives local governments a role to play in land development that is not observed in many other countries, particularly Western ones. Judging from the fact that local governments rely heavily on land revenues for public finance and play a dominate role in land markets, they can be viewed as land developers. This in turn makes land requisition a prominent policy issue as might be expected when the system of checks and balances to prevent governments from abusive actions towards the people is not fully established in China.

Pre-reform era

Under the central planning system, governments were in charge of establishing one-year and five-year socioeconomic development plans that laid out specific economic growth goals measurable mainly by industrial outputs. After examining existing capacities, governments determined the level of capital investment and improvements required to achieve their socioeconomic goals. Land development was considered to be an element of capital investment and improvement (*xiang mu gui hua*). However, since land was neither a commodity nor an asset capable of generating wealth, it was the last factor to be considered in the investments and industrial capacity expansion (Ding, 2003).

When socioeconomic development plans called for land development, municipal governments increased their land supply through land acquisition, a conversion of land ownership from the collective to the State. In these cases of land acquisition, the Constitution stipulates that municipal governments must compensate farmers for the loss of their land. Since there were no land markets, peasants were instead compensated with a package that included job offers in which farmers would work for the enterprises established on the acquired land, housing compensation (referred to as resettlement fees), compensation for the loss of crops and belongings connected to the land, and urban residency licenses (*hukou*).

It was common for large projects such as highways, railroads, and water projects to leave farmers with no land to farm. In these cases, the agency that had acquired the land from the farmers was responsible for job resettlement, and in the pre-reform era, State-owned enterprises were a dominant component of the labour force. Since output values were given greater weight than net profits in evaluating the performance of these firms, it was easy to place affected farmers in the State-owned enterprises. Job placement was applied to adults, whereas children and elders were not considered for these positions.

Although peasants were not paid market prices for their land, they were willing to strike deals with the government agencies. The relocation packages offered them non-agricultural jobs in accordance with the policy specifying that the government agencies purchasing the land should be responsible for job placement and urban *hukou* status. Granting of a city *hukou* was also very attractive to farmers. A *hukou* was a locality residence license that allowed the *hukou* holder to access social benefits as well as local public goods (including schools) and crops at subsidised prices (Ding, 2003). All social benefits and subsidised public goods were geographically bounded. Denying access to public goods and subsidised goods made it very difficult, if not impossible, for people without a city's *hukou* to live in that city. Thus, granting a city *hukou* to affected farmers made them eligible for the social welfare services – medical insurance, pension and retirement plans, high-quality schools, and subsidised agricultural goods – that were commonly provided in cities. Comparing direct compensation packages of resettlement, these intangible benefits may be more attractive. This was particularly true in the pre-reform era (before 1978) and in the early years of the post-reform era (after 1978).

Post-reform era

The reform eras started when China adopted its famous "open-door" policy in 1978. Since then, reforms gradually spread from rural areas to cities, from markets of consumption goods to input markets (land, labour, and capital), from the State-owned enterprises to institutional and legal systems. Perhaps the most influential reforms that were important to urban and land developments were the Constitutional Amendment and Land Administration laws of 1988 and 1986, respectively.

The compensation payable following compulsory land acquisition is primarily guided by the Land Administration Law that was first passed in 1986 and then amended in 1998. The Land Administration Law (1986) followed the old model used in the planned system to guide land acquisition compensation. It contained four main components: land compensation, resettlement subsidies, compensation for young crops and attachments on land, and labour resettlement. Under these provisions, land compensation should be 3–6 times the average annual output value of acquired land in the preceding three years, whereas resettlement subsidies should be 2–3 times the average annual output value. The sum of these two items should not exceed 20 times the average annual output value of acquired land in the preceding three years.

The Law further stipulated that compensation for young crops and land attachments should be given to farmers, whereas land compensation and resettlement subsides should be retained in collective communes that should use funds for the development and resettlement of affected labourers and for the assistance of unemployed farmers. The Department of Land Management at the county level was responsible for coordinating acquired communes, organisations or units that use acquired land, and related authorities to resettle affected farm labours. Any units beside the ones that use the acquired land were to be compensated for by offering employment opportunities to these affected farm labourers.

The scope of acquisition was widely defined. It should serve the need of land for State construction activities. Since the portion of the private economy was relative small, less than one-third in the 1980s, various developments such as infrastructure, expansion and the establishment of industrial firms, and housing were all justifications for land acquisition.

Rapid economic development and fundamental changes of economic structure prompted the nation to revise its laws governing land management. Thus, the 1998 Land Administration

Law (LAL) was passed. Compared to the 1986 version, this amendment is distinctive in three aspects with respect to compensation to be paid on compulsory land acquisition while maintaining the same, formula-driven framework. First, it raised compensation levels. Compensation for land taken was to be 6–10 times the average annual output value of acquired land in the preceding three years. Funds for resettlement should be 4–6 times the derived land productivity, a quantity determined through the following calculations. First, the affected population is established by dividing the total amount of acquired land by per capita cultivated land. Then the amount of resettlement subsidies per person is set to equal 4–6 times the average annual output value of acquired land in the preceding three years. The total amount of resettlement subsidies per hectare was not to exceed 15 times the average annual output value of acquired land in the three prior years. Upon approval from the provincial authorities, the combined amount of the resettlement and land compensation can increase but by no greater than 30 times the derived land productivity if needed to maintain a constant living standard for affected farmers.

Second, the LAL 1998 is silent on labour resettlement except that it encourages the development of village-owned enterprises. Finally, Article 51 of LAL 1998 states that the standard of compensation and resettlement following the requisition of land to build large or medium-sized water conservancy or hydroelectric projects shall be prescribed separately by the State Council. It requires public interests to justify land acquisition, although the definition of public interests is vaguely articulated.

According to these standards, the average land compensation and resettlement subsidies were 20,000–30,000 RMB[6] per mu in the fringe areas of the city Wenzhou in Zhejiang province (Ding, 2007).[7] This average is consistent with results from a 21 county and city survey conducted by the Zhejiang Department of Land and Resources on land acquisition in the first half of 2002 (Ding, 2007). The average compensation level was slightly over 28,000 RMB per mu, 8–10 times that for land compensation and 6–12.5 times resettlement subsidies. Interestingly, for every *mu* requisitioned, 1.83 farmers lost their land and 0.94 laborers lost the land on which they worked. A total of 9,203 farmers lost their cultivated land, and 60% of these people were labourers. This situation is representative of the impacts of land acquisition on farmers throughout China, and in particular throughout the eastern coastal areas where the economy is booming.

Farmland protection

Since the mid-1990s, the government of China had voiced concerns about its ability to continue feeding a growing population, when environmental analyst Lester Brown (1995) predicted that China would soon need to resort to grain imports on a scale massive enough to cause severe disruptions in world markets. Like Lester Brown, the government of China targeted the conversion of farmland to industrial and residential uses, especially in the most productive agricultural regions, which was the chief threat to the nation's continued capacity to produce adequate levels of staple cereals. According to official government statistics, China lost over 14.5 million hectares (35.8 million acres) of arable land between 1979 and 1995 (Lichtenberg and Ding, 2006).

The government of China responded to these food security concerns by introducing a number of measures aimed at protecting farmland, especially farmland with the greatest production potential. Two principal laws govern farmland preservation efforts in China: the Basic Farmland Protection Regulation, passed in 1994, and the New Land Administration Law, enacted in 1999.

The basic farmland protection regulation

The Basic Farmland Protection Regulation applies to five classes of land: (1) "cultivated land" currently planted with food grains, cotton, and oilseeds; (2) "cultivated land" with good irrigation, drainage, and erosion control, along with medium- and low-quality land on which irrigation, drainage, and erosion control measures are being installed; (3) land planted with vegetables; (4) experimental plots for agricultural research and development; and (5) other cultivated land as determined by the State Council. It is important to recognise that the term "cultivated land" does not correspond exactly to what would be defined as "farmland" in most countries. Instead, it refers only to land used to grow major food grains, feed grains, soybeans, and tubers. Not included is land used in other kinds of food production; in particular, the Basic Farmland Protection Regulation does not apply to tree fruits, viticulture, or fishponds.

The law requires governments at or above the county level to designate a basic farmland protection zone in every village or township. Determination of basic farmland and the designation of these farmland protection districts are subject to approval by higher government bodies up to the level of the State Council. There are two kinds of basic farmland protection districts. The first level consists of high-quality land with high productivity; the Law prohibits converting such land to nonagricultural uses. The second level consists of good-quality land with moderate productivity; the Law permits conversion of such land to nonagricultural uses under some circumstances, usually after a planned period of 5–10 years. The regulation further stipulates: (1) if the conversion of land within farmland districts is unavoidable in order to build national projects, such as highways, energy production, or transportation, the State must approve the conversion of land parcels of more than 500 mu while the provincial governments must approve those of less than 500 mu; and (2) the same amount of farmland lost to conversion must be replaced by new farmland somewhere else. The Act thus imposes a so-called dynamic balance (what in the USA would be termed a "no net loss") policy whose intent is to keep the total amount of basic farmland constant in the face of pressures from urbanisation and infrastructure construction.

The new land administration law

The 1999 New Land Administration Law is intended to protect environmentally sensitive and agricultural lands, promote market development, encourage citizen involvement in the legislative process, and coordinate the planning and development of urban land. Article 33 stresses the focus on the dynamic balance (no net loss) of farmland policy in the Basic Farmland Protection Regulation to all farmland. It states:

> People's governments of provinces, autonomous regions and municipalities directly under the Central Government should strictly implement the overall plans and annual plans for land utilisation and take measures to ensure that the total amount of cultivated land within their administrative areas remains unreduced. Where the total amount of cultivated land is reduced, the State Council shall order the government concerned to reclaim land of the same quality and amount as is reduced within a time limit.... Where individual governments of provinces or municipalities directly under the Central Government, for lack of land reserves, cannot reclaim enough land to make up for the cultivated land they used for additional construction projects, they shall apply to the State Council for approval of their reclaiming less or no land within their own administrative areas but of their reclaiming land in other areas.

The law reinforces farmland preservation efforts by requiring an approval from the State Council for any conversion of basic farmland, conversion of farmland larger than 35 ha, (86 acres) and conversion of other land larger than 70 ha. (172 acres). It further encourages land development in areas that are considered wasteland or that feature low soil productivity. Despite the stipulation that the dynamic balance (no net loss) of farmland policy be implemented at provincial levels, in practice this provision is actually carried out at the city, county, and sometimes township levels. Article 34 requires that basic farmland not be less than 80% of total cultivated land in provinces, autonomous regions, and municipalities directly under the central government. Articles 17–26 establish the mechanisms and principles of planning and implementing overall plans for land utilisation. A comprehensive scheme of urban development has been widely developed across Chinese cities in order to provide appropriate means to achieve balanced development between society, economy, and the environment. This scheme requires that urban development be coordinated through planning to eliminate redundancy and duplicated construction, rationalised in layouts so that land use is efficient, and provided with sufficient infrastructure. It is thus expected that urban development patterns will be different from those of the pre-reform period.

From the beginning of the 21st century to the present, China has achieved great advances in urbanisation and industrialisation, and the explosion in the expansion of urban land triggered widespread illegal use of arable land and many farmers lost their land without appropriate compensation (Hui et al., 2013). A series of policies and measures have been adopted by governments at all levels to address the land acquisition-induced problems, such as the *Regulations on Deepening Reform of Land Administration Decisions*, the *Guidelines on Improving Land Requisition Compensation and Resettlement System*, and the *Training and Social Security*. These policies or regulations were issued to improve the land acquisition system to achieve a more rational and acceptable compensation standard, within which there are several significant changes. First, the living standard of farmers should remain intact after land acquisition. As presented by the Regulation on Strengthening Land Administration, which was issued in 2006, the compensation for land-lost farmers should cover their social security. Second, the total value of compensation increases up to 30 times the previous three year's average yield, and the sources of funding should be clearly indicated. Thirdly, the annual yield or the equivalent price of the requisitioned land should be assessed under a unified standard and be transparent to the public.

Assessment of land institution and land requisition in China

Distinguishing land institution

The land institution system defined by China's Land Laws has profound implications on the ways China is urbanising as well as on the issues and challenges emerging from its rapid urbanisation.[8] First, land laws institutionalise city governments' dominant roles in land markets. Although land use rights can be transacted between users in land markets (in the second land markets), the total amount of land available in land markets is controlled by city governments, who act as representatives of the State in leasing out use rights. This is because lots should be leased out in the first land markets in which city governments are paid land conveyance fees upfront at the beginning of the leasing periods, and depending on land uses (it is 70, 40, and 50 years for residential, industrial, and commercial uses, respectively).

Second, city governments are given enormous institutional power in land requisition. Consequently, city governments take full advantage of it by pricing land for land requisition remarkably lower than land market prices for urban development. Anecdotal evidences show that land conveyance fees paid by developers to city governments are in the order of 10 times the costs paid by city governments to peasants in land requisition. The combination of the lump-sum nature of the payment of land leasing fees and the city governments' underpricing of land requisition enables local officials to generate outstanding off-budgetary revenues from land. Proceeds from land leasing remain with city (county) governments and become the most important source for off-budget incomes for cities (Ding, 2003; Ding et al., 2014).[9] For instance, land conveyance fees were 2.75 trillion RMB, which was about two-third of the GDP, in 2010. The ratio of land revenues to subnational governments' own revenues was 0.68 in 2010, indicating the importance of land-based public financing in China (Ding et al., 2014).[10] Proceeds from land leasing in Beijing and Shanghai, the two largest cities in China, for instance, were equal to 40–50% of total fiscal revenue in 2009 (Liu, 2010). In Hangzhou city, land conveyance fees contribute 60% of total revenues in 2004–2005 (Ding, 2007).

Thirdly, the non-market based method used in the determination of peasants' compensation on land requisition proves to be problematic and a source of social unrest. The LAL requires the same living standards for peasants after land requisition but does not provide concrete implementation guidelines to achieve it. The formula-based determination of compensation is static and does not include factors that capture the rapidly growing economy in China to address fairness in land taking over time. The formula might have been considered to be sufficient when it was first introduced but may not be so since, as living costs have increased along with China's economy. Further, with soaring prices (particularly for housing), the compensation package, which was considered to be appropriate once land is taken, may soon turn out to be insufficient for peasants to maintain the same living standards a few years after land requisition.

Fourth and finally, the central government is committed to adopting the so-called most rigid land management system, whose primary objective is to protect farmland for self-reliance in grain products. China's rigid land management system is characterised by the following features: (1) the mandated designation of no less than 80% of farmland as basic cultivated land that is prohibited from land development unless the State Council issues development permission;[11] (2) the strict implementation of the dynamic balance farmland policy, which is virtually a no-net loss of farmland policy, and which implies that land reclamation is mandated to offset farmland losses resulting from industrialisation and urbanisation; and (3) a vertical land use planning system in which land use and development quotas are allocated along the top-down administrative ladder, and land use master plans for cities and towns are approved by either the national or provincial governments. For instance, the State Council approves the land use master plan for cities with a population of over one million, while provincial governments grant approve for smaller cities (of less than one million).

Socioeconomic impacts and consequences of land requisition

The rapidly rising number of landless peasants from land requisition threatens social stability and is the predominant reason for rural social unrest. The accumulated number of landless peasants was estimated to be in the range of 40–50 million in 2011, and an additional three million is added annually.[12] Land requisition is the number one reason for peasants' letters of complaint and visits. Land-related disputes account for 40% of total complaint letters and visits and 60% of group complaints.[13] About 73% of peasants' complaints were related to land requisition (Lu et al., 2011). Peasants usually lack the skills necessary to compete for high-paid urban jobs, and land requisition compensation is not sufficient to generate income streams for daily spending over the long term. Traditionally, land has functioned as a safety net for peasants. Land requisition implies that peasants give up their economic safety net and have to migrate to cities. There are substantial differences between migrants and local residents in cities in terms of hourly wages, working hours, housing conditions, access to social insurance programmes, and poverty rates (Du et al., 2006; Park and Wang, 2010). This implies that land requisition generates a new (migrant) urban poor.

Chaotic and uncoordinated land use patterns become the norm of spatial expansion of urban built-up areas across Chinese cities and cause enormous loss of land resources. Prevailing and inefficient urban spatial structures take the forms of spatially sporadic, excessive designation of various Special Economic Zones (SEZs),[14] over-scaled land development projects, and a China style of urban sprawl that is largely derived by the ways in which farmland is protected. By the summer of 2004, there were 6,866 zones across the country, covering more than 38,600 km² (14,900 square miles). Land development costs are extremely high, and it was estimated that the basic infrastructure cost per square kilometre was 200 million RMB (nearly $25 million) in 2000. Because of the lack of investment funds, 24,900 km² (9,613 square miles) of planned development zones were eliminated in 2004, representing 64.5% of the total. More than 1,300 km² (502 square miles) have been returned to agricultural use (Cao, 2004). In Beijing alone, the number of SEZs was reduced from 470 to 28 in 2008; and 1,500 hectares (3,700 acres) of land was returned to agriculture.[15]

Excessive SEZs is a driving factor that causes over-capacity in many manufacturing sectors. The value of warehoused industrial goods in China, for instance, was estimated at $200 billion in 2006. For the steel sector, in 2005, the production capacity was estimated at 470 million tons, whereas the actual demand was only 370 million tons. The total capacity for steel production will top out at 600 million tons when all the projects planned and under construction are completed.[16] Overproduction in other industries can exceed 100% or even higher than the actual demand. The ratio of automobile production capacity to market absorption was 1.47:1 in 2005.

Inefficient patterns of land use and spatial growth may incur enormous socioeconomic costs. For instance, empirical studies on urban sprawl in US cities conclude that avoidable costs of time and fuel resulting from congestion were $78 billion in 2000; incremental costs of infrastructure services were, on average, $1.13 for every dollar of revenue generated; and development costs were calculated to be 7% more compared to compact and mixed land use alternatives (Green, 2006). Other negative impacts of urban sprawl cited include the loss of farmland, a rising tax burden, increasing racial and income segregation, and deteriorating public health (Soule, 2006; Victoria Transport Policy Institute, 2008).

Strict farmland protection policies prohibit land development in urban fringes if they are inside basic farmland districts. This generates two kinds of social welfare losses. One is related to urban sprawl, by forcing urban development to leapfrog over protected farmland at urban fringe areas. The other is related to the losses forgone in the land price premium. Land in urban fringes has a much higher land price premium than land further away from city cores. Overall, social welfares decrease if the price premium difference between two sites exceeds the gain output gaps. In other words, when gains from farmland protection in urban fringes cannot offset the losses in the land price premium, the result is a net reduction in social welfare (Ding, 2009). In addition, strict farmland protection policies make plans of incremental land supply for urban development impossible. As a result, local officials often use various large-scale SEZs to get an approval from central government on farmland development in order to circumvent strict farmland protection policies.

Land-based public finance imposes a huge risk. Land-based finance has caused skyrocketing local public debts. Lardy (2010) estimates that total local debts were 6 trillion RMB in 2009. Liu (2010) estimates that land-based financing of the public sector creates outstanding off-budget government liabilities that are more than 30% of GDP. Most of the liabilities are associated with land collaterals.

China has an extreme amount of off-budget revenues. Off-budgetary incomes, which are often associated with abuses, embezzlement, and the corruption of local officials, affect the efficiency of public finance as those spending patterns are different from that of on-budgetary revenues (Ding et al., 2014). Land revenues are the most important source for off-budget incomes in subnational governments in China. In 2013, total land conveyance fees were 4.1 trillion RMB, which was nearly 60% of the total revenues of subnational governments (including provinces, cities, counties, and towns). Since land conveyance fees are retained primarily by prefecture cities (provincial and county governments take a small part, depending on the intergovernmental fiscal arrangement), land revenues become more important to city governments. Proceeds from land leasing in Beijing and Shanghai, the two largest cities in China, for instance, were equal to 40–50% of their total fiscal revenues in 2009 (Liu, 2010).

Strong incentives for local governments to achieve land revenues is a major driver for excessive land conversion and rapid urban spatial expansion.[17] China's unique land institution empowers local governments to be able to rely on land to generate much needed incomes to alleviate rising fiscal pressure after the 1993/94 fiscal and tax reform. Local governments take advantage of their regulatory power in land requisition by compensating peasants at prices much lower than those they charge developers in monopolised first-level land markets. The price difference between land requisition compensation and land conveyance fees can be in the order of factor of tens (Ding, 2007). Local governments heavily rely on land either directly (land proceeds of land leasing) or indirectly (land used as collateral) in financing the provision and expansion of urban infrastructure such as roads. Land-based financing of urban road expansion is the only feasible mechanism for many Chinese cities (Ding, 2007).

One of the biggest consequences of aggressive land requisition perhaps is manifested in the incredible housing bubbles across Chinese cities. It is widely believed that the housing bubble in China has grown so big that its inevitable bust may have catastrophic impacts not only on the Chinese economy, but on the global economy as well. Three important indicators all point to the seriousness of the housing bubble. The first one is the rising housing price index. In Beijing, for instance, the average price of a new apartment flat in the inner city was 45,000 RMB in 2013, which had increased by a factor of 10 compared to the 2004 price. The second indicator is the ratio of annual rental values over the sale price of housing. It is estimated that the ratio fell to 3.81% in major cities like Beijing, Shanghai, Guangzhou, and Shenzhen. The ratio is well below the threshold of 4.5% widely used to indicate housing market bubbles. The third indicator is housing vacancy rates. A survey by the National Grid Company on 660 cities in 2010 revealed that there were 65.4 million new apartment flats that had zero electricity consumption for more than six months.[18] These vacant units have the capacity to house 200–250 million of the population, which is equivalent to the estimated total amount of rural-city migrants from urbanisation in the next 10–20 years. Vacancy rates are at 15–23% and inventories in third- and fourth-tier cities hold the equivalent of five year's demand.[19]

Housing bubbles are usually accompanied by land speculation and land hoarding. In 2003–2009, 40 well-known developers had acquired 270 plots through LURs; but less than half of land had been developed by the end of the period. In 2009, a Hong Kong-based company sold a lot whose land use rights were purchased from the Beijing government three years earlier and made a net profit of HK$ 235 million for doing nothing but land hoarding.[20] Land hoarding helps to accelerate housing price increases across major Chinese cities. Although it is mandated that lots should be developed within two years after being leased from governments, it is the potential of huge profits that encourages developers to hoard land.[21]

Case studies

Land requisition issues are often caused by below-market prices and unfairness in compensation. Many peasants were not sufficiently compensated to maintain the same living standards as mandated by the LAL. Taking land conveyance fees as a reference to land prices in markets, what peasants get from land requisition compensation may be just a fraction of land prices (for details see Ding, 2007; Siciliano, 2012; Zhang, 2007). The other type of unfairness is shown in cases of overcompensation, creating horizontal unfairness across land requisitions.[22] For example, at an informal dinner banquet in Zhengzhou, a well-dressed lady whispered to the lead author that she had received more than 10 million RMB from land requisition in 2009. In a land forum organised and funded by the World Bank in Beijing 2008, a deputy mayor of a Beijing district showed this author a peasant's text message in which the peasant earnestly requested the district government to conduct land taking as this was the last chance for him to become rich. This horizontal unfairness in land requisition compensation alters peasants' expectations, which in turn leads to their high demands in land requisition resettlement.

The literature has documented numerous cases of under-compensation of peasants in land requisition, but few cases of windfalls for peasants. Both extremes of under-compensation and windfalls represent social justice issues, in different perspectives. In the former extreme, the same living standard requirement by China's law on land requisition is not rigidly enforced/implemented, while in the latter one, State's asset in land is not fully protected and local governments are not able to recoup land value increases resulting from public actions such as in infrastructure investment. There are reports showing that peasants strongly protest and resist land requisition, leading to violence. Officials are often punished or sentenced to jail as the public outrages over deaths or personal injuries when force is used in land taking. As a result, windfalls are not uncommon in regions such as Beijing and Shanghai where political sensitivity on social unrests is extremely high.

In this chapter, we report those two extremes through two case studies.

Case one

Yingtan city is located in the northeast Jiangxi province of China, which is one of the important interregional transport hubs connecting the southeast coast and western areas of China. Nanjing is the capital of Jiangsu province, and is the regional central city in east China, next only to Shanghai. The survey covered 15 villages scattered in Yintang and Nanjing, and 401 farmers were investigated. The data were mainly collected through questionnaires and interviews in 2005. The average age of interviewees was 52 years, and 70% of them were householders with an average household income of 16,700 RMB of average household income (Xiao, 2008).

The average of compensation paid was 22,000 RMB per mu. As the average size of land requisitioned per household is 3.32 mu, on average, households got about 73,300 RMB in total. Taking the average size of households into account, this translates to 17,900 RMB per capita, which is high compared to the per capita annual living expenditure and per capita income, which are 2,135 RMB and 3,255 RMB, respectively, if judged simply by nominal value. However, they are very low if judged from the long-term perspective because cash compensation can only support these individuals for eight years even considering inflation.

As a result, 60.8% of interviewees stated that their living standards were substantially lowered (Xiao, 2008). Not surprisingly, 293 responses indicated that they would not want their land requisitioned, representing 76.7% of the total.

The main reasons for their opposition to land acquisition include (1) low compensation and the negative effects on their lives after land requisition; and (2) losing land, as the socio-economic safe net is extremely important because peasants are less educated and lack skills to compete in cities for high-paid jobs, which implies unemployment after land requisition leads to new urban poor.

The lack of transparency in land requisition and the absence of public participation is another main issue. For instance, 85.6% of interviewees reported that they were not fully informed about the scale of compensation, while 53.3% pointed out that no public hearing about land requisition had ever been organised. These suggest that village cadres may be corrupt by keeping a portion of the compensation themselves.

Recognising that their rights and interests may be infringed, land-lost peasants choose to appeal informally to the higher authorities such as municipal or provincial governments or to resort to violent protests against developers. The violent actions by peasants are not surprising as weak socioeconomic groups usually turn to violence. As expected, neither informal appeals nor violent protests has a positive impact on the outcome for land-lost peasants, as 88.4% of responses expressed their frustration at the absence of positive results from their protests.

Another important issue is associated with the distribution of compensation in villages. Commune villages used to be an integrated agricultural production unit under the planned system. In the pre-reform period, farmland of a village was equally divided and contracted out to all its members to encourage land investment and farmland productivity. The issue arises when some of village's households lost their land but not others. In this type of situation, there are two different ways to distribute the land requisition compensation. One is to equally distribute it among all the village members, and the remaining farmland repartitioned and contracted out to all members, as a reduced amount per capita. The other way is to distribute compensation to only those households whose land is affected by land requisition and would not have any land to farm after.

Survey responses indicate that about three quarters of interviewees were compensated in the first approach. Although only about one quarter were compensated by the second approach, responses suggest that there is a rising tension between land-requisitioned peasants and non-land-requisitioned ones.

Another interesting finding is that peasants living close to Nanjing tended to complain less and appeared happier about land requisition than peasants living in Yingtang. This may imply that the political status of a city matters. As the capital city of Jiangsu, Nanjing has a far more symbolic value politically than Yingtang. Social unrests in Nanjing may imply the termination of a political career for local officials. Wealthier Nanjing might also enable local officials to be more generous in land compensation than Yingtang.

Case two

Zitong County is located to the northeast of Mianyang, Sichuan province. It is 172 km (106 miles) from Chengdu, 49 km from Mianyang, and is regarded as a "pearl" on the economic development "golden line" in Sichuan. In recent years, the secondary industry of this county experienced development, which accounts for more than 40% in its economic structure. The development of manufacturing drives its urbanisation, so that an increasing area of arable land has been requisitioned and issues arose as a result which are perplexing the local government. Compared with the unusual situation of land acquisition where land-lost farmers are poorly compensated, the situation of Zitong County is quite the opposite.

According to the survey, by the end of 2015, 2,888.65 mu of rural collective-owned land had been accumulatively requisitioned over the last three years, and the amount fees paid for land acquisition have reached 127.69 million RMB. Meanwhile, the land acquisition in Wenchang, the capital of Zitong County, affected 11,237 villagers with 2,052.5 mu land over the past five years, and the compensation that those land-lost farmers received was 161.73 million RMB (Yong, 2016). Taking into account the amount of compensation paid and the area of land requisitioned, this translates to 78,796 RMB per mu and 14,393 RMB per capita, the latter being slightly higher compared with the rural per capital disposable income, which was 11,914 RMB.[23] However, the cash compensation was just a small part of the total compensation package, which together with the other parts, especially the rights granted to new homesteads being leased, traded, or used for other commercial purposes that had not been possessed by the old rural collective-owned land, enormously enriched the villagers.

One distinguishing feature of Wenchang is that there were a variety of compensation methods used in the land requisition process. Beside the normal compensation package that includes fees for land loss, resettlement, and compensation for crops and attachments on the requisitioned land, the local government planned/zoned land particularly for land-lost farmers where they could construct for commercial purposes or residential rental units, and from which they can generate stable income streams to live on after land requisition. Meanwhile, it could be expected that the value of newly constructed housing, compared with that of the rights-limited rural collective-owned land, would increase as a result of the improved location and clearer land property rights in the future. In fact, the average housing price of Zitong County in 2015 was 2,286.08 RMB/m².[24] Taking into consideration the amount of requisitioned land and the number of peasants who were adversely affected, 120 m² (1,290 sq ft) of housing area should have been offered as compensation to each land-requisitioned peasant, which, theoretically, means that the housing marketing value acquired by each land-requisitioned peasant would be 274,329 RMB.

The survey shows that farmers are highly satisfied with their living condition after land requisition (Yong, 2016). In fact, they are happy because others whose land is not requisitioned are jealous of their windfalls as a result of the land requisition process. In fact, this type of unusual high compensation has produced social conflicts. First, a new landlord class has been created, as peasants rent out extra space on land granted to them as a component in their compensation package. They can live very comfortably from rental incomes, which will definitely rise with urbanisation. This is good because peasants who are urbanised now can benefit from further urbanisation.

Second, windfalls from land requisition make peasants rich overnight, and the sudden wealth also changes their behaviours abruptly, including their consumption patterns. However, 30% of peasants lost their windfalls several years after land requisition and became poor again. The main reasons are (1) spending heavily without investment; (2) gambling; and (3) attitude changes toward working. A land-lost farmer, for instance, received 800,000 RMB in cash for land requisition, which is pretty high compared to the average earning of local peasants from farming. He spent 200,000 RMB immediately on a car and chose to stay at home doing nothing but gambling. A year later, he is living on a basic allowance from the village commune.

Sudden wealth changes land-lost peasants' working attitude. A township official said that 40% of land-lost peasants are aged between 40 and 50, and more than two-thirds are jobless. The local government arranged jobs for them as security guards, dustmen, and baby-sitters, but they chose to stay at home.

Third, windfalls from land requisition not only create a class of new landlord, which presents a new social issue, but more importantly increase land costs that then will push up housing prices. Skyrocketing housing prices in many Chinese cities contribute to housing market bubbles and threaten social stability.

Policy recommendations

The issues related to land requisition such as land-lost peasants have long been recognised in China. The central government has launched a series of efforts and policy initiatives to increase compensation levels, to pass laws that recognise and protect rights and interests of peasants in land, and to set up land requisition procedures for public participation and transparency. Those measures help alleviate the pressure of social unrest from land-lost peasants, but fail to address the aggressiveness of local governments in land requisition. At the same time, rising costs of land requisition are eventually passed on to housing consumers, further aggravating the already serious housing affordability problems in many Chinese cities.

The fact that land requisition plays a pivotal role in industrialisation and urbanisation in China underlies the difficulty in resolving land requisition issues. Land is used to promote urban growth (Ding and Lichtenberg, 2011; Lichtenberg and Ding, 2009). Land-based financing of urban transport networks is the driving force for rapid urban spatial expansion (Ding, 2007; Liu, 2010). Land is also used to attract industrial investment (Wu et al., 2014). Public land leasing helps facilitate the privatisation of State-owned enterprises.

Moving forward, however, China should undertake a radical and fundamental land policy reform, and land requisition reform is a part of it, to ensure that land institutions better serve socioeconomic reality and trends. Specifically, the radical and fundamental land reform should promote the following development. First, land markets should expand into rural areas to create one land market covering both urban and rural areas. This will be extremely challenging because land privatisation is politically impossible and there is a lack of theory and international practice to guide China towards generating a unified land market for two different land ownerships – public vs. commune (quasi-public). This is one of the main reasons that the call for one land market has been proposed, but little progress has been made so far.

Second, the protection of the rights and interests of peasants in rural land should underlie the development of one land market. The rural collective economic organisation has a mere nominal existence in many places of China. The farmers themselves are not the legal entities who claims land property rights, and this has been a prominent reason why their interests were often infringed in the process of land acquisition. In addition, they do not have a strong legal base from which to defend themselves (Tian, 2014). Peasants are a weak socioeconomic group, and this fact has been exploited by local governments in land requisition.

Third, local governments should withdraw direct involvement in land development and abandon their role as land developer. Instead, they can influence and control land development though zoning, planning, and building permits. In doing so, the scope of public interests that institutionalise compulsory land requisition by governments should also be redefined. Land supply for commercial housing (by private developers) is a justification for compulsory land requisition in China. Generalisation and enumeration are two popular methods adopted by Western countries for clarifying the range of public interest (Li, 2015). An eclectic method is recommended to be used in the context of China's land acquisition. Initially, the central government and local governments can articulate the matters which conform to the requirement of public interest. Then, the space and land use earmarked for future development can be generalised. Public interest should be articulated as specifically as possible, such as the land for national defence and the military, energy, transportation, water conservancy facilities, cultural relics and historic sites, public welfare establishments, and other urban infrastructure. Land acquisition for any purpose except the public interest should be stringently forbidden by law.

Fourth, fundamental land reform would not be successful unless it also resolves the problem of land-based public finance. Many land requisition issues are rooted in local governments' incentives behind the outstanding level of land proceeds from land development. Local governments should actively seek alternative sources to replace land revenues to minimise public finance risks as well as to seek long-term sustainable growth. This also requires China to gradually withdraw from its government-led growth mode that heavily relies on fixed investment.

Finally, these areas of reform would have profound impacts on land requisition that will also change dramatically. One land market implies that local governments would greatly reduce their involvement in land requisition as both the scope and scale of it will decline substantially. But at the same time, local governments should experiment with new approaches to land requisition to ensure due process and fairness in compensation. Both the extreme cases of under-compensation and windfalls should be avoided. It is of great importance to allow different approaches/modes to be developed in land requisition to acknowledge the vast variations across regions and the historical gradual reforms that complicate tenure systems and security secure, particularly in rural areas.

Final remarks

The issues surrounding China's land requisition process are complicated. They have historical origins and are "by-products" of the gradual land reforms undertaken in the pre-reform period. Resolving them requires both comprehensive solutions and policy instruments that also need to differentiate regions and cities. The former targets persisting issues, whereas the latter acknowledges that a one-size-fits-all approach has never worked and will not in the future. Comprehensive reform will need to focus on both reshaping the legal/administrative systems and on labour division between markets and government in the cause of rapid urbanisation. Legal aspects of land requisition involve land tenure and tenure security. Administrative restructuring needs to address the roles of local governments in land development and regional growth models. Both land policy and planning should include incentive structures to influence land use and development decisions. Finally, land requisition reforms demand strong political will in moving forward mainly because of emerging socioeconomic interest groups and that implies that the costs of reforms will be outstanding.

Notes

1 Source: www.ccud.org.cn/2017-03-28/115190230.html.
2 Source: https://wenku.baidu.com/view/7cf964ee998fcc22bcd10dda.html; Development and Reform Commission of China, "2015 China's New Urbanization."
3 Source: www.doc88.com/p-1961927130700.html.

4 Source: https://wenku.baidu.com/view/7b4ca8cf5a8102d277a22f23.html. Other factors causing farmland depletion is reforestation.

5 According to Xie and Zhou (2014), China's Gini coefficient is in the range of 0.53–0.55. This makes China to be on par with inequality levels in Colombia or Venezuela, which are both oil-based economies. Li and Wan (2015) showed that the wealth inequality (as opposed to income) reached 0.739 in 2010.

6 RMB is the acronym for the renminbi (the official currency of China), of which the basic unit is the yuan

7 1 hectare = 15 mu: 1 acre = 6 mu

8 China's Constitution (1988) and China's Land Administration Law (1986 and 1999) set up the current land institutions.

9 Land revenues include land conveyance fees, land use fees, and land taxation. Since land conveyance fees are dominant, city governments pay little attention to land use fees and land tax revenues. In some cities, land use fees and land tax revenues are so trivial that they are not collected. To make it simple, land revenues and land conveyance fees are interchangeable throughout the paper.

10 Land conveyance fees increases are associated with monopolized public leasing through land banking system, established in the middle of 1990s. All land leasing must be carried out through land banking, which deposits all lots that are planned for leasing. Land banking is administrated by land banking center of cities and countries (Wu and Jin, 2009).

11 The State Council approves land development on basic cultivated land for national projects such as transport networks, designations of various economic zones, and demonstration projects for policy reforms. Furthermore, without an effective mechanism to differentiate the percentage of basic cultivated land over the total farmland across administrative governments, the 80% minimum requirement is uniformly assigned to all subnational governments.

12 Source: www.caijing.com.cn/2011-08-09/110804337.html.

13 Source: http://news.sina.com.cn/c/sd/2013-10-14/085128427149.shtml.

14 SEZs include (1) high-tech industrial development zones; (2) economic and technological development zones; (3) free-trade zones; (4) export-process zones; and (5) others such as science-based industrial parks.

15 Beijing government work report, Beijing Municipal Government, 2005.

16 Industrial sectors with severely oversupplied capacities include electrolytic aluminum, ferroalloy, coke, calcium carbide, automobile, copper smelting, cement, electric power, coal, and textile goods. Sectors of petrochemical, paper box, chemical fertilizer, domestic electric appliances, micro-computers, and shipbuilding also have excessive capacity of production.

17 Yantai city of Shandong province, for instance, increased its built-up areas by nearly 200% from 2001 to 2004 (the built-up area increased from 120 km² to 340 km² in the period). Chongqing's urban built-up areas increased from 158 km² in 1994 to 175 km² in 2000. Beijing's urbanized areas increased nearly 30% in the 1990s. Guangzhou expanded its built-up areas by 7–8 km² per year in the second half of the 1990s (Ding, 2007).

18 Sources: Economist, May 4–10, 2013; http://house.ifeng.com/detail/2010_03_31/10444839_0.shtml; http://house.ifeng.com/detail/2010_07_06/11724747_0.shtml.

19 Recognizing the problem, the central government has introduced a series of measures to cool off housing and real estate markets since 2005. The strictest measure on housing markets was the housing purchase restriction introduced in 2010 that city residents with more than two flat units are prohibited from buying new one. The housing purchase restriction policy is rigidly implemented in 72 major cities since.

20 Source: www.legaldaily.com.cn/zmbm/content/2009-11/05/content_1177543.htm?node=7577.

21 Other related issues include embezzlement, corruption, money laundering, and fraudulent loans. There were more than 3,000 cases of illegal land leasing in 2010, and each case involved many officials of land and resources departments. A corrupted official underpriced a piece of land of 102 mu in land leasing, resulting in a loss of 9 million RMB in land conveyance fees in 2003. Source: http://cpws.flssw.com/info/41670547/.

22 Intuition is that the number of over-compensation cases might not be small since total affected farmers far exceed the number of farmers filing complaints or protesting. Social unrests and/or riots would have been much higher otherwise.

23 Source: Report on the Work of the Zitong Government in 2015.

24 Source: China Real Estate Association.

References

Bao, H. (2008). *Policies supply and institution organizatoin: fieldwork on the regulation evolvement of land acquisition*. Economy and Management Press, Beijing.

Brown, L., 1995. Who will feed China? Wakeup call for a small planet. WW Norton, New York.

Cao, D. (2004). 'China cancels 4800 developments zones', China Daily, 2004–08–24, www.china daily.com.cn/english/doc/2004-08/24/content36810.htm.

Ding, C. (2003). Land policy reform in China: assessment and protects. *Land Use Policy*, 20(2), 109–120.

Ding, C. (2007). Policy and praxis of land acquisition in China. *Land Use Policy*, 24(1), 1–13.

Ding, C. (2009). Policy and planning challenges to promote efficient urban spatial development during rapid transformation in China. *Sustainability*, 1(3), 384–408.

Ding, C., Lichtenberg, E. (2011). Land and urban economic growth in China. *Journal of Regional Science*, 51(2), 299–317.

Ding, C., Niu, Y. (2014). Spending preferences of local officials with off-budget land revenues of Chinese cities. China Economic Review, 2014(31), 265–276.

Du, Y., Gregory, R., Wang, X. (2006). The impact of the guest – workers system on poverty and the well-being of migrant workers in urban China, in Garnaut, R., Song, L. (eds), *The turning point in China's economic development*. Asia Pacific Press, Canberra, 172–202.

Green, H. (2006). *Urban sprawl costs: why we do not have more affordable Housing*. Santa Barbara News-Press—Affordable Housing Series, www.populareconomics.com/documents/urbanSprawlCosts.pdf.

Hui, E. C. M., Bao, H. J., & Zhang, X. L. (2013). The policy and praxis of compensation for land expropriations in China: An appraisal from the perspective of social exclusion. Land Use Policy, 2013 (32), 309–316.

Ji, X. Q., Qian, Z. H. (2011). Evaluation on land requisition system from urbanized land-lost farmers: based on the data collected from Jiangsu Province. *Journal of Agrotechnical Economics*, 2011(11), 4–15.

Li, X. T. (2015). *Study on collective land expropriation system in new urbanization process*. Anhui University, Anhui.

Li, S., Wan, H. (2015). Evolution of wealth inequality in China. *China Economic Journal*, 8(3), 264–287. doi:10.1080/17538963.2015.1110338.

Lichtenberg, E., Ding, C. (2009). Local officials as land developers: urban land expansion in China. *Journal of Urban Economics*, 66(1), 57–64.

Lichtenberg, E., Ding, C. (2006). Land use efficiency, food security, and farmland preservation in China. *Land Lines*, 2006(18), 2–7.

Lin, G. C., Li, X., Yang, F. F., Hu, F. Z. (2014). Strategizing urbanism in the era of neo-liberalization: state power reshuffling, land development and municipal finance in urbanizing China. *Urban Studies*, 20 (10), 1–21.

Liu, L. (2010). *Strengthening sub-national debt financing and managing risks*. World Bank, Washington DC.

Lu, Q. S., Liang, F. Y., Bi, X. L., Duffy, R., Zhao, Z. P. (2011). Effects of urbanization and industrialization on agricultural land use in Shandong Peninsula of China. Ecological Indicators, 11(6), 1710–1714.

Park, A., Wang, D. (2010). Migration and urban poverty and inequality in China. IZA Discussion Paper no 4877. http://ftp.iza.org/dp4877.pdf.

Qian, Z. H., Mou, Y. (2015). Land requisition system, land finance and reform of land market. *Issues in Agricultural Economy*, 2015(8), 8–12.

Siciliano, G. (2012). Urbanization strategies, rural development and land use changes in China: A multiple-level integrated assessment. *Land Use Policy*, 29(1), 165–178.

Soule, D. (2006). *Urban sprawl: a comprehensive reference guide*. Greenwood Press, Westport, CT.

Tian, X. (2014). *Research on distribution of land expropriation benefit with urbanization in China*. Liaoning UnivSersity, Liaoning.

Victoria Transport Policy Institute. (2008). TDM Encyclopedia: Smart Growth More Efficient Land Use Management. www.vtpi.org/tdm/tdm38.html.

Walker, A., Li, H. (1994). Land use rights reform and the real estates market in China. Journal of Real Estates Literature, 2(2), 199–211.

Wu, C., Jin, X. (2009). *30 years of China land reform*. Science Press, Beijing (in Chinese).

Wu, Y., Zhang, X., Skitmore, M., Song, Y., Hui, E. C. M. (2014). Industrial land price and its impact on urban growth: a centipede game model. *Land Use Policy*, 36 (1), 199–209.

Xiao, Y. (2008). *Study on the land-lost farmers' interest impairment and land expropriation system reform in China: an analysis from the property right perspective.* Nanjing Agricultural University, Jiangsu.

Xie, X., Zhou, X. (2014). Income inequality in today's China. *Proc Natl Acad Sci USA*, 111(19): 6928–6933. doi:10.1073/pnas.1403158111.

Yong, Z. K. (2016). Study on the land acquisition compensation managerial situation of land-lost farmers in the process of urbanization. *Focus on the Silk Road*, 2016(5), 31–32.

Zhang, J. X., Zhang, Y. H. (2007). Remote sensing research issues of the National Land Use Change Program of China. Journal of Photogrammetry and Remote Sensing, 62(6), 461–472.

12

Land acquisition for public purpose under Fiji Law

Abdul Hassan

Introduction

This chapter deals with the land acquisition for public use under Fiji Law. Under the Law, the right of the State and authorised statutory bodies to acquire or use private land for public purpose is protected the statute upon payment of just compensation to the affected owners. The origin of Law goes back a century, and the State's right to acquire land for public use has long been accepted. The current use of the Law includes both the right to acquire the land for public use and to pay just compensation. Some researchers claim that this right to acquire land for public use originates with the principle that the State owns all the property within its boundaries and the individual ownership and possession of property is always subject to reversion or repossession by the state. It is now generally accepted in many countries that the power to acquire land is not a property right but an attribute of the state. The powers of the state are broad enough to include the power to acquire land for public use, so the right does not specifically have to be given to the state by its constitution. However, the power to acquire land is limited by its very definition and cannot be exercised unless the proposed taking is for public purposes.

When dealing with land acquisition, one of the critical factors is just compensation. On many occasions court decisions have been given on this matter so as not to deprive the property owners of the monetary losses resulting from the land taken from their properties for public use. The basic premise is that the property owner must be compensated for the taking of the land, as opposed to being compensated for the land taken. It is generally recognised that property encompasses the entire bundle of rights inherent in the ownership of the real estate and that the acquisition of these rights often constitutes a taking, even if no part of the physical land is taken. The acquisition of all access rights is an example of such taking. In this case, the owners of land abutting onto a street cannot be deprived of all access to their premises without compensation. In this case, total deprivation of access is equivalent to a taking requiring compensation.

In this chapter a brief description of the land tenure system in Fiji is provided. In Fiji, the iTaukei (native) land is held under two different types of land tenure system: a 'western' land tenure system, and a 'traditional' land tenure system. Freehold, State, and a portion of Native

Lands that are leased out as 'Native Leases' operate under the 'western' land tenure system, while the communally held Native Lands operate under the 'traditional' land tenure system.

Land use planning policy, which has an impact on land acquisition for public purposes, is also investigated. A summary of the legislation that governs the land acquisition for public purpose is also discussed, noting the several changes made in the law over a period of time.

In 2016, an independent comparative study was completed by two international organizations, Asian Development Bank and World Bank, on the land acquisition policies they adopt for public purposes as compared to the Fiji Land Acquisition Law. This study was undertaken before major projects were funded jointly by these agencies, under the Transport Infrastructure Investment Sector. The finding provides strong grounds for Fiji to look into its policy on the resettlements of displaced property owners when the larger portion of their land is taken for public use.

Fiji Island

Fiji is an archipelagic in the South Pacific Ocean, comprising 322 islands, of which about 110 are inhabited. Located at 18 00 S, 175 00 E, Fiji has a total land area of 4,514,517 acres (1,826,960 hectares). Viti Levu and Vanua Leva are the largest of the islands, while the comparatively smaller ones are raised coral atolls, many of them unsuitable for habitation. In 1874, Fiji became a British Colony, gaining its independence in 1970, after nearly a century of British control.

Fiji's population mainly consists of two major ethnic groups. The indigenous population made up 51% of the population in 2007, Indo-Fijian comprising 44%, and the remainder being other ethnic groups. A broad category of age structure of the total population of 905,949 (Fiji Bureau of Statistics, 2008) is as follows: below 14 years (31.1%), 15–64 years (64.6%), and over 65 years (4.3%). The urban population of 424,846 comprises 51% of the total population. Of the total population, 41% live in the Central Division, which includes 58% of the total urban population. The national average household size is 4.91, which drops to 4.75 in urban areas.

Fiji's land tenure systems

The current Western land tenure system is based on the European-style, capitalist-oriented concepts, and is intended primarily to facilitate land conveyance and economic development. With its emphasis on individual land ownership, it applies in Fiji to Freehold, State, and Native Leases. It is based on the Torrens Title Registration System[1] and because it is oriented toward individualistic commercial enterprises, on an accurate Cadastral Surveying and Mapping System. Freehold lands are held individually or corporately in fee simple estates and are guaranteed by the government.

State lands are those that include land held by the State for public use, such as for roads, reservoirs, dams, drains, and leasing comprising residential, commercial, industrial, or agricultural leases. Also the State owns all lands below the high water mark, which includes mangrove swamps and all foreshores.

The Native land, owned by the iTaukei people, accounts for about 84% of all land in the country, with freehold and State or government land representing around 8% each. iTaukei land (Native Land) and State land cannot be bought or sold but is available on a long-term lease that often has a duration of up to 99 years, whereas freehold land can change hands in the open market. The freehold and State lands account for only 17.5% of Fiji's total land area, but as noted by Crocombe (2001), in terms of value, this category includes the best urban, commercial, industrial, and agricultural land, and sites for tourist resorts.

Native Leases are those lands that have been leased out largely to allow use for a fixed period of time and on payment of a ground rental. This land makes up a small proportion of accessible arable Native Land (31% of all Native Land, or 25% of Fiji's total land area), and is found, obviously, in the more valuable agricultural lands, such as the cane growing areas, and near the main urban centres. All legal dealings relating to Native Land, such as the issuing of leases, agricultural licenses, timber concessions, land subdivisions, and so on, are handled by the iTaukei Land Trust Board (TLTB). The TLTB was previously the Native Land Trust Board. The TLTB is a statutory body that was set up in 1940 as the Trustee of native owners under the Native Land Trust Act, to administer all Native Lands for the benefit of the indigenous Fijians and, paradoxically, for the nation as a whole.

As indicated earlier, at the national level, approximately 90% of land is Native Land, 6% is State land, and 4% is freehold. In urban areas, with the mixture of three types of tenure, comprising predominately Native Lands, the key trend is that the land market is distorted by informal land tenure arrangements. In fact, there is no shortage of land, but there is an inability to provide adequately serviced and affordable land to the market in a timely and serviced manner.

Use of customary land under special arrangement (Vakavanua)

Land is an important component of a healthy economy in the urban centres in Fiji. It regulates the performance of the development of any sector in the country. In the urban areas, Native Land is available through two systems: the formal sector and the informal systems. A large area of Native Land provides a supply of land through formal systems where the TLTB issues leases for certain duration and charges annual rentals. Under the informal arrangement, the native owners permit the occupation of their land (commonly known as a *Vakavanua*[2] arrangement) without the approval of TLTB. It is estimated that over 41% of the urban population live under this arrangement in informally developed areas in the urban centres (MLHSSE, 2004).

TLTB is the custodian of Native Land and administers all Native Land on behalf of landowning units. In urban areas, land that is available for development (MLHSSE, 2004) is owned by indigenous people. A very large proportion (80%) of such land in the greater Suva and other urban centres is leased informally or customarily (Vakavanua). Occupation of this land (without the consent of TLTB) represents unplanned commitments on large areas of land. It has been estimated that over 70–80% of the annual land development is available through the informal system. This is an important factor that needs to be resolved by the stakeholders. Most of the land with the potential for residential subdivision is taken up by informal systems of leasing (Vakavanua). It is important that a policy is formulated to develop this land for proper leasing that would provide a security of tenure to low-income people (MLHSSE, 2004). To facilitate this process, the TLTB must act urgently to develop vacant Native Land in urban areas.

Land planning policy in Fiji

The Town Planning and Subdivision of Land acts provide the legal framework for the physical planning of land in the declared towns and cities of Fiji (MLHSSE, 2004). Under the jurisdiction of the Ministry of Local Government and Director of Town and Country Planning, town planning schemes and land use plans are prepared. The existing planning systems have limited urban management capability to meet the current challenges. It has been noted that there are more than 10 legislations that deal with urban land use planning and development, and the local councils have to deal with 32 Acts in executing their daily business. Regulatory processes are cumbersome, centralised, and require lengthy approval processes. This has negative impacts on many proposed developments, particularly in the urban centres. It can also be concluded that the current policy and institutional framework for the urban development is outdated and not efficient to promote fast growth of the urban sector (NHP, 2011).

Land acquisition and compensation in Fiji

The Constitution of Fiji provides for the protection of private property against arbitrary expropriation, and the laws give protection to individual property owners against the arbitrary forcible taking of land for public purposes. The iTaukei land cannot be permanently alienated except for public use and that requires just compensation for all the land or rights relinquished to the government.

Acquisition of land in Fiji is governed by the State Acquisition of Lands Act (SALA), under the provisions of which, all categories of land can be acquired for public use. The legal title holders of the land have a right to demand compensation. The SALA also allows the owners to start legal proceedings in case of disputes and discontent with an amount of compensation offered. For the iTaukei land, the customary rights of the indigenous community are also protected.

The SALA guarantees compensation to persons that hold recognised legal rights or interest in the land. Compensation is paid under specific heads of claim at market value, effective as at the date of a sales and purchase agreement entered into between the State and the property owner. The affected structures are compensated on the basis of depreciated values. To comply with the Act, compensation is assessed for land, crops, structures, injurious affection, and severance. Changes in the use and restrictions on use of any non-acquired portions of land are also compensatable. Compensation may also include any reasonable expenses associated with the relocation of residences or places of business of the affected owner.

Section 12 (a) of the SALA specifically provides that a market value of the land be paid from the date of the notice of intention to take such land. Compensation is also paid for the standing crops or trees which were there when the land was taken for public use. In cases where a small portion of land is severed from the larger section of the same holding, a reasonable compensation is paid for the loss of value and use of the separated area. The SALA allows for compensation to be paid to the owner if by acquisition, other property (real, personal, or earnings) is adversely affected. If in the consequence of acquisition of land the owner is required to relocate a residence or business operation, then reasonable expenses must be paid. The SALA allows for the payment of compensation for the loss of rents and mesne profits for that period between the time the acquiring authority enters onto the land and the consideration due under an agreement has been paid. The SALA does not require the payment of compensation unless the acquiring authority has entered the land or has failed within one month of the order of the Court to decline to proceed with the acquisition.

Section 12 (b) of the SALA specifies the matters that shall not be considered by the Court when authorising the acquisition of the land for public use. These include the degree of urgency which has necessitated acquiring the land and the disinclination of the owner to move out of the acquired land. Also ignored is any damage caused to the land if caused by a private person and which would not result in such a person being liable to a suit; and any increase in the value of the acquired land resulting from the use of the acquired section. The affected owner will not be compensated for any improvement done on the acquired section after the date of the notice of the intention to take or an agreement is entered between the acquiring authority and the owner.

There is a penalty for impeding the taking of possession of the acquired land if the acquiring authority is molested, hindered, or obstructed from entering the land. In such an event, a person is liable to imprisonment for three months, a fine of 50 dollars, or both.

Fiji land acquisition Law and amendments

The current SALA (Cap 135) was enacted by an order of 8 October, 1970, just before Fiji became independent. Under British rule, land acquisition was governed by ordinances, and the first such Law was enacted under Number 24 of 1940. Subsequent amendments were undertaken by Numbers 11 of 1942, 15 of 1943, and 9 of 1955. Further changes completed by an order of January 1967 and October 1970. Final changes were completed by an Act of Parliament in 1998 (Act No. 1 of 1998).

The strength of the land acquisition Law in the country was tested when in 1966 (Privy Council, 1979), when the Suva City Council searched for an area of 50 to 70 acres (20 to 28 hectares) that could be a suitable site for an auxiliary power station to serve the city and possibly in due course to serve an area beyond the city boundary. The land was identified, and the landowners were approached to sell. It was freehold land (described as CT 8316), owned by Mukta Ben and Shanta Ben, located at Kinoya, Nasinu in the outskirts of Suva. Initially, the land owners agreed to make a gift of 5 acres (2 hectares) and were prepared to negotiate for the sale of additional land. The Suva City Council was interested in buying a larger area of the land, which the owners refused. After further negotiation between both parties, they could not agree to an area to be acquired nor the unit rate of compensation to be paid. Therefore the land could not be acquired by negotiation. After failing to buy the land by negation, on 1 March, 1967, the Governor in Council, under the Colonial Government, authorised the compulsory acquisition of 20 acres (8 hectares) for the power station.

Despite several negotiations and proceedings in the local courts, the dispute could not be resolved between the Suva City Council and the landowners. Finally, the City Council resorted to compulsory acquisition. The matter was then referred to the Privy Council (Privy Council Appeal Number 19 of 1997), and the judgment of the Lords of the Judicial Committee was delivered on 12 December, 1979.

While referring the matter to the Privy Council, the landowners sought to set aside as invalid the compulsory acquisition of the subject land with the claim that the Suva City Council had, from the outset, trespassed upon the land and erected and operated the power station and auxiliary building on it. Other specific grounds of the claims were that the notice of acquisition served by City Council lacked sufficient definition of the subject land and that it had no power to acquire the land compulsory outside the town/city boundaries. Other grounds stated that the City failed to publish notice of the acquisition of that particular land. The City Council, in addition to the actual power station, built on the subject land housing for employees and failed to purchase land by agreement on reasonable terms. The landowners further claimed that the Governor in Council was misled by the City Council, and they pointed out that the Council failed to offer access to the balance of the land to the west and that in the circumstances the requirements of natural justice were not observed. It was the contended that 20 acres (8 hectares) of land required by the City Council was an excessive area for the purpose. Their final challenge was based upon the provisions of the Subdivision of Land Ordinance.

In the judgment, the Privy Council asserted that if all the points were to be decided in favour of the landowners, it would still leave the appellants unable to assert, as they seek to do so, the invalidity of the compulsory acquisition. Their Lordships did not find it necessary to deal with all the facts relevant to that submission and considered it not necessary to rule upon it, as a result, the appeal was dismissed with costs.

Assessment of compensation under Fiji Law

The compensation is assessed under the provisions of the SALA having prepared the initial valuations using local market prices, and data in this regard are collected from the Valuation Office of the Ministry of Lands. The Fiji Road Authority (FRA) also involves the Department of Fisheries to assess compensation if traditional fishing rights are affected.

The FRA valuers undertake valuation and engage private valuers for affected landowners in case of any dispute on compensation. The FRA continues to provide private valuers under the project as a normal practice. The landowners are made aware of the availability of a private valuer at the beginning of the negotiation process provided the owners are prepared to pay fee to the valuer.

The basis of compensation to be offered is the replacement cost based on the actual market price of affected land and other assets. In a case where government policy prohibits the full replacement costs, the project's funding will include top-up payments or assistance to cover the full replacement cost.

Replacement cost is defined as the cost of replacing an expropriated asset of the same or better quality on the existing land or asset and comprises fair market value which can be determined by collecting sales data for the past few years for comparable properties. In many parts of Fiji, land values differ widely due to location, the availability of services and amenities, and the fertility and contour of land. Market value is the selling price of an asset in the arm's length transaction. In several places, no useful market exists, in which case baseline data are collected to value the asset. Transaction costs are also included in the compensation which includes legal and documentation expenses and an amount associated with registering property titles for the replacement of lands and houses. Where there is a lapse of time between the agreed schedule and the actual payment of compensation, interest on the amount outstanding that accumulates over that period is included in the compensation. In other cases, a short-term subsistence allowance is paid to the displaced persons throughout the period of income loss resulting from the project. Restoration costs are treated as the necessary improvements on the land or improvements to achieve the objectives of enhancing or reinstatement of livelihoods compared with pre-project levels.

Under the SALA procedure for land acquisition and compensation

In land acquisition for permanent use a preliminary alignment plan is prepared by the FRA and forwarded to the Director of Lands showing the estimated land-take together with a request to acquire the land. On receiving the plan from the FRA, the Director of Lands passes the alignment plan to its Statutory Section which identifies individual property owners and prepares the acquisition diagrams. These plans are then forwarded to the Valuation Section, which will engage in negotiation and obtain land clearance. Once the Valuation Section obtains the consent of the landowners, valuation reports are prepared by the government valuers based on their inventory of losses, using sales evidence as a basis to arrive at the total compensation.

In cases where iTaukei land is affected, meetings will be held with the members of the land owning unit (Matagali) arranged by the iTaukei Land Trust Board (TLTB), Trustee for the Matagalis and involving the FRA, the Provincial Council, and a representative of the Director of Lands. This meeting is held to negotiate and come to an agreed value on compensation. The land owning unit (Matagali) will have the final say to accept or reject the compensation offered by the Director of Lands. The landowners can also reject the recommendation of the TLTB if they do not agree on the amount of compensation or other conditions proposed to the acquiring authority.

A binding document, the Sale and Purchase Agreement, is executed by the TLTB on behalf of landowners and the Director of Lands. Having consented to the document upon payment of the relevant fee, compensation is paid based on the estimated area of land affected to be adjusted after the final survey and completion of the works. Leasehold Native Land follows a similar process, where the compensation is assessed and price agreement is executed. The Agreement is forwarded to the TLTB with the relevant fee for the Board's approval. If there is a registered lease, then a caveat is lodged against the title to protect the area acquired from the lease. The total compensation paid on the leasehold is divided between the tenants and the landowners. A similar process is followed to acquire land held on State leases, but compensation is paid only to the tenant for surrendering the affected area from the lease. On freehold land, the Valuation Section prepares the Sales and Purchase Agreement and negotiates the purchase price. After paying compensation, a Certificate of Transfer is prepared and sent for execution. At this stage, the FRA can enter onto the land to begin construction work.

The last stage is a final survey after the completion of the work that is carried out and approved. This survey plan is viewed against the original acquisition diagrams. If more land is affected, then compensation is adjusted to the exact area of land affected. In the leased land, the tenant is asked to provide lease documents for the registration of the surrender at the Registrar of Title's Office. The surrender document is then sent to the TLTB prior to registration. The caveat on the title is then withdrawn and the title is returned to the tenant.

Deficit in Fiji Law

The SALA was enacted in 1970 when the country gained independence from United Kingdom (UK). At that time, Fiji was still a developing country with limited infrastructures in urban and rural areas that would be affected when land was acquired for public use. In subsequent years, development has intensified in the country in all sectors. This necessitated the revision of SALA and the accommodation of the claims for other damages to a property. These include the recognition that the acquisition or use of land for public purposes can cause disturbance or inconvenience to landowners or to adjoining property. These disturbances can be in the form of loss of private property, business and economic losses or loss of profits, and can sometimes be a limitation on the usage of land. Other factors recognised as disturbance are noise, dust, smell, fumes, and vibration that in turn reduce the land value.

Provisions to pay compensation for such damages are not embedded in the SALA. A possible solution to these problems is to incorporate these provisions in the Act and to pay a fair compensation to the affected owners. In the case of disturbance caused by the construction of roads and other public works, compensation has to be paid to the occupiers of land or for the cost and expenses incurred to move away from the site. In other cases, the affected occupants may be provided with equitable accommodation. For example, in the UK, property owners can ask for additional compensation when they are not permitted a particular usage of the land. If the owners are prohibited from using the land for a specified period, then they are entitled to compensation for that period. In several countries, the owner is entitled to a home-loss payment and a specified amount is paid for such loss. If there are several owners, the home-loss payment is distributed equally between them.

In the process of land acquisition, the loss in value to the remaining land, particularly in a partial taking of a property, needs consideration. In other countries the method of paying compensation is the difference between the value of the whole property before the land was taken and the value of the remaining land after the land was acquired. This is the measure of the value of the portion of land acquired and the damages caused to the property retained. These types of damages can be recognised in two ways. First is the consequential damages, which arise as a result of the land taken or the effect of construction work on other properties. In those cases the owner will be compensated for the damage as a consequence of the change, for example, in the grade of a street, which adversely affects ingress to and egress from the affected property. Currently the owners are not compensated for the damages caused to the good will of a business which resulted from the land taken or from the construction work.

Fiji Law-advanced problem

In several countries there is a reasonable fear resulting from the taking or proposed construction of public works on a property. If the fear is well-founded, it has been universally accepted to compensate the property owner. Some jurisdictions have ruled that unfounded fear is a compensable item because that factor will have a detrimental effect on the market value of the remaining property. Others believe that unfounded fear is not a proper consideration because the anticipated damage was not done.

Much research has been completed recently concerning the effect of land acquisition on human health or its impact on real estate values (Eaton, 1995). For example, it has been established that there is a measurable effect on the value of real estate near electrical transmission lines. This reduces the market value of the property. Some countries have started to adopt land use regulations that require minimum building set-back from electrical transmission lines. These regulations have been prompted by the results of several health studies. If the property is affected by set-back requirement, then the acquiring authority must consider the land use regulation in both the highest and best use estimate and in the estimate of property value.

Rules of set-off not in Fiji Law

According to Eaton (1995), generally five separate benefits are derived from the various set-off rules in operation around the world. Normally, the benefits, whether special or general, which result from the acquisition and or development of land cannot be considered when assessing compensation, and the special benefits which result can only can be offset against the compensation paid for the damages to the land retained but not against the value of the land taken. Special benefits and general benefits can offset against compensation paid for the damages to the land retained, but not against the value of the land taken. Special benefits can be offset against both losses to the land retained and to the value of the land taken. Finally, special and general benefits can be offset against both losses to the land retained and the value of the land taken. In the USA, the Federal rule holds that benefits may be offset against the land taken and against damages to the remainder. In arriving at a just compensation, an offset should be made against the value of the land taken and the damage to the remaining property.

Easements – not specified in Fiji Law

The ownership of a property comprises a bundle of rights that can be held by one or several parties. When the bundle of rights is separated between parties, lesser estates are created. This is the case when a contractual limitation on freehold land is created by the formation of an easement. An easement is commonly a right to perform a specific operation on a particular piece of land without owning the land. An easement is an estate which can be separated from the bundle of rights and in specified terms of time and space. An easement can be temporary in nature, with a specific or an indefinite termination date (Eaton, 1995).

Permanent or perpetual easements in Fiji are acquired for electrical transmission lines, sewers, water, or fuel lines. Quite often an easement will have both temporary and permanent elements. For example, when an easement of 5 metres is required for the installation of a sewer, but only a 5-metre easement is required for its maintenance and operation, a 5-metre temporary construction easement is obtained in addition to a 5-metre permanent easement.

An easement can be classified as subsurface, surface, overhead, or a combination of these. All easement acquisitions are partial acquisitions because the fee, if it is raw land of no utility, will remain with the original owner. Damages resulting from the acquisition of an easement are measured by the loss of the salable utility in both the area encumbered by an easement and the unencumbered portion of the larger tract. Damages to the land area encumbered by the easement can range from nil to the total value of the land.

Comparison of Fiji Law (SALA) with Asian Development and World Bank policy

The Asian Development Bank and the World Bank, that have been funding projects in Fiji, have several additional requirements as compared to the current Law of Fiji (SALA) to acquire the land for public use. These requirements are focused on the social and economic impacts, permanent or temporary, caused by acquisition of land and other fixed assets, and the changes in the use of land or restrictions imposed on the land.

The merits of the policy are to avoid involuntary resettlement impacts, to minimise the effects by choosing alternative viable project options and to ensure that affected people receive compensation assistance for relocation including the provision of relocation sites with the necessary facilities and services. The rationale is to ensure that the affected owners will at least be put in the same position as they were before the project.

The Asian Development Bank has the policy to screen projects early to establish the past, present, and future involuntary relocation impacts and associated risks. After identifying risk, the Bank engages in consultations and informs the affected persons of their entitlements and resettlement options. Both banks are involved in the planning, implementation, monitoring, and evaluation of the relocation programmes. Special attention is paid to the needs of vulnerable people, particularly those below the poverty line, the landless, elderly women and children, indigenous people, and those without legal rights to the land. The banks take two options: (1) to restore the livelihoods of affected people through land-based resettlement strategies when affected livelihoods are land-based; or (2) cash compensation at replacement value of land when the loss of land does not undermine livelihoods, the replacement of assets with access to assets of equal value, and the payment of compensation at a full replacement cost if asset cannot be restored.

These international banks also provide physically displaced people with the needed assistance to secure land tenure on land identified, credit facilities, training, and employment opportunities. The banks develop all the procedures in a transparent, consistent, and equitable manner. The banks will pay compensation and provide other resettlement entitlements before the actual ground work or economic displacement start and will implement the resettlement plan and monitor the project throughout its implementation.

The banks seek to ensure that impoverishment risks resulting from involuntary resettlement are investigated and minimised. This action is taken to avoid resettlement when possible and to minimise it through alternative project designs. Resettlement is treated as a sustainable development programme, and affected people are consulted and assisted to improve and restore their livelihoods to pre-project levels. Broadly, the policy of the banks is to pay compensation to replace lost assets, livelihood, and income; provide assistance to the affected people for relocation; and offer rehabilitation to achieve at least the same level of well-being as before the project was implemented.

Requirement of Asian Development Bank, World Bank and Fiji Land Law

Several major projects in Fiji have been undertaken with the borrowed fund from the Asian Development Bank and the World Bank therefore, it is imperative to compare requirements and gaps between the land acquisition laws of these banks and Fiji. Both banks avoid and minimise involuntary resettlement wherever possible by redesigning projects, whereas in Fiji the Constitution and the SALA set out conditions under which land may be compulsorily acquired, i.e. the property is acquired for the public purpose with the payment of compensation. These banks have policies to restore the livelihoods of affected property owners relative to pre-project levels, and special attention is paid to vulnerable groups among those displaced. Under Fiji Law, the general principles of compensation for land and other assets are spelt out in the Act, but lack those provisions to restore the livelihood of the affected landowners.

Under the policies of the banks, the projects are screened earlier to determine the involuntary resettlement impacts and risks, whereas the Fiji, the Act sets out the process for land investigation which involves identification of affected landowners and their assets. The banks undertake effective consultation with other stakeholders and inform the displaced people of their entitlements and resettlements alternatives. Also they establish a grievances redress process to accommodate affected owners' concerns. Also the banks provide the necessary physical and economical assistance to the communities, whereas the Fijian law sets out the process of the notification of the proposed land acquisition and provides for an appeal against the declaration of public purpose. It sets out the process under which the affected person may claim the entitlement to an interest in the compulsory acquisition of land.

The banks have developed all their procedures in a transparent, consistent, and equitable manner and provide options to compensate affected people without title to land or any legal rights (Asian Development Bank and World Bank, 2016). They also conceive and execute an involuntary resettlement plan as part of a development project. Fijian laws have procedures for land acquisition by negotiation or purchase and have set out ways of advising landowners at different phases of the land acquisition procedures. They also set out the timing for the payment of compensation. The banks are involved in monitoring and assessing resettlement progress and their impacts on the standards of living for affected people. They also assess whether the objectives of the resettlement plan have been achieved. Fiji law does not have all these provisions in the relevant legislation.

Having compared two sets of provisions, there is a wide gap between those of the banks and Fiji laws when compensation matters are to be considered in relation to the affected property owners. There is no specific reference to the need for reducing resettlement impacts by looking at a range of alternatives. Fiji law does not take steps to restore or improve the standard of living of the affected people. The Fijian law does not have any specific require-ments for cut-off dates, impact assessments, and any resettlement planning. There are no specific provision for land acquisition and resettlement plans. There is a very limited griev-ance redress mechanism, and there is no specific requirement for land-based settlements, replacement of assets, compensation at replacement cost, and benefit sharing. Fiji laws do not have specific provisions on relocation and no provision for maintaining the livelihood status of affected people. The law does not have provisions to address the issue of a person who does not have a title or legal rights to the land. The law sets the timing for the payment of compensation within a specified period, but does not specifically state that this should occur before displacement. Generally, the policy is to pay 75% of the compensation before con-struction and 25% after the construction work is completed and the affected area is surveyed.

Major gaps in Fiji Law

Fiji law and its regulations do not compensate the affected persons who do not have a rec-ognised legal rights or interest in the land. The only payment would be made for the struc-tures on the basis of a depreciated value of those structures. Informal land users or squatters without land titles are not entitled to any compensation for the land they occupy. Under the policies of the banks, any non-titled people affected by the work at the time of the land survey to determine the cut-off date for eligibility for compensation and rehabilitation as-sistance, will be paid compensation for loss of structures, crops, or the income they obtain from the land despite not having formal title. All compensation, including for structures, is paid at replacement cost without any deduction of depreciation.

Fiji law does not allow the affected owners to provide alternative sites in the case of resettlement, and it also lacks provisions for the assistance for the resettlement of adversely affected people. The projects do not aim to avoid resettlement where possible and minimise damage through alternative project designs. In those cases where resettlements cannot be avoided, mitigation measures are not taken to restore livelihoods and standards living for the affected people to bring them back to pre-project levels. Nor are measures are taken to consult people in the planning and implementation of any sub-project resettlement plan.

While acquiring the land for public use, Fijian law does not provide any special assistance to vulnerable groups or to the poor people adversely affected, but it does not stop other in-stitutions from providing assistance to people adversely affected by the project. Under the banks Land Acquisition and Resettlement Framework there are provisions to ensure that affected people, especially vulnerable and disadvantaged groups, are assisted to improve their living standards.

Policy principles developed by Asian Development Bank and the World Bank

Having identified the gaps and deficiency in the land acquisition process in Fiji, both banks have drawn up policy principles under the Land Acquisition Resettlement Framework, which would apply to all projects. For the temporary use of land measures are taken to minimise resettlement impacts. The screening process identifies the need for a temporary use of land and its related impacts. As for permanent land acquisition attempts are made to avoid or reduce the negative impacts through careful engineering design during the planning stage of the project. Land acquisition and resettlement impacts are assessed after screening, based on a social assessment. The proposal is then disclosed to the affected people before the project appraisal.

The FRA and TLTB are responsible for public consultation and dissemination of information. Consultations and public participation are undertaken as ongoing processes throughout the project planning, designs, and implementation stages. The preparation of a land acquisition document is carried out after consultation with the affected peoples, and prior information provided in terms of compensation, relocation, and other assistance that would be provided. Also the affected persons receive rent or compensation at replacement cost from the contractor responsible for the civil works for the damages sustained with the temporary use of the land. The affected people receive compensation at replacement cost from the FRA for the permanent loss of land and assets such as houses, crops, trees, and other structures. This is to ensure that the affected people are restored to their pre-project standards of living. Additional compensation and assistance are granted in order to restore or improve the living standards of affected people including the compensation to non-title holders such as squatters and farmers engaged in share farming as at the cut-off date. Other expenses paid include the loss of livelihood or income, transaction costs (such as administrative charges, taxation, and registration), and titling costs and income restoration measures. All compensation is fully paid prior to the commencement of site clearance and subject to the issuing of a letter of 'no objection' from the banks. Having no formal title is not a bar to compensation and assistance to the affected people. Particular attention is paid to women and other vulnerable groups including those who are engaged in share farming or tenants without legal rights over the land. The impact of subprojects, including unforeseen damages and losses that take place during the construction period, is carefully assessed and remedial action taken as needed.

Eligibility for entitlements under Asian Development Bank and the World Bank

Under the banks' Land Acquisition and Resettlement Frame Work, the date of the land survey is the cut-off date for the eligibility to compensation and rehabilitation assistance. Landowners and users with documented claims to the affected land and other improvements are eligible for compensation and rehabilitation assistance in accordance with the project policy. The banks have categorised the displaced persons who are eligible for compensation, which include generally the customary landowners of iTaukei land or those with individual freehold ownership and leaseholders with formal legal rights as tenants. Others who are eligible for compensation include those whose rights are not formal or legal, but whose claims on the land or assets are recognised under national legislation, such as *Vakavanua* arrangements. The right to use the land is granted by the native owners (Matagali) to the individuals or to a community to use the land without formal title or lease. In the absence of title, the testimony from village chiefs and community leaders may be requested to determine eligibility for compensation, replacement land, or other resettlement assistance. Other groups that are compensated include sharecroppers, squatters, or labourers who depend upon the land acquired. These groups do not have legal rights or recognised ownership claims, but if the project land acquisition destroys their livelihoods, they are treated as displaced persons and are entitled to receive resettlement assistance. A detailed matrix of entitlement of compensation or assistance is prepared by the banks and made available to the affected persons which include employment during construction and maintenance period and cash assistance to the persons for the disturbance of their means of livelihood.

Grievance redress mechanism by Asian Development Bank and the World Bank

To deal with any resolution, concerns, and complaints by the affected people, a Grievance Redress Mechanism (GRM) is developed for the project, including for the subproject site. This mechanism is used in case of any complain and dispute. The GRM addresses these concerns and complaints promptly and transparently to avoid further delay on the construction work. The GRM is gender-responsive and readily accessible to all affected people at no costs. The GRM takes a traditional approach to conflict and dispute resolution, and every effort is made to resolve the dispute at the project level. The GRM will not, however, impede the affected landowners in their access to the Fiji judicial process.

Generally, the key function of the GRM is to record the types of grievances and settle the grievances in consultation with the complainants and other stakeholders. The GRM must inform the aggrieved parties about the solutions and forward the unresolved cases to higher authorities for further consideration and solutions. Generally, the subproject manager or engineer with the support of the FRA's social impact manager and consultants is responsible for the receipt of grievances and the review and management of project-related concerns. In doing this, they coordinate with government authorities and also make the affected people aware of their rights about land requirements. In the provision of this service, affected people are not charged any cost. Complaints are recorded and investigated by the FRA's social impact manager working closely with the relevant staff of the individual subproject. A complaints register is maintained which shows the details and nature of the complaint, name of complainant, and the date and the nature of the action taken to resolve the dispute. In the process the relevant Fiji agencies and in particular Director of Lands and TLTB are included in the process of the review the complaints and the advice on the FRA's performance for the redress of grievances.

Grievance redress mechanism on iTaukei land developed by Asian Development Bank and the World Bank

When dealing with iTaukei land, any affected person or village head/chief can take grievances to the FRA. After receiving the complaint, the FRA's, social impact manager on the relevant site/subproject enters the details in the complaints register. The complaint is recorded by date, name, contact address, and the reason for the complaint. If the complainants desire, then their identity is not revealed, but the nature of their concern is still recorded. A duplicate of the complaint is given to the complainant for the record, which shows the process that will be followed. For a simple grievance, the project engineer can make an on-the-spot decision to resolve the issue.

In a more complicated case, the FRA's social impact manager is expected to review and find a solution to the problem within two weeks, after liaising with village or traditional chief and other local agencies. The social impact manager reports back on the outcome of the review to the traditional chief and affected persons within one week. Failure to respond within a week, allows the affected persons to take grievance to the FRA, Chief Executive Officer, who coordinate with relevant national agency to review and report back to the affected person or chief regarding the outcome. Complainants can take the case to court if they are not satisfied, or if the matter is not resolved. In both the cases, successfully addressed complaints and non-responsive issues are reported to the Asian Development Bank and the World Bank by the FRA.

Conclusion

The SALA is the legal arm of the State and statutory bodies to acquire the land from private owners for public use. The SALA has survived in the past, allowing the State and statutory bodies to acquire land for public use. The strength of the legislation was tested when the Suva City Council exercised its powers to compulsorily acquire freehold land in 1966 for a power station site. Despite numerous attempts at various levels under the court jurisdictions, the landowners have not been successful in convincing the courts to set aside as invalid the compulsory purchase of the land by the acquiring authority.

The current SALA was enacted in 1970 just before Fiji gained independence from British rule. Subsequently, the country has developed, socially, economically, and politically, and the land acquisition process has become more sophisticated. Environmental laws have been enacted to protect the environment before any project is undertaken. In the past, several claims have been made by the landowners on the projects that have been completed under Fiji law to show their discontent on the amount of compensation paid. This is a clear indication that a revision is needed in the Act to reflect the challenging issues when land is needed for public purpose.

The Asian Development Bank and the World Bank who are the funding institutions for the major projects in Fiji have identified the weaknesses in the Fijian law when dealing with land acquisition cases. One of the major gaps noted is that Fiji legislation and its regulations do not pay compensation to affected persons who have no recognised legal right or interest in the land. It only allows for compensation on a depreciated/book value basis for structures. As a result, informal sharecroppers and squatters are not entitled to any kind of compensation for the land they occupy. Under the banks' policies, any non-titled people affected by the project at the time of the land survey to determine the cut-off date for eligibility for compensation and rehabilitation assistance are entitled for compensation for the loss of structures, crops, or income derived from the land.

Another critical issue is that the SALA does not allow for the provision of relocation sites to the affected people. There is no provision for assistance for the rehabilitation of adversely affected persons. Under the banks' policies, the projects aim to avoid resettlement where possible or to minimise the damage through alternative project designs. In cases where re-settlements cannot be avoided, mitigation measures to restore the livelihood and standards of the affected people are considered and implemented. An effective consultation is carried out with the affected people in the planning and implementation of a relocation plan.

The SALA does not have provisions to assist vulnerable groups or the poorest of those adversely affected. However, it does not prevent government agencies from providing assistance to people adversely affected by the project, including vulnerable groups. The banks under their Land Acquisition and Resettlement Framework have special provisions to ensure that affected people, particularly the disadvantaged and vulnerable, are assisted to improve their living standards. The banks undertake a social assessment, and if resettlement is anticipated for any subproject, the project authorities carry out an initial assessment to determine the potential social issues and their impacts on the subproject level. Based on this assessment, a decision is taken on the in-depth studies and field investigations needed and the preparation of necessary documents. The banks have policies that allow for close consultation, the participation of all key payers, and disclosures of information to the affected people. This is a very important process to maintain transparency, raise awareness, reduce potential conflicts, and minimise the delays in completing a project.

Notes

1 A system of land registration used in many countries in which the State issues title certificates covering the ownership of land, which serve as title insurance.
2 An informal system of leasing of land by indigenous landowners has persisted for many years, and it is based on traditional practices. These arrangements are in some cases a continuation of recognised land allocation systems in villages and in others. It is an alternative to leasing land by TLTB who is the custodian of all Native Land in Fiji.

References

Asian Development Bank and World Bank. (2016). Land Acquisition and Resettlement Framework, Fiji: Transport Infrastructure Investment Sector Project. http://www.fijiroads.org/wp-content/Land_Acquisition_and_Resettlement_Framework_.
Crocombe, R. (2001). *The South Pacific*, University of the South Pacific, Suva, Fiji.
Eaton, J. D. (1995). *Real Estate Valuation in Litigation*, 2nd edition, Appraisal Institute, USA.
Ministry of Local Government, Housing, Squatter Settlement and Environment (MLHSSE). (2004). "Urban Policy Action Plan", Stake Holders Workshop Held at Holiday Inn Hotel, Suva, Fiji.
Privy Council. (1979). Appeal Number 19 of 1977, Mukta Ben and Another v Suva City Council.
State Acquisition of Lands Act (Cap 135).

13

A fable and dialogue on taking the property of another under constitutional capitalism

Hong Kong

Lawrence W. C. Lai

"Thou shall not steal."

— The Fifth Commandment

A story[1]

Once upon a time, there was a beggar with a great name and a big, old, and gold-lined coat. Both belonged to his father, who was of some distinguished status. The coat was too big for him, but it was his sole possession and consolation. He sat outside the tall tower of a small and anonymous rich man who enjoyed himself daily in his tower. He made a living by begging anyone other than the rich man. He expected nothing from the resident of the lofty tower. The rich man paid no attention to the beggar and treated him as just another part of "the environment" – until one day he got a great idea after scrutinising the beggar's golden coat. He came out of his tower and impatiently asked the beggar to sell him the coat. The tramp refused, as that coat was not only his shelter, but his honour. The rich man told the beggar that he could use the money he would get from selling the coat to buy another old coat and celebrate. The beggar could not understand and declined. The rich man seized the beggar, stripped him of the big coat, and threw some money at his feet. "Take it or leave it and in any case go away, this coat is just too much for you!" It was complete darkness.

This story is repeated in the real world.

A dialogue on urban renewal[2]

When the sun is going down, G and C have a chat in a garden hanging about on a street.

G: Urban renewal by the government is a major contribution to society.
C: I agree that if the government did care about urban renewal, it would have done a great job of it!

G: What do you mean? Are you not the only person who does not know that we have an Urban Renewal Authority (URA)?[3]

C: The name does not matter. The URA used to be called the Land Development Corporation (LDC).[4] With all due respect, you cannot say that a change in the name of a government corporation alone would bring about urban renewal!

G: You are absurd. Look, the LDC or URA has completed so many urban renewal projects, which you can find on the URA website. It has replaced old buildings with new ones.

C: Well, it is not the number of projects, but their nature that is problematic. Demolishing old buildings and building new ones to replace them is not urban renewal. If it was, then all developers are undertaking urban renewal.

G: I know what you are trying to say. Are you saying that government urban renewal projects are no better than developer's projects? Note that there is private sector participation in LDC or URA projects. Some of them were not intended to make any profit.

C: Private participation in the sense that developers form partnerships with the LDC or URA to make money together is an even bigger problem, but the government deserves more blame. Please return to the point about replacing old buildings with new ones.

G: Oh, you have a list of complaints?

C: Sure. That no real government urban renewal has been done is just one of the major issues, but also one of the most important. Come on, redevelopment is not renewal. Agree?

G: Yes, but as the URA is a government body, it ensures that its projects are more than about demolishing buildings and building new ones. They make sure that both owners and tenants are compensated. Developers would not compensate tenants. Besides, there are also planning gains involved in these projects, such as conserving buildings with special architectural and historical values. Furthermore, some projects were scaled down in response to public comments.

C: Well, the only valid and perhaps unique benefit that the URA provides, as you mentioned, is compensation for tenants.

G: I am glad that you concede that the URA has made a contribution.

C: It could have done a lot more. The sadness is that when the tenants might have been happy with their compensation, the landlords would never be content. The value of the compensation at the moment is no more than the value of a similar seven-year-old property in the district.[5]

G: That is greed. You economists should know that humans have an "insatiable" desire. The properties taken back were often over 40 years old. The seven-year-old rule now used is far better than the existing market value of the units involved.

C: Wait, the desire to secure one's property for normal use is not greed, but those who appropriate it could be greedy. The urban renewal agency has appropriated the value of the development's potential.

G: The "public purpose"[6] is the heart of the matter. You cannot say a government body using public power to perform urban renewal is greedy. Such power is needed to overcome the tricky and practical problems of fragmented ownership and "holding out."

C: Is the construction of private office and apartment units on other's private land really a public purpose? They are "private goods," but do not re-accommodate the original residents or shop operators. *In-situ* re-settlement was never contemplated, even though the original initiator, the Housing Society, had that in mind. Therefore, such public power was not used to achieve any *bona fide* "public purpose," which is a real shame.

G: What in your mind is a "public use" but our written law is based on "public purpose," not "public use."

C: I say it again: the "public purpose" is the heart of the matter. This effectively means that whatever purpose of the government is a public purpose, so why isn't the expression, "government purpose," used? In any case, a man is a man, a woman is a woman. The law may call a man a woman and a woman a man. Yet it cannot alter reality by changing the meaning of words. Any use or purpose must be genuinely public, which is practically unavoidable for any appropriation to be considered legitimate in the eyes of the public besides the payment of fair compensation.

G: *In-situ* resettlement is impractical and the projects are necessary to remove dilapidated properties and use the land for modern buildings. That is good for Hong Kong. The property owners could not have undertaken such a project on their own. Besides, the URA did compensate the tenants.

C: The owners of the Queen's Street businesses and residential premises came up with a scheme of their own after LDC announced its scheme, but the former was discarded. Therefore, the claim to speed up urban renewal is a scam. To ignore private property rights this way is bad for Hong Kong. I must say that this is the worst colonial legacy for Hong Kong, especially when it was implemented by a government under a former leader of the Conservative Party.

G: Don't be so condescending and ironic! The so-called property owners in Hong Kong are actually tenants or owners of shares in multiple titled buildings on leasehold land. Leasehold properties are not permanent properties. They do not own the properties; the government does.

C: I am not trying to make things complicated, but I must point out that the nature of a leasehold interest in land is often misunderstood. Though they are limited in time with a pre-specified "terms of years" by the grantor, they are *bona fide* private property. Actually, the terms of years are a State-guaranteed period of the rights and liabilities of the lessees to use, derive income from, and alienate their leasehold interests. What the LDC and URA are doing is using government power under an ordinance to unilaterally and prematurely extinguish such rights. In other words, they take the leasehold interests back before the leases naturally expire. The government, in effect, is reneging on its promises regarding land sold by auction or tender. These promises were made in the conditions of the sale of land and are solemnly stated in the Crown leases.

G: Do not make a mountain out of a molehill. The interests of the existing owners are not those they purchased or inherited from the State from their previous owners!

C: That is no exaggeration about such legalised theft of private property. What is the difference? A lease is a lease. The current owners are legitimate owners of all rights (and duties) for the remaining years of their leases. The law protects property whether it was self-produced, purchased, inherited, or borrowed from others.

G: Do you realise that many buildings in Hong Kong are undergoing *urban decay*? These properties under multiple ownership would have serious problems if they were not reoccupied.

C: Wait a minute, I do not understand how the so-called "experts" borrowed the concept of "urban decay" from overseas, where urban decay means a *structural and secular fall in vitality and business*. Come on, please tell me the name of a district or neighbourhood in Hong Kong that is rampant with crime, unemployment, and depopulation. There is none! Depopulation of settlements has only happened in some remote outlying islands and pockets in the country parks. Urban decay was invoked to support the compulsory sale of private property[7] to supplement government urban renewal in the interest of developers. Many of the properties, including some in the Mid-Levels, that were ac-quired by developers in this way were hardly dilapidated.

G: Wait, please note that in deciding the *reserve price* for an auction, the Lands Tribunal will make sure that, "The reserve price will take into account the redevelopment value of the lot. Any person, including the minority owners, is free to bid at the auction of the lot."[8]

C: That sounds very nice, but there is no objective determination of redevelopment value by the Tribunal and minority owners have to hire experts to argue over this value. The law does not allow for the "merger value"[9] of redevelopment together with other lots. Above all, statistics have shown that developers usually avoid bidding for their rivals' properties: all auctions are settled at their reserve prices, which reflects no competition. Worse, urban renewal projects have generally depressed, rather than increased, the val-ues of neighbouring properties outside the renewal boundaries and such negative effects were greater for older buildings.[10]

G: In any event, the government has acted according to due process. Your views are only serving the interests of the landowners.

C: That might have been the case before 1997, assuming that Britain disregarded the United Nations Human Rights Declaration and the *Hong Kong Bill of Rights Ordinance*[11] had no relevance. To deny people the right to land they purchased from the government on State-planned layouts is hardly compatible with honouring basic human rights and is not a sign of paternal government or *laissez faire*. John Locke would not have agreed with this. Now we are under the *Basic Law*, which expressly protects private property rights. If these rights, sold as commodities to citizens, can be subsequently and loosely appropriated on some suspect grounds of the "public interest," as defined by the direc-tor of a government agency, in the name of urban renewal, then I question if the act is constitutional!

G: Your views are interesting, but purely academic. It may be worth writing papers or theses about, but no professional body[12] has ever complained about government-led urban re-newal, which is no more than private redevelopment with some cosmetic urban design.

C: This conspiracy of silence is due to vested interests. Indeed, other than one "whis-tleblower," there is nobody in academia who has criticised the LDC or URA for vi-olating private property rights. What is politically correct or smart is often morally decadent. Note, the sun always rises from the horizon and one day what is right will be vindicated.

Is it the same old story: some benefit, some lose?

In the famous book by the Friedmans, *Free to Choose*, there is a section on urban renewal:

In the United States, "Urban renewal was adopted with the aim of eliminating slums – "urban blight". The government subsidized the acquisition and clearance of areas to be renewed and made much of the cleared land available to private developers at artificially low prices. The program well deserved the names "slum clearance" and "Negro clear-ance"…The original occupants were forced to move elsewhere, often turning another area into a "blighted" one. The chief beneficiaries of public housing and urban re-newal have not been the poor people. The beneficiaries have, rather, been the owners of property purchased for public housing or located in the renewal areas; middle- and upper-income families who were able to find housing in the high-priced apartments or townhouses that frequently replaced the low-income housing that was renewed out of existence; the developers and occupants of the shopping centres constructed in urban areas....In the meantime, even where it was not deliberately destroyed, low-priced rental housing deteriorated because of rent control and similar measures."

(Friedman and Friedman 1990, 111–112)

The Friedmans' narrative, when adapted to Hong Kong's situation, is as follows:

In Hong Kong, urban renewal was adopted with the aim of eliminating the old urban fabric the owners of which have appeared to have *failed to exploit the development potential*. The government agency unilaterally terminates the leases for land sold to owners at artificially low prices and shares the profits with private developers the project partners for high rise office, shopping and housing. The program well deserves the name "*low buildings clearance*". The original occupants and family shops were forced to move elsewhere. The chief beneficiaries of urban renewal have not been the poor people. The beneficiaries have, rather, been the employees of the agency; the developer partners; middle- and upper-income families who were able to find housing in the high-priced apartments or townhouses that frequently replaced the low-income housing that was renewed out of existence; the owners and occupants of the shopping centres constructed in urban areas. In the meantime, even where it was not deliberately destroyed, low-priced rental housing deteriorated because of CDA zoning which is a measure similar to rent control (Cheung 1974).

To understand Friedman's narrative (as translated above), which shows that Hong Kong's situation is actually not unique and, therefore, is internationally contestable, the peculiar background of urban renewal in Hong Kong needs to be specified.

Since 1842, the Hong Kong Government has granted leasehold interests to purchasers by selling lots one by one for private development, according to a layout prepared by the Land Office (later the Public Works Department and, from 1982, the Lands Department). Each lot has a clearly delineated lot boundary drawn on a map.

The terms or covenants governing the rights and duties of the purchasers and their successors are specified in the conditions of sale and Crown leases for the lots.

This is a system of "planning and development by contract" (or "planning by contract") (Lai 1998b, 2022a, 2005, 2010)[13] between the State and individuals. The layout and individual lot maps, together with the covenants, serve as a mutually binding town plan for a neighbourhood or district. This plan can be altered lot by lot through consent (mutual agreement) upon the payment of a premium or compensation.

One covenant that is characteristic of the leases granted by sale is the term of years, which can be as long as 999 years or only 20–50 years, but is often 75 years plus another 75 years.

In the past, when there was no restriction in a lease against subdivisions, a large lot was invariably subdivided and sold as small lots along a street. Such a subdivision was a response to the demand for more housing, as well as commercial and industrial premises as Hong Kong's population and economy grew.

Multiple ownership by a large number of unit proprietors who owned shares in multistorey buildings erected on small lots was a product of subdivisions and typical of Hong Kong's urban development during the 1950s to late 1960s. That was before developers began to mimic public housing estates by producing comprehensively planned estates on large lots that used to be oil depots and docks (Lai 1998).

Starting in the 1980s and for the sake of statutory planning, these large lots under single ownership were zoned comprehensive redevelopment areas (CRAs). Many developers purchased these lots, relocated their facilities, and applied to modify their leases so that they could be redeveloped into self-contained housing estates with shopping malls and some commercial office space.

Due to the popularity of CRA estates since that time, the government applied the same concept of master layout planning suitable for CRA zoning to multiple titled properties with unexploited redevelopment potential by way of a zone type called a comprehensive development area (CDA), which it introduced in 1990.

A CDA can be considered an interventionist, top-down attempt to reverse the effects of subdivisions under market forces to provide more modern office space and housing units. Urban renewal that can inject some much-needed local open space and community facilities into Hong Kong's stock was often advanced as the rationale behind it. There has never been a scheme for public housing in the US mould criticised by Friedman and Friedman.

Once designated, individual lots zoned for CDA cannot be redeveloped on their own, but must be part and parcel of one master layout plan (MLP) approved by the Town Planning Board. Here, LDC and later its successor, the URA, emerged as the means to overcome the transaction cost problems involved in bringing about full consensus of owners of property shares in a large number of buildings within a CDA zone.

When property unit owners refused to sell their units to the LDC, they could be compelled to sell under the *Crown Lands Resumption Ordinance* (after 1997 *Lands Resumption Ordinance*) and compensated for the value of the existing property but no potential redevelopment value was taken into account. The URA, which also relies on the Lands Resumption Ordinance in case a negotiated price could not be reached, has improved the level of compensation to that for a unit of similar size to a seven-year-old flat in the same district. Like any other developer, it can force the owners of the remaining 20% shares to sell their properties at auction under another ordinance, the *Land (Compulsory Sale for Redevelopment) Ordinance*.[14] Like its predecessor, it does not plan for *in-situ* rehousing.

Both the LDC and URA schemes were/are in accordance with those sites identified by government planners after analysis.

The URA now operates according to an ordinance that is always subject to the *Basic Law*, which expressly protects private property rights and guarantees a capitalist market economy based on the freedom and privity of contract.

The ethical and economic issues of government urban renewal

The issue with government urban renewal (Lai 1993, 2002a, 2002b), not to mention the availability to developers of the option of using the forced auction mechanism, with great ethical and legal implications, are fourfold: (a) whether urban renewal, as such, is really a public purpose; (b) whether the expropriation of all redevelopment gains under the existing standard of compensation is fair and reasonable; (c) whether the premature unilateral termination of the land lease prior to its natural expiry, which certainly violates the principle of respect for private property rights and privity of contract, breaches the Basic Law's express protection of these rights; and (d) whether there is a solution for the problems in (a) and (b) so that (c) may be ameliorated or even avoided.

In the dialogue, G espouses the "official stance," whereas C is critical of this stance and his answers to Questions (a) and (b) are all in the negative, but affirmative for (c). To G, the implementation of a LDC or an URA MLP approved by the Town Planning Board is a public purpose, as it should bring about a new urban centre. The compensation paid out is fair, and any owner who is dissatisfied expects too much. To C, the government should be faithful to its promises to the proprietors based on the government lease, which, as explained above, is a town plan in its own right. G thinks this town plan is outdated. To him, the top planning or social value is more new floor space.

Any discussion of a violation of private property rights under the land lease by statutory CDA zoning cannot be complete if the method of their allocation is ignored. Unlike the case of other countries, these private rights were not grandfathered to attract migrants nor originated as squatter possessions. They were sold as commodities by the Crown at auction. As a change in use for a higher-value one requires a full premium payment, there is no reason why downzoning should not entail compensation. The term of years is like a warranty in any commercial sale that indicates the duration of a product's guarantee. To take away all rights before a lease *naturally expires* is a breach of contract, trust, and fidelity by the State.

The gold-lined coat in the story stands for the CDA zone designated for urban renewal by edict. It is too much for the beggar, while the proprietors affected by the resumption cannot on their own practically put their possessions to the highest valued uses.

In any event, neither the LDC nor URA has paid much attention to the concept of "subsidiarity,"[15] while paying no more than lip service to public engagement. A local community subject to "renewal" was actually eradicated, rather than empowered, and replaced by a major new anchor for global and regional capital investment and consumption. The result is "state-led gentrification" (La Grange and Pretorius). This gave an air of good taste for heritage branding, but is inauthentic.

Property rights and the common good

As a kind of planning by edict (Lai 1994, 1997, 1998a, 1998b), LDC or URA-led urban renewal violates the property owner's rights to exclusively use/not use, derive income/not derive income from, and alienate/not alienate one's property (Lai 2002a, 2002b, 2014).

Private property, personal or real (fixed), extends the freedom of a person and is essential for the common good. The person owes a "social mortgage" to society for being the custodian of such property, while the government should protect the common good as well. The common good refers to the respect and promotion of the fundamental rights of the person, the development of spiritual and material welfare of society, and peace and security of community and its members. Private property rights, especially those established by mutual agreement between the state and a citizen/citizens, are one of the fundamental group of rights that form the roots of material well-being and conditions of stability and prosperity (Hans 2013, 120). Henry George (1839–1897) was fundamentally wrong in advancing the extremist policy of a 100% land tax (George 1884). His ideas lent much support for reckless assaults on personal freedom by attacking private property in land (which is the basis of private housing) that is a physical extension and condition for that freedom.

Private property rights, as *de jure* rules that govern social relations in respect of such property, certainly do NOT constitute an absolute value, but this does not mean that they do not matter when those who are forced to sacrifice them are compensated for their losses, as dictated by an ordinance or "according to the law." The adverse effects on the dignity and welfare of the person deprived and on society as a whole, the common good so to speak, need to be ameliorated, if not totally avoided.

In discussing urban renewal as a government endeavour, due process (i.e., procedural justice) is not adequate and the following substantive principles should be observed. Otherwise, there would be uncertainty in the private property system and the government would lose credibility, not to mention face a deterioration in the society's social fabric and stability due to demoralised proprietors, and employees of shops, and produce uncertainty in the private property system. Thus:

a   Any government resumption (appropriation/taking) must be for "public use" rather than some broad and vague "public purpose."

b   Any violation of private property rights must be demonstrably necessary for the public good.

c   Those affected must be fairly compensated in light of the *redevelopment value* calculated with reference to the *actual amount of* Gross Floor Area.

d   Those affected should be given the greatest possible scope of participation in any project beyond formal notification and consultation.

e   Local reaccommodation should be an option for affected proprietors and tenants.

Possible "solutions" in which no proprietors' consent is given

Given that the URA is here to stay and the government is adamant about producing newer and larger buildings as one of its planning objectives, the way to address the violation of private property rights can follow the following broad principles:

a   All newly granted leases should have a condition which states that the property may be resumed according to a certain yardstick of compensation for urban renewal before the lease expires.

b   For new URA projects, affected proprietors should be given a transferrable entitlement to URA profits derived from redevelopment projects proportional to the area and type of property taken.

c   For completed URA projects, affected proprietors should be given a transferable entitlement to URA profits derived from redevelopment projects proportional to the area and type of property taken.

Principle (a) is *caveat emptor*, though it would affect the land bidder's willingness to pay for the land auctioned. Principles (b) and (c) are intended to balance the interests of the government and those of the proprietors. The entitlement mechanism can follow that for Letters A/B[16], which are a kind of "transfer of development rights" (TDR).

In any dispute between the State and an ordinary property owner, the latter is often the weaker one, especially when the voice of the owner's tenants is louder. Therefore, particular care on the violation of the owner's interest should be taken, even when there is no constitutional protection of private property.

Discussion

Any discussion of urban renewal as a government effort using its legal authority inevitably involves a conflict between a balancing of private and public interest. To deny that in public debate does not help formulate reasonable or legitimate polices that rally public support and hence are unsustainable, as social justice issues are denied as valid topics. The government should not recklessly compromise contracts it has entered into with citizens in respect of leasehold interests which it sold to them for money as a source of public revenue. This is so though there is no equivalent racially biased "Negro removal" agenda in URA projects but a growing discontent with "real estate oligarchs" partnering often with the government to grab land belonging to the less well-off people.

In the case of Hong Kong, an even more specific question that is relevant in terms of not only politics but also jurisprudence, is the constitutional validity of post 30 June 1997 (handover) taking of private land under the *Lands Resumption Ordinance* for urban renewal for an espoused "public purpose" rather than a genuine "public use" (whether or not necessary for government) is constitutionally valid under the *Basic Law* – which expressly protects private property rights and capitalism. It is true that legal battles under this British-born legal system had made little reference to US law cases in relation to that country's Fifth Amendment.

However, signs of legal development in favour of better protection for private property against town planning legislation, which generates and wings over urban renewal schemes, can be seen.

It is hoped that this work will stimulate debates over this important point, which has to do with the constitutionally required status of Hong Kong as a market economy, which, in turn, depends on the freedom and privity of contracts.

Conclusion

Economists define private property rights as three sets of exclusive, positive rights: (1) to use, (2) derive income from, and (3) alienate (sell, lease, let, mortgage, subdivide, etc.) a resource. They explain that an attenuation of any of these exclusive rights would inevitably alter the unaffected rights. Thus, economists should emphasise that these exclusive rights include the negative right to NOT use, derive income from, and alienate a resource, as private property rights would not be real without them.

Government-led urban renewal violates all three positive and negative rights. Once a CDA zone is designated, the owners of the land parcels enclosed by the zone lose their rights to carry out redevelopment on their individual lots and are forced to sell their land to the URA. Worse still, any developer that accumulates 80% shares of the land outside the zone can invoke an ordinance to force an auction of the remaining 20% of the shares.

The government's rationale behind all these measures is that urban proprietors in Hong Kong have no right to not maximise the gross floor area of their land, as not doing so would be, economically speaking, inefficient.

On the other hand, private property is not supreme and not just a matter of *de facto* exclusion for the sake of exclusion. Property rights have a social dimension. Exclusive rights are for the social purpose of the peaceful use of land in an environment in which investment, experimentation, and betterment (as a matter of the spatial division of labour) can take place and where useful social exchanges can occur without undue external interferences. Older urban areas have their own social exchange functions as the home bases of lower-income families and lower-technology production units, which have a useful role to play in any society.

The LDC and its successor the URA, as government corporations, are strange beings that represent the State when using their statutory power to take land, but also as private companies in their profit-making ventures.

The government has sold land for a set duration (a term of years) to landlords for money. Urban renewal in its present mode means that, later, before the promised term of years expires, the government effectively sold to the new landlords new floor space which the old landlords have failed to maximise. The logic and ethics of this, under the so-called due process, need to be examined and a proper solution identified for a society that claims to protect private property and is proud of its rule of law. The problem was not introduced into Hong Kong by socialist China, but by some bureaucrats in colonial Hong Kong trained in the British Commonwealth. Due process does not constitute effective valid laws, although the latter calls for due process to be effective.

Notes

1 This story is based on an essay published in Chinese in *Hong Kong Economic Journal* on 5 December 1991.
2 This dialogue is a sequel to Lai (2014). For the official history of urban renewal, see Town Planning Office (1988).
3 URA was established under the *Urban Renewal Authority Ordinance*, Cap.563, Laws of Hong Kong.
4 Established under the *Land Development Corporation Ordinance of 1987* No. 71 of 1987, Cap.15, *Laws of Hong Kong*. It was repealed by resolution of the Legislative Council (L.N.130 of 2007). For the differences between LDC and URA, see Planning, Environment and Lands Bureau, "Comparison of the Land Development Corporation Ordinance (Cap.15) and the *Urban Renewal Authority Bill* (White Bill)", 1999 [http://www.legco.gov.hk/yr99-00/english/hc/sub_com/hs01/papers/a398e02.pdf].
5 URA "URA issues acquisition offers for two Tai Kok Tsui projects":
    The URA acquires property interests by private agreements with individual owners. The acquisition offers are based on the Government's Home Purchase Allowance (HPA) policy plus a URA incentive of incidental cost allowance. HPA is the difference between the market value of a notional seven-year-old flat in a comparable quality building in a similar locality (commonly known as "seven-year rule") and that of the acquired property. Owner-occupiers will receive the full HPA amount whereas owners of tenanted and vacant domestic properties will receive a supplementary allowance up to half of the HPA.
    [2005.03.15, http://www.ura.org.hk/en/media/press-release/2005/20050315.aspx]
    See also Lands Department, "Land resumption and compensation in the urban area – guidelines of occupiers, owners and surveyors," July 2013. [http://www.landsd.gov.hk/en/images/doc/ulm_resumption.pdf].
6 S.3, *Lands Resumption Ordinance*, Cap.124, Laws of Hong Kong. Before 1 July 1997, it was the *Crown Lands Resumption Ordinance*.
7 Cap.545, *Laws of Hong Kong*.
8 Development Bureau. 2010. "Land (Compulsory Sale for Redevelopment) Ordinance (Chapter 545)", Legislative Council Brief DEVB (PL-UR) 70/41/85, January 2010.
9 See Lands Tribunal in *First Kind Ltd. v. Yuet Loong Investment Co. Ltd. and another* LDCS 12000/2014 on this value, which is also called "marriage value" by the Royal Institution of Chartered Surveyors. [http://www.rics.org/Global/red_book_2017_global_pgguidance_160617_rt.pdf].
10 Chau, K.W. and Wong, S.K. 2014. "Externalities of urban renewal: a real option perspective." *Journal of Real Estate Finance and Economics* 48(3), 546–560.
11 Cap.383, *Laws of Hong Kong*.
12 That would be the Hong Kong Institute of Surveyors, Hong Kong Institute of Planners, and Hong Kong Institute of Architects. Corray's (2002) book chapter on compensation is silent on property rights or their protection under the *Basic Law*.
13 The concept of planning by contract can be traced to Clawson (1960) and Roberts (1975).
14 Cap.545, *Laws of Hong Kong*. See also Legislative Council Secretariat (2016).
15 It is a concept adopted by the European Union. "The principle of subsidiarity is defined in Article 5 of the Treaty on European Union. It aims to ensure that decisions are taken as closely as possible to the citizen and that constant checks are made to verify that action at EU level is justified in light of the possibilities available at national, regional or local level. Specifically, it is the principle whereby the EU does not take action (except in the areas that fall within its exclusive competence), unless it is more effective than action taken at national, regional or local level. It is closely bound up with the principle of proportionality, which requires that any action by the EU should not go beyond what is necessary to achieve the objectives of the Treaties." [http://eur-lex.europa.eu/summary/glossary/subsidiarity.html?locale=en].

16 The Letters A/B were issued by the colonial administration to New Territories' private rural lot owners whose land government needed to implement layouts. These letters were transferrable and holders of them could use them to bid for urban lots in government land auctions or tenders at a rate of 5 units of farm land taken back by government to two units of urban land sold by government. (Lands Department 1991).

References

Cheung, S.N.S. 1974. "A theory of price control." *Journal of law and Economics* 17(1), 53–71.

Clawson, M. 1960. "Suburban development districts: a proposal for better urban growth." *Journal of the American Institute of Planners* 2, 69–83.

Corray, A. 2002. "Government as ground landlord and land use regulator; the Hong Kong experience." In Taking Land: Compulsory Purchase and Regulation in Asian-Pacific Countries, Kotaka, T. and Callies, D.L. (eds.). University of Hawaii Press, Honolulu: USA, 96–143.

Crown Lands and Survey Office (1977), *A Simple Guide to Crown Land Transactions*. Hong Kong, Government Printer.

Development Bureau. 2010. "Land (Compulsory Sale for Redevelopment) Ordinance (Chapter 545)", Legislative Council Brief DEVB (PL-UR) 70/41/85, January 2010.

Friedman, M. and Friedman R. 1990. *Free to Choose*. Harcourt Brace, San Diego: USA.

George, H. 1884. *Progress and Poverty: An Inquiry into the Cause of Industrial Depressions, and of Increase of Want with Increase of Wealth, the Remedy*. D. Appleton and Co., New York: USA.

Hans, S. 2013. *The Church: Sacrament of Salvation*. Midwest Theological Forum, Woodridge, IL: USA.

Lai, L.W.C. 1993. "Urban Renewal and the Land Development Corporation." In The Other Hong Kong Report, Choi, P.K. and Ho, L.S. (eds.). Chinese University Press, Hong Kong, 175–191.

Lai, L. W.C. 1994. "The economics of land use zoning – a literature review and analysis of the work of Coase." *Town Planning Review* 65(1), 77–98.

Lai, L.W.C. 1997. "The property rights justifications for planning and a theory of zoning." *Progress in Planning: Recent Research in Urban and Regional Planning* 48(3), 161–246.

Lai, L.W.C. 1998a. Zoning and Property Rights: A Hong Kong Case Study, 2nd ed. Hong Kong University Press, Hong Kong.

Lai, L.W.C. 1998b. "The leasehold system as a means of planning by contract: the Hong Kong case." *Town Planning Review* 69(3), 245–271.

Lai, L.W.C. 2002a. "Planning and property rights in Hong Kong under constitutional capitalism." *International Planning Studies* 7(3), 213–225.

Lai, L.W.C. 2002b. "'Fifty Years No Change?' Land Use Planning and Development in Hong Kong under Constitutional Capitalism." In Crisis and Transformation in China's Hong Kong, Chan, M. and So, A. (eds.). M.E. Sharpe, Armonk: USA and Hong Kong University Press, Hong Kong, 257–282.

Lai, L.W.C. 2005. "Planning by contract in Hong Kong: the leasehold foundation of a comprehensively planned capitalist land market." *Economic Affairs* 25(4), 16–18.

Lai, L.W.C. 2010. "A model of planning by contract: Integrating comprehensive state planning, freedom of contract, public participation, and fidelity." *Town Planning Review* 81(6), 647–673.

Lai, L.W.C. 2014 "Planning by contract: two dialogues." In Cities and Private Planning: Property Rights, Entrepreneurship and Transaction Costs, Andersson, D. and Moroni, S. (eds.). Edward Elgar, Cheltenham: UK, 135–152.

Lai, L.W.C. 2014. "Private property rights not to use, earn from or trade land in urban planning and development: a meeting between Coase and Buchanan." *Habitat International* 44, 555–560.

Lands Department (1991) "Land Exchange Entitlements (Letters A/B) and Modified Letter B" *Lands Instructions*, 13 May 1991.

Lands Department. 2013. "Land resumption and compensation in the urban area – guidelines of occupiers, owners and surveyors", July 2013. [http://www.landsd.gov.hk/en/images/doc/ulm_resumption.pdf].

Legislative Council Secretariat. 2012. "Implementation of the Land (Compulsory Sale for Redevelopment) Ordinance." Information Note, 13 April 2012.

Roberts, P.J. 1975. *Valuation of Development Land in Hong Kong*. Hong Kong University Press, Hong Kong.

Town Planning Office. 1988. Town Planning in Hong Kong. Buildings and Lands Department, Hong Kong.

14

Land based infrastructure development and ease of doing business in India

Poonam Kashyap and Anil Kashyap

Introduction

The rapid population growth has outpaced the planning interventions in most large Indian cities resulting in unplanned, leapfrogged physical development and considerable transport challenges for intra-city and regional traffic (Mittal and Kashyap, 2015). The role of infrastructure in economic growth has been widely recognised amongst authors (Sahoo and Dash, 2009), and it is described as being the backbone of a nation upon which the economy, competitiveness and the nation's standard of living depend. The World Development Report (1994) states that infrastructure represents, if not the engine, then the 'wheels' of economic activity (Mishra et al., 2013). Urban infrastructure systems play a pivotal role in any development including mobility, accommodation, energy, potable water, sanitation and communication. Energy, water, transport, digital communications, waste disposal networks and facilities are seen as essential ingredients for the success of a competitive modern economy (Manesh and Karimani, 2017). Research demonstrates that improvements in transport infrastructure (e.g. road density network, air transport, railways, ports and logistics) have resulted in increased trade flows. Information and communications technology (ICT) infrastructure has also enhanced trade as the numbers of telephone lines, mobile phones, broadband access, internet users and secure internet servers are found to have positive effects for importers and exporters (Ismail and Mahyideen, 2015). The infrastructure sector is a key driver for the Indian economy, evident in the country's plans to spend USD 1 trillion on infrastructure development in the 12th Five-Year plan 2012–2017, and it is expected that 40% of it will come from the private sector (IBEF, 2017; Kumar, 2013). Increased investment in infrastructure is not only critical for the country's growth and to sustain the battle against poverty, but also to lay the foundations for stronger economic growth in the future (Mishra et al., 2013).

The flow of investment hinges largely on the policy and regulatory environment. Although there has been a significant level of institutional investment flow into the infrastructure sector, the delays in regulatory approvals and acquisition of land for projects have remained a major impediment in countries like India. Developing countries are facing major obstacles to achieving sustained high growth (Spence, 2016). Barriers to infrastructure development include weak and unstable investment and regulatory investments as well as corruption and a lack of transparency. Such issues not only deter investment but make it more expensive to deliver infrastructure (Banks, 2014). There also remain barriers to financing, such as the unintended consequences of financial regulation, underdeveloped local currency capital markets and the limited availability of appropriate, standardised instruments to align projects' risk and return profiles with investor needs. Delays in land acquisition and bureaucracy issues together with ineffective resolution of disputes are huge bottlenecks to implementing infrastructure projects in India and often result in time and cost over-runs, stalling projects for years (McKinsey, 2009).

Land acquisition refers to the process where a government acquires land from landowners for any purpose; generally, it is related to development projects conducted by public sector units or the private sector (Tyagi and Shinde, 2016). Economies are facing serious challenges in creating development processes that generate economic growth while being socially inclusive, ecologically sustainable, politically feasible and in accordance with the rule of law (CPR, 2017).

This chapter considers the key challenges in terms of land and land acquisition issues which are critical for building confidence among foreign institutional investors in terms of the ease of doing business. These are land and land rights, land administration and legislation, compulsory purchase versus market acquisition and finally the policy on the rehabilitation of a displaced population in a democracy where it is important to understand the political economy of land.

Resources and development challenges

In the 21st century land has emerged as a critical resource with respect to the management of economic development, urban expansion and industrialisation (Samanta and Shireesh, 2015). Globalisation and liberalisation of economies have brought up land as an important policy issue as various stakeholders lay claims to it like never before (Singh, 2016). Cities in developing countries are witnessing a rapid increase in the size of their population; this urban growth demands more space for industrial estates, commercial centres, communication and transportation systems and so on (Mishra, 2014). Land continues to remain important for production and rural livelihoods in developing economies like India. However, the land and natural resources that millions depend on worldwide are routinely stolen or are under constant threat of expropriation as a result of a lack of legal recognition. An estimated 80% of the global population does not have access to formal systems to protect their land rights, and in many countries the majority of the land area is not legally recognised (Haki, 2017). Farmers cannot invest in their land for fear of dispossession; women are denied their rightful inheritance; the lack of legal ownership depresses credit and investment markets; trees, water, minerals and other resources are taken from community lands with no compensation; and large investment projects displace entire villages (Haki, 2017). Land and land rights have become increasingly contentious issues over recent decades as demand for valuable land intensifies and land relations are becoming more transnational (IIED, 2015). In a globalised world, where land governance is increasingly shaped by international regulation, securing land rights at the grassroots level is essential. Investment treaties are often negotiated with little public or parliamentary oversight. However, spaces for citizen engagement are evolving rapidly as people become more aware of the stakes and avenues for influence. Investment treaty negotiations are being increasingly scrutinised by civil society and social movements, and community perspectives are being brought in to investor-state arbitration (IIED, 2015).

The development of infrastructure projects typically requires land, and often very large tracts of land (Vanclay, 2017). Sustained economic growth hinges on alternative uses of land, such as for industries, infrastructure (roads, railways, power, telecoms, mining), housing, commercial buildings, social infrastructure (health and education) and other economic activities. This need for land can result in the physical displacement of the people living there. The World Bank Environment Department (WBED) has estimated that 60% of development-induced displacement every year – about six million people – is as a result of urban infrastructure and transportation projects (FMO, 2011). Even in situations where people are not required to physically move, the project may still impact their livelihoods or income-generating activities, either temporarily or permanently (i.e. economic displacement) or cause other environmental and social impacts that make it untenable to continue living there. The acquisition of land and other assets for development projects deprives people of their livelihood; some of them are displaced and others are alienated from their livelihood without physical relocation (Fernanades et al., 2012 cited in Karmakar, 2017). Resettlement can be defined as the comprehensive process of planning for and implementing the relocation of people, households and communities from one place to another for some specific reason (Vanclay, 2017). The process of resettlement is complex due to the varying vulnerabilities, capacities, positionings and interests of the people being resettled. It has become evident that resettlement practice has mainly focused on providing cash compensation or addressing the need for replacement housing, with inadequate attention being paid to all the other dimensions of life that are affected by being resettled. The problematic aspects of resettlement practice include unrealistic time frames and inadequate budgets for undertaking the resettlement, inadequate compensation arrangements, poor engagement with impacted communities and a failure to manage land speculation and the opportunistic behaviour of various stakeholders, including the affected communities.

The disruption to people's lives and livelihoods can create harm, sometimes on a long-term basis, especially when there is no adequate restoration of the livelihoods and/or income-earning activities of the resettled people (Vanclay, 2017).

Streamlining land procurement and fair compensation

There have been a number of different legislations in India including the Land Acquisition Act of 1894, the National Rehabilitation and Resettlement Policy of 2007, the Land Acquisition, Rehabilitation and Resettlement Act of 2013 and the different state legislations on land acquisition (Naika, 2016). Until the enactment of 2013, compulsory acquisition of land was regulated by the Land Acquisition Act of 1984. This Act was based on the colonial presumption that the State had the absolute sovereign right over all land, therefore there was little scope in that Act for any consultation or negotiation with the affected people. It received much criticism for lacking transparency, breeding corruption and insufficiently protecting landowners and local communities (Jenkins, 2013). The Act of 1894 was amended twice, in 1962 and 1984, both of which increased the state's taking powers, and the essential arbitrariness of the acquisition and compensation process remained unaltered (Chakravorty, 2016; Bajaj, 2015). Since independence, millions of people have been dispossessed of their lands and displaced from their homes to make way for various development activities (Figure 14.1). It is possible that upwards of 20 million hectares (50 million acres) of agricultural and non-agricultural land was converted to different uses in independent India. As a result of these land use conversions, it is believed up to 60 million people were affected (Chakravorty, 2016). In the majority of cases, the amounts of compensation and

State	Period	Water	Transp.	Welfare/Admin	Environ	Industry	Mines	Other	Total
Andhra Pradesh	1951–1995	1865	47	38	136	540	101	490	3216
Assam	1947–2004	449	169	746	265	58	41	191	1919
Goa	1965–1995	6	43	7	0	1	0	3	61
Gujarat	1965–1995	2379	1356	45	26	141	4	124	4075
Jharkhand	1951–1995	233	0	0	510	88	403	314	1548
Kerala	1947–2000	134	152	17	15	223	0	12	552
Odisha	1947–2000	800	0	0	108	158	300	100	1466
West Bengal	1947–2004	1724	1164	1674	785	404	418	775	6944
TOTAL		7590	2931	2526	1845	1613	1267	2009	19781
Share (%)		38.4	14.8	12.8	9.3	8.2	6.4	10.2	100.0

Figure 14.1 Number of displaced and project-affected persons for selected States and major categories

the associated resettlement and rehabilitation efforts have been highly inadequate, leaving large numbers destitute and in a state of distress. Since the 1990s, massive public outrage and civil society movements over the increasing visibility and severity of the land conflict have translated into legislative efforts (Wahi et al., 2017). It was in this climate of rising tensions, protests and rebellions that the new Land Acquisition Act was enacted with the support of the entire political establishment (Bajaj, 2015).

In September 2013, the Government of India adopted the legislation 'The Rights to Fair Compensation and Transparency in Land Acquisition, Resettlement and Rehabilitation Act' (LARR), in an attempt to resolve disputes relating to land acquisition (Agrawal, 2015). The law was created by the United Progressive Coalition (UPA) led by the Congress party and was supported by all major political parties (Chakravorty, 2016). This legislation was historic because for the first time, it addressed the concerns of displacement caused by land acquisition. It was termed 'pro-people' and viewed as a more competent, consultative and participatory rights-based Act which addressed the major drawbacks of the 1894 Act (Karmakar, 2017). The law helps farmers who have been exploited by promising to pay them four times the existing market price for their land, and requires the approval of 80% of the landowners in the affected area, making it much more difficult for corporations to acquire land (Agrawal, 2015). It includes compensation provisions for landless households like tenants and farm workers who depend on the farming activities on acquired land, and an automatic rehabilitation and resettlement (R&R) package is applicable if the acquired land is more than 40 hectares (100 acres) in rural areas and 20 hectares (50 acres) in urban areas. Furthermore, irrigated and multi-cropped land can be acquired only as a last resort and only up to a small percentage of the total of such land in a given location, for example, not more than 5% in multi-crop districts. It also includes annuities, land for land exchange, a transportation allowance, a portion of capital gains from resale, the construction of alternative housing and communal amenities in the event of loss of a homestead, tightens the definition of 'public purpose' and provides for a social impact assessment (Ghatak and Ghosh 2011, cited in Singh, 2016).

However, within a year of its coming into force there was an attempt to amend the LARR Act by the Right to Fair Compensation and Transparency in Land Acquisition Rehabilitation and Resettlement (Amendment) Ordinance, 2014, proposed by the Bharatiya Janata Party (BJP) (Chakravorty, 2016). The main aim of the Ordinance and the corresponding bill was to exempt five specified categories of projects from the provisions regarding consent, social impact assessment and the safeguarding of food security (Bajaj, 2015). According to the new bill, a mandatory social impact assessment and a consent clause – 70% consent from landholders for public private partnerships (PPP) and 80% for private projects – were done away with in the case of five categories of projects which included defence, rural infrastructure, affordable housing, industrial corridors and infrastructure (Balachandran and Punit, 2015). The amending Ordinance and bill were seen as positive measures offering enhanced compensation, rehabilitation and resettlement benefits to people and families affected by land acquisition undertaken through 13 acts (Bajaj, 2015). The Ordinance was repromulgated on April 3, 2015. However, 10 days later, the LARR Ordinance was challenged before the Supreme Court as constituting an 'abuse of power' on the part of the government. As a result, no law was passed to implement the Ordinance in two successive sessions of parliament. On May 30, 2015, the LARR Ordinance was promulgated a third time. A bill to replace the Ordinance was referred to a joint parliamentary committee which comprised legislators across party lines in June 2015. A few months later, at the close of the monsoon session of Parliament, the Ordinance lapsed. Following this lapse, in September 2015 the Supreme Court dismissed the challenge to the LARR Ordinance as infructuous. In December, the Joint Parliamentary Committee was given an eighth extension to submit its report. The government's inability to garner parliamentary support to pass the LARR Amendment Bill 2015 into law is a testament to the intense and continued political dispute regarding this subject (Wahi et al., 2017).

With regards to more recent changes to the Act and its impact, the Planning Commission of India's recommendations relating to land acquisition and rehabilitation and resettlement advocate that indiscriminate land acquisition should be halted and land acquisition for public purposes should be confined to public welfare activities and matters of national security. It has been recognised that amendments must be made to India's benchmark land acquisition law in order to make it easier to buy land for defence and development projects in the fast-growing economy, whilst also ensuring the rights of farmers (Chandran, 2017). According to a secretary of the Department of Land Resources, one of the biggest issues faced is the pace of land acquisitions; it takes, on average, 59 months to acquire land under this law. Conflicts related to land and resources are the main reason behind stalled industrial and development projects in India, affecting millions of people and jeopardising billions of dollars of investment, according to a recent study (Chandran, 2017). Prime Minister Modi has highlighted the need for the cooperation of all parties, stating that 'in a democracy there should be dialogue, discussion and positive outcome' (Times of India, 2015).

Demand for land by non-agricultural sectors has increased phenomenally, and incidents of State-driven land acquisition have become far more numerous than ever before following the liberalisation and globalisation of the Indian economy (Roy, 2016). Since 2006, Singur in West Bengal has been the centre of controversy over land acquisition for a Tata Motors car manufacturing unit, bringing to light the contested nature of development in contemporary India. The West Bengal Government acquired around 405 hectares (1,000 acres) of land for Tata Motors to manufacture the Nano (the world's cheapest car) (Chakravorty, 2016). The land in Singur was the preferred choice of the auto manufacturer because of its railway and highway links, as well as its proximity to the city of Kolkata (Ray, 2015). A local rural movement challenging the land acquisition soon attracted the support of various activist groups and political parties from across India, and in late 2008, it succeeded in forcing Tata Motors to abandon the site (Nielson, 2010). Although West Bengal was once India's industrial powerhouse, it has witnessed a significant decline in industrial production since independence. This gathered speed during the mid-1960s when West Bengal was hit by reductions in central government investments intended to hold back drought-induced inflation (Nielson, 2010).

The opening of the Tata factory was to be the first in a series of new industrial ventures, expected to create an estimated 10,000 jobs and bring in investments worth INR 10 billion). The Chief Minister believed this would set in motion the other wheels of industrial progress in the State and would change the face of not only Singur but of the entire State. However, following the announcement of the project, criticism of and opposition to the land acquisition soon surfaced. Around 403 hectares (996 acres) of multi-crop farmland was forcibly acquired under the LAA 1894, provoking anger among the local population who depend on the land for agriculture (Bommakanti, 2016). Owners of approximately 137 hectares (338 acres) out of the total targeted for expropriation in Singur refused to hand over their land and did not accept compensation. The farmers protests were not against industrialisation led by private capital; instead, they stressed the importance of not undermining pre-existing livelihood strategies as part of the development process by completely replacing a regenerative resource (land) with a perishable one (money) (Nielson, 2010). Within months, the project was abandoned at Singur and operations were moved to the business-friendly State of Gujarat (Ray, 2015).

The State of Bihar has also experienced serious issues with land acquisition, with a report stating that land transactions are more complex and chaotic in Bihar than in other Indian states. This is largely due to the fact that land records have not been updated. The first and only comprehensive land study was carried out in British India in 1915 (Choudhary, 2017). The lack of up-to-date records of land rights and a lack of proper infrastructure is thought to have contributed to several land disputes in the State. Samanta et al. (2013) conclude that an up-to-date record of land rights is needed to ensure individual tenure rights and their recognition as well as the completion of a land survey map and record of rights along, with its access to people to reduce conflict over land and land-related disputes.

Innovative mechanism for land procurement

Changing demographics has created greater demand for housing and the need for more serviced urban land (Mathur, 2012). The enormity of the pressure on growth, the limited availability of serviced urban land, combined with cash-strapped state governments and municipal authorities, has led to urban growth preceding any planning intervention in most Indian cities. The net result of this is visible in urban growth being fragmented, leapfrogged, and ad hoc in most cities with a million-plus population. Since it is the civic authority's responsibility to provide for infrastructure, the budget-constrained municipal authorities attempt to devise various innovative tools to finance urban development. In the current economic climate, India's infrastructure deficit is creating significant challenges for the country's continued economic growth (KPMG, 2012). India's infrastructural investment up to 2030 is estimated at USD 690 billion (HPC Report, 2011). The magnitude of the infrastructural investment challenge runs far beyond the capacity of the public sector alone. Therefore, interventions in the form of innovative land development and monetisation techniques are required to create the conditions conducive for the implementation of mega infrastructure projects, such as ring roads and express highways.

The land-based financing techniques such as land readjustment work on the principle that the benefits of infrastructure projects are capitalised into land values, which could then generate upfront revenues for the local authority. The theory supports the notion that the value created by public infrastructure investment is an 'unearned increment' and therefore should flow to the community, rather than to individual landowners (Peterson, 2009, 71). This technique then reduces the financial dependence of the implementing agency on alternative strategies such as debt financing and related fiscal risks (Peterson, 2009) or budgetary outlay.

Land readjustment is used for peri-urban or suburban land development and combines several elements – the pooling of property rights, physical reorganisation of land parcels and the preparation of a layout plan, with an aim to provide planned urban growth and the development of urban infrastructure in a self-financing way. A certain percentage of each participating landowner's original holding is appropriated to contribute towards the provision of land for roads, rights-of-way, lots for public amenities such as parks and a number of lots which are reserved for sale. A fixed percentage of the final land lots kept aside for sale purpose is added to the implementing agency's land bank, which, once sold, pay for the costs of the infrastructure development (Ballaney and Patel 2008; Gautam 2012; Mathur 2012, and Sorensen 2000). When irregular shaped, rural lots are converted into urban lots and are provided with public infrastructure and amenities, lots become more marketable and gain greater market value. Land readjustement techniques involve greater public participation and the distribution of the financial costs and benefits and thus share the betterment between private landowners and the public agency (Home, 2002).

Land readjustment is used in many countries to reconfigure underperforming land parcels and, after pooling land and servicing areas with basic infrastructure, achieve coordinated planned development. Land readjustment is an area planning tool, commonly employed at the neighbourhood scale for the redevelopment of an 80 to 160 hectares (200 to 400 acres) land area. It is a self-financing tool and does not involve land acquisition for roads and other infrastructure. In a land readjustment scheme, the land is first pooled, then the use of the area is redesigned, next the land is serviced with urban infrastructure and finally the land bank is created that financially supports the new development. A percentage of the land is appropriated from the landowners to create rights of way for public infrastructure and lots for public amenities.

The states may acquire land for private companies to set up large industrial projects supposedly to provide benefit to the local economy including employment opportunities. Landowners have always contested land acquisition on the grounds of arbitrariness in the process and inadequate compensation, causing delays and sometime the abandonment of the land acquisition proceedings in the judicial review, for example, the Tata Nano project discussed earlier.

Summary

The land readjustment technique involves greater public participation and distributes financial costs and benefits to share betterment between private landowners and the public agency. A pro-rata share of serviced land is given back to the owners after making provisions for roads and other public amenities. Thus, unlike land pooling via direct acquisition such as by negotiated purchase or eminent domain, which involves a permanent change in the landownership and the transfer of a land parcel from a passive to an active landowner, land readjustment allows continuous landownership and inspires owners to actively participate in the new development. However, there are challenges in making land available for the implementation of mega infrastructure projects, or the setting up of large industries, through implementation of master plans, and development schemes because of litigations and prolonged disputes in taking of clear ownership of land. Professional bodies are now getting involved in setting global standards for the measurement of land to make it easy for reporting agencies to document it in consistent manner, particularly for the benefit of overseas investors.

References

Agrawal, P. (2015). Infrastructure in India: Challenges and the Way Ahead [online]. Available from: www.iegindia.org/upload/publication/Workpap/wp350.pdf. [Accessed 30 August 2017].

Bajaj, J. K. (2015). Land Acquisition Bill: The Core Issues. Available from: http://indiafacts.org/land-acquisition-bill-the-core-issues/. [Accessed 30 August 2017].

Balachandran, M. and Punit, I. (2015). Timeline: 200 Years of India's Struggle with Land Acquisition Laws. Available from: https://qz.com/471117/timeline-200-years-of-indias-struggle-with-land-acquisition-laws/. [Accessed 30 August 2017].

Ballaney, S. and Bimal, P. (2009) Using the 'Development Plan—Town Planning Scheme' Mechanism to Appropriate Land and Build Urban Infrastructure. India Infrastructure Report. Oxford Press.

Banks, B. (2014). Guest Post: Barriers to Infrastructure Investment and How to Tackle Them. Available from: www.ft.com/content/48a336ea-ba07-36de-9406-35526d2cbeef. [Accessed 14 September 2017].

Bommakanti, U. (2016). Singur Tata Nano Controversy: How Agriculture Paid the Costliest Price for the World's Cheapest Car. Available from: www.newindianexpress.com/nation/2016/sep/02/Singur-Tata-Nano-controversy-How-agriculture-paid-the-costliest-price-for-the-worlds-cheapest-car-1515294.html. [Accessed 12 September 2017].

Chakravorty, S. (2016). Land Acquisition in India: The Political-Economy of the Changing Law. *Area Development and Policy*. [online] 1 (1), pp. 48–62. [Accessed 11 September 2017].

Chandran, R. (2017). For Faster Growth in India, Change the Land Acquisition Law: Official. Available from: www.reuters.com/article/us-india-landrights-lawmaking/for-faster-growth-in-india-change-the-land-acquisition-law-official-idUSKBN1781M4. [Accessed 11 September 2017].

Choudhary, A. (2017). In One Bihar *Village*, *A Snapshot of How Corruption is Derailing a Bid to Acquire Land for Industry*. Available from: https://scroll.in/article/825811/it-isnt-resistance-but-corruption-thats-derailing-bihars-attempts-to-acquire-land-for-industry. [Accessed 12 September 2017].

CPR. (2017). CPR Conference on Land Rights and Land Acquisition. Available from: https://indconlawphil.wordpress.com/2017/02/28/cpr-conference-on-land-rights-and-land-acquisition/. [Accessed 12 September 2017].

FMO. (2011). Types of Development Projects Causing Displacement. Available from: www.forcedmigration.org/research-resources/expert-guides/development-induced-displacement-and-resettlement/types-of-development-projects-causing-displacement. [Accessed 14 September 2017].

Gautam, I. P. (2012). A Presentation on Land Use and Urban Transport. ICRIER's Program on Capacity Building and Knowledge Dissemination. *ICREIR*. Available from: http://icrier.org/pdf/IP_Gautam_GOG_IPG_Program.pdf [Accessed on 13 Sept 2017].

Haki. (2017). Global Land Rights Index [online]. Available from: https://static1.squarespace.com/static/53f7ba98e4b01f78d142c414/t/58f966b9579fb3435963448b/1492739775286/Global+Land+Rights+Index_Brief+2017.pdf. [Accessed 14 September 2017]. Home R K (2002) "Why was land readjustment adopted in British India but not in Britain? A historical exploration. Unpublished paper to workshop on Land Readjustment. Boston. Lincoln Institute of Land Policy.

HPC (2011). Urban Infrastructure and Services – Report of High Powered Expert Committee. Planning Commission of India. Available at: http://icrier.org/pdf/FinalReport-hpec.pdf [Accessed on 13 Sept 2017].

IBEF. (2017). Infrastructure Sector in India. Available from: www.ibef.org/industry/infrastructure-sector-india.aspx. [Accessed 30 August 2017].

IIED. (2015). Investment Treaties, Land Rights and a Shrinking Planet. Available from: www.iied.org/investment-treaties-land-rights-shrinking-planet. [Accessed 30 August 2017].

Ismail, N. and Mahyideen, J. (2015). The Impact of Infrastructure on Trade and Economic Growth in Selected Economies in Asia [online]. Available from: www.adb.org/sites/default/files/publication/177093/adbi-wp553.pdf. [Accessed 14 September 2017].

Jenkins, R. (2013). Land, Rights and Reform in India. *Pacific Affairs*. [online] 86 (3), pp. 591–692. [Accessed 12 September 2017].

Karmakar, P. (2017). Politics of Development: Land Acquisition and Economic Development in India. *Journal of Land and Rural Studies*. [online] 5 (2), pp. 164–182. [Accessed 11 September 2017].

KPMG. (2012). Infrastructure 100: World Cities June Edition Online. Available from: https://assets.kpmg.com/content/dam/.../infrastructure-100-world-markets-report.pdf [Accessed on 13 September 2017].

Kumar, A. (2013). CIRC Working Paper: Infrastructure Investment A Trillion Dollar Question [online]. Available from: www.circ.in/pdf/Infrastructure_Investment_A_Trillion_Dollar_Question.pdf. [Accessed 30 August 2017].

Manesh, M. and Karimani, F. (2017). Differences Between Monopoly and Perfect Competition in Providing Public Transportation (Case Study: Lane No. 10 and 96 of Mashhad Bus System).

International Journal of Economics and Management Sciences. [online]. Available from: www.omicson line.org/open-access/differences-between-monopoly-and-perfect-competition-in-providing-public-transportation-case-study-lane-no-10-and-96-of-mashhad-bu-2162-6359-1000416.pdf. [Accessed 14 September 2017].

Mathur, S. (2012). Self-financing urbanization: Insights from the use of Town Planning Schemes in Ahmadabad, India. *Cities* 31, p. 308.

McKinsey. (2009). Building India: Accelerating Infrastructure Projects [online]. Available from http://www.csdcindia.org/sites/default/files/Building_India-Accelerating_infrastructure_projects.pdf. [Accessed 30 August 2017].

Mishra, R. (2014). Displacement: A Socio-Economic Rights Perspective. *Vikalpa: The Journal for Decision Makers*. [online] 39 (4), pp. 11–21. [Accessed 30 August 2017].

Mishra, K A., Kunapareddy, N. and Kar, P. B. (2013). Growth and Infrastructure Investment in India: Achievements, Challenges and Opportunities. *Economic Annals*. [online] 58 (196), pp. 51–68. [Accessed 30 August 2017].

Mittal, J. and Kashyap, A. (2015). Real Estate Market Led Land Development Strategies for Regional Economic Corridors – A Tale of Two Mega Projects. *Habitat International*. 47, pp. 205–217.

Naika, B. (2016). Land Acquisition and Development Induced Displacement: India and International Legal Framework. *ILI Law Review*. [online]. Available from: www.ili.ac.in/pdf/p6_balaji.pdf. [Accessed 30 August 2017].

Nielson, K. B. (2010). Contesting India's Development? Industrialisation, Land Acquisition and Protest in West Bengal. *Forum for Development Studies*. [online] 37 (2), pp. 145–170. [Accessed 11 September 2017].

Peterson, G. E. (2009) Unlocking land values to finance urban infrastructure. Trends and policy options: no. 7. The World Bank and PPIF. Washington, DC. Available from https://www.ppiaf.org/sites/ppiaf.org/files/publication/Trends%20Policy%20Options-7-Unlocking%20Land%20Values%20-GPeterson.pdf [Accessed on 13 September 2017].

Ray, S. (2015). On the Question of Land Acquisition for Private Development: Lessons from United States, India and China. *Emerging Economy Studies*. [online] 1 (1), pp. 71–89. [Accessed 13 September 2017].

Roy, A. (2016). Land Acquisition and Rural Transformation: A Case Study from West Bengal. *Chinese Sociological Dialogue*. [online] 1 (1), pp. 32–47. [Accessed 11 September 2017].

Sahoo, P. and Dash, R. K. (2009). Infrastructure Development and Economic Growth in India. *Journal of the Asia Pacific Economy*. [online] 14 (4), pp. 351–365. [Accessed 30 August 2017].

Samanta, D. and Shireesh. (2015). Social Impact Assessment of Projects involving Land Acquisition in India: Implications of RFCTLARR Act, 2013. *Journal of Management and Public Policy*. [online] 7 (1), pp. 27–35. [Accessed 11 September 2017].

Samanta, D., Jha, J. and Dinda, S. (2013). *Assessment of Land Governance in Bihar* [online]. Available from: https://mpra.ub.uni-muenchen.de/64095/1/MPRA_paper_64095.pdf. [Accessed 12 September 2017].

Singh, S. (2016). Land Acquisition in India: An Examination of the 2013 Act and Options. *Journal of Land and Rural Studies*. [online] 4 (1), pp. 66–78. [Accessed 30 August 2017].

Sorensen, A. (2000). Conflict, consensus or consent: implications of Japanese land readjustment practice for developing countries. *Habitat International* 24, 51–73.

Spence, M. (2016). *Michael Spence: There are Major Obstacles to Economic Growth, But There's Still Hope*. Available from: www.weforum.org/agenda/2016/07/michael-spence-there-are-major-obstacles-to-economic-growth-but-theres-still-hope. [Accessed 14 September 2017].

Times of India. (2015). *Land the Bill: Changes in Land Acquisition Law a Test Case for Modi, Government Must Stick to Its Guns*. Available from: https://blogs.timesofindia.indiatimes.com/toi-editorials/land-the-bill-changes-in-land-acquisition-law-a-test-case-for-modi-government-must-stick-to-its-guns/. [Accessed 12 September 2017].

Tyagi, V. and Shinde, R. (2016). Government Policies and Difficulties in Land Acquisition: A Questionnaire Survey. *International Journal of Innovative Research and Development*. [online] 5 (8), pp. 75–77. [Accessed 12 September 2017].

Vanclay, F. (2017). Project-Induced Displacement and Resettlement: From Impoverishment Risks to An Opportunity for Development? *Impact Assessment and Project Appraisal*. 35 (1), pp. 3–21.

Wahi, N., Bhatia, A., Gandhi, D., Jain, S., Shukla, P., and Chauhan, U. (2017). *Land Acquisition in India: A Review of Supreme Court Cases 1950–2016*, Centre for Policy Research [online]. Available from: http://cprindia.org/sites/default/files/policy-briefs/Land%20Acquisition%20Report.pdf. [Accessed 13 September 2017].

15

Compulsory land acquisition in Malaysia

Critical challenges, approach and success stories

Dzurllkanian Daud, Fauziah Raji, Salfarina Samsudin, Wan Ibrisam Fikry Wan Ismail, Mohd. Nadzri Jaafar and Ismail Omar

Introduction

Land activities are essential to meet human needs to ensure proper social, economic and ecological functions. Equally, as a crucial economic and social resource (Bandeira et al., 2010) with limited supply (Nzioki et al., 2009), land requires the best management practices (Williamson et al., 2010). Land administration systems contribute to managing land rights and facilitating the property market (Barnes, 2003), primarily through land registration, land mapping, property valuation and land development subsystems (Kalantari et al., 2008). In Malaysia, separate laws regulate land use, land tenure, administration, land development, land acquisition and environmental matters, such as the National Land Code (NLC) 1965; Strata Titles Act 1985; Town and Country Planning Act 1976; Street, Drainage and Building Act 1974; Local Government Act 1976; and the Environmental Quality Act 1976. For compulsory acquisition, land is acquired in Malaysia under the Land Acquisition Act (LAA) 1960. Since land is a state matter[1], there are still differences over state land policy implementations (Samsudin et al., 2011). This situation provides further challenges in the development of uniform land policies to be applied by the different states (Azimuddin, 2008).

Compulsory acquisition of land is an extreme form of governmental intervention which affects the constitutional rights of landowners. According to Ghimire (2017), land acquisition involves the compulsory taking of land, often against the will of the landowners. The process involves a legal procedure for the public sector in acquiring any land for development projects that benefits the country (Musaddiq and Singh, 2016). The process acquires land from landowners which is needed for a public purpose or for a project beneficial to the nation. It involves an extensive process and the procedure commences with the issuance of gazetted forms, notices and a follow-up by survey of the affected land. The acquisition process must comply with every provision stated by the NLC 1965 and the LAA 1966 in observing legal actions relating to the acquisition. Landowners are invited to attend a hearing during the enquiry proceedings, and if agreeable and satisfied, they will receive the compensation resulting from the dispossession and exclusion rights of landowners from their properties (Hashim, 2017).

The issues such as land valuation, assessment of compensation, violation of rights, loss of ownership and the loss of livelihood of the affected people come together during the land acquisition process (Ghimire, 2017). Land acquisition has always been considered a sensitive issue, and it may cause controversies and create dissatisfaction amongst the people (Mohd Afandi Mat Rani and Mohamed Azam Mohamed Adil, 2014). Acknowledging these effects, stakeholders should consider their possible approaches to land acquisition and adapt best practices in order to achieve their desired outcomes. The next part of this chapter discusses the practice of land acquisition in Malaysia.

Policy contexts and practice of land acquisition

In Malaysia, the Land Acquisition Act 1960 (LAA 1960) is the tool used by the government to synchronise and develop land for public purposes and for the provision of economic benefits to the country (S3.1(a), S3.1(b) & S3.1(c)). With the existence of the LAA 1960, nobody can question the process of land acquisition by the state authority on the appropriation and dislodgment of private property owners from their properties. Property owners have to agree and are considered unwilling sellers.

The LAA 1960 is an Act of Parliament that outlines the procedures for land acquisition, the making and dealing with objections to compensation, and other related matters, reference to court, court procedures and the assessment of compensation. For objections on a point of law, the appellant needs to apply for a judicial review. The LAA 1960 only allows for reference to court on matters of compensation, the area of the scheduled land, persons of interest (POI) and the apportionment of compensation amongst POI (S37 LAA 1960). (See Figure 15.1 for graphical illustration).

Section 69 of the LAA 1960 allows the minister in charge to make rules for the provisions under the Act. Such rules are as described in the second and third schedule of the LAA 1960, and relate especially to the purpose of acquisition under S3.1(b) and 3.1(c). In 2016, Section 69 of the LAA 1960 was amended to allow for rules to be made in respect of any form, fee or deposit to be charged in connection with any matters related in the LAA 1960. In short, the LAA 1960 is comprehensive and encompassing, and has been amended several times to tighten procedures to meet current development demands. The Malaysian Federal

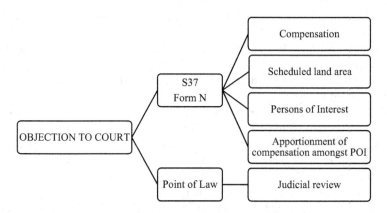

Figure 15.1 Objections to court for land acquisition

Constitution provides for the protection of the right of an individual to own property. Article 13 of the Federal Constitution reads as follows:

1   No person shall be deprived of property save in accordance with the law;
2   No law shall provide for the compulsory acquisition or use of property without adequate compensation.

The LAA 1960 flows from these provisions and is a tool to "process land acquisition and pay equitable compensation". Although land may be purchased from the owner for development purposes, the government prefers compulsory acquisition for the following reasons:

•   It is difficult for both the landowner and the party that needs the land to come to an agreement over the price of land;
•   The land purchased is subject to a condition contrary to the use that is intended. Therefore, the condition needs to be changed. This can cause a lot of inconvenience;
•   The land bought may also be subjected to encumbrances like a charge, lien and tenancy that are exempted from registration;
•   Upon acquisition, an Acquiring Authority does not pay Stamp Duty nor do affected property owners pay Real Property Gains Tax (RPGT).

Through compulsory acquisition, the land can be obtained even though the proprietor does not agree to sell it, and no bargaining over the price is necessary. All encumbrances on the land can be nullified upon the Acquiring Authority taking possession of the land, because all persons of interest would have been adequately compensated.

While the LAA 1960 is Federal Law, land is a state matter, hence only the State Authority (SA) is empowered to acquire land (Federal Constitution 1957, 9th schedule list ii). By and large, all procedures pertaining to land acquisition have to adhere closely to the provisions of the LAA 1960. It is not possible to take shortcuts to speed up the land acquisition process. However, the states do have a say in the administrative procedures and measures undertaken. In light of this, administrative procedures amongst the states in Malaysia can vary for land acquisition purposes. In line with this, the Department of Director General of Lands and Mines (JKPTG) has also developed a Standard Operating Procedure (SOP) for land acquisition by the Federal Ministries and Departments. This SOP can be adopted by other non-Federal government agencies as well (JKPTG 2010).

Figure 15.2 aptly illustrates the land acquisition process from the Federal government to the SAs. According to the LAA 1966, there are 17 forms; ranging from Forms A to Q, some of which must be used, while some are optional, depending on situations and circumstances (Hashim, 2017).

Several disputes in land acquisition have arisen when the Federal government and the state government do not see eye to eye on projects, which involve land acquisition. Noteworthy is the KIDEX highway (or the Kinrara-Damansara Expressway) that was planned by the Federal government of Malaysia. The proposed highway was to weave through a very dense urban area in Selangor and would have involved the acquisition of 3,700 properties. There was very strong opposition to the project. Although the acquisition was gazetted, the resulting powers lapsed, and the Selangor State Government did not consent to it being regazetted. In the end, this project was shelved (Kamal, 2016) Of late, Malaysia has been actively expanding and improving its infrastructure with the construction of a Mass Rapid Transit (MRT) system and the expansion of its Light Rapid Transit (LRT) line. The constructions of these modes

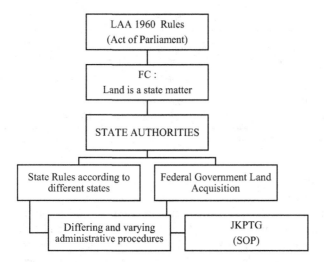

Figure 15.2 Role of federal government and state authorities in land acquisition
Source: Uni Technologies (2015).

of public transport involve tunnels and underground stations; hence, these new developments require the acquisition of underground land. Initially, the LAA 1960 was not fully equipped to cater for this. Thus, the Act was amended in 2016 to allow for innovative and creative development, be it infrastructure or otherwise. In 2008 (Circular No 1/2008), the Directorate of Land and Mines developed guidelines about the minimum ground depth that can be enjoyed by the landowner (Zaini et al., 2014). However, the minimum depth is valid only for the fresh alienation of surface land, while for the alienation of surface land without the minimum depth, the underground land can still be alienated but only by the surface landowner. The circular specifies that the depth of the ownership shall not be less than 6 metres (20 feet) in the case of agricultural lands, and in case of the building or industrial categories it shall not be less than 10 and 15 metres (32.8 and 49.2 feet), respectively; these guidelines, however, do not apply to alienations granted before 2008. Thus, for the moment unless the circular is gazetted or made into law, lands alienated prior to 2008, will have to be compensated even though the underground portion of the land is needed for underground tunnels or similar (Table 15.1).

In tandem, Section 92B (3) (b) (NLC1965) stipulates that underground land can be used independent of the surface of the alienated land in terms of category of land use. Therefore, the substrata land can be used in whatever way the landowner wishes after obtaining the approval of the State Authority. Interestingly, Section 92C (2) (a) (NLC1965) also allows different uses for different parts of the underground land.

Although substrata development in Malaysia is not growing as rapidly as in other countries, Malaysia's pioneer case, the MRT project, has raised many issues and has alerted all the relevant parties, especially those involved in the legal aspects. Even with the provisions regarding the development of underground land and the supporting circulation, it still cannot be implemented directly. In the case of the MRT system, because some of the underground alignment is proposed to be developed under alienated land, issues arise, especially in relation to land ownership, the landowners' rights and the implementation of legislation (Land Public Transport Commission, 2011; Zaini et al., 2014). If these issues are not clearly defined, Malaysia's future underground land development will continue to be facing the same problem, and this will delay progress, which will complicate other related factors.

Table 15.1 Minimum depth for underground land disposal

Type of stratum application	Categorise of land		
	Agriculture	Building	Industry
Section 92(b) NLC 1965	6 metres	10 metres	15 metres
Section 92(e) NLC 1965	6 metres	10 metres	15 metres

Source: Strata Title Section, JKPTG (2008).

Land ownership is the generic concept used in land administration theory to explain how people approach and think about land. It includes land at surface level, buildings held in separate ownership, a cube of airspace as in condominiums and the substrata. For underground land cases, if the surface land is state land, the underground land can be alienated to whoever applies for it. But, it becomes more complicated when the surface landowner is a different party from the underground land developer. This is because the legislation (Section 92D (1), NLC 1965), states that only the landowner can apply the stratum title if the minimum depth is not issued in the surface land title. Even though the JKPTG Circulation No 1/2008 has provided the number of minimum depths the surface landowner can enjoy, it is only applicable to fresh alienations.

The Natural Resources and Environment Minister has said that changes to the Land Acquisition Act 1960 (enacted in the Acquisition of Land (Amendment) Act 2016 (LAA(A) 2016) are necessary, especially for infrastructure development, to retain the country's competitiveness in its progress toward being a developed nation (Anon. 2016). He further said the amendments covered important areas like underground work such as the building of tunnels, drainage systems and underground infrastructure. The Minister did caution that "Acquisition of land for Malaysia's economic development and for a locality however must meet stringent conditions so that the interests and welfare of the people are not affected."

In retrospect, the amendments to the LAA 1960 are timely, because they expand the ambit of the 1960 Act to include the right of compulsory acquisition to subdivided buildings (parcels or provisional blocks) as well as underground land which previously only expressly addressed the compulsory acquisition of surface land. In addition, in respect of the temporary occupation or use of land under the original Act, the LAA (A) 2016 introduces amendments to the LAA 1960 which allow landowners or lessees to object if aggrieved by the compensation offered by the Land Administrator and to refer their dispute to the court. This is a significantly change from the previous wording of the 1960 Act and arguably brings more fairness compared to the previous situation.

Section 57 of the LAA 1960 was amended to clarify the provisions relating to the temporary occupation or use of land. The amendment sought to broaden the factors that allow these provisions to be applied and introduces the requirement to endorse notes of temporary occupation and use of land on the document of title or other documents stipulated under (subparagraphs 57(9)(2)*(a)* and *(b)* of) the LAA 1960. With this amendment, the Land Administrator, as directed by the State Authority, can now also procure the temporary occupation or use of private land for a period not exceeding three years for the following purposes:

a   For any purpose specified in subsection 3(1);
b   In order to carry out public works on any land; or

c   As indicated in a development plan under the law applicable to it relating to town and country planning, the State Authority may direct the Land Administrator to procure the occupation or use of any such land for such term as he thinks fit, not exceeding three years from the date of commencement of such occupation or use, in the manner prescribed by this part.

The amendment to S.57 is in tandem with the thinking of the Natural Resources and Environment Minister who theorised that in the case of the acquisition of land for underground development, the technical aspects and the safety of those above must be considered before a project can be implemented. The Minister said that "If there is a need for [occupiers] to vacate their premises temporarily for their safety while the underground project is carried out, compensation will be paid." In going for temporary occupation under the LAA 1960, the residents of the scheduled land can move back once the specified term is up. "This way compensation paid could be less and there should be less disgruntled POI" (Anon. 2016). In retrospect, temporary occupation under the LAA 1960 is an alternative to compulsorily acquiring land and in the long run can be beneficial to the nation as a whole. There would be savings in compensation paid, and landowners could resume their occupation after the maximum three years. It was reported in the *The Star* that a property developer had received notice of compensation for the temporary occupation of its land for the construction of Light Rail Transit Line 3 project from Bandar Utama to Johan Setia in Selangor (Anon. 2017).

Approach and success story in two project cases

This section discusses the actions taken, the best approaches and the success stories from two selected project cases. The discussion focuses on critical issues associated with or derived from land acquisition projects. It also includes a review on the best approach taken and highlights valuable lessons behind the projects. The selected land acquisition cases are the Pengerang Oil and Gas Hub project and the Klang Valley MRT project.

The Pengerang Integrated Petroleum Complex (PIPC) Project

The country's transformation plans (Government Transformation Programme (GTP) and Economic Transformation Programme (ETP)) are seen as major milestones in Malaysia's progress toward its 'Vision 2020' as a developed nation. To achieve this goal, the government has also launched a rural transformation plan which involves the local and regional authorities, under the Ministry of Rural and Regional Development. Pengerang, Johor, a southern tip of Peninsular Malaysia, is being developed by the Malaysian government as a hub for oil and gas, with an investment value almost RM60 billion in 2011. It is expected that this mega project will be fully completed by 2023. With the development of the oil and gas hub, about 21,500 acres (8,700 hectares) of land has been taken back or acquired to provide infrastructure and related facilities. The land acquisition for the project involves 10 villages, affecting about 4,000 people from 1,268 families (Salleh Buang, *Utusan Malaysia*, 24 February 2012). The development of the oil and gas hub provides prospective effects to the occupiers of the land: owners, dealers, retailers, the owners of hotels etc.

In a nutshell, the regional development authority (RDA) of the Regional Area of Pengerang and the Lembaga Kemajuan Johor Tenggara (KEJORA) is expected to achieve potential growth, especially from the socio-economic aspects of the development. Lembaga Kemajuan Johor Tenggara (the RDA of KEJORA) was established on 1 June 1972 under the Lembaga Kemajuan Johor Tenggara Act 1972 (Act 75) and the enactment (assignment of duties) of the Lembaga Kemajuan Johor Tenggara Act 1972 (enactment No. 7, Z1972). The RDA of KEJORA is under the authority of the Ministry of Rural and Regional Development Malaysia, and KEJORA serves as a regional development agent for the southeastern part of the State of Johor. The area under KEJORA amounting to 300,111 hectares (741,590 acres), which is 16% of the entire area of the State of Johor, and includes Johor Tengah (149,009 hectares or 368,210 acres) and Pengerang (151,356 hectares, some 374,000 acres). In the context of the transformation of this development, the Lembaga Kemajuan Johor Tenggara (KEJORA) is not left behind in the move to improve efforts and to implement the programme in order to transform the rural areas.

Pengerang is located approximately 45 kilometres (28 miles) east of the city of Johor Bahru. A large part of the area, almost 70%, are Federal Land Development Authority (FELDA) settlements and agriculture, while 30% comprise traditional villages. The main activity of the Pengerang's population is agriculture and fisheries, while the main attraction for tourists is the resort of Desaru. However, the area has yet to reach the level of its highest and best use (Uni Technologies, 2015). Nevertheless, construction of the Senai-Desaru Expressway, the development of Bio-Desaru and the construction of the Integrated Petroleum Complex Pengerang (PIPC) on a 8,700 hectare (21,500 acre) site have started. The complex will house the Integrated Oil Refining and Petrochemicals Development Projects (RAPID) developed by Petronas and the Deep Sea Petroleum Terminal by Dialog Group and Royal Vopak in collaboration with the State Secretary of Johor Incorporated. When these two projects (the completion of which is anticipated in 2017) start operation, Pengerang will change the face of oil and gas hub in Asia Pacific, and perhaps become comparable to Rotterdam in the Netherlands and Jurong in Singapore with its concept of eco-friendly and green technologies.

Land acquisition and resettlement plan

The issue of the acquisition of traditional lands is more than just a matter of law and compensation; it is a matter of justice between society and the people (Alias et al., 2010). For projects involving large spatial areas such as in the area of Pengerang, various issues and problems may arise in relation to the local community, environment and so on. One of the issues highlighted concerns the occurrence of land acquisition and resettlement areas. Land acquisition and resettlement for those affected by the development in the area has caused some issues in Pengerang, such as the transfer of the population to new settlement areas, a loss of local natural resources, psychological and emotional effects on the community and new employment opportunities. As explained earlier, about 4,000 people from 1,268 families situated in 8,700 hectares (21,500 acres) including 10 traditional villages are involved (Buang, 2012).

Another issue raised is the infrastructure and social facilities offered. Sufficient facilities such as education, health, transportation and roads, electrical power supply and water supply in Pengerang area must be provided. This is necessary because, in the future, it is anticipated that this area will attract more residents for jobs and business opportunities and to meet the needs of current and future residents.

The project also involves the extension of the development of the municipality. Among the areas that are experiencing rapid growth in the Pengerang area is Bandar Penawar and its surrounding communities. This is because of the availability of the proposed construction of more government complexes, educational and training centres and health services. In the vicinity, there will be rapid growth in the housing and business sectors, as well as tourism and recreation

The outlying areas of the oil and gas hub of Pengerang, such as Punggai, Gugusan FELDA Adela, Belungkur, Sebana Cove and Ladang Sungai Papan are expected to become new growth areas. Therefore, suitable and careful planning should be undertaken so that employment opportunities can be exploited by the locals.

Socioeconomic impact of the projects

The implementation of the projects involved certainly has both negative and positive socioeconomic impacts on the local residents and the surrounding areas. In terms of the economy, it has a big and positive impact boosting the economy, especially in Johor, and in Malaysia in general. For the RAPID projects, Petronas will invest RM60 billion to build two oil filter centres that would be able to produce 450,000 barrels per day. It has been announced that the oil and gas industry in Pengerang will receive a total investment of RM120 billion in the next five to six years. The government has also estimated that RAPID would contribute RM17.7 billion to the country's gross domestic product (GDP) by 2020.

The development of mega projects in each region has influenced economic activities within the surrounding areas, as well as the environmental and social aspects. As a whole, it brings changes in the demographic structure, the demand for public facilities, changes in social values, as well as other side effects. The high-impact projects such as the development of the oil and gas hub declared in 2011 will inspire a large prospective socioeconomic impact in the Pengerang area and its surroundings. Thus, a study was needed to identify the benefits from the development of such a high-impact project to the local and surrounding communities, as well as giving any necessary protection to the environment and thus stimulating the economic development for the local society.

An industrial and gas hub can make an impact on local and surrounding communities in terms of their regional income and employment growth. Among the positive effects of the project is the increased taxes and royalties that could be used by the whole society. As a result of the oil- and gas-based industries in Pengerang, income will be generated not only for the local authority (LA), but also for the State and Federal governments. Normally such increased revenue is used for the development of the local community through an increased supply of infrastructure and public facilities.

The Pengerang development will change the pattern of economic and employment opportunities in the entire district of Kota Tinggi and the State of Johor when fully completed. The anticipated job opportunities will probably emerge from various types of businesses. For the oil and gas industry, it is expected that 40,000 employment contracts will be produced at the construction stage, many of which will benefit the local population. For this purpose, the local population should be given training opportunities to maximise the local skilled personnel so that they can participate in developing Pengerang, rather than simply hiring workers from outside the area.

Generally, it is found that majority of the population in Pengerang is from the Malay community. As a result, the development of the oil and gas industry has an impact on their socio-cultural and economic activities. The population required appropriate forms of employment opportunities after their lands were taken, and in addition, they have experienced problems with their new jobs as compared to their previous occupations as self-employed individuals and fishermen. Because the majority of the population are from the area, their sensitivity to any development project was relatively high and there was reluctance to accept the changes that were to occur in their settlement area.

In the area, it is found that there was a small active workforce (population between the ages 21–40 years) as a result of migration out of the area. This situation can lead to lack of human resources accessible to the new employers in Pengerang. But with the availability of the industry-based hub for oil and gas, it is likely to be able to attract the interest of those who have migrated to return to work. Because the area is able to attract the population by offering job opportunities, adequate and affordable housing needs are to be provided by the authorities. For the development of Pengerang, more skilled and trained labourers are needed. Thus, this region needs more skills training centres in order to meet the human resource demands that can serve the province and reduce the intake of external labourers. The technical skills programmes that should be introduced include electrical, mechanical, instrumentation, processing, production and so on.

Generally, it is found that the residents of Pengerang are independent in seeking employment opportunities, with the majority (65.7%) being self-employed with an uncertain income flow. With the availability of high-impact projects in the region, local citizens have the opportunity to upgrade their economic status within the various fields of employment that will be offered. In this area, the majority of the population has an income of below RM2,000 (about 500 USD) per month. With the availability of high-impact projects in the region, the level of their income is expected to increase if they are able to secure new jobs. This situation becomes a challenge to the authorities to provide skills training, particularly in the oil and gas industry which can generate better income. Training centres around the city should be equipped with a range of new programmes in accordance with the nature of employment opportunities emerging Pengerang. A large part of the population in Pengerang anticipates negative effects more than positive impacts in various aspects. One of them is its anticipated effect on housing prices in the area. For residents who have yet to own a home, especially the second-generation, they see the increased difficulty of owning a home in the future because of the anticipated increase in housing prices as one of the negative impacts of the development of high-impact projects in the province.

With the entry of many new residents to work in the new industries, the authorities need to pay attention to the systems and structures for better roads and the effectiveness of public transport. In addition, the transport system in the city and the region should be planned in a systematic manner to assist the movement of the residents.

On balance, it seems that the majority of the population in Pengerang is affected positively by the employment opportunities that will be generated based on the new industrial developments. However, the authorities must give priority to the locals before offering opportunities to outsiders, particularly foreign investors. In addition to the job opportunities in the industrial area in the region, the opportunities for economic activities such as small and medium industries should be given support to help local people increase their income. In addition, the Bio-Desaru project should also offer additional opportunities to the locals. Downstream oil and gas also has the potential to be developed further. In addition, the manufacturing sector is expected to make more jobs available to local residents, and the emergence of an investment sector can be anticipated in the future.

The cost of living is also likely to go up as high-impact projects begin operating in the region. Other problems that worry the residents include pollution, health, social problems and the safety element. To reduce these problems, public facilities should be supplemented from time to time. The Federal and the State governments should provide various facilities, ensure smooth development, to see that pollution is minimised, that jobs are prioritised for the local population and the support from various parties, especially the private sectors, is enlisted.

Another sector that has an indirect impact on this project is that of tourism. The development of tourism will boost the economy of Pengerang. Opening up an attractive area will provide business opportunities and jobs to the local residents to venture into the hospitality sector of the economy in the form of hotels and other accommodation. The business sector is also expected to have an impact on the residents in the region, in particular in the catering sectors of food and restaurants. Thus, the Bumiputera community of Pengerang should take full advantage of the opportunity to enter into these business sectors. It is also anticipated that the government and the financial institutions will also diversify their credit facilities, business advisory services, as well as other measures to provide various incentives to support these economic opportunities.

The Klang Valley MRT (KV-MRT) Project

Public transport remains inadequate in Kuala Lumpur, as it is fragmented and often congested and unreliable. The public transport modal share stood at just 12% in 2009 compared to other major metropolitan areas, such as Singapore, Hong Kong and Tokyo, which typically have public transport modal shares over 50% (Performance Management and Delivery Unit, 2011). Therefore, under the ETP, the Urban Public Transport National Key Results Area has initiated a programme of enhancing urban rail capacity, to achieve a 50% public transport modal share by 2020.

The KVMRT project is one of the largest transport infrastructure projects in Malaysia, and is an Entry Point Project (EPP) of the Economic Transformation Programme (ETP) aimed at acting as a 'spark plug' to fire up the Greater Kuala Lumpur/Klang Valley National Key Economic Area (NKEA) engine of growth (Mass Rapid Transit Corporation, 2012a). The ETP is being implemented by the Performance Management and Delivery Unit of the Prime Minister's Department. This project involves the construction of a rail-based public transport network, which is aimed at providing a major boost to the integration and efficiency of urban public transport. The KV-MRT project spans 141 kilometres (some 88 miles) with three major routes MRT lines, namely, MRT Line 1, MRT Line 2 and MRT Line 3, and will cover a radius of 20 kilometres (some 12.5 miles) from the city centre. Financing for the project will come entirely from government funds (ERE Consulting Group, 2003).

The construction of the MRT is currently ongoing, and it is the country's largest construction in the development of underground land (Jamalludin et al., 2016). The project was approved by the government in December 2010, and has involved land acquisition in prime areas. Preliminary estimates show a total funding requirement of around RM47 billion with potentially an additional RM2 billion for expedited land acquisition (Performance Management and Delivery Unit, 2011). First proposed in early 2010, and included as an EPP in the final ETP, the MRT was one of the highest priorities in the first stages of the programme. The timetable set was ambitious: from approval in principle in 2010 to the operation of the 51 km (31.6 miles) Line 1 by 2017, at a total investment of RM 23 billion, or roughly US$5.6 billion (Sabel and Jordan, 2015).

The main objective of the MRT is to increase the number of people using public transport, to alleviate traffic congestion and decrease travel time from one place to another (ERE Consulting Group, 2003). Apart from achieving the objective of improving passenger mobility, the Mass Rapid Transit Corporation (2012b) reported that there are several spillover benefits, namely:

i   Generating economic value – an increasing productivity from greater mobility;
ii Generating RM3 - 4 billion gross national income through construction activities and operations between 2011 and 2020;

iii Generating a further RM8 - 12 billion in gross national income from spillover effects. In total, an average of RM21 billion gross national income per annum will be generated over the next 10 years;

iv Creating 130,000 jobs, pushing up the value of property through better connectivity which will also result in property appreciation, especially in the vicinity of MRT stations;

v Spurring new property developments – including the Rubber Research Institute development in Sg Buloh, Warisan Merdeka, Kuala Lumpur (KL) International Financial District;

vi Boosting commerce because improved connectivity will bring more commuters to the city centre, and stations will contain hubs for commercial activity; and

vii Reducing carbon emissions by removing cars from the roads.

Rail transit systems have both a positive and negative impact on the value of residential property (Moorthy and Jeronn, 2014). The Real Estate and Housing Developers' Association of Malaysia (Rehda) consider that the Greater KL and KV-MRT project will generally have a positive impact on the property market and the economy. The property rental levels have increased in other countries such as Singapore and Taipei where properties are located close to the MRT stations. With over 30 stations, the development of the MRT will promote a lot of business opportunities as the stations will have a wealth creation effect. There will also be higher density developments in the areas which the MRT reaches.

MRT Sungai Buloh – Kajang

The KV-MRT from Sg. Buloh to Kajang (SBK Line) is one of the major infrastructure projects launched in 2011 by the government and managed by MRT Corporation Sdn Bhd. It is the first MRT project in Malaysia (Tan et al., 2016), and it is one example of the dynamics of integrated land and transit use (Malaysia Institution Development Finance, 2017). The project comprises a total of 9.8 km (6 miles) long twin tunnels from Semantan to Maluri, with seven underground stations and associated structures such as portals, ventilation shafts, escape shafts and crossovers to be constructed over the Klang Valley and KL city areas (Tan et al., 2016). Table 15.2 shows the summary of land acquisition on the SBK Line. It involved 303 lots in KL and the Selangor area, with total compensation estimated at around RM 1.5 million.

Table 15.2 MRT Sungai Buloh-Kajang line land acquisition summary

	Acquisition		
	Kuala Lumpur	*Selangor*	*Total*
Number of acquired lots	74	227	301
Acquisition of additional lots in progress	2		2
Compensation paid for acquired lots	RM943,009,287.78	RM613,836,926.38	RM1,556,846,214.16
	Form N (objection)		
Cases concluded	30	103	133
Compensation paid	RM117,089,216.46	RM21,899,030.00	RM138,988,246.46

Source: (Mass Rapid Transit Corporation, 2015).

MRT Sungai Buloh – Serdang – Putrajaya

The MRT Sungai Buloh – Serdang – Putrajaya (SSP Line) is the second MRT line. In February 2014, the government gave its approval for its implementation, stretching from Sungai Buloh to Putrajaya via Serdang (Mass Rapid Transit Corporation, 2015). The preliminary process for land acquisition for the project began with the gazetting of 1,210 lots in the areas of KL, Putrajaya and Selangor which may need to be acquired under Section 4, LAA 1960. Referring to Table 15.3, the number of lots to be compulsorily acquired under Section 8 is lower than those gazetted under Section 4. The total of lots under Section 8, LAA 1960, from phase 1 to phase 3, is 495.

As a mega infrastructure project, its design and construction have created a series of issues to be resolve, involving multiple states, regulatory bodies and complex financial and technical decisions (from funding models to tariffs) (Sabel and Jordan, 2015). The rule of law, fair compensation and stakeholders participation in the process of land acquisition are the major determinant issues (Ghimire, 2017). The rail transit of two of the MRT lines (SBK Line and SSP line) encountered many issues and challenges. Interestingly, it involved many new cases of compulsory inquisition for infrastructure development. The first line was the earlier case for strata title acquisition which involved the acquisition of the Ampang Park Shopping Center to make way for the MRT project. The Shopping Centre owners were not satisfied and made a bid to challenge the acquisition in March 2016. However, 39 strata owners and tenants of Ampang Park lost their appeal in January 2017. This challenge and the subsequent appeal caused a delay in the land acquisition for SBK line. According to Musaddiq and Singh (2016), the factors that cause delays in the land acquisition for the MRT projects are changes in the alignment scheme, poor handling of land records, the sentimental value of the land for the landowners, inaccurate information of the measurement of lots by land surveyors, insufficient numbers of land officers and untraced and unnumbered lots.

Table 15.3 MRT Sungai Buloh-Serdang-Putrajaya line land acquisition summary

| | Aquisition | | | |
	Kuala Lumpur	Putrajaya	Selangor	Total
Section 4, LAA 1960				
Gazette date	21 July 2015	14 August 2015	4 June 2015	
Number of lots	675	31	513	1219
Section 8, LAA 1960				
Phase 1	2 September 2015	8 August 2016	22 February 2016 (Petaling district) 22 February 2012 (Gombak district) 3 March 2016 (Sepang district)	
Number of Lots	45	6	142	193
Phase 2	7 April 2016			
Number of lots	268			268
Phase 3	Date not determined			
Number of lots	34			34
Total	**347**	**6**	**142**	**495**

Source: Sumber: Mass Rapid Transit Corporation, 2016.

Realignment in Jalan Sultan/Jalan Petaling

The impact of the MRT project is huge in the country in which the estimated gross national income will be in the range of RM21.3 billion per year by 2020, and approximately 20,000 jobs will also have been created as a direct and indirect result. However, in order to make it successful, there are several things that need to be considered, including the final alignment of the rail track. For example, in Jalan Sultan/Jalan Petaling, the final alignment was determined using the proper strategic process. It covered a three-step process, as shown in Figure 15.3.

The first step involved the establishment of fixed points along the corridor which the MRT alignment must serve. These points are densely populated areas, activity centres such as the Central Business District, shopping centres, office blocks or areas where there is potential for future growth. The second step is the process of alignment to connect these fixed points. Several factors need to be considered including the need to minimise negative social impacts and the amount of land to be acquired, the optimising of the journey time, constructability and the integration with existing and future public transport. Finally, after several discussions and feedback from the public, the final alignment has been proposed.

The legal framework of the LAA 1960 allows for the compulsory acquisition of land and does not provide for flexibility with regard to the acquisition of land underground. Under these provision, all land on the surface needs to be acquired in order to acquire the substrata, even if only the underground portion of the land is required (ERE Consulting Group, 2003). Therefore, in the case of the Jalan Sultan/Jalan Petaling area, to ensure the safety of MRT tunnel below, the first proposal was to acquire the whole of all of the land to allow for total control of surface land as well as the substrata. However, after many objections, recall and discussion with the parties involved, especially the landowners, the government decided to find a more effective solution to satisfy landowners and achieve the success of the project.

Almost all owners attach sentimental value to their residential properties, and the district of KL involved in this acquisition is the earliest commercial area of the city, generally consisting of double storey shop houses carrying out retail and other trading activities. For a win-win situation, the MRT Corporation decided to avoid land acquisition and the disruption to the lives of the property owners there (ERE Consulting Group, 2003) This was made possible because, according to the soil structure at this location and the nature of the work to be done, there was no a need to demolish surface structures nor acquire the surface land. Therefore, by mutual agreement, landowners were allowed to retain their occupation of the surface land, and the substrata was taken and used for the MRT tunnel.

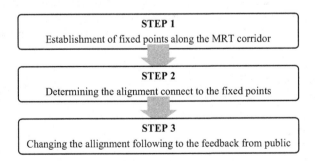

STEP 1
Establishment of fixed points along the MRT corridor

STEP 2
Determining the alignment connect to the fixed points

STEP 3
Changing the allignment following to the feedback from public

Figure 15.3 The process of MRT final alignment in Jalan Sultan/Jalan Petaling
Source: (Mass Rapid Transit Corporation, 2012b).

Mutual agreement and compensation

The practice of land acquisition is different between countries because of the different legal, economic, social and political conditions. Different countries have different legal instruments, different procedures for land acquisition and land valuation approaches (Ghimire, 2017). The MRT Corporation chose to adopt another process instead of using compulsory acquisition for this project. The process of mutual agreement was applied to a scheme which enables the coexistence of privately owned land with the MRT alignment in limited situations (Mass Rapid Transit Corporation, 2013). This option has allowed some of the owners whose lands were originally the subject of compulsory acquisition under LAA1960 to be removed from the provision. The landowners were given a chance to retain their ownership while reflecting the presence of the MRT structures (Mass Rapid Transit Corporation, 2013). For this option, the MRT Corporation has had to deal with the landowners on specific terms and conditions. More than 20 lots were identified for the scheme under which the landowners would continue to own their properties while allowing tunnels to be constructed underneath their properties. After signing the agreements with landowners, the MRT Corporation examined the properties and carried out structural strengthening works (Mass Rapid Transit Corporation, 2015).

A total of 50 lots were subject to this kind of mutual agreement by the end of 2014 (Mass Rapid Transit Corporation, 2014). Thus, existing properties above the tunnel at Jalan Sultan/Jalan Petaling will not be acquired nor demolished. However, their occupants will have to relocate temporarily for an expected maximum period of six months, and the buildings above the tunnel will need to be reinforced prior to tunnelling work, which were expected to start in 2014. Vacating the buildings during the six-month period while the tunnelling work are being carried out will cause hardship to the affected residents and businesses. Chattels will need to be moved and businesses will have to close during this period. The temporary evacuation is purely for the safety of the occupants of the properties, and also to minimise the inconvenience to them. Compensation will be provided to business owners for loss of business during this period when their premises are vacated, a formula worked out to establish the quantum of compensation, and those affected will be fairly compensated for whatever costs are incurred and losses sustained.

Summary

Land acquisition involves the compulsory taking of land rights. Different countries have different legal instruments, procedures for land acquisition and land valuation approaches depending upon social, political and economic condition of the country. As for Malaysia, the government has its own strategies and concerns in tackling problems of land acquisition, depending on the issues that exist at the time of each acquisition, such as those presented in the above two cases. The law in Malaysia requires actions undertaken by the authorities to be consistent with the nation's rules and laws, particularly for land taken by force or without the valid consent of the land owners, by taking into account the principles of adequate compensation as guaranteed in Article 13 (2) of the Federal Constitution.

The MRT system in Kuala Lumpur is an example of how the compulsory acquisition is not being implemented as a whole. One of the significant realignment objectives is to minimise the land acquisition. The MRT Corporation introduced another scheme which respects the right of landowners, and their method of mutual agreement has proved to be very successful for the project. The scheme has allowed some of the owners whose lands were originally to be acquired under the Land Acquisition Act 1960 to retain ownership of their lands subject to the land titles reflecting the presence of the MRT structures. The 2016 amendments to the National Land Code 1965 and the Strata Titles Act 1985 should assist the mutual agreement arrangements because there will be better clarity for the implementation of stratum title for substrata land.

Another big project that involves land acquisition is the PIPC project. The project has had both positive and negative socioeconomic impacts. Generally, the impact of this project is likely to be positive, with the provision of more jobs and an increase in the level of residents' economic situation through business opportunities and investment in the province of Pengerang. However, the authorities and the government should take proactive measures to address the issues and problems of local residents who may be marginalised by the mainstream development of Pengerang. Mitigation programmes and new approaches and strategies in administration and management, improvements by KEJORA in accordance with the aspirations of the economic transformation agenda, economic empowerment plans and so on can be undertaken.

Note

1 Malaysia consists of thirteen states and three federal territories.

References

Alias, A., Kamaruzzaman, S. N., & Daud, M. N. (2010). Traditional lands acquisition and compensation: the perceptions of the affected Aborigin in Malaysia. International Journal of the Physical Sciences, 5(11), 1696–1705. Retrieved from www.academicjournals.org/IJPS.

Anon. (2016) Dewan Rakyat passes Land Acquisition (Amendment) Bill (www.thesundaily.my/news/1813597).

Anon. (2017) Titijaya gets compensation (www.thestar.com.my>2017/10/24).

Azimuddin, B. (2008) The National Land Policy – the way forward for a sustainable economic, environmental and social development in Malaysia. The International Real Estate Research Symposium. INSPEN.

Bandeira, P., Sumpsi, J. M., & Falconi, C. (2010). Land use policy evaluating land administration systems: a comparative method with an application to Peru and Honduras. Land Use Policy, 27, 351–363.

Barnes, G. (2003). Lessons learned: an evaluation of land administration initiatives in Latin America over the past two decades. Land Use Policy, 20, 367–374.

Blakely, Edward J., Leigh, Nancey G. (2009). Planning Local Economic Development: Theory and Practice. SAGE.

Buang, Salleh. (2012). Tempias Projek Hab Minyak dan Gas di Pengerang. Utusan Malaysia. February 24, 2012.

ERE Consulting Group. (2003). Klang Valley Mass Rapid Transit: S. Buloh – Kajang Line Environmental Impact Assessment. https://doi.org/https://doi.org/10.1142/9781848161269_0001.

Ghimire, S. (2017). Governance in land acquisition and compensation for infrastructure development. American Journal of Civil Engineering, 5(3), 169. https://doi.org/10.11648/j.ajce.20170503.17.

Hashim, H. (2017). Land Acquisition Procedure: A Case Commentary on Ee Chong Pang & Ors v. The Land Administrator of the District of Alor Gajah & Anor. Legal Network Series, (Current Law Journal) (2017). Available at SSRN: https://ssrn.com/abstract=2973959.

Jamalludin, N. A., Zaini, F., & Hussin, K. (2016). Development of underground land in Malaysia: the need for master plan of urban underground land development. Procedia - Social and Behavioral Sciences, 219, 394–400. https://doi.org/10.1016/j.sbspro.2016.05.061.

JKPTG 2010. Land Acquisition. www.jkptg.gov.my/en/guidelines/land-acquisition: 16 October 2017

Kalantari, M., Rajabifard, A., Wallace, J., & Williamson, I. (2008). Spatially referenced legal property objects. Land Use Policy, 25(2), 173–181.

Kamal, Shazwan Mustafa (2016) Kidex is dead, or is it? Another elevated highway rises in Selangor. www.maylaymail.com.

Land Acquisition Act 1960 (Act A1517 as amended 2016).

Malaysia Institution Development Finance. (2017). *Malaysia Equity Transit-Oriented Development* (Vol. 2013).

Mass Rapid Transit Corporation. (2012a). *Annual Progress Report 2012*.

Mass Rapid Transit Corporation. (2012b). *MRT Project construction along Jalan Sultan*. Retrieved from www.mymrt.com.my/cms/upload_files/reportfile/reportfile_file_000001.pdf.

Mass Rapid Transit Corporation. (2013). *Annual Progress Report 2013*.

Mass Rapid Transit Corporation. (2014). *Annual Progress Report 2014*.

Mass Rapid Transit Corporation. (2015). *Annual Progress Report 2015*.

Mass Rapid Transit Corporation. (2016). *Annual Progress Report 2016*.

Rani, Mohd Afandi Mat, & Adil, Mohamed Azam Mohamed. (2014). The Implementation of Land Acquisition Act 1960 and its Negative Impact on the Development of Waqf (Endowment) Land in Malaysia. *Islam and Civilisation Renewal*.Vol 5 No 3 pp 375–393.

Moorthy, R., & Jeronn, N. (2014). Public transportation effect on the rising of property prices in Malaysia : a correlation study of MRT project. *Review of Integrative Business & Economics Research, 3*(2), 350–357.

Musaddiq, M., & Singh, B. (2016). Land acquisition for Klang Valley Mass Rapid Transit Line 1 Project. *Construction Managament and Transportation, 2*, 27–39.

Nzioki, N., Kariuki, C., & Murigu, J. (2009). Implementing land reform policies in Eastern African countries: the case study of Kenya. *Property Management, 27*(4), 267–278.

Performance Management and Delivery Unit. (2011). *Economic Transformation Programme: A Roadmap for Malaysia*.

Sabel, C., & Jordan, L. (2015). Doing, learning, being: some lessons learned from Malaysia's national transformation program. *Competitive Industries and Innovation Program, The World Bank*, (January), 1–96.

Samsudin, S., Lim, L. C., & McCluskey, W. (2011). A review of organizational arrangements in Malaysia Land Administration System towards good governance: issues and challenges. *FIG Working Week* 2011, (May), 1–15.

Tan, Y., Chow, C., Koo, K., Nazir, R., Paper, F., & Bhd, G. S. (2016). Challenges in design and construction of deep excavation for KVMRT in Kuala Lumpur lomestone formation. *Jurnal Teknologi. 78*(8–5), 97–107.

The Malay Mail, Accessed 24 October 2017 www.themalaymailonline.com/280714.

The Star Property, 24 October 2017, www.thestar.com.my/business/business-news/2017/10/24/titijaya-gets-compensation/#b1J1diw8xIHppwk3.99.

The Sundaily, Accessed 20 October 2017 www.thesundaily.my/news/1813597.

Uni Technologies. (2015). Laporan Akhir Penilaian Impak Sosioekonomi bagi Pembangunan Berimpak Tinggi di Wilayah Pengerang. UTM Johor.

Williamson, I., Enemark, S., Wallace, J., & Rajabifard, A. (2010). Land administration for sustainable development. In FIG Congress 2010. Sydney: International Federation of Surveyors.

Zaini, F., Hussin, K., Zakaria, S. R. A. (2014). "*Legal and Administrative Issue for Underground Land Development In Malaysia*" IRERS 2014, 29–30 April 2014, Kuala Lumpur, Malaysia.

16

Real estate expropriation in Russia

Statutory regulation and enforcement

Nadezhda B. Kosareva, Tatyana K. Baykova,
and Tatyana D. Polidi

Introduction

Real estate expropriation for public needs is quite a common practice in Russia. Over the past 30 years, as private ownership of land and other real estate has developed in Russia, an objective need also developed for such expropriation, including forced real estate expropriation, based on judicial decisions, subject to "fair" compensation for the owners. Over the period, a regulatory environment emerged for handling cases, establishing grounds and procedures for real estate expropriation for State and municipal needs, and a certain enforcement practice was developed.

It should be noted that Russian law denotes a fairly large number of varied cases and respective dedicated legal institutions for the forced divestiture of real estate from an owner. They include requisition,[1] confiscation,[2] nationalisation,[3] forced divestiture due to a breach of law,[4] forced divestiture due to a breach or specific regulation of contractual obligations,[5] and several other institutions.

This chapter, focuses only on analysing the statutory regulation and practice of real estate expropriation for State and municipal needs (hereinafter, expropriation also real estate expropriation,) applied to the development of public infrastructural facilities and in certain other circumstances.

Until the Russian Soviet Federative Socialist Republic Law "On Property" was passed in 1990,[6] private land ownership had been banned in the Union of Soviet Socialist Republics (USSR), while private ownership of other real estate was allowed only with respect to detached homes (and only with numerous restrictions). In the light of this, to understand the scale of development in the private ownership of land and other real estate in Russia, several introductory figures should be cited (Table 16.1).

On the whole, private land ownership has developed rather slowly in Russia (only 7.8% of the country's land was privately owned in early 2016), although much more intensively in populated areas (on average, 23.2% of this land category was privately owned in early 2016[8]).

Private property has become most common within the housing sector, as a result of the gratuitous privatisation of tenant apartments owned by the State or a municipality, the removal of restrictions on the construction of detached homes, and the development of the housing market. In early 2016, around 90.0% of Russia's housing stock was privately owned (of which 87.1% was owned by individuals), as compared with 35.0% in 1987.

Table 16.1 Breakdown of All Land, Populated Area, and Housing Stock in Russia by Form of Ownership

Form of Ownership	Breakdown by Form of Ownership, % in Respective Year	
Land	*1989*	*2015*
Total, including:	100.0	100.0
publicly owned (state or municipal)	100.0	92.2
privately owned	0.0	7.8
of which owned by individuals	0.0	6.7
Populated area	*2005*	*2015*
Total, including:	100.0	100.0
publicly owned (state or municipal)	81.5	76.8
privately owned	18.5	23.2
of which owned by individuals	17.8	20.2
Housing stock[7]	*1987*	*2015*
Total, including:	100.0	100.0
owned by state	42.0	3.2
owned by municipalities	22.0	5.7
privately owned	35.0	90.3
of which owned by individuals	38.0	87.1
other	0.75	0.40

Source: State (National) Report (2016), Federal Statistical Observation Form No. 1-zhilfond (2016).

The need for, and the practice of, real estate expropriation affected mainly settlements, mostly large Russian cities and their surrounding areas, where most housing construction takes place and where new public infrastructure is built. Real estate expropriation mechanisms are also widely used in developing certain areas in Russia, as part of special government programmes, regulated by special expropriation mechanisms prescribed by law. Russia also has a special process for real estate expropriation as part of removing unsafe apartment buildings. A search is underway for legal mechanisms to support the redevelopment of deteriorating urban areas, as exemplified by a newly launched programme in Moscow for renovating the housing stock built during the first prefab construction period.

This chapter briefly reviews all such cases of using real estate expropriation mechanisms for State and municipal needs, including the most recent innovations in this field.

General statutory regulation of real estate expropriation for state or municipal needs

A mechanism for expropriating land plots and other real estate is commonly used when a need arises to use such land for important statewide or municipal construction or reconstruction projects (primarily infrastructural facilities), or pursuant to international treaties. The Russian Federation Constitution stipulates a general provision under which *"No one may be deprived of property otherwise than by a court decision. Forced confiscation of property for state needs may be carried out only on the proviso of preliminary and complete compensation."* (Part 3, Article 35).

This constitutional provision was reflected in subsequent regulations on real estate confiscation in Russia, including expropriation for State and municipal needs. First of all, the Russian Federation Civil Code (hereinafter, the Russian Civil Code) sets out a limited list of cases of forced termination of property rights, including those in real estate, and the applicable legal mechanisms (Article 235). Matters concerning the forced termination of titles to land plots are regulated by the Land Code of the Russian Federation (hereinafter, the Russian Land Code), and those related to residential premises are regulated by the Housing Code of the Russian Federation (hereinafter, the Russian Housing Code). Special grounds for real estate expropriation and the specifics of such expropriation are established by numerous other federal laws.

The grounds for real estate expropriation for State or municipal needs

Land plots are expropriated for State and municipal needs based on the common grounds listed under Article 49 of the Russian Land Code. Common grounds primarily include the need to construct or reconstruct facilities of Statewide (federal, regional) or local importance, the types of which are not specifically defined, and Russia's compliance with international treaties.

In general, expropriation of a land plot is antecedent and in accordance with the Russian Civil Code which provides grounds for the forced divestiture of other real estate located on that land plot (buildings, structures, objects of unfinished construction, etc.). Exceptions may exist with respect to such facilities, e.g., structures (including objects of unfinished construction) located on an expropriated land plot that are not subject to expropriation if their deployment does not contradict the objective of the land plot expropriation.

The primary common grounds for real estate expropriation and the general procedures for such an expropriation are contained in Table 16.2.

The expropriation of a land plot and the forced divestiture of real estate located thereon are carried out concurrently according to the rules established for land plot expropriation. The amount of compensation for the expropriated land plot includes the market value of the facilities located on it (or the market value of other rights to those facilities).

The Russian Land Code allows for establishing special grounds for expropriating land plots through other federal laws.[9] A review of those laws shows that individual cases where real estate expropriation is permitted are established either in accordance with the special purposes of expropriation (e.g., for special governmental projects) or with respect to certain categories of expropriated real estate (e.g., residential premises).

It should be noted that the Russian Land Code, along with grounds for expropriation, also sets basic conditions applied to land plot expropriation:[10] *the exceptional nature of the case*, calling for the termination of the title to the real estate, and in cases of expropriation for purposes of constructing or reconstructing facilities of Statewide or local importance, *the unavailability of other options for constructing and/or reconstructing such facilities.* Unfortunately, those conditions did not spread further, either in regulation or in practice.

Procedures for real estate expropriation for state or municipal needs

The general real estate expropriation procedures are primarily set within the Russian Land Code. Some of the expropriation procedures according to the law are additionally regulated by the Russian government.[11] Special real estate expropriation procedures established by other federal laws with respect to specific purposes for expropriation or certain types of real estate also have their specific features.

The statutory regulations of the general real estate expropriation procedure requires that an expropriation be initiated by public authorities (state or local authorities, depending on

Table 16.2 Common grounds and procedures for real estate expropriation for state or municipal needs

Common grounds	General procedures
I Expropriation of land plot for state or municipal needs (Russian Civil Code, Articles 279–282; Russian Land Code, Article 49 and Section VII¹).	

Common grounds	General procedures
1 Russia's compliance with international treaties.	1 The substantiation of land expropriation, reservation, and the identification of rights holders of real estate.
2 The following construction or reconstruction projects with statewide (federal, regional importance) or local importance:	2 Real estate expropriation decisions by a state or municipal authority.
a federal and regional energy systems and facilities;	3 Prior notification of rights holders of the real estate expropriation decision.
b nuclear energy facilities;	4 Real estate is expropriated subject to agreement between the rights holder and a state or municipal authority.
c national defense and security facilities, including technical structures and communication lines built for the defense and security of the Russian state border;	5 If no agreement is reached, expropriation is carried out based on a court decision following a claim by a state or municipal authority.
d important federal transportation and communication facilities, important regional transportation and communication facilities, and public railway transportation infrastructure;	6 In exchange for the expropriated real estate, the rights holder shall be paid prior and commensurate reimbursement.
e facilities used for space operations;	7 Expropriated real estate is transferred into state or municipal ownership.
f important federal and regional linear facilities that support the activities of natural monopolies;	8 A resolution on real estate expropriation, a real estate appraisal report drawn up to calculate the amount of reimbursement, and a court decision on forced real estate expropriation for state or municipal needs may all be contested in court.
g electric supply, gas supply, central heating system facilities, hot and cold water supply, and water discharge facilities of federal, regional, and local importance;	
h automobile roads of federal, regional (inter-municipal), and local importance.	
3 Other grounds provided by federal laws.	

Common grounds	General procedures
II Divestiture of real estate due to the expropriation of a land plot for state or municipal needs (Russian Civil Code, Article 2392; Russian Land Code, Section VII¹).	
Expropriation of a land plot under a real property for state or municipal needs.	The expropriation of real estate located on an expropriated land plot is carried out concurrently with the expropriation of the land plot and according to the procedures established for the expropriation of that land plot.

whose needs the real estate is expropriated for). Certain specific traits of such an expropriation are established for land plot expropriations initiated by third parties.

General procedures

The general procedures for real estate expropriation (allowing for the exceptions reviewed below) consist of several steps.

1 *Substantiating an expropriation*. According to the general rule, either urban planning regulation documents providing for the deployment of facilities of federal, regional, or local importance, or an international treaty are required.

2 *Land reservation*. A reservation decision must be adopted by a public authority (generally, for a period not exceeding three years), citing substantiating documents, the borders of the reserved land, the period and purpose for the reservation, limitations on rights to the real estate subject to reservation, and other information accompanied by a reservation chart. The decision is subject to the official publication and State registration in the Unified State Register of Real Estate (hereinafter – EGRN). Land reservation puts a limitation on the respective land plots in terms of transactions and use.

3 *Identifying real estate rights holders.*[12] An agency authorised to make real estate expropriation decisions for State or municipal needs (hereinafter, also an authorised agency) requests the details of the real estate rights holders from the EGRN, archives, other public authorities, and the purported real estate rights holders, and publishes notifications on the planned real estate expropriation. If no rights holders are identified following the prescribed procedure, the real estate is identified as publicly owned according to the court decision. Thereafter, such rights holders are entitled to compensation from the respective treasury.

4 *Passing a resolution on real estate expropriation*. An authorised agency passes a resolution on the expropriation of land plots, citing substantiating documents, the purpose of the expropriation, a list of land plots subject to expropriation, the structures and easements preserved on such land plots, and, if necessary, including a layout of the land plots to be allotted. A resolution is valid for three years, may be contested in court, and is subject to official publication and the sending to the rights holders of real estate to be expropriated and to the agency in charge of State registration of real estate rights for the recording of such a resolution at the EGRN. The lack of details from the EGRN on the rights holders of the expropriated real estate and the real estate itself, on the borders of expropriated land plots, the overlap between the borders of the land plots, or any current land disputes or disputes related to the rights to the real estate is not an obstacle for the passing of a resolution on expropriation.

5 *Evaluating the amount of compensation for real estate subject to expropriation*. An authorised agency acts as the customer of the service for evaluating the amount of compensation to be paid and, if necessary, the customer of the required cadastral actions. For example, on behalf of the rights holder the agency performs actions for the cadastral accounting of the land plot to be expropriated, if such a land plot was not previously accounted for or was accounted for improperly.

The amount of compensation for the real estate to be expropriated is determined as follows:

i compensation for land plots (or other terminated rights to land plots) includes:

a the market value of privately owned land plots or the market value of other private rights to land plots subject to termination, owned by the State or a municipality (lease rights and other special rights to such land plots[13]), subject to the following conditions:

the market value of the lease rights to the land plot is determined based on the term of the lease agreement;

the market value of other special rights to State or municipal land plots is determined according to specific rules in relation to the value of the land plot or the value of the lease rights to the land plot;

b losses caused by the expropriation of land plots, including losses arising due to the rights holders' failure to meet their obligations to third parties, including those based on contracts signed with such third parties;

c loss of profits;

ii the amount of compensation for the expropriation of a part of a land plot (or the termination of rights to part of a land plot) are determined as the difference between the respective market value of the total original land plot and that of the portion retained by the rights holder;

iii compensation for other real estate located on expropriated land plots or for the termination of rights to such real estate is included in the amount of compensation for the expropriated land plots (or the termination of the rights thereto) and is determined as the market value of such real estate or other rights thereto subject to termination;

iv the market value of real estate or other rights to real estate is based on the permitted use of the real estate as of the date preceding the date of the resolution on the land plot expropriation, i.e., without taking into account any planned change in the permitted use;

v the amount of compensation is determined no later than 60 days prior to the sending of the real estate expropriation agreement to the rights holder;

vi the following shall not be included in the compensation:

real estate and any permanent improvements made in contradiction to the permitted use of a land plot to be expropriated or in contradiction to the agreements for using a land plot owned by the State or a municipality;

real estate and any permanent improvements made after the rights holder is notified of the effective resolution on expropriation (except for permanent improvements made for purposes of the safety of the real estate, preventing extraordinary circumstances, and mitigating their consequences, and except for construction or reconstruction pursuant to a construction permit issued prior to the notice of such a decision);

transactions signed by the rights holder of real estate after being notified of an effective resolution on expropriation, if such transactions entail an increase in the amount of losses to be included in the amount of compensation;

vii an appraisal of the market value of the real estate to be expropriated is to be carried out by a professional appraiser (an individual who is a member of a self-regulated organisation of appraisers and who has liability insurance in accordance with Federal Law No. 135–FZ "On Appraisal Activity in the Russian Federation").

6 *Signing an expropriation agreement.* The authorised agency sends the expropriation agreement to each rights holder for the real estate to be expropriated containing the purpose of expropriation, the cadastral numbers of the real estate to be expropriated, real estate transfer dates, the amount of compensation,[14] and the payment procedure. The agreement is accompanied by the cadastral 'passports' for the real estate to be expropriated, and a report on the amount of compensation. The rights holder may send proposals to the authorised agency to amend the agreement, including the compensation amount, to be accompanied by supporting documents. In this case, the authorised agency may amend the agreement.

7 *Filing a claim on forced expropriation in court.* This is a contingent step taken if the rights holder of the real estate refuses to sign the expropriation agreement, or if a

countersigned copy of the agreement is not received by the authorised agency by a certain date. In this case, an authorised agency may, during the effective period of the resolution for the expropriation, file a claim in court on the forced expropriation of the real estate. The dates, compensation amount, and other terms of a forced real estate expropriation shall be determined by the court in this case.

8   *Compensation.* Compensation is paid to the rights holder of the real estate to be expropriated, provided that the authorised agency has received a copy of the expropriation agreement countersigned by the rights holder, or that a court decision on the forced expropriation has taken effect, subject to the following:

- compensation shall be paid out of the respective budget;
- payment of compensation shall be certified with a payment instruction to deposit cash into the rights holder's account or a notary account, or with other documents evidencing such payment according to the law.

The rights holders of the real estate to be expropriated are required to work out their own settlements with any third parties whose rights or contracts (as well as encumbrances for their benefit) are subject to termination or are no longer possible due to the real estate expropriation.

9   *Terminating and transferring real estate rights.* The final step consists of transferring the expropriated real estate from the private owner to public ownership, and terminating all other rights to the expropriated real estate. The previous rights holders of the expropriated real estate are required to unilaterally terminate all of their contracts with third parties which will be rendered impossible to perform as a result of the expropriation. The public title to the expropriated real estate is created on the State registration for the transfer of the real estate rights.

Procedure features for real estate expropriation by third-party motions

In certain circumstances, the initiation of the procedure for real estate expropriation for State or municipal needs is permitted by a motion of a third party which, in this case, acts as a third party in the expropriation process and plays quite an active role. This right usually arises with third parties because of the specifics of their activities, which includes the construction of facilities of public importance that are partially or fully funded by such third parties.

In the case of real estate expropriation by a third-party motion, additional formalities are included in the expropriation procedure:

1   the motion for expropriation and decision-making on the motion. Motions may be filed to expropriate a land plot for State or municipal needs by national monopolies (for deploying facilities with Statewide importance and those that support the operations of such monopolies), subsoil users (for subsoil use works), State organisations (for deploying facilities with Statewide importance in accordance with a targeted investment programme), entities which have signed an agreement on the comprehensive development of an area of land, carried out at the initiative of a local authority, and other organisations authorised to conduct operations which may require real estate expropriation for State or municipal needs, in accordance with the Russian Land Code. However, the expropriation of real estate for deploying facilities of Statewide or local importance, funded in part or in full by a natural monopoly, is strictly subject to a motion by that monopoly.

The motion is filed with an authorised agency and should contain reference to supporting documents, the purpose of the expropriation, details of the real estate to be expropriated, and, if necessary, a layout of the land plots to be allotted.

The authorised agency may reject the motion if the need to expropriate is not confirmed by substantiating documents, or if no valid grounds exist in accordance with federal laws, or if the layout of the new land plots to be allotted does not meet the requirements established by land laws. Expropriation for regional or municipal needs may be denied in other circumstances, as established by laws of Russian Federation subjects. Otherwise, the authorised agency begins the procedure to identify the rights holders of the real estate to be expropriated;

2   additional documents may be filed to substantiate an expropriation (e.g., a subsoil user license, a contract for comprehensive development of a territory initiated by a local authority, targeted investment programme);

3   the reservation of land in cases where land is expropriated for subsoil use purposes should be based on government subsoil exploration, the restoration of the mineral base, and rational subsoil use programmes;

4   the identification of real estate rights holders is to be conducted within a reduced time period and at the expense of the petitioner (organisation which submits a motion);

5   the resolution on real estate expropriation should contain additional details about the petitioner, which should be provided with a copy of the resolution, details about the rights holders of the real estate to be expropriated, and copies of their title documents;

6   the organisation applying for an expropriation makes its own arrangements with regard to appraising and executing a real estate expropriation agreement, and carries out the initial negotiations with the rights holders;

7   the expropriation agreement is prepared by the petitioner jointly with the authorised agency, and may list the obligations of the petitioner to provide the rights holder with other real estate in exchange for the real estate to be expropriated, and contain clauses for offsetting the compensation amount based on the market value of the transferred real estate. The agreement is signed between the rights holder of the real estate to be expropriated, the authorised agency, and the petitioner. The petitioner is responsible for all actions related to the execution of the agreement;

8   the petitioner files a claim on forced expropriation in court and pays the compensation;

9   the petitioner's title to the expropriated real estate arises subject to the payment of full compensation (except when the expropriated real estate cannot be privately owned and is transferred into public ownership).

Specific regulations for real estate expropriation for State or municipal needs with respect to certain types of real estate and for various purposes of expropriation

This section deals with specific aspects of real estate expropriation for State or municipal needs with respect to certain types of real estate (residential premises) and for certain end uses (including the relocation of residents from unsafe apartment buildings, and as part of special government programmes or projects). Later text considers issues regarding real estate expropriation for State and municipal needs, including new legal mechanisms, for large-scale urban redevelopment.

Specific aspects for expropriating residential premises, including relocating residents from unsafe apartment buildings

The grounds for expropriating residential premises is the requirement of the land plot under these premises, for State or municipal needs. Article 32 of the Russian Housing Code contains certain provisions regarding the expropriation of residential premises, which primarily include:

1 the expropriation of residential premises is to be carried out either by the authorised agency, for whose needs the land plot is being expropriated, purchasing the residential premises, or, subject to agreement with the owner, by providing the owners with other residential premises (the latter being the most common in practice);
2 in the case of expropriating residential premises by purchase, the following components of the compensation for the residential premises are established:
   a the market value of the residential premises and the market value of the common property in the apartment building, subject to the share owned by the owner of the residential premises in such property, including the land plot under the apartment building;[15]
   b all losses incurred by the owner of the residential premises as a result of the expropriation, including losses related to the change of residence, the temporary use of another residence prior to purchasing new residential premises, removal costs, searching for new residential premises to purchase, registration of the title to new residential premises, and the termination of the owner's obligations to a third party early, including loss of profits;
3 in the case of expropriating residential premises by purchase, unless the owner owns other residential premises, the owner may request to retain the right to use the residential premises to be expropriated, but for no longer than six months after receipt of compensation.

The expropriation of residential premises, along with regular expropriation cases, has been widely used to solve the pressing problem of removing unsafe apartment buildings constructed in Russia during the Soviet period, or even earlier. The proportion of dilapidated and unsafe housing stock in the country is 2.1% (Federal Statistical Observation Form No. 1-zhilfond. 2016).

Between 2014–2017, a special programme was adopted aimed at removing 10.82 million sq. m. (116 million sq. ft.) of unsafe housing and relocate 689,590 people from apartment buildings found to be unsafe as of 1 January 2012, which accounted for only 60% of the old and unsafe housing stock as of the beginning of 2016.[16] The programme is being implemented by a State Corporation - the Fund for Supporting Housing and Utility Reform (hereinafter, the Fund), which uses a federal budget and co-finances regional and local budget funding.[17]

A special procedure was established for relocating residents from unsafe buildings at the Fund's expense, including the following:

1 financial support from the Fund is subject to an approved regional targeted programme for relocating residents from unsafe housing stock, and which must contain a detailed justification and parameters;
2 the resources of the Fund, regional budgets, and (or) local budgets are used to purchase and construct residential premises, and to compensate owners for the expropriated residential premises;
3 the residential premises provided to the residents following relocation may be located within the limits of that settlement or, subject to a resident's consent, in another settlement in the same constituent entity of the Russian Federation.

Without dwelling on the programme's mechanism and evaluating its effectiveness, it should be noted that, from a legal perspective, it relies on a mechanism for expropriating all apartments and non-residential premises in unsafe apartment buildings for municipal needs. The expropriation of residential premises in such buildings is subject to certain provisions according to the Russian Housing Code:

- the grounds for expropriation are the decisions recognising the apartment building as unsafe and subject to demolition or reconstruction;
- this recognition provides the grounds for requiring the owners of premises in an unsafe building to demolish or renovate it within a reasonable period. The residential premises may not be expropriated prior to the expiration of that period;
- if the owners have not demolished or renovated the building within that period, the land plot under that building becomes subject to expropriation for municipal needs;
- as a result of the expropriation of the land plot under the unsafe building, every housing unit within that building becomes subject to expropriation for municipal needs;
- the other stages in the procedure for expropriating residential premises in an unsafe building are the same as the general procedure for expropriating residential premises, as described earlier.

As part of the programme, 655,310 people were relocated between 1 January 2014, and 1 September 2017, from 10.2 million sq. m. (110 million sq. ft.) of unsafe housing, which accounted for 94.3% of the unsafe housing designated as such prior to 1 January 2012. The programme is nearing completion, and new parameters and mechanisms for a subsequent relocation programme are being discussed.

Specific aspects of real estate expropriation as part of certain special government programmes and projects

In recent years, Russia has implemented large-scale government programmes and projects which, for certain reasons, required a special approach to the expropriation of privately owned real estate in certain regions of the country. Applying that special approach required adopting special federal laws[18] that provide for roughly the same procedures to expropriate the land plots required for such programmes and projects. These include:

1 the organisation and the holding of the Sochi 2014 Winter Olympic Games and Paralympic Games. The first special federal law, which was adopted in 2007, as part of the preparation for the games, established a special procedure for expropriating real estate, including residential premises, for State and municipal needs in the Krasnodar Territory from 1 January 2008, until 1 January 2014, for the purposes of deploying Olympic facilities;[19]

2 the organisation and the holding of the 2012 Asia-Pacific Economic Cooperation Forum summit for the heads of states and governments of member countries, and the development of Vladivostok as a centre for international cooperation in the Asia-Pacific region. A special federal law was passed in 2009, allowing the expropriation of real estate and other property to deploy facilities required for the summit until 31 July 2012, in accordance with a special procedure;

3 the organisation and the holding of the 2018 International Federation of Association Football (FIFA) and 2017 FIFA Confederations Cup in Kaliningrad, Kazan, Nizhny Novgorod, Rostov-on-Don, Samara, Saransk, Volgograd, and Yekaterinburg. A special

federal law was passed in 2013, providing for specific real estate expropriation procedures for the deployment of infrastructural facilities[20] in the Russian Federation constituent entities (subjects) hosting the matches until 31 December 2017;

4   the inclusion of new territories within Moscow, a subject of the Russian Federation and city of federal importance, for which a special federal law was passed for development purposes at the beginning of 2013, establishing specific grounds for real estate expropriation and expropriation procedures; and

5   an incentive for Russia's socioeconomic development, providing for support in the creation of proactive socioeconomic development areas. A special federal law was passed in 2014, with certain specific provisions for real estate expropriation.

The principal common features of the real estate expropriation procedures, established for implementing the majority of the aforementioned government programmes and projects, include:

- listing the deployment of facilities required for accomplishing the goals of such programmes and projects, and included in lists approved by the executive authorities, as grounds for real estate expropriation;
- listing the approval of site design plans as sufficient grounds for expropriation (without the approval of urban planning documents and without public hearings, as prescribed by the general procedure);
- excluding certain stages of the common expropriation procedure (most often, the stage involving the identification of rights holders of the real estate to be expropriated, where the rights holders would have an opportunity to be acquainted with the notice of the planned expropriation in advance);
- excluding certain duties of authorised agencies that require additional time (most often foregoing the requirement for State registration of the expropriation resolution);
- significantly decreasing the expropriation procedure time frame (at any stage);
- restricting a rights holder's freedom to negotiate with respect to the text of the real estate expropriation agreement (most often regarding the amount of compensation);
- a simplified procedure for terminating the rights of rights holders for land plots owned by State or municipality (leaseholders and others);
- in certain cases, transferring the compensation obligation on the organisation performing construction on the expropriated land plot, concurrently with the transfer of the expropriated real estate title to a public authority;
- reducing the subject matter and period for contesting the expropriation procedure, including setting special provisions for enacting and contesting court decisions (allowing only the amount of compensation to be paid for the expropriated real estate to be contested, prompt execution of the court decisions, and reducing the periods for filing and considering appeals and cassation appeals).

For example, in the preparations for the Sochi 2014 Winter Olympic Games and Paralympic Games, the expropriation agreement had to be signed within one month of the date on which the rights holder of the real estate to be expropriated had the opportunity to read the draft of the agreement; there was no opportunity for a reciprocal proposal from the rights holder regarding the amount of compensation. The expropriation agreement might have provided for the replacement of the expropriated residential facility with other housing to be constructed in the future, and any resident had to vacate the expropriated housing within 10 days from receiving the notice of title transfer.

As part of the preparations for the 2018 FIFA and 2017 FIFA Confederations Cup in Russia, it was established that a judgment by the court of first instance should take effect within 10 days from the award, appeals were to be filed within 10 days from the award, and appeals and cassation appeals considered within 10 and 5 days, respectively, from the expiration of the contested period.

The assumed main objectives for establishing such specific expropriation procedures are to make the expropriation procedure as simple as possible, and the duration of the procedure as short as possible, in order to reduce the duration of large-scale government programmes, even to the prejudice of the interests of private owners and other real estate rights holders.

Specific real estate expropriation regulations in the new territories adjoining Moscow (New Moscow)

The project called the New Moscow is an example of special real estate expropriation regulations for the purposes of large-scale government projects.

On 27 December 2011, the Federal Assembly of the Russian Federation approved the Agreement on Changing the Borders between Russian Federation subjects: Moscow and Moscow Region, which provided for the merging with Moscow of 21 municipalities adjoining to the southwest and three territories to the west of Moscow. Thus, in 2012, through the addition of the less densely populated Moscow Region areas, the land area of Moscow increased 2.5 times, whereas the city's population increased by only 250,000. The project and the newly adjoined territory were named the New Moscow.

A special federal law established additional grounds for expropriating land plots and other real estate within the New Moscow: being expropriation for the purposes of deploying facilities of Statewide importance intended to develop engineering, transportation, and social infrastructure, or other State objectives subject to the inclusion of such facilities in the special federal list or Moscow's special list.[21]

Also, a special urban planning procedure was established with respect to facilities of Statewide importance, for the deployment of which expropriating privately owned real estate in the New Moscow may be permitted:

- the deployment of facilities of Statewide importance and changes to the permitted use of land plots required for deploying these facilities are established in the site design plans (according to the general rule, the deployment of such facilities must be stipulated in the urban planning documents, including the general plan and changes of permitted use for land plots must be stipulated in land use and development regulations, as zoning documents are named in Russia);
- public hearings are no longer required to approve site design plans in the New Moscow.

At the same time a special procedure was used for urban planning in Moscow, previously established in 2012, by the Federal Law 'On the Enactment of the Urban Planning Code of the Russian Federation':

- prior to 1 July 2017, the preparation of site design plans was allowed in the absence of the general plan of Moscow (including the New Moscow), i.e., the deployment of facilities of statewide importance for which real estate expropriation is allowed was not reflected in urban planning documents (the general plan) or discussed at public hearings;

- the preparation of site design plans and urban planning documents (with respect to the New Moscow) is permitted without taking into account urban planning documents, urban zoning documents, and the New Moscow area site design plans, which were previously considered at public hearings (before those areas were adjoined to Moscow).

In view of the special procedure, there is a strong likelihood of expropriating privately owned real estate for deploying facilities of Statewide importance in the New Moscow, the planning for which citizens have not been involved at any stage and of which they became aware only once the expropriation procedure for their real estate started.

The specific aspects of the expropriation procedure for the New Moscow itself are as follows:

- a real estate expropriation resolution may only be contested in court within two months from the passing of that resolution, whereas according to the general rule, a three-year period is established for contesting a real estate expropriation resolution;
- in the case of a forced expropriation according to a court procedure, the amount of compensation for the real estate to be expropriated is determined by the court based on an appraisal of the real estate to be taken ordered by the authorised agency (whereas according to the general procedure, the court is not restricted to such an appraisal and may order a separate appraisal);
- the compensation amount determined based on the appraisal ordered by the authorised agency may be contested in court by the rights holder in a separate claim, while the presence of such a legal dispute is not an obstacle for a court order on forced expropriation, payment of compensation or the transfer of title to the expropriated real estate (no such restrictions exist in the general procedure).

Also, a special procedure was established for expropriating residential premises: a ban was imposed (not stipulated in the general procedure in the Russian Housing Code) on providing new residential premises to residents in exchange for expropriated residential premises, if the value of the residential premises provided exceeds the value of the expropriated residential premises by 30% or more, although this does not apply to the expropriation of a housing unit which is the citizen's sole residence.

Currently, the development of areas in the New Moscow is underway, and the main goals include increasing the population in the area (from 455,800 to 1.5 million), generating more employment (from 84,800 jobs to 1 million), increasing the housing stock (from 18.9 million sq. m. (203 million sq. ft.) to 52.0 million sq. m. (560 million sq. ft.)), increasing non-residential real estate (from 5.1 million sq. m. (55 million sq. ft.) to 48 million sq. m. (517 million sq. ft.)), utilising the area's recreational potential (forests represent over 50% of the territory), developing transportation infrastructure, and creating an energy-efficient technical infrastructure. In the period from 2012 to 2016, 7.6 million sq. m. (82 million sq. ft.) of residential real estate and 2.8 million sq. m. (30 million sq. ft.) of non-residential real estate has been built in New Moscow, and over 0.5 million jobs created from 2012 to 2015 (Moscow Department for Urban Planning and Construction Web-site 2017).

Using the mechanism of real estate expropriation for State or municipal needs and the new legal mechanisms for large-scale urban redevelopment projects

The issue of redeveloping run-down urban areas is quite topical for Russia, in part because of the constant growth of the accumulated deficit of restorative investments in the residential segment (i.e., investments in the reconstruction and capital repairs of residential buildings, modernisation of the utility infrastructure, and the construction of new housing in place of demolished and depreciated residential buildings). This accumulated deficit was estimated at RUB 2.3 trillion (31.4% of the GDP) in 2000, and as much as RUB 22.6 trillion (36% of the GDP) in 2012 (Kosareva et al. 2015, 302).

At the same time, a survey of city representatives conducted by the Institute for Urban Economics in 2014, showed that, in reality, only around 20% of territories requiring transformation are actually involved in redevelopment projects in large cities (with populations exceeding 250,000), whereas the new residential construction potential in all those areas is around 260 million sq. m. (2,800 million sq. ft.) of the total area (Legal Regulation 2014).

Legislation in various countries differs in how they treat the matter of whether redevelopment projects in run down urban areas are a public need, and whether their implementation may involve the mechanism of real estate expropriation for public needs. Russian legislation is still in a formative stage in this respect. In particular, an initiative which was called "development of built-up areas" has been tested over the past 10 years. Quite recently, a new initiative called "comprehensive development of territories" was introduced into legislation; however, that has not yet been implemented in practice. In 2007 Moscow started a renovation programme with respect to the housing stock from the first prefab construction period. Certain significant regulatory novelties have been introduced for the purposes of the programme.

These approaches are considered in detail in the following section.

Real estate expropriation for State or municipal needs as part of projects for developing built-up areas

The purpose of the built-up area development (BAD) initiative regulated by the Russian Urban Planning Code, is mainly focused on redeveloping the areas occupied by old and unsafe apartment buildings at the expense of a private developer selected by the municipality through an auction, rather than being funded by the State or municipal budgets.

To define the BAD borders, municipalities should be guided by the presence of apartment buildings in that location (within the borders of the site planning structure unit, adjacent units, or parts thereof) recognised as unsafe and subject to demolition according to the formal procedure for such recognition, as well as apartment buildings planned for demolition or reconstruction based on municipal targeted programmes. The BAD area may also accommodate technical infrastructure intended exclusively for such apartment buildings, as well as the utility, social, and transportation infrastructure required for residents. No other capital facilities may be located in that area.

Until recently, the Russian Urban Planning Code also allowed capital facilities to be located within a BAD area where their permitted uses and threshold parameters did not correspond with the land use regulations (e.g., dilapidated detached homes located in zones intended for apartment building construction). However, this opportunity was abolished on 1 January 2017, which appears to have been a mistake, because it has resulted in considerable difficulties in identifying redevelopment projects which may be of interest to private investors without considerable budgetary support (Trutnev et al. 2016).

Since it is the intention that BAD projects be financed by private investments, including those connected with the relocation of residents from unsafe apartment buildings, the Russian Housing Code and Russian Urban Planning Code provides specific procedures for expropriating land plots under such buildings and the residential premises in such buildings. The main specific feature is that, although decisions on expropriating a land plot and the residential premises in an unsafe apartment building are made by the local authority, it is the developer in charge of the BAD project who pays compensation to the owners (or provides other residential premises to them). It should be noted that uncertainty about the deadlines for reaching an agreement with the owner of the residential premises regarding the amount of compensation (purchase amount) places the successful implementation of a BAD project by a developer at substantially higher risk than the costs associated with that compensation. Accordingly, in practice, in most cases developers provide residents other residential premises to replace the expropriated facilities, instead of compensation.

One of the main problems with implementing BAD projects is that, with respect to other land plots and real estate, including residential premises in apartment buildings, the demolition and reconstruction of which are planned as part of municipal targeted programmes, the law stipulates no conditions for a forced sale (if common grounds do not apply in accordance with Article 49 of the Russian Land Code). The developer is expected to negotiate with the owners, which often creates insurmountable obstacles for implementing a BAD project (there is a high risk of project suspension if one or more owners in the building do not agree to sell their premises voluntary).

Real estate expropriation for State or municipal needs as part of projects of comprehensive development of areas initiated by local authorities

Quite recently, the legislator made an attempt to regulate the redevelopment of deteriorating urban areas, including former industrial zones, based on applying the right to expropriate any real estate in that area according to a special procedure.

After the Soviet era, many Russian cities were left with areas of land occupied by large industrial facilities which are not in operation today. Those areas are deteriorating while occupying very valuable land in median and even central districts of cities. Although the law is trying to generalise the approach and does not directly focus on the nature of those areas, a new regulatory tool to redevelop those areas was introduced in the Russian Urban Planning Code on 1 January 2017, which was called "comprehensive development of territory." Under normal circumstances, the law provides for two types of comprehensive development of lands: at the initiative of a local authority or at the initiative of real estate rights holders. The tool for real estate expropriation for municipal needs is regulated with respect to the comprehensive development of territory (CDT) initiated by local authorities.

The generalisation of enforcing the CDT tool is still premature. However, many questions arise with respect to the law's criteria for determining the borders of the CDT area and, accordingly, the opportunity for real estate expropriation for municipal needs in that area. As a criterion for determining the borders of a CDT area, it has been established that at least 50% of the total area of that territory should consist of:

1   land plots occupied by capital facilities (except for apartment buildings) recognised according to a formal procedure as unsafe and subject to demolition, or capital facilities

(except for apartment buildings) planned for demolition as part of municipal targeted programmes approved by a representative local authority;

2   land plots used for other purposes not in accordance with urban zoning regulations and/or land plots on which capital facilities are used other than in accordance with urban zoning regulations;

3   land plots on which unauthorised structures are located.

While the criteria and procedure for identifying capital facilities as unsafe and subject to demolition are established by the Russian government, grounds for including facilities in municipal demolition and reconstruction programmes are not specified (in fact, it seems that any facility may qualify, except for apartment buildings). However, with respect to the second criterion (conflict with urban zoning regulations), CDT borders may also encompass residential buildings, including apartment buildings. The other part of the CDT area (the remaining 50%) may accommodate any facilities.

The resulting conclusion is that, notwithstanding the attempt to regulate the criteria for 50% of a CDT area, ultimately the CDT area may accommodate any real estate which may be expropriated for municipal needs. No additional protection is established by the law for the rights of real estate owners in that area, including housing rights.

CDT projects also use a special procedure for expropriating real estate for municipal needs:

*   justifying the need for real estate expropriation in a CDT area consists of the planning design and the delineation design documents. Public hearings have been abolished for the planning design documents for such locations, and real estate owners no longer even have an opportunity to discuss development options for the area.
*   a special expropriation procedure has been introduced, according to which any court decision on the expropriation of land plots and/or other real estate located thereon for the purpose of CDT shall be subject to *immediate execution*, and a court decision on expropriation may be contested only with respect to the amount of compensation for the expropriated real estate;
*   reduced deadlines have been established for real estate expropriation (e.g., the expropriation agreement should be signed by the rights holder of the real estate within one month, rather than within 90 days as prescribed by the general procedure).

New legal mechanisms used to implement the housing stock renovation programme in Moscow

In 2017, Moscow started a large-scale, socially significant housing stock renovation programme which required the adoption of not only a special federal law, but also a special Moscow law and decree by the Moscow government.[22] This programme does not provide for the application of the mechanism of real estate expropriation for State or municipal needs with respect to residential premises, but achieves the same goal by using other legal methods which the authors consider to be more effective.

The programme is relevant for the following reasons. A substantial portion of Moscow's housing stock was built during the first prefab construction period from 1951 through to 1960. During that period, standard designs were used to build panel and block buildings, mostly five-storied (they came to be called "khrushchevky," after Nikita Khrushchev who was the Soviet leader during that period). Apartments in those buildings are usually small, with small kitchens and lavatories.

Currently, the technical condition of those buildings is causing many problems; however, their structural features make capital repairs, including utility system replacements, either impossible or excessively expensive. A total of 1,671 such buildings were demolished in Moscow during the first period (1999–2017). As part of that programme, the city administration engaged private developers, while the programme itself followed the principle of voluntariness, i.e., the developer was required to reach agreement on relocation with all owners in such buildings, which was time-consuming and not always successful.

In the light of the poor technical condition of those buildings and their social obsolescence, it was decided to start the next stage and launch a renovation effort with respect to this kind of housing stock in Moscow, aimed mostly at preventing the massive emergence of unsafe housing stock and at adjusting the disparities in Moscow's urban development that have accumulated over previous years. It should be noted that the idea of a renovation programme in Moscow appears justified both in terms of improving the living conditions of residents in those buildings and in terms of the urban development of Moscow's median areas occupied by those socially and physically obsolete, low-density developments, increasing the supply in the modern housing market, and creating a comfortable urban environment in those areas.

The programme has a large number of interesting features, however, only those related to the issue of real estate expropriation are considered here.

First, the implementation of the programme was preceded by a survey of the population regarding the demolition of the apartment buildings they live in. Voting was organised for every building; the programme covered only buildings in which owners and tenants (only the votes of tenants in State-owned or municipal apartments were counted) of at least two-thirds of the apartments voted to join the programme. The voting was organised in several formats for residents to choose from: on the Active Citizen web portal managed by the Moscow government, by voting in person at multi-functional State and municipal service centres, and at general meetings of the owners of the premises in the building.

This preliminary stage resulted in a vast number of questions and disputes. Numerous public discussions were held, and explanations were provided to the media. Finally, in almost 90% of the buildings on the voting list (4,073 out of 4,539), the residents voted "for" and were included in the renovation programme (Moscow Government Web-site for Housing Stock Renovation Program 2017).

Second, attractive and diverse relocation options were offered to the residents, which included providing an equivalent apartment in a new building in the same district (whereas the number of rooms in the new apartment should be the same as in the old one, its floor area is estimated to be at least 20% larger); providing an equivalent apartment (based on the value); or compensation. The value of an equivalent apartment or the amount of compensation are determined according to the general principles applied to calculating the purchase price in the event of expropriating residential premises for State or municipal needs.

The procedure for providing residential premises or compensation required a mandatory procedure and dates for the signing of a respective agreement (pursuant to Article 445 of the Russian Civil Code) between the apartment rights holder and the authorised Moscow executive agency. If no agreement is signed within 90 days from its receipt by the rights holder, the authorised agency is entitled to file a claim in court to compel the signing of the agreement and to ensure that the residential premises are vacated, and its transfer into the ownership of the City of Moscow, as well as the State registration of the transfer of the title to the residential premises.

The approach described in the programme appears to arrive at effectively the same result as that for expropriating residential premises for State and municipal needs, while providing the opportunity to the owners of residential premises in the building to make a collective decision, which increases their involvement in redevelopment projects and lowers social tension.

It should be noted that the aforementioned aspects of the programme only apply to apartments within apartment buildings. Non-residential premises in those buildings included in the resolution on renovation are subject to expropriation for Moscow's public needs, subject to prior and commensurate compensation to the owners, or by providing equivalent non-residential premises. The amount, procedure, and conditions for compensation are determined in accordance with the common federal laws. The tenants of non-residential premises owned by the city of Moscow (small and medium enterprises) in apartment buildings covered by the renovation programme retain their right to sign a new lease agreement with respect to equivalent non-residential premises.

Review of legal practices concerning matters of real estate expropriation for state or municipal needs

An analysis of legal practice materials has shown that the most common disputes related to real estate expropriation for State or municipal needs are disputes regarding the amount of compensation for the real estate to be expropriated. Disputes on the legality and justification of the real estate expropriation *per se* are much rarer.

Claims regarding the amount of compensation for real estate to be expropriated can be divided into two groups: claims to increase the amount of compensation (the rights holder of the real estate being the plaintiff) and claims to reduce the amount (the authorised agency being the plaintiff).

The first group includes most of the disputes associated with the expropriation of residential premises, when a court commissions an independent examination of the appraisal, based on which the compensation for the real estate to be expropriated is determined.

The second group of litigations mainly includes disputes associated with real estate expropriation pursuant to special federal laws (e.g., the Federal Law "On the FIFA Cup in Russia"). The subject matter for those disputes is the appraisal carried out at the behest of the authorised agency by an independent appraiser, or the appraisal examination of the court of first instance. Courts typically dismissed claims by authorised agencies to reduce the compensation amount in those disputes.

It should be specifically noted that uncertainty around the very concept of State and municipal needs is a huge legal issue. The Russian Supreme Court stated its opinion on the matter,[23] in which it noted that State or municipal needs may mean the needs of a public legal entity, which must be satisfied in the interests of society, and which is impossible without the expropriation of private property. This is why such an expropriation may not be carried out solely or substantially for the benefit of other private entities whose businesses only indirectly serve the interests of society.

The analysis of legal practice yielded the following findings:

- in court disputes to increase the amount of compensation for real estate to be expropriated, courts usually side with the plaintiffs who are the rights holders of the real estate filing such claims;
- in disputes to decrease the amount of compensation, courts usually dismiss the plaintiff (authorised agency) claims to reduce the amount of compensation;
- disputes regarding the legal grounds for real estate expropriation are less common than disputes regarding the amount of compensation;

- in the few cases where expropriation resolutions passed by authorised agencies are contested, courts mostly side with the authorised agencies, as the plaintiffs typically have no clear arguments to defend their position in the absence of a clear concept of State and municipal needs.

Issues with Russian general statutory regulations on real estate expropriation for State or municipal needs

The first issue, as evidenced by a review of legal practices, is the uncertainty around the very notion of "State or municipal needs," which is not defined in the legislation. Notwithstanding that the courts are trying to formalise the parameters and criteria for this concept, the development of statutory regulation, on the contrary, is constantly extending the list of grounds for real estate expropriation and the confines of State and municipal needs. Moreover, the legislation appears to be moving even further away from the general requirement to prove that publicly significant goals cannot be achieved by means other than through the expropriation of real estate at that particular location.

For example, the principal conditions for possibly applying the real estate expropriation mechanism (the exceptional nature of the case and the absence of other options for constructing or reconstructing facilities of Statewide or local importance), which are established in the Russian Land Code, have not been reflected in subsequent regulations of the expropriation procedures. In justifying an expropriation, the procedure boils down to verifying one of the grounds for expropriation, formulated quite vaguely in the laws, and to the availability of a certain document approved by a public authority. The very availability of such a document confirms *a priori* the exceptional nature of the case and the absence of other options for realising the facilities. For example, the designation of areas for the facilities of Statewide or municipal importance planned for deployment in the federal, regional, or municipal territories planning schemes, including the general plans of municipal territories, is considered to be sufficient grounds, and in this case there is no need to prove the existence of other options for realising the facilities.

Also unclear is the concept of "facilities of federal, regional, or local importance," for the construction or reconstruction of which land plots may be expropriated. According to the definitions of the terms "facilities of federal importance," "facilities of regional importance," and "facilities of local importance" in the Russian Urban Planning Code, attribution to a category of the aforementioned facilities is determined as the necessity of that facility for executing State or municipal powers and for the exerting of substantial influence of that facility on the socioeconomic development of the respective area. In the authors' opinion, both are evaluation categories admitting to various interpretations. As a result, public authorities are virtually unrestricted in using the available grounds and in establishing new grounds for real estate expropriation; in practice, public authorities make individual decisions for every facility.

Another crucial problem, in our opinion, is the insufficient attention given to organising public discussions involving interested residents and rights holders in making urban planning decisions, which entail, *inter alia*, real estate expropriation (an exception is the aforementioned housing stock renovation programme in Moscow). Advanced discussion of those decisions could ensure protection from unreasonable expropriation of privately owned real estate; however, such discussions are not established practice in Russia.

Generally, according to the Russian Urban Planning Code, public hearings should be held with respect to adopting and amending general plans, land use and development rules, site planning design, and site delineation design documents. However, first of all, there are no clear legal consequences determined for the negative opinion of public hearing participants, and second, the negative trend in recent years is for the reduction in the legislative list of cases requiring public hearings.

For example, recent amendments to the Russian Urban Planning Code negated the requirement for public hearings:

a   in the case of amending municipal land use and development rules (LUDR) to ensure the deployment on the territories of settlements of facilities of Statewide importance and local importance for the municipal district (private real estate may be expropriated for purposes of their deployment), provided for in the urban planning documents of the Russian Federation, a subject of the Russian Federation, and a municipal district;

b   with respect to site planning and site delineation design documents during redevelopment of built-up areas or during comprehensive development of new, undeveloped territories. Such projects should be implemented within the borders of special territories (so-called territories intended for activities related to the comprehensive and sustainable development of the territory) designated on the urban zoning map in the LUDR. In this case, public hearings are conducted only in the first stage, during the delineation of the borders of such areas of the LUDR. Taking into account that the law stipulates no clear reasons or conditions for establishing the borders of such areas, including the separation of the zones for redevelopment or zones for new development on the urban zoning map in the LUDR, public hearings on the LUDR in this first stage may include discussion of the general borders of an area where something has been planned at some time only, without specific information regarding where, when, what exactly, and under what conditions it will be deployed in the area. Finally, residents and real estate rights holders become aware of the beginning of a particular large-scale project, including the one requiring real estate expropriation, only after the site design plans have been approved and the expropriation procedure has started with respect to their real estate.

Conclusions

On the whole, it can be stated that the Russian legal framework regulating the expropriation of land plots and other real estate for State or municipal needs, while existing and tested in practice, is still far from being perfect:

- on the one hand, to build a facility required by a public authority where the expropriation of real estate is required, public authorities face uncertainty in the legislation regarding the concept of "state or municipal need," which entails both a very broad interpretation of the concept and the risk of the failure of such projects;
- on the other hand, an exclusive system of urban planning regulation is being introduced for certain areas and national programmes, providing for unrestrained expropriation of practically any real estate for unrestricted public needs. Under such circumstances, the risks of investments in real estate will grow, as there is no guarantee that an individual's real estate will not be expropriated in the future;
- among State and municipal needs, legislation has not yet identified a case for the need to renovate deteriorating areas, including residential areas, nor a clear and effective procedure for such situations (except for the demolition or reconstruction of unsafe apartment buildings and special statutory regulations for the housing stock renovation programme

in Moscow), although the need for such renovation in Russian cities is quite high and this is despite several attempts by the legislator to provide the regulation;

- a trend has been identified toward reducing cases where urban planning decisions, including those requiring real estate expropriation, should be preceded by public hearings, including those for the purposes of protecting private real estate from unreasonable expropriation.

Notes

1 According to the Russian Civil Code and Russian Land Code, *requisition* means the expropriation of property from the owner subject to compensation, in the interests of society and on the basis of a decision by public authorities in cases of natural disasters, emergencies, epidemics, and epizootic and other extraordinary circumstances.

2 According to the Russian Civil Code and Russian Land Code, *confiscation* means the expropriation of property from the owner based on a court judgment, such as a penalty for a crime or other offense.

3 According to the Russian Civil Code, *nationalisation* means the transfer of property owned by individuals and legal entities into public ownership pursuant to a special law and subject to compensation for the value of the property and other losses.

4 Divestiture of property which cannot be owned by a respective person by operation of law; the purchase of mismanaged cultural valuables, pets; divestiture of construction in progress due to the termination of a land lease owned by the state or municipality; divestiture of a land plot used in a breach of Russian law; divestiture of real estate due to the divestiture of the land plot resulting from improper use; termination of the title to a mismanaged residential premises; removal from circulation of counterfeit physical media used in violation of intellectual property rights; subject to a court judgment, realisation for the benefit of the Russian Federation of property purchased in exchange for corruption-related or illicit funds; subject to a court judgment, realisation for the benefit of the Russian Federation of property related to acts of terrorism.

5 Seizure of property against obligations; loss of title to a share in jointly owned property subject to reimbursement; loss of title to real estate abandoned by the owner on a land plot which the owner has ceased to use; mandatory signing of a contract.

6 The law was repealed in 1994, following the enactment of Part 1 of the Russian Civil Code.

7 The breakdown of the housing stock according to Russian Federal State Statistics Service (Rosstat) data was determined based on the total area of residential units (apartments in apartment buildings and detached homes).

8 In 2015, the total populated area in Russia accounted for 1.2% of Russia's total land. (https://rosreestr.ru/site/activity/sostoyanie-zemel-rossii/gosudarstvennyy-natsionalnyy-doklad-o-sostoyanii-i-ispolzovanii-zemel-v-rossiyskoy-federatsii/).

9 Such special grounds established by specific federal laws include:
   a) the expropriation of residential premises due to the expropriation of a land plot for state or municipal needs (Russian Housing Code, Article 32, Parts 1-9);
   b) the expropriation of residential premises in an apartment building found to be unsafe and subject to demolition, due to the expropriation of the land plot under such a building for state or municipal needs (Russian Housing Code, Article 32, Parts 10 and 12), including cases involving a decision on the development of a built-up area in which the unsafe building is located (Russian Housing Code, Article 32, Part 11; Russian Urban Planning Code, Article 46^2);
   c) the expropriation of land plots for purposes of subsoil use activities (Federal Law "On Subsoil");
   d) the expropriation of land plots for protected natural territories (Federal Law "On Protected Natural Territories ");
   e) real estate expropriation as part of redevelopment projects, including:
      – comprehensive development of territory (Federal Law "On Amending the Urban Planning Code of the Russian Federation, Certain Legislative Acts of the Russian Federation with Respect to Regulating the Preparation, Agreement, and Approval of Site Design Plans and the Documentation of Comprehensive and Sustainable Development of Territories, and Negating Certain Provisions of Legislative Acts of the Russian Federation");

- the renovation of Moscow's housing stock (Federal Law "On Amending the Russian Federation Law 'On the Status of the Capital City of the Russian Federation' and Certain Legislative Acts of the Russian Federation to Establish Special Regulations for Certain Legal Relations for Purposes of Renovating the Housing Stock of Moscow, a Subject of the Russian Federation, and City of Federal Importance");

f) real estate expropriation as part of large-scale special government programmes, including:
- the construction of public infrastructural facilities in areas of former Moscow regions that were incorporated into Moscow on 1 July 2012 (Federal Law "On Specific Regulations on Certain Legal Relations Related to the Incorporation of Certain Territories into Moscow, a Subject of the Russian Federation, and City of Federal Importance, and on Amending Certain Legislative Acts of the Russian Federation");
- the construction of Olympic facilities in Krasnodar Territory (Federal Law "On Organizing and Holding the Sochi 2014 Winter Olympic Games and 2014 Paralympic Games in the City of Sochi, Development of Sochi as a Mountain Resort, and on Amending Certain Legislative Acts of the Russian Federation");
- the construction of facilities required for the summit of heads of states and governments for the member countries of the Asia-Pacific Economic Cooperation Forum in Primorsky Territory (Federal Law "On Organizing and Holding a summit of heads of states and governments for member countries of the Asia-Pacific Economic Cooperation Forum in 2012, on the development of Vladivostok as a centre for international cooperation in the Asia Pacific, and on Amending Certain Legislative Acts of the Russian Federation");
- the deployment of infrastructural facilities in subjects of the Russian Federation which will host matches for the FIFA 2018 and FIFA Confederations Cup 2017 (Federal Law "On Preparing and Holding the FIFA 2018 World Cup, FIFA Confederations Cup 2017 in the Russian Federation, and on Amending Certain Legislative Acts of the Russian Federation");
- the deployment of infrastructural facilities of federal and regional importance, intended for transport communication between the Tamansky and Kerchensky peninsulas, and technical infrastructure of federal and regional importance on the Tamansky and Kerchensky peninsulas (Federal Law "On Specific Regulations on Certain Legal Relations Arising Related to the Construction and Reconstruction of Transportation Infrastructure of federal and regional importance, intended for transport communication between the Tamansky and Kerchensky peninsulas, and technical infrastructure of federal and regional importance on the Tamansky and Kerchensky peninsulas, and on Amending Certain Legislative Acts of the Russian Federation");
- the deployment of infrastructural facilities for proactive socioeconomic development (Federal Law "On the Areas of Proactive Socioeconomic Development in the Russian Federation").

10 According to Article 49 of the Russian Land Code, "*In exceptional cases*, land plots may be expropriated for state or municipal needs based on grounds related to:
1 Russia's compliance with international treaties;
2 the construction or reconstruction of the following facilities of statewide importance (facilities of federal importance, facilities of regional importance) or facilities of local importance *in cases where other options for constructing and/or reconstructing such facilities are absent:*...
3 *other grounds provided for by federal laws.*"

11 In particular, the Russian government regulates specific procedures related to reserving land for state and municipal needs, as well as a list of organisations entitled to file petitions for expropriating land plots for federal needs.

12 Hereinafter the term "rights holders" means "owners of real estate in private property as well as private persons holding real estate in state or municipal property under lease agreements or other special rights for land plots or residential premises."

13 Such special categories of rights that allow for providing land plots owned by the state or a municipality to a limited number of persons, include the right of permanent (indefinite) use, the right of lifelong (inherited) possession, and the right of gratuitous use (Russian Land Code, Articles 39^9 and 39^{10}).

14 A cadastral passport is the extract from the land register for an individual unit of real estate.

15 According to the Russian Housing Code, the land plot under an apartment building is owned in shares by the owners of premises in that condominium and forms part of the common property, subject to special regulatory treatment.

16 Russia has a procedure for officially recognising apartment buildings to be unsafe and subject to demolition or reconstruction, which was established by a Russian government decree based on the

Russian Housing Code. In 2013, the Russian government, in executing the Presidential Decree, approved a set of measures to address matters related to liquidating unsafe housing stock that was designated as such as of 1 January 2012.

17 The Fund was established in 2007, pursuant to the Federal Law "On the Fund for Supporting Housing and Utility Reform."

18 A list of the laws is provided in Footnote 10, Paragraph *e*.

19 Olympic facilities are those facilities included in the Olympic facility construction programme approved by the Russian Government Decree "On the Olympic Facility Construction Programme and Development of Sochi as a Mountain Resort."

20 The list of those facilities was approved by the Russian Government Decree "On the Programme for Preparing and Holding the World Football Championship in Russia in 2018."

21 The federal list of facilities of federal importance was approved by the Russian Government in 2015, and Moscow's list of facilities of regional importance was approved by the Moscow Government in 2013.

22 The legal grounds and procedures for implementing the housing stock renovation programme in Moscow were established by: the Federal Law "On Amending the Law of the Russian Federation 'On the Status of the Capital City of the Russian Federation' and Certain Legislative Acts of the Russian Federation to Establish Special Regulations for Certain Legal Relations for Purposes of Renovating the Housing Stock of Moscow, a Subject of the Russian Federation, and City of Federal Importance"); the Moscow Law "On Additional Guarantees for the Residential and Property Rights of Individuals and Legal Entities in Renovating the Housing Stock in Moscow"; the Moscow Government Decree "On the Housing Stock Renovation Programme in Moscow."

23 Russian Supreme Court Ruling No. 309-KG15-5924, dated October 27, 2015 (Case No. A07-21632/2013).

References

Federal Statistical Observation Form No. 1-zhilfond. 2016. *Russian Federal State Statistics Service (Rosstat)*. www.gks.ru/wps/wcm/connect/rosstat_main/rosstat/ru/statistics/population/housing/

Kosareva, N., Polidi, T., Puzanov, A. 2015. *Housing Policy and Economics in Russia: Results and Development Strategy*. Moscow, Russia: Publishing house of National Research University – Higher School of Economics.

Legal Regulation for the Built-up Area Development. Stage 1. The Concept of Improving the Built-up Area Development Institute. 2014. *The Report of the Institute for Urban Economics*. www.urban economics.ru/sites/default/files/koncepciya_rzt_01_04_14_itog-1.pdf.

Moscow Department for Urban Planning and Construction Web-site. 2017. https://stroi.mos.ru/new-moscow.

Moscow Government Web-site for Housing Stock Renovation Program. 2017. https://mosrenovacia.ru/kak-vyiyti-iz-programmyi-renovatsii/.

State (National) Report on the Status and Use of Land in the Russian Federation in 2015. 2016. *Russian Federal Service for State Real Estate Registration, Cadastre and Cartography (Rosreestr)*. https://rosreestr.ru/site/activity/sostoyanie-zemel-rossii/gosudarstvennyy-natsionalnyy-doklad-o-sostoyanii-i-ispolzovanii-zemel-v-rossiyskoy-federatsii/.

Trutnev, E., Polidy, T., Safarova, M., Igumenov, E. 2016. *City for Living*. Moscow, Russia: The Institute for Urban Economics Press.

17

Compulsory acquisition compensation issues in Australia

David Parker

Introduction

Australia is in the midst of an infrastructure boom with the development and provision of infrastructure being a key government policy for not only the Commonwealth Government but also for most of the State governments. The former Federal Prime Minister Abbott built his successful 2013 election campaign on the development and provision infrastructure, famously stating:

> If elected, I want to be known as an infrastructure prime minister.
>
> *(Liberal Party of Australia 2013)*

Indeed, the development and provision of infrastructure across Australia is now so topical that it has its own 30-minute satirical television show on the national broadcaster (Parker 2015):

> Utopia: A satire about the difficult process of taking grand, uncosted, inadequately planned, fundamentally flawed schemes – and passing them off as "Nation Building".
>
> *(Utopia 2015)*

Prime Minister Turnbull, the successor to Prime Minister Abbott, continued the focus on the development and the provision of infrastructure across Australia in the 2017 Federal Budget, providing a further A\$20 billion in capital spending in addition to the A\$50 billion announced the previous year (Norington 2017). The Commonwealth's most high-profile infrastructure project is a A\$5.3 billion investment over 10 years to build a new West Sydney Airport at Badgery's Creek, a project that has been 50 years in the planning and site amalgamation, together with the building of an \$8.4 billion east coast inland rail freight line, stretching 1,700 km (1,056 miles) from Melbourne to Brisbane, to efficiently deliver goods and take the pressure off traditional road transport routes (Norington 2017).

   In addition to the development and the provision of Commonwealth infrastructure, the Commonwealth government also works with State governments in the joint development and provision of infrastructure. The Commonwealth government is investing A$1 billion in regional rail networks in Victoria, A$1.4 billion in road upgrades in Queensland, and A$1.2 billion in passenger rail networks and A$337m in road upgrades in Western Australia (Norington 2017).

Simultaneously, the Queensland State Government's 2017 budget included a focus on the development and provision of infrastructure with a A$42.75 billion capital works programme over four years including the high-profile Cross River Rail Project (Caldwell 2017), A$488.8m for the Toowoomba Second Range Road Crossing and the widening of the Gateway Motorway, A$250m for a sports stadium in Townsville, A$120m for port widening and deepening in Cairns and A$200m for the expansion of the Capricornia Correctional Centre (jail) (Queensland Budget 2017).

In comparison, the New South Wales Government's 2016–2017 budget included a focus on the road and rail infrastructure, with a A$73.3 billion capital works programme over four years, including A$44.6 billion in one year alone (2016–2017), of which approximately half will be spent on road and rail. Major projects included A$2.9 billion for WestConnex, a major road programme linking Sydney's west with the Central Business District (CBD), airport and Port Botany, A$2.7 billion for the Sydney Metro rail project, A$1.5 billion to continue the duplication of the Pacific Highway between Brisbane and Sydney, A$338m to build roads in western Sydney to support the new Commonwealth West Sydney Airport (Rostron 2017), A$7.77 billion for hospitals, A$4.2 billion for schools, A$160.5m for a sports stadium in Parramatta, A$244.3m for the NSW Art Gallery, A$19m for the Sydney Opera House renewal programme and A$3.8 billion for two new jails (NSW Government 2017).

Accordingly, with a massive government investment in the development and provision of infrastructure, ranging from rail and roads to schools, hospitals and jails, the extent of compulsory acquisition of private land and interests by government over the next four years is likely to be unprecedented in the history of Australia. This will place enormous pressure on the various acquiring authorities and an intense focus on the specific wording of the various statutes governing compulsory acquisition and compensation payable by the Commonwealth government and the respective State governments.

Statutory framework at Commonwealth and state levels

While both the Commonwealth and each of the States and Territories have their own statutory framework, there is considerable conceptual commonality though with some small differences in detail.

Principal statutes

The principal Commonwealth, State and Territory statutes for compulsory acquisition and compensation include:

Commonwealth and the Australian Capital Territory (ACT)	*Lands Acquisition Act 1989*
New South Wales (NSW)	*Land Acquisition (Just Terms Compensation) Act 1991*
Victoria	*Land Acquisition and Compensation Act 1986*
Queensland	*Acquisition of Land Act 1967*
South Australia	*Land Acquisition Act 1969*
Western Australia	*Land Administration Act 1997*

Tasmania   *Land Acquisition Act 1993*
Northern Territory   *Lands Acquisition Act 2016*

In this chapter, the NSW *Land Acquisition (Just Terms Compensation) Act 1991 (NSW Act)* is used for the purposes of illustration of the concepts and principles of compulsory acquisition and compensation.

Effect of compulsory acquisition

Upon the publication of a notice of compulsory acquisition as required under the respective statutes, all specified interests of specified persons in the land are thereupon vested in the acquiring authority (Hemmings 1997).

The acquiring authority is vested with an estate in fee simple, discharged and freed from all trusts, obligations and interests, contracts, licenses, rates, charges, easements and all other restrictions and encumbrances whatsoever (Hemmings 1997).

The effect of the compulsory acquisition is to convert an interest in land into a claim for compensation, assessable in accordance with the statute as at the date of acquisition (Hemmings 1997). Effectively, therefore, the landowner cannot hold up the project for which the land is being acquired as the concept of acquisition is severed from the concept of compensation. Acquisition and dispossession are instant, though some statutes allow continued occupation in certain circumstances, while compensation may be agreed at a later time. In the event that compensation is disputed and a protracted period is likely before agreement is reached, certain statutes allow for a large proportion of the compensation (potentially up to 90% in NSW (s48, NSW Act)) to be paid in advance. It is, however, not unusual following litigated compensation disputes for the dispossessed to be required to pay back a portion of the compensation advanced.

Most statutes make provision for the acquisition of land after an acquiring authority has determined that the land is required for a public purpose. However, if there is a delay between the identification and acquisition, hardship may be caused to the landowner as the land may become unsalable or blighted and so reduced in value. Accordingly, some statutes provide for a landowner to compel the acquiring authority to acquire the land or remove the public purpose designation, though this may limit the heads of compensation claimable (Hemmings 1997).

Usque ad coelum et ad inferos

Generally consistent with the principles of land ownership applying in many Commonwealth countries, Australia recognises land ownership, and therefore that which is acquired, as stretching from the centre of the earth to the outermost parts of the heavens, the usual restrictions applying.

Land may also comprise a lot under strata title or community title, with land usually including not only buildings and crops thereon but also all interests and estates in the land (Hemmings 1997).

Just compensation

Compensation for compulsory acquisition is not a right vested by common law, but is solely a matter of statutory entitlement in Australia, and its assessment is limited by that legislation. All acquisition legislation seeks to provide the dispossessed owner with the full money equivalent of the property acquired by compulsion (Hemmings 1997).

Significantly, as Hemmings (1997) notes, early statutes such as the NSW *Public Works Act 1912*, enacted not long after the great railway acquisitions in the United Kingdom (UK) in the late 1800s, provided only for compensation upon resumption for *"the value of the land taken"* (Hemmings 1997, p. 435).

The current statutory framework is premised on compensation, having regard to all relevant matters permissible under the legislation, being an amount that will justly compensate (Hemmings 1997). Section 54(1) of the NSW Act specifies:

54 Entitlement to just compensation

1   The amount of compensation to which a person is entitled under this Part is such amount as, having regard to all relevant matters under this Part, will justly compensate the person for the acquisition of the land.

The principle that, in the assessment of compensation, doubt should be resolved in a more liberal estimate in favour of the dispossessed has been established for over 60 years (*Commission of Succession Duties (SA) v Executor Trustee Agency Co of SA Ltd* (1942) 74 CLR 358 at 374).

This is of particular importance in the compulsory acquisition of land from indigenous groups, where the spiritual significance of the land may be contended to require reflection in the principle of just compensation. Section 54(2) of the NSW Act seeks to address this issue.

54 Entitlement to just compensation

2   If the compensation that is payable under this Part to a person from whom native title rights and interests in relation to land have been acquired does not amount to compensation on just terms within the meaning of the Commonwealth Native Title Act, the person concerned is entitled to such additional compensation as is necessary to ensure that the compensation is paid on that basis.

Nevertheless, the extent to which money may be equivalent to land for dispossessed indigenous groups remains contentious and unsettled.

Disregard of the public purpose

The respective compulsory acquisition and compensation statutes follow the principle established in *Pointe Gourde Quarrying Transport Co v Sub-Intendent of Crown Lands (Trinidad)* 1947 AL 568 that the purpose for which the land is being compulsorily acquired is disregarded in the assessment of compensation.

Such a public purpose disregard is specified in s56(1)(a) and (b) of the NSW Act (see below)

Generally, in a "before and after" valuation approach to the assessment of compensation, regard may not be had to the public purpose in the "before" scenario but regard may be had to the public purpose in the "after" scenario (Hemmings 1997).

Alternative heads of compensation available

By way of an indicative example, the NSW Act specifies the following alternative heads of compensation which are generally mirrored in the other relevant statutes:

55 Relevant matters to be considered in determining amount of compensation

In determining the amount of compensation to which a person is entitled, regard must be had to the following matters only (as assessed in accordance with this Division):

a   the market value of the land on the date of its acquisition,

b   any special value of the land to the person on the date of its acquisition,

c   any loss attributable to severance,

d   any loss attributable to disturbance,

e   the disadvantage resulting from relocation,

f   any increase or decrease in the value of any other land of the person at the date of acquisition which adjoins or is severed from the acquired land by reason of the carrying out of, or the proposal to carry out, the public purpose for which the land was acquired.

The alternative heads of compensation may be considered as follows:

Market value

By way of indicative example, the NSW Act specifies the payment of market value for the interest in land acquired, on a prescribed basis and definition, with consequential adjustment to any compensation for disturbance:

56 Market value

1   In this Act: **"market value"** of land at any time means the amount that would have been paid for the land if it had been sold at that time by a willing but not anxious seller to a willing but not anxious buyer, disregarding (for the purpose of determining the amount that would have been paid):

a   any increase or decrease in the value of the land caused by the carrying out of, or the proposal to carry out, the public purpose for which the land was acquired, and

b   any increase in the value of the land caused by the carrying out by the authority of the State, before the land is acquired, of improvements for the public purpose for which the land is to be acquired, and

c   any increase in the value of the land caused by its use in a manner or for a purpose contrary to law.

2   When assessing the market value of land for the purpose of paying compensation to a number of former owners of the land, the sum of the market values of each interest in the land must not (except with the approval of the Minister responsible for the authority of the State) exceed the market value of the land at the date of acquisition.

3   If:

a   the land is used for a particular purpose and there is no general market for land used for that purpose, and

b   the owner genuinely proposes to continue after the acquisition to use other land for that purpose,

the market value of the land is taken, for the purpose of paying compensation, to be the reasonable cost to the owner of equivalent reinstatement in some other location. That cost is to be reduced by any costs for which compensation is payable for loss attributable to disturbance and by any likely improvement in the owner's financial position because of the relocation.

As the definition of market value is central to compulsory purchase compensation, it is considered further later in the chapter. However, fundamental to the definition is the assumption that a sale will occur with the existence of a buyer at a fair price (Hemmings 1997), as stated in *Minister of Public Instruction v Turner* 1955 20 LGR (NSW) 85 at 91:

> a voluntary bargain between a vendor and a purchaser each willing to trade but neither of whom was so anxious to do so that he would overlook ordinary business considerations.

Also fundamental to the definition is the assumption that the value of the land is that of its highest and best use or *"most advantageous purpose"* (*Minister of State for Home Affairs v Rostron* 1914 18 CLR 634), the property being valued at the relevant date in its existing condition with all its *"potentialities"* (*Yates Property Corporation Pty Ltd (in liq) v Darling Harbour Authority* (1991) 24 NSWLR 156 at 175–176). While not specified, the International Valuation Standards (IVS) elements of physically possible, legally permissible and financially feasible may be considered likely to be applicable, with such use being probable and not merely speculative. This has been of particular significance in recent NSW rail compulsory acquisition cases where rural land, which would ultimately, at some undefined point in the future, become residential development land, was acquired at various stages of that journey. In *Chircop v Transport for NSW* [2014] NSWLEC 63, it was held that such land must be *"ripe"* (para. 10) for such potential higher and best use in order for that to be compensable, with *"ripe"* in this case being likely to occur within 15–18 months of the acquisition.

Special value

By way of an indicative example, the NSW Act specifies the payment of special value, significantly in addition to market value, where there is financial value for an advantage incidental to the person's use of the land:

57 Special value
In this Act:
> **"special value"** of land means the financial value of any advantage, in addition to market value, to the person entitled to compensation which is incidental to the person's use of the land.

In *Peter Croke Holdings Pty Ltd v Roads and Traffic Authority of NSW* (1998) 101 LGERA 30 at 38, Bignold J said:

> Special value is an element of the concept of 'value to the owner', and is the additional sum above market value which the owner would have given for the land sooner than fail to obtain it at the time of the hypothetical sale.

The benchmark example for special value in NSW is generally considered to be the decision by Callinan J in *Boland v Yates Property Corporation Pty Limited [1999] HCA 64; 74 ALJR 209; 167 ALR 575* where His Honour cited the example of a blacksmith's shop adjacent to a racetrack:

> 292 The special value of land is its value to the owner over and above its market value. It arises in circumstances in which there is a conjunction of some special factor

relating to the land and a capacity on the part of the owner exclusively or perhaps almost exclusively to exploit it. None of the examples given by the Full Federal Court are true examples of special value. There will in practice be few cases in which a property does have a special value for a particular owner. Obviously neither sentiment nor a long attachment to it will suffice. The special quality must be a quality that has an economic significance to the owner. A possible case would be one in which, for example, a blacksmith operates a forge in the vicinity of a racetrack on land zoned for residential purposes as a protected non-conforming use, the right to which might be lost on a transfer of ownership or an interruption of the protected use. Such a property will have a special value for its blacksmith owner, and perhaps another blacksmith who might be able to comply with the relevant requirements to enable him to continue the use but to no one else.

While this fulfils the tests of incidental to the use of land and an advantage of financial value, the example is rare and unusual, consistent with the concept of such value being "special". Essentially, special value is a notion of worth or value to the owner, rather than a notion of value between a hypothetical vendor and purchaser, which may ground payment of compensation greater than that payable for market value provided the statutory tests can be met, especially that the property is put to some use for which it is specially well suited.

As the Courts have extensively explored and clarified the concept of market value, it may be anticipated that future applicants may be keen to explore the potential for claims under special value.

Severance

By way of indicative example, the NSW Act specifies payment for the reduction in market value of land retained by the landholder as a result of the acquired land being severed:

55 Relevant matters to be considered in determining amount of compensation
In determining the amount of compensation to which a person is entitled, regard must be had to the following matters only (as assessed in accordance with this Division):
(f) any increase or decrease in the value of any other land of the person at the date of acquisition which adjoins or is severed from the acquired land by reason of the carrying out of, or the proposal to carry out, the public purpose for which the land was acquired.

58 Loss attributable to severance
In this Act:
"**loss attributable to severance**" of land means the amount of any reduction in the market value of any other land of the person entitled to compensation which is caused by that other land being severed from other land of that person.

The assessment of compensation is usually based on a "before and after" method, whereby the value in the "before" acquisition scenario is assessed and the value in the "after" acquisition scenario is assessed and the difference determined. Such a difference may be negative, resulting in compensation being payable, or positive resulting in a windfall gain or betterment which is deducted from compensation paid for severance or disturbance (*G&R Wills & Co Limited v Adelaide City Corporation* 1962 HCA 61; *Moloney v Roads and Maritime Services (No 2)* [2017] NSWLEC 68) (Hemmings 1997).

Related to severance, where compensation may be payable for the effect on the retained land of being severed from the parent parcel, is the notion of injurious affection where compensation may be payable for the negative effect on the retained land of the public purpose. Similarly, the assessment of compensation is usually based on a "before and after" method, whereby the value in the "before" acquisition scenario is assessed (disregarding the public purpose) and the value in the "after" acquisition scenario (having regard to the public purpose) is assessed and the difference determined. Such difference may be negative, resulting in compensation being payable such as arising from the development of a sewage plant (Hemmings 1997).

Disturbance

By way of indicative example, the NSW Act specifies payment for specified forms of disturbance:

59 Loss attributable to disturbance
1   In this Act: **"loss attributable to disturbance"** of land means any of the following:
   a   legal costs reasonably incurred by the persons entitled to compensation in connection with the compulsory acquisition of the land,
   b   valuation fees of a qualified valuer reasonably incurred by those persons in connection with the compulsory acquisition of the land (but not fees calculated by reference to the value, as assessed by the valuer, of the land),
   c   financial costs reasonably incurred in connection with the relocation of those persons (including legal costs but not including stamp duty or mortgage costs),
   d   stamp duty costs reasonably incurred (or that might reasonably be incurred) by those persons in connection with the purchase of land for relocation (but not exceeding the amount that would be incurred for the purchase of land of equivalent value to the land compulsorily acquired),
   e   financial costs reasonably incurred (or that might reasonably be incurred) by those persons in connection with the discharge of a mortgage and the execution of a new mortgage resulting from the relocation (but not exceeding the amount that would be incurred if the new mortgage secured the repayment of the balance owing in respect of the discharged mortgage),
   f   any other financial costs reasonably incurred (or that might reasonably be incurred), relating to the actual use of the land, as a direct and natural consequence of the acquisition.

Each of the heads of disturbance has been subject to extensive litigation with myopic focus on the exact wording of the NSW Act. For example, legal fees and valuation fees generally need a clear connection with the compulsory acquisition itself rather than fees attributable to advice on related issues or issues arising. Relocation costs and stamp duty costs need to be reasonably incurred with a case-specific debate about whether losses are costs.

As may be anticipated, s59(1)(f) is generally the most contentious, being that sub-section within which a wide range of costs (or losses) could potentially be claimed. Despite the NSW Act clearly requiring a series of hurdles to be overcome for a successful claim for compensation, including that such costs be financial, reasonably incurred, relating to the actual use and arising as a direct and natural consequence, the creativity of claims under s59(1)(f) has increased since the common law around compensation for market value became more settled.

As Hemmings (1997) notes, disturbance is an element of personal loss not related to the market value of the land. Disturbance may include costs incurred in the purchasing of comparable property, bridging finance, increased rents, increased building costs, removal expenses, diminution in the value of fixtures, loss of goodwill, loss of profit reinstatement, repairs and alterations to buildings and repairs to fences.

Solatium – disadvantage resulting from relocation

By way of indicative example, the NSW Act specifies the payment of solatium where the acquisition concerns the principal place of residence:

60 Disadvantage resulting from relocation

1   In this Act: "**disadvantage resulting from relocation**" means non-financial disadvantage resulting from the necessity of the person entitled to compensation to relocate the person's principal place of residence as a result of the acquisition.

2   The maximum amount of compensation in respect of the disadvantage resulting from relocation is $75,000. Schedule 1A provides for the amendment of this section to enable the maximum amount of compensation to be increased by regulation and for the automatic indexation of the maximum amount in line with inflation.

3   In assessing the amount of compensation in respect of the disadvantage resulting from relocation, all relevant circumstances are to be taken into account, including:
   a   the interest in the land of the person entitled to compensation, and
   b   the length of time the person has resided on the land (and in particular whether the person is residing on the land temporarily or indefinitely), and
   c   the inconvenience likely to be suffered by the person because of his or her removal from the land, and
   d   the period after the acquisition of the land during which the person has been (or will be) allowed to remain in possession of the land.

4   Compensation is payable in respect of the disadvantage resulting from relocation if the whole of the land is acquired or if any part of the land on which the residence is situated is acquired.

5   Only one payment of compensation in respect of the disadvantage resulting from relocation is payable for land in separate occupation.

6   However, if more than one family resides on the same land, a separate payment may be made in respect of each family if:
   a   the family resides in a separate dwelling-house, or
   b   the Minister responsible for the authority of the State approves of the payment.

7   If separate payments of compensation are made, the maximum amount under subsection (2) applies to each payment, and not to the total payments.

It is interesting that, in principle, the NSW Act recognises that dispossession from the family home is a separate head of compensation, presumably reflecting the connection between the dispossessed, their family home, its memories and significance to the family unit. This may be contrasted to the dispossession of indigenous Australians where their land may be acquired but where, unless there is a family home upon the land, such aspects of spiritual connection are not specified as a separate head of compensation.

Recent developments in the interaction between alternative heads of compensation

Hemmings (1997) states the principle underlying the law of compulsory acquisition in Australia to be:

> It is well established that the dispossessed owner is entitled to not only market value of the land but its value to the owner (whichever be the greater).
>
> *(p. 436)*

Epstein (1985) notes that it was common practice in England until the 1950s to pay 10% higher than the estimated value of the acquired property for incidental losses:

> This bonus can be justified, first, as a balm for the infringement upon autonomy brought about by any forced exchange and, second as an effort to correct the systematic under-estimation of value in the market value test.
>
> *(p. 184)*

The challenge in Australia, however, lies in the wording of the respective compulsory acquisition statutes. Early statutes, such as the NSW *Public Works Act 1912*, provided only for compensation upon resumption for *"the value of the land taken"* and not for the value to the owner (being a notion of worth) (Hemmings 1997, p. 435). Subsequent compulsory acquisition statutes have continued this basis, leaving the dispossessed to seek compensation for worth from among the other available heads of compensation.

Hemmings (1997) notes that compensation for matters such as disturbance, special value and injurious affection originally were not separate heads of consideration and therefore could only be recovered under Judge-made law as part of the concept of *"value to the owner"* (p. 436), though significantly limited as total compensation could not exceed the value of the land.

A trend is emerging in compulsory acquisition litigation in Australia whereby the dispossessed seeks to optimise the claim for market value and maximise any possible claim under any other head of compensation in order, presumably, to be compensated for a notion of worth as well as for the compulsory nature of the dispossession – effectively seeking compensation based on a notion of worth to the forcibly dispossessed owner rather than a concept of value to the market.

With the common law around compensation for market value being generally well settled, dispossessed owners are now seeking to try and fit broader claims for worth within the specific requirements of the statute, leading to an intense focus on the precise wording of the statutory provisions. Using the NSW Act as an example, recent cases have included:

- *Hua and Anor v Hurstville City Council* [2010] NSWLEC 61 which considered the distinction, for the purposes of disturbance, between the relocation of an acquired business and the reinstatement of an acquired business, particularly in the context of a small family business (being a bakery) where the baker's oven, various shop fittings and the electrical and plumbing infrastructure necessary for the operation of the business cannot be economically removed from the acquired property and relocated to an alternative property, such items requiring replacement by new items in alternative premises to effect the relocation and/or reinstatement. While extinguishment of the business would result in a lower compensation payment than relocation/reinstatement, the Court applied latitude in the case of a family business and awarded compensation on the basis of relocation to include reinstatement of the Applicants' bakery business under the disturbance provision of s59(c);

- *George D Angus Pty Limited v Health Administration Corporation* [2013] NSWLEC 212 found the correct construction of s 59(f) of the Just Terms Act to be that the expression *"financial costs"* includes financial losses and is not limited to expenditure. This decision was challenged on appeal (*Health Administration Corporation v George D Angus Pty Ltd* [2014] NSWCA 352), with the appellant unsuccessfully contending that the expression *"financial costs"* in s 59(f) meant only expenditure and did not include financial losses, with any loss or potential loss of income only assessable as special value of the land under s 57 of the Just Terms Act; and

- *Allandale Blue Metal Pty Ltd v Roads and Maritime Services (No 6)* [2015] NSWLEC 18 which considered the value of a rock resource in a quarry and found that, on the construction of the case brought by the Applicant, the Applicant received compensation for the rock resource as market value even though the Applicant's tenant had already received compensation for the same rock resource as disturbance.

Valuation methodology within the statutory framework

For over a century, the approach to the valuation of land for compulsory acquisition matters in Australia has been overshadowed by the High Court decision in *Spencer v Commonwealth* (1907) 5 CLR 418 (*Spencer*). The decision in *Spencer* not only explicitly determined the basis of market value but also implicitly determined the comparable sales method of valuation to be the preferred method for application in compulsory acquisition matters.

Despite the widespread acceptance of the hypothetical development method, the capitalisation method and the discounted cash flow (DCF) method of valuation by the property profession and the property industry for decades, the Courts find enormous difficulty adopting such methods if there is even the remotest possibility that the comparable sales method of valuation could be applied.

The spectre of Spencer v Commonwealth

The basis of market value, for the purposes of compulsory acquisition matters in Australia, was determined by the High Court decision in *Spencer*, with the following drawing heavily upon Parker (2016).

Following the cessation of colonial status with the creation of the Commonwealth of Australia upon Federation on 1 January 1901 and the separation from the UK, the High Court of Australia was only 4 years old when three Judges heard an appeal on a compulsory acquisition matter. The bench was particularly notable, comprising Griffith CJ who was generally claimed to be the principal author of the Constitution of Australia and the first Chief Justice of Australia, Barton J who had previously been the first Prime Minister of Australia from 1901 to 1903 and Isaacs J who became the first Australian-born Governor General of Australia in 1930.

The appeal concerned the acquisition by the Commonwealth of 6 acres, 1 rood and 2 perches (some 2.534 hectares) of land in North Fremantle for the construction of a fort in anticipation of a Japanese invasion, being described as follows:

> The land consists of sand-hummocks overlooking the Indian Ocean. It has no grass; and it is useless in its present condition for any purpose of production.

with Mr Spencer claiming compensation of £10,000 and the High Court awarding the sum of £3,000, being that which had previously been admitted and paid into Court.

The significance of the decision lies in the way in which the Judges constructed the concept of market value:

> In my judgement, the test of value of land is to be determined, not by inquiring what price a man desiring to sell could actually have obtained for it on a given day, ie, whether there was in fact on that day a willing buyer, but by inquiring "What would a man desiring to buy the land have had to pay for it on that day to a vendor willing to sell it for a fair price but not desirous to sell?" It is, no doubt, very difficult to answer such a question, and any answer must be to some extent conjectural. The necessary mental process is to put yourself as far as possible in the position of persons conversant with the subject at the relevant time, and from that point of view to ascertain what, according to then current opinion of land values, a purchaser would have had to offer for the land to induce such a willing vendor to sell it, or, in other words, to inquire at what point a desirous purchaser and a not unwilling vendor would come together.
>
> *(Griffiths CJ)*

> And I should say, in view of the many authorities cited and upon the sense of the matter, that a claimant is entitled to have for his land what it is worth to a man of ordinary prudence and foresight, not holding his land for merely speculative purposes, nor, on the other hand, anxious to sell for any compelling or private reason, but willing to sell as a business man would be to another such person, both of them alike uninfluenced by any consideration of sentiment or need.
>
> *(Barton J)*

> To arrive at the value of the land on that date, we have, as I conceive, to suppose it sold then, not by means of a forced sale, but by voluntary bargaining between the plaintiff and a purchaser, willing to trade, but neither of them so anxious to do so that he would overlook any ordinary business consideration. We must further suppose both to be perfectly acquainted with the land, and cognizant of all circumstances which might affect its value, either advantageously or prejudicially, including its situation, character, quality, proximity to conveniences or inconveniences, its surrounding features, the then present demand for land, and the likelihood, as then appearing to persons best capable of forming an opinion, of a rise or fall for what reason soever in the amount which one would otherwise be willing to fix as the value of the property.
>
> *(Isaacs J)*

together with:

> In order that any article may have an exchange value, there must be presupposed a person willing to give the article in exchange for money and another willing to give money in exchange for the article.
>
> *(Griffiths CJ)*

> … value implies the existence of a willing buyer as well as of a willing seller…
>
> *(Griffiths CJ)*

Prosperity unexpected, or depression, which no man would ever have anticipated, if happening after the date named, must be alike disregarded.

(Isaacs J)

... the all important fact on that day is the opinion regarding the fair price of the land, which a hypothetical prudent purchaser would entertain, if he desired to purchase it for the most advantageous purpose for which it was adapted. The plaintiff is to be compensated; therefore he is to receive the money equivalent to the loss he has sustained by deprivation of his land, and that... cannot exceed what such a prudent purchaser would be prepared to give him.

(Isaacs J)

Within the Judges' construction of the concept of market value, the following elements may be identified that are consistent with the IVS definition of market value (Parker 2016):

- an estimated amount: *could actually have obtained for it, have had to pay* (Griffith CJ), *value of the land, the fair price of the land* (Isaacs J);
- an exchange: *a man desiring to buy the land have had to pay for it... to a vendor willing to sell, may have an exchange value* (Griffith CJ), *willing to trade* (Isaacs J);
- a valuation date: *on a given day, on that day* (Griffith CJ), *on that date, prosperity unexpected, or depression,... if happening after the date named* (Isaacs J);
- a willing buyer: *a man desiring to buy the land, a desirous purchaser, willing buyer* (Griffith CJ), *voluntary bargaining, willing to trade, hypothetical prudent purchaser* (Isaacs J);
- a willing seller: *a vendor willing to sell it for a fair price, a not unwilling vendor* (Griffith CJ), *voluntary bargaining, willing to trade* (Isaacs J);
- a knowledgeable and prudent buyer and seller: *to a man of ordinary prudence and foresight, willing to sell as a business man would be to another such person* (Barton J), *perfectly acquainted with the land, hypothetical prudent purchaser* (Isaacs J);
- an absence of compulsion: *but not desirous to sell* (Griffith CJ), *nor, on the other hand, anxious to sell for any compelling or private reason, uninfluenced by any consideration of sentiment or need* (Barton J), *not by means of a forced sale, overlook any ordinary business consideration* (Isaacs J); and
- an assumption of highest and best use: *the most advantageous purpose for which it was adapted* (Isaacs J).

While *Spencer* has assumed almost mythical status in Australian litigation and case law and forms the foundation for the IVS definition of market value, it should be recognised as constrained by its context and circumstances:

- it concerned a block of vacant, undeveloped land rather than a high-rise building in the CBD or other form of property;
- it occurred at a time when the currency of conversation in the community was the sale of blocks of land providing extensive comparable evidence, not of land upon which income-producing structures were built and acquired for investment purposes which may sell infrequently;
- it occurred at a time when the hypothetical parties were private individuals in a local market, not international multi-billion investors acting in a global market;

- it requires conversance, perfect acquaintance with the subject property and cognisance of circumstances affecting value, being a vacant block of land, not comprehensive knowledge or concepts of market efficiency.

Accordingly, while very useful as a statement of principal, it is often challenging to apply to modern investment property where the vendors, purchasers, marketing process, role of information in price formation and so forth differ radically from that for a vacant block of undeveloped suburban land.

As Hemmings (1997) notes, it is premised on a *"selling approach"* (p. 438), being the price achievable on an appropriately conducted hypothetical sale, clearly rejecting notions of worth (*what price a man desiring to sell could actually have obtained*) and so distinguishing claims for market value from other forms of claims for value to owner.

Valuation methodology within the statutory framework

The decision in *Spencer* not only explicitly determined the basis of market value but also implicitly determined the comparable sales method of valuation to be the preferred method for application in compulsory acquisition matters. Despite the unsuitability of the comparable sales method of valuation for certain properties, the Courts have been reluctant to embrace hypothetical development or income methods, including DCF, except as a last resort.

Though Wells J stated a general principle of willingness to consider alternative methods:

> ... I am not disposed to reject any method of valuation adopted by either valuer on the ground that it is not worth considering; it seems to be that if Spencer's case is to keep its practical worth in this jurisdiction, this court should be slow to reject any method that, in expert hands, is capable of yielding a result within bounds that are not unreasonable. The limitations of every method must, of course, always be kept clearly in mind.
>
> *(Bronzel v State Planning Authority (1979) 44 LGRA 34v at 38)*

while Hemmings (1997) observes:

> Valuation based upon proper analysis of comparable sales must always be preferred to any hypothetical or capitalisation approach.
>
> *(p. 439)*

Comparable sales method of valuation

Hemmings (1997) describes the comparable sales method of valuation as follows:

> Value may be best ascertained by inference from the price at which "comparable" land has been sold in the market. Whilst no sales of identical land are likely to be available the test is prices obtained in arms' length recent sales on usual terms of land "capable of being compared" with the subject land. An expert is entitled to apply adjustments to take account of differences, unusual or unique features and special potentialities of the acquired land.
>
> *(p. 439)*

While the comparable sales approach may appear straightforward, the Courts have attached a range of conditions to its application:

- concerning offers, while not evidence of a concluded sale, may be taken into account as evidence of a market and some evidence of value, being at least evidence of the interest of the owner in selling and others in negotiating the sale of the land (Hemmings 1997);
- concerning subsequent events, while not impacting value at the date of acquisition, may be admissible if confirming a foresight (*Housing Commission of NSW v Falconer* 1981 1 NSW LR 547);
- concerning sales to the acquiring authority, whilst not impermissible as evidence, should be treated with considerable caution (Hemmings 1997);
- concerning the process of adjustment of comparable sales:
  - a preference for as few adjustments as possible in a consistent manner (*Holcim (Australia) Pty Ltd v Valuer General* [2009] NSWLEC 225 at 31);
  - caution where large explicit and/or implicit adjustments are required, with particular caution required for large implicit adjustments (*Graham Trilby v Valuer General* [2008] NSWLEC 217 at 36);
  - a preference for separately itemised and reasoned explicit adjustments to an implicit process comprising a single adjustment (*Tomago Aluminium Company Pty Ltd v Valuer General* [2010] NSWLEC 4 at 45);
  - a preference for a transparent process of explicit adjustment leading to an explicable assessment of value rather than an opaque process of implicit adjustment leasing to an assertion of value (*Jessica Investments Pty Ltd v Valuer General* [2008] NSWLEC 1375 at 6);
  - a preference for an adjustment process that works forwards from the comparable sales to derive an opinion of value, rather than working backwards to justify an opinion of value previously formed (*Graham Trilby v Valuer General* [2008] NSWLEC 217 at 35); and
  - an acknowledgement that insufficient transparency in the adjustment process risks rejection of the valuation evidence (*Tomago Aluminium Company Pty Ltd v Valuer General* [2010] NSWLEC 4 at 45) (Parker 2015).

While such an extensive range of conditions might be expected to bring transparency to the application of the comparable sales valuation process, the continued simple unsupported assertion of value by expert witnesses led to a series of decisions in the NSW Land and Environment Court commonly identifying four steps in the comparable sales valuation process, summarised in *Adams v Valuer General* [2014] NSWLEC1005:

1   accumulation – the accumulation step seeks to identify and establish a pool of relevant comparable sales from which information may be deduced concerning the value of the subject property (at 32);
2   analysis – the analysis step provides a common basis of measurement by seeking to convert all potentially comparable sales to a common basis of expression such as a unitary rate (rate per square metre, rate per hectare, etc) improved or unimproved (through allowance for the absence of existence of improvements, etc) (at 38);
3   adjustment – the adjustment step acknowledges the fact that no two properties are ever identical and seeks to convert those analysed potentially comparable sales to a hypothetical expression of value as a unitary rate in the context of the subject property through

the reflection of differences (such as size, location, use, date, etc) between the respective potentially comparable sales and the subject property (at 40); and

4   application – the application step seeks to determine the value of the subject property through a consideration of the relevance (such as being limited, indirect or direct) of the unitary rate derived from those adjusted comparable sales relative to the subject (at 56).

Capitalisation of income method of valuation

The capitalisation of income method was accepted by Mitchell J for the valuation of income producing land and property:

> [I]t was necessary to fix the net rental value of the premises on the basis of a rack-rent, taking from that rack-rent proper deductions to arrive at a net annual value to the owner, and then to choose a rate of capitalisation.
>
> *(Hill v Commissioner of Highways (1966) 13 LGRA 369 at 375)*

Hypothetical development method of valuation

Being dependent on the assessment of numerous interactive variables, the hypothetical development method of valuation is relatively controversial, being described by Sugarman J as the derivation of land value through the assumption that a party:

> ... erects a hypothetical building upon the subject land, capitalises the anticipated net return therefrom, and subtracts the estimated building cost from the capitalisation, the balance being treated as the value of the site.
>
> *(AG Robertson Ltd v Valuer General (1952)*
> *18 LGR (NSW) 261 at 262)*

with a preference, where possible, for valuation by comparable sales:

> It has been said that because many estimates and assumptions must be made the hypothetical development method ought not be used where some use can be made of a comparable sale.
>
> *(Gwynvill Properties Pty Ltd v Commissioner for Main Roads (1983)*
> *50 LGRA 322 at 326)*

and:

> ... the residual approach involves a higher risk of reaching unrealistic results than the direct comparison approach.
>
> *(Graham Trilby Pty Limited v Valuer General [2008]*
> *NSWLEC 217 at 32)*

but may be considered in *"the absence of directly comparable sales"* (*Graham Trilby Pty Limited v Valuer General* [2009] NSWLEC 1087 at 41) or the very limited availability of relevant comparable sales evidence (*Gwynvill Properties Pty Ltd v Commissioner for Main Roads* (1983) 50 LGRA 322) (Parker 2015).

Discounted cash flow method of valuation

While DCF may be used as an income method of valuation or as a dynamic hypothetical development method of valuation and despite its global use in property valuation, the Courts are disinclined to accept it if any other alternative may be available.

The source of such disinclination may be found in a common misunderstanding of the findings in *Albany v Commonwealth* 1976 60 LGRA 287 where Jacobs J considered and rejected the use of DCF in the valuation of urban and residential development land. However, His Honour clearly stated:

> However, I would not consider it safe to adopt the indicated figure as a correct valuation of the lands, because I am not satisfied of the suitability in this case of a method of valuation based on discounted cash flow.

such that DCF methods were not rejected in principle but only "*in this case*". The decision, however, constrained the acceptability of DCF methods of valuation by the Courts for the next two decades.

In more recent years, DCF has become more common and has been accepted as a method of valuation of land and business, including by Talbot J in *Collex Pty Ltd v Roads and Traffic Authority of New South Wales* [2006] NSWLEC 579, His Honour commenting at para 82:

> 82 Although Courts have clearly experienced difficulty from time to time in accepting the DCF method due to the unreliability of the assumptions made for the purpose of the analysis, it is nonetheless a method which can be accepted where the special facts and circumstances pertaining to the subject land make it appropriate to do so.

This was supported by Pain J in *Allandale Blue Metal Pty Ltd v Roads and Maritime Services (No 6)* [2015] NSWLEC 18, a case concerning the valuation of a quarry, where Her Honour commented at para 304:

> 304 The Court accepts that the DCF method can be usefully applied to value the resource in the land in the before and after scenarios.

Accordingly, while the principal of acceptability of the DCF method of valuation appears settled, the comparable sales method of valuation remains the Court's preferred approach.

Alternative dispute resolution

Within the principal Australian jurisdictions, alternative dispute resolution has become a popular approach to the just, quick and cheap disposal of compulsory acquisition proceedings, avoiding the need for a full Court hearing.

Alternative dispute resolution is particularly useful where the dispossessed is self-represented or of limited funds, where there is ambiguity or misunderstanding between the parties concerning facts, opinions, calculations or reliance on certain comparable sales or where the difference in dispute is disproportionate to the cost of litigation.

Conversely, alternative dispute resolution may not be useful where there is a genuine difference between the parties concerning the interpretation of a point of law or where the parties have fundamentally different approaches to the matter, necessitating resolution by a full Court hearing.

The most common approaches adopted to alternative dispute resolution in Australia include neutral evaluation, mediation and conciliation:

Neutral evaluation

Neutral evaluation is a process of evaluation of a dispute in which an impartial evaluator seeks to identify and reduce the issues of fact and law in dispute. The evaluator's role includes assessing the relative strengths and weaknesses of each party's case and offering an opinion as to the likely outcome of the proceedings, including any likely findings or the award of damages (LEC Annual Review 2017).

Mediation

Mediation is a process in which the parties to a dispute, with the assistance of an impartial mediator, identify the disputed issues, develop options, consider alternatives and endeavour to reach an agreement. The mediator has no advisory or determinative role in regard to the content of the dispute or the outcome of its resolution, but may advise on or determine the process of mediation whereby resolution is attempted (LEC Annual Review 2017).

By way of example, the NSW Land & Environment Court may refer matters to mediation at the request of the parties or of its own volition, with Table 17.1 showing the number of matters referred to mediation over the last 5 years in Class 3, being the rating valuation and compulsory acquisition class, with the numbers being relatively low because of the ready availability and use of conciliation by the Court (LEC Annual Review 2017).

Conciliation

Conciliation is a process in which the parties to a dispute, with the assistance of an impartial conciliator, identify the issues in dispute, develop options, consider alternatives and endeavour to reach agreement. The conciliator may have an advisory role on the content of the dispute or the outcome of its resolution, but not a determinative role. The conciliator may advise on or determine the process of conciliation whereby resolution is attempted, and may make suggestions for terms of settlement, give expert advice on likely settlement terms and may actively encourage the parties to reach agreement (LEC Annual Review 2017).

By way of example, the NSW Land & Environment Court may refer a compulsory acquisition matter to conciliation under s34 of the NSW Act, to be conducted by a Commissioner with valuation expertise, prior to going to hearing. The parties have a duty to participate in the conciliation conference in good faith (s34(1A)). If the parties are able to reach agreement

Table 17.1 Land and environment court of NSW matters referred to mediation 2012–2016

	2012	2013	2014	2015	2016
Total referred	9	9	4	2	5
Number finalised pre-hearing	9	9	3	1	5
Finalised pre-hearing (%)	100	100	75	50	100

Source: LEC Annual Review (2017).

Table 17.2 Land and environment court of NSW matters referred to conciliation 2012–2016

	2012	2013	2014	2015	2016
S34 conferences	911	899	1,169	1,500	2,035

Source: LEC Annual Review (2017).

following conciliation, being a decision that the Court could have made in the proper exercise of its functions, then the Commissioner may record the decision as a decision of the Court and dispose of the proceedings (s34(3), s34(8)). If the parties are unable to reach agreement, the Commissioner terminates the conciliation conference (s34(4)) and may only adjudicate a later hearing with the agreement of the parties (s34(13)) (LEC Annual Review 2017).

Table 17.2 shows the number of matters referred to mediation over the last 5 years in all Classes, including, but not limited to, rating valuation and compulsory acquisition matters, with the total number of matters being relatively high, reflecting the popularity of this form of alternative dispute resolution (LEC Annual Review 2017).

Summary and conclusion

With the Australian Commonwealth and State governments investing hundreds of billions of dollars in infrastructure projects over the next few years, the extent of compulsory acquisition activity in Australia may be expected to increase exponentially.

Therefore, the increasing trend to the adoption of alternative dispute resolution processes, either by the choice of the parties or by compulsion of the Courts or statute, is to be commended to facilitate the just, quick and cheap disposal of compulsory acquisition disputes, so avoiding the need for a full Court hearing.

It is understandable, where there is a genuine difference between the parties concerning the interpretation of a point of law or where the parties have fundamentally different approaches to the issues, that a matter may not be resolvable by alternative dispute resolution and may require resolution by a full Court hearing. However, such matters may be relatively few and so consume relatively little of the various Courts' time.

A greater risk to consumption of the various Courts' time in compulsory acquisition matters may be expected to arise from parties and their legal advisors seeking to explore all opportunities to secure some form of value to the owner (being notions of worth as well as attempting to recognise the compulsory nature of the dispossession), through innovative interpretations of the disturbance or special value provisions of statutes, given that the common law on market value is now relatively well settled. Accordingly, it may be anticipated that a range of matters may be litigated at first instance, then appealed, over the next decade that either settle or expand the interpretations of disturbance and special value within the precise wording of the respective statutes, providing a dynamic era for compulsory acquisition law and valuation in Australia.

References

Caldwell, F. 2017. "Queensland budget 2017: Jobs, infrastructure spending and surpluses", *Brisbane Times*, 13 June 2017, available at www.brisbanetimes.com.au/politics/queensland/queensland-budget-2017-jobs-infrastructure-spending-and-surpluses (accessed 4 December 2017).

Epstein, R.A. 1985. *Takings: Private Property and the Power of Eminent Domain*, Harvard University Press, Cambridge.

Hemmings, N. 1997. *Compensation in Valuation Principles and Practice*, First Edition, Australian Institute of Valuers and Land Economists, Deakin.

LEC Annual Review 2017. *Land & Environment Court of NSW Annual Review 2016*, State of NSW, Sydney.

Liberal Party of Australia 2013. "Only the coalition will deliver the infrastructure of the future", *Media Release*, 5 September 2013, available at www.liberal.org.au/latest-news/2013/09/05/only-coalition-will-deliver-infrastructure-future (accessed 18 May 2015).

Norington, B. 2017. "Budget 2017: Turnbull to embark on ambitious infrastructure spending program", *The Australian*, 9 May 2017, available at www.theaustralian.com.au/budget-2017/turnbull-to-embark-on-ambitious-infrastructure-spending-program/news-story (accessed 4 December 2017).

NSW Government 2017. NSW Budget 2017–18, Budget Paper No. 2, Infrastructure Statement, NSW Government, Sydney.

Parker, D. 2015. "The 2012 metamorphosis of the common law of compulsory acquisition valuation in Australia", *Common Law World Review*, Vol. 44, No. 3, pp. 175–191.

Parker, D. 2016. *International Valuation Standards: A Guide to the Valuation of Real Property Assets*, Wiley Blackwell, Chichester.

Queensland Budget 2017. https://budget.qld.gov/budget-highlights/infrastructure/ (accessed 4 December 2017).

Rostron, S. 2017. "NSW Budget 2016–17: $20bn infrastructure spend for roads and rails", available at https://blog.plantminer.com.au/nsw-budget-2016-17-20bn-infrastructure-spend-for-roads-and-rails (accessed 4 December 2017).

Utopia, 2015. www.abc.net.au/tv/programs/utopia/ (accessed 18 May 2015).

18

Challenges in compulsory acquisition of land in Kenya[1]

Owiti Abiero K'Akumu and Washington H.A. Olima

Introduction

This chapter explores the challenges encountered in the use of compulsory acquisition of land as an instrument of land policy. A timeline approach is adopted where the challenges are sequenced into three legal regimes that are historical: the colonial era (1895–1963), the independence constitution era (1963–2010), and the 2010 Kenya Constitution era (from 2010). In the colonial era, the main challenge was the absence of a legal regime for acquisition. This was created by borrowing the Indian Land Acquisition Act of 1894.

During the independence constitution era, the main challenge was litigation for registered land and the lack of a cadastre for unregistered land. These challenges have remained even in the current era of the 2010 Kenya Constitution. The chapter therefore proceeds as follows: the policy environment covering the legal and constitutional provisions, historical challenges during both the colonial era and the independence constitution era, and the emerging new challenges in the 2010 Kenya Constitution era. The chapter finally presents recommendations and conclusion.

The policy environment

The legal and constitutional provisions for compulsory land acquisition are both historical and contemporary. There are three epochs in the time line of compulsory acquisition in Kenya: the imperial or colonial era, the independence constitutional era, and the 2010 Kenya Constitution era.

During the imperial period, the Kenyan territory formed part of the larger British Empire circa 1889–1963. The process of transforming Kenya, hitherto a patchwork of stateless tribal communities, into a nation-state took place mainly in the decade of 1895–1904, what Lonsdale (1989) termed as "The conquest state". It is within this period that compulsory acquisition of land was first applied in Kenya. The territory was declared the British East Africa Protectorate on 15 June 1895 (Okoth-Ogendo 1991).

The independence Constitution brought in a new legal regime of land use and ownership management and it made express provisions for the applications of compulsory land acquisition. Section 75 (1) i) of the Constitution provided that the State could take possession of private land if it was necessary in the interest of defence, public security, land use planning, among others, or where the development and utilisation of property was to promote the public benefit. This section specifically applied to private lands with titles registered under the land registration statutes. However, there is another category of land, the communal land or land held under African customary tenure, that was not registered, also known as Trust land.

Sections 117 and 118 of the Constitution applied where Trust land was concerned. Section 117 empowered the relevant county council in which the land was vested in trust for the inhabitants to compulsorily acquire the land if it was required by a public body for public purposes or if it was required by a person or private entity for a purpose that would bring benefit to local inhabitants.

Sections 75 and 117/118 were implemented by relevant statutes i.e., the Land Acquisition Act Chapter 295 and the Trust Land Act Chapter 188 of the laws of Kenya, respectively. Chapter 295 was the postcolonial reincarnation of the Indian Land Acquisition Act, while Chapter 288 was of the Native Lands Ordinance.

In 2010, Kenya introduced a completely new Constitution that totally repudiated the Independence Constitution. In terms of nomenclature, the 2010 Kenya Constitution converted Trust land to Community land, while land that was acquired under the Land Acquisition Act is now known as "Private Land". To implement the provisions of Article 63(5) of the Constitution on the management of Community land, the Community Land Bill of 2015 is being processed into law. At section 5(4), the Bill has made it clear that Community land can be compulsorily acquired if needed for public purpose subject to prompt payment of just compensation in full to the rights holders. However, the Bill has not made provisions on how the acquisition is to be undertaken, unlike its predecessor, the Trust Land Act. Part VIII of the Land Act No. 6 of 2012 made provisions for compulsory acquisition of interests in land, but this generally refers to registered land and may not exactly apply to former Trust land that is essentially unregistered.

Challenges during the colonial era

When the British colonialists came to Kenya, the first imperial development project they embarked on was the construction of the Uganda Railway necessary for connecting the source of River Nile to the East African coast for the territorial protection of Egypt against the Germans and for opening up the hinterland for trade and agriculture (K'Akumu 2002). Hardinge, the first Commissioner of the Protectorate, faced the challenge of acquiring land for the construction of the railway in a territory where the British Crown did not own title to land. At this time, the Protectorate consisted of two parts: the dominions of the Sultan of Zanzibar comprising of the Island of Zanzibar and the 10-mile strip of the main land; and beyond the 10-mile strip into the hinterland.

The Commissioner was forced by circumstances to invoke the Indian Land Acquisition Act of 1894 to acquire land owned by British nationals within the Sultan's dominions and beyond the 10-mile strip (Okoth-Ogendo 1991). Sorrenson (1967) noted that compensation was not paid for the latter except in Kikuyu country. Lands belonging to the subjects within the Sultan's dominions were acquired through fetwa—a device in Muslim law similar to a compulsory acquisition edit—issued by the Sultan (Okoth-Ogendo 1991).

Challenges during the independence Constitutional era

Litigation

The main challenge to the compulsory acquisition of land during the period of the independence Constitution was litigation especially in relation to dissatisfaction with the quantum of compensation. Generally, the condamnees were dissatisfied with the level of compensation awarded because of their high expectations. A development project usually involves a huge outlay of money, and the expropriatees expected to benefit from this fund. Nevertheless the levels of compensation awarded are usually below market values because of the method of valuation the government used to arrive at the compensation awarded. The practice is that compensation is calculated by the government valuer. For the purposes of documentary evidence, the valuer would rely on declared sales in the land register in order to arrive at the market value. Unfortunately, the sales recorded in the register are usually understated in order to reduce the financial burden of stamp duty usually pegged at a percentage of the declared sale price (4% for urban and 2% for rural lands). Data from private treaty sales are usually not reliable even where they are be available.

The challenge of litigation was prominently in the case of Thika Dam component of the Third Nairobi Water Supply Project that was scheduled for construction in 1991, 1992, and part of 1993. However, litigation delayed possession of the project site by 126 days (K'Akumu 1996) and led to a contractor's claim for 'idle time' of Kenya Shilling (Ksh) 55,571,868 or US$ 551,434 (Olima and K'Akumu 1999). In this case, about 80 landowners contested the awards in the High Court, claiming that the compensation of Ksh 52,595,299 awarded by the government was too low and demanding instead Ksh 158,606,031. The gap between the amount claimed and the amount awarded was clearly over Ksh 100 million, thereby making it very difficult to reconcile the parties. The stalemate lasted for some time, thereby causing delays in project implementation. Unfortunately, the land of the claimants in question was in the very centre of that required for the dam construction, and work therefore could not continue before the settlement of their case.

There was an attempt to take possession of the site before compensation was paid. However, this move was quashed when the landowners applied for and were granted a court injunction to maintain the *status quo* until when the case was determined. The attempt also resulted in more litigation. The people also brought an action of contempt of court against those involved in the attempt to take possession of the site.

In the end the court awarded the claimants a flat rate of 22% of the original compensation offered in addition to the government's award regardless of whether the claims were on land or improvements. The claimants accepted this and agreed to vacate the site for construction to begin. The most important cause of litigation here therefore clearly concerns adequate compensation. The landowners felt that the compensation offered was inadequate.

The 1990 amendments

The litigation partly arose from the constitutional provision that gave property owners direct access to the High Court to challenge issues of compulsory acquisition. Subsection (2) of Section 75 provided safeguards for the property owners by granting them direct access to the High Court for:

i   the legality of the taking of possession or acquisition of the property interest or right; and
ii the purpose of obtaining prompt payment of that compensation.

Following the experiences of the Thika Dam project, to reduce litigation and hence eliminate legal disruption to the acquisition process, the government introduced the 1990 amendments to the Land Acquisition Act. The amendment introduced the Land Acquisition Compensation Tribunal to deal with cases against the Commissioner of Land's decision under section 19. Under this new arrangement, claimants were not granted direct access to the High Court for the following, as previously provided by the Act:

i   the determination of their interest or right in or over land; nor for
ii the amount of compensation paid or offered; subsection (8) now provides for the public body benefiting from the acquisition to contest compensation awarded to claimants in the tribunal.

A party dissatisfied with the decision of the tribunal was given the right to appeal to the High Court on any of the following grounds:

i   if the decision of the tribunal is contrary to law or to some usage having the force of law;
ii   if the decision failed to determine some material issue of law or usage having the force of law; or
iii if a substantial error or defect in the procedure provided in the Act has produced an error or defect in the decision of the case upon its merits.

The third provision made it possible for claimants to appeal over a wide range of issues. The amendment allowed for an appeal against the High Court's decision to the Court of Appeal only on a point of law.

The creation of the tribunal is within the Constitutional provisions, and a similar tribunal (the Lands Tribunal) existed in Britain. However, so far it has not been tested. The tribunal may be of some help because it will be made up of experts, a triumvirate of one advocate and two valuers. Hence, technical cases regarding compensation matters will be heard by specialists, not ordinary judges who might not understand them. Only matters akin to the interpretation of law would be referred to the latter.

Delayed payment of compensation

The inability of the government to pay prompt compensation to the claimants as stipulated in the Constitution was another major challenge. The government's contribution to the project was to assist in the provision of land for the implementation of the project. According to the initial estimates, the government had to provide Ksh 86 million for the purpose of land acquisition. Normally, the Commissioner of Lands would not begin the acquisition process without a written commitment that compensation cash was available. Since there was no money forthcoming from the Treasury, the City Council of Nairobi decided to provide an initial Ksh 50 million to avoid delays in the acquisition, with the understanding that the Treasury was to provide the remaining amount and also reimburse the City Hall. At a time of critical shortage, the Treasury was only able to release Ksh 20 million. By this time the costs had increased to Ksh 120 million because of an increase in acreage to be acquired for the project.

Fortunately, the litigation temporarily stalled the critical need for compensation funds. Toward the end of the interlude, the Commissioner of Lands requested that "Now that the Court cases are to be determined soon I fear that there will be no money to effect the determined compensation. Could you please take action towards provision of the required funds to avoid further litigation and possible delays in execution of the project" (K'Akumu 1996, p. 97). Unfortunately, in the end there was no money available to pay the court-determined compensation. Out of the total of Ksh 70 million so far provided, the Commissioner of Lands had paid out Ksh 56,156,477 to landowners who had accepted the awards leaving only Ksh 11,843,523 against a compensation sum of Ksh 63 million to be paid to the 80 landowners who had litigated (K'Akumu 1996, p. 97). The question is if there had been no litigation, how could the problem of the inadequacy of funds have been resolved?

By this time, the City Council was losing millions of shillings in contractual claims as a result of the non-availability of the site. The Water and Sewerage Department, the consulting engineers, and Commissioner of Lands tried to save the situation by paying for the land necessary for work to begin. The total amount required for this purpose was Ksh 18,844,968. The City Council provided a further Ksh 6,844,968 in addition to the balance from earlier payments. However, the claimants marched on Ministry of Lands Offices and vowed not to accept piecemeal compensation. Later, the Treasury managed to release Ksh 30 million to add to the funds already deposited with the Commissioner of Lands, but this still left a shortage of Ksh 10.7 million, which again was provided by City Council to help settle the claims (Table 18.1).

Note that the release of funds spanned a period of 27 months. This was a long a time for compensation which was expected to be 'prompt'. The Commissioner of Land's office had tried to invoke section 19 of the Land Acquisition Act so that construction could commence. The valuation office had asserted that "Payment of compensation is not a precondition for the taking of possession" (K'Akumu 1996, p. 98). However, this did not work out because of the assertive nature of the claimants who refused the piecemeal settlement of compensation.

Resettlement

A resettlement challenge arose earlier than the actual land acquisition in this project. According to the *Nation* newspaper, "The project affects about 300 families and over 3,000 individuals. They would be happier to be allocated with a single piece of land equal to what you are taking rather than being asked to look for alternative land individually" (K'Akumu 1996, p. 92). The Interim Committee of Thika Dam Affected Families (in a letter copied to local and national administrative organs), wrote to the Commissioner of Lands in conjunction with City Council of Nairobi that "We are… beseeching you because you hold our

Table 18.1 Schedule of the release of compensation

Date of release of check	Payer	Amount in Ksh
June 30, 1988	CCN	50,000,000
August 9, 1989	GOK	20,000,000
August 23, 1990	CCN	4,436,869
September 3, 1990	CCN	2,408,099
September 19, 1990	GOK	30,000,000
September 14, 1990	CCN	10,700,000
Total		127,544,968

Source: K'Akumu (1996, p. 98).

future and… lives in your hands, to consider giving alternative settlement in form of land even if it means at least 2 acres [0.8 hectares] per family in a potentially good area" (K'Akumu 1996, p. 92). According to the Interim Committee, this was necessary because:

a   any compensation in the form of money only would not be of much benefit because of the difficulties in finding, acquiring, and developing an alternative piece of land; and
b   some heads of families might misuse all the cash given as compensation.

The profile given to resettlement in these two instances moved certain government departments into action. The issue of resettlement was considered as purely administrative and was left to the Permanent Secretary (Local Government) and the Provincial Administration. They managed to identify suitable land i.e., the portion of Samar Farm in Murang'a District which had been sold to Mbo-i-Kamiti and Murang'a County Council (K'Akumu 1996).

Initially, the government expressed its willingness to purchase the land for the purposes of resettlement (K'Akumu 1996). However, the advice from Lands Department was that the government should not be directly involved in resettlement issues as this would create a serous precedence whereby a landowner would expect to be compensated in kind for land acquired (K'Akumu 1996). The advice was agreeable to all concerned. Resettlement was to be dealt with as a policy issue. The Permanent Secretary (Local Government) had noted that "I have addressed the question of resettlement… to the Head of Civil service since this matter requires policy decision by the Government" (K'Akumu 1996, p. 93).

Since the Ministry of Lands was the technical arm of the government and well-versed with issues of land, its advice and guidance was followed in this case. It was agreed that the government would only facilitate resettlement by ensuring that land was available for purchase by the expropriated landowners. The landowners were on the other hand expected to pay for land at its market price. However, it was up to the relevant government institutions to pay prompt compensation to the land owners so that they did not lose the chance of buying the land for resettlement. In the end, however, compensation was not paid promptly, and the chance was lost.

Resettlement as a problem was acute in the very beginning when the Commissioner of Lands first attempted to obtain the Minister's approval in order to go ahead with the acquisition. The Commissioner of Lands had noted that "I had prepared a draft of the Minister's instructions but the then Minister had some reservations regarding the people who were to be displaced" (K'Akumu 1996, p. 94). This demonstrated the conflict in the treatment of resettlement issues by different facets of the government, and in the process of resolving this conflict time was lost—to the disadvantage of the project implementation programme.

This chapter has discussed challenges experienced when registered land is acquired under the Land Acquisition Act. Now attention is focused on unregistered land acquired under the Trust Land Act. These challenges were experienced in yet another dam project—the Kiambere Hydro-Electric Power Dam Project—implemented along the Tana River course in the Embu and Kitui districts.

Cadastral challenge

The main challenge here related to the incomplete or non-availability of a cadastre. For instance, the land on the Embu side had been adjudicated; however, it was treated as Trust land. This is because registration had not been undertaken. Consequently, the people were not able to effectively assert their rights. As has been noted, in Trust land, rights are less defined. This is confirmed by the Provincial Land Adjudication officer who he wrote that:

> Actually Riachina and Mutitu Adjudication section are not registered, subsequently, they both fall within the jurisdiction of Land Adjudication Department and not the Department of Lands. You should therefore regard your 3 pieces of land as your own property and it is you who should make every endeavour to check their existence and do all you can to have them assessed by whoever is acquiring them.
>
> *(K'Akumu 1996, p. 61)*

This treatment of Trust land or 'African' land as 'inferior' is a reflection of the colonial hang-over that continues to beset land rights in Kenya. The fact that Trust land falls within the definition of "lesser rights" means that compensation cannot be adequate in terms of achieving a replacement livelihood for the occupants. People on the other hand are deeply aware of their innate rights to land, and this sets the scene for protests which may result in litigation.

On the Kitui side where no adjudication had been done, the adjudication machinery had to be put in place to accomplish its mission before the valuers went in to determine compensation. The procedure therefore is that the Compulsory Acquisition Act compensation schedule applies to both Trust and registered lands. The setting apart of Trust land and the compulsory acquisition of registered land therefore follows the same procedure. In the case of Trust land, rights have to be ascertained through adjudication, and the only stage that remains is just registration before acquisition is effected. This stage is, however, only procedural.

The problem with this process is that the work is quite demanding in terms of time and human resources, and it cannot be accomplished within the short time pending acquisition. The result is a host of mistakes/errors in the computation of areas and the quantum of compensation. This again is a potential ground for complaints and litigation. In the case of Kiambere, however, the claimants never resorted to the latter.

Assessment of market value

Although the Constitution and Land Acquisition Act stipulate adequate compensation as a condition for acquisition, compensation here seemed far from adequate. 'Adequate compensation' means amount of compensation that will put the expropriatees in the same position after acquisition as they were before. The people themselves seemed to understand this, as expressed by the Nthawa Mutitu Lands Committee:

> We the undersigned on behalf of the above committee kindly request you to consider in your compensation to us award a value which will enable us to buy alternative land within the district equivalent to the land taken by the above project [sic]. This is to avoid creating landlessness to those of us who are affected by the project.
>
> *(K'Akumu 1996, p. 64)*

The implication of this statement is that adequate compensation must be based on market value. Market value is defined as the value which a property is expected to realise in the open market under three main assumptions (Syagga 1994):

i   the transaction is between willing buyer and willing seller;
ii both are perfectly aware of the market/price situation concerning similar properties; and
iii reasonable time is given to expose the property in the market to as many buyers as possible.

All these conditions are hypothetical. Note that the expropriatee is not a willing seller, but this does not negate the concept of market value as far as compulsory acquisition is concerned. Since the Government's intention is not to negotiate with the "unwilling seller", the expropriatee is well shadowed by the "willing seller" in the open market.

In Kiambere, the determination of market value, which is stipulated as the base value for compensation in the schedule of Land Acquisition Act, did not conform to the aforementioned principles. There was difficulty in determining the value of land per acre because:

i   there was no established land market in the area; and
ii land was sold in block in exchange for goats, cows, etc.

In one of the pre-acquisition meetings attended by the District Officer (member of the local Land Control Board), Clerk to County Council (also represented in the Land Control Board), [sic] Government valuers and representatives of TARDA (Tana & Athi Rivers Development Authority) (beneficiary of acquisition), the land value was determined reportedly through balloting: "... all present obtained a paper slip on which they wrote down what they thought was the fair price of land per acre in the area" (K'Akumu 1996, p. 66).

It was reported that the suggested units prices ranged from Ksh 400 to 700. The meeting agreed that Ksh 600 be taken as an average, and to this Ksh 100 (1 USD) was added "to cater for items not quantifiable for compensation which nevertheless were financially beneficial to land owners" (K'Akumu 1996, p. 66). The final figure therefore rested at Ksh 700 per acre (some Ksh 1,730 per hectare). About the same year, an environmental impact assessment study group had placed it at Ksh 300 per acre (Ksh 740 per hectare), which was argued to be "the value of other ranches in the country" (K'Akumu 1996, p. 66).

The value was disputed by local MPs for some time. The Provincial Commissioner of the area wrote that "... I understand that the local members of parliament have not yet accepted the figure of Ksh 700 and this has been made known to the land owners" (K'Akumu 1996, p. 66). The letter is written to indicate that they were to accept sooner or later. Indeed, they "accepted" because the figure was never changed. The former landowners disputed the market value in a Memorandum of Complaint. One of the grounds was that "There was a committee which deliberated the nature and mode of compensation. We were not represented in this committee and neither were our view sought" (K'Akumu 1996, p. 66).

It was noted that those present in this meeting were only government officials (not accountable to the public) and the official "buyer" (TARDA). There was no market value in effect; what the meeting did was to negotiate the price on the table. Whereas the "buyer" was represented in the negotiations, the "seller" was not. The result was an unrealistic value. The claimants' criticism was therefore genuine. The Managing Director of TARDA wrote a response to this memorandum but virtually failed to address the gist of the argument.

One of the greatest determinants of land value in an area is its use. In the project area, land was either under natural vegetation or cultivation. However, no values were given to the indigenous trees, contrary to the expectation of the claimants. Such trees were useful to the claimants for fuel, building, beekeeping and their medicinal value.

In the memorandum of complaints, the landowners pointed out that "Trees which rightfully belonged to us were also felled in the process of cleaning the ground. These items that normally go into determining the value of a piece of land were not addressed ..." (K'Akumu 1996, p. 67). However, earlier, the Commissioner of Lands officers had written to one of the claimants who had expected compensation for "land and trees therein" saying that "The

Table 18.2 Land acquired for sand harvesting

District	Place	No. of Plots	Area in HA
Embu	Maribwe Valley	100	328.00
Kitui	Masaa Valley	80	251.02
Total		180	579.02

Source: K'Akumu (1996, p. 68).

Government is not to pay for the indigenous bush although the value of well-tended trees shall be reflected in the assessment". Thus, it becomes apparent that the Ksh 700 per acre (1,730 per hectare) was a flat rate awarded to any piece of land regardless of whether it is cultivated, vegetated or barren, which is inequitable.

In the Maribwe and Masaa Valleys, land was temporarily acquired for the harvesting of sand to be used in dam construction, as indicated in the table (Table 18.2).

Again compensation was not paid for the indigenous trees (K'Akumu 1996, p. 68). However, in this case, compensation for land was awarded at Ksh 1,000 per acre (Ksh 2,470 per ha) in contrast to Ksh 700 per acre (1,730 per ha) awarded for land in the dam area. The reason for this is that it was thought sand that had greater economic value. This, nevertheless, is only one instance of land value differentiation in the entire acquisition spectrum.

The claimants were left in a quandary as to what method was used to arrive at the quantum of compensation. Indeed, it is clear that no method was used. One of the claimants put it very clear in his letter in which he pointed out the reasons of his dissatisfaction to be (K'Akumu 1996, p. 68) as follows:

i   that his plot gives more yield than the amount of compensation given;
ii   that he had tried to buy other plots of the same size but was charged more.

Another dissatisfied claimant asked the valuers to "Kindly revalue those items bearing in mind that replacing them is going to cost me more than double their original value" (K'Akumu 1996, p. 69).

These two letters indicate the main methods of valuation which should have been used. The investment value of land in (i) of first letter; the comparable sale value of land in (ii) of first letter; and the replacement cost value of property in second letter. The latter might have been used throughout the valuation exercise for valuing improvements while the first two were largely ignored. The result is that market value was not reflected in the values returned by the Commissioner of Lands. The effect of this was a plethora of complaints.

Challenges facing the 2010 Kenya constitutional era

The challenges of the Independence Constitution have remained unresolved by the 2010 Constitution. These are likely to be aggravated by new challenges set in during the 2010 constitutional era. For instance, after the acquisition of land for the Standard Gauge Railway project, a new thinking came about that land acquisition was too costly and thus has sponsored a Bill in Parliament that seeks to cap the quantum of compensation to be paid to property owners. Additionally, the Bill was prompted by litigation that occasioned a Court injunction during the construction of Standard Gauge Railway project.

Land Value Index (Amendment) Bill 2016

The Bill was introduced as an Act of Parliament to amend the Land Act, the Land Registration Act, and the Prevention, Protection and Assistance to Internally Displaced Persons and Affected Communities Act to provide for the assessment of a land value index in respect of compulsory acquisition of land and for concerned purposes (ROK 2016). As a reaction to litigation, the law is similar to the 1990 amendments.

Kenya has an ambitious development programme – Vision 2030 – that aims to propel the country into a middle-income economy by 2030. The execution of this programme involves the implementation of several flagship projects including the Standard Gauge Railway and the Lamu Port-Southern Sudan-Ethiopia Transport corridor. The implementation of some of the pioneer projects, such as the two aforementioned, has run into problems as a result of land disputes, where Courts have issued injunctions halting the works pending the resolution of such disputes. For instance, the High Court in Mombasa halted the construction of the railway in July 2016, after the Africa Gas and Oil Company sought such orders over a compensation dispute to the tune of Ksh 500 million.

Of course, court injunctions lead to time and cost overruns that eventually become a bigger financial burden to the State. Another difficulty the government is facing with the compulsory acquisition practice in Kenya is that it is a long and protracted process that does not make available land in time for development purposes. So part of the objectives of the amendment is the shortening of the time to court or the speeding up of the court process which implies curtailing of the court's powers. It is believed that getting land for development purposes in Kenya is difficult and that this could be the reason why the Ugandan government decided to relocate the construction of its oil pipeline through Kenya to Tanzania.

The government also is wary that the cost of land is very high in Kenya, forming up to 30% of total project costs. For this reason the law has made provisions that compensation for land taken shall be based on a land value index to be calculated by the government itself (the buyer). Hence, this is the government's way of controlling the price of land it is buying from private owners.

There are many debatable issues in the amendment law. These three issues, the banning of court injunctions, the establishment of a tribunal and the capping of land price for compensation, are notable highlights for this chapter. Overall, it is important to remember that although it is a reaction to the challenges of litigation, the law itself presents various challenges in the land acquisition process.

Conclusion

Kenya has faced challenges in the application of compulsory acquisition of land in the dozen decades of its existence, starting from 1895. During the colonial time, there was the problem of land rights. Particularly the land rights of Native Africans were not clearly defined or recognised, and thus, in some instances, their lands were acquired arbitrarily. The colonial administration developed the Native Lands Ordinance that defined Native African lands whose tenure was customary and this land largely remained unregistered. This was carried over to the independence period under the Trust Land Act. This land is more problematic in the case of acquisition, as the case of the Kiambere Dam project has illustrated. Such land is un-surveyed, un-inventorised and is without a cadastre. The other type, the registered lands, presents a totally different challenge in the case of acquisition—the challenge of litigation. The government has reacted to the challenge of litigation on two occasions by introducing legal amendments, but it seems these attempts to resolve the problem are not adequate.

Note

1 The material for the case studies of the Thika Dam and the Kiambere Dam is reproduced from 'The Impacts of Land Acquisition Problems on Plan/Project Implementation' Masters Thesis submitted by Owiti Abiero K'Akumu, to the University of Nairobi, August 1996. Available at: http://ere pository.uonbi.ac.ke/bitstream/handle/11295/28783/K%27akumu_The%20impacts%20of%20 land%20acquisition%20problems%20on%20plan/project%20implementation%EF%BB%BF. pdf?sequence=3&isAllowed=y.

References

K'Akumu, O.A. 2002. Expropriation of land for urban development in Kenya, in Kreibich V. and W.H.A. Olima, *Urban Land Management in Africa*, Ch. 23 pp. 322–334. Spring Centre, Dortmund.

K'Akumu, O.A. 1996. The impacts of land acquisition problems on project implementation, unpublished Master Thesis, University of Nairobi, Nairobi.

Lonsdale, J. 1989 The conquest state of Kenya. in J. de Moor & H. Wesseling (eds) *Colonial Warfare*, Brill, Leiden, 87–120.

Okoth-Ogendo, H.W.A. 1991. *Tenants of the Crown: Evolution of Agrarian Law and Institutions in Kenya*, ACTS Press, Nairobi.

Olima, W.H.A. and K'Akumu, O.A. 1999. Problems of project implementation: A post-mortem study of Thika Dam Project, *Habitat International*, 23(4): 467–479.

ROK (Republic of Kenya) 2016. The Land Value Index Laws (Amendment) Bill, 2016, Kenya Gazette Supplement, The Government Printer, Nairobi.

Sorrenson, M. P. K., 1967 Land reform in the Kikuyu county: a study in government policy. East African Institute of Social Research (Makerere University College) Oxford University Press.

Syagga, P. M. 1994. *Handbook of Real Estate Valuation*, Nairobi University Press, Nairobi.

19

Compensation for expropriation in Botswana

Issues and transformative suggestions

Donald Mengwe

Introduction

Public authorities in Botswana, when undertaking projects which require land for the public good and where there subsists a private interest or right to use the land, may exercise powers of eminent domain under the terms of the Constitution of Botswana, 1966, the Acquisition of Property Act, 1955, the Tribal Land Act, 1968 and the Tribal Land (Amendment) Act, 1993. As expropriation is seldom resisted, controversies often emanate from the issue of compensation. This is hardly surprising in a society that is increasingly literate, human rights-conscious and litigious, and where property owners are asserting their disapproval of inadequate compensation. Protests are pervasive in respect of tribal land rights because compensation offers from the government are based on the statutory interpretation that such rights do not have a market value, and communal land rights are awarded little, if any, compensation. Compensation assessment for tribal land rights under the Tribal Land (Amendment) Act, 1993 has received a public backlash, and the government has responded by proposing a Tribal Land Bill, 2017 that seeks to apply the statutory rules for computation of compensation for private land enshrined in the Acquisition of Property Act, 1955 in order to address public perceptions of injustice. As for freehold land acquired during the colonial era, the government has been forced to shelve land redistribution plans to augment tribal grazing land and State land for urban expansion, on the grounds of budgetary constraints, and on account of the excessive monetary compensation demanded by the property owners.

Expropriation and compensation does touch a raw nerve because it leads to displacement and has negative effects on livelihoods. This chapter describes the compensation laws and the evolution of land tenure which are essential ingredients for determining the quantum of compensation. It also explores different perspectives on the purpose of the constitutional property clause and approaches articulated in commentaries on assessing just compensation. Problems with the current compensation system are highlighted and recommendations for improvement are suggested. It concludes by suggesting a legislative reform which would put the question of the assessment of compensation in the political arena subject to judicial review, and a paradigm shift from the individual to an approach that puts an individual in a societal context where the proportionality test plays a dominant role in the assessment of compensation.

The legal framework

Constitutional property clause

In tandem with the principles of equity and equivalence, the constitutional property clause, section 8, guarantees the right to prompt and adequate compensation albeit without defining or stating the criteria for determining the amount of compensation, and leaving the details to the law applicable for the taking of possession. It further secures the right to access the High Court either directly or on appeal from any other authority for the determination of the amount of compensation the owner is entitled to and for the purpose of obtaining prompt payment of compensation.

Acquisition of Property Act, 1955

This statute makes provision for authorising the acquisition of property for public and other purposes, and for settling the quantum of any compensation due or any matter in dispute. It further provides for the President to acquire any real property without the willing consent of the owner in the public interest and also allows flexibility in that the acquisition may be attained through private treaty. In the case of private treaty, consideration or compensation is as agreed or determined under the provision of the Act. The critical provision for the assessment of compensation is section 16. Section 16 (1) states that:

In determining the amount of compensation to be given for the property acquired or to be acquired under this Act, a Board shall assess what is adequate compensation therefor, and for such purpose shall have regard to;

a   the market value of the property at the date of service of notice of acquisition under section 5;

b   any increase in the value of any other property of any person interested likely to accrue from the use to which the property acquired will be put;

c   the damage, if any, sustained by any person interested by reason of the severing of any land from any other land of such person;

d   the damage, if any, sustained by any person interested, by reason of the acquisition injuriously affecting any other property of such person; and

e   the reasonable expenses, if any, incidental to any change of residence or place of business of any person interested which is necessary in consequence of the acquisition;

Provided that the Board shall not have regard to the;

i   the fact that the acquisition is compulsory;

ii   the degree of urgency which has led to the acquisition;

iii   any disinclination of any person interested to part with the property to be acquired;

iv   any damage sustained by any person interested which, if caused by a private person, would not be a good cause of action;

v   any increase in the value of the property to be acquired which is likely to accrue from the use to which it will be put when acquired; or

vi   any outlay on additions or improvements to the property to be acquired, which has been incurred after the date of service of the notice of acquisition under section 5 unless such additions were in the opinion of the Board necessary.

353

Section 16 (2) states that:

> if the market value of the property has been increased by means of any improvement made within one year immediately preceding the service of the notice of acquisition under section 5, such increase shall be disregarded unless it is proved that the improvement was made *bonafide* and not in contemplation of such property being compulsory acquired under the provisions of this Act.

There are also procedural matters for the compulsory acquisition regarding the quantum of compensation and the nature of the interest at the Board of Assessment constituted in terms of the Act. In terms of the Act, the Board of Assessment may regard as evidence of value of property or any buildings or trees or crops, the written reports of any officer of an appropriate or admissible government agency and sworn appraisement of a sworn appraiser. Further, any party in the Board of Assessment proceedings or the representative of the President may call upon such officer or sworn appraiser as a witness and may also cite any other evidence as to value. Despite the Board having quasi-judicial and judicial powers, aggrieved parties may appeal its decision on both matters of fact and law. There is also an express provision that real property shall not include Tribal Territories as defined by the Tribal Territories Act, 1933. The Act also makes express provision for any person aggrieved by delay in the payment of compensation due to appeal to the High Court for the purpose of obtaining prompt payment.

The Acquisition of Property Act, 1955 is a legacy of British colonial rule when the High Commissioner realised that there was a need for legislative powers of expropriation in respect of land allocated to the settler community under freehold and leasehold titles (Ng'ong'ola 1989). The BSA Company and Tati Concession Ltd were the biggest beneficiaries of private land allocated to the settler community. On discerning the apparent weakness of provisions for expropriation and compensation in the proclamations granting land to the aforementioned entities, the Bechuanaland Protectorate Acquisition of Property Proclamation No. 80 of 1954 was promulgated in 1955, which has traces of the English Land Clauses Consolidation Act, 1845. "Property" meant interests in immovable property and it excluded tribal land as chiefs were circumspect in giving sovereignty over tribal land holdings to the High Commissioner. Ng'ong'ola (1989) reveals that amendments followed after its promulgation until the enactment of the Acquisition of Property (Amendment) Law of 1966 aimed at harmonising it with Bill of Rights in the independence constitution.

Arguably, the Acquisition of Property Act, 1955 in its form and embodiment were influenced by the British compensation code designed for post-first and second world wars reconstructions which envisaged large scale property acquisition, and introduced statutory rules for the assessment of compensation to make the system efficient, uniform, simpler, and cost effective by removing complexities. Rowan-Robinson (1990) suggests that the Reports of the 1918 Scott Committee dealing with the Acquisition and Valuation of Land for Public purposes and 1942 Uthwatt Expert Committee on Compensation were instrumental in ushering in the reform of the legislative system.

Evolution and aspects of legislation dealing with compensation of tribal land

The Tribal Land Act, 1968 has undergone a number of amendments as a result of land tenure reforms since independence. The Tribal Land Act, 1968 established Land boards to give them authority over tribal land administration. In order to give effect to this land administration system, it repealed the chiefs' powers under customary law in relation to tribal land. It is worth emphasising that the intention of this Act was not to change customary land tenure but to provide common law leases with the consent of the minister.

Regarding compensation, in terms of section 33 of Tribal Land Act, 1968, the State is required to grant alternative land of *equivalent value* and also to settle adequate compensation reflecting the value of standing crops and improvements, including the value of any clearing and preparation of land for agricultural or other purposes. The value of compensation should be adequate; however, "adequate compensation" is not defined and the criteria for its determination are not expressly prescribed in the subject statute. Aggrieved parties may make application to the High Court or to the magistrate of the competent jurisdiction for the purpose of ascertaining the amount of any compensation to which they are entitled, whether or not such compensation is adequate in the circumstances of the case and, if not, what is adequate compensation. The court may make such order in the matter as it thinks fit.

The Report of the Presidential Commission of Inquiry in Land Problems in Mogoditshane and other Peri-Urban Villages (1991) led to the enactment of the Tribal Land (Amendment) Act, 1993. Of particular note is that the Tribal Land (Amendment) Act, 1993 sought to entrench customary values in tribal land administration to address concerns of the illegal sale of tribal land. The informal land market was premised on the interpretation of Section 10(2), meaning that tribal land can be held in a private and personal capacity. This section was deleted. Section 18 of the Tribal Land (Amendment) Act, 1993 amends section 33 of the Tribal Land Act, 1968 which deals with compensation following expropriation. The deletion of the requirement to grant the affected occupier the right to use alternative land of "equivalent value" is an acknowledgment of the difficulty of implementing the code in the midst of a shortage of land for different classes of use as a result of the fast growing population, particularly in peri-urban villages. Instead, the Legislature preferred an approach that grants the right to use alternative land, *if available*, as part of the compensation award, and adequate compensation reflecting improvements on land. In this respect the following claims were added in amendments: costs of resettlement and the loss of user rights over such land. The loss of user rights component in compensation arises only when alternative land is not available.

The legislative intent in the Tribal Land and Deeds Registry Bills of 2017 is embodied in the Botswana Land Policy (2015). Clause 32 (1) of Tribal Land Bill, 2017 deals with compensation payable as a result of expropriation for public purposes. This clause is a replication of section 16 of the Acquisition of Property Act, 1955 with the additional proviso that in determining the amount of compensation it has to be taken into account that the claimant has been granted the "right to use" other land, and for appeals to be settled by the Land Tribunal, a quasi-judicial body. In this context, the amount of compensation should, *inter alia*, be determined considering the "right to use" other land allocated for resettlement and the market value of the property expropriated. However, the express statement "right to use" serves to emphasise the customary nature of the land tenure system which is incongruent with market value, which implies commoditised private land rights, and "market value" and "property" are not defined in the proposed legislation. This, notwithstanding, may be a deliberate move to "equate" compensation standards with that of private land as detailed in the Acquisition of Property Act, 1955.

Land tenure system in Botswana

The concept of property rights

Land tenure is the manner in which land is held by an individual and by groups. It relates to social relations, legally or customarily defined, among people in a society with respect to land or resources (Abdulai 2006; UN Habitat 2008). Land tenure is an institution and the concepts of land tenure are generally an expression of the value system which that society upholds. The UN Habitat publication, *Secure land rights for all,* enunciates property rights as

> recognised interests in land or property vested in an individual or group and can apply separately to land or development on it. Rights may apply separately to land and to property on it. ... A recognised interest may include customary, statutory or informal social practices which enjoy social legitimacy at a given time and place.
>
> *(UN Habitat 2008:5)*

Antwi (1998) observes that property rights are defined by formal and informal rules, customs and regulations of a society. A system of property rights is visibly authoritative or assured not because of the coercive power of the State or other supreme power, but because the majority of individuals aspire to be governed and organised in the chosen system (Alchian 1965, as reported by (Antwi 1998)). A system of property rights in the land of a given society is the product of or is derived from economic, legal, social, political circumstances or evolution (Antwi 1998; Ebohon et al. 2002).

Macpherson (1975) in his article "Capitalism and the Changing Concept of Property" in the book *Feudalism, Capitalism and Beyond* attests that changes in the concept of institutions and property in democratic society were compelled by and naturally the consequence of capitalism, and that as capitalism matures and is exposed to new forces, further advancements in the concept and institutions of property are required. In giving a historical account on the evolution of the concept of property, he states that

> In pre-capitalist England, property had generally been seen as a right to a revenue ... rather than as a right to specific material things ... the great bulk of property was then property in land, and a man's property in a piece of land was generally limited to certain uses of it and was not freely disposable.
>
> *(Macpherson 1975:110)*

He goes on to assert that

> The change ... to treating property as the things themselves, came with the spread of the capitalist market economy, which brought the replacement of the old limited rights in land by virtual unlimited rights ... As rights in land became more absolute, and parcels of land became more freely marketable commodities, it became natural to think of the land itself as the property. ... with these changes the state became more and more an engine for guaranteeing the full right of the individual to the disposal as well as use of things.
>
> *(Macpherson 1975:111)*

Antwi (1998) is alert to the fact that property rights exist because resources are scarce relative to competing claims. He further opines that it is because resources are scarce that there is need to define a system that stipulates who has authority to exercise rights that lead to the utilisation of resources at any given time. He also notes that in the absence of scarcity, there would be no need for property rights and that economic efficiency is not the only force guiding societies in choosing a specific property rights system.

Land tenure in pre-colonial era

In the pre-colonial era in territories that later came to form the nation-state called Botswana, most ethnic groups showed a disposition toward egalitarian principles in terms of land allocation and utilisation. Land was the source of livelihood and the main economic activity of people living at subsistence level was engagement in arable and pastoral farming. The Chief was the custodian of the land, holding it in trust for the benefit of the tribe. The main ingredient of the pre-colonial land tenure system was the "right of avail," that is every member of the community was entitled or had a birthright to be allocated residential, arable and grazing land. Each family was granted exclusive user rights to residential and arable land, but grazing land was used on a communal basis. The rights in land were limited to user rights and were not traded for commercial gain, but reverted to the tribe when they became surplus to requirements. Transfer among tribesmen and the right to revenue, normally in the form of cattle, and from improvements were permitted. Security of tenure derived from kinship and from being a member of the tribal society. The concept of private ownership was unknown. This is the customary land tenure system based on customary law and is noticeable in the vast expanse of sub-Saharan Africa.

Land tenure in the colonial era (1885–1966)

During the colonial era, the customary land tenure system remained intact in areas declared as native reserves. In areas carved out of tribal lands, the British colonial administration declared Crown and freehold land to serve their political and economic interests. The concept of private property was introduced with respect to new lands carved out of tribal land. It has been the cornerstone of Western democracies for the past two centuries which upholds the primacy of the individual and is inextricably linked to civil liberties subject to the limitation of "eminent domain" (Payne 1996). The concept of civil liberties can be traced back to the Magna Carta, arguably Europe's first written constitution, drafted by rebel nobles in England to curtail the power of their tyrannical King John (1166–1216). In Botswana, freehold land was allocated to white settlers for cattle ranching mainly around the borders of the newly established colony to curb Boer expansion from South Africa and a German incursion from South West Africa (Namibia), so that British Imperial commercial interests were safeguarded. Crown land was introduced as an appropriate tenure for township development along a capitalist market-oriented system, in contrast to the egalitarian system preferred in the native reserves. This required the institution of private property or the commodification of land rights as an incentive to yield economic growth. The main objective of the privatisation of tribal land was to facilitate the development of land and property markets for the efficient allocation and use of land subject to legislative restrictions.

Land tenure since independence to present

After independence, attained in 1966, the new government retained the edifice of customary land tenure. It fortified this by promulgation of the Tribal Land Act, 1968 which converted native reserves into tribal land. Under this Act, chiefs were replaced by decentralised Land Boards, as body corporates, which were given powers or authority over customary land administration, and also certificates were introduces as evidence of customary grants. In order to meet the changing attitudes or values to land by the indigenous people influenced by the modern capitalist economy, which required the institution of private property, the

Act provided for the granting of common law leases within tribal territories. It was envisaged that this innovation would facilitate the development of property markets and greater investments in rural areas as it would enhance access to credit.

The State Land Act, 1966 converted Crown lands to State land to ensure public ownership of land in urban areas and also conferred on the President the power for its disposal. State land is allocated to citizens on a rationed and subsidised basis, for residential use on a 99-year fixed period State grant and for commercial and industrial uses the grants are for 50 years. All fixed period state grants (FPSGs) are registered in accordance with the Deeds Registry Act, 1960. The allottees are given the right to transfer plots at will for consideration provided they have complied with the development covenant to avoid land speculation. The government also introduced a Certificate of Rights (COR), in urban centres as a land tenure system designed for low-income households in residential areas; however, the COR are not registered at the Deeds Registry. This land tenure system is perpetual and designed to mitigate dispossession and improve access to land. It has been discontinued by government in favour of FPSG and those with COR are encouraged to convert to FPSG of their own volition.

Freehold land was left intact after independence, but the government imposed restrictions, particularly for farms, on their disposal by enacting the Land Control Act, 1975, which gave citizens the right of first refusal.

Land tenure in Botswana since independence has evolved in a gradual and cautious manner to avoid social and economic disruptions. In 1975, the government introduced land tenure reform in grazing areas through the tribal grazing land policy (TGLP) to address land degradation and overgrazing and to provide greater equality of income in rural areas by curbing land grabbing by the rich. This introduced exclusive lease rights for the duration of 50 years as bankable interests that would facilitate the development of credit markets and commercialise the cattle industry. TGLP also addressed the concerns of the smaller farmers by reserving communal grazing areas to be utilised in accordance with traditional practice. The Report of the Presidential Commission on Land Tenure (1983) constituted a major milestone of Botswana's land tenure as the Commission was given the major task of reviewing the existing land tenure system and advising the government on the necessary improvements and the removal of obstacles holding back developments. The Commission recommended the granting of tribal land leases for residential use for 99 years, and for industrial and commercial use for 50 years with automatic rights of inheritance, and for subletting, hypothecation and transfer to be subject to the land board's consent. FPSG and COR were proposed as appropriate tenure forms for State land. The recommendations were approved by the government.

The Report on the Review of the Tribal Land Act, Land Policies and related Issues (1989), the Report of the Presidential Commission of Inquiry into Land Problems in Mogoditshane and other Peri-Urban Villages (1991) and the White paper on Land Problems in Mogoditshane and other peri-urban villages (1992) were also instrumental in land tenure reform in the country. The major issues addressed by the reports were primarily illegal tribal land transactions and informal tribal land markets in major urban villages which are conurbations of the cities of Gaborone and Francistown. This competition for land rights stemmed from population growth and increased demand as result of migration from rural to urban areas. The weak land administration system for State land caused low-income earners to be priced out of the urban land market. In respect of the tribal land, the system was not responsive to increased demand for land by expeditiously allocating land and executing effective land use planning. Some individuals who held tribal land rights before the enactment of the Tribal Land Act, 1968 traded their rights relying on section 10 (2), which they interpreted to permit tribesmen to hold tribal land in a personal and private capacity. Others devised legal personal contractual arrangements to circumvent government regulations for statutory restrictions on transfer. The decision of the Court of Appeal in the case between *Kweneng Land Board v Kabo Matlho and Another* (1992) was a watershed in defining the nature of the tribal land interest. It firmly established that private ownership of tribal land, as customary law, evolves with the changing conditions of society. In response to these developments, the government promulgated the Tribal Land (Amendment) Act, 1993, which restored customary land tenure by deleting section 10 (2) and imposing restrictions on transfers and land markets.

In 2002, the government appointed a consultant to conduct a comprehensive review of land policy which culminated in the White Paper on Botswana Land Policy (2015). The policy thrust is that the current land tenure system should be retained and improvement made to management processes and systems to ensure efficient land administration in the interest of social and economic development. It acknowledges that land squatting, informal and illegal land transactions and insecurity of tenure are symptomatic of an inefficient customary land administration system under pressure from increased competition in land rights as a result of urbanisation and population growth. Regarding tribal land, it was to be planned, surveyed and registered in terms of the Deeds Registry Act, 1960 and the Tribal Land Act, 1968 would be amended to give effect to this pronouncement. In a nutshell, Botswana land policy (2015) arguably progressively extends land markets into rural areas, by promoting land titling in respect of customary land tenure to facilitate credit market linkage and intervention that enhances security of tenure for weaker segments of society who are vulnerable to increased competition for land rights.

Nature of the interest for acquisition and customary law

In order to determine adequate compensation after the notice of intention of acquisition, it is of critical importance to evaluate the nature of the property interests subject to expropriation. As stated earlier, Botswana has a three-tier land tenure system comprising State land, freehold land and tribal land.

State land is allocated on fixed period State grants, which are effectively leaseholds registered in accordance with Deeds Registry Act, 1960. This gives the registered owner limited ownership of the land, and the rights to use, dispose, alienate the land subject to State restrictions, whilst the State retains the reversion. A land registration system has been deliberately created to address information asymmetry, by keeping a record of all State grants and deed transfers by registered owners, and these are guaranteed by the State to simplify or facilitate transactions of property rights in respect of State land and improved market efficiency. Real estate markets exist in urban areas, and the leaseholds are also pledged as collateral to banks to suggest that such property interests are marketable commodities.

Regarding the freehold tenure, it gives the owner absolute ownership and the right to transfer, bequeath and dispose of the property interest at will. It is a form of private ownership of land in perpetuity which permits unrestricted exchange of property supported by the State's guaranteed land registration system.

Communal land rights, a form of customary tenure, mainly for grazing purposes, are recognised and relate to common goods or commonage where every member of the community has a right to use independently. In economic terms, common goods such as common pastures are non-excludable and rivalrous. The rights are limited to use and are not subject to personal ownership. In the context of expropriation, it is fairly easy to determine the nature of the rights, but they present a serious challenge when determining adequate compensation.

Regarding the tribal land allocated for residential and arable (ploughed fields) use in terms of the Tribal Land Act, 1968, there are two competing schools of thoughts as to the exact nature of the tribal land rights. It is beyond doubt that the Tribal Land Act, 1968, Tribal Land Grazing Policy (1975), National Land Policy on Land Tenure (1985), White Paper on Land Problems in Mogoditshane and Other Peri-Urban Areas (1992), Tribal Land (Amendment) Act, 1993 and Botswana Land Policy (2015) are evidence of a desperate endeavour to delicately balance the various socioeconomic needs of a modern urbanised society and the forces of conservatism in retaining traditional custom rules and procedures governing tribal land rights.

One perspective asserts that tribal land held under customary tenure is not held in a private capacity or ownership and the grantee has user rights to the exclusion of other members of the community. A major feature of customary tenure is that the tribal land does not belong to the individual but to the community, and the beneficiary of user rights is only entitled to gain financially from the proceeds of the disposal of the improvements on it.

The other perspective is that the policy pronouncements that have introduced land tenure reform (such as Tribal Land Grazing Policy (1975), National Land Policy on Land Tenure (1985), White Paper on Land Problems in Mogoditshane and Other Peri-Urban areas (1992), Tribal Land (Amendment) Act, 1993 and Botswana Land Policy (2015)) undermined the customary basis for land administration in favour of the recognition of the changing attitudes to land. This inclination has been driven by the quest for national development powered by urbanisation, technology and economic growth, as well as the demands of a market-oriented economy. The Tribal Land Act, 1968 and its amendments introduced customary grants of individual rights on arable land and residential plots and the granting of common law leases subject to the consent of the Land Board. The Tribal Land (Amendment) Act, 1993 went further by providing that the Land Boards' consent is not required in the case of a sale in execution to citizens, hypothecation, or the inheritance of land which has been developed to the satisfaction of the Land Boards. This has led to the emergence of informal land markets in tribal territories, and indeed prices are observable of rights in tribal lots being traded as a result of either outright sale or mortgage foreclosures. Economic agents in the tribal land market consider customary grants to use and occupy land as potentially equivalent to perpetual interests and common law leases, conferring rights to use land for a definite period of time. This view finds support in the White Paper on Land Problems in Mogoditshane and Other Peri-Urban areas (1992), on page 17, which states that "on the basis that the Landboard retains reversionary right on any land granted, such grant is in fact equivalent to a leasehold." Further, there is also a State-guaranteed land registration system, which allows grantees to upgrade their "intermediate" title of a certificate of customary grant to a "title deed" by registering their common law leases under the terms of the Deeds Registry Act, 1960 by of their own volition. This facilitates proof of title and tribal land transactions. As transactions in land deal so much in legal rights rather the land *per se,* it is argued that the tribal land rights held under customary grant or common law are a commodity that may be traded in the market place. Further, to give credence to this perspective, it is asserted that the reality is that the country has undergone social and economic transformation in tribal territories and as result the property rights system has evolved to be in harmony with the prevailing circumstances of a modern cash-based economy, despite State interventions to curb land speculation and commodification. To support this point, it is averred that social relations among individuals in urban villages demonstrate the individualisation of tribal land rights, through the existence of an informal land market where transactions are designed to circumvent the legal regulatory system through personal contracts. Further, the legislative intent of the Tribal Land and Deeds Registry Bills resembles a bold expression to introduce market forces into tribal land; although there are contradictions. For example, clause 27(1) stipulates that tribal land may only be granted in ownership to the State and there is a restriction on transferability in clause 33(1) which is a disincentive in the commercialisation of tribal land. The Tribal Land Bill, 2017 provides for the compulsory registration of all tribal land rights nationwide, and the Deed Registry Act, 1960 is amended to give effect to this pronouncement. It is evidently clear that it is the government's conviction that land registration would improve tenure security and create bankable interests for credit market linkages, improve productivity and investment in rural areas. Considering the long enduring view that customary land rights are not a commodity, this may be considered a recognition of the idea that a market-oriented economy depends and requires well-defined private property rights. The use of the expression "land transactions" in the Tribal Land Bill, though there are clear provisions for their restrictions, is a direct resignation to and recognition of the fact that social and economic changes have rendered commercial dealings in tribal land inevitable.

Nature of customary law: Kweneng Land Board v Kabo Matlho and Another and Kweneng Land Board v Mpofu and Another

The expected reaction of the valuer in the midst of contradictory perceptions as to the nature of tribal land rights is to refer to case law for guidance. *Kweneng Land Board v Kabo Matlho and Another* and *Kweneng Land Boad v Mpofu and Another* are Court of Appeal cases which effectively dealt with the substantive issue of whether tribal land can be held in a private and personal capacity or whether it belongs to the community under the terms of customary law. The subject matter of these cases was not compensation at all but rather issues arising from sale agreements in respect of tribal land situated in Mogoditshane which had not been authorised by the Kweneng Land Board (KLB), and the subsequent erection of residential building thereon. However, it is beyond doubt that they serve as useful reference material to direct any proceedings regarding the valuation of tribal land for compensation purposes as they deal with the issue of customary tenure.

In *KLB v Matlho and Another*, the High Court held that the "ownership of the land fell fairly and squarely within the exception to the vesting of the land in the appellant; and that the land was private property of the second respondent." It relied on its interpretation of section 10(2) of the Tribal Land Act, 1968, which provides that

> Nothing in this section shall have the effect of vesting in a landboard any land or right to water held by any person in his personal and private capacity.

KLB appealed the matter, and it was dismissed with two judges concurring and one dissenting. The majority of the Court held that

> customary law is not static but has developed, and has continued to develop to meet the demands of modern society. Whatever the customary law might have been in the past in the area concerned in this case, the law has apparently developed to permit private ownership of tribal lands. On the evidence the second respondent had capacity to hold land in his personal and private capacity and that he acquired title to the land in question in his personal and private capacity. Consequently he had lawfully transferred it to the first respondent.

Kweneng Land Board v Mpofu and Another (2005), is an appeal against the decision of the High Court in which the court held that it was bound by the decision of the Court of Appeal case in *Kweneng Land Board v Matlho and Another (1992)*, as to the interpretation of section (10) 2 of the Tribal Land Act. In this case, the Court of Appeal decided in favour of the KLB. The Court of Appeal, in analysing the judgment in the *Matlho* case, revealed that the difficulty was caused by the interpretation of section 10(2), specifically what was the object of the government enacting it. Judge Tebbut JP in this case cited Lord Atkinson in *Cape Brandy Syndicate v Inland Revenue Commissioners (1921) 2 KB 483* where he stated that where an earlier Act is "fairly and equally open to diverse meanings," the aims and provisions of the subsequent statutes may serve a useful purpose in unraveling its meaning. He went on to say that he had "no doubt that the interpretation of the words ('land or right to water held by any person in his personal and private capacity') in the context of the Tribal Land Act, 1968 is obscure ('fairly and equally open to diverse meanings')"... and

> Whatever lay behind the object of the legislature in enacting s 10(2), I cannot accept that it intended to create a class of private ownership within the customary law. It would fly in the face of all the tenets of customary law, which from all the authoritative text writers specifically excluded it.

Judge Tebbut JP also stated that by considering the latter statute, (Tribal Land (Amendment) Act, 1993) there is nothing that suggests that the legislature intended to create a class of private ownership in land that was previously allocated under customary law before the commencement of the Tribal Land Act in 1970. The court also observed in the government White Paper No 1 of 1992 titled "Land Problems in Mogoditshane and Other Peri–Urban Villages" that the issue concerning the sale of tribal land was being discussed, and the culture of not selling tribal land was recognised and interventions to curb the sale of tribal land through legislation was proposed.

The *Matlho* case, it could be argued, firmly establishes that tribal land is a commodity, if not wholly across the country but in certain instances or areas where it can be adequately proven that such land falls outside the ambit of the Tribal Land Act or that customary law has evolved to permit private ownership. The difficulty with *Mpofu* case is that it is not of great help from a valuation perspective, when one considers section 38(1) in juxtaposition with the judgment. It would seem reasonable that the position of the government in the White Paper No.1 of 1992, (which informed the Amendment of Tribal Land Act, 1968 to restrict what is regarded as illegal land market), is an acknowledgment that attitudes toward tribal land have changed to something akin to a commodity that can be traded as result of social and economic transformation. Judge Amissah in the *Matlho* case expressed that the view that the White Paper intended to put the matter as to whether tribal land cannot be held in private capacity beyond doubt once and for all. Judge Tebbut JP, with respect to this, states

> In August 1993 the Tribal Land Act (Amendment) Act 14 of 1993 was passed. This contained a number of provision which it would seem, were designed by the legislature to underline the customary law restriction on the private ownership of tribal land.

However, the effect of section 38(1) is to allow the gradual development of land markets in tribal areas and at the same time is a desperately attempt to entrench customary law to ensure the equitable distribution of land or to regulate land transfers. An essential feature of a market-oriented economy is the institution of private property, where individuals have the right to own, control and dispose of natural or man-made resources. Section 38 requires that the rights of any person in respect of any tribal land grant shall be transferred, whether by sale or otherwise, to citizens without the approval of the land board in the case of land developed to the satisfaction of the land board, via a sale in execution or hypothecation. Arguably, for any transfer by a person to be regarded as a sale, what is exchanged should be exclusive private property. The land board is also required to scrutinise sale transactions and, in terms of natural justice, consent for the transaction should not be unreasonably withheld. On that account, it is therefore debatable whether the *Mpofu* case can still be taken as an absolute authority on the nature of tribal land interests.

What is adequate or just compensation?

The issue of compensation continues to intrigue and bemuse commentators and naturally concerns those who have to bear the brunt of expropriations, as resistant to the eminent domain is uncommon. In contrast to other human rights such as life, liberty and protection from slavery or forced labour, the right to property is no doubt one of the most controversial and complex. The primacy of property is subject to more qualification and limitation and has other implications in relation to other social and economic rights such as rights to education and adequate housing. It is therefore true that most revolutions and the worst abuses of human rights in the twentieth century have centred around the issue of property. Among the worst violations are the disenfranchisement or dispossession of native Africans under the Apartheid regime in South Africa and the collectivisation of agricultural land in Ukraine during the Stalin era, which led to massive famine and as result a catastrophic loss of life during 1932–33.

In western democracies, the protection of property is considered sacrosanct and an essential ingredient of a market economy and the security of the freedom of the individual despite its controversies and complexity. In Africa, the right to property is protected under Article 14 of the African Charter on Human and peoples' rights or the Banjul Charter, and in Europe under Article 1 of Protocol No. 1 to the European Convention on Human Rights. Other international instruments such as the Universal Declaration of Human Rights also recognises the right to property, but controversies remain on the degree of protection to be accorded to private property against expropriation and intrusive regulation.

du Plessis (2009), in his doctoral thesis *Compensation for Expropriation under the Constitution*, extrapolated the inextricable theoretical link between the amount of compensation due after the occurrence of expropriation and the reason for the payment of compensation. This was based on American literature, which developed in the last century, and which focused on takings and on the conditions to be met for the payment of compensation. His observations and the works of Michelman (1981), Alexander (2003), Radin (1982), Wyman (2007), Fee (2006) and Allen (2004) are summarised below to present diverse expositions or commentaries on the purpose of compensation and on compensations standards.

Purpose of compensation

Generally, compensation is required to indemnify the individual from harmful government interference and to distribute the burden of government interference. Regarding the proposition that the individual is thus protected from harmful interventions, there is a dichotomy in the analysis of the scholarly debate. Preference for the liberal notion of property, which upholds private property and conceptualises it as something exclusive which promotes individual freedom, propagates the view that any government interference must be accompanied by compensable expropriation save under police powers (see Epstein 1985 as cited by du Plessis 2009). The conception of property is a "Lockean" right which is justified under the social contract theory of John Locke based on his "state of nature" abstraction. Property should not be insubordinated to other constitutional rights in the lexical order. The taking of one of the sticks in the bundle of rights leads to the reciprocal obligation for full indemnification of the owner, which makes government regulation expensive, and severely limits its powers. By requiring expensive compensations and thus curbing government regulatory powers governments are compelled to opt for market solutions as opposed to political solutions. Expropriating property without compensation would lead to inefficient outcomes or uses, which is in stark contrast to conditions under a market discipline. From a societal perspective, which views property rights as manifestations of social relations, the individualisation of property rights serves to frustrate government redistributive actions in its mediating role between individual rights and government power. The liberal conception of property is thus an affront to democratic process and does not take into account the social origins of property. By its nature, property is underpinned by society's value judgments in that property rights are dynamic and determined by political and social circumstances. On this basis, the assertion that compensation prevents harmful social inefficient expropriation is untenable. The works of Nedelsky (1990), Singer and Beerman (1993) and Serkin (2004) as cited by du Plessis (2009) provide material for this exposition.

Sax (1964, 1971), as cited by du Plessis (2009), stresses that the purpose of compensation is not so much to safeguard existing economic values against government interference but rather a deterrent against arbitrary government action or its abuse of power. His theory is that because property is a result of a competitive process, the question of when compensation is due is determined by consideration of whether the government acts in an enterprising capacity, where it is a participant in the competition for property interests or a mediator of competing interests, where it does not accrue any benefit. Compensation is required where the government acts in an enterprising capacity by acquiring resources to discourage the profit motive which demands foresight, whereas where it is exercising its police powers in the interest of the public welfare, compensation is not due.

The notion that property has its roots in social relations, and thus that private property is inextricably linked with social obligations which are the outcome of democratic community or/and state decisions on the usage of property, assumes that the purpose of a constitutional property clause is to guarantee liberties through its compensatory effects in the spirit of fairness. This view is anchored on John Rawls Theory of Justice, as fairness which proposes a conception of society as a fair system of cooperation between free and equal persons (Spring 2008). According to Rawlsian theory, a just and fair society or social order encapsulates two principles, which are the basic terms of social cooperation deduced from the abstract original position, being Equal Liberty and Social and Economic Inequalities. In this vein, interference that burdens an individual disproportionately to the benefit of society or unequal impairment of liberties requires adequate compensation.

For Michelman (1981), what is protected under the constitutional property clause is a political right that entitles an individual to participate in democracy. This in sync with Rawls's Theory of Justice in that the fundamental values, such as liberty, freedom of thought and association, and dignity, which are essential ingredients for an individual possessed of moral powers to lead a self-governing life or to pursue self-determination and happiness, thus allowing the individual to participate in social and political life, are effectively political rights. Property is also a political right but uniquely so in relation to other rights within a political constitution, in that it can be understood to serve other social, moral and political values or substantive interests. By extension, the protection is for the maintenance of conditions necessary for fair and effective participation in politics, meaning that it entails far more than ownership in its strict sense. Just compensation is therefore owed when expropriation will impede effective participation in societal politics alongside other members. It plays a mediating role to address the contradictions between individual worth and popular rule. This line of argument means that some properties may not be subject to takings at all since deprivation means political marginalisation and monetary just compensation for presumed economic loss would not suffice, which arguably enunciates the case that the substance of property is more than ownership but a "right to property." Generally the theme that recurs in his work is that compensation serves to "equalise" the redistributive effect in the reallocation of resources or the distribution of wealth among members of society, where one member loses the beneficial use of property.

Alexander (2003) in his article "Property as a fundamental Constitutional Right? The German example" offers an flawless discussion on constitutional property law. Thus, under German Basic law, the institution of private property is guaranteed in positive terms and the right to private ownership (even extant ownership) is also protected on the well-established interpretation that the moral purpose of the law is to uphold the principle of human dignity. He asserts that property is socially bound and subject to prevailing limitations essential for public order requirements as demanded by society. In his exposition, he opines that the German constitution strongly protects property interests to the extent that they serve primary constitutional values, particularly those of human dignity and self-governance, and this derives from its most basic commitment in its entirety, that is the commitment to the principle of human dignity. The corollary then is that property interests would be relegated to an inferior status, thus receiving little protection if held for solely or largely for wealth maximisation or speculative purposes. Property is not treated only as a market commodity, which implies that in certain circumstances, for some property interests, the compensation solution may be unfeasible and should therefore be immune from government interference, while others may be expropriated at no compensation or at less than full market value. According to Alexander (2003), in the German approach, the constitution proclaims a social relationship between the individual and community of nature, where the individual is dependent on the community but without violating individual worth. It thus follows that in the case of the deprivation of property and the assessment of compensation, the principle of proportionality is convenient.

Radin (1982) suggests, intuitively, that there is an emotional bond between an object and a person, and its value strength can be tested based on the pain visited in the event of loss. Objects which churn out distress in the event of loss are related to personhood and are personal property. These objects are irreplaceable as opposed to fungible property which can easily be replaced with other goods of equal market or functional value. In this discourse, she further states that in that intuitive understanding it is possible that personal property may be associated with autonomy and liberty, and if that is the case, it is a necessity or *indispensable* (author's emphasis) for the person, and therefore deprivation will be detrimental to autonomy and liberty. The concession that a person can be bound to an object demands that there should be provision for greater protection to permit great liberty regarding control over the object. In this respect, she makes the observation that on moral grounds there is a possibility for fetishism or bad object relations as well as good attachment to objects, so it would be inappropriate to hold that all such attachments warrant equal treatment in terms of legal protection. To clarify, *supra*, *verbatim*, she states "At the extreme, anyone who lives only for material objects is considered not to be a well-developed person, but rather to be lacking some important attribute of humanity" (Radin 1982). Applying this theory to the murky area of expropriation, she makes the case that monetary compensation cannot adequately "replace" the personhood element of property, particularly a home interest (Radin1982). Therefore, there are instances where the power of eminent domain cannot be exercised. For her, because property is critical for individuals to take control of their lives or define their psyche, the government should be sensitive and assess whether property subject to expropriation deserves high protection which may require compensation at higher cost than market value. Property functions in a societal aspect, the personhood is conditioned by the environment which includes things and people, and the purpose of compensation is to burden members of society equally (Radin 1982). By her own admission, she is at odds with the liberal concept of property, which is accommodated by the courts, that private property protects individuals. She is of the view that fungible property does not deserve the same degree of protection as personal property.

Wyman (2007) also rebuts the idea that compensation protects private property against socially inefficient expropriation by stretching the budget; as a result, it forces the decision-makers to internalise the costs of their actions, which motivates efficient decision-making regarding takings. She elucidates that there are a host of factors that may lead to opposition of this myth, one being that the government is more responsive to political costs than monetary costs. The other reason is that the risk aversion of a government agency may prevent it from undertaking an otherwise efficient action. According to Wyman (2007), the obligation to pay compensation is an activity that seeks to achieve *corrective* justice by making the victim or expropriatee whole by restitution to a pre-expropriation level, and is not an exercise of distributive justice. Expropriations are not appropriate for *distributive* justice for the simple reason that they are not typically targeted at particular needs in ways that allow compensation for the takings to systematically redistribute resources.

Wyman (2007) also critically examines the presumption that compensation should serve to make expropriatees subjectively indifferent in the spirit of making them whole. This "subjective view" sits well with the liberal concept of property and the liberal society which generates a limited role of the government and for the state to exercise neutrality and focuses instead on promoting the satisfaction of individual preferences. She draws on the debate in egalitarian political philosophies relating to the appropriate yardstick of distributive justice when making public policy decisions. These philosophies attempt to obliterate the notion that distributive justice should be based solely on the satisfaction of individual preferences—the idea that the metric of preference satisfaction is instrumental, in that societies would allocate things to permit individuals to have an equal ability to realise their own preferences. Wyman's (2007) inference from the normative critiques of this approach enunciates her objections to the idea that expropriatees should be made subjectively indifferent. She asserts that the peculiarity with this approach rests on the fact that there are offensive, expensive and adaptive preferences. In a case where preference is discriminatory in nature and detrimental to human dignity, a victim (i.e. expropriatee) who holds this view, expressed for instance by residing in a neighbourhood attractive for racists because it is not integrated, would translate into compensating an unpleasant preference. Further, if fair market value serves as a basis for compensation, these distasteful preferences are imputed in pricing, which questions the objectivity of market value. Compensating for expensive tastes at fair market value may create a moral hazard in that expropriatees may be motivated to pursue expensive tastes in the full knowledge that there is no risk that they will not be indemnified for their opulence. The adaptive critique is premised on the proposition that individual preferences are conditioned by individual circumstances in life. She suggests that a possible solution is that compensation should be paid to make expropriatees objectively whole. This objective measure would be determined by societal value judgments on what generates wholeness in an individual—such that the person is paid compensation to enjoy things that society commonly values to the same extent that the person enjoyed pre-expropriation. The second possible basis proposed by Wyman (2007) for an objective measure of compensation draws on Sen's capability theory which suggests that enjoyment of capabilities, which are basically freedoms, resembles quality of life. Therefore, in terms of this theory, the measure of compensation would be the quantum required so that the same capabilities valued by society are the same as prior to expropriation. Wyman cements her views based on the United States (US) Supreme Court decision *Kelo V City of New London* that upheld the authorities' decision to expropriate residents' properties under the auspices of economic regeneration or renewal in the public interest, despite resistance and public outrage. The gist of her argument is the futility of the subjective measure of compensation as those who resist eminent domain naturally cling to the concept of the sanctity of "home." *A priori,* there are cases where it may not be morally appropriate to expropriate and where it may be justified to pay more (or less) compensation in relation to market value depending on personal characteristics rather than on focusing on the property subject to expropriation.

In "Eminent Domain and the Sanctity of Home" Fee (2006) argues that the obligation to pay compensation is geared to correct the fiscal illusion by compelling the government to internalise the cost to society. This is in alignment with the view that the requirement for compensation protects private property by making socially inefficient expropriation expensive, thus severely restricting government interference. For Fee (2006), this intention is not realised regarding "homes," when the government is allowed to compulsorily acquire solely based on market value. In such circumstances, under fiscal illusion, the costs of government actions are underestimated, which gives the impression that a public investment project amasses social benefits, whereas the public interest, on the basis of fully transparent social costs, would be served best by aborting it. This distorts government decision-making. Fiscal illusion, therefore, encourages the government to overuse eminent domain rather than engage in private treaty for the acquisition of "homes" to the detriment of homeowners. Fee (2006) is not sanguine about the reform efforts that seek to protect "homes" by the removal of ambiguity and increasing legitimacy through an emphasis on the "strict" public interest requirement and the failure to make no distinction between owner-occupied "homes" and other kinds of property. The focus is instead on the factors that characterise public interest rather than on the root cause of the inadequate protection of "home." Business owners fare better in the whole scheme of compensation for expropriation as the appraisal for their commercial properties is in sync with the market value concept and other claims, such as loss of profits and goodwill, are entertained. As compensation is the fundamental reason for the inadequate protection of "home," Fee (2006) proposes that compensation should in such cases be greater than market value, as many owners value their "homes" considering the personal benefits that develop over time in residency. This confirms that a "home" is more than an exchangeable commodity or fungible, because there are personal attachments relating to memories, and such factors as the proximity to community of friends and family. He asserts that there is nothing untoward in reviewing compensation law to take into account non-transferable subjective values, as this is consonant with the pattern of expanding tort law, where damages relating to emotional loss are permitted, whereas historically the emphasis was on pecuniary losses. Further, eminent domain circumvents a situation where an owner is able to exploit a monopoly situation by requesting exorbitant sums because the government is desperate for

367

the property, risking bargaining failure. In most long-established expropriation cases, value to the government is always higher than the value to owner. The owner therefore should be compensated for subjective value and not allowed to extract surplus from the budget, as this would result in an unequal distribution of the burden. The ideal measure of just compensation in respect of "homes" should take into consideration the owner's reasonable subjective value. Fee (2006) is alive to the fact that some owners may make unjustified or unreasonable demands of subjective value, and in this sense there is no system that can leave owners subjectively whole. The answer lies in a proposed statutory formula that takes into account horizontal equity.

Compensation standards

The discourse *supra*, on the purpose of compensation no doubt can serve as a useful guide in an attempt to answer the question on the compensation standards which the government should apply in exercising its powers of eminent domain. It may also be worthwhile to refer to commentaries on the international experiences of selected countries for a comparative analysis.

Most constitutional property clauses guarantee the right to compensation for expropriated property. Generally, the criterion for determining the quantum of compensation is not specified in constitutions. Where the nature of compensation is stated, various adjectives are used: that compensation must be "adequate," "fair," "just," "full" and "just and equitable." In the US, the compensation standard must be "just," and this is normally accepted as market value (Wyman (2007). In terms of German Basic Law, compensation payable upon expropriation must "….reflect a fair balance between the public interest and the interest of those affected" and demand the application of the proportionality principle, meaning every case be judged on its own merit. Market value in most cases has achieved the balance (du Plessis 2009).

The European Convention on Human Rights, Article 1 of the first Protocol, guarantees the right to peaceful enjoyment of possessions, but it does not guarantee compensation for every interference with property rights (Allen 2004). The European Court of Human Rights (ECtHR) applies a balancing test to evaluate whether the expropriation strikes a fair balance between community interests and the protection of the expropriatee's property rights. Compensation is one of the factors amongst others taken into consideration in determining whether there is a fair equilibrium. It "is merely a means of ensuring a fair balance" (Allen 2004). There are circumstances where the nature of the public interest may justify or lead to a situation where the property owner receives less compensation than market value or where compensation is denied. In some situations the availability or absence of procedural rights may influence the balance, such as where claimants had insufficient legal remedies to protect themselves against interference with their property. Generally, although there is no express provision for compensation in Article 1, expropriation of property without the payment of compensation reasonably related to its value is normally considered disproportionate interference, which is a violation of Article 1 (Sluysmans and de Graaff 2013).

The South African constitutional property clause, section 25(3), requires "just and equitable" compensation, in that assessment should not only consider the element of market value but also seek an equitable balance of private and public interests. It bears similarities to the proportionality test or approach by the ECtHR. It further includes a list of inexhaustible circumstances to be taken into account in determining "just and equitable" compensation.

In his book *The Right to Property in Commonwealth Constitutions,* Allen (2004) observes that in the Commonwealth, the general trend or pattern is one that reflects the interpretation of the constitutional guarantee of compensation as a guarantee of full compensation. As most of the countries were former colonies of the UK, this predisposition resonates with the *Ricket principle,* which relates to an English judicial decision in *Ricket v Metropolitan Rail Co. (1867)* where it was established that "compensation is the amount required, so far as money can do so, to put the owner in the same position as if his property had not been acquired," that is full indemnification for the loss suffered by the expropriated owner (Baum and Sams 1997). Allen (2004) stresses that there is a strong focus on the individual, and judicial decisions show an inclination to ensure that the owner is treated fairly, and that this is prioritised over the protection of public funds. This predisposition leads the Courts to assume that the award of compensation should not be less than market value.

Allen (2004), to demonstrate judicial inflexibility on compensation, draws on the Supreme Court of India's interpretation of Article 31(2) of the Constitution. Basically Article 31(2) provides that no law should authorise expropriation unless it provides for compensation or specifies the principles on which compensation is to be assessed and awarded. He states that:

> The Constitutional Assembly was informed that the courts would not 'question the adequacy of compensation from the standard of market value; they will not question the judgment of Parliament unless the inadequacy is so gross as to be tantamount to a fraud on the fundamental right to own property'.
>
> *(Allen 2004:224)*

Despite the aforementioned assurances that the Supreme Court will not challenge the legislature to acquire property at below market value, the court in *State of West Bengal v Bela Banerjee* (1953) interpreted Article 31(2) as giving the legislature a narrow discretion and required that compensation be assessed such that there is full indemnification of the expropriated owner. Allen (ibid., 225) further states that in response the Indian Parliament followed by Fourth Amendment of the Constitution, however, the court countered in *Vajravelu v Special Deputy Collector, West Madras* (1964) where it was held that the legislature had no power to acquire property unless the relevant legislation provided that compensation is, "a just equivalent of what the owner has been deprived of." Allen (2004) opined that the tussle continued, with the ruling party blaming the court for blocking economic reforms, and the court at one point ruling that the right to property formed an impregnable core of the constitution. In the *State of Gujarat v Shantilal Mangaldas* (1969), the Supreme Court softened its attitude, by accepting that the fourth amendment provided that the legislation could only be questioned on the basis that compensation is not sufficient but not on the fact that the quantum of compensation specified in the legislation or the principle for the assessment of compensation therein is contrary to the "just equivalent" of the loss suffered by the expropriated owner. However, subsequently, the court showed lesser deference to parliament and reverted to the "just equivalent" approach. Several amendments and shifts in approach ensued as result of conflicts or power play between the courts and the government. The Indian example reveals different interpretations of fair compensation, and Allen (2004) suggests it can also serve as a warning to other Commonwealth countries intent on comprehensive economic reform.

Allen (2004) emphasises that most Commonwealth courts continue to hold on to the notion that "compensation" means "full compensation." But within this perspective there is room for the legislature to opt for either the subjective valuation which takes into consideration market value and other claims related to disturbance or sentimental values, or objective valuation which is strictly confined to market value. He observes that modern statutes show a proclivity from subjective valuation to objective valuation, and that courts regard objective valuation as the constitutional minimum, Botswana is an exception in the light of *Attorney General v Western Trust (Pty) Ltd* (2006), where the High Court relied on the older statutory principle of full indemnification for loss, though on a questionable basis.

Allen (2004) further observes that in the application of an objective valuation to determine full compensation, there is a need for judgment to be exercised in relation to the assumptions which should underpin the assessment of market value, e.g., whether to value an asset by itself or as part of larger asset. According to him, the constitutional issue is how the choice of assumptions is limited or controlled by the requirement of full compensation, and he cites the Indian and Caribbean courts as an illustration that courts are often unwilling to allow discretion to the legislature and executive in making assumptions for the determination of market value. Normally, in applying the general principles of judicial review, courts are often inconsistent; as for a review of "public purpose" there is a high degree of deferment, whilst for the meaning of "property" and the compensation issue there is a very low degree of deferment.

Generally Allen's (2004) analysis is that courts focus typically on the loss suffered by the expropriatee, which reflects the dominance of the liberal conception or theories of property and the constitution which stress a limited role of government. The liberal conception of property upholds private property rights and seeks to protect it from government interference, but the courts have not examined whether the current emphasis on full compensation is the best means of achieving this. According to Allen (2004), courts still have other different options of "characterising" loss which they rarely consider, even when focusing strongly on the individual; that is, there are other alternatives of denoting and measuring loss that might be regarded as fair and adequate.

Allen (2004) also presents Frank Michelman's views as articulated in his article "Property, Utility, and Fairness: Comments on the Ethical Foundations of 'Just Compensation' Law" as an alternative to measuring loss where compensation is required. In terms of Michelman's approach, a rational government would exercise powers of eminent domain if the benefits outweigh the costs. In this vein, compensation would only be awarded when "settlements costs" of compensation are less than the "demoralisation costs" of denying compensation. Generally, the objective is to reach a level where the monetary value of settlements costs required is adequate to avoid the demoralisation costs (see Allen 2004, for definitions of "settlements costs" (at page 236) and "demoralisation costs" (at page 235)). Therefore, Michelman's general rule is not prescriptive in nature as to the level of compensation to be applied wholesale to every compensation case nor for a "one size fits all" solution. The rule does not suggest that compensation be set at an equivalent of market value nor for full indemnifications of property owners. All that is required is an amount to eliminate demoralisation costs, which may be less than fair market value. du Plessis (2009) reiterates Michelman (1967) views that the question of redistribution is ideally placed within the political arena and that it is inappropriate to rely on the Judiciary for the assessment of compensation; the reason being that "fairness" is a value judgment subject to political decision-making, and the calculation of compensation is a difficult question for the courts to assess. The assumption is that the legislature when deciding on what is fair compensation bases its view on objective information about the system of compensation and distribution, while judicial decisions are made on a subjective formulation of "fairness" to the affected individual in court (Michelman (1967) as cited by du Plessis (2009)). The other reason is that it is impossible to assess fair compensation based on the "yes or no" method of constitutional adjudication. Singer and Beerman (2009) (as cited by du Plessis (2009) also suggest that the realm of public policy making is best suited for parliament, and that the judiciary should decline to rule when the regulation of takings requires just compensation.

Issues and recommendations

Kirby (2017) in his article "Conditional on a Bill of Rights: Race and Human Rights in the Constitution of Botswana" argues that the constitutional foundations of modern-day Botswana were to a large degree designed to reflect the needs of Europeans, who insisted on the protection or preservation of their private property rights and liberal democratic values. As a matter of fact, the constitutional guarantee of compensation under the property clause, Section 8, has been interpreted by the High Court as a guarantee for full indemnification of the owner in line with western democratic values that promote the protection of private property and emphasise the primacy of the individual. In terms of the liberal conception of property, what is protected under the constitutional property clause is private ownership, and private property is treated as market commodity. The High Court decision in the only judicial precedent (*Attorney General v Western Trust (Pty) Ltd*) relating to a dispute on the adequacy of compensation is the one confirming the aforementioned judicial clarification, and the rules or principles for the assessment of compensation under the Acquisition of Property Act, 1955 which may give credence to the value system proposition by Kirby (2017). In the judicial precedent, *supra*, O' Brien Quinn CJ stated that "reading section 16 of the Acquisition of Property Act, 1955 in conjunction with the Constitution, and South African and English authorities on the point, the only fair method of valuation is one based on the principle that the expropriatee should be compensated adequately for the land, and, insofar as money can do it, be put back into the same position as he would have been, had the land been not expropriated." This resonates with the *Ricket principle* established in the English case *Ricket v Metropolitan Rail Co (1867)*. Further it is also in line with Epstein's view that the constitutional guarantee of compensation protects private owners from government interference by limiting government powers by demanding full indemnification.

Admittedly, there is nothing amiss with this arrangement if this is what is demanded by popular rule or the democratic process; however, serious issues have been revealed by Ng'ong'ola (1989) in the aforementioned case (*Attorney General v Western Trust (Pty) Ltd*), who doubts whether it can be taken as an absolute authority in determining the quantum of compensation. This case related to the compulsory acquisition of Bonnington Farm (which was in close proximity to the city of Gaborone) for urban development. It was stated that "… valuation on the basis of market value is first of all too narrow, secondly, it ignores the subjective element of loss that might be suffered by the expropriatee…." According to Ng'ong'ola (1989), this restrictive interpretation of market value was based on the explanation of the court that the market value does not take into account the potential value of the property subject to expropriation. Further, the failure of the court to offer an explanation of what "subjective element" entails led it to awarded expenses such as transfer and consultancy fees under the heading of "subjective element" when such losses could be easily recovered under Section 16 as reasonable expenses necessary in consequence of the acquisition. According to his perspective, a "subjective element of loss," if it is construed to mean "solatium," will have violated Section 16 which clearly provides that in assessing compensation no account should be taken to the fact that the acquisition is compulsory. Ng'ong'ola (1989) makes the reasonable point that the authority of the case is questionable, in that no effort was made to dispel the common law authorities that the compensation standard is strictly market value, not value to the owner or a subjective valuation, and because of the confusion or lack of clarity in the application of the "subjective element." This he attributes to the fact that "adequate compensation" and the concept of market value are not defined in the legal framework, leaving room for speculation and conjecture.

The analysis by Ng'ong'ola (1989) brings to the fore the problems observed by Allen (2004) and Michelman (1967) (as cited by du Plessis (2009)) of allowing the judiciary to assess compensation, and the potential for judicial activism. Allen (2004) has disclosed that even where courts have decided that full compensation can be determined through objective valuation, there is still discretion in choosing the assumptions on which the valuation should be based. He cites the Indian case[1] as an illustration that Commonwealth courts are often unwilling to allow parliament and the executive room in making assumptions necessary for determining market value. It thus follows that the valuation process for determining market value cannot be likened to a scientific process and casts doubt on relying the judiciary to assess compensation when it does not have the budgetary and objective policy information on the redistribution of resources nor about the system of compensation, as stated by Michelman (1967) (as cited by du Plessis (2009). Judicial decisions within the Commonwealth show a strong proclivity to the expropriatee and are essentially based on the formulation of fairness to the affected individual in court. The question of compensation as "fairness" is a normative issue and may thus be better placed in the political arena and subject to political decision-making. In the light of the abovementioned observations, it may be important to reform the compensation law in Botswana such that the National Assembly is the final authority in settling disputes over compensation and the principles for the assessment of compensation but subject to judicial review. Further, the National Assembly compensation award should not be questionable in court on the basis of adequacy. In these circumstances, it might be sensible to borrow from the German model. Although under German law the proportionality test plays a dominant role in the assessment of compensation, in that the quantum of compensation must reflect an equitable balance between the public interest and the interests of those affected, it gives the legislature considerable freedom to set compensation standards. The courts' powers are limited to review as to whether the calculation of compensation is proportional or not.

The assessment of compensation for tribal land interests remains a controversial issue in Botswana, especially when juxtaposed with that for private property such as freehold interests. It does not fare well in terms of the quantum of compensation and there is generally a public outcry that it attracts less monetary compensation. The reason for this is that, the government considers tribal land held under customary tenure granted in accordance with the Tribal Land Acts as not "owned," but rather the grantee is afforded user rights over the land to earn a livelihood. This perception is derived from traditional custom rules governing land administration in the pre-colonial era. As stated earlier, tribesmen were entitled to land without giving anything for it and the concept of individual ownership was unknown. Land was not regarded as a commodity, and this mindset still persists in land boards.

As stated earlier, compensation in terms of Section 33 of the Tribal Land (Amendment) Act, 1993 is assessed using a Depreciated Replacement Cost (DRC) for building improvements and a market-derived value for standing crops. Prior to the amendment of Tribal Land Act, 1968, the expropriatee was given alternative land for resettlement, but after 1993 disturbance costs and a standard value applicable for all tribal territories as compensation for the loss of user rights, where alternative land was not available, was paid to expropriatees. The standard value disregards location and bears no relation to the market value of expropriated land, and its calculation is arguably based on conjecture. The norm for disturbance is 10% of the aggregate of DRC and the standard value. A valuation conundrum arises where a common law lease is registered in respect of a parcel of tribal land. In this instance, there are two possible approaches in practice, depending on the perception of the nature of the tribal land interest. Where it is held that a common law lease does not change tenure, Section 33 of Tribal Land (Amendment) Act, 1993 applies. In a case where it held that a common law lease confers a leasehold interest with the landboard holding a reversionary interest, and that considering that the Tribal Land Act, 1968 and Tribal Land (Amendment) Act, 1993 facilitate trading in tribal land rights albeit restrictively, it is unconstitutional if the market value of the interest in the tribal land is disregarded. It is apparent then that the assessment of compensation for interests in tribal land subject to expropriation is complicated by a tangle of governing statutory law. This is partly the result of desperate attempts to blend market libertarian principles with the conservatism for customary law system, in tribal land administration. In any case both these approaches confirm that the statutory rules for assessing compensation were influenced by the historically prevailing liberal market economic system or liberal conception of property where the purpose of the constitution property clause is to protect private ownership. In this case the tribal land compensation standards or guidelines suggest that what is protected is "ownership" of improvements and loss of user rights. Ironically, the Tribal Land Bill, 2017 has replicated Section 16 of the Acquisition of Property Act, 1955 in an attempt to "equalise" the compensation standard with that of private land. The difficulty is that though this legislation shows an appreciation of the role of effective and efficient land administration in sustainable economic development and the symbiotic link between private property and market-based institutions, there is still a preference to retain customary land tenure and ownership in the State, which is akin to a marriage of incompatible partners. The uncomfortable truth that requires effective intervention is that customary land tenure is undergoing pressure from, amongst others demographic growth, the monetisation of the economy and urbanisation.

In this context, there is a need for a flexible compensation system to deal with these complexities. Michelman (2012) in his article "The Property Clause Question" has highlighted that the "Property Clause Question" is not identical to the "Property Question." This explanation is again provided *verbatim*:

> A country may or may not feel itself committed, in general, to private-property and market-based institutions, and therefore to providing and upholding the sorts of civil and regulatory laws and transactional facilities required to support such institutions ... Our question, quite specifically, is whether the country's entrenched, supreme law is to invest in every individual a trumping right to be significantly shielded against a wide range of redistributive aims and effects of state legislative and other actions. The two questions—of a country's sustaining private-property and market—style institutions and practices, and of its having a property clause in its constitutional law—are obviously different."
>
> *(Michelman 2012)*

His proposition then on those contemplating the inclusion of a property clause in their supreme law is that a constitutional property clause can support both a market libertarian and a social democratic system, or leftist and rightist ideologies. Thus, in the context of this paper, it can support both private property rights and tribal land rights held under customary tenure.

In this sense he affirms;

> There is no liberally basic individual right against state-engineered impairments of asset-holdings, considered just as such and without regard to ramification to 'other' liberally cognizable basic rights such as those to liberty, dignity, equality, and legality. Thus, a constitutional property clause—insofar as it has anything at all to do with vindication of basic rights of individuals—must be understood as secondarily supportive of those other basic rights… Not only, then, will the best judicial answers to contested property-clause applications vary with the circumstances; but even *given* the circumstances, the questions will often be ones on which relatively left-leaning liberal adjudicators and relatively right-leaning adjudicators will not always agree."
>
> *(Michelman 2012)*

In this respect he presents as an illustration of the Hungarian case where Parliament, in the name of economic reform, scrapped some well-established entitlement programme, and when this was brought for judicial review, the Hungarian constitutional court relied on the constitutional property clause and rule of law doctrine as enshrined in its Constitution. For Michelman's (2012) perspective, it is easy to comprehend this as resistance to reform but instead the court based its decisions on a liberal-style guarantee of property rights and the rule of law rather than the "social rights" guarantee in the constitution. It is thus clear that the obstacle to liberal economic reform in Hungary is not likely to be the lack of State guarantee of private property but its excessive protection. He also relates a South African case where Parliament on the basis of the constitutional guarantee for everyone "to have access to adequate housing" enacted strong legislation restricting judicial evictions of squatters even based on the owners' valid legal claims for immediate possession of the property. In simple terms, all these examples suggest that the concept of property is liable to different interpretation, depending on where one stands. In these cases, "social rights" have been characterised as "property."

Why relate Michelman's philosophical proposition in the context of the application of the constitution property clause in respect of tribal land rights and communal land? The major characteristic of customary tenure is that land is not regarded as a market commodity but as belonging to a whole social group or community. User rights are transferable within the community, which does not require a formal land registration system to address information asymmetry. This has obviously evolved over time to reflect changing social, political and economic circumstances. But land in this system of property rights is sacred, a "social right," not an asset, and is also a social system. It creates relations and is intertwined with the entire area of human relationships such as kinships. Land is life and without land livelihoods are impeded. Where customary tenure is recognised by the government or given legal protection, what is protected under the constitutional property clause can also be construed, not as private ownership, but as a social right to prevent landlessness or political marginalisation, especially for those with insecure rights. This perspective can be likened to the constitutional guarantee for access to adequate housing in the South African context. Thus, a just compensation solution or compensation standards which respect the liberal notion of property are at odds with the conception of property under customary tenure.

Therefore, a paradigm shift in the Botswana compensation system is required that conceptualises property as socially bound and subject to limitations essential for public order as demanded by society. That is, the focus should shift from the individual, as is the trend being upheld by commonwealth courts, to society. This could be something akin to Michelman's view that what is protected under a constitutional property clause is a political right to participate in society. The protection is for the maintenance of conditions necessary for a fair and effective participation in politics. Just compensation plays a mediating role to address contradictions between individual worth and popular rule; it is due when expropriation of private property and tribal land will impede effective participation in societal politics alongside other members. The German model may also be useful in that the moral purpose of the constitutional property clause is to uphold human dignity. It is to enable an individual to lead a self-governing life. As stated earlier under the German model, the constitution proclaims a social relationship between an individual and the community of such a nature that the individual is dependent on the community but without violating individual worth.

Under the Michelman and German approach, there are cases where some private properties or tribal land interests may not be subject to expropriation at all since the takings mean political marginalisation or will adversely affect livelihoods, self-governance or human dignity. Property rights held for commercial or speculative purposes would receive lesser protection and just compensation would not be solely for economic loss. This also tallies with Radin's (1982) view that property is critical for individuals to take control of their lives and the government should always be wary and sensitive as to whether property subject to expropriation deserves high protection, which may require higher compensation at a higher cost than market value. Personal property associated with autonomy and liberty deserves higher protection relative to fungible property. Wyman's (2007) proposition that the obligation to pay compensation is an effort that seeks to achieve corrective justice by making the victim objectively whole by restitution to the pre-expropriation level is also useful. The objective measure of compensation is therefore based on societal value judgments on what generates wholeness in an individual; thus, individuals are paid to enjoy things society commonly values to the same extent that they did pre-expropriation. For example, goods worth having may include autonomy and liberty, deep and meaningful relationships, enjoyment, all of which are in line with the human welfare conceptions at the heart of the Universal Declarations of Human Rights. Fee's (2006) view particularly on the "home" interest is also relevant, in that a "home" is more than an exchangeable commodity because there is personal attachment in the form of memories, proximity to friends and family, for example; thus, compensation should reflect such non-transferable subjective values of owners to protect their "homes."

How then should adequate compensation be calculated for tribal land rights where expropriation is justified or is considered a last resort after discarding all viable alternative proposals? It is clear that under customary tenure, land is life, sacred and creates social relations. It is not treated as an asset, but it allows personhood and a basis for livelihood. This runs contrary to the idea that compensation should only be payable if there is formal registered legal title to the land even if the land rights are recognised by custom or the informal rules of a community. The fact of the matter is that involuntary resettlement or displacement of people without compensation or social support for rehabilitation is a violation of human rights and can lead to impoverishment, especially to vulnerable members of the community. Determining monetary compensation where there are no land markets or a restricted market, or for shared resources such as communal pastures, is obviously a difficult task. Therefore, the viable practical approach which would mitigate conflict would be one that requires consultation with the affected owners or community where various options as to the form of compensation, such as alternative land, cash payments, share in project benefits, provision of social amenities such as schools and clinics, are considered to improve their livelihoods and standards of living. For example, alternative land for resettlement may be the only solution for vulnerable members of community, as loss of land effectively means loss of livelihood, and because they are unable to use financial resources to find new ways of earning a living or purchasing alternative land. To ensure that affected people receive equitable compensation when customary tribal land is acquired, legislation should envisage such possibilities and devise mechanisms for fair conflict resolution. In this instance, the World Bank's operational manual within its Policy on Involuntary Resettlement (2002) may be of great assistance.

Further, all grants of tribal land rights are allocated *gratis*, State land is allocated on a subsidised basis, whereas some freehold has been acquired through conquest. In this respect, the proposition that market value should be the dominant factor in assessing just compensation does not reflect an equitable balance between the interest of the owner and the public interest. It might be helpful to take a cue from the South African constitutional property clause, Section 25, and Article 14.3.3 of German Basic Law where the proportionality test plays a dominant role in the assessment of compensation. In cases where proportionality is applicable, there must be a balancing act where the interests of both parties are weighed such that there is equilibrium, and where there is no balance compensation plays an equalisation effect. Equalisation relieves an individual owner of an undue burden where there is disproportionate interference. The balancing act may reveal situations where compensation may be less than market value or entirely denied. Under this approach, each individual case is treated on its own merit, thus making it a flexible principle which the legislature and executive should firmly adhere to when setting procedures or guidelines for compensation assessment. Judgment on the principles for assessment of compensation is better placed at a parliamentary level. The courts may then apply the ECtHR approach of a proportionality test in determining whether deprivation should be permitted.

Conclusion

What is protected under the constitutional property clause in Botswana is interpreted as private ownership, and the assessment of compensation reflects the application of the liberal concept of property with a strong emphasis on the individual. The case *Attorney General v Western Trust (Pty) Ltd* exhibits the problem of allowing the judiciary to assess compensation. There is also discrepancy in the assessment of compensation for private land compared to that of tribal land. Further, even the assessment of compensation in respect of tribal land, in practice, reveals the operation of two regimes which do not lead to same award of compensation for the same interest in tribal land. Communal land rights such as for grazing areas are awarded little, if any, compensation on the basis that the claimants do not hold land title. All these raise legitimate constitutional questions of fairness within the compensation system. The law is rather complex, ambiguous and disadvantageous, especially for the vulnerable members of the community who lack the mettle to assert their right to adequate compensation. A comprehensive and simplified law should reduce time expended on interpretation and reduce the number of contentious matters. It is recommended that the settlement of disputes of compensation and the determination of principles of compensation should be confined to the ambit of Parliament subject to judicial review. The award of Parliament should also not be questioned in court on the basis of adequacy. Further, the proportionality test, used in the human rights approach, should be used to determine whether expropriation should be allowed, as well as in the assessment of compensation in the interest of justice.

I would like to end with this note: that law must reflect changing circumstances in society, and the constitution is also not cast in stone—tribal land constitutes a large land mass of over 70% of the country land area, sustaining the livelihoods of a huge proportion of the population. Undoubtedly it plays a major role in the social organisation of communities, and land rights are pivotal to other civil or socioeconomic rights such as housing. The constitutional property clause and socioeconomic rights are thus strong candidates for long overdue constitutional reform.

Note

1 Vyricherla Narayana Gajapativaju v The Revenue District Officer, Vizagapatan [1939] AC 302, 312.

References

Abdulai, R. 2006. "Is Land Title Registration the Answer to Insecure and Uncertain Property Rights in Sub – Saharan Africa?" RICS research paper series. 6(6).

Allen, T. 2004. *The Right to Property in Commonwealth Constitutions*. Cambridge. University Press.

Alexander, G. 2003. Property as a Fundamental Constitutional Right? The German Example. *Cornell Law Faculty working papers*. Paper 4.

Antwi, A. 1998. *The Property Rights Question: The Economics of Urban Land Management in Sub – Saharan Africa*. Our Common Estate. RICS. London.

Baum, A. and Sam, G. 1997. *Statutory Valuations*. International Thomson Business Press. London.

De Graaff, R. and Sluysmans, J. 2013. *Land Reform in the Case Law of the European Court of Human Rights. Lessons for South Africa?*, Paper presented at the Conference on 'Land Divided: Land and South African Society, in Comparative Perspective', University of Cape Town, 24–27 March 2013.

du Plessis, E. 2009. *Compensation for Expropriation under the Constitution*. Unpublished dissertation for Degree of Doctor of Law. Stellenbosch University.

Ebohon, O., Field, B. and Mbuga. 2002. A conceptual analysis of the problems associated with real property development in sub – Saharan Africa. *Journal of Property Management*, 20(1). 7–22.

Fee, J. 2006. Eminent domain and the sanctity of Home. *Notre Law Dame Review*, 81(3). 783–819.

Government of Botswana.1985. *National Land Policy on Land Tenure*. Government Printer. Gaborone. Botswana.

Government of Botswana. 1989. *Report on the Review of Tribal Land Act, Land Policies and Related Issues*. Government Printer. Gaborone. Botswana.

Government of Botswana. 1992. *Report of the Presidential Commission of Inquiry into Land Problems in Mogoditshane and other Peri – Urban Villages*. Government Printer. Gaborone, Botswana.

Government of Botswana.2015 *Botswana Land Policy*. Government Printer. Botswana.

Kirby, J. 2017. 'Conditional on a bill of rights': Race and human rights in the constitution of Botswana, 1960–1966. *Law and History*, 4(1). 30–61.

Macpherson, C. 1975. "Capitalism and the changing concept of property" In *Feudalism, Capitalism and Beyond*, Kamenka, E. and Neale, R. S. (Ed.), Edward Arnold Publishers. London.

Michelman, F. 1981. Property as a constitutional right. *Washington and Lee Law Review*, 38(4). 1097–1114.

Michelman, F. 2012. "The Property Clause Question". Public Law and Legal Theory Working paper series. Paper No.12–07. Harvard Law School.

Ng'ong'ola, C. 1989. Compulsory acquisition of private land in Botswana: The Bonnington farm case. *Comparative and International Law Journal of Southern Africa*, 22(3). 298–319.

Payne, G. 1996. Urban Land Tenure and Property Rights in Developing Countries. A Review of the Literature. Overseas Development Administration.

Radin, M. 1982. *Property and Personhood*. 34 Stan.L. Rev.957.

Rowan-Robson, J. 1990. *Compulsory Purchase and Compensation, The Law in Scotland*. W Green & Sons. Edinburgh.

Spring, D. 2008. *John Rawls's Theory of Justice*. Notes for Philosophy 167.

UN Habitat. 2008. Secure Land Rights for all. Global Tool Land network. Nairobi. Kenya.

Wyman, K. 2007. The measure of just compensation. *UC Davis Law Review*, 41(1). 239–287.

Legislation

Acquisition of Property Act, 1955
Constitution of Botswana, 1966
Constitution of Republic of South Africa, 1996
Deeds Registry Act, 1960
Deeds Registry (Amendment) Act, 2017
English Lands Clauses Consolidation Act, 1845
German Basic Law of 1949
Tribal Land Act, 1968
Tribal Land (Amendment) Act, 1993
Tribal Territories Act, 1933
Tribal Land Bill, 2017

Cases

Botswana

Attorney General v Western Trust (Pty) Ltd (1981) BLR 1 (HC)
Kweneng Land Board v Matlho and Another 1992 BLR 292 (CA)
Kweneng Land Board v Mpofu and Another 2005 (1) BLR 3 (CA)

South Africa

Cape Brandy Syndicate v Inland Revenue Commissioners (1921) 2 kb 483
Pillay v Krishna and Another1946 AD 946

India

West Bengal, State of v Bela Banerjee A.I.R. 1954 S.C. 170
Vajravelu v Special Deputy Collector, West Madras A.I.R. 1965 S.C. 1017
Gujarat v Shantilal Mangaldas A.I.R. 1969 S.C. 634

United Kingdom

Ricket v Metropolitan Rail Co. (1867) LR 2 HL 175 192–3, 202, 214

United States of America

Kelo v City of New London 843 A 2d 500 (2004)

20

The valuation profession and compulsory acquisition and compensation in Africa with special reference to Zimbabwe

Maxwell Mutema

Overview of the valuation profession in Africa

In Africa, in general, the valuation profession and valuation practice are still evolving except in a few countries such as South Africa, and to some extent in countries like Zimbabwe. Otherwise, for most of Africa, the profession can best be described as being in its "infancy" in countries such as Botswana, Namibia and Rwanda.

Countries like Mozambique and Angola have literally no valuation institutions of their own. Ironically, these two countries are currently witnessing some of the fastest real estate development growth rates in Africa.

While countries like Kenya, Uganda, Ghana and Nigeria have valuation professions and practices dating back four decades or so, several authors from these countries who are experienced in the valuation profession have written about the serious challenges they face in these countries. Most of the challenges are generic and are discussed in the next section of this chapter.

However, it is encouraging to note that most African countries are now making concerted efforts to improve the valuation profession landscape in their respective countries by either setting up or promoting new valuation institutions and professional bodies where they are non-existent, or strengthening existing ones. Such efforts are commendable given that professional property valuation is a key element in the smooth functioning of land and property rights. Vibrant and functional property markets play a vital role in national economic development, wealth creation and a nation's prosperity. The absence of such land and property markets has partly been blamed for the lagging behind of the economic development of Africa and other developing countries in general. This has led to many economic and development analysts describing such land as "dead capital", the leading one on this subject being de Soto, the revered Peruvian economist. Active and functional land and property markets can be regarded as the foundation (bedrock) of all other economic activities for any nation.

In Africa, the negative effects of the "dead capital" nature of prime land has been exacerbated not only by the poor state of the valuation profession but also that of other supporting institutions that are related to land and real estate, such as land registration and administration, rural and town planning and land surveying, among others.

Challenges of the valuation profession in Africa

The challenges are multi-faceted and multi-dimensional. They include poor professional education and training, the absence of or weak professional institutions, a lack of reliable property price information, issues to do with ethics and, in some instances, complexities surrounding real estate ownership, land administration and tenure under African traditional customary land tenure.

In most universities in Africa, real estate and valuation degree programmes are still new, ill-equipped, undeveloped and experience severe shortages of well-qualified teaching staff. For example, when both the University of the Copper Belt in Zambia and Namibia Polytechnic started offering real estate and valuation programmes, not so long ago, they had to rely on expatriate teaching staff.

To fill the vacuum created by the absence of qualified valuation and real estate professionals, people of various professional backgrounds assume the role of a "valuer", and these range from lawyers, financial professionals, engineers, rural planners and quantity surveyors, and because they lack the right skills, the work of such professionals could fall short of the expected standards.

Some indicators of the state of the valuation profession in Africa and pointers to challenges

Country	Indicator/valuation challenge pointer			
	Year the representative professional body was formed	Existence of property price/ data index	Number of valuers	Affiliation to international valuation professional organisations such as IVSC* and RICS*
Ghana	1969	None	44 fellows, 279 members	
Kenya	1969	None	<400	Institution of Surveyors of Kenya
Malawi	2012	None	<20	
Namibia	2011	None	<10	Namibia Institute of Valuers, Ministry of Estate Surveyors and Valuers
Nigeria	1969	None	—	Nigeria Institution of Estate Surveyors and Valuers
Rwanda	2011	None	77	
South Africa	1909	Yes	2030	SACPVP*, SAIV*
Tanzania	1997	None	74 fellows, 217 associate members, 43 corporate members	
Uganda	2002	None	62	—
Zimbabwe	1945	None	143	—

Source: Compiled from feedback from key informants compiled data sheets, 2016, IVSC2015.

*Key to Acronyms

IVSC   International Valuation Standards Council
RICS   Royal Institution of Chartered Surveyors
SACPVP South African Council for Property Valuers Profession
SAIV   South African Institution of Valuers

Poor professional standards have also been cited as widespread in most countries in Africa.

Valuation challenges of selected African countries

Rwanda

The valuation profession in Rwanda is still in its infancy. The law to establish and organise the property valuation profession was enacted in 2010, and in the same year, a council to regulate the real property valuation profession was appointed. The Institution of Real Property Valuers of Rwanda was launched in 2011 and, by the end of 2012, it had 77 members.

Ghana

Among the challenges bedevilling the valuation profession in Ghana are unqualified valuers hijacking the profession, the absence of transparent property transactional market information, unstable prices which are sometimes exacerbated by periodic unannounced flashes of high inflation and interest rates, land tenure issues, social factors and variations in demand.

Kenya

Comparable sales data are not readily available. What is supposed to be comparable is hardly comparable as information on the nature of real estate sales, improvements and incomes generated is not readily available.

There is gross under-declaration of values when registering properties for the determination of stamp duty. While the Collector of Stamp Duty requires valuations to be carried out by a government valuer where under declaration is suspected, this is often riddled with corruption.

As for rural valuation, the state agricultural marketing boards (such as those for tea and coffee) have a tendency to manipulate the prices of these commodities, and therefore they do not have or keep true returns from the land; thus, any comparison of the market value of land obtained through using the income approach and sales data in unreliable.

Uganda

The major challenges that the valuation profession faces in Uganda include those associated with a high level of property value speculation, limited public knowledge of the services of valuers, high levels of valuation variance as a result of "opaque" property market price information, inadequate research on pertinent valuation issues, a lack of professional integrity and gaps in the curricular of courses of the major universities offering valuation-related degrees.

Namibia

Until 2012, Namibia did not have legislation to regulate the valuation profession. This meant that valuation activities was almost a free for all, that is, literally, anyone could call themselves a "valuer".

Even before the laws that came to existence in 2012, the Central Bank of Namibia, had been vocal in raising concerns over the lack of consistency when banking institutions conducted valuations, especially for mortgage lending.

Most institutions involved with valuation in Namibia are fairly new and still going through a learning curve. For example, the Directorate of Valuation and Estate Management in the Ministry of Lands and Resettlement needs to be strengthened with regard to human and Information and Communications Technology (ICT) resources.

Malawi

One of the major challenges the valuation profession is experiencing in Malawi stems from being represented by a main professional body whose focus is land surveying and not valuation. While the Survey Institution of Malawi (SIM) is identified by the International Valuation Standards Council (IVSC) as a Valuation Professional Organisation (VPO), the key mandate of the SIM has more to do with land surveying, specifically the geoinformatics aspects of land surveying, such as geodesy, cadastre and photogrammetry, than valuation, at least according to the stated functions of the SIM.

The situation of the representation of the valuation profession by a non-valuation professional body is also common in other countries in Africa.

Addressing the challenges

The challenges tend to be interrelated and addressing them requires comprehensive, multi-pronged and elaborate measures centred on a programme of human capital capacity building and not piecemeal measures.

Globalisation of valuation standards as an additional dimension of valuation challenges in Africa

Related to the aforementioned challenges is the issue of the globalisation of valuation standards. Regardless of the circumstances surrounding the valuation profession in Africa, there is a growing trend toward "globalisation" in real estate practice, and one of the key issues is the desire to standardise valuation practice. Thus to keep pace with the rest of the world Africa has a lot to do in terms of valuation in order to not miss out from global real estate markets and cross real estate trading which demands transparency and consistency in the use of valuation approaches. Investors, especially the major institutional real estate investors, require the assurance of valuations prepared on a basis which is similar to that which they are used to, in order to make informed real estate investment decisions; hence the call for uniform global valuation standards.

The valuation profession in Zimbabwe

In Africa, outside South Africa, Zimbabwe traditionally had one of the oldest and most advanced valuation profession and other real estate-related professions such as rural and town planning, engineering and land surveying. The origin of these expertises was based on the British system, because most of these started as affiliates or offshoots of similar British professional institutions, such as the Royal Institution of Chartered Surveyors, the Chartered Institute of Arbitrators, the Royal Town Planning Institute and the various engineering institutions, such as the Institution of Civil Engineers. Inevitably, this also resulted in Zimbabwe once having one of the most developed, vibrant and functional real estate markets in Africa.

However, since 2000, the situation has significantly changed as a result of a massive skills "brain drain", which was triggered by an unprecedented economic crisis resulting in the collapse of the economy.

The Real Estate Institute of Zimbabwe (REIZ), formerly called the Southern Rhodesia Institute of Estate Agents and Valuers, was formed in 1945. Similarly, a sister or rather a complementary institution (now called the Zimbabwe Institute of Rural and Urban Planners (ZIRUP)) was formed in 1951 by members of the British Town Planning Institute (now called the Royal Town Planning Institute) resident in Central Africa as a Central Africa Branch and this continued to operate as such until it became defunct in 1982 after being replaced by the ZIRUP.

As for the REIZ, until 1996 it was responsible for the regulation of both the valuation profession and estate agency. From 1996 a separate public statutory entity to regulate and govern the valuation profession called the Valuers Council of Zimbabwe was created, and the two institutions have continued to work together, given that most of the valuers originally came through a REIZ qualification route. Today, the two institutions complement each other to ensure the smooth functioning of the valuation profession in Zimbabwe.

The specific functions of these two key institutions in relation to the valuation profession in Zimbabwe are presented below.

Functions of the Real Estate Institute of Zimbabwe

The Real Estate Institute of Zimbabwe seeks to unite in one body all persons practising the various disciplines of the profession of real estate including estate agency, valuation, auctioneering and property management.

It also seeks to secure the advancement and to facilitate the acquisition of knowledge by real estate professionals including valuers practising in Zimbabwe and to maintain and promote the usefulness of these professionals for the public advantage.

It is the Institute's mission to protect and promote the general interest of its members, the profession and the highest standards of ethics and conduct.

The functions of the Valuers Council of Zimbabwe

According to Zimbabwe's Valuers Act, 1996 the function of the Valuers Council is to:

> hold inquiries for the purposes of this Act and to do all things required to be done by the Council in terms of this Act and such other things as... are necessary for ensuring that the competence and conduct of valuers practising in Zimbabwe are of a standard sufficiently high for the protection of the public.

The statutory and legislative framework that affects valuation in Zimbabwe

Some of the key statutes and legislation pertaining to real estate and valuation in Zimbabwe include the following: Estate Agency Act, Valuers Act, Regional Town and Country Planning Act (Chapter 29:12), Urban Councils Act (Chapter 29:15), Rural District Councils

Acts, Deeds Registries Act (Chapter 20:05), Land Acquisition Act (Chapter 20:10), Environmental Management Act (Chapter 20:27), Land Survey Act (Chapter 20:12), Capital Gains Tax Act (Chapter 23:01), Electricity Act (Chapter 13:05), Estate Duty Act (Chapter 23:03), Fencing Act (Chapter 20:06), Forest Act (Chapter 19:05), Housing Standards Control Act (Chapter 29:08) and Mines and Minerals Act (Chapter 21:05).

Compulsory land acquisition and compensation in Zimbabwe

Since 2000 Zimbabwe has found itself in probably one of the biggest compulsory land acquisition programmes for resettlement purposes to occur in Africa, if not in the world, in recent years. It has involved 6,214 large-scale commercial farms covering nearly 10 million hectares (24.7 million acres). Out of the total of 6,214, less than 250 farms (>4%) have been paid compensation nearly 20 years after the government acquired the farms. This means that compensation is one of the key outstanding issues of Zimbabwe's Land Reform Programme.

The programme was heavily criticised internationally in terms of the manner in which it was conducted, in particular for the failure by the government to compensate the farmers whose land was expropriated.

From 1980 to 1990, Zimbabwe conducted an organised and orderly compulsory land acquisition programme accompanied by fair compensation based on market value for the same purpose.

The key highlights and dates in the evolution of compulsory land acquisition and compensation in Zimbabwe can be summarised as follows:

1971: Under the Land Acquisition Act, the Compensation Court was established which fixed the standard of compensation as the market value applicable assuming a willing buyer and willing seller immediately prior to the acquisition

1980: The Independence Constitution permitted compulsory acquisition of "underutilised land" for agricultural resettlement purposes and required "prompt and adequate" compensation to be paid on a willing buyer-willing seller basis for agricultural land, with the option for the sellers to expatriate their compensation. Both these provisions were "entrenched", that is, they were not practically capable of being amended.

1985: The amended or New Land Acquisition Act reserved "the right of first refusal" to the State in respect of every proposed sale of private "rural land" and permitted it to acquire land compulsorily under resumption clauses in title deeds.

1992: Amendments were made to the Land Acquisition Act which provided in Part IV for the "designation" of rural land for resettlement and other purposes. "Fair compensation" was payable for such land in accordance with guidelines issued by the responsible Minister to the Compensation Committee. The Minister was also empowered under the Act to limit the size and number of pieces of land that any person might own for farming purposes and to restrict the ownership, leasing or occupation of land by foreigners in Zimbabwe.

The land acquisition and compensation process followed prior to 2000 (between 1980 and 1999), which was based on a willing buyer-willing seller, market-value and fair compensation, is illustrated diagrammatically below. Note that in the diagram, CONEX stands for the Department of Conservation and Extension which was the main institution then providing technical agricultural advisory, extension and soil and land conservation services and has since been renamed AGRITEX (Department of Agricultural Technical and Extension Services) (Figure 20.1).

2000: Major amendments were made to the original Land Acquisition Act with respect to Clause 57 on compulsory acquisition and compensation. In this Clause, provisions were

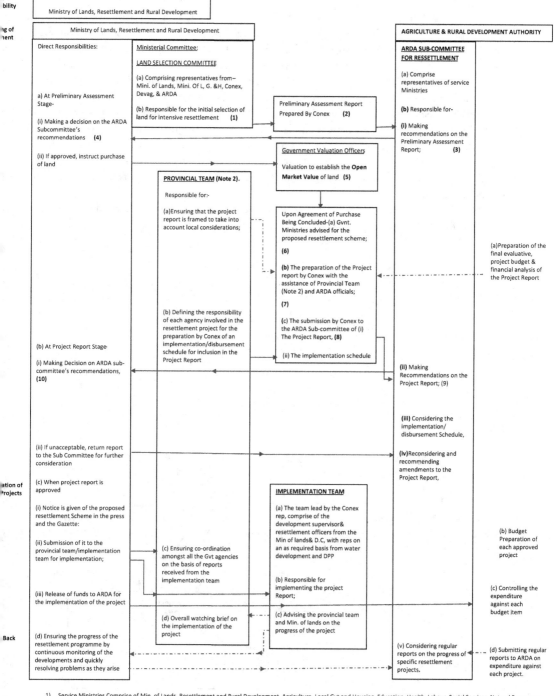

The following text appears within the organogram:

Responsibility

Minister of Lands, Resettlement and Rural Development

Ministry of Lands, Resettlement and Rural Development

ng of ment

Ministry of Lands, Resettlement and Rural Development

AGRICULTURE & RURAL DEVELOPMENT AUTHORITY

Direct Responsibilities:

Ministerial Committee:

LAND SELECTION COMMITTEE

(a) Comprising representatives from– Mini. of Lands, Mini. Of L, G. &H, Conex, Devag, & ARDA

(b) Responsible for the initial selection of land for intensive resettlement **(1)**

ARDA SUB-COMMITTEE FOR RESSETLEMENT

(a) Comprise representatives of service Ministries

(b) Responsible for-

(i) Making recommendations on the Preliminary Assessment Report; **(3)**

a) At Preliminary Assessment Stage-

(i) Making a decision on the ARDA Subcommittee's recommendations **(4)**

(ii) If approved, instruct purchase of land

Preliminary Assessment Report Prepared By Conex **(2)**

Government Valuation Officers

Valuation to establish the **Open Market Value** of land **(5)**

PROVINCIAL TEAM (Note 2).

Responsible for:-

(a)Ensuring that the project report is framed to take into account local considerations;

Upon Agreement of Purchase Being Concluded-(a) Gvnt. Ministries advised for the proposed resettlement scheme;

(6)

(b) The preparation of the Project report by Conex with the assistance of Provincial Team (Note 2) and ARDA officials;

(7)

(b) Defining the responsibility of each agency involved in the resettlement project for the preparation by Conex of an implementation/disbursement schedule for inclusion in the Project Report

(c) The submission by Conex to the ARDA Sub-committee of (i) The Project Report, **(8)**

(ii) The implementation schedule

(a)Preparation of the final evaluative, project budget & financial analysis of the Project Report

(b) At Project Report Stage-

(i) Making Decision on ARDA sub-committee's recommendations, **(10)**

(ii) Making Recommendations on the Project Report; (9)

(iii) Considering the implementation/ disbursement Schedule,

(ii) If unacceptable, return report to the Sub Committee for further consideration

(iv) Reconsidering and recommending amendments to the Project Report,

ation of Projects

(c) When project report is approved

(i) Notice is given of the proposed resettlement Scheme in the press and the Gazette:

(ii) Submission of it to the provincial team/implementation team for implementation;

(iii) Release of funds to ARDA for the implementation of the project

IMPLEMENTATION TEAM

(a) The team lead by the Conex rep, comprise of the development supervisor& resettlement officers from the Min of lands& D.C, with reps on an as required basis from water development and DPP

(c) Ensuring co-ordination amongst all the Gvt agencies on the basis of reports received from the implementation team

(b) Responsible for implementing the project Report;

(b) Budget Preparation of each approved project

(c) Controlling the expenditure against each budget item

(d) Overall watching brief on the implementation of the project

(c) Advising the provincial team and Min. of lands on the progress of the project

Back

(d) Ensuring the progress of the resettlement programme by continuous monitoring of the developments and quickly resolving problems as they arise

(v) Considering regular reports on the progress of specific resettlement projects.

(d) Submitting regular reports to ARDA on expenditure against each project.

1) Service Ministries Comprise of Min. of Lands, Resettlement and Rural Development, Agriculture, Local Gvt and Housing, Education, Health, Labour, Social Services, Natural Resources and Water Development and Roads and Road Traffic

2) The Provincial Term is under the following of Provincial Commissioner and Comprises representatives of the service Ministriesat local level

3) Key to the Organogram ———▶ Progress of Resettlement Project
- - - - - ▶ Inputs for the Project Report Preparation
——— ▶ Report Back Procedures

0.1 The original compulsory land acquisition and purchase process for the Land Resettlement Programme in Zimbabwe.

added stating that if "the former colonial power" did not pay compensation for agricultural land required for resettlement purposes, the Government of Zimbabwe had no obligation to do so and that if the Government of Zimbabwe chose to pay compensation in respect of such land, it might choose by Act of Parliament to pay for improvements to the land only. This has continued to be the basis for compensation up to this date. However, this provision mainly applies to compensation for land which belonged to former white farmers and as such has been criticised as selective, vindictive and discriminatory. Land with freehold title deed, which remained private land, had never been acquired by the government for resettlement purposes; land which belongs to any indigenous person and land which is under a Bilateral Investment Promotion and Protection Agreement (BIPPA) is compensated on the basis of fair and full open market value and compensation is for both land and improvements.

The process of compensation under Zimbabwe's statutes can be summarised diagrammatically as follows (Figure 20.2):

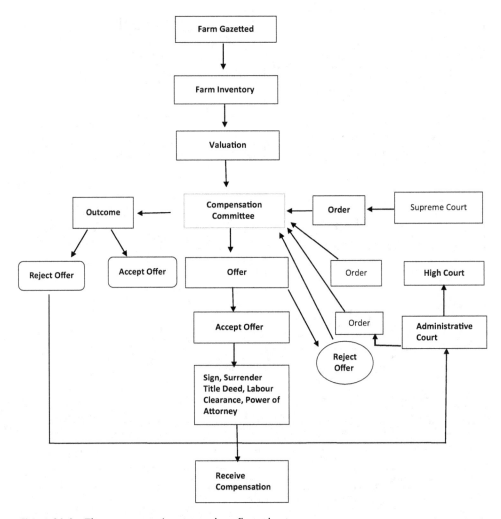

Figure 20.2 The compensation procedure flow chart

Criticism of compensation for improvements-only approach

The compensation based on an improvements-only approach has been largely criticised as flawed as it excludes the land and this is contrary to best international practice. According to the Food and Agriculture Organisation of the United Nations (UN FAO) (2009) and the International Federation of Surveyors (FIG) (2010) compensation should reflect all the assets that were affected by the compulsory acquisition or purchase, including the land and improvements Other criticisms which have been levelled against this approach include a lack of transparency in the manner in which it is conducted by the government—the parameters used by the government to determine the value, the failure by government to consult and engage with the former farmers to be compensated, the arbitrary nature of the award of compensation (take it or leave it) without a genuine and credible appeal mechanism, the lack of capacity resources to carry out timely valuations and the time lapse without compensation amounting to nearly two decades since government acquired the land.

The time lapse factor also gives rise to other complications such as missing information and assets, time value of money and loss, among many others.

Questions have been raised on the impartiality and transparency of the Compensation Committee when making decisions on the final compensation value. The Compensation Committee is a legally constituted body that makes the final approval of the amount of compensation based on valuation reports by government valuers.

It has also been suggested that there should be an Arbitration Committee to separate responsibilities so that not one committee is responsible for awarding the compensation as well as for mediation when a disagreement on the amount of compensation arises.

These criticisms imply that the approach falls short of the minimum international best practice on compulsory acquisition and compensation which, according to the FAO and FIG, must have the features described in the preceding section.

The universal basis and purpose for compensation

Payment or settlement of compensation for property, business or an asset that has been compulsorily acquired by the state or any other public institution acting on behalf of public good is a fundamental requirement of international law.

In the interest of civilisation and in the eyes of the international community, compensation signifies acceptance of responsibility by the state and its agencies for its actions and policies.

Regardless of the circumstances that result in the justification of the compulsory acquisition of an asset, business or property by the state or any of its agencies acting on its behalf, if compensation is not paid, this is deemed unacceptable.

Customary international law provides the legal foundation for the compensation of victims (claimants) of the compulsory acquisition of property, business or an asset by the state. Compensation is part of international humanitarian law. Article 8 of the Universal Declaration of Human Rights states that everyone has a right to an effective remedy (in this case, compensation).

Compensation serves a variety of important functions:

- It helps claimants to manage the material aspect of their loss—to bring immediate economic relief and to fulfil the basic survival needs of claimants. In many cases monthly payments are crucial to ensure the claimants' survival.
- Compensation is also about making crucial repairs to individuals' psyches, social and political institutions.

- Compensation helps to restore the claimant's dignity and is an important component and focal point in the claimants' healing process.
- Compensation helps to deter the abuse of state power. It prevents the reoccurrence of acts which require compensation—policies and powers that give rise to the need to pay compensation are only used when absolutely necessary.
- Compensation helps claimants move beyond the desire for revenge and makes it possible to repair relationships that have been damaged by the compulsory acquisition process.
- Compensation signifies a move to make amends and to take responsibility and is some form of symbolic apology.

General international principles and recommendations for good practice

According to the UN FAO and FIG general principles and recommendations for good practice, the processes for compulsory acquisition and compensation should be based on the following:

- Assistance should be provided so that the people to be compensated participate effectively in negotiations on valuation and compensation.
- The affected parties should have the right to represent themselves and/or use a lawyer, expert or agent.
- The government should take possession of the land after owners have been paid at least partial compensation, accompanied by clearly defined compensation guarantees.
- Participatory planning processes should be used ensuring that all the affected people are involved.
- The right to appeal to an independent court must be assured.
- The acquiring agency should be accountable for its actions and personal discretion should be limited.
- Compulsory acquisition should not be the preferred tool for the acquisition of land. The land to be acquired should be kept to a minimum.
- The due process should be defined in law with specified time limits.
- Procedures should be transparent and undertaken in good faith.
- Notice should be clear in written and oral form.

What may be compensated for under international good practice

- The land: The land must also be included, but in the particular case of Zimbabwe, the position of the government on land is outlined under Section 72 of the Zimbabwe Constitution of 2013. Section 72 Rights to Agricultural Land, subsection (7) (c) (i) and (ii) states that: (i) the former colonial power has an obligation to pay compensation for agricultural land compulsorily acquired for resettlement, through an adequate fund established for this purpose; and (ii) if the former colonial power fails to pay compensation through such a fund, the Government of Zimbabwe has no obligation to pay compensation for agricultural land compulsorily acquired for resettlement.
- Improvements including crops.
- The value of any financial advantage other than the market value of the land that the landowner may enjoy by virtue of owning that land.
- Interest on unpaid compensation from the day of acquisition.
- Costs incurred as a direct and reasonable result of the acquisition.

- Loss in value to any other land owned by the affected person as a result of the acquisition of the land. In some jurisdictions the compensation is reduced if the retained land increases in value as a result of the project. This is referred to as betterment.
- Professional, arbitration or legal expenses including the costs of obtaining advice and of preparing documents to be submitted.
- Costs of moving and acquiring alternative accommodation.
- Expenses associated with reorganising farming operations when only a part of the property or business is acquired.
- The loss in value of the business displaced by the acquisition or when the business is permanently closed as a result of the acquisition.
- Temporary loss of earnings.
- Personal hardships.
- Any other losses or damages suffered as a result of the acquisition.

Pertinent international good practice issues

The principle of equivalence

Affected persons should receive compensation that is no more or no less than the loss resulting from the compulsory acquisition of their land. Appropriate measures should be taken to ensure that those affected are not disadvantaged.

Valuation method

A valuation method or approach refers to generally accepted analytical methodologies to establish the value of an asset, property or service.

There are various methods or approaches to calculate market value, but the most common ones used in practice and academic writing are the market approach (or the sales comparison approach), the income capitalisation approach (including the discounted cash flow analysis), and the asset-based valuation approach (or the cost approach). Depending on the situation, the type of property, business, asset or service to be valued, any of these methods can be chosen to provide a relatively reliable measure of market value.

The criteria for choosing a valuation method include:

- The nature of the property being valued, as different methods or approaches are better suited for certain assets than others.
- Whether the asset is a going concern with future prospects of profitability or in liquidation.
- The quantity and quality of information available to the valuer is important.
- Perceptions also play an important role in the choice of valuation method.

Market value

The market value is the most reliable indicator of the actual value of an asset at a determined date. A good measure of the market value is the evidence of a prior arm's length transaction involving a willing seller and a willing buyer involving similar property units made close to the date of valuation. The market value is often calculated by reference to the business as a going concern. Normally, the market value of a going concern with a history of profitable operations and anticipated future profits can be estimated.

Where there are no markets

The absence of a market for a property, business or an asset to be compensated may be encountered in some instances. In such cases, things to consider include comparable sales, replacement costs, cost of obtaining a functional substitute, income produced by the property, chances of gains and risks of loss as well as any other data for constructing this missing or substitute market. This helps to give a hypothetical market for the asset or improvement in question when a directly demonstrable market is not available.

The valuation date

The choice of the valuation date can materially affect the amount of compensation to be awarded or paid, and as such it is important for the valuation of compensation and damages under international compensation law. The value of an asset changes over the course of time. In addition, social, economic and political developments also have a direct impact on value.

It is often the case that a considerable amount of time elapses between the acquisition that gives rise to the claims and the award of the compensation or damages. This makes the valuation date an important factor for consideration in terms of international good practice on compensation settlements.

The valuation date is important both for the relevant condition of the asset and for the information available and its usability. The valuation date should be determined either on the basis of the agreement between the two parties or on the law applicable. In principle, the valuation date in expropriation is generally accepted to be the expropriation date. However, information breakout about proposed compulsory acquisition measures before this date can significantly affect the value. As a result, the decisive valuation date under international law effectively lies immediately before the acquisition or before the date at which the decision to compulsorily acquire becomes publicly known. This helps to avoid diminishing the value of the asset or property just before the expropriation.

Timing of compensation payments

International good practice requires that the payment of compensation for expropriation be made "promptly", "without delay", "without undue delay" or "without unreasonable delay".

Payments may be made in instalments in case of difficulties in mobilising payment resources, or in the case of a payment crisis (as in the case between Sierra Leone and UK in 1981). Where compensation payments are delayed, interest on the outstanding amount may be applied.

Interest

When a party does not pay a sum of money when it falls due, the party to be compensated is entitled to interest upon that sum from the time when payment is due to the time payment is made, whether or not the non-payment has been explained.

A number of issues affect the rate of interest on the awarded sum, and these include:

- Fixed or floating interest rate;
- Compounding;
- Beginning dates for interest accrual;

- Legal sources of interest computations (calculations);
- The currency of the interest rate; and
- The day count (e.g. actual/360 or 30/365).

Date from which interest accrues

Date from which interest should accrue provides that the obligation to pay interest starts "from the date when the principal sum should have been paid until the date the obligation is fulfilled" (Sabahi 2011 at page 149). The time period between the two dates may be divided into pre-award and post-award stages. The obligation to pay interest extends across these periods starting from the date of an action and continuing until the date of payment. If the day of the action and valuation are not the same, the latter sets the starting date. All awards adjudicated under international tribunals accrue post-award interest.

Rate of interest

The rate at which interest accrues should be 'appropriate' or equal to the 'prevailing commercial rate'. The task of setting the rate of interest can be left to an agreed independent committee on a case-by-case basis or can be negotiated amicably between the two parties. A general guiding principle can be that it is the interest rate the aggrieved party could have earned if the action had not been committed. Depending on the circumstance, it may also be taken to be the hypothetical rate that the claimants could have obtained if they had repatriated the compensation sum to their country to invest in a suitable investment vehicle.

Simple or compound interest

Until recently, the norm has been to award only simple interest. However, this seems to be changing in favour of awarding compound interest. From 1993 to 2004, out of 21 international cases in which monetary compensation was awarded, 10 of the cases were awarded simple interest. However, from 2006 to 2009, 18 out of 26 cases were awarded compound interest.

Currency of compensation

During relatively stable economic times, when exchange rates between various currencies do not fluctuate radically, it does not matter in which currency the compensation has been awarded as there would be no financial or economic harm to the recipient of the award. The choice of currency of compensation in this case may not have any practical significance.

However, during times of economic or financial uncertainty or turmoil when the currency of one country substantially loses value against other major currencies, the difference between receiving compensation in the former or the latter where large sums of money is involved may be significant. In such cases the claimant or aggrieved party must be protected against such risks.

The choice of compensation currency should be motivated by the objective of protecting the person to be compensated against currency devaluation. Thus, compensation can be paid in the currency in which the investment was made, or the currency of the claimant's home state or otherwise.

Transferability and convertibility of compensation currency

International good practice also generally requires that payments be made transferable and in a freely convertible currency. Payment should be freely transferable to the country designated by the claimant and must be effectively realisable. It must also be paid and made freely transferable to a foreign bank account and in the currency of the country of which the claimant is a national or any freely convertible currency agreed upon by the two parties.

The principle of highest and best use

One of the principles underlying the determination of fair market value for compensation is the concept of highest and best use (HABU).

Fair market value is not a measure of the value of the asset as it has been used, but rather it is a measure of the value of the asset if the asset is put to its most valuable potential use.

In the *Santa Elena v Costa Rica Case*[1], for example, the claimant's beach front property was to be developed into a resort and residential complex, when, in 1978, the Costa Rica Government expropriated it. In 2000, during arbitration, the claimant argued that the best use of the property would have been as a resort and residential complex, while Costa Rica argued that its best use was as a conservation area. The tribunal's valuation decision took the property's potential for touristic development into account in its award of compensation.

Review and arbitration

The amount of compensation must be subject to prompt review by a judicial authority or another competent and independent authority.

Deductions and reductions

In determining the amount to be paid by way of compensation, deductions or reductions can be made on liabilities owed by the claimant, such as an outstanding loan to the government or a financial institution.

Efforts toward reaching consensus on compensation between former farmers and the government

The government has since realised the importance of constructive engagement and consultation with the former white commercial farmers to bring to a close the outstanding issue of compensation in order to move the country's land reform agenda forward and subsequently its overall economic recovery and growth. As a result, a joint *ad hoc* committee comprising government officials and representatives of the former farmers has been created to build consensus on compensation. The committee is chaired by the Head of the Legal Department in the Ministry of Land and Rural Development.

The initial meeting of the joint committee has already taken place. The major outcome of the inaugural meeting was an agreement to form a technical subcommittee comprising valuers representing the government and those representing the former farmers. The subcommittee focuses on the technical issues relating to valuation, such as valuation parameters and the sharing of price information (Figure 20.3).

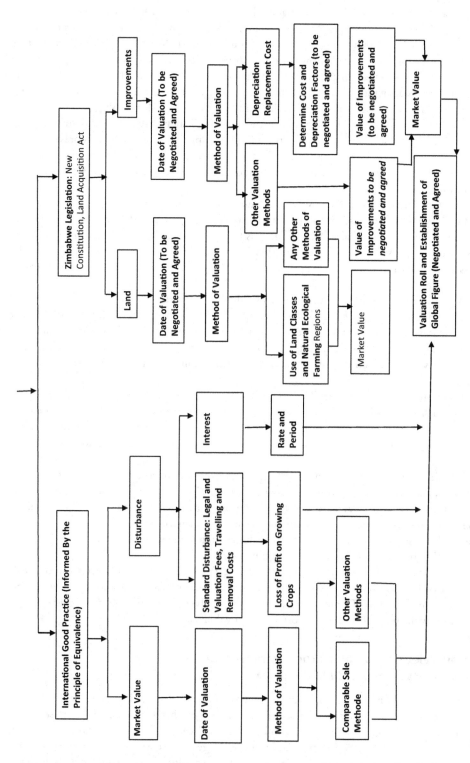

Figure 20.3 Conceptualised consensus-based valuation and compensation framework for Zimbabwe

So far, steady progress has been made, although there are still outstanding contentious issues, such as the land. Overall, the engagement so far has been harmonious and constructive; it is hoped that this trajectory will continue and that the compensation issue will be resolved amicably. There is determination from both sides to see this happening. If indeed this comes to pass, a new chapter would have been opened to unlock the potential and value of Zimbabwe's agricultural land, which is one of the country's treasured natural resources. Zimbabwe's agricultural land is almost the equivalent of what oil is to Nigeria.

To ensure the success of this process, the former farmers have formed a fully constituted Compensation Steering Committee (CSC), comprising five members representing all the major former farmer representative groups such as the Commercial Farmers Union, Southern Africa Commercial Farmers Alliance, Agriculture Recovery and Compensation Committee.

The Committee has a chair who is a high-profile figure in the farming community and society and is deputised by a vice chair who is also a past president of the Commercial Farmers Union of Zimbabwe. The composition is completed by three other members who are of high standing and credibility within the echelons of the farmers to be compensated, including one who was once awarded the accolade of 'Cattleman of the Year of Zimbabwe'.

With advice from professional legal and valuation experts, the specific function of the Compensation Steering Committee is to engage, lobby and advocate with the Government of Zimbabwe and other stakeholders on behalf of the commercial farmers of Zimbabwe who suffered losses during the Fast Track Land Resettlement Exercise to achieve full, fair and effective compensation/restitution and the restoration of rights in a framework of rural reconstruction and development.

The valuation expert group that advises the former farmers to be compensated is called Valuation Consortium (Valcon). Valcon was set up to deal with all technical valuation matters pertaining to the compensation of the farmers. Valcon is also the representative of the farmers on the joint government-farmer technical subcommittee under the current arrangements.

Initially, Valcon compiled and developed a state-of-the-art asset database register or inventory of all assets which existed on the farms at the time of the acquisition by the government. It maintains the database and continuously improves its functionality. The database contains the most authentic, accurate and credible information on the farms that were acquired. Valcon's work is world class and combines high database functionality and the use of Geographic Information System (GIS) technology.

The Valcon was formed at the onset of the Fast Track Land Reform Exercise on the realisation that it was crucial to keep a reliable record of all assets for the purpose of future compensation negotiations. The formation of Valcon involved bringing together eight reputable valuation firms with good track records of farm valuations.

An overview of valuation for compensation of compulsory acquired land in Africa

Valuation for compensation of land that is compulsorily acquired is more complex than normal or ordinary valuation and requires more experienced valuers, which poses more challenges and difficulties than valuation in Africa is already facing. The rapid urbanisation, the many infrastructure projects underway and large-scale natural resources investments (such as in oil and gas), and large-scale commercial agricultural investments currently being witnessed in many countries in Africa have also added to the problems as they displace people and communities who need to be compensated.

Just to give a snapshot of some of the large-scale developments in Africa today, they include large-scale commercial agricultural investments in countries like Zambia, Mozambique, South Sudan and Angola, the oil and gas discoveries in, for example, Ghana, Uganda, Kenya, Mozambique and the large infrastructure projects in many African countries.

The new era in Zimbabwe

As the author of this chapter had just finishing writing it, President Mugabe resigned after a six-day house arrest by the military. The news of his political demise was received with euphoria and a great sense of hope by the Zimbabwean population. The new President Cde Mnangagwa, his former deputy, has since been sworn in and has promised to take the country in a different direction from that of his predecessor to ensure economic revival and recovery. One of the key issues that President Mnangagwa has identified as top priority in his inaugural speech was that of the compensation of farmers whose land was acquired by the government for resettlement purposes. The following are excerpts of that speech on compensation.

"... given our historical realities, we wish the rest of the world to understand and appreciate that policies and programmes related to land reform were inevitable. ... the principle of repossessing our land cannot be challenged or reserved. Dispossession of our ancestral land was the fundamental reason for waging the liberation struggle. ... Therefore, I exhort beneficiaries of the Land Reform Programme to show their deservedness by demonstrating commitment to the utilisation of the land now available to them for national food security and recovery of our economy....

My government is committed to compensating those farmers from whom land was taken, in terms of the laws of the land. As we go into the future, complex issues of land tenure will have to be addressed both urgently and definitely, in order to ensure finality and closure to the ownership and management of this key resource, which is central to national stability and to sustained economic recovery. We dare not prevaricate on this key issue"

(from Scoons, 2017)

Without doubt the President is absolutely right to recognise the urgency to resolve this one issue as the major stumbling block in the cog of the wheel to redeem Zimbabwe's economic fortunes. The President's development and economic agenda, the dream and the vision can only move forward in earnest once the issue of compensation has been satisfactorily resolved.

Conclusion

There are a number of challenges currently bedevilling the valuation process across Africa. Efforts are underway to deal with them, but it will take a while to build a strong and formidable valuation process supporting institutions and frameworks. Africa can benefit immensely by collaborating and partnering with valuation institutions and professional bodies from those countries with developed valuation profession and practice, such as the UK, Europe, Australia, New Zealand, Singapore and the USA, global institutions like RICS and the IVSC.

Valuation for compensation for compulsory purchased or such acquired land requires more experienced and skilled professional valuers than the normal (market) valuation, and this puts most countries in Africa in an even more difficult position given the already existing challenges. The situation is made worse by the rapid urbanisation and the large infrastructure projects currently underway across the continent, which in most cases involves compulsory acquisition of large tracts of land which thus requires compensation of the affected people and communities.

As for Zimbabwe, the country has had previous experience of handling compensation for compulsorily acquired land for resettlement purposes and one hopes that the current engagement and involvement of the former farmers will yield a positive outcome. This experience from Zimbabwe, in future, may also become useful reference for the rest of Africa.

There are also large-scale land reform programmes in South Africa and Namibia involving the acquisition and compensation of large tracts of land for resettlement purposes, and these can also be reference points for Zimbabwe and the rest of Africa. In the particular case of Zimbabwe, compensation of land acquired by the government's fast track land reform programme needs to be resolved as a matter of urgency in order to unlock the value of the country's fertile agricultural land. As the saying goes 'When agriculture sneezes the rest of the economy catches the cold' Agriculture is the backbone of Zimbabwe's economy.

Note

1 *Compañía del Desarrollo de Santa Elena S.A. v The Republic of Costa Rica* 2000.

References

Food and Agriculture Organisation of the United Nations (UN FAO) (2009) Compulsory Acquisition of Land and Compensation, FAO Land Tenure Studies Number 10, FAO, Rome.

International Federation of Surveyors (FIG) (2010) Compulsory Purchase and Compensation, FIG, Copenhagen.

Sabahi, Borzu (2011) Compensation and Restitution in Investor-State Arbitration. Principles and Practice. International Economic Law Series. General Editor John H Jackson. Oxford University Press. Oxford.

Scoons, Ian (2017) Two Speeches for New Era Zimbabwe. Zimbabweland https://zimbabweland. wordpress.com/2017/12/11/two-speeches-for-new-era-zimbabwe/.

21

An economic analysis of compulsory acquisition in selected Caribbean states

Tina Beale

Introduction

Compulsory acquisition is a sociolegal phenomenon that affects individuals with property rights across the globe. In the Caribbean, it is governed by the Land Acquisition Act for individual island states. Although expropriation is not a recent phenomenon in the region, there appears to be nascent academic literature on its undertaking in the small island economies of the Caribbean. In a bid to begin the process of filling the aforementioned gap, the purpose of this chapter is threefold.

The chapter begins with an overview of the principal compulsory purchase legislations in Antigua and Barbuda, St. Lucia and St. Vincent, Jamaica and Trinidad and Tobago. Thereafter, an economic analysis of compulsory acquisition in the selected territories is undertaken, with a view to illustrating the socio-economic problems associated with the phenomenon in the selected territories. The chapter concludes with a theoretical framework of expropriation in the territories and provides recommendations on how to improve the equitability of compensation.

An overview of compulsory purchase legislations in the selected territories

In this subsection, the principal land acquisition statutes of Antigua and Barbuda, St. Lucia, St Vincent and the Grenadines (the Eastern Caribbean), Jamaica and Trinidad and Tobago will be presented in unison. The principal statutes of the islands are as follows:

*   Antigua and Barbuda – The Land Acquisition Act (CAP 233) 1958
*   St. Lucia – The Land Acquisition Ordinance (CAP 101) 1946
*   St. Vincent – The Land Acquisition Act (CAP 241) 1947
*   Jamaica – The Land Acquisition Act (CAP 204) 1947 and
*   Trinidad and Tobago – The Land Acquisition Act (CAP 58:01) 1996

The legislations for the territories are generally, similar in nature. As a result, similar administrative procedures are applied in the islands. Their legislations may be arranged in three sections as follows:

1   the acquisition of land and abandonment of the acquisition;
2   the appointment and powers of the Board of Assessment and the Commissioner of Lands; and
3   the determination and assessment of compensation.

A description of each category is provided hereinafter.

The acquisition of land and abandonment of acquisition

Under the legislations, when any land may be needed for a public purpose, a notice outlining the government's intention to acquire the land is published in the Gazette and posted in the locality where the land is situated. Upon publication of the notice, authorised officers and/ or their agents may enter the land, demarcate it and conduct preliminary investigations on the site. Where access is needed to buildings, permission must be obtained from the owner.

Whenever it is apparent that the land will be needed for the intended public purpose, a declaration is published in the Gazette and posted on buildings where the land is located. Subsequently, the authorised officer has the authority to take possession of the subject. Where any land acquired has not been demarcated or cannot be identified by reference to any plan, the authorised officer or Commissioner may have the land demarcated, and have a copy of the notice of acquisition served personally on persons with compensable interests (persons interested) or delivered to their homes or businesses.

Negotiations between the landowner and authorised officer may commence before the publication of a declaration or immediately after its publication. All persons interested should appear in person or be represented by an attorney/agent before the officer to explain the nature of their interest. They may also be required to submit in writing the details of their interests or the interest of other persons in a period stipulated by the authorised officer or outlined in the declaration.

In the Eastern Caribbean Territories, the officer has three months to acquire the land or to abandon the acquisition. If the acquisition has not been declared by that time, persons interested may serve a notice on him, requiring feedback on the status of the acquisition. Subsequently, if the acquisition is still incomplete within a month, it should be construed as being abandoned. The governor-general also has the right to declare an acquisition abandoned. In Trinidad and Tobago, if the acquisition has not been declared within six months after the conclusion of preliminary investigations and the Commissioner has not taken possession, persons interested may serve a notice on the Cabinet Secretary requiring that one of the following be undertaken:

1   An order declaring that the land is needed for a public purpose;
2   An order authorising the Commissioner to take possession; or
3   An order declaring that the acquisition be abandoned.

Additionally, the President also has the power to declare an acquisition abandoned. On the other hand, the Jamaican legislation does not indicate a time frame in which the declaration has to be made.

Acquisition in special cases in Trinidad and Tobago

The Trinidadian legislation enables highway authorities, municipal and statutory corporations and private entities or individuals (promoters) to expropriate lands, in accordance with the requirements outlined in the Acquisition in Special Cases Schedule in the Act. Highway authorities and municipal/statutory corporations can acquire lands in performance of their statutory duties. The Acquisition in Special Cases Schedule states that a Minister with responsibility for public works and municipal corporations is regarded as a highway authority.

Municipal and statutory corporations need a resolution from the municipal council and corporation in order to acquire land compulsorily. Thereafter, a notice outlining the intention to conduct preliminary investigations will be published by the highway authority or corporation. When the Minister with responsibility for public works is the highway authority, it is the Minister who will publish the notice. If the land is suitable, then the acquisition will be declared. Any land acquired by municipal or statutory corporations vests absolutely in the corporation. When the Minister acquires land, it vests absolutely in the Crown. Persons interested will be required to provide the details of their interests and submit their claims for compensation and costs to:

1   the Permanent Secretary for the Minister with responsibility for public works, when the acquisition is being undertaken by a Minister who is the highway authority; or
2   the town clerk or chief executive officer when the municipal council is the highway authority; or
3   the corporation when any land is being acquired by a statutory corporation.

All costs normally undertaken by the Commissioner will be covered by the highway authority and corporation. The corporation will need approval from the President to sell any land it has acquired.

When a promoter wishes to acquire land under the Act, an application has to be made to the Cabinet Secretary. The application should include all details related to the intended use of the land. Subsequently, an inquiry is undertaken by the Cabinet Secretary and the costs associated with it are covered by the promoter. Next, a recording of the inquiry is submitted to Parliament for a decision to be made. If the application is approved, the promoter will cover all costs associated with the acquisition.

Subsequently, the promoter will enter into an agreement, with the government, which outlines the terms on which the company or individual will hold the land, the type and duration of works that will be conducted and maintained, how the public will be entitled to use the land and the benefits they will receive. Thereafter, the Parliament will approve the acquisition. If a promoter defaults on the terms of the agreement, the land will be forfeited to the State.

Appointment and powers of the Board of Assessment and the Commissioner of Lands

In the Eastern Caribbean Territories, the Board of Assessment consists of three members – a High Court Judge who will serve as its chair, a member who is nominated by the governor-general and a member who is nominated by the owner of the acquired land. If the owner fails to nominate an individual within a reasonable time, the Board will consist of the chair and the governor-general's nominee.

The authorised officer is required to provide the Board with an opinion of a proper description of the land and the amounts that are to be awarded in compensation to each party. The Board is mandated to:

1   hold an inquiry with persons interested; and
2   make a determination on the award for compensation.

Where two board members have decided on the same figure for compensation, their decision will be the award for compensation. However, where each member has proposed different figures, the mean between the chair's proposal and the amount proposed by another member whose figure is closer to the chair's proposal will be the award for compensation. Persons interested have the right to lodge an appeal against the Board's decision at the Appellate Court.

In Jamaica, the Commissioner of Lands performs a similar role to the Board of Assessment. The Commissioner has the power to enquire into any objections persons interested may have and determine the amount of compensation payable to them. The Commissioner also has the power to:

1   order persons interested to attend the enquiry; and
2   oblige them to produce documents that will be important for the determination of an award.

The Commissioner's award will be final provided that persons interested have not appealed their award.

The assessment and determination of compensation

The assessment and determination of compensation in the territories are predicated on the *Point Gourde Principle (Pointe Gourde)*, established in the Privy Council case *Pointe Gourde Quarrying and Transport Company Limited v Sub Intendent of Crown Lands* 1947.

The valuation date for the determination of compensation in the Eastern Caribbean islands is one year before the date of possession. In Jamaica and Trinidad and Tobago, the valuation date is the date possession was taken by the Commissioner. In the Eastern Caribbean states and Jamaica, disputes are settled by the Appellate Court. However, in Trinidad and Tobago, disputes are settled by the Land Tribunal.

Toward an economic analysis of compulsory acquisition in the selected territories

The enactments of the islands possess two similarities which form the bedrock of their legislations. These similarities may also be considered to be the most fragile aspects of expropriation in the region. The first issue relates to the public purpose-public use requirement in expropriation law. The second centres around the efficacy of the *Pointe Gourde* Principle and its application in the islands. The analysis explores the intricacies of each issue by evaluating the legal code and case law in the selected territories.

The public purpose-public use requirement

The compulsory purchase legislations of St. Lucia, St. Vincent and Jamaica do not define or outline the term "public purpose". However, the Trinidadian and Antiguan statutes define the term broadly, which suggests their governments have wide powers when expropriating land. The Antiguan legislation defines "public purpose" as "a purpose determined to be a public purpose…" (Laws of Antigua and Barbuda, Land Acquisition Act, 3). However, the Antiguan constitution outlines "a use is public if it is intended to result or results in a benefit or advantage to the public and,…includes any use affecting the physical, economic, social or aesthetic well-being of the public" (Section 9 (6), 12). On the other hand, the Trinidadian Act states "public purposes include the purpose of fulfilling any obligation of the State under any treaty or agreement made by the Government with the Government of any other country … and any purpose pertaining or ancillary thereto" (Section 2 (3), 6). In light of the manner in which the terms "public purpose" and "public use" are used in the Antiguan and Trinidadian legal codes, it may be argued that both terms are used interchangeably, which suggests there is no distinction between them.

Nicholson and Mota (2005) defined "public use" as the taking of private power for use by the public. Simply put, expropriated land will be used by the public for the benefit of the public. Therefore, a "public use" should increase social welfare in a society. In *Thompson v Consolidated Utilities Corporation 1937*, the court ruled "[T]his court has many times warned that one person's property may not be taken for the benefit of another private person without a justifying public purpose, even though compensation be paid" (cited in Nicholson and Mota, 2005). In the light of the court's judgement, one may ask what constitutes a "justifying public purpose". The judgement implies a "public purpose" is derived from a third-party transfer of expropriated land. As a result, ownership rights of the benefit which emerge from the acquisition are not owned by the public or a public corporation. Rather ownership rights rest in private hands that will earn economic rent from those rights. It should therefore follow that expropriations which involve third-party transfer(s) require more careful scrutiny by the judiciary.

Slade (2014) argued that "public purpose" is more limited in scope than "public use". He contended that this distinction is important when a taking includes a third-party transfer. In this regard, Kelly (2006) opined that any expropriation which involves a third-party transfer is unnecessary because promoters can avoid the strategic holdout problem by using secret agents to purchase lands on their behalf. As a result, government intervention would not be required even if the intended use of the land will result in a public benefit. In the light of the aforementioned arguments, the application of the public purpose requirement in the Caribbean needs examination.

It is clear that the public purpose requirement enables Caribbean governments to expropriate lands for "public use" and "public purposes". However, the constitutions of the Eastern Caribbean islands and Jamaica imply a compulsory purchase will only involve a transfer of private rights to the government. However, the Trinidadian act explicitly facilitates expropriation with third-party transfers.

The provisions of the Jamaican and Eastern Caribbean legal codes collectively presuppose, third-party transfers are not involved in a compulsory purchase, and in consequence neither of their constitutions nor their statutes have outlined what constitutes a third-party transfer. They are also not explicit on whether property rights (such as ownership rights, use rights, the right to earn and the right to enforce property rights) in any acquired land will be transferred to third parties, in order for the intended public benefit to be achieved. Where ownership rights are retained by the government, but use rights, the right to earn an income and the right to enforce property rights are transferred, promoters will possess the right to earn economic rent from the public benefit. Similarly, if ownership rights are transferred, promoters will possess the right to earn economic rent from the public benefit. Regardless of the type of third-party transfer that is involved or associated with an expropriation, the outcome is the same. Both transfers enable promoters to earn profits from the expected benefits and/or ownership rights in the expropriated land. This issue brings two questions to the forefront of the analysis:

1   Who will be the main beneficiary of the expropriation – the promoter or the public?
2   Is expropriation the only means by which the public benefit can be achieved?

By using two cases, one in Antigua and another in Jamaica, the importance of these questions is highlighted.

The Antiguan Case of the Half Moon Bay Resort

The Half Moon Bay Resort was built in Antigua in the 1950s. In 1971, seven American investors formed HMB Holdings Limited (HMB) to own and operate the resort. In 1995, the hotel was severely damaged by Hurricane Luis. Subsequently, the hoteliers tried to re-build their resort, but its reconstruction was delayed by insufficient insurance and a dispute between the shareholders.

In 1998, the Antiguan government investigated the reasons for the hotel's continued closure, and, as a result, the legislature passed a resolution, which authorised the government to intervene with the restructuring of HMB and to grant economic incentives to the company. Subsequently, in January 1999, HMB's representative advised the government that its lender was seeking various concessions, namely, a waiver of stamp duty on property transfers and company shares. The Cabinet decided not to grant the concessions, and in June 1999, the government decided to compulsory acquire the Half Moon Bay Resort.

In August 1999, HMB advised the public that the hotel would be reopened in November that year. In September, the Tourism Minister sought confirmation from HMB and this was received. HMB's new joint venture partner also sought concessions from the government. Of importance to them was an exemption from stamp duty. The waiver was granted in May 2000 on the condition that re-construction works commenced within six months, leading to a re-opening of the hotel on July 1, 2001. This new partner withdrew because it lost support from its financial backer.

In November 2000, HMB entered into negotiations with another investor, who requested a non-citizen land holding licence that would serve as collateral for a loan over the property. In December 2000, the Antiguan government decided to acquire the resort. Thereafter, HMB obtained an *ex parte* injunction against the Attorney General and Cabinet not to proceed with the expropriation. The outcome of this case was an agreement between HMB and the Government of Antigua and Barbuda. Under this agreement, the hoteliers were required to provide proof of their financial ability to undertake the project, settle all debts to former staff and workers at the hotel, develop and present proposals for the construction and operation of a four- or five-star hotel and to commence construction in six months, starting February 1, 2001.

In March 2001, the Permanent Secretary for the Ministry of Tourism advised HMB that all the concessions requested by its investor would be granted, but two months later, the government made changes to the terms of the agreement. Soon after, the investor's bank forfeited the loan in the belief that HMB did not have support from the Antiguan government. HMB's agreement with the government expired on July 31, 2001. In January 2002, the government moved a resolution authorising the Cabinet Secretary to declare the acquisition of the Half Moon Bay Resort.

In the light of the events associated with the acquisition, HMB sought a judicial review of the acquisition on the basis that:

1   the procedure adopted by Cabinet was incorrect; and
2   the acquisition was a breach of HMB's constitutional right to the protection of the law.

After reviewing the evidence presented, the Privy Council ruled that the conclusive nature of the declaration in the legislation prevented any form of judicial scrutiny, but nothing prohibited decisions made under the Act from being reviewed. As such, HMB's claim that the acquisition was a breach of its constitutional right could be heard by the court. In their judgement, the Law Lords held that the agreement between HMB and the government stressed the commencement of construction works in a six-month period, and this condition was not satisfied by the claimant. Further, it was undisputed that purpose for which the hotel was being acquired was a public purpose. As a result, the government had the right to proceed with the acquisition. The appeal was dismissed. The government took possession of the property in July 2008.

Moncrief-Scott (2009) reported that a former Antiguan Prime Minister offered to broker the sale of the Half Moon Bay Hotel to a private investor. Moncrief-Scott (2009) also wrote that it was no secret that the hotel was acquired, with the intention to transfer title to this investor, to whom the Antiguan government owed EC$230 million by 2004. This investor also owned Guiana Island that is located northeast of the coast of Antigua. Some months after taking possession in 2008, it was reported that the investor had plans to present to the Cabinet his proposal for the Half Moon Bay Hotel. However, fraud charges that were lodged against the investor in 2009, prevented the sale of the hotel (Moncrief-Scott 2009). The property remained unoccupied until a new investor acquired the hotel in January 2016.

The Jamaican Case of the North-South link of Highway 2000

The Jamaican government acquired 14 parcels of land in Charlemont, St. Catherine, for the construction of the North-South Link of Highway 2000. Negotiations between persons interested and the Commissioner were unsuccessful. As such the Commissioner made an award for compensation to each party, but these were rejected and were brought to the Appeal Court for determination.

It was reported in a local newspaper that the Jamaican government had signed a 50-year concession agreement, which enables the investor to recoup its investment by being the toll operator of the highway (Thompson 2015).

In an open statement published by the Office of the Contractor General (OCG) on May 1, 2012, the OCG opined that the unsolicited proposal for the construction of the North-South link by the contractor was not financially viable. This position was supported by the grantor, which is the state-owned National Road Operating and Construction Company (NROCC). The OCG reported on NROCC's position on the viability of the North-South link as follows:

> the project was not viable in terms of the rate of return on investment over the life of the proposed 50-year toll concession…the contractor would not, on the basis of the Government's projections, and its consultant's advice, recoup the overwhelmingly majority of its US $270 million investment on the project.
>
> *(Office of the Contractor General 2012)*

The North-South link of Highway 2000 was opened to the public on March 9, 2016.

In both case studies, lands were acquired with the intention of producing public benefits such as increased employment and productivity levels, foreign exchange earnings and an improved transportation network.

Since the Antiguan government took possession of the Half Moon Bay Resort in 2008, the intended public benefits have not been realised. In the case of Highway 2000, the reported unviable nature of the 50-year concession agreement between the Jamaican government and contactor raises questions in relation to when or how will the public benefits be fully realised. Cumulatively, both cases demonstrate the need for answers to questions such as who are the primary beneficiaries of these expropriations – promoters or the public – and could secret buying agents be used instead to mobilise land and deliver these public benefits.

The cornerstone of an acquisition is the taking of private rights for the benefit of communal needs. If there is uncertainty surrounding the expected public benefits of the exercise, then its rationale becomes questionable. The case studies imply there is a need for the contractual arrangements/agreements between governments and promoters to be analysed, before a declaration is made.

The conclusive nature of the declaration

The certainty of a declaration makes a successful case for judicial review an uphill task. The broad definition of "public purpose" in each statute suggests, when a regional government declares any use to be a "public purpose", the declaration serves to validate that the intended use is one that will benefit the public and increase public welfare in the society. Therefore, if expropriations are misguided, the conclusiveness of a declaration can assist with masking improper motivations behind an acquisition. In such a case, the end result is a taking of private rights for a purported public purpose.

It is therefore important for persons interested to be given an opportunity to challenge the validity of a taking, especially when expropriations involve any third-party transfers. What needs to be addressed is how the legal codes of the Caribbean territories facilitate this opportunity to affected parties.

The Trinidadian constitution does not outline the grounds on which an acquisition can be brought before the court. Nonetheless, the island's Land Acquisition Act infers that only matters related to compensation may be heard by the Land Tribunal or Court of Appeal. By contrast, the constitutions of Antigua, St. Lucia, St. Vincent and Jamaica are explicitly clear on the grounds on which an intended acquisition can be brought to the court. Namely:

1 to determine the nature and extent of the claimant's interest;
2 to determine if the acquisition was undertaken in accordance with the law;
3 for determining a party's award for compensation; and
4 for ensuring the right of an interested person to receive compensation.

In lieu of the aforementioned, in order to successfully challenge an acquisition, the claimants must prove that the taking is unconstitutional or unnecessary. Case law from the region suggests the claimants will only achieve their desired outcome, if they demonstrates that:

1 **Alternative sites were not considered before expropriating the property**. This guiding principle was established in F. *Wattley v The Attorney General of St. Lucia 2004*. In this case, the claimant received planning approval on May 24, 2001, to undertake development on a parcel she inherited from her deceased father. On February 9 and 26, 2002, the St Lucia Government published two notices in the Gazette, which indicated that the land was needed to develop a school. The claimant found this surprising since she recently received planning approval from the government. She subsequently met with the Minister of Planning and advised him of similar lands in the area that were for sale and suitable to construct a school. On August 12, 2002, the acquisition was declared and published in the Gazette. As a result, the claimant filed a twofold motion against the Attorney General. The grounds of her challenge were: (1) she had an expectation that the property would not be acquired since she recently received planning approval; and (2) the procedure for the acquisition was defective since alternative sites were not considered. In the ruling, the court determined that the claimant's statement that other lands were for sale amounted to hearsay evidence and therefore it was unreliable. The court also held that allegations such as accusing the Cabinet of not considering alternative sites require conclusive evidence. In other words, the provision of suitable alternative sites to the Government did not mean the site that was initially identified will not be acquired. The judge maintained that it may be the case that the government considered alternative sites but stuck to its original plan.

2 **The intended acquisition infringes a claimant's constitutional rights**. R. *Toussaint v the Attorney General of St Vincent and the Grenadines, 2007* highlighted this principle. In this case the claimant purchased 12,957 square feet (1,203 square metres) of land in Canouan from the Vincentian government, through the Development Corporation in 1990. The Deed of Conveyance to Toussaint contained restrictive covenants. The restrictive covenants governed the sale and development of hereditaments, subject to approval from the Development Corporation. In 1993, Toussaint sought an extension to comply with the restrictions. This was approved. Thereafter, on April 23, 1996, he applied for a waiver to the restrictions. This was also approved by an indenture dated March 5, 1996. There was a change of government on March 20, 2001. On March 26, the Attorney General wrote Toussaint outlining that the land was sold to him at a low price because of his close relationship with the previous government. Toussaint ignored the letter. Subsequently, he tried to resell the land, but when the Valuation Department received the Deed of Conveyance for the sale, they kept the document and failed to return it. In December 2002, in the House of the Assembly, the Vincentian Prime Minister described

the sale of the land to Toussaint as an injustice…a scandal that needs to be corrected. As a result, the Cabinet published the declaration in the Gazette on the same day. In response, Toussaint challenged the acquisition. The Prime Minister's statement was the central plank of Toussaint's application for judicial review. The Privy Council held that the Government's action was unconstitutional because the purpose of the acquisition was a sham that was being used to dispossess Toussaint.

3   **The land is not needed for the intended public purpose**. This guideline would be applicable to Jamaica as the island's Land Acquisition Act does not outline the grounds on which an acquisition may be abandoned. In *The Commissioner of Lands v Homeway Foods Limited and S Muir 2012*, a property belonging to Homeway Foods was acquired by the Commissioner for the relocation of the Students Loan Bureau (SLB) in May 2006. The Commissioner and Homeway were unable to agree on the award for compensation, but throughout the court proceedings, the defendant's attorney argued that the acquisition should be abandoned because the land was no longer needed for the intended public purpose. In her counter arguments, the Commissioner's attorney contended that the defendant's submission requires an Order of *Certiorari*. The judge agreed the claimant's argument was correct but underscored that the defendant's submission can be allowed based on the nature of the case. On March 9, 2012, it was published in local newspapers that the SLB had acquired another building for its offices. It further stated that the SLB used funds from the sale of a property which adjoins the defendant's land to purchase the new property. The court held that all proceedings for the acquisition were to be abandoned. Homeway was, therefore, entitled to take possession on or before 3 August, 2012.

The conclusiveness of the declaration ensures that a government's decision on what is a "public purpose" is not justiciable. Inherent in this position is the assumption that a decision-maker will always act in a law-abiding manner which ensures the realisation of expected public benefits. The stance adopted by the law may be viewed as naive, because the wide powers vested in the decision-maker presents the opportunity to increase societal welfare or create moral hazards or a combination of both.

In order to reduce the likelihood of moral hazards, *ex ante* analyses of the contractual terms between governments and promoters must be undertaken, the results of which should be subject to public scrutiny. Presently, the introduction of such matters in the court will be regarded as a rudimentary argument (B. *Spencer v The Attorney General of Antigua and Barbuda, L. Bird and Asian Village Antigua Limited 1997*). Therefore, if an acquisition is guided by illegitimate motivations, the probability of curtailing a disastrous outcome may be low. The legal code does not facilitate a judicial review of the declaration and high litigation costs operate as a barrier, which prevents a greater number of landowners from requesting judicial reviews. The analysis suggests the legal disposition in most of the islands closes the stable door after the horse has bolted.

On the matter of compensation

The Pointe Gourde principle

Pointe Gourde is at the heart of compensation in the islands. The Principle is underpinned by six rules which contextualise the exchange between persons interested and the government. Its guiding principles are provided as a reminder to the reader. Subsequently, the analysis is presented. The rules are as follows:

1   The compulsory nature of the acquisition should be ignored.
2   The value of the land is the amount which it would fetch on the open market assuming a willing seller and a willing purchaser.
3   Any special suitability of adaptability of the property should be disregarded if such a use could only be realised in pursuant of statutory powers or if the statutory body undertaking the acquisition is the only purchaser who would have an interest in acquiring the property.
4   Any change in the land value as a result of the expropriation is to be ignored.
5   The land value of lands for which there is no market is to be determined by the depreciated replacement cost approach.
6   Any assessment of compensation for damages, disturbance, injury etc. should not be affected by Rule 2 (Vaughan and Smith 2014).

Pointe Gourde requires the valuer to place the transaction between persons interested and the government in a no-scheme world. To this end, the valuer must assume that the landowner is a willing seller. Intuitively, this may appear to be unrealistic as the exchange involves a compulsory taking of private land rights from its owner. However, within the system of representational government (adopted in the islands) is an implicit theory of consent. At the crux of representational government is the delegated power the citizens give to the legislature, to speak and act on their behalf. As such, the legislature may give consent on a citizen's behalf that property rights may be taken for a public use or public purpose.

Under the aforementioned conditions, a taking does not involve the compulsory removal of property rights from a landowner, but rather a willing resignation of those rights (Stoebuck 1972). The aforementioned forms the bedrock of Rules 1 and 2. Therefore, the taking has been contextualised as a transaction between a willing buyer and a willing seller. Rules 3, 4, 5 and 6 serve as a buttress for Rules 1 and 2 ensuring that the basis of compensation is market value.

The statutes of the Eastern Caribbean Territories and Jamaica confirm that open market value is the basis of compensation. However, Section 12(7) of the Trinidadian act suggests where landowners have not obtained a certificate from the planning authority indicating the permitted ways in which their land could be used in a no-scheme world, the basis of compensation will be hope value. Simply put, after determining the land value, the valuer must make adjustments for the fact that approval for the land to be used for its highest and best use (HABU) is a possibility and not a certainty. In Trinidad and Tobago, the planning authority's certificate ensures that the HABU of the land to be acquired will be considered when determining the award for compensation.

Lord Collins in *Transport for London v Spirerose Limited 2009* stressed that the basis of compensation for expropriated land is the value to the seller and not the purchaser. "The question is not, what the persons who take the land will gain by taking it; but what the person from whom it is taken will lose…" (The Principles of the Law of Compensation, 1881, 144 cited in *Transport for London v Spirerose Limited 2009*, 33). In lieu of the aforementioned, it must be examined whether open market value or hope value can arrive at the value to the seller.

How fair is market value?

The International Valuation Standards Council (2016) defines market value as follows:

> The estimated amount for which an asset or liability should exchange on the valuation date between a willing buyer and a willing seller in an arm's length transaction, after proper marketing and where the parties had each acted knowledgeably, prudently and without compulsion.

407

This definition assumes that the HABU of the subject will be considered in the value determination process.

Each parcel of land is unique, and this feature distinguishes the land market from any other economic market. Burdsal (2005) argued that the only feature the land market shares with the traditional market is the presence of a myriad of purchasers. Burdsal (2005) contends that the valuer inspects a property and tries to determine what a willing buyer would offer. This suggests that market value represents value to the purchaser and not the value to the seller.

In the field of property valuation, value to the seller is known as value in use (use value). It is a term that contrasts with market value, because no consideration is given to the HABU of land when determining its use value. To this end, it is the value a property has for a specific use. Although it is quite likely that the use value and market value may be synonymous for some properties, for specialised properties the distinction is important. The use value of specialised properties is driven by cost and not the behaviour of market participants. As a result, if a specialist property such as a hospital is being acquired and market value is the yardstick that will be used to determine compensation, the landowner's award will not be equivalent to the loss sustained. It is often difficult to convert specialist properties into an alternative use. Thus, where the use of a specialist property is not its HABU and it is being sold on the open market, there may be very few buyers who could utilise the building as it is designed. In such an event, market value will be below the use value of the property.

Other shortcomings of utilising market value as the primary means of determining compensation are as follows:

1   Property rights and externalities are like kindred spirits (Demsetz 1967). Typically, expropriation is a negative externality that is not desired by landowners. By utilising market value as the basis of compensation, the full costs of this externality are not being absorbed by the government, because market value represents value to the purchaser and not value to the seller.

2   Governments utilise the power of eminent domain to exact taxes and property rights in land. Whether it is the taking of property rights in money or land rights, both assets are taken for a public benefit. The distinction between the two is how the exaction is undertaken (Stoebuck 1972). With taxation, the burden of the taking is shared among all members of society. With expropriation, the burden is borne primarily by the landowners. On the other hand, market value represents the consensus of market participants who are not adversely affected by the taking. How fair is it to use a standard, which represents the perspective of individuals who are not negatively affected by the taking, to determine compensation for a landowner who has been placed in the unfavourable position of having land acquired? It is difficult for the purchaser to truly understand the landowner's position, as the realities of both parties are in stark contrast to each other.

3   The statutes of the islands suggest that market value is a function of the willingness of a seller. However, the acts provide no indicator(s) that may be used to measure a seller's willingness. Therefore, if market value is the outcome of a seller's willingness, how will an unknown measure of the independent variable enable a valuer to (accurately) determine the unknown dependent variable?

4   For expropriation cases where the Depreciated Replacement Cost method is used to determine building values, there may be some uncertainty surrounding the extent to which the technique can place a landowner in a position of pecuniary equivalence. It is a method in which a valuer uses building construction costs, experiential judgement of

the depreciation rate of a building and the market value of land in order to provide an estimate of value. In property markets where construction costs are (extremely) high, the application of a property's perceived depreciation rate may result in a value that is higher than the price the property would have fetched if placed on the open market. It also follows that the method may produce a value outcome that places the landowner in a lower financial position. When a landowner is dispossessed, it is reasonable to assume that another property will be needed to replace the one acquired. As a result, the landowner has the task of finding and purchasing a comparable property, with a market value that is equivalent to the replacement cost of the previous property. When a landowner is unable to find comparable properties with market values that are less than or equivalent to the replacement value of the previous property, demoralisation costs will be incurred that are not included in the award for compensation.

The arguments presented suggest that market value has not brought us close enough to the actual position of the landowner in the transaction. An essential ingredient to improving the suitability of market value is aligning the purchaser's position to the actual realities of the seller. This suggests the guiding principles of the conjecture, which underpin the exchange, need amending in order to produce compensation that reflects the actual value to the landowner.

The determination of compensation by Caribbean courts

The previous subsection demonstrates that the most likely remedy that may be obtained by a landowner is compensation. Thus, the determination and payment of compensation is a critical aspect of acquisition cases in the Caribbean. This subsection focuses primarily on how the award of compensation for land is determined and how expeditiously payment is made to persons affected

Antigua and Barbuda

In 1997, the Antiguan government acquired 5 acres (some 2 hectares) of land leased by Guiana Island Farms Limited (Guiana Farms) to Cyril and Lona Eileen Bufton (the Bufton's) for 99 years at a peppercorn rent. Guiana Farms also agreed by contract to purchase a bungalow for the Bufton's upon termination of their employment or sale of the island.

Cyril Bufton was employed by Guiana Island Farms to manage the farm operations on Guiana Island between 1965 and 1976. In 1983, he was appointed as the Wildlife Conservation Officer for Guiana Island and served in this capacity until December 1997 when the land was acquired.

At the time of the acquisition, the lease had an unexpired term of 77 years. After the acquisition, the Antiguan and Barbudan Legislature passed the Cyril Thomas Bufton and Lona Eileen Bufton (Resettlement and Maintenance) Act 1997. The Act was promulgated on the basis that it would have been operational until the Bufton's were compensated for the loss of their right to remain on the property for 77 years. The legislation mandated the Cabinet to provide the Bufton's with the following:

1   5 acres (2 ha) of land and a two-bedroom house;
2   a monthly stipend of EC$[1]1,700, that should be paid from the Consolidated Fund; and
3   a vehicle for their daily commute.

After passing the Act, the Government provided the Bufton's with temporary accommodation inclusive of utilities, a vehicle and a monthly stipend of EC$1,200. The Bufton's refused to occupy the house.

Two valuers testified on behalf of the government with conflicting valuations. The Chief Lands Officer testified that similar lands (to that being acquired) were available in Antigua for EC$30 per acre (some EC$74 per hectare), which made the value of the Bufton's land in the region of EC$11,500. In comparison, the Government's Chief Evaluation Officer outlined that he used an internationally accepted formula which produced a value of EC$93,525 as at March 2004. In his testimony he explained that his valuation was based on evidence from comparable agricultural land which was rented at a rate of EC$1,500 per acre (some EC$3,700 per hectare).

The Bufton's assessor valued the leasehold at EC$1,550,000 as at late 2003. He explained that he valued the subject as land with development potential for the Tourism Industry. In response, Counsel for the Government argued that the Sales Comparable Approach is an incorrect method of valuation under the Act, but cited no substantial evidence for such a claim.

The Court agreed with valuation provided by the Bufton's assessor but discounted the value by 51.6% to comply with Section 19 (a) of the Antiguan legislation. The relevant section specifies that the valuation date is one year prior to the date of acquisition. In this regard, the Bufton's were awarded EC$800,000 for their leasehold interest.

Cheong (2015) argues that the difference between a 60- and 99-year lease and a freehold is so small that it can safely be disregarded. As such, the application of the Sale Comparison Approach by the Bufton's assessor is not alarming. On the other hand, it is unclear how the Government's assessors arrived at the values they quoted, as no evidence presented in the judgement clearly supported those value outcomes. The testimonies of the Government's valuers imply that the Income Approach was used to arrive at their leasehold value, but the yield rates that would have been used to arrive at these values were not provided in the judgement. Similarly, the discount rate applied by the Judge to arrive at the Court's determination was also not provided. Therefore, the processes used to calculate the values presented were not explicit.

The previous subsection demonstrated that *Pointe Gourde* needs to be more equitable in order to provide an outcome which reflects the value to owner. However, in the Eastern Caribbean Territories, the market value of expropriated land is assessed as at one year before the date of acquisition. Such a statutory requirement further reduces the likelihood of a landowner being placed in a position of pecuniary equivalence, especially under the circumstances where capitalisation and discounts rates of unknown quantities are being applied to determine the compensation for land taken.

Jamaica

In the case *The Commissioner of Lands v Worman* 2002, 805.352 square metres (some 8,670 square feet) of land belonging to the respondent was taken for the development of a bridge to ease traffic congestion in a locality. The Commissioner offered $4,323,664 JMD[2] as compensation for the subject land. However, the respondent's claim to compensation was $45,206,968 JMD. In its submission, Worman provided a statement of claim, a schedule of claim and a valuation report which included compensation for the acquired land and the loss of rental income.

The valuation report the Commissioner relied on indicated that the property had several planning breaches. Thus, a claim for compensation under those circumstances was viewed to be inappropriate. The valuer also explained that the acquisition could result in an increase of 15% or more in the value of the land retained. It was also noted that confirmation of such an increase could only be obtained by conducting an appraisal before the acquisition.

In contrast, the Court's assessor determined the market value of the subject land on two bases. The first was on actual sales evidence which produced a value of $6,487,125, and the second on asking prices which amounted to a value of $7,611,560. The assessor recommended the former value but noted that the respondent should have been offered the value based on asking prices (per square foot) subject to adjustments based on the condition and location of the property. However, he did not explain how or on what basis the adjustments should have been made.

The Count agreed with the land value produced by the assessor and awarded compensation in the sum of $6,487,125 JMD.

In reviewing the facts surrounding the case, it appears that the valuation report provided by the Commissioner observed the criteria for determining market value. Namely, the Commissioner's valuer opined that the acquisition would have resulted in an increase of the value of the retained land. Such a consideration is mandated by 14 (1) (i) (b) of the Act. Interestingly, the court rejected the Commissioner's valuation on the basis that it included "preliminary observations with conclusions based on incorrect assumptions" (*Commissioner of Lands v Worman*, 9). It was also observed that the judgment made no mention of the evidence, which assisted the Commissioner in arriving at the offer of $4,323,664. On the other hand, it was noted that the Court's assessor used sale prices to arrive at market value.

In light of the Commissioner's offer, it was deduced that compensation was being offered at a rate of $499 JMD per square foot (some $5,370 JMD per square metres). However, the court provided compensation at $748 JMD per square foot (some $8,050 JMD per square metre). Although it appears that the Commissioner's valuation followed the criteria outlined in Jamaica's Land Acquisition Act correctly, the arguments presented by the Judge suggest that the Court's assessor provided a better rationale for his determination of value. The relatively wide disparity in values presented in this case highlights one of the primary weaknesses of *Pointe Gourde*.

Pointe Gourde is a principle written in absolute terms, which requires an assessor to arrive at market value by making assumptions, bearing in mind the planning regime and the HABU of the subject. Thus, depending on the assumptions made by a valuer, *Pointe Gourde* could produce a market value that is inconsistent with market values for similar properties. Lord Nicholls (2004) in *Waters v Welsh Development Agency 2004*, commented:

> *Pointe Gourde* should not be pressed too far...it should be applied to produce a fair result. A valuation result should be viewed with caution when it will lead to a gross disparity between the amount of compensation payable and the market values of comparable adjoining properties.
>
> *(cited in Vaughan and Smith 2014, 186)*

Delayed payment of compensation

As outlined previously, the payment of compensation is an integral aspect of land acquisition in the islands. To this end, expropriation cases in St. Lucia and Trinidad and Tobago are used to illustrate the lengthy delays can be associated with the payment of compensation in the territories.

St. Lucia

In 1990, the St. Lucian government acquired 94 acres (some 38 hectares) of land owned by Jerome Montoute in Gros Islet. In 2007, the claimant filed a constitutional motion against the Attorney General because compensation was not paid. In the case it was revealed that the Board of Assessment was not established. The Judge also outlined that in a case of this nature, a rigid interest rate cannot be applied to the claimant's award. He opined that the Board needs to determine an appropriate interest rate to ensure that the claimant receives just compensation. In the court decision, the Judge ruled that Montoute was entitled to the value of his land at the date of assessment along with interest at a reasonable rate.

On April 21, 2016, the claimant's daughter wrote an open letter to members of the St. Lucian government, the West Indian Legal/Judicial Committee and selected human rights organisations such as Amnesty International, Human Rights Watch, the Caribbean Community (CARICOM) and the Organisation of Eastern Caribbean States (OECS). Her letter outlined that compensation had not been paid to the estate of Jerome Montoute (deceased). She also explained that the Chief Justice expressed her concern with the undue delays with the payment of compensation to the deceased (Montoute 2016). In response to Ms. Montoute's letter, the President of the Caribbean Court of Justice provided an undertaking to personally resolve the matter (VP Digital 2016).

In *Jerome Montoute v the Attorney General of St. Lucia 2008*, the judge deliberated on whether the payment of interest at the rate outlined in the Act was suitable, in light of the 18-year delay in the payment of compensation. The case also illustrated that the only remedy a landowner receives is the payment of interest at a fixed rate of 5%.

When compensation has been delayed by so many years, the value of a landowner's compensation erodes over time. This is especially true when the country's inflation rate is higher than the interest rate provided in the Act. Economic data on St. Lucia suggest that the island's average inflation rate for the period 1990–2016 was 6.04%. Over the period, the island's annual inflation rate ranged from a high of 7.18% (in 2008) to 1.67% (in 2009) (The World Bank 2017 cited in the Global Economy 2017).

Trinidad and Tobago

The case presented was taken from an article that was published by Felmine (2017) in the Trinidad Guardian Newspaper.

The National Gas Company (NGC) rented lands belonging to a Trinidadian couple in 2004 for the laying of 56″ (1.422 metre) gas lines, during its island-wide pipeline project. In 2006, they received notification from the Ministry of Land and Marine Affairs that the lands were listed for compulsory acquisition. The couple agreed to sell the government two parcels of lands, but the Planning Authority advised them to sell their third parcel because there would be no access to the other areas.

In 2006, Parcels One and Two were valued at TT$370,000 and TT$300,000, respectively. However, they contend, the Ministry of Land wanted to compensate them TT$16,000 for one parcel. A cheque was issued to them in this amount but the couple refused it. The couple also complained about "getting the run-around by several state bodies with respect to payment for the three parcels of land…" (Felmine 2017, para 3).

Subsequently, the landowners made contact with the NGC and the Land Settlement Agency (LSA). After submitting new valuations for their parcels to the LSA, they were advised that compensation was provided for one parcel, so there would be no further settlement for it. They were also told that documents for the other two parcels could not be found.

This case raises the matter of what is a reasonable time in which compensation should be paid. It was observed that the legislations for the islands do not provide a specific or general sense of how soon compensation is to be paid. Based on the nature of compulsory acquisition, it is understandable why a stipulated time period has not been specified in the legislations. That is, under normal circumstances, compensation will not be paid until the award has been determined. Therefore, payment delays arise for two reasons:

1   Tardiness by landowners and/or government; and / or
2   A lengthy award determination process as a result of external factors such as trial dates set by the courts.

Generally, the negotiation process is initiated by the government when persons interested are asked to submit their claims for compensation. The case as reported by Felmine (2017) suggests the process was initiated and the couple provided their claim. Additionally, the compensation offered for one parcel was not accepted, but the government maintains that the settlement for that parcel has been concluded.

Section 11 of the Trinidadian legislation outlines that disputes will be settled by the Land Tribunal, but unlike the other statutes, it is not explicit on whether:

1   landowners should request the authorised officer to refer the matter to the Land Tribunal; or
2   landowners should file a submission to the Land Tribunal; or
3   the authorised officer should refer the matter once there is a dispute.

Further checks with the Land Tribunal Act 2000, never resolved this issue as the relevant sections (Sections 7 and 8) only speak to landowners being required to submit their appeals and claims to compensation under the Land Adjudication and Registration of Titles to Land Acts. Nonetheless, given the nature of expropriation and the importance of landowners being compensated, it may be construed that the State has a role to play in ensuring that disputes are settled and compensation is paid.

Huggins et al. (n.d.) lamented that the compensation process in Trinidad and Tobago can be lengthy and exhaustive. They opined "many of the cases show that claimants have waited decades to be compensated..." (Huggins et al., n.d., 8). It may be argued that the lacuna identified in the legislation complements a drawn out compensation process, because there is no clear identification of the individual (landowner or Commissioner of State Lands) who has the responsibility of bringing disputes to the Land Tribunal. The aforementioned suggests that the unclear delineation of the roles and responsibilities of each party contributes to the free rider problem, as landowners and state officials can adopt two contrasting positions, which result in a coordination failure.

Concluding remarks

Within the context of compulsory purchase, the transaction between persons interested and the government occurs in a bilateral monopoly (Korobin and Ulen 2000). As a result, the government faces the strategic holdout problem and will need to reduce its costs of transacting. The principal-agent relationship between citizens and the government is underpinned by a unique delegated power, which enables the agent to provide consent on the principal's behalf. Thus, this unique power assists the government with resolving the strategic holdout problem, thereby reducing its transaction costs. In a world of zero or low transaction costs, the allocation and delineation of property rights is immaterial, whether a transaction is efficient or not (Coase 1960).

The economic analysis suggests that all the costs associated with the negative externalities faced by landowners are not absorbed by the purchaser. In this regard, the decision to acquire for a public purpose is not justiciable and compensation is paid at market value. In some cases, payments are received decades after the purchaser has taken possession.

Land markets in the islands consist of the following:

1   registered lands with registered and unregistered interests;
2   unregistered lands with unregistered interests; and
3   family land tenure, which can coexist with registered and other types of unregistered interests on registered and unregistered lands.

The complex nature of these land markets makes the costs of transacting between persons interested and the purchaser high. There can be several persons interested for a parcel, who may be unknown to the purchaser. This validates the inclusion of sections in the expropriation statutes, which mandate the authorised officer or Commissioner to obtain details of all persons interested from any person interested for a subject property. If the purchasers had the obligation to absorb all the negative externalities of all persons interested, their transaction costs could be insurmountable.

The aforementioned underpins the rationale for making market value the basis of compensation and not the value to the seller. Burdsal (2005) asserted that the use of market value as the underlying foundation for compensation created a seller's paradox. To this end, Burdsal (2005) proposed two willingness models to determine a landowner's willingness to sell. The first utilised a macro approach, which obtained a seller's willingness through the adoption of data farming techniques, such as surveys. However, he argued that data findings may be affected by the moral hazard problem. They may also be too costly. On the other hand, the second approach is dependent on the implementation of a self-assessment property tax. Burdsal (2005) affirmed that property values reported by landowners represented value to the seller. This is ideal from the standpoint of accountability, because annual values reported by landowners would be the basis of compensation, if their property was being acquired. However, the costs associated with transitioning to a self-assessed property tax system could potentially be too costly for the islands.

In order to resolve the seller's paradox, the asking prices of different property types in various localities could be analysed statistically. The asking prices for all property types in each territory could be obtained from real estate firms and be included in databases that contain data such as market values, land values, land size, building values, building size, the number of habitable rooms, bedrooms, proximity to various amenities, measurable variables related to soil quality, crop quality, age of crops. With this database, valuers could develop hedonic price models of asking prices for different property types in a myriad of localities. This provides valuers with a robust approach to determining value to the seller and can bridge the gap between theory and practice. Alternatively, probit or logit regression models could be created from observations in the dataset in a bid to bring us closer to value to the seller.

The economic analysis has examined compulsory purchase in the territories, with the aim of understanding the nature of the exchange between the government and persons interested. The chapter also highlighted the problems with the unclear delineation of property rights in the principal-agent relationship. More importantly, it has illustrated the socio-economic problems associated with compulsory purchase in the islands. Hopefully, this chapter will spur more elaboration on this and other topics, with the intention of addressing socio-economic problems affecting the region.

Notes

1 Eastern Caribbean Dollar
2 Jamaican Dollar
3 Trinidad and Tobago Dollar

References

Burdsal, N. 2005. "Just Compensation and the Seller's Paradox". Brigham Young University Journal of Public Law 20(1): 79–102.

Cheong, A. 2015. "Leasehold versus Freehold: An Argument that will go on Until the Cows Come Home." Available from: www.edgeprop.sg/property-news/leasehold-versus-freehold-argument-will-go-until-cows-come-home [Accessed 12th October 2017].

Coase, R. 1960. "The Problem of Social Cost". The Journal of Law & Economics 3: 1–44.

Demsetz, H. 1967. "Toward a Theory of Property Rights". The American Economic Review 57(2): 347–359.

Felmine, K. 2 June 2017. "Decade Long Wait for NGC Land Deal". The Trinidad Guardian Newspaper. Available from: www.guardian.co.tt/news/2017-06-02/decade-long-wait-ngc-land-deal [Accessed 22nd October 2017].

Huggins, E., Roach, K. and Jessemy, G. (n.d.). "Land Acquisition in the Context of Institutional Problems in the Legal and Administrative Framework in Trinidad and Tobago". Ministry of Food Production, Land and Marine Affairs Land Management Division, Trinidad and Tobago. Available from: https://sta.uwi.edu/conferences/11/landtenure/documents/EsricHugginskRoachGJessemy-Landacquisitionprocess.pdf [Accessed 5th October 2017].

International Valuation Standards Council. 7 April 2016. "IVS 104: Bases of Value Exposure Draft." Available from: www.ivsc.org/files/file/view/id/646 [Accessed 12th November 2017].

Kelly, D. 2006. "The Public Use Requirement in Eminent Domain Law: A Rationale Based on Secret Purchases and Private Influence". Cornell Law Review 92(1): 1–66.

Korobin, R. and Ulen, T. 2000. "Law and Behavioral Science: Removing the Rationality Assumption from Law and Economics". California Law Review 88(4): 1053–1144.

Moncrief-Scott, I. 20 July 2009. "Antigua and Barbuda: Stanford's First Major Victim – Half Moon Bay Hotel, Antigua". Available from: www.mondaq.com/x/77544/Corporate+Commercial+Law/Stanfords+First+Major+Victim+Half+Moon+Bay+Hotel+Antigua [Accessed 4th November 2017].

Montoute, T. 21 April 2016. "Open Letter regarding Jerome Montoute land expropriation case in St. Lucia". Caribbean News Now. Available from: www.caribbeannewsnow.com/topstory-Open-Letter-regarding-Jerome-Montoute-land-expropriation-case-in-St-Lucia-30116.html [Accessed 2nd November 2017].

Nicholson, B. and Mota, S. 2005. "From Public Use to Public Purpose: The Supreme Court Stretches the Takings Clause in Kelo v. City of New London". Gonzaga Law Review 41: 81–101.

Office of the Contractor-General, Government of Jamaica. 1 May 2012. "Open Statement by the OCG Regarding the Proposed Highway 2000 North South Link and the Container Transshipment Hub Projects". Available from: www.ocg.gov.jm/ocg/releases/open-statement-ocg-regarding-proposed-highway-2000-north-south-link-and-container [Accessed 15th October 2017].

Slade, B. 2014. "Public Purpose or Public Interest and Third Party Transfers". Potchefstroom Electronic Law Journal 17(1). Available from doi:10.4314/pelj.v17i1.042014.

Stoebuck, W. 1972. "A General Theory of Eminent Domain". Washington Law Review 47(4): 553–569.

The Global Economy. 2017. "Saint Lucia: Inflation". Available from: www.theglobaleconomy.com/Saint-Lucia/Inflation/ [Accessed 12th November 2017].

Thompson, M. 4 December 2015. "CHEC Gets Special Assurances for Highway Compensation". The Gleaner. Available from: http://jamaica-gleaner.com/article/business/20151204/chec-gets-special-assurances-highway-compensation [Accessed 4th November 2017].

Vaughan, D. and Smith, L. 2014. "An introduction to compulsory purchase valuation principles spanning 150 years". Journal of Building Survey, Appraisal & Valuation 3(2): 184–189.

VP Digital 21 May 2016. "Campaign Underway to Settle Land Claim Against Gov't". Available from: http://thevoiceslu.com/2016/05/campaign-underway-settle-land-claim-govt/ [Accessed 2nd November 2017].

Legal cases

Baldwin Spencer v The Attorney General of Antigua and Barbuda, Lester Bryant Bird and Asian Village Antigua Limited [1998].

Francisca Jules Wattley v The Attorney General [2004]

Jerome Montoute v The Attorney General [2008]

HMB Holdings Limited v Attorney General of Antigua and Barbuda [2012]

Pointe Gourde Quarrying and Transport Company Limited v Sub Intendent of Crown Lands [1947] AC 565.

Randolph Trueman Toussaint v The Attorney General of Saint Vincent and the Grenadines [2015]

The Attorney General of Antigua and Barbuda v the Estate of Cyril Thomas Bufton and Lona Eileen Bufton [2006]

The Commissioner of Lands v Clifford Armstrong, Raymond Ellis (In the estate of Walford Ellis, deceased), Delbert Francis, Headley Graham. Fitzroy Green, David Harrison, Donald James, Julet Murphy, Loxley Murphy, Lenford Parker, Authur Smith (In the estate of Winchester Smith, deceased), Winston Taffe, Ronald Watkiss and Ralph Weir [2012] JMSC Civ. 115

The Commissioner of Lands v Homeway Foods Limited and Stephanie Muir [2012]

The Commissioner of Lands v Worman Limited [2002]

Transport for London (London Underground Ltd) v Spirerose Ltd [2009] UKHL 44

Legislation

The Land Acquisition Ordinance 1946 (CAP 101)

The Land Acquisition Act 1947

The Land Acquisition Act (CAP 241) 1947

The Land Acquisition Act (CAP 233) 1958

The Land Acquisition Act (CAP 58:01) 1996

22

The United States' experience with expropriation and the lessons yet to be learned

Lawrence Walters

Introduction

Most if not all national legal systems allow for the public expropriation of private land and property for public purposes. Debates around expropriation generally centre around the definition of public purpose, property valuation, and compensation standards (Lamoreaux, 2011; Scheiber, 1973). This chapter explores expropriation as it has been used in the United States (US). The US experience suggests that there is much yet to learn about fair and just applications of the power to require landowners to relinquish possession of their property. In particular, the constitutionally required standard of "just compensation" for expropriated property seems unattainable in practice. If this is the case, it is essential that alternatives to expropriation be found. One possibility used widely in other countries is considered here.

To explore these issues, the next section provides a brief summary of the history of expropriation in the US. The literature and case law are vast and can only be superficially considered here. However, the principal trends and issues are presented. The focus then shifts to the issue of compensation, and it is argued that the usual standard of fair market value falls well short of what is ethically required to make property owners "whole." This point is explored further in a consideration of recent studies of the relationship between a person's sense of self-identity and the places they frequent. In an effort to provide an alternative to expropriation, international experiences with land readjustment are next briefly described. The chapter ends by offering a few concluding thoughts.

Expropriation in the United States

The US Constitution provides that private property cannot be "taken" for public use without "just compensation" (US Constitution, Amendment V). Despite this clear and succinct statement, the history of expropriation in the United States has been described as a "massive body of case law, irreconcilable in its inconsistency, confusing in its detail and defiant of all attempts at classification" (Note, 1949, pp. 605–606). There are, however, a few patterns of policy and practice that can be discerned.

By the early 1820s, state courts within the United States had settled on three concepts which were considered part of constitutional law even when state constitutions were not explicit:

- Expropriation or eminent domain powers were an inherent attribute of sovereignty, so that private property was held subject to takings by the state.
- This power could be used legitimately by the state only for "public use" or a "public purpose."
- When property was expropriated, property owners must be paid "fair" or "just" compensation (Scheiber, 1973).

Scheiber (1973) also describes what he terms "expediting doctrines" adopted by early state courts and justified on the grounds that expropriated property was of extraordinary public importance. One such doctrine was that compensation was limited to property that was physically taken. For example, an 1823 Massachusetts court decision ruled that a homeowner had no right to compensation when the city re-graded the street, exposing the home's foundation and destroying accessibility. In the court's view, those who buy land on hills or slopes are presumed to anticipate such changes. In 1857, the US Supreme Court upheld similar interpretations of the compensation requirement arguing that "private interests must yield to public accommodation" (Scheiber, 1973, p. 236).

Another expediting doctrine limited access to a jury trial as long as defined procedures provided for appropriate valuations, appeals of valuations and timely payment of compensation. The final doctrine identified by Scheiber permitted state legislatures to partially offset the cost of compensation with benefits to the remaining property for owners who were forced to give up only part of their property. As Scheiber notes, this "offsetting" doctrine is mentioned often enough in court records and other sources to suggest the subsidy thus required from private landowners was substantial (Scheiber, 1973). Indeed, Nichols writing in 1917 makes the following observation regarding whether benefits to the remaining land should at least partially offset the value of land taken:

> Upon this subject there is a greater diversity of opinion and more different and inconsistent rules have been laid down than upon any other point in the law of eminent domain ...
>
> *(Nichols, 1917, p. 761)*

Scheiber goes on to suggest that the most important single development in early US expropriation law was the "wholesale transfer of these doctrines over to the private sector, in aid of incorporated companies on which legislatures devolved the power of eminent domain" (Scheiber, 1973, p. 237). The power of eminent domain was granted to turnpike, bridge, canal and railroad companies in every state. The result was that railroad companies were able to acquire land at virtually no cost, arguing that the benefits to landowners' remaining land entirely offset the value of property taken. Further, having once exercised eminent domain, these companies were free to use the power again to expand their adjacent land holdings based almost exclusively on their own judgment regarding company needs.

Courts also drew on the precedents established by legislatures regarding grain mills. Gristmills were of importance in many farming communities and legislatures had granted them special privileges, including the right to install dams and inundate adjacent property in order to provide the necessary water power. To compensate owners of the flooded land, mill-dam statutes provided either for an annual assessment of lost income or a one-time damage judgment. From the mid-1830s through the civil war period, many states extended this mill-dam principle to manufacturing facilities in need of water power for purposes other than grinding grain (Scheiber, 1973).

These extensions of the power of eminent domain were resisted by some stakeholders, though they did not find much support in the courts. By the 1850s, opponents began to push through reforms in state constitutional conventions. Ohio was one of the first states to amend its constitution to require corporations to provide compensation to property owners, with compensation to be determined "irrespective of any benefit from any improvement proposed by such corporation, ... by a jury of twelve men" (Scheiber, 1973, p. 241). Other states began to follow suit.

Despite efforts to curtail the use of expropriation, especially by private interests, Scheiber summarises the period following the civil war as follows:

> The heyday of expropriation as an instrument of public policy designed to subsidize private enterprise can probably be dated as beginning in the 1870's and lasting until about 1910. During that era of alleged *laissez-faire* (which in fact was a period of broad-ranging public subsidies for business), all the constitutional stops were pulled out.
>
> *(Scheiber, 1973, p. 243)*

A 1906 ruling by the Idaho court was typical of the reasoning used, particularly in western states: unless the eminent domain power was interpreted very broadly and extended to private industrial interests, "a complete development of the material resources of our young state could not be made" (Scheiber, 1973, p. 246).

By about 1910, the shape of expropriation laws in the US had begun to change. As noted, state constitutions were being amended requiring jury trials, narrowing the range of permissible "offsetting" procedures and requiring prior compensation payments. In addition, eminent domain powers were being employed in city planning and public improvements. The topic of "excess condemnation" was emerging as a central issue, debated both in legislatures and courtrooms. With large regional development projects, federal urban renewal and highway programmes, the main focus of eminent domain in the US had shifted to government projects and their social consequences (Scheiber, 1973).

While the excesses of expropriation in subsidising private ventures has slowed, the shift to more extensive government use of eminent domain has not addressed some of the more fundamental concerns with its use. Three examples from the past 50 years serve to demonstrate this point. These cases also frame most of the current law and practice related to expropriation in the United States. The cases involve urban renewal, land reform and economic development.

Berman v Parker (348 U.S. 26 1954) centred on the use of expropriation as a tool in urban renewal. The US Congress created a local redevelopment land agency in Washington DC, with the power to expropriate land for the purposes of urban renewal. The agency determined that one section of the city was "blighted" and initiated eminent domain proceedings. Some landowners sued, arguing that beautification was not a legitimate public use under the Constitution. Their claims were rejected in a unanimous Supreme Court decision. The majority opinion stated in part "If those who govern the District of Columbia decide that the Nation's Capital should be beautiful as well as sanitary, there is nothing in the Fifth Amendment that stands in the way" (Lavine, 2010). Under the guise of city beautification and renewal, approximately 5,000 urban black residents were displaced (Somin,

2015a). Following *Berman*, hundreds of thousands of Americans were removed from their homes across the country and their homes replaced with more modern architecture and highways (Lavine, 2010). While on its face, urban renewal may be a worthy public purpose, the practice in the US has tended to displace minorities and the poor much more frequently than other social and economic groups.

In *Hawaii Housing Authority v Midkiff* (467 U.S. 229 1984), the issue was land reform. In 1967, 91 percent of all privately owned land in the state of Hawaii was held by just 72 land-owners. Almost all residents leased their property. The Hawaii Land Reform Act of 1967 gave the Hawaii Housing Authority the power to use eminent domain to acquire and then sell land to lessees. Over the next decade, the authority took control of 30 tracts (about 5,000 house lots) and redistributed the land. In 1979, one of the largest landowners sued arguing that redistribution in this manner did not constitute a legitimate public purpose. The case was originally decided in favour of the State, but the decision was overturned on appeal. The Court of Appeals found that the Hawaii Land Reform Act was "a naked attempt on the part of the state of Hawaii to take the private property of *A* and transfer it to *B* solely for *B*'s private use and benefit" (Lamoreaux, 2011, p. 294). The Supreme Court did not agree. In a unanimous decision, the Court reversed the Court of Appeals ruling. The High Court found instead that the constitution did not preclude the judgment by a state legislature that land reform was a legitimate public purpose. Such judgments were legislative in nature and not within the purview of the courts (Lamoreaux, 2011).

> Taking land from A and giving it to B ("redistribution of fees simple") was constitutional if its purpose was "to correct deficiencies in the market determined by the state legislature to be attributable to land oligopoly."
>
> *(Lamoreaux, 2011, p. 295)*

As surprising as it may seem, the *Hawaii Housing Authority* case generated little public interest or comment at the time.

The most recent case however generated the most public outcry. In the 2005 case of *Kelo v City of New London* (545 U.S. 469 2005), The City of New London, Connecticut, acting through its private development agency, sought to expropriate a block of 90 middle-income residential properties in good repair as part of its plan to redevelop the area into more mixed-use commercial and high-end residential land use. Thus, the housing was to be expropriated from one set of private middle-class owners and given to another private development interest. Both the Connecticut Supreme Court and the US Supreme Court upheld the action. The courts reasoned that the general benefits a community enjoyed from economic growth qualified as a permissible "public use" (Somin, 2015a).

The public response to the *Kelo* decision was marked but not necessarily consistent. Both the *New York Times* and the *Washington Post* published editorials agreeing with the court's decision. But groups as diverse as the American Association of Retired People and the National Association for the Advancement of Colored People expressed opposition to the ruling. Many small farmers feared the ruling could pave the way for local governments to expropriate their land for private developments. In the end, 43 states amended their laws governing eminent domain in response to the ruling, though in a number of cases the changes were little more than cosmetic (Gold & Sagalyn, 2010). Less than half of these reforms place significant restrictions on the use of expropriation for economic development purposes (Somin, 2015a). In addition, then-President George W. Bush issued an executive order instructing the federal government to limit the use of eminent domain (Bush, 2006). The impact of this order is also restricted since most expropriation actions are taken by local and state governments. But the reform efforts have tended to limit economic development as a rationale for using eminent domain (Hudson, 2010).

As worrying as it may be, it is still the case that from concepts such as "blight" (often used to justify eminent domain) and "public use/purpose" to the procedural rights of property owners, there is still much confusion in US eminent domain law (Gold & Sagalyn, 2010; Hudson, 2010). But most troubling is the fact that Scheiber's observation from 40 years ago is still very apt:

> Hence perhaps the most important continuity in public debate over expropriation, coming down to our own day, is the widely shared sense that the appalling technical complexities of eminent domain law, troublesome enough in themselves, are but the surface manifestation of serious social inequities associated with it.
>
> *(Scheiber, 1973, p. 249)*

Lamoreaux (2011) argues that property rights for the majority in the United States are reasonably secure against expropriation because property ownership is so widespread. Property rights are protected for most landowners, in this view, because when the application of expropriation is seen as threatening middle-class landowners, voters mobilise and demand reforms. At the same time, expropriations that affect mainly the poor or members of minority groups are particularly likely to go unchallenged. Neither is the expropriation of narrow business interests as in the *Berman* case likely to stir public outcry. But Lamoreaux argues that the principal protection of property against expropriation relies on voters rather than any constitutional or statutory limitation.

> Security of property rights in the United States depends on the mass of voters and so does not offer the same degree of protection to those at the bottom or top of the wealth distribution as it does to those in the middle.
>
> *(Lamoreaux, 2011, pp. 300–301)*

Kaldor-Hicks and compensation

Recognising the social inequities that Scheiber referred to and that continue to persist in the US system, it is useful to step back and consider the underlying principles in play regarding expropriation. In particular, the ethical justifications for compensation resulting from expropriation are worth revisiting.

In essence, expropriation is nearly always justified using what amounts to a cost-benefit calculation. Society as a whole is better off, so the argument goes, if the specific private property interest is repurposed to some particular public use. The benefits to society are larger than the private costs to current landowners. From this perspective, compensation becomes simply an application of the Kaldor-Hicks criterion which allows winners (society) to compensate losers (landowners) and still be better off (Miceli, 1997). Society is, in the aggregate, better off. In particular, no one is worse off since the payment of compensation took place, and aggregate social welfare is improved.

Clearly, there are several strong assumptions being made in applying this logic in expropriation. Perhaps most obvious is that the compensation paid must equal the value of the loss to the landowners. In concept, Kaldor-Hicks does not actually require that compensation be paid at all, but in the context of expropriation, compensation is required. A frequently contentious issue is therefore the calculation of the compensation due landowners.

Compensation nearly always involves valuation of the property interest at stake. Valuation theory argues that the estimated value of a property will depend on the purpose of the valuation exercise. Properties have different "values" when viewed from different perspectives (Appraisal Institute, 1992). In the context of expropriation, "[c]hoosing the appropriate measure of compensation for eminent domain inevitably involves selecting among imperfect alternatives" (Wyman, 2007, p. 245). In the US, the generally accepted valuation standard is that of "fair market value," or the price at which a property would sell if the transaction were between a willing buyer and willing seller, neither of whom are required to enter into the transaction (Wyman, 2007). In the event that only part of the property value is taken, say for a public easement, the compensation should reflect the overall impact on total value.

> It is well settled that, when part of a tract of land is taken for the public use, the just compensation to which the owner is entitled by the constitution includes the damages to the remainder of the tract resulting from the taking as well as the value of the land taken.
>
> *(Nichols, 1917, p. 721)*

After the *Kelo* decision, some have argued that just compensation standards should change, and that compensation should aim to make property owners subjectively indifferent to whether the expropriation took place or not. Wyman argues that such a proposal is both impractical and undesirable, since it is imprudent to base public policy choices on individual preferences (Wyman, 2007). The US Supreme Court has recognised the difficulty in adopting subjective indifference as a standard. For example, Justice Marshall provided this explanation for the fair market value standard:

> In giving content to the just compensation requirement of the Fifth Amendment, this Court has sought to put the owner of condemned property "in as good a position pecuniarily as if his property had not been taken." However, this principle of indemnity has not been given its full and literal force. Because of serious practical difficulties in assessing the worth an individual places on particular property at a given time, we have recognized the need for a relatively objective working rule. ... The Court therefore has employed the concept of fair market value to determine the condemnee's loss.
>
> *(United States v. 564.54 Acres of Land, 441 U.S. 1979, pp. 510–511)*

It must also be acknowledged that fair market value is often difficult to determine for many expropriated properties because they are unique properties in the path of a road or economic development project for which there is no easily obtained market price comparison (Wyman, 2007).

Wyman (2007) also notes that "just compensation" under the fair market value standard does not require governments to compensate certain kinds of losses that property owners may experience. Judge Posner makes this point in the following passage from *Coniston Corp. v Village of Hoffman Estates*, 844 F.2d 461, 464 (7th Cir. 1988):

> Compensation in the constitutional sense is... not full compensation, for market value is not the value that every owner of property attaches to his property but merely the value that the marginal owner attaches to his property. Many owners are "intramarginal," meaning that because of relocation costs, sentimental attachments, or the special suitability of the property for their particular (perhaps idiosyncratic) needs, they value their property at more than its market value (i.e., it is not "for sale"). Such owners are

hurt when the government takes their property and gives them just its market value in return. The taking in effect confiscates the additional (call it "personal") value that they obtain from the property.

Posner's point bears further exploration. In particular, what Posner calls "sentimental attachments" and "special suitability" deserve greater explication. In land policies internationally, there are two dominant views of the relationship between people and their property, but Posner's comment seems to suggest a third view as well.

People-place relationships

The view that seems to underlie many expropriation regimes sees land as most fundamentally an economic commodity, and land rights are characterised in terms of economic potential (Assies, 2009; Borras & Franco, 2010; Payne, 2001). Since economic commodities are largely interchangeable, as long as the market value of a property is paid in compensation, the property owners can readily replace their holdings in the market place. To be sure, there are relocation costs which should be factored in, but from this perspective, the value of property is reflected in its price. With adequate compensation, a property owner will be able to replace any given property by entering the market place and bidding on a comparable property. As noted, disputes will certainly arise regarding the appropriate level of compensation. But these can in principle be resolved by reference to the market.

Increasingly, however, scholars and policy makers are coming to recognise that "rights to land" differ markedly from "land rights." Rights to land and property are seen as essential to the achievement of human rights. Access to land and security of tenure are regarded as an important "means to achieve human rights, as defined by international conventions" (EU Task Force on Land Tenure, 2004, p. 4; Franco, Monsalve, & Borras, 2015). The *EU Land Policy Guidelines* further argues that "land titling is not always the best way of increasing tenure security, and nor does it automatically lead to greater investment and productivity" (EU Task Force on Land Tenure, 2004, p. 6; Keith, 2002). Access to land in this view is an inseparable ingredient in a poor household's ability to survive, earn, thrive and lift itself out of poverty (UN-Habitat, 2008a).

> [Secure land tenure and rights to property] are fundamental to shelter and livelihoods; as such, they are an important foundation for the realisation of human rights and for poverty reduction. Secure land rights are particularly important in helping to reverse three types of phenomena: gender discrimination; social exclusion of vulnerable groups; and wider social and economic inequalities linked to inequitable and insecure rights to land.
>
> (UN-Habitat, 2008b, p. 3)

Importantly, tenure security in this context is in the first place "the right of all individuals and groups to effective government protection against forced evictions" (UN-Habitat, 2008b, p. 5).

From this perspective, expropriation is much more difficult to justify unless there is both adequate compensation and sufficient land available for acquisition by the dispossessed land holder. Adequate compensation in this sense would provide the land holder with sufficient resources to obtain the same standard of living obtained prior to expropriation. Note that this view requires both compensation and the opportunity to replace lost property.

These are the two dominant views in the international development community. Posner's statement identifies a third aspect of the person-property relationship that merits consideration. This third view is currently being explored most fully by scholars in environmental psychology and human geography under the headings of place attachment and place identity. In a recent review article, Lewicka notes the increasing interest in the subject of person-place relationships in these and other fields. By her account, over 400 papers have been published within the last 45 years in more than 120 different journals on these and related subjects, with the greatest activity in the past decade or so. These publications represent all branches of the social sciences, including environmental psychology, sociology, community psychology, human geography, cultural anthropology, gerontology, demography, urban studies, leisure sciences and tourism, ecology, forestry, architecture and planning, and economics (Lewicka, 2011).

The central notion of relevance here is the observation that a person's identity is often defined in part by places encountered on a daily basis.

> In effect, the subjective sense of self is defined and expressed not simply by one's relationship to other people, but also by one's relationships to the various physical settings that define and structure day-to-day life.
>
> (Proshansky, Fabian, & Kaminoff, 1983, p. 58)

Admittedly, this is a field of study that is still struggling to find a strong theoretical framework (Lewicka, 2011; Raymond, Brown, & Weber, 2010). Essentially, it is argued that people form an emotional bond with their environments, and this bond is manifest both as place dependence and place identity. Place identity is most simply defined as the physical setting's importance for a person's identity (Anton & Lawrence, 2014; Scannell & Gifford, 2010; Wester-Herber, 2004). The concept of place identity has been shown to be of importance for both self-identity and the processes that guide action in relation to the environment (Wester-Herber, 2004).

Two examples from the *Kelo* case provide helpful examples. Wilhelmina Dery was one of the plaintiffs in the *Kelo* case. At the time of the case, she was in her 80s and had lived in the same house her entire life. Her wish was to continue living in the house for the remainder of her life. A second plaintiff, the Cristofaro family had lived in their home about 30 years, having purchased their property in the 1970s after their previous home had been expropriated as part of an urban renewal project. These individuals had deep roots in the community and strongly resisted being forced out (Somin, 2015b). They were attached to their location, but their personal identities were also linked to those places. Disrupting such relationships can have significant repercussions for individuals and families (Fullilove, 1996).

Speller (2000) conducted a longitudinal study of Arkwright Town, North East Derbyshire, UK, a mining community of 177 households forced to relocate when the local mine was reopened. The old village consisted of five straight rows of terraced houses without front gardens and limited or no back gardens, and limited public facilities. The replacement homes were semi-detached houses or bungalows with front and rear gardens and all public facilities were replaced. There was strong support from residents for the village relocation. Speller's extended study of participants suggested that there are five important factors which, when present, facilitate the development of an emotional bond with place. These, she argues, are aspects of place attachment. Her list includes a sense of security, a sense of autonomy, the desire and ability to engage in appropriation, an optimal level of internal and external stimulation, and place congruence. She argues that place can thus be an integral part of identity (Speller, 2000; Speller, Lyons, & Twigger-Ross, 2002).

Another way to make the case regarding the role of places in identity is to consider the importance of place for cultural and ethnic groups. Consider the following statement from the United Nations publication *State of the World's Indigenous Peoples*:

> The importance of land and territories to indigenous cultural identity cannot be stressed enough. The survival and development of indigenous peoples' particular ways of life, their traditional knowledge, their handicrafts and other cultural expressions have, since time immemorial, depended on their access and rights to their traditional lands, territories and natural resources. But land is not only the basis of the indigenous economy. Indigenous peoples also have a deep spiritual relationship with the land; they feel at one with their ancestral territory and feel responsible for the healthy maintenance of the land—its waters and soils, its plants and animals—for both themselves and future generations. Land is where their ancestors are buried and where sacred places are visited and revered.
>
> Very often, *people identify themselves by taking the name of the place to which they belong.*
>
> *(Kipuri, 2009, p. 53, emphasis added)*

As a consequence, the expropriation of traditional lands held by indigenous peoples in the United States has had devastating effects which persist to this day (Wallace, 1993).

To more fully appreciate the importance of place identity in the expropriation discussion, consider the following example offered by Wyman as part of her discussion on compensation for expropriation:

> Consider, for instance, a long-time homeowner whose house is expropriated. She would be compensated to allow her to re-establish herself after the taking in a neighborhood where she could enjoy valuable goods, such as community and autonomy, to roughly the same extent that she enjoyed them in her old neighborhood.
>
> *(Wyman, 2007, p. 244)*

Now replace "a long-time homeowner" with "Palestinians." Is it conceivable that the Israeli-Palestinian conflict could be resolved if we simply got the compensation right? Could either Palestinians or Israelis be convinced to accept compensation and relocate to another plot of land, say in Brazil, where they could enjoy their "community and autonomy" to roughly the same extent they did in their "old" neighbourhood? The Palestinian "right of return" and the Jewish "next year in Jerusalem" would seem to suggest such a resolution to the conflict misses the importance of place in their respective identities.

This example also serves to point out one of the ambiguities in place identity. Studies show that "place" may refer either to the home as the strongest contributor to identity, or to the city/village, often only a slightly weaker source of identity. Results relating to other scales (neighbourhood, state, region, country, etc.) are more mixed (Lewicka, 2010, 2011). In some instances, people may identify with a community rather than a specific parcel of land, and they may be largely indifferent between one location and another within the community.

More study of the nature of the person-place relationship is required to understand how place identity and expropriation interact. But if it can be demonstrated that a specific location is an important contributor to a person's sense of identity, it is hard to see any ethical justification for a forced disruption of that person-place relationship. To be justified, any disruption would require the participation and agreement of the persons affected.

425

An alternative to expropriation

It should be clear from this brief summary of the vast literature and case law on expropriation that the tool has a long but rather sordid history in the United States. As often as not, expropriation has been used to promote special commercial interests at the expense of the poor and minorities. Compensation levels remain contentious even when market value is the agreed standard. The concepts of public use and public purpose have been stretched far beyond normal parlance. Federal executive orders have been issued directing the national government to avoid all expropriation actions (Bush, 2006; Scheiber, 1973). And influential members of the judiciary acknowledge that we simply are not able to fairly and consistently make people "whole" who are subject to expropriation.

And yet there are legitimate instances in which privately held land is needed for important public uses, or when the particular configuration of private interests impedes repurposing land for valid public purposes. What alternatives exist for meeting these legitimate needs while minimising or avoiding altogether the use of expropriation? The answer currently in the United States is, not many. But the US could benefit significantly by learning from other countries. One tool in particular could prove valuable in the US context: land readjustment. Much of the following discussion draws heavily on *Leveraging Land*, a recent joint UN-Habitat/GLTN publication (UN-Habitat, 2016a).

Land readjustment consists of pooling all land parcels within the area of interest, joint planning for servicing the land, and the redistribution of parcels in an orderly configuration, making room for public improvements. Land readjustment has been widely used in a number of countries for many years to address primarily three challenges: (1) a disorderly plot pattern, (2) insufficient public space or space for public services, and (3) lack of funding or ability to expropriate private land to create the needed public space. Through the pooling and reallocation of plots, new public space can be created, avoiding the financial and political costs of expropriation.

Additionally, land readjustment can raise funds through the creation and sale of extra plots. This funding usually feeds back into the improvements associated with the readjustment project and can be used to repay borrowing for capital improvements. Such revenues from the sale of extra plots typically do not go to the government's general revenues. Therefore, land readjustment is not considered a revenue tool, but can be used to allow neighbourhood upgrades to be self-financing.

A land readjustment project is usually only approved if a minimum number of participating landholders are in favour. The approach benefits landholders by providing their plots with access to new public space and services, thereby increasing the value of their land. While the surrender of some land for infrastructure and public spaces is a key characteristic, the land retained by the original land owners as a result of the readjustment process is assumed to be inherently more valuable as a result of improved services and development potential (UN-Habitat, 2014; Yau & Cheng, 2010).

Brief history of land readjustment

Land readjustment has different names in different countries: "land readjustment" in Japan and South Korea, "land pooling" in Australia and Nepal, "land consolidation" in Taiwan and Indonesia, and "land re-plotting" in Canada (Karki, 2004). But the approach has been used as a development tool since at least 1791 when it was used in the United States for planning the Washington DC area. Unfortunately, that was also about the last time it was used in the US. Nonetheless, the tool, in its different forms, has become widely popular today in countries such as Australia, Germany, France, Netherlands, Sweden, Israel, Japan, Thailand, South Korea, Indonesia and others (Mittal, 2014).

> The success of land readjustment in [these] countries is also attributed to the fact that cities in these countries were largely fiscally constrained, and were experiencing rapid population growth. The real estate values were high and land markets were significantly active causing demand for urban infrastructures and serviced urban land to accommodate new growth. In many cases, land readjustment was chosen as the land development tool, because of its self-financing nature and its greater social and political acceptability.
>
> *(Mittal, 2014, p. 315)*

In the international literature, Germany's examples of the land readjustment process are some of the oldest and most often cited examples. In fact, in the early 1900s, Japan adopted Germany's land readjustment model. Currently, Japan is Asia's example for land readjustment schemes (Lozano-Gracia, Young, Lall, & Vishwanath, 2013). Another prominent Asian example of land readjustment use is in Indonesia where about 132 projects in 70 cities have used land readjustment for urban development since 1982 (Andre Sorensen, 2000).

The land readjustment variations in the countries of Germany, France, and Japan are described here to provide a clearer picture of the different types of land readjustment schemes.

Germany

As stated previously, Germany's land readjustment model (*Umlegung*) is possibly the oldest and most pervasive example in the literature. The process is carried out by local authorities, and all landowners within the boundaries of the land readjustment area have no option to leave the programme. They can express their views and have a right to appeal but have very little formal power. Maps are drawn up and a common share is taken out of the landowner's properties for streets and other public spaces. In the reduced area of private ownership, every landowner receives a share of land back in proportion to their original holdings, either in area or in value. Land readjustment in Germany is an important and recognised means for building in Germany. It is probably the most common method used for the implementation of new dwelling plans (Davy, 2007; Larsson, 1997).

France

In France, land readjustment can be initiated by landowners or the government. The responsibility mainly is given to landowners. Normally, two-thirds of the owners *and* those who own two-thirds of the total area, need to agree on the project. After the area for public use has been deducted from each individual property, the landowners receive a redistribution of land with at least the value of the land they owned before the project. In some cases, land can be exchanged for cash. The French method takes longer than Germany's approach and requires more commitment from and risk for the landowners (Larsson, 1997).

Japan

The model in Japan is called the *Kukaku Seiri* and has developed into the approach used in about 50 percent of all new development areas. This model is not designed for either the public or private sector specifically (Larsson, 1997). Projects in Japan can be either privately or publicly initiated, and can include (1) individuals, (2) land owner associations, (3) local governments, (4) government agencies, and (5) housing and town corporations. Because of the range of executors, Japan is often seen as having one of the most participatory land readjustment processes in the world (André Sorensen, 2007; Lozano-Gracia et al., 2013).

If initiated by the private sector, then two-thirds of owners and leaseholders must agree on the project. The cost sharing between the private and public sectors is determined in each project by mutual agreement. This method is sometimes criticised, however, because there is no deadline for completion nor is it always combined with formal building plans (which results in buildings with very different appearances in the same neighbourhood) (Larsson, 1997).

Basic conditions required for successful land readjustment

Based on the literature, there are nine conditions repeatedly seen that are required for a successful land readjustment regime. These are listed here with only a brief description of some, and the reader is referred to the UN-Habitat publication *Remaking the urban mosaic* for a more detailed discussion (UN-Habitat, 2016b).

Need for an appropriate legal framework

In order to apply many land readjustment principles successfully, a legal framework needs to be established. This framework would most likely be articulated at the state level in the United States. Land readjustment provides an alternative to expropriation, but the law must still address a fundamental question: if a given land owner resists providing land for public purposes, what options exist? The land readjustment legal framework must specify what options exist in a land readjustment project including the principles and procedures to be followed (Turk, 2008).

Additionally, the enabling legal structure can regulate when and why land readjustment will occur in an urban area. To increase the possibility of implementation, legal regulations should also stipulate which entities can initiate a land readjustment project. This could be limited to a public agency (Germany), the landowners (France), or any of a variety of entities (Japan and South Korea) (Turk, 2008).

It is also desirable to spell out how property valuation will be determined. In Germany, for example, the law mandates setting up valuation committees, the definition of standardised market values, and the method for collecting purchase price data (Lozano-Gracia et al., 2013, p. 10).

Finally, the legal framework should provide guidance regarding the status of land titles. Since in land readjustment, the land titles are readjusted, ownerships are switched, and property-lot boundaries are altered. Having clear land titles and property records expedites this process (Mittal, 2014, p. 316).

Shared project benefits and costs

Transparency and certainty in sharing both the costs and the benefits among the public entity and the landowners are important. This does not necessarily mean that the municipality and the landowners share costs or benefits equally. For example, in Germany, the municipalities initiate land readjustment and little power is given to landowners in the process. In these models, the municipality assumes the majority of the cost of the project. Muñoz-Gielen (2014) describes a policy in Spain that allows local governments to share a significant portion of the incremental land value created through land readjustment. When the landowners are the active participants in the land readjustment process, then they should also share more of the risk of the project (Turk, 2008).

Furthermore, equity and fairness need to be maintained among landowners. At the beginning of the land readjustment process, each landowner's property has a different value. During the project equity needs to be maintained, as some might be able to use their property during the process while others will not. Even more important, at the end of the land readjustment project, fairness should be achieved between landowners when reallocating property to the original owners in proportion to the previous value of their property. During this "'distribution" stage, estimates must be made of new market values resulting from the project. Formulas can be used to aid the process, but using a skilled land appraiser is the best approach (Turk, 2008).

Participation of landowners

Given the importance of land and tenure security in all cultures, the participation of landowners is important to the success of any land readjustment project. Recognition of the vital role land owners play has led UN-Habitat to initiate a specialised version of land readjustment, with particular focus on participation (UN-Habitat, 2014, 2016b). Landowners who are (1) more educated about the project and its benefits, (2) feel like they have a voice, and (3) who are well informed about the land readjustment process, are more likely to agree to the project without bringing court action against the project or otherwise seeking to delay progress (Turk, 2008). Furthermore, landowner satisfaction is crucial to the success of any current or future projects. The more examples of agreement there are for land readjustment projects, the more willing landowners will be to engage in such projects (Mathur, 2013).

In general, opponents to land readjustment projects take one of two positions. First, and most common, there are those who do not believe they will gain any benefit and may in fact be worse off as a result of the project. The second group tends to have plans of their own for the land and may resist subordinating their plans in a land readjustment project. This second group often tends to encourage other land holders to oppose the project as well (Turk, 2008). In order to gain support from a majority of the landowners and promote landowner satisfaction with both the process and the outcomes, landowners should:

- Be well informed and know how the land readjustment project benefits them;
- Know the different channels (informal and formal) available to express their views;
- Be given a time frame for commitment;
- Be allowed to participate in as many land readjustment exercises as possible; and
- Be given plenty of public notice about the progress of the project.

In addition, discussions of meetings should be well documented, so landowners know their voice is being heard and is important (Yau & Cheng, 2010).

Other requisites for success in land readjustment include:

- Projects should be self-financing to the extent practical, including construction costs where possible;
- Sufficient land use, infrastructure and financial planning resources should be available and used;

- Project management and technical personnel should be available and used;
- Quality cadastral maps and map updates are extremely helpful; and
- A favourable real estate market which greatly eases the process.

Conclusions

The chapter began with a review of the history of expropriation in the United States. While the power to expropriate private property for public use has been assumed since the country's inception, the principles on which appropriate use of the eminent domain process can be grounded have never been adequately articulated and agreed upon. The only meaningful check on the expropriation power has been public resistance to perceived abuses. As a result, expropriation in the United States in the past has been used largely to benefit special commercial interests at the expense of the poor and minority groups. Currently, the use of eminent domain tends to be strongly resisted by the public. State and local governments are frequently reluctant to use the power because it is financially and politically expensive and because litigation often delays needed projects for years.

One of the major flaws in the use of expropriation is the supposition that the market value standard for compensation provides adequate compensation for condemned land. As explained earlier, the assumptions needed for this condition to hold are very strong and would be true only if landowners are indifferent between their current land holdings and any other comparable land in any location. It is the case, however, that people form attachments to places, and over time, their individual identities become wrapped up in those places. It is not clear that there are any ethical grounds for disrupting this sense of place identity without the consent of the people involved.

But there is a better way. Many countries make successful use of land readjustment to avoid the pain of expropriation and still achieve needed public use of private lands. States in the US would be well advised to learn from these international examples and update their legal structures to encourage land readjustment for needed projects.

Since land readjustment involves active engagement with all landowners, and the agreement of a super majority, there is a greater likelihood that the excesses of past expropriation events can be avoided. And by securing the agreement of landowners, concerns about forced disruption of place identity can be circumvented. Of course, land readjustment is not a panacea. There will still be instances in which individual landowners resist participation. In such cases, patience may prove the best course of action.

References

Anton, C. E., & Lawrence, C. (2014). Home is where the heart is: The effect of place of residence on place attachment and community participation. *Journal of Environmental Psychology, 40*, 451–461.

Appraisal Institute. (1992). *The appraisal of real estate*, 10th ed. Chicago, IL: Appraisal Institute.

Assies, W. (2009). Land tenure, land law and development: some thoughts on recent debates. *The Journal of Peasant Studies, 36*(3), 573–589.

Borras, S. M., Jr., & Franco, J. C. (2010). Contemporary discourses and contestations around pro-poor land policies and land governance. *Journal of Agrarian Change, 10*(1), 1–32.

Bush, G. W. (2006). *Executive order: Protecting the property rights of the American people*. Washington, DC: The White House.

Davy, B. (2007). Mandatory happiness? Land readjusment and property in Germany. In Y.-H. Hong, & B. Needham (Eds.), *Analyzing land readjustment*. Cambridge, MA: Lincoln Institute of Land Policy.

EU Task Force on Land Tenure. (2004). *EU land policy guidelines*. Retrieved from Brussels: https://ec.europa.eu/europeaid/sites/devco/files/methodology-eu-land-policy-guidelines-200411_en_2.pdf.

Franco, J. C., Monsalve, S., & Borras, S. M. (2015). Democratic land control and human rights. *Current Opinion in Environmental Sustainability, 15*, 66–71.

Fullilove, M. T. (1996). Psychiatric implications of displacement: Contributions from the psychology of place. *The American Journal of Psychiatry, 153*(12), 1516.

Gold, M. E., & Sagalyn, L. B. (2010). The use and abuse of blight in eminent domain. *Fordham Urban Law Journal, 38*(4), 1119–1173.

Hudson, D. Z. (2010). Eminent domain due process. *The Yale Law Journal, 119*(6), 1280–1327.

Karki, T. K. (2004). Implementation experiences of land pooling projects in Kathmandu Valley. *Habitat International, 28*(1), 67–88.

Keith, S. (2002). Rural property tax systems in central and Eastern Europe. FAO Land Tenure Studies 5. Rome Food and Agriculture Organization of the United Nations.

Kipuri, N. (2009). *Culture State of the world's indigenous peoples* (Vol. ST/ESA/328). New York, NY: United Nations.

Lamoreaux, N. R. (2011). The mystery of property rights: A US perspective. *The Journal of Economic History, 71*(2), 275–306.

Larsson, G. (1997). Land readjustment: A tool for urban development. *Habitat International, 21*(2), 141–152.

Lavine, A. (2010). Urban renewal and the story of Berman v. Parker. *The Urban Lawyer, 42*(2), 423–475.

Lewicka, M. (2010). What makes neighborhood different from home and city? Effects of place scale on place attachment. *Journal of Environmental Psychology, 30*(1), 35–51.

Lewicka, M. (2011). Place attachment: How far have we come in the last 40 years? *Journal of Environmental Psychology, 31*(3), 207–230.

Lozano-Gracia, N., Young, C., Lall, S. V., & Vishwanath, T. (2013). *Leveraging land to enable urban transformation: Lessons from global experience.* Policy Research Working Paper 6312. Washington, DC: The World Bank.

Mathur, S. (2013). Use of land pooling and reconstitution for urban development: Experiences from Gujarat, India. *Habitat International, 38*, 199–206.

Miceli, T. J. (1997). *Economics of the law: Torts, contracts, property, litigation.* New York, NY: Oxford University Press.

Mittal, J. (2014). Self-financing land and urban development via land readjustment and value capture. *Habitat International, 44*, 314–323.

Muñoz-Gielen, D. (2014). Urban governance, property rights, land readjustment and public value capturing. *European Urban and Regional Studies, 21*(1), 60–78.

Nichols, P. (1917). *The law of eminent domain: A treatise on the principles which affect the taking of property for the public use* (Vol. 2). Albany, NY: Matthew Bender & Company.

Note. (1949). The public use limitation on eminent domain: An advance requiem. *The Yale Law Journal, 58*(4), 599–614.

Payne, G. (2001). Urban land tenure policy options: Titles or rights? *Habitat International, 25*(3), 415–429.

Proshansky, H. M., Fabian, A. K., & Kaminoff, R. (1983). Place-identity: Physical world socialization of the self. *Journal of Environmental Psychology, 3*(1), 57–83.

Raymond, C. M., Brown, G., & Weber, D. (2010). The measurement of place attachment: Personal, community, and environmental connections. *Journal of Environmental Psychology, 30*(4), 422–434.

Scannell, L., & Gifford, R. (2010). Defining place attachment: A tripartite organizing framework. *Journal of Environmental Psychology, 30*(1), 1–10.

Scheiber, H. N. (1973). Property law, expropriation, and resource allocation by government: The United States, 1789–1910. *The Journal of Economic History, 33*(1), 232–251.

Somin, I. (2015a). *The grasping hand: Kelo v. new london and the limits of eminent domain.* Chicago, IL: University of Chicago Press.

Somin, I. (2015b, May 29). The story behind Kelo v. City of New London - How an obscure takings case got to the Supreme Court and shocked the nation. *The Washington Post.* Retrieved from www. washingtonpost.com/news/volokh-conspiracy/wp/2015/05/29/the-story-behind-the-kelo-case-how-an-obscure-takings-case-came-to-shock-the-conscience-of-the-nation/?utm_term=. cb1a1567b212.

Sorensen, A. (2000). Conflict, consensus or consent: Implications of Japanese land readjustment practice for developing countries. *Habitat International, 24*(1), 51–73.

Sorensen, A. (2007). Consensus, persuasion, and opposition: Organizing land readjustment in Japan. In Y.-H. Hong, & B. Needham (Eds.), *Analyzing land readjustment.* Cambridge, MA: Lincoln Institute of Land Policy.

Speller, G. M. (2000). A community in transition: A longitudinal study of place attachment and iden-tity processes in the context of an enforced relocation. (PhD), University of Surrey, Guildford, UK.

Speller, G. M., Lyons, E., & Twigger-Ross, C. (2002). A community in transition: The relationship between spatial change and identity processes. Retrieved from www.researchgate.net/publication/266883861_A_Community_in_Transition_The_Relationship_between_Spatial_Change_and_Identity_Processes

Turk, S. S. (2008). An examination for efficient applicability of the land readjustment method at the international context. *Journal of Planning Literature, 22*(3), 229–242.

UN-Habitat. (2008a). *Quick guide 3: Land: A crucial element in housing the urban poor. Housing the urban poor in Asian cities.* Nairobi, Kenya: United Nations Human Settlements Programme.

UN-Habitat. (2008b). *Secure land rights for all.* Nairobi, Kenya: United Nations Human Settlements Programme.

UN-Habitat. (2014). *Participatory and inclusive land readjustment (PILaR).* Nairobi, Kenya: United Na-tions Human Settlements Programme.

UN-Habitat. (2016a). *Leveraging land: Land-based finance for local governments-A reader.* Nairobi, Kenya: United Nations Human Settlements Programme and Global Land Tool Network.

UN-Habitat. (2016b). *Remaking the urban mosaic: Participatory and inclusive land readjustment.* Nairobi, Kenya: United Nations Human Settlements Programme and Global Land Tool Network.

Wallace, A. F. C. (1993). *The long, bitter trail: Andrew Jackson and the Indians.* New York, NY: Hill and Wang.

Wester-Herber, M. (2004). Underlying concerns in land-use conflicts—the role of place-identity in risk perception. *Environmental Science & Policy, 7*(2), 109–116.

Wyman, K. M. (2007). The measure of just compensation. *UC Davis L. Rev., 41*(1), 239–287.

Yau, Y., & Cheng, C. Y. (2010). Applicability of land readjustment in urban regeneration in Hong Kong. *Journal of Urban Regeneration and Renewal, 4*(1), 19–32.

23

Toward responsible land governance in the expropriation process

A case study of the Northern Coastal Highway and Highway 2000

Cadien Stuart and Susanne Lyon-Josephs

Introduction

From time to time it becomes necessary for the government to take land in private ownership for public use. In Jamaica, this process is termed compulsory acquisition. Elsewhere, it is referred to as condemnation (Eminent Domain); in the United States and the United Kingdom it is known as expropriation.

The two conditions which must be met for the government to exercise eminent domain/condemnation are:

a   that the taking of the land must be for public use; and that the
b   holders of interests in or rights over the property must be paid "just compensation."

Generally speaking, "just compensation" is the market value of the property, if all of the land is taken, or the value of all financial loss, if partially taken. The value of a property is based on its highest and best use (HABU) at the time it is taken, not necessarily its current use. "Just compensation" is the amount that restores the property owner to a financial position equivalent to that existing before the property was taken (Ling and Archer, 2005).

The power of compulsory acquisition can be abused. Unfair procedures for the compulsory acquisition of land and inequitable compensation for its loss can reduce land tenure security, increase tensions between the government and citizens, and reduce public confidence in the rule of law. Unclear, unpredictable, and unenforceable procedures create opportunities for corruption. Good governance is necessary to provide a balance between the needs of the government to acquire land rapidly, and the need to protect the rights of people whose land is to be acquired (FAO guidelines, 2008).

Source of power

In Jamaica, the Land Acquisition Act 1947 ("the Act") governs the process by which the Government of Jamaica is enabled to compulsorily acquire/expropriate land. As is the case with many Commonwealth countries, the law is a derivative of the old English Act of the same name. Note, however, since Jamaica's independence in 1962, the Act has not been updated in parallel with the UK version.

The Act outlines the process which ought to be observed and followed in the acquisition. The process as outlined in the various sections of Act is as follows:

Section 3: The power to enter and survey, and carry out such works as necessary;
Section 5: Declaration that land is required for a Public Purpose;
Section 6: Direction to begin proceedings of Acquisition;
Section 7: Requirement for a Survey to be undertaken;
Section 8: Power to Value land and to negotiate for private treaty;
Section 9: Invitation to a hearing extended to persons with interest in land (Where no agreement has been reached by private treaty);
Section 14: Determination of the Compensation to be paid;
Section 15: Taking possession of land Section 16: Vesting of land in the Crown.

The problem

Compulsory acquisition is taken to mean, in simple terms, the power of the government to acquire private rights in land without the willing consent of its owner or occupant in order to benefit society (FAO guidelines, 2008). That is to say, this is where the government acquires the whole or a portion of a land parcel from its private owner and compensates the owner for the ownership interest in that parcel, along with other elements of loss. Yet in many places, including Jamaica and other developing countries, this simple model encounters a wide range of exemptions and complications, often poorly or incompletely addressed in national legislations.

In many countries, weak expropriation laws open the door for governments and companies to take land for private interests without adequately compensating or resettling displaced people. Compulsory acquisition is inherently disruptive. Even when compensation is generous, and procedures are generally fair and efficient, the displacement of people from established homes, businesses, and communities still entails significant human costs. Where the process is designed or implemented poorly, the economic, social, and political costs may be enormous.

All affected owners and occupants may be at a disadvantage when their land is being compulsorily acquired, but the burden is particularly hard on the poor. They may not know their rights nor how to safeguard them during negotiations with experienced officials who are supported by all the powers and resources of government (FAO guidelines, 2008).

Historically, the courts seem to have succumbed to the pretense that the adequacy requirement may be achieved by giving sufficient monetary rewards in exchange.

The problem then is to find out:

- What are the rights and interests in the property that need to be valued?
- Who are the persons holding those rights and interest?
- What is their entitlement to compensation?

- What methods should be used to assess compensation?
- What are the tests of adequacy?

Chapter questions

The chapter seeks to address:

Question #1: What is the definition of public purpose?
Question #2: How can transparent and participatory expropriation processes be established?
Question #3: Who is entitled to compensation?
Question #4: What is Adequate Compensation (just compensation)?
Question #5: How should compensation be assessed?

In answering these questions, interviews were conducted and documents were reviewed, including the Land Acquisition Act as well as the Constitution of Jamaica which became source documents to determine what governs and what should govern the administration of the compulsory acquisition process.

Some of the indicators when answering the question of expropriation and "just compensation" are outlined below:

Indicator #1: Is "public purpose" clearly defined to allow for judicial review?
Indicator #2: Is the procedure transparent and participatory?
Indicator #3: Prior to expropriation, must the government identify and inform all affected populations?
Indicator #4: Are customary tenure holders/occupiers with formally recognised tenure rights entitled to compensation?
Indicator #5: Is there a payment for injurious affection?
Indicator #6: Is there a payment for severance and disturbance?
Indicator #7: Must compensation reflect the economic activity associated with the land?
Indicator #8: Must compensation reflect the improvements on the land?
Indicator #9: Is compensation payable in addition to relocation? (i.e., market value plus costs)
Indicator #10: Can affected populations negotiate compensation levels?
Indicator #11: Can affected populations challenge compensation in court or before a tribunal?
Indicator #12: Are displaced persons legally entitled to a relocation allowance?

Methodology

Primary data and secondary data are considered. The research employed case studies and interviews. The interviews were wide-ranging in their scope as they included valuers, property owners, tenants/occupants (informal settlers), administrators, and attorneys involved with the Land Acquisition Act as respondents.

Theoretical framework

The road to the development of a country is through the development of its infrastructure.

It is also said that when undertaking the physical development of any country, the land acquisition process is perhaps the single major deterrent to its expeditious growth.

The Government of Jamaica saw the need to implement the North Coast Highway Development Project which introduced a corridor as an initiative to improve communications along the entire stretch of north coast road from Negril in the West, to Port Antonio in the East of the island.

The entire project consisted of approximately 287 km (178 miles) of roadway and was divided into three segments. Segment 1 – Negril to Montego Bay (approx. 71 km (44 miles)), Segment 2 – Montego Bay to Ocho Rios (approx. 97 km (60 miles)), and Segment 3 – Ocho Rios to Fair Prospect (approx. 119 km (74 miles)). (JNHT, Archives)

Research has shown that the construction of the Northern Coastal Highway was a project of great significance in Jamaica for many reasons.

- The acquisition process, in undertaking the Northern Coastal Highway, provided the first occasion that the Act was used over such an extensive area, with a large number of affected properties, ownerships and other tenure rights, and varying land uses.
- The Northern Coastal Highway, especially in Segments 1 and 2 of the project, provided an opportunity for "regularising" of the ownership.
- It was primarily out of this project that a Resettlement Unit was established by the Ministry of Transport of Works to oversee the entire process.
- Note that the project also provided an opportunity for the honing of the skills of the land management professionals whose role is vital to the development of the built environment and related infrastructure.

It is generally agreed that the operation of the Land Acquisition Act was perhaps most tested in Segments 1 and 2 of the Northern Coastal Highway for the construction of new roads, whereas Segment 3 primarily involved the widening of (existing) roads.

In Segments 1 and 2, much of the activity revolved around the acquisition of many parcels of land for the construction of new roads. The Land Acquisition Act was utilised because it allowed for the acquisition of land by negotiation by the government for this public purpose, while also allowing the issues of ownership, rights to, and the quantum of compensation to be addressed with those persons claiming an interest in the land to be acquired.

Indicator #1: is "public purpose" clearly defined to allow for judicial review?

> Section 5 of the Land Acquisition Act 1947 states: "Whenever it appears to the Minister that any particular land is needed for a public purpose a declaration shall be made to that effect under his signature."

When the minister declares that property is needed for a "public purpose," the declaration is deemed to be conclusive evidence that the land is needed for a "public purpose."

Without a clear definition of "public purpose" in law, executive bodies may misuse or abuse expropriation power by arbitrarily justifying an expropriation decision under the pretext of a "public purpose" when the actual purpose will not serve public interests. Ambiguous definitions of "public purpose," or laws that grant broad discretion to executive bodies to determine what constitutes a "public purpose," limit the potential for effective judicial oversight (Tagliarino, 2016).

The Voluntary Guidelines on the Responsible Governance of Tenure of Land, Fisheries, and Forests in the context of National Food Security[1] (VGGTs) are the first comprehensive global instruments on the governance of tenure. They establish best practices that "are backed by international consensus of governments, international NGOs, civil society, and the private sector." The VGGTs were prepared through extensive intergovernmental negotiations launched in 2009 by the Food and Agriculture Organization of the United Nations (FAO). (Tagliarino, 2016).

The FAO handbook (2008) provides an established inventory of permissible purposes beyond which the government may not expropriate land. This inventory provides criteria that people can use to challenge proposed justification decisions in court. Laws with clear lists of "public purposes" (e.g., public infrastructure projects, national defense) provide courts with better guidance when ruling on expropriation cases and diminish the potential for conflicting court decisions.

The FAO VTTG guidelines have adopted some examples of commonly accepted "public purposes":

- Transportation uses including roads, canals, highways, railways, bridges, wharves, and airports;
- Public buildings including schools, libraries, hospitals, factories, religious institutions, and public housing;
- Public utilities for water, sewage, electricity, gas, communication, irrigation and drainage, dams, and reservoirs;
- Public parks, playgrounds, gardens, sports facilities, and cemeteries.

In countries where courts have reviewed "public purpose" justifications, they have often proved lenient and refused to second-guess the executive and legislative branches' rationale for an expropriation. In contrast, some courts have taken a more active approach to reviewing justification decisions. In Sri Lanka, for example, the Supreme Court overruled a decision to expropriate land for a private golf resort in the Water's Edge case (2008).

The common definition of a "public purpose" is a governmental action or direction that purports to benefit the populace (Ling and Archer, 2005). Historically, "public purpose" was defined in practice in the context of land being made available for public access, for example, the construction of a highway or building of a bridge. Therefore, the taking of private property for the use of another private citizen was not considered a public purpose, except in the case of private railroad companies, because railroads serve as common carriers openly available for public use.

The definition has been expanded to include instances where there is a clear public benefit or public purpose. Thus property for civic centres, cultural centres, trade facilities, and sports facilities may be deemed public uses. In a 1954, a ruling of the US Supreme Court further expanded the definition of public benefits to allow for the condemnation of blighted areas for aesthetic benefit (Ling and Archer, 2005).

In Jamaica, is it clear as to what constitutes a "public purpose"?

It is noted that under the Land Acquisition Act (1947), the term "public purpose" is not defined. The Commissioner is empowered to acquire land either by way of private treaty or by compulsory acquisition following a gazetted declaration of intent. The Jamaican government has for the most part not strayed from what is understood as the textbook definition and understanding of "public purpose."

In many cases, the omission of a definition for "public purpose" is deliberate, providing much greater flexibility for the exercise of discretion and interpretation. It provides for the flexibility of innovative programmes of urban renewal and expansion, and allows for public/private partnerships (PPPs) that yield benefit to the public, but may not have been possible if "public purpose" was prescribed in the legislation. Jamaica has not yet faced the issue as even in the case of PPPs, with several housing projects over the past two decades, the Government has been able to make land available out of its own land bank, or developers have proposed the development on land already in their ownership, with partnership with the Government being in the form or reduced cost on titling and other infrastructure costs. With the possibility of the development of poverty alleviation programmes and various other social justice programmes, "public purpose" could well extend beyond road works or public infrastructure to new town development and land assemblage for PPP development that is commercial in nature but provides wide-scale public benefit that justifies the need for compulsory acquisition to facilitate the partnership. Under the Land Development and Utilization Act 1966, the Government has expropriated land under the provisions of the Land Acquisition Act for agricultural resettlement and land lease programmes. It is noted that in these instances, the owners are often absentee landowners and compensation has been by way of Land Bonds.

Internationally, there seem to be some but not much evidence of case law addressing this area of land acquisition legislations and this is very limited in Jamaica. There appears to have been very little evidence, if any, of abuse of the Land Acquisition Act for appropriating land for activities that would not readily be defined as a "public purpose," such as road works, school projects, and other infrastructure works that the public would readily attribute to being within the purview of the government and constitute a "public purpose."

However, in Jamaica, there has been one instance involving lands located at Orange Grove Trelawny, in which the Court of Appeal upheld a ruling that barred the Minister of Housing from compulsorily acquiring privately owned land, by saying the takeover did not serve a public purpose as required by law, but was done for the benefit of squatters. The lands had housed an informal settlement and the owners sought to recover possession. It was the view of the Court of Appeal that

> The Housing Act and The Land Acquisition Act do not provide for the compulsory acquisition of privately owned land in order to transfer an interest to a community of persons who have occupied those lands despite the efforts of the owner to evict, and in defiance of orders of the Supreme Court.

It was further upheld that "the Constitution protects private property, and does not provide justification for the acquisition of private property in order to regularize the unlawful occupation of squatters."

In the United States, the concept of "public use" has evolved to one no longer requiring actual physical use by the acquiring agency. The case, often cited in connection with the definition of public purpose, is *Kelo v City of New London* (2005); however, many see this case as the Supreme Court of the United States stretching the Taking Clause. The US Supreme Court concluded that the fact that expropriations for "economic development" benefit private parties and produce only incidental public benefits did not render the expropriation unconstitutional. This decision gave to the government additional rights of appropriation by extending the previously understood and practiced definition of "public purpose."

It may be argued that a clear definition of "public purpose" remains an issue for governments.

Indicator #2: is the procedure transparent and participatory

In Jamaica, the expropriation process is outlined in the Land Acquisition Act. Note that the decision to use the Act to acquire land is not immune from judicial review. It may be challenged on the grounds of illegality, irrationality, or procedural impropriety. So if the procedure set down in the Act is not followed or if the decision to use the land for a public purpose is illegal or outside of the realms of what a reasonable decision maker would do, it may be successfully challenged in court (Robinson, 2016).

The process starts either with a notice published in the Gazette indicating that the minister is of the opinion that the land is likely to be needed for a public purpose (Section 3 notice, which triggers powers to enter and survey the land) or with a declaration published in the Gazette (Section 5) stating that the land is needed for a public purpose, where certain requirements have been met in relation to the source of the compensation funding. The land is then valued by the Commissioner (Section 8), who then begins negotiations with the landowners for the purchase of the land by private treaty (though the negotiations may predate the publication of the declaration in the Gazette).

If the negotiation stage is unsuccessful, interested persons are given at least 21 days' notice of a hearing before the Commissioner where the objections, respective interests and values of the land are the subject of enquiry (Section 9). From the date of the service of the notice of the hearing, the Commissioner may take possession of the land, if the minister so directs (Robinson, 2016).

The Act provides for public notice, which allows for transparency and provides the opportunity for participation, not only by those likely to be affected but by the general public. In the case of the North Coast Highway project, the provision of a public notice meant that public utilities and other government agencies' project managers were alerted to other affected interests not initially considered. For example, the Jamaica National Heritage Trust was able to get involved early in the process as a result of the public notice of the project. The Jamaican National Heritage Trust's Archaeology Division was recruited to manage the archeological component of the North Coast Highway project. Forty sites were directly affected in Segment 1 and 16 in Segment 2. These sites included settlements, caves, plantations and sugar factory complexes. In addition Anglo and African-Jamaica vernacular houses and other historic and contemporary monuments were affected. Archeological assessments was also completed on 10 areas chosen for the resettlement of affected individuals. The involvement of the utility company allowed for this private entity to make the necessary bid for budgetary support and the cost of relocating poles and power lines as well as preparing a schedule of work.

Indicator #3: prior to expropriation, must the government identify and inform all affected populations?

It is understandable that compensation would not be paid to persons having temporary use of the property who could have been required to vacate by the owner by way of a 30-day notice or eviction. The period between the Section 3, Section 5, and Section 8 notices under the Land Acquisition Act, could be deemed to be providing more than adequate notice to persons without substantial interests or rights in the property to find alternative accommodation. Additionally, the Surveyor under the Land Surveyors Act (1944) gives notice to the person(s) who is the reputed owner and all adjoining owners, again providing notice to the community of the intent and interest in the property for a public purpose.

Not only are they made aware through the service of the Sections 3, 5, and 9 notices, but the government of Jamaica through its promotion and project advertisement alerts parties to pending actions, the possibilities of actions and the need to be prepared to present documentation of proof of ownership for compensation purposes. Notwithstanding the many advances in the evolution of the Jamaican land market, there are still various informal interests in real estate and interests which are not properly documented.

The Government will also often give to those with agricultural crops adequate time to harvest that produce. The loss of community assets and common resources like grazing grounds and forests, which again may be critical for the livelihood of the poorest, are not compensated for under the acquisition process. Long-term crops planted by a squatter will not be compensated for in the acquisition process. Time is allowed for the person to harvest the crops, but long-term benefits may not be fully addressed.

The Commissioner of Lands can take possession of the property at any time after service of the notice under subsection 1 of Section 9. Compensation at this point is only offered to interested persons for the loss of standing crops and fruits. This will pose a problem where the person in possession of the land, the party who derives an income from the standing crops and fruits, is not the person with an interest in the property to be acquired as determined in the administration of the Act.

Regarding possession of the land by government, the FIG guidelines state:

- Possession should not be taken unless at least a substantial percentage of the agreed upon compensation offer has been paid. If the remainder is unpaid, interest on the remainder should accrue from the date of possession.
- People should be given a reasonable time to vacate, while respecting the need to keep to the project schedule.
- Farmers should be allowed time to harvest that year's crops, or receive full compensation for the crops.
- A clear time-limit should be placed to ensure that the acquisition process is not unduly long.

Determination of interest and rights to be compensated and valued

Section 8 of the Jamaican Act essentially instructs the Commissioner to begin negotiations to purchase the property to be compulsorily acquired. Two critical issues need first to be established before private treaty negotiations can commence:

What are the rights and interest in the property that need to be valued; and
Who are the persons holding those rights and interest?

Where, for example, the land to be taken includes improvements that may be in commercial use or is subject to a land lease or sometimes, more importantly, in Jamaica, is an estate that has not been administered, the various interests to be appraised for compensation need to be determined so that the Commissioner may provide proper instruction to the valuer assigned to determine value or compensation. The Commissioner also needs to be aware of the individual with whom to negotiate and the nature of the interest or right the person holds to ensure that equitable and adequate compensation is negotiated.

Section 16.1 of the VGGTs states, "[States] should respect all legitimate tenure rights holders, especially vulnerable and marginalized groups, by... providing just compensation in accordance with national law."

The VGGTs do not explicitly define the term "legitimate tenure rights holders." However, Section 3.1 provides that states "should... respect legitimate tenure rights holders and their rights, whether formally recorded or not."

While the VGGTs call for states to look beyond formally recognised rights, states are presumably permitted to develop their own interpretations of what constitutes "legitimate tenure."

Definitions of "legitimate tenure" can be found in other international instruments. According to the UN Special Rapporteur on the Right to Adequate Housing (2013), for example, the concept of legitimate tenure rights extends beyond mainstream notions of private ownership and includes multiple tenure forms deriving from a variety of systems. The Special Rapporteur goes on to state that legitimate tenure rights can derive from statutory, customary, religious, or hybrid tenure systems.

Customary tenure holders

The recognition and protection of customary tenure is particularly important given that indigenous peoples and local communities are estimated to hold as much as 65 percent of the world's land area under customary systems. However, research shows that only 18 percent of the world's land is formally recognised as owned or controlled by local communities and indigenous peoples.

The World Bank estimates that more than 90 percent of rural land in Africa is undocumented and informally administered, making it susceptible to land grabbing and expropriation without fair compensation. Recognition of these territories is crucial given that up to 2.5 billion people inhabit and depend on community land.

While Section 16 is silent on whether customary tenure holders must receive compensation, the VGGTs place special emphasis on the protection of vulnerable and marginalised groups, a category of tenure holders that presumably includes indigenous peoples and local communities who hold land under customary tenure.

Informal interests in Jamaica

In Jamaica the law recognises the fee simple owner. The Act does not recognise squatters or the customary rights/family lands. Therefore, they have no legal rights. This is really the interpretation of the legislation with respect to the provision of Section 9, subsection 2, which states:

> Every such notice shall state the particulars of the land and shall require all persons interested therein to appear personally or by agent before the Commissioner at a time and place to be specified in such notice, such time not being earlier than twenty-one days after the date of publication of the notice, and to state the nature of their respective interests in the land the amount and particulars of their claims to compensation for such interest and their objections, if any, to the survey made under section 7. The Commissioner may in any case require such statement to be made in writing and signed by the party or his agent.

Subsection 3 further states:

> The Commissioner shall also serve notice to the same effect on the occupier, if any, of such land and on all persons known or believed to be interested therein, or to be entitled

to act for persons so interested, as reside or have agents authorized to receive service on their behalf, within the parish in which the land is situated, provided that if any such person resides elsewhere and has no such agent the notice may be sent to him by registered post if his address can be ascertained after reasonable enquiry.

It may be argued that both these subsections address those persons who have an interest in the property being acquired by compulsory purchase. Note, however, that there is no clear definition given to the nature of that interest in property. The wording of the legislation allows for some flexibility in practice and the possibility of more innovation to allow for the various secondary and informal interests in property in the local context to be addressed.

Long-term leaseholds, certificates of occupancy, concessions or other arrangements are examples of the various forms in which land may be held. Additionally, there may be multiple layers of rights held by any number of rights holders, leasehold, mortgages, rights of way for utilities or transportation, concessions, rights of traditional or other uses, rights to forest products, etc. Ownership of land, trees, buildings and other improvements may all be separately held. Each of these separate interests may represent a significant loss to its holder if the land parcel is acquired by the government and the rights terminated.

Existing compulsory acquisition, legislations and practices may not be well adapted to cover all relevant interests in a land parcel. Laws target land owners without mentioning the array of other potential rights that may also be relevant and affected by the acquisition. A more frequent scenario is that even where the legal framework clearly recognises subsidiary or secondary rights, the processes put in place for identifying, notifying and compensating interest holders are not well designed to discover the existence of such rights in a context in which the holder is not in physical possession, or to bring the holder of those rights into the discussion about compensation. This is particularly the case with respect to customary rights.

It is not unusual for compulsory acquisition laws to presume a level of documentation of rights, which may, in fact, not exist. Some laws, for example, tie eligibility for compensation narrowly to whether the land right is registered in accordance with the country's land registration system. This can be problematic. Frequently, the case is that only a fraction of a given country's land has been registered.

Informal occupation of land in many cases is not so much a matter of choice but one of necessity. Informal occupation very often forms part of the practice of dealing with land assets as part of an inheritance, exacerbated by inaccessible land markets and poorly functioning planning regimes. In some cases this is condoned and encouraged by authorities. Hence, while a full legislative embrace of the nation requiring that squatters should be compensated is perhaps unlikely to occur in most countries, there is a growing trend on the part of governments to adjust the law and practice to deal with the individual and societal consequences associated with the displacement of informal occupants.

Jamaica, like many countries, has modern registration laws, but implementation frequently suffers from financial or other capacity constraints or a lack of political will. In many cases, registration does not capture the all important secondary rights that are present, nor address the rights that attach to an estate that may not have been administered or probated, or where land has been divested without formal documentation. In such contexts, given these situations and circumstances, too strict an application of a registered interest-only rule to compensation would result in many interests being uncompensated or under-compensated. To deal with the problem realistically could place an additional burden on the government. A more desirable approach would be to explore the possibility of building flexibility into legislative design where needed. In practice, the government may, in fact, rely on alternate forms of evidence in the implementation of compulsory acquisition laws, relaxing the rule to accommodate the facts on the ground. The issue of registration touches upon the broader problem of official records that are inaccurate or out of date. Geographic data may wrongly define the size or location of the parcel, and legal data may list the wrong person as the holder of the land rights. The failure to administer estates and the illegal subdivision of land parcels without the relevant planning approvals, documentation and completion of registration leads to the persistent problem of determining the interest in land. Additionally, there is the issue of squatter and prescriptive rights to land. In Jamaica, the Facilities for Titles Act (1955) provides one alternative vehicle to prove ownership rights over land. However, this alternate vehicle has limited application since this Act is really only used where persons applying for a loan for an approved purpose are unable to show title under the Registration of Titles Act.

There are many instances of undocumented right-of-way easements over land in Jamaica that is often affected by compulsory acquisition. Frequently the informal practice is continued if the subservient landowner retains most of the property after acquisition, but where all of the land is taken, and the dominant landowner does not respond to the Section 9 notice, the subservient landowner has no recourse but to respond to the Section 9 notice and throw themselves at the mercy of the Commissioner. Unfortunately, most are left to resolve the issue on their own, resulting in resentment and anger, not only with the land acquisition process but also with the project that prompted the compulsory acquisition in the first instance.

The Commissioner of Land in practice, usually in the hearings facilitated by the Section 9 notices, provides the opportunity to look at documentations and adjudicate on the nature of interests in the land to be taken being claimed by the representative claimants.

This aspect is broken down into:

a   compensable interest and rights (addressed below); and
b   non-compensable interests, e.g., squatters, which need to be addressed in a different way and which resides outside the purview of the Commissioner or the Act.

In Jamaica, the situation is even worse as regards squatters. This situation was raised in the recent Highway 2000 acquisition. These groups may be seen as vulnerable and marginalised.

Unregistered or inaccurately documented rights

Section 18 of the Constitution of Jamaica states:

18 (1) No property of any description shall be compulsorily taken possession of and no interest in or right over property of any description shall be compulsorily acquired except by or under the provisions of a law that –

a   prescribes the principles on which and the manner in which compensation therefor is to be determined and given; and
b   secures to any person claiming an interest in or right over such property a right of access to a court for the purpose of –
  i   establishing such interest or right (if any);
  ii   determining the amount of such compensation (if any) to which he is entitled; and
  iii   enforcing his right to any such compensation.

The provision of the Constitution with respect to the Land Acquisition Act provides for the Commissioner of Lands to be the first point of adjudication of the interest or rights over such property as being taken, thus giving the Commissioner of Lands the opportunity to determine if in fact the person responding to the Section 9 notice has a compensable interest or right. To address the matter of a squatter or persons occupying family land, all the other relevant legislations addressing land rights become applicable including the Facilities For Titles Act (1955) and the Prescription Act (1882).

Payment of compensation for rights that are not legally recognised raises difficult policy questions. The policy of international organisations for the most part includes squatters and other informal occupants or users as among those entitled to receive resettlement assistance, but this is an area in which international norms and national law frequently diverge. Many governments object to the idea that even those who are clearly occupying land illegally are entitled to some level of compensation. To do so, it is argued, creates perverse incentives for people to ignore the rules when they occupy land, and rewards illegal behaviour to the detriment of the rule of law. These objections are compounded when the illegal occupier in question is not poor and vulnerable but a relatively well off and well-connected investor. On the other hand, it needs to be recognised that a resettlement approach that focuses only on those with formal legal rights to their occupation could have detrimental development consequences.

Also instructive in addressing the issue of compensable interest is the World Bank document "Jamaica – Inner City Basic Services for the Poor Project: resettlement plan: Land acquisition and resettlement policy framework" which provides additional insight into the matter of what is considered a compensable interest or right and just compensation. The document looks at what it perceives to be gaps in the Land Acquisition Act and points to Section 10, subsection 1, under which the Commissioner may also require any person interested to deliver to the Commissioner the name of any other person possessing any interest in the land or any part thereof as co-owner, mortgagee, sub-lessee, tenant or otherwise, the nature of such an interest, and details of the rents and profits, if any received or receivable on account thereof, for three years immediately preceding the date of the statement. This requirement of the Act is sometimes overlooked in practice, but should also provide an opportunity for the Commissioner to address those who benefit economically from the property with undisturbed occupation and whose interest has not been formalised but could be formalised with the exercise of the provisions of any other relevant statutes relating to land.

Methods of compensation

It is customary to adopt several methods of awarding compensation. The usual methods have included resettlement or relocation, land swaps, payment of grants and land bonds. Research has shown that of those affected, generally compliance or cooperation with the requirements is high. However, occasionally, there are delays. The greatest delays and deterrent to the projects often come from the following:

- geographical and topographical obstacles; and
- having to ascertain ownership and therefore rights to compensation.

Additionally, the problem is not always necessarily with the poor and dispossessed, because there have been instances of protests and stalling by the wealthy. Note though that the protests by the wealthy, though they may often result in attempts to delay the projects, are unsuccessful in trying to avoid the project.

Research demonstrates that sometimes the rich will put up a good fight but eventually will cooperate when they are made to realise that ultimately and in the long term they will benefit, more so directly than indirectly, from the project.

The decision as to whether compensation should be through resettlement or in monetary terms may be difficult and complex. Caution must be taken to ensure that a proposed solution is not an attempt to avoid paying equivalent compensation, i.e., to propose financial compensation even if it is not equitable when the cost of resettlement is high; or to propose resettlement when financial compensation would be above the existing use values of the land to be acquired. In addition, displaced families may have their own reasons for preferring one option over another (FAO guidelines, 2008).

In many instances, the funding agencies such as the Inter-American Development Bank (IADB) and World Bank stipulate conditions of disbursement as to how non-legal interests are to be protected, i.e., non-legal ownership to be relocated. Indeed, there is a clear obligation to those who have formal interests but there is no such obligation to those having an informal interest.

Relocation

The Northern Coastal Highway

Research has shown that the practice has been as outlined below.

> According to Commissioner of Lands, Elizabeth Stair: If the occupier does not have a title to the land but they have a house on the land which is to be demolished, a recommendation is made that the structure is rebuilt on another section of the land or on another property which they own. They will not receive compensation for the land until a title is provided.
>
> She further states: If they are tenants, for example, they can be given a rental grant to assist them to relocate. This is under the control of the National Works Agency (NWA).
>
> In the case of occupiers, in some cases, persons do have to be relocated as it can be very costly for the works to be held up because persons/buildings are in the way. Relocation sites are not normally provided for displaced persons but they are not made homeless.

In the case of the Northern Coastal Highway, where persons who were in possession of the property have constructed improvements on the land, there is an attempt to separate structures/improvements from the land in its unimproved state so that payment can be appropriated accordingly. For example, where there is a lease there will be a distinction between the owner and the tenant.

In the above-mentioned project, the general policy adopted was one where assistance was granted to the informal occupier by way of the payment of a grant. That is to say, the general policy is to provide material and resources but no money is awarded as compensation. Grants in kind rather than cash are made. Note that there is no relocation.

Highway 2000

Highway 2000 involves the construction of a multi-laned tolled highway from Kingston to Montego Bay and a spur from Bushy Park to Ocho Rios. The total length of the project is approximately 230 km (143 miles). The construction and operation of the project is the purview of the National Road Operating and Constructing Company (NROCC). This agency of the government has been mandated to:

- arrange for toll road construction;
- protect the government's participation in the process; and
- protect the assets.

Although the compensating authority is the Commissioner of Lands, the National Road Operating and Constructing Company assumes a practical, yet non-legal role. The Company states that there is a Quality Management Manual which provides guidance on the treatment of relocation. It sets out a relocation plan, which is used to establish guidelines as to the amount of compensation to be paid and the percentage of market value applied to structures.

Research has shown that it is not uncommon that in whole communities consisting of hundreds of individuals there is not one registered title to be found. As a result, great care has to be taken when treating with these persons who possess informal interests only.

The research further states that affected persons are encouraged to make arrangements to relocate themselves, that is, persons are provided with the opportunity to vacate and relocate. This is strongly encouraged. Also, the opportunity is given to these persons to secure elements of the structure as well as their relocation themselves. The affected persons are allowed to rebuild. It is felt that it is in their interest to make their own arrangements.

Note that actual payments are made toward arrangements for those affected to relocate themselves.

Notwithstanding, the State is, however, mindful of international guidelines.

According to VGGT guidelines:

> 10.6 Where it is not possible to provide legal recognition to informal tenure, States should prevent forced evictions that violate existing obligations under national and international law, and consistent with relevant provisions under Section 16.

From this it is clear that the government is not required by law to resettle persons who have been disrupted/uprooted/displaced as a result of land acquisition. In fact, under the scenario where a property has been legally acquired but vacant possession is not provided, the Government of Jamaica will evict squatters pursuant to the provisions of the Land Acquisition Act, 1947. The law nobly requires that they be compensated. In addition, only those persons who can show either a registered Certificate of Title or some other means of legal ownership are entitled to compensation. Illegal occupants/squatters are not so entitled.

In practice, however, research has shown that there is a preference not to use the full weight of the law but to instead exercise empathy. Every effort must be made not to bring about delays which are both time-consuming and costly to the project.

Land Bonds and Land swaps

According to Commissioner Stair, Land Bonds are a financial instrument which can be used to pay for lands acquired. They can give annual interest payments with the principal paid after 5 or 10 years or whatever period is stated by the Ministry.of Finance. They were used mainly in the 1990s to pay for lands acquired. Some persons prefer to be paid cash for lands acquired and others were happy to receive the land bonds as the interest rates were favourable.

Adequate compensation

The principle which is applied states that the affected party should not be left in a worse position after the acquisition. FAO guidelines (2008) state that compensation is to reimburse them for these losses, and should be based on principles of equity and equivalence. The principle of equivalence is crucial to determining compensation: affected owners and occupants should be neither enriched nor impoverished as a result of the compulsory acquisition.

In addition to equivalence, the guidelines further seek to balancing the interests and achieve flexibility. It states that by balancing the interests, the process should seek to safeguard the rights of persons and that the law should provide clear guidelines whilst at the same time should be flexible enough to allow for the determination of appropriate equivalent compensation in special cases.

Financial compensation on the basis of equivalence of only the loss of land rarely achieves the aim of putting those affected in the same position as they were before the acquisition: the money paid cannot fully replace what is lost.

In one instance when relocating residents at Vanity Fair, Linstead, St. Catherine, one resident stated "Moving affects our lives... they should give us compensation to start over our lives." She said the relocation will cost her and her family more money to go about their daily business, pointing to a $300 increase in taxi fare she now faces, to make her point (Observer, July 2014).

In some countries, there is legal provision recognising this in the form of additional compensation to reflect the compulsory nature of the acquisition. In practice, given that the aim of the acquisition is to support development, there are strong arguments for compensation to improve the position of those affected wherever possible.

Internationally, the most common appeals are about compensation. They are generally based on the perception of people that the compensation offered to them for their land is inadequate. Those who appeal do not challenge the constitutional power of the government to acquire their land for the project, but they simply seek more money or other forms of compensation. Appeals may claim that incorrect principles of valuation have been used, or that the compensation offered is unjust and should be recalculated (FAO guidelines, 2008).

As Alias and MD Nasir, (2006), referenced, the term "adequate compensation" is not defined. It is totally abstract; it has no meaning from a practical standpoint, unless it is related to something which has a concrete value (Graham, 1984 in Khong, 1996).

- Just compensation is the amount that restores the property owner to a financial position equivalent to that existing before the property was taken.
- The issue of the appraisal not considering the reason for or market impact of the acquisition has often been raised by affected persons especially where the purpose would otherwise yield further economic benefit for the person being compensated. Often, the government of Jamaica and appraisers ignore this provision in private negotiations, but should this really be disregarded?

   "The social costs which can be imposed by compulsory purchase should not be ignored. Clearly the owners do not feel that the market price would fully compensate them for the loss of their land otherwise there would be no need to compel them to sell. Because of these social costs – the difference between the owner's use value and the exchange value – the law usually provides for some compensation over and above the market value of land to be paid to occupiers or owners by organizations allowed to purchase land compulsorily." (Evans, 1985)

How should compensation be calculated?

Market value remains the basis of the valuation. Valuation methods, which rely on the use of the direct comparison method, are usually preferred (Denyer- Green).

As a basic principle of expropriation law, market value is calculated on the basis of the highest and best use (HABU) of the property. This may not be the current use of the property. This principle is considered when determining whether a parcel of land has been injuriously affected and in particular whether there is a decrease in market value of any remaining parcel.

According to Commissioner of Lands, Elizabeth Stair, the Land Acquisition Act speaks to the calculation of the compensation. She further states that the law sets out the matters that can be considered in arriving at the compensation payable. These and no other matters can be included.

Section 14 states that in determining the amount of compensation to be awarded for land acquired under this Act:

i   the following and no other matters **shall** be taken into consideration-

   a   the market value at the date of the service of the notice under subsection (3) of section 5;

   b   any increase in the value of the other land of any person interested likely to accrue from the use to which the land acquired will be put;

   c   the damage, if any, sustained by any person interested at the time of the taking possession of the land by the Commissioner by reason of the acquisition injuriously affecting the actual earnings of such person;

   d   the reasonable expenses, if any, incidental to any change of residence or place of business of any person interested which is necessary in consequence of the acquisition.

ii   The following matters **shall not** be taken into consideration

   a   the degree of urgency which has led to the acquisition;

   b   any disinclination of the person interested to part with the land acquired;

   c   any damage sustained by the person interested which, if caused by a private person, would not be a good cause of action;

   d   any damage which is likely to be caused to the land acquired after the date of the publication of the declaration under section 5 by or in consequence of the use to which it has been put;

   e   any increase to the value of the land acquired which is likely to accrue from the use to which it will be put;

   f   any outlay on additions or improvements to the land acquired, which was incurred after the date of the publication of the notice under section 5, unless such additions or improvements were necessary for the maintenance of any building in a proper state of repair;

   g   the fact that the land has been compulsorily acquired;

   h   whether or not compensation is to be paid in whole or in part by the issue of land bonds in accordance with the provisions of the Land Bonds Act.

It should be noted that the Act does not define "market value." This leads to various issues with respect to the determination of compensation. The International Valuation Standards (IVS) and the Royal Institution of Chartered Surveyors (RICS) Valuation Standards (the so-called "Red Book") provide definitions of "market value."

On receipt of instruction from the Commissioner to determine the market value of the land to be taken, the valuer is to do the following:

- determine the market value of the fee simple interest in the property to be taken regardless of any other interests or rights that may exist over the property if these were unknown or have changed from the time of the service of the section 5 notice and the date when the valuer was asked to perform the appraisal;
- prior to completing the appraisal, investigate all the interests and rights to be affected by the acquisition of the property and to determine the value of each interest; and
- where only a portion of the property is to be taken, the value of the site remaining should be appraised to determine any increase in the value of this portion because of the use to which the land being taken is put.

While the Act says that this must be considered in the valuation (subsection (i) (b)), there is no indication as to how this should be done. The suggestion is that this increase or betterment should be used to reduce the quantum of compensation paid to the landowner.

The considerations under this statutory valuation give rise to several assumptions that may in some instance be considered contradictory. It leads to conclusions that are more difficult to defend on appeal. Consideration of the increase or loss of value because of the use/public purpose promotes assumptions and a forecast of value that may be nebulous, especially in the circumstances of road infrastructure works, as in the recent projects of the North Coast Highway and Highway 2000 projects. These projects open up otherwise inaccessible lands and reduce traffic in some areas, on what were once more trafficked roadways, thus affecting income in both cases. The valuer has the task of determining through market evidence the impact these activities will have on the parcel being appraised and then making the necessary adjustments for those considerations that reduce compensation to a statutory value, rather than a market value as the Act requires. The techniques and procedures of valuation are often difficult to explain to the layman. Additionally, the client requiring the appraisal is the Commissioner, who determines the compensation based on the valuation but who has no obligation to explain how that compensation was arrived at. Parties, whose land is being taken by compulsory acquisition, will in many cases feel aggrieved at the compensation being paid. Many will feel obliged to settle for the compensation being offered if:

- they do not have the funds to employ their own independent valuation professional to adequately defend their position with respect to compensation claim; and if
- the protracted time in negotiation is having and continues to have a damaging effect on the economic position of the party.

Injurious affection, severance and disturbance and its application

Valuation Surveyor, Lloyd Davis, states that injurious affection is not a matter for consideration since it was removed from the Act in 1968. Thus, the law states that compensation is payable only in the situation where land is taken. However, injurious affection occurs when income has been adversely affected but there is no corresponding taking of land. This loss of income is therefore treated as disturbance.

The following outlines the acquisition of land for the Mount Rosser segment of Highway 2000 and the impact on the operators/occupants of shops located at Faiths Pen.

In the early 1990s, when a Bauxite Company first relocated, the group of vendors who had an informal service stop along the roadside suffered loss of income. The vendors were not compensated monetarily; however, the company relocated the vendors to structured facilities and with formalised tenancies. The Bauxite Company employed a more compassionate approach to the question of compensation to these then informal users of the road easement that were to be affected by its then acquisition programme. They had discussions and came to a solution that did not involve compensation but resulted in the relocation and formalisation of the tenure of the parties affected. The vendors of Faiths Pen again face loss of income with the current Highway 2000 project that reroutes the traffic away from Faiths Pen. These vendors now have a formal tenure and will suffer injurious affection because of the project. However, their land is not being compulsorily acquired by the government, and therefore they are not entitled to any compensation. This is an example of the consideration of the profit and loss assessments of public projects that should be entertained prior to these projects commencing.

What of severance and its application?

Commissioner Stair states: If a parcel of land is acquired which results in the remaining parcel being severed, then a decision is made as to whether there is utility in the severed sections. If they are unusable, then a decision is likely to be made to acquire the entire parcel.

Disturbance

Section 14 (d) of the Act states that: the reasonable expenses, if any, incidental to any change of residence or place of business of any person interested which is necessary in consequence of the acquisition shall be taken into consideration.

Commissioner Stair continues: Under the Land Acquisition Act disturbance is paid where a business is in operation at the time of the acquisition and so the reasonable removal expenses are paid. This will also include fitting out the building in which they will relocate.

Conclusions

Public Purpose: "Public purpose" is not clearly defined in the Act.

The Jamaican government has for the most part not strayed from what is understood as the textbook definition and understanding of "public purpose". Internationally, there seems to be some case law, but not many address this area of land acquisition legislation and it is very limited in Jamaica. The definition of "public purpose" requires further clarification.

Interest vs Rights: Note that although interests may have been valued, other property rights also need to be identified and addressed. For example, prescriptive rights where in the property has been used by the party in excess of 20 years.

"...any profit or benefit, or any way or easement, or any watercourse, or the use of any water, a claim to which may be lawfully made at common law, by custom, prescription or grant ...enjoyed over or any land or water of Her Majesty the Queen, or of any person, or of anybody corporate, by any person claiming right thereto, without interruption for the full period of twenty years." (Prescription Act, 1882)

Market Value: The use of market value is agreed. However, "market value" is varied in its interpretation and its application. The Act states that the considerations in the valuation process should establish a statutory value, with market value as its basis. There are areas of adjustments that need to be quantified and applied to ensure that the items to be considered and not considered (as stipulated in the Land Acquisition Act) are in fact addressed by the valuer. There appears to be inconsistencies in the application, and consistency is required in the valuation of parcels. This often leads to the disagreement between landowner's valuers and those instructed by the Commissioner. Great care has to be taken in the valuation of parcels being acquired.

Recommendations

Recommendation #1

Those whose land is being compulsorily acquired should be given help to understand every aspect of the process. They may need assistance contesting the decisions and actions of the acquiring agency, getting second opinions on the value of their land, and ensuring that compensation is paid.

Recommendation #2

- The posting of a Section 3 notice should be the signal for persons who have an interest in the property to be acquired to begin to formalise that interest where there is no registered title. This includes seeking Letters of Administration, any utilisation of the Facilities for Title Act, Prescription Act and Deed Registration or any other documentation that may facilitate establishing an interest in the property to be acquired.
- As soon as the minister commences any project which involves the administering of the Land Acquisition Act, assistance should be given, wherever possible, to persons who need to formalise their interest in land that may be acquired. Funds could be set aside to achieve this. This is where the role of the Land Administration and Management Project (LAMP) could be further empowered and consolidated. LAMP is a government initiative to help all owners of land in Jamaica to obtain Certificates of Title for their land and to update the information on existing Land Titles.

Recommendation #3

Compensation could be payable to persons whose livelihood depends on the land. The Commissioner of Lands can take possession of the property at any time after service of the notice under subsection 1 of Section 9.

- Compensation at this point is only offered to persons having an interest in the land, and for the loss of standing crops and fruits. The delay in the payment of compensation poses a problem where the person in possession of the land derives an income from using the property other than for standing crops and fruits.

The taking possession of the property and depriving the interested party of use of the property by the Commissioner should be a signal for compensation. The Land Acquisition Act should be made consistent with the intent of the Constitution, and compensation should not be a payment only for the asset primarily as it is currently, but also for all the other rights lost as a result of the acquisition, particularly compensation for the loss of utility.

Recommendation #4

"Market value" should be defined within the context of the relevant Valuation Standards being applied in Jamaica. Although market value is not in dispute, however, there are various interpretations of it. For example, compensation for disturbance might be confusing. A definition of "market value" will eliminate any ambiguity.

- It is necessary to ensure that not only are valuers clear as to the value to be determined for compensation purposes but also to allow for better explanation of the context and criteria for arriving at the relevant opinion of value.
- In cases of an appeal, it sets in context the value or the logic and criteria for the opinion of value for litigants and judicial personnel.
- The determination of value for interests other than the fee simple interest more readily fit into the traditional definition of market value. These are leasehold interests, ground leases and other rights and easements that should not be confused with "fair value," "fair market value" or other values that fall within the definition associated with market value.

The considerations under this statutory valuation give rise to several assumptions, but may in some instance be considered contradictory. This leads to conclusions that are more difficult to defend on appeal. Consideration of the increase or loss of value because of the use/public purpose promotes assumptions and forecasts of value that may be nebulous. This should have been a prime concern in the Highway 2000 acquisitions, where previously inaccessible land was being opened up, giving rise to increases in value at the same time that other areas would be seeing less traffic and therefore could experience loss of value, or a change in utility.

Recommendation #5

All professionals should be brought into the process at the same time. The valuer could be introduced to the process much earlier since such professions are skilled in negotiations. The valuer could be brought in, for example, prior to the survey being carried out (Section 7), bearing in mind that the valuer's introduction at this stage would be more in terms of a property consultant so issues of values would be delayed until the survey is actually conducted and the parcel to be taken defined at which point all relevant attributes affecting value would be known.

Note

1 Available at: www.fao.org

References

Davis, L, (2017) Allison, Pitter and Company
Ling D and Archer W. (2005), Real Estate Principles: A Value Approach, McGraw-Hill /Irwin series (2005), Library of Congress Cataloging ISBN 0-07-282463-8
Madden, W. (2017), National Land Agency
Myers P. (2017) National Road Operating & Constructing Company (NROCC)
Patterson, E. (2017), National Works Agency,
Tagliarino N. (2016), Encroaching on Land and Livelihoods: How National Expropriation Laws Measure Up Against International Standards, World Resources Institute, Working paper (2016)
Tagliarino N. (2016): 6 Ways to Bring Land Expropriation Laws Up To International Standards. World Resources Institute, (2016)

Concluding comments and thoughts

Frances Plimmer and William McCluskey

Compulsory acquisition, with its various terminologies, is global, and, as the chapters in the book demonstrate, so are the problems for which the process is perceived as a solution, as well as the problematic results generated. It is an instrument within the arsenal of all governments, with the exception of a very few (geographically) small states, such as Monaco.

Yet, as McDermott,[1] Ding and Wu[2] and Kashyap and Kashayp[3] indicate, the so-called developing nations rely on the power of compulsory acquisition to achieve their ambitions to modernise their infrastructure and thus boost their economies. For more developed countries, it allows for the redevelopment of the existing built environment, which may be obsolete, and which in turn allows for modernisation and economic growth (as discussed by Parker[4] and Lai[5]).

However, there is evidence of unanticipated harmful outcomes of the process. Ding and Wu discuss[6] the negative consequences of compulsory acquisition and its resulting development, which include housing bubbles and inefficient and chaotic land development.

The chapters in this book demonstrate compulsory acquisition and associated rights to compensation across a global range of jurisdictions (so-called developed, emerging and developing, large and small states, with long and short experiences of its implementation). It is well recognised (see, for example, Daud et al.[7]) that the subsequent development of the land taken is seen as a vital means to securing solutions to the increasingly global problems of inadequate infrastructure necessary to support the growing global population and its expanding urban habitat. In addition, there is the problem of the shortage of suitable residential accommodation in large cities, particularly the growing megacities and the associated informal settlements. The clearance of large tracts of poorly used land allows for large-scale planning and redevelopment to ensure a more efficient (residential) use and the reduction of poor living accommodation and homelessness, as well as the related economic, health and social problems.

Origins

There is evidence[8] that the commoditisation of land was exported from Europe during the 16th and 17th centuries in its waves of colonisation around the world. The early European enclosure movement turned common land into private property, and thereby generated (amongst other things) the emergence of different forms of rights to land and a real estate market in which they could be traded. A range of supporting systems and institutions, including the registration of rights to real estate, planning policies, valuation professions and the culture of land ownership developed, and the definition of "*wealth*" changed forever.

The tension between customary land rights (where land is a common asset which no one individual can "*own*") and the colonial spread of the concept of land ownership and trading in land rights originated from these very different philosophies which underpin each system of land tenure. Such issues are discussed by Stuart and Lyon Josephs in their chapter[9] on Jamaica, while K'Akumu and Olima[10] outline the history of expropriation in Kenya. It also has major implications for the valuation of the land rights of the so-called Indigenous people (see for example Mengwe[11]) – discussed further below.

"Public Benefit"

It is well recognised that the sole justification for the state's use of its compulsory acquisition powers is that the rights of the individual (property) owner should be sacrificed in favour of the wider "*public benefits*" which accrue from the development for which the land and other property is being acquired. At its most basic and extreme, rights of individual landowners can be overridden by the needs of the country for defence against external threats and, for this purpose, real estate may be taken without invoking the normal legal procedures.

There is, however, a major problem in that there is no one definitive definition of "*public benefits*" within this context. Where it has been subject to judicial interpretation,[12] the term may include the wider economic advantages which result from the development of job-creating industries on the land taken. In others, such a purpose is specifically excluded from the definition of "*public benefits*". Murphy, McCord and Davis[13] discuss this issue in relation to recent cases in the UK.

Different jurisdictions use different terminology to describe the needs of the wider community to justify the use of compulsion in land and property rights acquisition. Thus, terms such as "public benefit", "public interest", "public use" and "public purpose" may be used although, according to Lai,[14] "public use" and "public purpose" may not be synonymous.

However, Daud et al.[15] recognise that compulsory acquisition is an extreme form of government intervention in the constitutional rights of landowners and a contravention of the Universal Declaration of Human Rights which provides protection of the rights of an individual to own property (real estate) without interference.[16] While compulsory acquisition can be and is justified on the grounds of the wider "*public benefit*" which accrues to the community at large, Grover provides evidence[17] that it is in the implementation of compulsory acquisition powers that further human rights infringements may arise as a result corruption, abuse of office and ineffectual implementation policies. Stuart and Lyons-Josephs[18] also discuss the importance of good governance in this and other land rights issues.

Indeed, Lai[19] opines that the real driving force of urban renewal in Hong Kong is the capturing of unexploited development potential by the State, and that a justification of "*urban decay*" is merely a pretext.

Principles of natural justice (duty to act fairly)

While it can be accepted that different jurisdictions implement compulsory acquisition procedures in different ways, there are certain principles which they are expected to observe in terms of both the process and the outcomes of acquisition. These principles of natural justice (also called the "*duty to act fairly*") demand, for example, the right of a citizen to a "*fair hearing*" and the right to legal representation.

Thus, within the terminology of the compulsory acquisition provisions which each state enshrines within its own legislation, such principles are unlikely to have any basis in law, unless they are specifically and clearly incorporated into the legislation. Consequently, the fact that the processes, rights and obligations are expressed in legal jargon and that their interpretation may run contrary to the generally understood principles of "*fairness*", it is the wording of the law which matters in each individual case, even if the outcomes are clearly contrary to the principles of natural justice or the apparent intention of the legislators.

In some jurisdictions, achieving its "*duty to act fairly*" may require a more proactive, and potentially expensive, acquisition process for the government than is enshrined in legislation. In, for example, rural areas of the so-called developing countries, understanding of the legislation and the legal processes which underpin compulsory acquisition may be minimal. It may even be that the legislation is not written in the language of the local community.

In such a situation, natural justice requires that the government undertakes the responsibility (and the cost) to provide "*experts*" who can explain in a balanced manner to the landowners and to the wider community in terms they can understand, what is being proposed and why, how it will proceed and their rights (if any) to object to the acquisition in principle, the process to be undertaken, the level of compensation offered and how and when it will be paid. Such "*experts*" should perceive themselves as responsible to the community rather than to the government or the acquiring authority, and their involvement should occur at a time when the community has a chance to alter the proposed acquisition by negotiation, either to prevent it, or to amend it in such a way that any damage to their community is minimised.

Such consultation should involve the entire community, including women and young people, who will be affected by the acquisition and the subsequent development. Their individual rights to compensation should also be secured within the legislation.

This, of course, increases governments' costs and may be seen as a (potential) hindrance to their plans to achieve their goals, to benefit the wider public and provide much needed development. As stated earlier, the principles of compulsory acquisition require a balance to be struck between those from whom land is taken and the wider public benefit. Yet, if such consultation and educational procedures are not enshrined in the law, it may be seen to be acceptable to ignore them. This inevitably increases levels of confusion, dissatisfaction and potentially hostility in the affected community.

In principle, what really matters is that the process is undertaken in an equitable, transparent and consistent manner in which all parties are satisfied with the outcome. This has implications for both the "*why*" and the "*how*" of compulsory acquisition, because the failure to achieve community satisfaction risks social unrest[20] and major long-term problems.[21]

Legislation and governance

Compulsory acquisition is a creation of statute - it does not exist within either customary or judicial law. Thus, for the rights, obligations, procedures etc. of compulsory acquisition to exist, they must all be laid down in legislation. A failure to mention, for example, a right to compensation for a particular loss within the legislation means that such a right cannot be assumed (as Stuart and LyonJosephs[22] explain), and the law must be amended to specifically secure such rights for the future. In the meantime, no compensation is payable for any losses for which compensation provision is not specifically made in law. This makes the letter (rather than the spirit) of the law the source of all compulsory acquisition powers and responsibilities for the payment of compensation and its inadequacy may result in the impoverishment of affected communities.

Walters[23] provides a brief historical overview of the confusing and inconsistent judicial interpretations of expropriation.

Where legislation is poorly drafted, is out of date, misleading or ambiguous, or where the process of acquisition fails to reflect the legislation and is not transparent, the risks of an unsatisfactory outcome are huge (Grover,[24] see also Tannvermiş and Aliefendioğlu[25]).

The rights to appeal both the taking of the land and the use of compulsion as well as the level of compensation assessed, also need to be enshrined in legislation. Timely and effective judicial decisions benefit both parties. However, it is well recognised that litigation can be costly. Parker[26] explores the role of alternative dispute resolution as a just, quick and cheap route to the resolution of compensation claims.

Therefore, clear, detailed, well-drafted legislation, incorporating unambiguous provisions for all eventualities, including the right of the dispossessed to compensation which fully reflects all of their losses, and which is implemented in an equitable, effective and efficient manner for all parties, provides the ideal basis for the exercise of compulsory acquisition powers, and thus the economic modernisation which so many governments seek. Sadly, as many of these chapters demonstrate, such legislation and its equitable implementation are rare commodities. However, Radvan and Neckar[27] review the expropriation legislation operating in the Czech Republic and conclude that there is no need for amendments to the existing law.

In the worst-case scenarios, governments have been reported to employ enforced evictions in order to clear land for redevelopment, which involve no consultation with and no compensation for the affected communities.[28] Such a practice clearly can have no legitimacy nor can it have any moral or ethical validation.

Alternatives to compulsory acquisition

There are, of course, alternatives to compulsory acquisition. It is not always necessary, nor is it always legal, for a government authority to use compulsory powers to acquire land. For example, in Estonia,[29] Tiits and Tomson discuss the process of acquiring land on the basis of voluntary acquisition. In some jurisdictions and for certain stated purposes,[30] land can be acquired only by the mutual agreement of seller and buyer. Legislative powers to force the transaction are simply not available. This puts both seller and buyer on an equal footing and can therefore be said to be truly "*fair*", assuming that the operation of the property market is active, healthy, transparent etc.

The wider use of land readjustment[31] is discussed, for example, by Hong and Chen[32] to facilitate land assembly, public and private partnerships and good governance. The authors use case studies to demonstrate the wider potential for the use of such processes instead of eminent domain in order to achieve land assembly for redevelopment. Similarly, Kashyap and Kashyap[33] discuss models for land development using land pooling.[34] Opportunities for land readjustment, land exchange or land pooling should be explored to avoid the negative connotations, adverse publicity, costs and potentially disastrous consequences associated with the enforced legislative process of compulsory acquisition. Genuine community involvement in the process is likely to result in an outcome which increases local satisfaction and reduces government costs.

Nevertheless, there are likely to remain situations where, because of the scale of the project, compulsory acquisition is the only practicable method of land assembly, as, for example, that discussed by McDermott.[35] In such circumstances, attention should be paid to good governance and the timely payment of adequate compensation to the dispossessed,[36] and to the potential public private partnership models[37] to achieve major developments.

Some of the authors provide case studies, including those within China,[38] Fiji,[39] Jamaica,[40] Kenya,[41] Moldova,[42] Poland,[43] Malaysia,[44] Russia,[45] and Turkey.[46]

Compensation

It is anticipated that the taking of land under statutory compulsory acquisition powers triggers the right to compensation from the acquiring authority to the dispossessed for all losses, and it is usual for national legislation to include a statement both as to the rights to compensation and some definition of the quantum at which it should be fixed.

However, once the balance has been struck at the moment when government overrides the private individual's property rights in favour of the wider public benefit, (i.e. at the point of implementing compulsory acquisition powers), no further concession should be given to the acquiring authority, and certainly not within the level of compensation paid. Arguments for reducing the level of compensation, such as "*being fair to the taxpayer*" who is funding the land purchase, are neither "*acting fairly*" nor moral. Such an argument may be presented to justify a relatively low level of compensation for the former landowner, but instead, it merely indicates that the state cannot afford to pay for the full loss of the dispossessed and therefore cannot afford to purchase and develop the land. In such a case, the acquisition (and future development) of the land should not proceed (see Tannvermiş and Aliefendioğlu[47]).

The rights to, and the definition of the level of compensation payable, should also be enshrined in legislation,[48] and almost invariably, it is anticipated that compensation will take the form of a monetary payment. Once again, regardless of "*acting fairly*", governments constrain themselves by providing a legal definition of compensation,[49] the interpretation of which can achieve a less than satisfactory outcome for the dispossessed, and these definitions do vary.

While recognising the need for the quantum of compensation (and the method of assessment) to be enshrined in legislation, the essential principle of the rights to and the level of compensation payable is to ensure that the dispossessed are put back in the same economic and social position they enjoyed prior to the acquisition.[50] After all, they can be regarded as "*blameless*" victims of their government's initiation of the compulsory acquisition process and the wider community's needs for and benefits from the resulting improved infrastructure and facilities.

Some jurisdictions define the compensation to be paid in a form other than monetary and instead allow for land swap. There are jurisdictions which use the term "*market value*",[51] to define the basis of compensation payable. Such a criteria may be acceptable where there is an active, healthy and transparent market within the locality of the property(ies) being acquired. The assumption is that a "*market value*" level of compensation is sufficient for the dispossessed to go into the market and purchase an equivalent property which allows them to continue their lifestyle, whether in terms of residential or economic activities. Where this is the case, "*market value*" can be regarded as "*fair*" to the claimant who, with the exception of the disruption, cannot be said to have lost as a result of the process, provided, of course, that all costs incurred are also included in the compensation paid.

However, this is not always the case. For example, the UK does not allow the dispossessed to benefit, within the compensation paid, for any increase in market value which results from the acquisition and (future) development for which the real estate was taken. Thus, if the government's acquisition and development of the land taken increases property values in the market, the UK's definition of "*market value*" for land taken excludes such an increase in the compensation paid.[52] This means that the dispossessed is not provided with sufficient compensation to purchase a similar property within the same location. Given the terminology used in the legislation, a member of the general public can be forgiven for assuming that there can be only one "*market value*" for the property taken and that compensation at that level will allow for the purchase of an equivalent property within the same location. The failure of this principle causes understandable dissatisfaction.

Another term used to define the level of compensation payable is *"just compensation"*. The implications of this are also clear, but again, what matters is how the term is interpreted within the legislation. In the USA, *"just compensation"* is translated by the courts as *"fair market value"*. However, it seems that the Supreme Court has acknowledged that, as defined, *"fair market value"* falls short of what a willing seller would accept in a true open market sale.[53]

In addition to the (mis)interpretation of the legislation which may or may not fully compensate the dispossessed for all their losses, it is the use of the term *"fair"* which also contributes to the confusion and frustration for members of the public within the process of expropriation and the resulting compensation.

"Fair", and indeed *"just"*, are highly subjective terms and can mean different things to different participants in the process. Ideally, such terms should not be used within the context of either compulsory acquisition or the assessment of compensation, because both sides can argue that what is *"fair"* to one party is highly *"unfair"* to the other. It tends not to be a term defined in the legislation, yet it is frequently used as part of the description of the level of compensation to be paid. Often, therefore, there may be little or no *"fairness"* involved, either in the compulsory taking of the land of an individual (which by its very occurrence demonstrates that the property owner is an unwilling and therefore a dissatisfied seller[54]), or in the payment of compensation which may be seen as the *"enrichment"* of one or several individuals at the expense of the taxpayer. Indeed, Ding and Wu[55] unusually discuss "windfalls" in compensation payments. Specific principles contained in individual national legislation may also add to an outcome perceived as *"unfair"*, usually to the claimant.

Several chapters demonstrate the inadequacy of either the legislation underpinning the level of compensation to be paid, or the practice of its implementation, with both Walters[56] and Mengwe[57] advocating that compensation should reflect personal values.

While legislation may define the level of compensation in terms of *"market value"* (or similar), if there is no healthy, active property market for a full range of property types within the location where acquisition is being undertaken, compensation needs to be assessed other than by the use of sales transactions of similar interests in comparable properties. Bozu[58] explains the use of "normative" pricing in Moldova, while K'Alumu and Olima[59] discuss a project which has prompted the Kenyan government to enact legislation to control the price of land and curtail litigation. Mutema[60] states that customary land ownership is characterised by informal land sales, with the resultant price information asymmetry challenges. Beale[61] opines that land markets in different regions of the Caribbean are arguably synonymous with a lattice with a myriad of interwoven formal and informal tenures, resulting in acquiring authorities facing a strategic hold-out and insurmountable costs.

In addition, to undertake the assessment of any form of market-based assessment, a reliable, competent, ethical valuation profession which is supported by relevant technical and institutional systems is vital. Such a profession should be adequate (in terms of numbers and training) and adhere to international valuation standards and practice, in order to achieve (and to be seen to achieve) the level of compensation stated in the legislation. Mutema[62] discusses the paucity of academic training, lack of local valuation standards, evidence of professional malpractices and virtual absence of competent local professional representative bodies to give professional advice in Zimbabwe and other African states. Tannvermiş and Aliefendioğlu[63] also note the lack of qualified human resources, as well as the technical infrastructure and valuation databases in Turkey. The availability of comprehensive and up-to-date data (regarding both land values and land ownership rights), databases which allow for data sharing with all relevant institutions, is also crucial to the achievement of appropriate real estate valuations.

Mengwe[64] proposes that, in Botswana, the question of the assessment of compensation should be placed within the political arena, subject to judicial review, and that a paradigm shift is necessary from the individual to an approach which puts the individual within a societal context where proportionality plays a dominant role in the assessment of compensation.

For some individuals, particularly in isolated rural settings, a monetary form of compensation may be inappropriate. In certain situations, particularly where farming is the main occupation, compensation should be based on the provision of alternative land, which is capable of providing a similar yield, and located in the same community thereby retaining the individuals' social standing. Thus, it should be the replacement of the dispossessed's livelihood which be the measure of compensation payable. Indeed, in extreme cases, money may have a limited meaning or value within the community. Consequently, dispossession of their lands leaves farmers impoverished in a way which they are unlikely to be capable of remedying. Such individuals, particularly those with a long history of family farming of the land, can lose much more than its monetary value.

> ... land for a rural farmer is a strong base and an unshakable life security. It provides the means by which he and his family, and perhaps generations to come, subsist.
>
> *(Ambaye, 2009: 20)*

In countries where the state has retained ownership of all land in its territory, compensation will not include any form of land value. Instead, individuals can only expect compensation for loss of their user rights.

> In rural areas [of Ethiopia], the value of the land expropriated is based on the previous five years' average annual income of the farmer. This annual income shall be multiplied by ten and that is the value of the land to be given as compensation. The problem of this system is that it does not adequately compensate the farmer's loss. The farmer has a life time right in the land with life-long income and also the right to pass it onto generations to come. The argument is that ten year's annual income will not adequately compensate the loss of all the rights mentioned above.[65]

In locations where there is no form of property market, there are very few options available for the objective and realistic assessment of "*market value*" of the land taken, with the major risk that compensation fails to permit the dispossessed to reinstate their livelihood. In addition, in such locations, there is unlikely to be a valuation or appraisal profession to assist in the assessment of compensation. A similar outcome is likely in jurisdictions where the state owns all the land and the population have merely user rights.

> In cases of an undeveloped real property market in [Ethiopia], the valuation method followed tends to be the replacement cost approach. This may be partly attributable to the state ownership of land. In such a situation the "market price" of houses and buildings tends to be based on the price of construction materials, instead of the value and location of the land, where the building is situated. During expropriation, in urban areas, land has no value. Expropriated people are not compensated for their losses associated with the location, which by itself affects their businesses, living conditions and standards, means of transportation, and access to facilities. The law provides that they should be given the replacement **cost** of the building and a land replacement to

build their home on it. Moreover, there is no guarantee to get [an] equal area of land, since it is the municipality that decides the location as well as the size of the land to be given to the expropriated person. Hence, expropriation in this respect has an adverse effect on the owner, and this shows that the constitutional guarantee for commensurate compensations is not observed and respected. The holder of the land does not get a share of the benefit of his investment on the land, which is… being reaped by municipalities.[66]

In extreme cases, the acquisition of land belonging (or perceived as belonging) to "*indigenous*" populations of larger countries involves an assessment of the "*value*" of the land which has far more than a monetary value to the inhabitants. Such land is increasingly recognised as including the nebulous (but no less real) historical, cultural and spiritual importance to the people, which is impossible to monetise. It is progressively accepted that the acquisition of rights over or of such land itself involves a huge degree of sensitivity on the part of an acquiring government.[67]

Walters[68] discusses recent research into "*place identity*" - the importance people give to specific places - which brings into question the possibility of full and just compensation. Tannvermiş and Aliefendioğlu[69] also discuss the impacts of compulsory acquisition on natural and cultural assets in Turkey.

Large-scale land acquisitions (land grab)

In order to secure food sources for their domestic market, it has become increasingly popular for foreign governments or transnational companies to purchase or lease large tracts of land (including sources of water) from within the territories of other governments. The term "*land grab*" has very negative connotations, yet not all such international arrangements have negative consequences - on the contrary.[70] Nevertheless, because of the associated controversy, it is hard to provide definitive information, for example, on the geographical extent of the problem, but a 2011 World Bank report[71] estimated that it involves some 56 million hectares (138 million acres) worldwide.

It seems that the largest (in terms of land acquired) "*destination countries*" are Brazil, Sudan, Madagascar, the Philippines, Ethiopia, Mozambique and Indonesia, while the "*investor countries*" are the USA, United Arab Emirates, China, India, Egypt, UK, South Korea, South Africa, Saudi Arabia, Singapore and Malaysia. Drivers include such commodities as bio fuels, sugarcane and palm oil.

Although not significant (in terms of hectares taken), certain African countries are popular "*destination countries*". Because in many of the countries within Africa, land is state-owned (and occupiers of land have only user rights), and with the lack of a comprehensive and reliable system of registering title, the promises of economic development, infrastructure provision and job creation have encouraged many such states to consider foreign investment within their territory in a positive light.

There is a major issue involving the balance of cash crops and the rejection of traditional methods and the produce of agricultural operations which benefit the local community. Nevertheless, there is evidence[72] of local benefits, with investors employing local workers and training them to increase the production within their own communities.

One of the problems with large-scale land acquisition is that the negotiations and the decisions often take place between the foreign investor and the national government, which bypass the local community, both in terms of consultation and compensation. In some cases, negotiations do take place between investors and local chiefs. Nevertheless, where investors gain approval for their projects in advance of local consultations, they lack any incentive to carry out promises made to the local population.[73]

However, it is the complexity and opacity of the negotiations, approval, and post-contract processes which have resulted in much of the criticisms levelled against the procedure. Alongside this are the issues of the displacement of local people and the environmental consequences of large-scale agriculture.

A 2009 Report[74] to the United Nations General Assembly focused on the issue of human rights associated with the large-scale acquisition of land:

> The human right to food would be violated if people depending on land for their livelihoods, including pastoralists, were cut off from access to land, without suitable alternatives; if local incomes were insufficient to compensate for the price effects resulting from the shift towards the production of food for exports; or if the revenues of local smallholders were to fall following the arrival on domestic markets of cheaply priced food, produced on the more competitive large-scale plantations developed thanks to the arrival of the investor.

The Report includes a list of *"minimum human rights"* principles applicable to large-scale land acquisitions or leases.

Further thoughts

The issue of compulsory acquisition and the assessment of compensation continue to be matters of political, public (see, for example, Tannvermiş and Aliefendioğlu[75]) and professional debate, despite (in some countries) centuries of application.

At an international workshop held in Helsinki[76] in 2007, on the subject of compulsory acquisition and compensation, it was proposed that there should be no compulsory acquisition at all (and therefore no requirement for any legal provisions for the payment of compensation). Instead, all land required for public infrastructure and facilities should be purchased in the open market, and governments should act as private purchasers negotiating terms and conditions of purchase, in the same way as any other individual, with no enforcement rights *"in the background"*.

Initially, perhaps, something of a Utopian aspiration, but, as shown earlier, there are alternatives to compulsory acquisition and all that it entails.

More realistically, the outcome of the 2007 Workshop and the subsequent policy statement[77] from the International Federation of Surveyors (FIG) recommend that compulsory acquisition should not be the preferred option for acquiring land. However, for large projects involving complex land ownership patterns, the use of compulsion may be the only realistic option.

Issues of legitimacy, transparency, impartiality and rights of appeal should all be clearly explained in any legislation, and should ensure that all reasonable costs are borne by the expropriating authority. The FIG statement reinforces the need for a genuine *"public interest"* justification for the expropriation, and the establishing of (and adherence to) a strict timetable with additional compensation penalties for a dilatory acquiring authority.

Regardless of how the relevant state legislation defines the level of compensation to be paid on expropriation, there should be certain recognised and legally binding principles which should accompany the payment of compensation. For example: compensation should be paid promptly, although there is evidence (K'Akumu and Olima[78] and Mutema[79]) that delays may be lengthy.

The FIG statement also recognises the potential for compensation to take the form of other land or land swap, subject to the agreement of the dispossessed. Also recommended is that the measure of compensation ensures:

> … that the affected party's financial position is not weakened… This means that the primary focus in determining the basis and amount of compensation is in the financial status of the affected party both in advance of the compulsory purchase and after."[80]

Several authors highlight to need to develop acquisition procedures and the assessment of compensation in the light of 'international best practice'. FIG statements and the FAO's voluntary guidelines (VGGT[81]) are identified by, for example, Mutema[82] and Stuart and Lyons-Josephs[83] as significant. Also relevant are the standards imposed by international donor organisations, such as the World Bank. Hassan[84] discusses how Fiji's principles and practice might change in the light of the standards set by such bodies. Increasing globalisation and its effects on the knowledge and expectations of populations raises expectations which increases the risk that national norms may be seen to be inadequate when compared to international standards, and countries may be forced to revise their laws, procedures and practices accordingly.

Despite international principles, standards and experiences regarding the payment of compensation, recent developments in South Africa have highlighted both the political desire to remove the rights to compensation from landowners whose land is earmarked for acquisition as part of a land reform policy as well as the unintended consequences of such actions.

In February 2018, an *ad hoc* Constitutional Review Committee was established to reconsider the relevant section of the South African Constitution to make it possible for the State to expropriate land without paying the dispossessed compensation.[85] Apparently, provided that zero compensation can be seen to be "just and equitable", the Constitution already makes provision for this.

It seems that one of the underlying drivers for this amendment is the desire for the State to be the "custodian of all South African land". As Hall[86] points out, this is a totally different matter to zero compensation on compulsory acquisition.

The South African proposal for zero compensation is aimed entirely at land in rural areas and not at such properties as residential homes. As the debate progresses, one of the issues to be determined is whether different standards can be applied to owners of different property types.[87]

This is clearly a major political and social change for the country, but there are lessons which can be learned from its neighbour, Zimbabwe, which implemented a similar policy. The price of such a policy has been "… eight consecutive years of economic decline that led to job losses, deindustrialization and a loss of agricultural export revenues".[88] It is reported[89] that the Zimbabwe's land reform has cost an estimated $20 billion, which includes lost export revenues, a loss of food aid imports and the reduction in economic growth. In addition, there has been a rise in the unemployment rate to 90%, and some $10 billion wiped off the country's land value, which also affects the value of the assets of banks holding land as security. Such outcomes have caused the Zimbabwean government to decide recently to reverse its policy and to compensate farmers, at an estimated cost of $11 billion. As the authors put it:

The moral of the story is if the government declines to directly compensate its commercial sector for land improvements, at the very least, then someone else will have to pay for it, indirectly.

Full circle?

It is clear that failure to provide adequate compensation - in terms which fully compensate the dispossessed for their loss, particularly by the failure to provide adequate means for the dispossessed to reinstate an alternative or equivalent livelihood - results in poverty for the dispossessed and, often, in their enforced removal from their community. The losses affect both the individuals displaced and their future generations. Such individuals tend to gravitate to large population centres and fuel the rapid and extreme population increases, which contribute to overcrowding, a failure of existing infrastructure, the expansion of informal settlements and, basically, aggravate some of the urgent urban problems which compulsory acquisition is perceived as being necessary to resolve. History bears out this pattern,[90] yet it continues.

Regardless of the legal provisions underpinning both the taking of land and the assessment of compensation, research[91] has also shown there to be *"greedy"* and *"corrupt"* practices in their operation. Dissatisfaction with the principles and practices of compulsory acquisition and inadequate compensation can fuel social unrest, which is the ultimate human cost and tragedy.[92]

The chapters in this book discuss contemporary issues associated with compulsory acquisition and compensation experienced around the world. They demonstrate that there are global issues with the unsuitability of compulsory acquisition legislation and inequity in its implementation, and the inadequacy and dissatisfaction with the level of compensation paid. There are global similarities in the extent and severity of the different issues and the various outcomes of the process and there are less confrontational alternatives, yet the draconian processes continue.

It can be argued that the international community has a duty to use its knowledge and experience to the benefit of the global society, in particular for those who are disadvantaged as a result of what should be a process which provides major *"public benefit"* and social improvements with minimal individual disadvantages. However, it is only by revealing the nature and magnitude of the problem and generating a genuine global debate that satisfactory solutions can be found. This book is part of that process.

Notes

1 See Chapter 3.
2 See Chapter 11.
3 See Chapter 14.
4 See Chapter 17.
5 See Chapter 13.
6 See Chapter 11.
7 In Chapter 15.
8 Buck, A. R., McLaren, J., Wright, N. E. (Eds.) (2001). *Law Property Rights and the British Diaspora.* Aldershot: Ashgate.
9 See Chapter 23.
10 See Chapter 17.
11 See Chapter 19.
12 See, for example, Jacobs, Harvey M., Bassett, Ellen M. (2010). After "Kelo": Political Rhetoric and Policy Responses. *Land Lines.* Lincoln Institute of Land Policy. www.lincolninst.edu.
13 See Chapter 9.
14 See Chapter 13.
15 See Chapter 15.

16 See, for example, Article 1 of Protocol 1 of the European Convention of Human Rights.
17 See Chapter 1.
18 See Chapter 23.
19 See Chapter 13.
20 See Ding and Wu, Chapter 11.
21 See, for example, Kakulu, Iyenemi Ibimina (2007) Assessment of Compensation in the Compulsory Acquisition of Oil and Gas Bearing Lands: The Niger Delta Experience. Paper presented at the FIG Seminar on Compulsory Purchase and Compensation. 6–8 September, Helsinki.
22 See Chapter 23.
23 See Chapter 22.
24 See Chapter 1.
25 See Chapter 7.
26 See Chapter 17.
27 See Chapter 4.
28 See, for example, du Plessis, Jean (2005). Growing Problems of Forced Evictions. *Environment and Urbanization,* 17, 123.
29 See Chapter 5.
30 For example, in the UK, under the Open Spaces Act 1906.
31 See, for example, Home, Rob (2007) Land Readjustment as a Global Land Tool: Focus on the Middle East. Findings in Built and Rural Environments (FiBRE) RICS www.rics.org; Müller-Jökel, Rainer (2004) Land Readjustment - a Win-Win-Strategy for Sustainable Urban Development. FIG Working Week, 22–27 May 2004; Seppänen, Heikki (2004). Land Acquisition and Compulsory Means - Cooperation Creates Satisfaction. FIG Working Week, 22–27 May, 2004.
32 See Chapter 2. See also Chapters 17 and 22.
33 See Chapter 14.
34 See, for example, Connellan, Owen (2002) Land Assembly for Development. The Role of Land Pooling, Land Readjustment and Land Consolidation. FIG XXII International Congress, Washington DC USA. 19–26 April, 2002; Oli, Punya P. (2010). Land Pooling / Readjustment Programmes in Nepal. FIG Congress 2010. Sydney, Australia, 11–16 April, 2010.
35 See Chapter 3.
36 ibid.
37 See Kashyap and Kashyap in Chapter 14.
38 See Chapter 11.
39 See Chapter 12.
40 See Chapter 23.
41 See Chapter 18.
42 See Chapter 6.
43 See Chapter 8.
44 See Chapter 15.
45 See Chapter 16.
46 See Chapter 10.
47 See Chapter 7.
48 See Chapter 23.
49 See, for example, Chapters 6, 11, 12, 13, 18, and 22.
50 See, for example, McDermott, in Chapter 3, Mengwe in Chapter 19, and Walters in Chapter 22.
51 *"Market value"* is defined as

> the estimated amount for which a property should exchange on the date of valuation between a willing buyer and a willing seller in an arm's-length transaction after proper marketing wherein the parties had each acted knowledgeably, prudently, and without compulsion.
>
> *IVS 1, International Valuation Standards, 7th Edition*

52 See, for example, the *Pointe Gourde* Principle.
53 For example: United States v. 50 Acres of Land, 469 U.S. 24 (1984); United States v. Pewee Coal Co., 341 U.S. 114 (1951); Olsen v. United States, 292 U.S. 246 (1934).
54 Otherwise the authority would have negotiated the purchase without resorting to time-consuming (and therefore expensive) legislation.
55 See Chapter 11.

56 See Chapter 22.
57 See Chapter 19.
58 See Chapter 6.
59 See Chapter 18.
60 See Chapter 20.
61 See Chapter 21.
62 See Chapter 20.
63 See Chapter 7.
64 See Chapter 19.
65 Ambaye, Daniel, Weldegebriel (2009). Land Valuation for Expropriation in Ethiopia. Valuation Methods and Adequacy of Compensation. 7th FIG Regional Conference. Hanoi, Vietnam, 19–22 October, 2009.
66 Ambaye (2009). *op. cit.*
67 See, for example, McNeil, Kent (2004). The Vulnerability of Indigenous Land Rights in Australia and Canada. *Osgood Hall Law Journal*, 42.2, 271–301; Fortes, Raewyn (2005) Compensation Models for Native Title. Pacific Rim Real Estate Society Conference. 23–27 January. Melbourne, Australia.
68 See Chapter 22.
69 See Chapter 10.
70 FAO (2012) Large Agricultural Investments and Inclusion of Small Farmers: Lessons of case studies in 7 countries. Food and Agriculture Organization of the United Nations. Land Tenure Working Paper 23. www.fao.org.
71 "Rising Global Interest in Farmland" The World Bank, March 2015.
72 See, for example, FAO (2012), *op. cit.*
73 Deninger, Klaus, Byerlee Derek (2010) "Rising Global Interest in Farmland: Can It Yield Sustainable and Equitable Benefits?" The World Bank.
74 Report of the Special Rapporteur on the Right to Food, Oliver de Schutter. 2009. U.N. General Assembly. A/HRC/13/33/Add. 2.
75 See Chapter 7.
76 Involving experts from 35 countries.
77 Refer Viitanen, Kauko, Falkenbach. Heidi, Nuuja, Katri (2010). Compulsory Purchase and Compensation. Recommendations for Good Practice. FIG Policy Statement. Publication No. 54. www.fig.net Resources. Publications. ISBN 978-87-9090-89-1.
78 See Chapter 18.
79 See Chapter 19.
80 Ibid. Section 3, Recommendation 19.
81 Voluntary Guidelines on the Responsible Governance of Tenurre of Land, Fisheries and Forests in the context of National Food Security. www.fao.org
82 See Chapter 20.
83 See Chapter 23.
84 See Chapter 12.
85 Hall, Ruth (2018). Land expropriation Without Compensation: What Does It Mean? www.news24.com/Columnists/GuestColumn/land-expropriation-without-compensation-what-does-it-mean-20180304-5
86 Hall, Ruth (2018). *op. cit.*
87 Hall, Ruth (2018). *op. cit.*
88 Kirsten, Johann, Sihlobo, Wandile (2018). Expropriating Land Without Compensation Is Impossible - Take It from Zimbabwe. Quartz Africa. 1 March 2018.
89 Kirsten, Johann, Sihlobo, Wandile (2018). *op. cit.*
90 Buck et al. (Eds.) (2001). *op cit.*
91 See, for example, Kakulu (2007). *op. cit.* and Chapters 1, 3 and 11.
92 See Chapter 11 and du Plessis (2005) *op. cit.*

Index

Printed in the United States
by Baker & Taylor Publisher Services